Practical Aspects of

RAPE INVESTIGATION

A Multidisciplinary Approach

Fifth Edition

CRC SERIES IN
**PRACTICAL ASPECTS OF CRIMINAL
AND FORENSIC INVESTIGATIONS**

VERNON J. GEBERTH, BBA, MPS, FBINA *Series Editor*

**Practical Homicide Investigation: Tactics, Procedures, and
Forensic Techniques, Fifth Edition**
Vernon J. Geberth

**Practical Homicide Investigation Checklist and Field Guide,
Second Edition**
Vernon J. Geberth

Practical Bomb Scene Investigation, Third Edition
James T. Thurman

Analyzing 911 Homicide Calls: Practical Aspects and Applications
Tracy Harpster and Susan H. Adams

**Practical Aspects of Rape Investigation: A Multidisciplinary Approach,
Fifth Edition**
Robert R. Hazelwood and Ann Wolbert Burgess

**Munchausen by Proxy and Other Factitious Abuse: Practical and
Forensic Investigative Techniques**
Robert R. Hazelwood and Ann Wolbert Burgess

Forensic Footwear Evidence
William J. Bodziak

**Practical Analysis and Reconstruction of Shooting Incidents,
Second Edition**
Edward E. Hueske

**Gunshot Wounds: Practical Aspects of Firearms, Ballistics,
and Forensic Techniques, Third Edition**
Vincent J. M. DiMaio

**Informants, Cooperating Witnesses, and Undercover Investigations:
A Practical Guide to Law, Policy, and Procedure, Second Edition**
Dennis G. Fitzgerald

Practical Military Ordnance Identification
Tom Gersbeck

Practical Cold Case Homicide Investigations Procedural Manual
Richard H. Walton

Autoerotic Deaths: Practical Forensic and Investigative Perspectives
Anny Sauvageau and Vernon J. Geberth

Practical Crime Scene Processing and Investigation, Second Edition
Ross M. Gardner

The Counterterrorism Handbook: Tactics, Procedures, and Techniques, Fourth Edition
Frank Bolz, Jr., Kenneth J. Dudonis, and David P. Schulz

Practical Forensic Digital Imaging: Applications and Techniques
Patrick Jones

Practical Crime Scene Investigations for Hot Zones
Jacqueline T. Fish, Robert N. Stout, and Edward Wallace

Sex-Related Homicide and Death Investigation: Practical and Clinical Perspectives, Second Edition
Vernon J. Geberth

Handbook of Forensic Toxicology for Medical Examiners
D. K. Molina

Practical Crime Scene Analysis and Reconstruction
Ross M. Gardner and Tom Bevel

Serial Violence: Analysis of Modus Operandi and Signature Characteristics of Killers
Robert D. Keppel and William J. Birnes

Bloodstain Pattern Analysis: With an Introduction to Crime Scene Reconstruction, Third Edition
Tom Bevel and Ross M. Gardner

Tire Tread and Tire Track Evidence: Recovery and Forensic Examination
William J. Bodziak

Officer-Involved Shootings and Use of Force: Practical Investigative Techniques, Second Edition
David E. Hatch and Randy Dickson

Practical Drug Enforcement, Third Edition
Michael D. Lyman

Cold Case Homicides: Practical Investigative Techniques
Richard H. Walton

Principles of Bloodstain Pattern Analysis: Theory and Practice
Stuart James, Paul Kish, and T. Paulette Sutton

Global Drug Enforcement: Practical Investigative Techniques
Gregory D. Lee

Practical Investigation of Sex Crimes: A Strategic and Operational Approach
Thomas P. Carney

Principles of Kinesic Interview and Interrogation, Second Edition
Stan Walters

Practical Criminal Investigations in Correctional Facilities
William R. Bell

Practical Aspects of Interview and Interrogation, Second Edition
David E. Zulawski and Douglas E. Wicklander

Forensic Pathology, Second Edition
Dominick J. DiMaio and Vincent J. M. DiMaio

The Practical Methodology of Forensic Photography, Second Edition
David R. Redsicker

Quantitative-Qualitative Friction Ridge Analysis: An Introduction to Basic and Advanced Ridgeology
David R. Ashbaugh

Footwear Impression Evidence: Detection, Recovery, and Examination, Second Edition
William J. Bodziak

The Sexual Exploitation of Children: A Practical Guide to Assessment, Investigation, and Intervention, Second Edition
Seth L. Goldstein

Practical Aspects of Munchausen by Proxy and Munchausen Syndrome Investigation
Kathryn Artingstall

Practical Fire and Arson Investigation, Second Edition
David R. Redsicker and John J. O'Connor

Interpretation of Bloodstain Evidence at Crime Scenes, Second Edition
William G. Eckert and Stuart H. James

Investigating Computer Crime
Franklin Clark and Ken Diliberto

Practical Investigation Techniques
Kevin B. Kinnee

Friction Ridge Skin: Comparison and Identification of Fingerprints
James F. Cowger

Tire Imprint Evidence
Peter McDonald

Practical Gambling Investigation Techniques
Kevin B. Kinnee

Practical Aspects of
RAPE INVESTIGATION
A Multidisciplinary Approach

Fifth Edition

Edited by
Robert R. Hazelwood
Ann Wolbert Burgess

CRC Press
Taylor & Francis Group
Boca Raton London New York

CRC Press is an imprint of the
Taylor & Francis Group, an **informa** business

CRC Press
Taylor & Francis Group
6000 Broken Sound Parkway NW, Suite 300
Boca Raton, FL 33487-2742

First issued in paperback 2020

ISBN-13: 978-1-4987-4196-5 (hbk)
ISBN-13: 978-0-367-77840-8 (pbk)

Library of Congress Cataloging-in-Publication Data

Names: Hazelwood, Robert R., editor. | Burgess, Ann Wolbert, editor.
Title: Practical aspects of rape investigation : a multidisciplinary approach / edited by Robert R. Hazelwood and Ann Wolbert Burgess.
Description: Fifth edition. | New York : CRC Press, 2017. | Series: Practical aspects of criminal and forensic investigations | Includes bibliographical references and index.
Identifiers: LCCN 2016028976| ISBN 9781498741965 (hardback : alk. paper) | ISBN 9781315316369 (ebook)
Subjects: LCSH: Rape--Investigation. | Rape--United States--Investigation.
Classification: LCC HV8079.R35 P7 2017 | DDC 363.25/95320973--dc23
LC record available at https://lccn.loc.gov/2016028976

Visit the Taylor & Francis Web site at
http://www.taylorandfrancis.com

and the CRC Press Web site at
http://www.crcpress.com

Dedication

This book is dedicated to the victims of rape and to those law enforcement, mental health, and medical professionals who work on behalf of the victims.

In Memoriam

To Roy Hazelwood and Contributor Teresa Scalzo.

Spring 2016 brought the very sad news that we had lost two key contributors in the field of sexual violence: the editor of this book Robert (Roy) Hazelwood whose career clearly advanced the practical investigation of sexual violence crimes and Teresa Scalzo, a chapter contributor who furthered the successful prosecution of cases of sexual assault, particularly those committed by someone known to the victim and/or facilitated with drugs and alcohol.

Remembering Roy Hazelwood

The professions of law enforcement, investigative science, and victim services mourned the loss of Robert (Roy) Hazelwood on April 18, 2016. It is rare that an individual has a significant impact on investigative practice and research but in Roy Hazelwood, we have an even more remarkable occurrence—his influence can be identified in three separate fields of study—law enforcement, investigative science, and profiling. Roy had great energy, compassion, and dedication to the field. In our estimation, his attempts to foster interactions and intellectual exchange among academics, forensic scientists, and practitioners across different fields of study represent perhaps his greatest intellectual legacy.

A History of the Relationship between the Co-editors, Ann and Roy

The story of how I became involved with the Behavioral Sciences Unit (BSU) at the FBI starts with Roy. In 1978, he was teaching sexual assault at the National Academy (250 officers from throughout the United States and Europe), and Rita Knecht was in the class. Rita was an LA detective and ER nurse. After class one day, she suggested to him that I would be a great resource for the topic. She gave Roy my number and he called my office at Boston College and invited me to come to the Academy to speak on rape victimology. After the lecture, Roy told me about his interest in researching a new type of case the BSU was seeing on dangerous autoeroticism. In fact, Roy had counted over 100 cases that had come in over the years on this topic. Sometime later Roy was speaking in Boston and I invited him to my home to meet psychologist Nick Groth and by 1981 we three of us had co-authored an article from the data on autoerotic fatalities. That article was evidence that we could work and write together.

Roy traced his interest in sexual violence to the Harvey Glatman case. Glatman was the first serial killer to take pictures of his victims and it was his case that lead Pierce Brooks to develop the Violent Criminal Apprehension Program (VICAP). Pierce was the homicide detective on the case and was also the first director of VICAP at the BSU at Quantico.

Two additional cases have historical meaning to the BSU. The first was the Robert Hanson case out of Alaska. It was a serial murder case that John Douglas worked on and it was the first time an analysis/profile assessment was used to establish the probable cause in a search warrant. Another case that Roy was initially involved in with John was the Atlanta child killing case. This case put criminal profiling on the map both nationally as well as internationally particularly the prosecution cross-examination strategies of Wayne Williams.

By the mid-1980s, Roy was lecturing and consulting nationally on rape and sexual assault cases.

Concurrently, homicide detective Vernon Geberth was lecturing at the BSU and was also looking for someone to write a textbook on investigating rape cases. Roy talked with Vernon and agreed to write a book for the series *Practical Aspects of Criminal and Forensic Investigation*. I joined Roy to bring the victim component to the book and the 1st edition was published in 1987, the 2nd in 1995, the 3rd in 2001, and the 4th in 2009. Vernon Gebarth said that he considered Roy a friend and colleague, and that he was down-to-earth and genuine. He was particularly impressed that Roy did his own research for his writings and the textbook. When Roy died, everything was already complete for the 5th edition. He was always thinking of other people. He was devoted to his family and loyal to his professional friends, of which there were many. He touched many lives and the legacy of his writings will continue to benefit future generations.

Contributor's Tributes to Roy

Roger Depue published this tribute for the Academy Group where Roy was a cofounder.

I have known and respected Roy Hazelwood for about 40 years. Roy came to the Behavioral Science Unit to take over sex crimes training which at the time was primitive to say the least. In a relatively short time he had the course improved until it eventually became one of the best programs at the FBI Academy.

Roy went on to become a world-renowned authority in the field of interpersonal violence and sexual assault crimes. He was regarded as a singular expert and his opinion was sought after in the criminal, civil, and political domains worldwide. He became an excellent researcher obtaining information never before known in the investigative, scientific, and academic communities. He personally interviewed scores of violent criminals of every sort and their surviving victims. He constantly wanted to know more and formulated research instruments allowing for answers to age-old questions about criminal behavior. He was a prolific author publishing books, journal articles, and scholarly papers held in the highest regard in professional arenas. His knowledge of the behavior of the criminal and the victim gave him the ability to interpret behaviors and solve cases when all hope for solution had been lost for law enforcement officers and the family members of victims. His sympathetic approach made him an advocate for victims and their families.

Roy was a consummate teacher able to communicate with the toughest detectives as well as the most skeptical scientists. He wanted his students to understand and use the information he had developed through his years of research, training and operational (case) support. Some people would describe him as a 'workaholic' but he did it without neglecting his family and friends. Roy's innovations changed investigative practices throughout the world. He wanted to share his knowledge with all law enforcement so he instituted the 'Police Fellowship Program' at the FBI Academy allowing sophisticated police investigators to travel to the academy and stay for a year to learn these new techniques.

Upon retirement he was cofounder of the Academy Group, Inc. Roy was an astute businessman and soon became the Chairman of the Board of Directors for the Academy Group. He was a caring and compassionate friend who quietly visited homebound and hospitalized associates bringing heightened levels of mood and humor. Two weeks before his death Roy visited Ed Sulzbach a dying FBI agent in the hospital, who then died only days before his own death. He was an excellent judge of character and managed to marry a woman who was his equal in ability but considerably more lovely, fortunately. His only fault that I know of (if it can be called a fault) was that he did not like to exercise. I don't think he ever set foot in the gymnasium. And then there was his love for grilled cheese sandwiches and tomato soup which he consumed on a daily basis for years at the FBI Academy. Roy, we loved you in so many ways. We will never forget you. I hope the soup is hot and the cheese is flavorful as you enjoy your well-earned reward in heaven.

Many of us may be along in the not too distant future, I suppose.

Roger Depue

He was a supremely authentic, dedicated role model who led a brilliant life in the service of others. He will always guide my thinking and teaching of others.

James Knoll

Roy Hazelwood and I were partners for many years in the FBI Behavioral Science Unit where he shared with me his extensive experience and knowledge concerning the criminal aspects of deviant sexual behavior.

Ken Lanning

Roy was an honest, loyal, and generous man who was always thinking and trying to use his talents to protect others.

Janet Warren

How does one briefly or adequately speak about someone like Roy Hazelwood. Just a few remarks: For more than 30 years Roy Hazelwood has appreciably impacted my life. His sincere willingness to always help others with any problem was a hallmark of his character. Through his sharing of knowledge he has made such a huge difference in this world. His logical talents, structural approach, work ethic, and generosity in time and efforts to help resolve major problems were also trademarks of his character. Roy's appreciable understanding of the criminal and the victim afforded him tremendous insight allowing him to properly interpret their behaviors and in turn help resolve violent crime cases for law enforcement officials around the world. He will be a person sorely missed but never forgotten.

Steve Mardigian

Michelle Ortiz, Forensic Healthcare Coordinator and NMCP SAFE Program Manager at Naval Medical Center Portsmouth Virginia quoted Evan Esar when learning of the passing of Roy Hazelwood: "You can't do anything about the length of your life, but you can do something about its width and depth."

Remembering Teresa Scalzo

Contributor Teresa Scalzo, JD, passed away on May 23, 2016. At the time of her death, she served as the deputy director of the Navy Judge Advocate General (JAG) Corps Trial Counsel Assistance Program (TCAP), where she provided training, case consultation, and assistance to the navy's prosecutors. She previously served as the senior policy advisor for the Office of the Secretary of Defense Sexual Assault Prevention and Response Office (OSD SAPRO).

Teresa advanced the prosecution of violence against women in the United States in countless ways. She provided technical assistance and trial support to thousands of criminal justice professionals throughout the nation, published numerous influential works, and served on a number of national committees dealing with sexual assault and domestic violence. She also served as the chief of the Sexual Assault Unit in the Northampton County, Pennsylvania District Attorney's Office, where she was recognized by the Crime Victims Council of Lehigh Valley, Pennsylvania, with an *Allied Professional Award for Outstanding Commitment to Victims' Services*.

On a personal level, she was one of the brightest, kindest, and most generous people you could ever hope to meet with a fierce intellect and insatiable curiosity that drove her to continually learn and grow. She will be greatly missed by all of us who worked with her and knew her.

When I was looking for an attorney to write a chapter on prosecuting rape cases, Kathy Brown suggested I call Teresa Scalzo who at the time was working.

One of my best memories of Teresa was her serving as the Panel Chair for a presentation to the nursing and medical school students at the Uniformed Services University of the Health Sciences in

Bethesda, Maryland. The presentation was on the murder of Petty Officer Amanda Snell and Teresa, at the time, was a consultant to the Navy JAG. She was superbly skillful in abstracting the key points of everyone's presentation and then fielding questions from the students. You could count on Teresa to complete any task assigned to her, to produce a quality product and to be gracious in all interactions and meetings.

Ann Burgess

Kathleen Brown remembers Teresa as her mentor in her first expert testimony case. She said,

The first time I ever testified was for Teresa. She met with me in planning phase and relieved my anxiety. She was fearsome in the courtroom. I will never forget it. At first, I wasn't sure the woman in the courtroom was the woman I met the week before in preparation! She fought for the victim! My testimony was well received because she prepared me well. The accused was found guilty and the victim was connected to all the services she needed post trial. I am very fortunate that Teresa introduced me to the prosecutor's role and the responsibilities of testifying as a nurse for victims of crime.

Kathleen Brown

Roy Hazelwood and Teresa Scalzo will be missed by many in the fields they cultivated, but their contributions will not be forgotten by their colleagues and students.

Contents

Series Editor's Note xvii
Preface..xix
Acknowledgments...xxi
Editors xxiii
Contributors xxv

SECTION I   The Victim

Chapter 1   Rape and Its Impact on the Victim..3

               Ann Wolbert Burgess and Carrie M. Carretta

Chapter 2   Victim Services and SANE/SART Programs 19

               Annie Lewis-O'Connor, Ann Wolbert Burgess, and Carol Anne Harvey Marchetti

Chapter 3   Youth, Social Media, and Internet Crime 35

               Elizabeth Burgess Dowdell

Chapter 4   Elder Sexual Abuse Victims...45

               Ann Wolbert Burgess

SECTION II   Investigation

Chapter 5   The Relevance of Fantasy in Serial Sexual Crimes Investigation...............................67

               Robert R. Hazelwood and Janet I. Warren

Chapter 6   The Behavioral-Oriented Interview of Rape Victims: The Key to Profiling.............79

               Robert R. Hazelwood and Ann Wolbert Burgess

Chapter 7   Analyzing the Rape and Profiling the Offender 97

               Robert R. Hazelwood

Chapter 8   Interviewing the Rapist 123

               Michael R. Napier

Chapter 9   Collateral Materials in Sexual Crimes 139

               Robert R. Hazelwood and Kenneth V. Lanning

Chapter 10 Linkage Analysis: MO, Ritual, and Signature in Serial Sexual Crimes 149

  Robert R. Hazelwood and Janet I. Warren

Chapter 11 False Rape Allegations 159

  Robert R. Hazelwood and Ann Wolbert Burgess

Chapter 12 Interrogation and False Confessions in Rape Cases 177

  Richard A. Leo

Chapter 13 Rape Escalating to Homicide 187

  Robert R. Hazelwood and Janet I. Warren

Chapter 14 Cold Case Investigation 199

  R. Stephen Mardigian and Roger L. Depue

SECTION III   Forensics and Court

Chapter 15 Physical Evidence in Sexual Assault Investigations 211

  Tara Crider

Chapter 16 Medical Evaluation of Sexually Abused Children 241

  Andi Taroli

Chapter 17 Injury and Forensic Examination of the Victim 269

  Kathleen P. Brown and Marilyn S. Sommers

Chapter 18 Prosecuting Rape Cases: Trial Preparation and Trial Tactic Issues 287

  Teresa Scalzo

SECTION IV   Offender Populations

Chapter 19 Sexual Victimization of Children: Rape or Molestation 305

  Kenneth V. Lanning

Chapter 20 The Sexual Crimes of Juveniles 319

  John A. Hunter

Chapter 21 Female Sex Offenders 337

Janet I. Warren and David A. McLeod

Chapter 22 Drug-Facilitated Sex Assault 355

Michael Welner and Barbara Welner

Chapter 23 The Criminal Sexual Sadist 373

Robert R. Hazelwood, Park Dietz, and Janet I. Warren

Chapter 24 Sexual Sadists: Their Wives and Girlfriends 385

Robert R. Hazelwood

Chapter 25 Sex Offenders of the Elderly 393

Ann Wolbert Burgess, Robert A. Prentky, and Mark Safarik

Chapter 26 Educator Sexual Misconduct: Grooming Patterns and Female Offenders 407

James L. Knoll, IV

Chapter 27 U.S. Military Sexual Assault.. 421

Cynthia T. Ferguson

Chapter 28 Campus Sexual Assault... 433

Raina V. Lamade, Ann Wolbert Burgess, Sarah M. Chung,
Shannon W. Spencer, and Robert A. Prentky

Index..449

Series Editor's Note

This textbook is part of a series titled "Practical Aspects of Criminal and Forensic Investigations." This series was created by Vernon J. Geberth, a retired New York City Police Department lieutenant commander, who is an author, educator, and consultant on homicide and forensic investigations.

This series has been designed to provide contemporary, comprehensive, and pragmatic information to the practitioner involved in criminal and forensic investigations by authors who are nationally recognized experts in their respective fields.

Preface

One of the most startling aspects of sex crimes is how many go unreported. The most common reasons given by women for not reporting these crimes are the beliefs that they are private or personal matters and fears of reprisal from the assailant. The FBI estimates that only a third of all rapes are reported to the police. U.S. Justice Department statistics are even lower, indicating that only 26% of all rapes or attempted rapes are reported to law enforcement officials.

These figures become even more critical when we realize that, despite the increased focus on criminal investigation of rape and sexual assault crimes, in 2014, only 39.3% of all known forcible rape offenses were cleared by arrest—a figure that has not changed over the past four decades. An overwhelming majority of rape victim service agencies believe that public education about rape, as well as expanded counseling and advocacy services for rape victims, would be effective in increasing the willingness of victims to report rapes to the police.

Concurrent with the numbers of victims and suspects arrested, there has been a burgeoning of research into myriad factors interwoven with sexual violence and its aftermath. Substantial contributions have been made to advancing the state of knowledge for law enforcement agents, health professionals, rape crisis staffs, and criminal justice professionals.

Although most people working with sexual crimes see either the victim or offender, the investigator and prosecutor frequently encounter both the victims and offenders of sexual assault. Thus, it becomes crucial that these two groups have the benefit of research results in the fields of victimology, criminology, behavioral sciences, forensic sciences, and criminal justice. Such information can substantially impact the effectiveness of the investigative interview, the collection of forensic evidence, and the prosecution of cases.

The aim of this fifth edition of *Practical Aspects of Rape Investigation* is to present current research findings and new forensic techniques and to acquaint the reader with current information about special populations of victims and offenders.

The book is divided into four sections. Section I includes four chapters specific to the victims of rape and sexual assault. In the first chapter, Burgess and Carretta outline the short- and long-term consequences of rape and sexual assault. In Chapter 2, Lewis-O'Connor, Burgess, and Marchetti describe victim care services, including history and the SANE and SART programs. A new chapter, Chapter 3 by Dowdell, is included on youth, social media, and Internet crime, and Chapter 4, by Burgess, on elder sexual abuse provides insightful information on the sexual abuse of elderly victims.

Section II includes 10 chapters on the investigation of rape and sexual assault cases. Chapter 5, by Hazelwood and Warren, addresses the relevance of fantasy in serial sexual crime investigations, proposing that fantasy is the link between the underlying motivation for sexual assaults and the behavior exhibited during the crime. Chapter 6 deals with the behavioral-oriented interview of rape victims, and Hazelwood and Burgess describe interviewing the victim to determine the verbal, physical, and sexual behavior exhibited by the offender during the commission of the crime. In Chapter 7, Hazelwood describes his process for analyzing rape and presents such an analysis via an extensive case history. Chapter 8, by Napier, is on interviewing the rapist. He presents basic steps and techniques of the interview process, taking into account the type of rapist being interviewed. In Chapter 9, Hazelwood and Lanning define the concept of collateral material in sexual crimes and identify the various types of such material.

In Chapter 10, Hazelwood and Warren contrast impulsive and ritualistic behavior in the sexually violent offender and illustrate with case examples how analyzing and comparing behavior can demonstrate the likelihood that the same offender is responsible for the crimes in question.

One of the thorniest problems in rape investigation is a false allegation. An inherent conflict arises between the investigator's obligation to accept the victim's complaint as legitimate and his duty to develop the facts of the case. Chapter 11, by Hazelwood and Burgess, reviews the literature on rape allegations and proposes a model to understand the concept. This chapter includes a discussion on motivation and red flags for false allegations. In Chapter 12, written by criminologist attorney Leo, who has studied how and why innocent people confess to crimes that carry potentially lengthy sentences; he describes how law enforcement may avoid such situations.

Two new chapters in Section II include Chapter 13, by Hazelwood and Warren, on rape escalating to homicide and Chapter 14, by retired FBI agents Mardigian and Depue, on cold case analysis.

Section III deals with forensics and the court. In Chapter 15 on physical evidence in sexual assault investigations and evidence recovery by Crider provides a solid background and framework for recovering and processing physical evidence in rape and sexual assault cases. The forensic scientist discusses the collection and observation of physical and trace evidence of the victim, the offender, and the scene of the crime, and the presentation of evidence in court. Chapter 16, by Taroli, presents the methodology of complicated medical examinations of sexually abused children. Brown and Sommers, in Chapter 17, present the injury research and forensic examination of the adult victim. Medical treatment for the victim is also outlined. Chapter 18, by attorney Scalzo, deals with the prosecution of rape and sexual assault cases.

Section IV deals with special populations. In Chapter 19, Lanning proposes a discussion on rape or molestation in the sexual victimization of children. In Chapter 20, forensic psychologist Hunter writes on the sexual crimes of juveniles and provides insights on juvenile sex offenders and their classifications. Chapter 21, by Warren and McLeod, concerns female sex offenders and presents relevant information on a little understood population of women who sexually offend. Chapter 22, written by forensic psychiatrist Michael Welner and forensic nurse Barbara Welner, presents current findings and insights on the serious problem of drug-facilitated rape. Chapter 23, by Hazelwood, Dietz, and Warren, deals with the criminal sexual sadist and contains findings from their study of 30 men who sadistically raped and/or murdered their victims. In Chapter 24, Hazelwood discusses findings from his interviews of the female partners of sexual sadists. Chapter 25, by Burgess, Prentky, and Safarik, follows up on the topic of elder sexual abuse by discussing a study and classification system of those who offend against the elderly. Chapter 26 written by forensic psychiatrist James Knoll is about educator sexual misconduct and discusses the patterns of female educators who "groom" their students for sexual abuse.

Two new chapters complete the book. Chapter 27 by Ferguson discusses a current issue of rape in the military and Chapter 28 on sexual assault on college campuses is written by a team Lamade, Burgess, Chung, Spencer, and Prentky.

This book represents a major commitment by its authors to present the most current knowledge for the investigation and prosecution of rape and other sexual assault cases.

Acknowledgments

We wish to thank the many people who helped in the first, second, third, fourth, and latest editions of this text. We especially wish to thank the following individuals, without whose efforts this book would not have been possible.

For their encouragement and support: Peggy Hazelwood, Allen G. Burgess, retired assistant director James D. McKenzie (FBI), retired deputy assistant director James A. O'Connor (FBI), and retired unit chief Roger L. Depue (FBI).

Others deserving special thanks are retired supervisory special agent Howard D. Teten (FBI) and professor emeritus Carol R. Hartman (Boston College) for their insight and professional advice over the years.

A very special appreciation goes to Stefan Treffers, a PhD candidate in the Sociology Department at York University who spent many hours *meticulously* researching articles to update the chapters. His editorial skills were especially outstanding. A special word of thanks to CRC Press senior editor Mark Listewnik and project editor Richard Tressider for their patience and scrupulous attention to detail.

Editors

Robert R. Hazelwood, MS, a retired supervisory special agent of the Federal Bureau of Investigation (FBI) who served 22 years in the FBI, 16 of which were in the Behavioral Science Unit at the FBI Academy. He also served 11 years in the U.S. Army, attaining the rank of Major. He earned a BS degree in sociology and an MS degree in counseling, and attended a 1-year fellowship in forensic medicine from the Armed Forces Institute of Pathology. Hazelwood has edited one book, co-authored four books, published more than 45 articles in peer-reviewed journals, and contributed chapters in 10 books. He has lectured in all 50 states, every Canadian province, several European countries and Caribbean nations. He has testified as an expert witness in civil and criminal cases in city, county, state, military, and federal courts. Hazelwood has conducted and published research on autoerotic fatalities, serial rape, juvenile sexual offenders, police attitudes on rape, sexual sadists, sexually sadistic serial killers, staged crimes and former wives and girlfriends of sexual sadists, and child molesters. He twice was awarded the Jefferson Award for Research from the University of Virginia.

Ann Wolbert Burgess, DNSc, APRN, BC, FAAN, is a professor of psychiatric mental health nursing at Boston College Connell School of Nursing and professor emerita from the University of Pennsylvania. She was educated at Boston University and the University of Maryland. She, with Lynda Lytle Holmstrom (Boston College), cofounded one of the first hospital-based crisis intervention programs for rape victims at Boston City Hospital. She served as chair of the first Advisory Council to the National Center for the Prevention and Control of Rape of the National Institute of Mental Health, was a member of the 1984 U.S. Attorney General's Task Force on Family Violence, on the planning committee for the 1985 Surgeon General's Symposium on Violence, served on the National Institute of Health National Advisory Council for the Center for Nursing Research 1986–1988; and a member of the 1990 Adolescent Health Advisory Panel to the Congress of the United States Office of Technology Assessment and Chair of the National Institutes of Health AIDS and Related Research Study Section (ARRR 6), 1992–1994. She was elected to the American Academy of Nursing in 1977, the National Academy of Sciences Institute of Medicine in October 1994, and chaired the 1996 National Research Council's Task Force on Violence against Women. She helped write an online course in military sexual trauma as a visiting professor at the Uniformed Services University of the Health Sciences in Bethesda and recent funded project included campus sexual assault and developing a college warrior athletic initiative.

Contributors

Kathleen P. Brown, RN, NP, PhD, is a practice associate professor and nurse practitioner in women's health in the School of Nursing at the University of Pennsylvania. She is the director of the forensic program at Penn Nursing. Educated at the University of Pennsylvania, Dr. Brown's clinical work and her research focus on victims of sexual assault. She consults with law enforcement and health care professionals regarding effective responses to sex crimes and has testified in courtrooms throughout the country. She has published her research on domestic violence, genital injury, sexual assault teams, and sexual assault nurse examiners.

Carrie M. Carretta completed her PhD at Vanderbilt University and is currently employed in Medical and Clinical Affairs, managing consultancy projects as well as medical science liaison and clinical teams in the pharmaceutical industry. In addition to her experience in Medical Affairs, Carrie has experience as a principal investigator running numerous clinical trials. She is nationally board certified as both a family psychiatric nurse practitioner and advanced holistic nurse. Dr. Carretta's research encompass forensics; specificity homicide/suicide, psychopathy, rape and sexual assault, and general trauma, and violence and abuse.

Sarah M. Chung, BS, RN, received her BS in 2016 from the William F. Connell School of Nursing at Boston College. She has worked as an undergraduate research fellow with Dr. Burgess for 2 years. She will continue as a research fellow and focus her graduate education on psychiatric–mental health nursing.

Tara Crider, MFS, is a crime scene investigator with 9 years of experience who works for the Arlington County Police Department in Virginia. She has a BS in biochemistry and genetics from the University of Minnesota and a MS in forensic science from George Washington University. She is a graduate of the Virginia Department of Forensic Science Academy and lectures in various colleges and at universities and the Northern Virginia Criminal Justice Training Academy.

Roger L. Depue, PhD, is retired from the Federal Bureau of Investigation where he last served in the positions of chief of the Behavioral Science Unit and administrator of the National Center for the Analysis of Violent Crime. Following his retirement he founded the Academy Group, Inc., a forensic behavioral science services company located in Manassas, Virginia. He then studied philosophy and theology in a seminary adding spiritual perspective to his background in the behavioral sciences. He is a former marine, infantry weapons armorer, county juvenile officer, chief of police, SWAT team member, university professor, business CEO, and a noted author and speaker on criminal behavior. He has testified in criminal and civil cases and on law enforcement matters before both houses of the U.S. Congress. Dr. Depue is currently responsible for a block of police leadership instruction at the University of Virginia National Criminal Justice Command College.

Park Dietz, MD, MPH, PhD, is a clinical professor of psychiatry at the UCLA David Geffen School of Medicine, a distinguished fellow of the program in psychology and law at the University of California, Irvine, and the founder and president of both Park Dietz & Associates, Inc., and Threat Assessment Group, Inc., of Newport Beach, California. He was educated at Cornell, Johns Hopkins, and the University of Pennsylvania, served as an assistant professor of psychiatry at Harvard Medical School, and as a professor of law and professor of behavioral medicine and psychiatry at the University of Virginia. He often appears as an expert witness in trials involving homicides and sex crimes and has been named one of the 10 most famous psychiatrists in history by biography.com. He created the specialty of workplace violence prevention and has been named one of the "Top 25 Most Influential People in the Security Industry" by *Security* magazine.

Elizabeth Burgess Dowdell, PhD, RN, FAAN, is a professor of pediatric nursing at Villanova University, College of Nursing in Pennsylvania. She was educated at Vanderbilt University, Boston College and the University of Pennsylvania. As a nurse scientist she has worked to identify the inter-relationships among various forms of electronic aggression, including cyber-bullying and sexting, in addition to the new phenomena of sleep texting. She has been published in the areas of health-risk behaviors, caregiver burden, issues of foster care placement, and high-risk Internet behaviors.

Cynthia T. Ferguson, Navy CDR (Ret.), is an advanced forensic nurse and certified nurse midwife with 24 years of experience working in women's health, and over 16 years of experience working in forensics. She obtained her master's degree at Case Western Reserve University in 1998. In 2009, she graduated from George Washington University's Masters of Public Health program after analyzing sexual assault prevention and response policy in the military. She earned a PhD in public health from Walden University in 2015 after focusing her research and dissertation on violence prevention and response programs and policy in the military while on deployment in Afghanistan. The U.S. Navy and Department of Defense have relied on her to serve as a sexual assault subject matter expert, forensic exam trainer for health care personnel, and consultant/expert witness in many sexual assault cases. CDR (Ret.) Ferguson currently works at the Fluvanna Correctional Center for Women (FCCW), in Virginia, as a primary health care provider, where she is focusing on improving medical practices and health care policy regarding incarcerated women in the jail and the prison system.

John A. Hunter, PhD, is a clinical psychologist with more than 30 years of clinical and research experience in the field of sexual trauma, including the etiology, evaluation, and treatment of juvenile, and adult sexual offenders. He has published over 40 articles or book chapters on the subject of juvenile sexual offending and/or sexual trauma and has been the recipient of seven federal research grants. Dr. Hunter has directed both community-based and residential treatment programs for juvenile sexual offenders and is a former member of the board of directors for the Association for the Treatment of Sexual Abusers (ATSA). He has served on the Kempe Center's National Task Force on Juvenile Sexual Offending, the University of Oklahoma National Center on Sexual Behavior of Youth's National Advisory Committee, and the Center for Sex Offender Management's National Resource Group.

James L. Knoll, IV, MD, is the director of forensic psychiatry and professor of psychiatry at SUNY Upstate Medical University in Syracuse, New York. Dr. Knoll also served as the medical director of psychiatric services for the New Hampshire State Prison system before becoming training director of the SUNY Upstate forensic psychiatry fellowship training program. He is the emeritus editor-in-chief of the *Psychiatric Times* and contributing editor for the *Correctional Mental Health Report*. He has authored over 150 publications in journals and book chapters. He has served as vice president of the American Academy of Psychiatry and the Law (AAPL), and teaches in the annual AAPL forensic psychiatry board review course. He has worked as a forensic evaluator for state and federal courts, corrections, and the private sector. His main areas of research interest include suicide, violence prevention, mass murder, and analysis of inappropriate communications.

Raina V. Lamade, PhD, is the co-project manager of a Department of Justice SMART Office grant to develop a treatment program for students found responsible of sexual misconduct. She also serves as a consultant, conducting psychological evaluations for the Mental Health Courts within New York City. Dr. Lamade received her PhD in clinical psychology with a concentration in forensic psychology from Fairleigh Dickinson University, under the mentorship of Dr. Robert Prentky.

She serves as an ad hoc reviewer for two professional journals. She has taught clinical and forensic psychology courses at the undergraduate and graduate levels, has been published in professional journals, and has presented at various conferences.

Kenneth V. Lanning is currently a consultant in the area of crimes against children. Before retiring in 2000, he was a special agent with the FBI for more than 30 years. He was assigned to the FBI Behavioral Science Unit and the National Center for the Analysis of Violent Crime at the FBI Academy in Quantico, Virginia, for 20 of those years. He is a founding member of the Board of Directors of the American Professional Society on the Abuse of Children (APSAC) and is a former member of the APSAC Advisory Board. He is a former invited member of the Advisory Board of the Association for the Treatment of Sexual Abusers (ATSA). Lanning is the 1990 recipient of the Jefferson Award for Research from the University of Virginia, the 1996 recipient of the Outstanding Professional Award from APSAC, the 1997 recipient of the FBI Director's Annual Award for Special Achievement for career accomplishments in connection with missing and exploited children, and the 2009 recipient of the Outstanding Service Award for lifetime achievements from the National Children's Advocacy Center. He has testified on seven occasions before the U.S. Congress and many times as an expert witness in state and federal courts. Lanning has authored numerous publications and consulted on thousands of cases involving sexual offenses, especially those against children. He has lectured before and trained tens of thousands of law enforcement officers, prosecutors, social workers, mental health and medical personnel, judges, and other professionals.

Richard A. Leo, PhD, JD, is the Hamill Family professor of law and psychology at the University San Francisco School of Law, and a fellow in the Institute for Legal Research at the University of California, Berkeley School of Law. Dr. Leo is one of the leading experts in the world on police interrogation practices, the impact of *Miranda*, psychological coercion, false confessions, and the wrongful conviction of the innocent. Dr. Leo has authored more than 100 articles in leading scientific and legal journals as well as several books, including the multiple award-winning *Police Interrogation and American Justice* (Harvard University Press, 2008). Dr. Leo has won numerous individual and career achievement awards, as well as prestigious fellowships (Guggenheim, Soros, and others) for research excellence and distinction. Dr. Leo has been featured and/or quoted in hundreds of stories in the national print and electronic media, and his research has been discussed and cited by numerous appellate courts, including the United States Supreme Court on multiple occasions. He is regularly invited to lecture and present training sessions to lawyers, judges, police, forensic psychologists, and other criminal justice professionals. Dr. Leo is also often called to advise and assist practicing attorneys and has served as a litigation consultant and/or expert witness in hundreds of criminal and civil cases.

Annie Lewis-O'Connor, PhD, is a board certified nurse practitioner. She is the founder and director of the Women's CARE Clinic (Coordinated Approach Recovery & Empowerment) which provides patient informed health care to women who have been intentionally harmed by gender-based violence. Annie is committed to addressing gender-based violence from a research, policy, education, and clinical perspective. She holds faculty appointments at Harvard Medical School and Boston College. Dr. O'Connor has published in peer-reviewed journals and academic books on the topic of violence against women and children. She is currently the primary investigator in a National Institute of Justice grant addressing domestic violence homicide and risk reduction and is the chair of the National Health Collaborative on violence and abuse. In 2012, she was recognized by the *Boston Business Journal* as a champion in health care. She received her masters in nursing from Simmons College in Boston, her masters in public health from Boston University, and her PhD from Boston College.

Carol Anne Harvey Marchetti, PhD, PMHNP-BC, is a clinical associate professor at the William F. Connell School of Nursing at Boston College. Carol has been affiliated with the Massachusetts Sexual Assault Nurse Examiner (SANE) Program for over 12 years and currently serves as the SANE Program's Psychiatric-Mental Health Consultant and Educator. Additionally, she practices as a nurse at Colony Care Behavioral Health in Wellesley, Massachusetts.

R. Stephen Mardigian served for 31 years as an FBI supervisory special agent. As a violent crime assessor and administrator for the FBI's National Center for the Analysis of Violent Crime (NCAVC), he has conducted detailed evaluations on violent crime cases to assist criminal justice agencies faced with the most baffling and vicious violent crimes. He has provided a broad range of investigation and analysis on hundreds of cases involving homicide, sexual assault, child abduction and molestation, arson, bombing, extortion, product tampering, stalking, workplace violence, domestic and international terrorism, and threat assessment. Currently, Mardigian serves as the president and CEO of the Academy Group, Inc., the largest privately owned forensic behavioral science firm in the world with over 300 years of collective investigative and analytical experience in understanding, interpreting, and managing criminals, violent crime, and violent criminal behavior. As a consultant to corporations, Mardigian specializes in crime scene and communicated threat analysis, and in providing human resources, employee assistance programs, security, corporate, and legal professions with behavioral threat assessments, analyses of aberrant and criminal behavior, and incidents which affect workplace safety and security. As a violent crime expert witness, he continues to serve law enforcement in criminal cases and assists insurance carriers in matters involving premises liability and negligence cases.

David A. McLeod, PhD, MSW, is an assistant professor with the Anne and Henry Zarrow School of Social Work at the University of Oklahoma. He holds affiliate faculty status with multiple departments and research centers at the University of Oklahoma, including Women's and Gender Studies, the Center for Social Justice, and the Knee Center for Strong Families. He is a former police detective and forensic mental health clinician whose current research is broadly focused on forensic psychopathology and criminal behavioral development as they intersect with trauma and gender. For more on his professional endeavors, visit www.damcv.com.

Michael R. Napier, BS, retired from the Federal Bureau of Investigation as a supervisory special agent after nearly 28 years of service. At the time of his retirement he was assigned to the Critical Incident Response Group and the National Center for the Analysis of Violent Crime, both at the FBI Academy. He is currently a vice president and violent crime consultant for the Academy Group of Manassas, Virginia. Napier was an FBI-certified polygraph examiner and graduated from the Department of Defense Polygraph Institute. He has specialized in the study of interviewing and interrogation and the analysis of violent and sexually violent crimes.

Robert A. Prentky, PhD, is a professor in the School of Psychology at Fairleigh Dickinson University (Teaneck, New Jersey) and the director of forensic training. He received his PhD from Northwestern University and completed National Institute of Mental Health postdoctoral fellowships from the University of Rochester Medical Center, the University of York in England, and the University of Massachusetts. He has practiced as a forensic psychologist for more than 30+ years, and in that capacity has assessed or supervised the assessment of 2000+ offenders. He has been conducting research on sex offenders for 30+ years, and has been the principal or coprincipal investigator on 17 state and federal research grants (12 years as a principal investigator). His research has focused predominantly on taxonomic systems, risk assessment models, Internet child victimization, childhood antecedents of juvenile/adult outcomes, and most recently campus sexual violence. He has served as an ad hoc reviewer for 18 professional journals, and has chaired two conferences on sexual offenders for the New York Academy of Sciences (1988 and

2002). He has presented hundreds of times in the United States, Europe, Canada, and Israel, and published 80+ papers/chapters and 6 books. His most recent book, on sex offender risk assessment, was published in 2015. He was elected a fellow of the American Psychological Association in 2003 and the Association for Psychological Science in 2006.

Mark Safarik, MS, VSM, is the president of Forensic Behavioral Services. He retired from the FBI after 23 years having served for the last 12 years as a supervisory special agent criminal profiler in the FBI's elite Behavioral Analysis Unit. He specializes in the analysis of complex violent crimes with an expertise in sexual homicide. His research and investigative specialty is the sexual homicide of elder females. He is a lecturer at the University of Pennsylvania and Boston College. He has cold case homicide television series in both the United States and Europe.

Teresa Scalzo, JD, graduated from Temple University School of Law and held various positions, including chief sex crimes prosecutor in Northampton County, Pennsylvania; policy attorney for the National District Attorneys Association; director of the National Center for the Prosecution of Violence Against Women; senior policy advisor for the Department of Defense Sexual Assault Prevention and Response Office; and deputy director of the Navy Judge Advocate General Corps Trial Counsel (Prosecutor) Assistance Program. Scalzo provided training, technical assistance-and-trial support to criminal justice professionals throughout the nation on the prosecution of sexual assault. She designed the curricula for several courses on the investigation and prosecution of sexual assault, including sexual assault trial advocacy for the National Advocacy Center and numerous courses for military investigators and prosecutors. In addition, she oversaw the creation of the National Institute on the Prosecution of Sexual Violence. Scalzo authored numerous articles and was a contributing author for the *Pennsylvania Bench Book on Crimes of Sexual Violence.*

Marilyn S. Sommers, RN, PhD, is professor emeritus at the University of Pennsylvania School of Nursing. She is known for her research and publications in the area of injury related to sexual assault and risk-taking behaviors. Her clinical background is in trauma and surgical intensive care unit nursing. Dr. Sommers's current research is studying the sensitivity of colposcope examination to determine sexual assault.

Shannon W. Spencer received a BA from the University of Washington–Tacoma, graduating magna cum laude, and an MA in forensic psychology from Fairleigh Dickinson University. She is currently teaching as an adjunct instructor, and working in Dr. Robert Prentky's research lab at Fairleigh Dickinson University. She is an Air Force veteran, and flew as a loadmaster on the C-17 cargo aircraft for nearly 7 years.

Andi Taroli, MD, who was an early proponent of children's advocacy centers and forensic interviewing, became board certified in Child Abuse Pediatrics, and has provided extensive education and training on the medical aspects of child abuse for law enforcement, protective services, and other nonmedical investigators. She authored a chapter for the previous edition of this textbook, is a contributing author to the OJJDP's *Portable Guides to Investigating Child Abuse* 2014 revision of *Recognizing When a Child's Illness or Injury Is Caused by Abuse,* and also contributed to Hazelwood's research on *Wives of Child Molesters within the Family* (2015, SpringerBriefs in Behavioral Criminology). Dr. Taroli now enjoys a farm life in Pennsylvania with her loving family, ill-mannered dogs, lazy chickens, and aging horses.

Janet I. Warren, DSW, is a professor of psychiatry and neurobehavioral sciences at the University of Virginia where she serves as a teaching and research faculty at the Institute of Law, Psychiatry, and Public Policy, a multidisciplinary policy center organized under the auspices of the School of Law and the School of Medicine. Over the years, Professor Warren has worked with the FBI's

Behavioral Sciences Unit in developing paradigms relevant to the criminal investigative analyses of sexual offenders, including distinctions between impulsive versus ritualistic sex offenders and the elements of modus operandi, ritual, and the signature displayed in an offender's crime scene behavior. She has published in peer-reviewed journals on topics including forensic evaluation and opinion formation for the courts concerning competency to stand trial and sanity, and in 2013 she published a book entitled *Risk Markers for Sexual Predation and Victimization in Prison*, which explored risk markers for coerced, bartered, and consensual sex in prison for both male and female inmates. Professor Warren has a BSW and a MSW from the University of Manitoba, Canada, and a doctorate in social welfare from the University of California, Berkeley. She is a clinical social worker licensed by the Virginia Board of Social Work (1988), a sex offender treatment provider licensed by the Virginia Board of Psychology (1994), and a psychoanalyst accredited by the Contemporary Freudian Society, New York, and Washington, DC (2001).

Barbara Welner, RN, is a registered nurse and consultant with The Forensic Panel. Her experience spans six decades and most recently has focused on misconduct involving health care professionals, specialization in geriatric issues and nursing home standards, and elder abuse.

Michael Welner, MD, a forensic psychiatrist, is the chairman of The Forensic Panel, a forensic science consultation practice of psychiatry, neuropsychology, pathology, toxicology, and medicine. The Forensic Panel, which Dr. Welner founded, was the first of its kind to optimize prospective peer review to enhance the integrity, objectivity, and quality of forensic assessment. Dr. Welner has been the lead examiner in numerous highly sensitive and precedent setting court cases in various jurisdictions across America, including claims of drug-facilitated sex assault, ambiguous death, and a range of other sex and violent crimes. He developed typologies for classifying drug-facilitated sex assault offenders through the first research of such convicted offenders. Dr. Welner is perhaps best known for his groundbreaking research to standardize the distinction of the worst of crimes, known as the Depravity Standard (www.depravitystandard.org). He has been a central influence in important legislative advances, including landmark crisis mental health reform legislation that recently passed the United States Congress.

Section I

The Victim

1 Rape and Its Impact on the Victim

Ann Wolbert Burgess and Carrie M. Carretta

CONTENTS

Introduction..3
Rape Trauma Syndrome..3
History of Psychological Trauma..4
The Psychobiology of Trauma..5
Anxiety-Based Disorders..5
Depression...6
Substance Abuse 6
Psychosocial Adaptation 6
Childhood Sexual Abuse 7
Physical Health Effects of Rape...7
    Pregnancy...7
    Sexually Transmitted Diseases (STDs)..7
    Perception of Health...8
    Utilization of Health Services 8
    General Health Effects 8
    Genital Injury 8
Specific Populations...9
Global Perspectives..11
Overview of Culture and Its Relevance to Sexual Assault...11
    Cultural Values and Sexual Assault..12
    Research Related to Rape and Culture..12
Global Reports of Rape and Sexual Assault 13
Investigative Implications 14
Updated Disclosure Findings..14
Summary...14
References..14

INTRODUCTION

Rape affects the lives of victims and their significant others with various physical and emotional consequences. While some women and men are able to successfully manage the experience of rape in a timely manner, the majority of victims report psychological symptoms that were not present prior to the rape. This chapter discusses the mental health, physical health, and cultural components of rape and its effect on the victim.

RAPE TRAUMA SYNDROME

Prior to the work of Burgess and Holmstrom (1974), research on rape focused on the perpetrator as opposed to the victim. Through work with numerous rape survivors at a Boston hospital, the short- and long-term symptoms of rape trauma syndrome (RTS) were identified. RTS consists of an acute and long-term reorganization process that occurs at an actual or attempted sexual assault. During the assault victims experience fear of being raped and of being killed or hurt. The emotions of fear and anxiety may continue to be experienced by women for years after the attack. The acute phase is marked by major life disruption and disorganization. The individual goes through an emotional reaction that includes symptoms such as fear, anger, self-blame, shock, guilt, embarrassment, anxiety, and shame. Physical reactions include trauma from injuries, headaches, sleep disturbances, stomach pains, nausea, and vaginal pain or discomfort.

Women often demonstrate the impact of the assault in either an expressed or a controlled way. The expressed style includes overt behaviors that are commonly associated with trauma victims. Expressed behaviors include crying, hysteria, tenseness, confusion, and volatility. A controlled style involves more ambiguous behaviors that are not frequently associated with trauma survivors. Controlled behaviors include calmness, shock, and subdued appearance. Long-term reorganization occurs for a longer time and includes many symptoms. Common manifestations of this stage include fears and phobias, increased emotional lability, increased motor activity, and intrusive thoughts.

The major emotional symptoms include fear and anxiety. Immediately after the rape, physical symptoms—for example, generalized physical soreness or pain and gastrointestinal and genitourinary disturbance—are reported. Sleep and eating disturbances may also be present. Feelings of humiliation, degradation, guilt, anger, self-blame, and revenge are common. Fear of injury, mutilation, and death also predominate. Long-term reactions include dreams, nightmares, and phobias. Many women make lifestyle changes with the intention of avoiding the possibility of rape. Women may move or change their phone numbers or jobs. There is difficulty carrying out the normal routines of life. Preoccupations with recollections or flashbacks of the rape and a global fear of sex, men, and being alone in crowds are common. Recovery from rape trauma takes longer than recovery from other types of crimes and crises.

As part of the model of RTS, a continuum of sexual trauma sequelae exists relative to the type of sexual injury experienced (rape, pressured sex, stress) Burgess and Holmstrom (1974). Recent research added to this by uncovering a fourth category of sexual trauma, now classified as multiple rape type (Carretta & Burgess, 2013).

In 2013, the American Psychiatric Association (APA) revised the post-traumatic stress disorder (PTSD) diagnostic criteria in the fifth edition of its *Diagnostic and Statistical Manual of Mental Disorders* (DSM-5). Diagnostic criteria for PTSD include a history of exposure to a traumatic event that meets specific stipulations and symptoms from each of four symptom clusters: intrusion, avoidance, negative alterations in cognitions and mood, and alterations in arousal and reactivity. The sixth criterion concerns duration of symptoms; the seventh assesses functioning; and the eighth criterion clarifies symptoms as not attributable to a substance or co-occurring medical condition. Two specifications are noted including delayed expression and a dissociative subtype of PTSD, the latter of which is new to DSM-5. In both specifications, the full diagnostic criteria for PTSD must be met for application to be warranted (APA, 2013).

HISTORY OF PSYCHOLOGICAL TRAUMA

The concept that a person may develop symptoms following an accident has a long tradition; psychological trauma has been noted in literature as far back as the writings of Homer (van der Kolk, McFarlane, & Weisaeth, 1996). In Shakespeare's *King Henry IV*, Lady Percy describes the nightmares that Hotspur was suffering, particularly dreams of war. Samuel Pepys's *Diary* chronicles the effects of the September 2, 1666, Great Fire of London (Daly, 1983). Pepys outlines the gradual progression of the fire toward his home and the terror he sees in other people fleeing their homes; he subsequently develops "dreams of the fire and falling down of houses." Six months later he was still unable to sleep "without great terrors of fire." Charles Dickens was involved in a railway accident on June 9, 1865, and in a letter described the horrifying scene of the dead. Sometime after the accident he wrote of not feeling quite right, developed a phobia of railway travel, and described feeling weak as if recovering from a long illness (Forster, 1969).

Nostalgia was the diagnosis given to Swiss soldiers in 1678 by Dr. Johannes Hofer. In 1761, Austrian physician Josef Leopold Auenbrugger wrote about the widely diagnosed condition of nostalgia in his book *Inventum Novum*, writing that soldiers "become sad, taciturn, listless, solitary, musing, full of sighs, and moans. Finally, these cease to pay attention and become indifferent to everything which the maintenance of life requires of them. This disease is called nostalgia" (Anders, 2016).

THE PSYCHOBIOLOGY OF TRAUMA

The mental health field has long been interested in the aftermath of trauma; the debate has been over whether trauma was biophysiologically based or psychologically based. As early as 1859, French psychiatrist Briquet described symptoms of hysteria that he linked to childhood histories of trauma in 381 out of 501 patients. However, his belief was that the symptoms reflected a personal weakness in the person's ability to deal with the traumatic event. This notion continued and came to characterize soldiers suffering from post-trauma stress during World Wars I and II (van der Kolk et al., 1996). In fact, the term *shell shock*, as coined by British military psychiatrist Meyers, could be explained as part of the soldier's makeup. Even Freud supported the notion and argued that trauma symptoms were a "flight into illness by subconscious intentions … [and] that at the end of the war the war neurosis would disappear" (cited in van der Kolk et al., 1996, p. 55). Freud believed the symptoms were consciously incited and motivated by the individual's unconscious desire to get out of the war and that, once the war was over, the symptoms would disappear. This amelioration of symptoms, of course, did not occur (van der Kolk et al., 1996).

In 1889, Pierre Janet noted the psychobiological link to trauma response. He suggested that the psychological effects of trauma are stored in somatic memory and expressed as changes in the biological stress response. To quote psychiatrist van der Kolk (1994), "The body keeps score." Janet emphasized that intense emotional reactions make events traumatic by blocking the usual information processing into existing memory paths (Janet, 1889). He also observed that traumatized patients reacted to environmental cues reminiscent of the trauma, were unable to put the trauma behind them, had trouble learning from their experiences, became fixated on the past or obsessed with the trauma, and behaved and felt as if they were traumatized all over again without being able to determine the origins of the feelings (van der Kolk & van der Hart, 1991).

Another group of researchers looking at stress and its physiological effects has contributed to the knowledge base of trauma. Hans Seyle (1956) suggested that some stress experiences were growth enhancing. In contrast, repetitive, continuous, escalating, and uncontrollable stressful experiences may put the person at risk for illness. Stress has been shown to be mediated by the hypothalamic–pituitary–adrenocortical (HPAC) biologic stress systems. Stress that challenges homeostasis stimulates secretion of glucocorticoids, which are catabolic hormones that help mobilize stored energy to support the body's physiologic response to stress for use in the "flight or fight" response (Cannon, 1932; Seyle, 1956; van der Kolk, 1994).

ANXIETY-BASED DISORDERS

The emotional picture depicted with RTS is consistent with the symptom pattern of PTSD. This may be an immediate or chronic response to physical or sexual violence. PTSD is diagnosed in individuals who have experienced, have witnessed, or were confronted with a traumatic event and have characteristic resulting symptoms. Resulting symptoms include persistent reexperiencing of the event, persistent avoidance of stimuli associated with the trauma, and symptoms of increased arousal (APA, 2013). Rape victims may experience flashbacks, nightmares, or some experience in which the traumatic event is reenacted. They may also feel the need for safety rituals, such as extensive checking of locks. Sexual violence is associated with behavior categorized as that of avoidance or of increased arousal (Flack et al., 2007). Avoidance behaviors are efforts to avoid anything associated with the rape. This can include efforts to avoid feelings, thoughts, activities, places, and people. Other victims may have symptoms of increased arousal. Arousal symptoms include being extremely watchful of the environment, insomnia, anger, and rage. These behaviors may persist for years after the attack and usually cause some disruption in the individual's interpersonal, social, or occupational functioning.

Individuals who have a history of depression or alcohol abuse or who experienced injury during the rape are at greater risk for experiencing PTSD. Past experiences of violence predict future experiences of violence. This is important because each additional traumatic event increases the risk of an individual's developing PTSD (Breslau, 2002b). A delay in disclosing the assault is associated with the development of PTSD (Ullman & Filipas, 2001).

Additional findings of relevance include recent research examining a group of 242 women who reported their most recent unwanted sexual experience to have occurred within the past 5 years. Findings from this study showed that PTSD was significantly higher in those who had experienced a forcible rape or multiple rape-type trauma ($p = 0.044$). Further, no differences in respondents with PTSD over a 5-year period relative to delayed onset, symptom duration, or severity of symptoms, suggesting the permanency of the trauma narrative being encoded and stored in memory (Carretta & Burgess, 2013).

DEPRESSION

After the experience of sexual trauma, depression is a common consequence. Symptoms of depression include significant weight loss or gain, sleep disturbances, increased or decreased motor activity, loss of energy, loss of pleasure in activities of life, decreased concentration, feelings of worthlessness, depressed mood most of the day, and recurrent thoughts of death or suicidal ideation. Symptoms of current depression were three times higher among those who reported experiencing sexual assault than those who did not experience sexual assault. Sexual violence is associated with severe depression in young women (Csoboth, Birkas, & Purebl, 2005). Adult victims of sexual assault also reported current hopelessness and suicidal ideation (Masho, Odor, & Adera, 2005). An online study also supported a statistically significant difference ($p = 0.013$) in symptoms of depression based on Beck Depression Inventory II scores (BDI-II) (Carretta & Burgess, 2013). *Post hoc* analysis of the overall difference in depression revealed that the multiple rape type (newly identified group from this study) ($p = 0.010$) and the forcible sex group ($p = 0.016$) had higher levels of depression than did the group experiencing sex stress.

SUBSTANCE ABUSE

A number of research articles have documented an association between rape and sexual assault and substance abuse. A high incidence of substance abuse was reported among female veterans who presented requesting help for sexual trauma. Current alcohol abuse was two times higher among those who reported sexual assault than among those who did not report experiencing sexual assault. Data from a 2-year longitudinal study suggest that after women were sexually assaulted, the odds of both alcohol abuse and drug use were significantly increased (Kilpatrick, Whalley, & Edmunds, 2002). Similarly, women who reported a history of forced sex, compared with those who never experienced forced sex, were more likely to drink alcohol four or more times a week and use illicit drugs (Masho et al., 2005). It was also suggested that PTSD seems to serve as a mediator between childhood rape and subsequent alcohol use.

PSYCHOSOCIAL ADAPTATION

Sexual assault report is associated with emotional trauma and psychological distress. Women who were sexually assaulted report fears and phobias of being alone and associated with the site or other characteristics of the assault. For example, a woman who was raped outdoors may fear being outdoors. Many women experience disruptions to their sexual functioning, feeling an inability to feel intimacy in their sexual relationships. Lowered self-esteem is often associated with victimization. After experiencing sexual assault it is common for women to report self-blame in the form of feeling embarrassed, ashamed, or guilty (Ruch & Wang, 2006). Self-blame after rape has also been associated with psychological distress (Burgess & Holmstrom, 1974). Past victimization also seems to put one at risk for subsequent victimization (Field & Caetano, 2005). While much research has identified patterns of repeated victimization of individuals, the cause is likely to be a complex interplay of multiple factors.

Carretta, Burgess and DeMarco reported a significant difference between groups citing first time disclosure versus those who had previously disclosed their rape in rates of seeking treatment for emotional injuries with both medical providers ($p = 0.003$), and nonmedical therapist/counselors ($p < 0.001$). In both cases, a higher proportion of those admitting to first time disclosure reported never seeking treatment for emotional injuries from medical provider (52 of 58, 90%) or a therapist/counselor (46 of 58, 79%) than those who had previously disclosed (65% and 42%, respectively). The overwhelming majority of those citing first time disclosure ($n = 46$, 70.3%), cited they had never seen a nonmedical therapist/counselor for emotional injuries, whereas the majority (57.8%) of those citing prior disclosure reported seeing a therapist/counselor more than five times (Carretta, Burgess, & DeMarco, 2015).

CHILDHOOD SEXUAL ABUSE

Women who were sexually abused as children are vulnerable to many of the same consequences as women who were raped as adults. Women who were raped as minors were twice as likely to report rape as an adult than women without abuse histories (Tjaden & Thoennes, 2006). Adult survivors of child sexual abuse have been known to experience PTSD in addition to difficulty in relationships, guilt, low self-esteem, inability to trust others, and flashbacks (Breslau, 2002a). Depression, suicidal thoughts and behaviors, extreme anger, and mood swings are also present. Childhood sexual abuse has also been associated with depression, self-destructive behaviors, alcohol use, and substance abuse.

PHYSICAL HEALTH EFFECTS OF RAPE

Sexual assault of a woman produces many undesired physical and psychological effects. In the immediate aftermath of rape, a woman may be injured on the genitals and on other parts of her body. Initial medical care is essential. Other direct concerns are the prevention of sexually transmitted disease and pregnancy. Some groups, such as elderly or homeless women, are at greater risk of physical injury following sexual assault.

PREGNANCY

Researchers have estimated the incidence of pregnancy among rape victims of reproductive age to be significant, about 3–5% (Holmes, Resnick, Kilpatrick, & Best, 1996; Masho et al., 2005). Holmes et al. used a national probability sample of 4,008 adult American women surveyed longitudinally over a 3-year period. Among the 34 cases of pregnancy that resulted from rape, most of the women were adolescents and assaulted by a known assailant. However, Lathrop (1998) noted that pregnancy resulting from rape was more prevalent than generally recognized due to underreporting of sexual assaults leading to underestimated crime statistics. Limited research has addressed the impact of rape on a pregnant woman.

SEXUALLY TRANSMITTED DISEASES (STDs)

Generally, researchers have studied the relationship between rape and transmission of gonorrhea, chlamydia, trichomoniasis, bacterial vaginosis, syphilis, and HIV. However, one case has been reported where acute hepatitis A occurred 4 months after multiple rape (Crowell & Burgess, 1996). Forced sex is associated with increased incidence of developing pelvic inflammatory disease and reoccurrence of STDs (Champion, Piper, Shain, Perdue, & Newton, 2001; Upchurch & Kusunoki, 2004). Contracting a sexually transmitted disease is one factor that prompts women to seek health care after rape. Limited research documents occurrence of STDs; however, as many as 2% of women report contracting an STD as a consequences of sexual violence (Masho et al., 2005). Exact numbers that document the presence of HIV infection after rape do not exist.

PERCEPTION OF HEALTH

Women who have been sexually assaulted are more likely than women who have not been assaulted to report poorer health perception (Masho et al., 2005). Health fears, such as worry of disease or injuries from the assailant, are commonly reported by women after sexual violence (Ruch & Wang, 2006). Survivors of trauma often report lower health-related quality of life (Schnurr & Green, 2004). Determination of one's perception of health is important as it can serve as a predictor of the use of health care services.

UTILIZATION OF HEALTH SERVICES

Survivors of sexual assault have been found to be disproportionately frequent users of health care services due to the acute and chronic physical, somatic, and psychological consequences of assault (Schnurr & Green, 2004). Survivors have been found to have increased medical service usage even when perceptions of health and somatic symptoms are no longer elevated, reflecting the insidious and long-term effects of sexual violence. The number of medical visits increased significantly during the year of the crime and was most pronounced in the second year after the crime (Koss, 1993).

GENERAL HEALTH EFFECTS

Women suffer from acute and chronic physical symptoms and health effects after sexual violence. These health symptoms may persist for years after the initial trauma. A third of sexual assault victims in the National Violence against Women Survey reported physical injury, most often scratches, bruises, and welts (Tjaden & Thoennes, 2006). In the acute phase, genital and nongenital injuries, sexually transmitted diseases, and pregnancy are immediate health concerns. Sexual assault is a major assault on the body and the body reacts by bringing on a range of physical symptoms. Physical force and bodily injury are present in most sexual assault cases (Riggs, Houry, Long, Markovchick, & Feldhaus, 2000).

Women who have been sexually assaulted may also have gynecological symptoms such as chronic pelvic pain, painful urination, bladder infection, and painful intercourse (Campbell, Lichty, Sturza, & Raja, 2006). Sexual violence has also been associated with headaches, back pain, gastrointestinal symptoms, and premenstrual symptoms as well as a host of other physical health consequences (Campbell, 2002).

In a study of 298 African-American women recruited through the VA hospital women's clinic, sexual victimization was associated with more frequent gynecological health symptoms (Campbell et al., 2006). Women with histories of physical and sexual abuse were much more likely to report more somatic symptoms and functional disability (Eby, Campbell, Sullivan, & Davidson, 1995). In women who returned for follow-up, Holmes, Resnick, and Frampton (1998) reported that the common concerns were disturbances in sleep, sexual function, and appetite.

GENITAL INJURY

While general body trauma is common, many women experience genital injury. In a study of rape victims seen in an emergency department, genital trauma occurred in 57% of cases (Riggs et al., 2000).

Genital trauma was more common in women younger than 20 and older than 49 (Sugar, Fine, & Eckert, 2004). Although genital injury does not occur in all sexual assault cases, conviction rates are higher when genital injury is sustained (Palmer, McNulty, D'Este, & Donovan, 2004). Forensic evidence of genital injury strengthens the legal claim of force.

SPECIFIC POPULATIONS

Some specific populations have been determined to be more at risk for physical injury with sexual assault. Rape of elderly women is underreported and the needs of these victims are often neglected (Burgess, Dowdell, & Brown, 2000). As previously stated, women over the age of 49 are more likely to sustain genital injury (Sugar et al., 2004). Genital trauma, abrasions, or edema were more common in postmenopausal women than in younger women. Authors have written about the necessity of age-related assessment techniques (Burgess et al., 2000).

Decades of research on violence have indicated that violence against women is most often partner violence (Tjaden & Thoennes, 2000). Sexual assault often occurs from a known perpetrator, most often a current or former partner. Limited research includes multiple forms of violence. Sexual assault by a date was associated with physical assaults, sexual assaults, and stalking by an intimate partner (Slashinski, Coker, & Davis, 2003). Battered women who were both physically and sexually abused had higher levels of PTSD than women who experienced only physical abuse (Bennice, Resick, Mechanic, & Astin, 2003). Sexual violence is associated with an increased risk of femicide, or homicide of a woman by her abusive intimate partner (McFarlane, Campbell, & Watson, 2002).

Findings from the National Violence against Women survey suggest that younger women are at greater risk of sexual victimization than older women (Tjaden & Thoennes, 1998). In addition, experts have asserted that women on college campuses are at greater risk for sexual victimization than other women of the same age group and women in the general population. Fisher, Cullen, and Turner (2000) report that 2.8% of college women surveyed in a large nationally representative sample had experienced a completed or attempted rape during the past 6.91 months and those women were more likely to have been raped or sexually assaulted by someone who is known to them than by a stranger (Fisher et al., 2000). Johnson and Sigler (2000) reported that 19% of college women surveyed said that they were forced to have sex at some point during their lives, most commonly in dating situations. Wolitzky-Taylor, Resnick, Amstadter, McCauley, Ruggiero, and Kilpatrick (2011) interviewed a national sample of 2,000 college women about rape experiences in 2006 and found 11.5% of college women in the sample reported their most recent/only rape experience to authorities, with only 2.7% of rapes involving drugs and/or alcohol reported (Wolitzky-Taylor et al., 2011). Minority status (i.e., nonwhite race) was associated with lower likelihood of reporting, whereas sustaining injuries during the rape was associated with increased likelihood of reporting.

Currently, there is a developing published evidence on rape reporting and disclosure.

Data from the 2004 crime victimization survey suggest that women are more likely to be raped by a friend or acquaintance and that sexual victimization is reported by 36% of women (Catalano, 2005). As in adult women, college women also may experience sexual violence within the context of a known perpetrator, most commonly an acquaintance or a current, former, or potential partner. Following nonstranger sexual assault, victims feel blame, guilt, and emotional distress (Fisher, Cullen, & Daigle, 2005; Fisher et al., 2000; Flack et al., 2007). Secrets, especially those involving incest, rape, and abortion, are closely aligned with nondisclosure. Georg Simmel defines secrets, as "consciously willed concealment" (1950:449) that involve a tension that when revealed breaks its power that can result in positive or negative outcome (Simmel & Wolff, 1950). Secrecy sets barriers. A secret disclosed may advance to betrayal. Simmel describes a secret being surrounded by temptation and possibility of betrayal; and the external danger of being discovered is interwoven with the internal danger of giving oneself away (Simmel & Wolff, 1950:334). As long as the rape remains cloaked in secrecy, the victim only has to manage that information internally; once the rape is disclosed, the victim has to manage the external reactions.

Alcohol is often associated with sexual violence in college students (Abbey, Zawacki, Buck, Clinton, & McAuslan, 2006). Alcohol use may be seen as both a risk factor for sexual victimization and an outcome of sexual victimization. Other outcomes are mental health symptoms and physical injury (Amar, 2007a). Other health risk behaviors associated with sexual violence include unhealthy weight control, arrest for sex crimes and prostitution, teen pregnancy, multiple partners, and HIV-related risk behaviors (Silverman, Raj, Mucci, & Hathaway, 2001; Wordes & Nunez, 2002). As past experiences of violence predict future occurrences, it is important to identify adolescent and young adult victims. Youths, women who are homeless, and survivors of gang rape are other at-risk populations. Runaway youths frequently report sexual abuse within the family as a reason for leaving home.

Male on male rape is a form of sexual violence that, despite worldwide prevalence, remains vastly underreported and unrecognized. Society is becoming increasingly aware of male rape. However, experts believe that current male rape statistics vastly under-represent the actual number of males age 12 and over who are raped each year. Rape crisis counselors estimate that while only one in 50 raped women report the crime to the police, the rates of under-reporting among males are even higher. The lack of tracking of sexual crimes against men and the lack of research about the effects of male rape are indicative of the attitude held by society at large—that while male rape occurs, it is not an acceptable topic for discussion.

This type of sexual violence is cloaked in stigma and shame. Male rape, as similar to male-female rape, is predominantly an assertion of power and aggression rather than an attempt on the part of the perpetrator to satisfy sexual desire. The effect of the attack is to damage the victim's psyche, rob him of his pride, and intimidate him.

It is not uncommon for a male rape victim to blame himself for the rape, believing that he in some way gave permission to the rapist. Some assailants may try to get their victim to ejaculate because for the rapist, it symbolizes their complete sexual control over their victim's body. Since ejaculation is not always within conscious control but rather an involuntary physiological reaction, rapists frequently succeed at getting their male victims to ejaculate. This aspect of the attack is extremely stressful and confusing to the victim as it misidentifies ejaculation with orgasm, and the victim may be bewildered by his physiological response during the sexual assault.

Military sexual trauma (MST) is the term used by Veteran Affairs (VA) to refer to experiences of sexual assault or repeated, threatening sexual harassment that a Veteran experienced during his or her military service. This definition comes from Federal law (Title 38 U.S. Code 1720D) and is "psychological trauma, which in the judgment of a VA mental health professional, resulted from a physical assault of a sexual nature, battery of a sexual nature, or sexual harassment which occurred while the Veteran was serving on active duty or active duty for training." Sexual harassment is further defined as "repeated, unsolicited verbal or physical contact of a sexual nature which is threatening in character." In 2003 the U.S. Air Force Academy was also accused of systemically ignoring an on-going sexual assault problem on its campus. More than 50 cases of sexual assault were identified as having occurred at the US Air Force Academy between January 1993 and December 2002 (Mullen & O'Connor, 2011). An online study by Burgess, Carretta, and Lee (2016) examined a subset of the sample who affirmed having experienced one or more episodes of rape either while actively serving in the military, or while on a military property. Of the 60 cases analyzed, 11 (18.3%) were male.

Individuals with disabilities also compose a high-risk and neglected group of sexual violence victims. Developmental disabilities represent a cluster of disorders that are usually present in early childhood and represent some impairment in the acquisition of developmental milestones. For example, not walking or speaking at the appropriate time in childhood would be failure to meet a developmental milestone. Mental retardation represents deficits in the general intellectual function and adaptive functioning of an individual. The disorder is characterized by deficits in communication, self-care, home living, and social and interpersonal skills, and an IQ of 70 or below. Communication skills range from limitations in speech in the moderate mental retardation population to little, if any speech development in the profoundly mentally retarded population. It is estimated that mental retardation exists in about 1% of the general population.

The pervasive developmental disorders are a group of conditions in which expected social skills, language skills, and behavioral repertoire do not develop appropriately or are lost in early childhood. Autistic disorder, the best known of the disorders, is characterized by markedly abnormal or impaired communication and a markedly restricted repertoire of activity and social interest. Language may be totally absent or characterized by immature structure or idiosyncratic utterances. Nonverbal communication is either absent or socially inappropriate.

Autistic disorder occurs at a rate of two to five cases per 10,000 (0.02–0.05%) under age 12. About 40% of autistic children are moderately, severely, or profoundly mentally retarded, and retarded children may have behavior symptoms that include autistic symptoms.

Individuals who have developmental disabilities are vulnerable to sexual assault and abuse. As compared with women without disabilities, women with disabilities were four times more likely to be sexually assaulted (Martin et al., 2006). Women with health or emotional impairments may be less able to recognize impending danger and successfully fight off or evade an attack. In the aftermath, individuals with learning disabilities may not have the language to express and explain what has happened to them. Individuals with disabilities may be dependent upon others for their care, which could increase their vulnerability for abuse. Behavioral changes, such as acting out, may be the only clues that something is wrong with the individual.

GLOBAL PERSPECTIVES

Research conducted in industrialized countries has shown that the likelihood of a woman being raped or having to fight off an attempted rape is high. In developing countries, research suggests that rape is an ever present threat and a reality for millions of women. In different parts of the world, at least one in five women suffers rape or attempted rape in her lifetime. It is also well known that rape and sexual torture are systematically used as weapons of war. Violence against women is present in every country, cutting across boundaries of culture, class, education, income, ethnicity, and age. Even though most societies denounce violence against women, the reality is that violations against women's human rights are often sanctioned under the garb of cultural practices and norms, or through misinterpretation of religious tenets (World Health Organization, 2001). Child sexual violence is reported in many countries across the globe, including Kenya, Madagascar, and Congo (Salah, 2005). The history and continuing tradition of the United States as a melting pot society, wherein many individuals of various cultural, racial, religious, and ethnic backgrounds coexist, make knowledge of cultural considerations of rape and sexual assault essential.

OVERVIEW OF CULTURE AND ITS RELEVANCE TO SEXUAL ASSAULT

Culture provides a strong influence on one's perceptions, behaviors, and attitudes. Cultural perceptions affect the way people are viewed and expected to act in certain situations. Cultural values are unique to a group and guide actions and decisions. The importance of culture to rape and sexual assault is affected then by the cultural values and norms related to sexual behavior and the social organization determining roles and responsibilities of men and women. These two factors are closely intertwined. In a culture that values patriarchy and diminished social status and rights of women, the forcible rape of women may not be a crime of major importance. While in a matriarchal society or even one that is matrilineal or matrilocal, abuse of a woman would result in public humiliation, ostracism, and loss of honor (Bohn & Holz, 1996). In the Muslim community, families' honor lies in the virtue of women. Modesty is emphasized by the use of the veil, and chastity is seen as protecting the virtue of women (Amar, 2007b). Norms for sexual behavior may include the double standard of prized virginity of women and an emphasis on male experience with sex. While researchers have articulated the importance of the relationship between the concepts of sexuality and culture, limited research exists in this area. It must be acknowledged that not all members of a particular group are alike and this is not intended to provide an "all Latina women will do this" kind of approach. Not only do cultural and ethnic factors operate in varying degrees in the lives of people, but also the diversity within a culture may be greater than between cultural groups.

CULTURAL VALUES AND SEXUAL ASSAULT

The way a cultural or ethnic group defines gender roles and the woman's place in society impacts how rape will be perceived. In the United States, multiple examples of male superiority and female subjugation exist in popular literature, media, fashion, art, and language. These cultural symbols help us to form our attitudes and beliefs that are then further translated into laws, court proceedings, police behavior, educational curricula, and social service programs. Society sends a strong message that a woman's value is related to her sexuality and that rape decreases that value. This is highlighted in the message that the rape of a virgin is worse than that of a nonvirgin. Myths that blame victims for rape and broad conceptualizations of sexual assault are influenced by ethnic-specific cultural values and norms (Neville & Heppner, 1999). Cultural values are the underpinnings of our beliefs and attitudes and assist the victim, friends, family, police, and any helper in deriving meaning of the experience.

While the overarching beliefs of a patriarchal society affect all women within the society, special concerns exist for women of color or of other ethnic backgrounds. Stereotypes such as the following prevail:

- African-American culture is a culture of violence.
- Latin cultures are based on brutal machismo.
- Asian cultures train women to pleasure their men.
- Historically, African-American women have been stereotyped as sexually uninhibited women who could not be raped because they welcomed sexual advances.

Within the various ethnic groups, issues related to gender and power further affect women. For example, in the traditional Hispanic family, the authority figure is the husband and the woman holds the subjugated roles of wife and mother (Torres & Han, 2000). In many Latino families, adolescents recognize a double standard in that the dating rules are more restrictive for boys than for girls. In South Asian countries, the family structure, in which the man is the undisputed ruler of the household and activities within the family are seen as private, allows physical and sexual violence to occur at home (Niaz, 2003). Similarly, in research with women in South Africa, it was observed that abuse and sexual assault of women are rampant because of the endemic culture of violence and the customs, culture, and tradition that tend to objectify women and make them feel like male property (Dangor, Hoff, & Scott, 1998). Recent study findings suggest that the majority of participants in research relative to sexual assault continue to be Caucasian (Carretta et al., 2015) making it difficult to understand how the needs of ethnically diverse groups can best be served.

RESEARCH RELATED TO RAPE AND CULTURE

Much of the available research attempts to provide for cultural diversity by using samples from ethnically, culturally, and racially diverse populations. However, limited research attempts to provide results that have been evaluated using a culturally sensitive approach. Much of the research reflects a middle-class European–American perspective that may not be applicable to women of various cultural backgrounds.

Researchers have attempted to increase our understanding of the cultural definition of rape. An interesting study by Lira, Koss, and Russo (1999) described the differences in meaning of words that are regarded as similar by Americans. Focus groups with seven Mexican immigrant women revealed that a distinction was made between rape and violation. Violation was regarded with strong disapproval and disgust. It was viewed as a human violation of rights and freedom. Rape, however, was viewed as distinctly different. The woman involved was perceived as "loose" and was seen as having complicity in and blame for the rape. However, if rape was defined according to the traditional Mexican definition of kidnapping or holding a woman by force, then the participants viewed the act as undesired by the victim. These findings illustrate the importance of clarifying culture-specific meanings and of thorough review of instruments and data collection tools for culture biases and ambiguities.

Sexual abuse and rape by an intimate partner are not considered crimes in many countries around the globe, and women in many societies do not consider forced sex to be rape (World Health Organization, 2001). Culturally sanctioned beliefs about the rights and privileges of husbands have historically legitimized a man's domination over his wife and warranted his use of violence to control her (Crowell & Burgess, 1996). However, women who have been forced into sex by an intimate partner are at risk for the same risks and consequences—for example, sexually transmitted diseases, physical trauma, and emotional consequences—as women who are sexually assaulted by a stranger (Campbell & Soeken, 1999).

GLOBAL REPORTS OF RAPE AND SEXUAL ASSAULT

According to a report on violence against women issued by the World Health Organization (2001), women who are the victims of sexual violence are often reluctant to report the crime to police, family, or others. In countries where a woman's virginity is associated with family honor, unmarried women who report a rape may be forced to marry their attacker. As a way of restoring family honor, shamed fathers or brothers may murder some women. In some countries, a woman who has been raped may be prosecuted and imprisoned for committing the "crime" of sex outside marriage, if she cannot prove that the incident was in fact rape. To offer proof would mean to present witnesses to the act. In some Middle Eastern cultures, witnesses must be males. In reporting sexual violence, a victim is admitting an offense. If the victim cannot provide witnesses that she was raped, she will be punished.

Starzynski, Ullman, Filipas, and Townsend (2005) emphasized that deciding who to tell about sexual assault is an important and potentially consequential decision for sexual assault survivors. A diverse sample of adult sexual assault survivors in the Chicago area was surveyed about sexual assault experiences, social reactions received when disclosing assault to others, attributions of blame, coping strategies, and PTSD. Women disclosing to both formal and informal support sources experienced more stereotypical assaults, had more PTSD symptoms, engaged in less behavioral self-blame, and received more negative social reactions than those disclosing to informal support sources only.

The military practice of rape for the purpose of genocide practiced in Bosnia-Herzegovina and Croatia involved rape leading to forced pregnancy. Women were held in rape camps until they passed the time frame for a safe abortion. The genocidal aspects of the pregnancy lie in the view of the rapist that the child is viewed as Serbian with no ethnicity being derived from the mother. Sexual violence is used as a tool of war to demoralize entire communities. News reports tell of sexual crime in wars in Darfur, Sudan, Sierra Leone, Burundi, and Congo. The demoralization results from a vicious attack on women that attacks the dignity of the individual and her entire community (Goldstein, 2001). Victims are stigmatized by the attack and male members of the community are made to feel helpless in protecting their women.

What is important about knowledge of the rape and sexual assault of women from around the world is that, when immigrants present in the United States, they still carry with them the beliefs, attitudes, and perceptions of their native land. Their family members also view them from within the same lens. Rape is often an unforgivable offense within a culture. When the cultural values and norms are different for two individuals, much discussion and reflection are needed by the helper to provide help that is congruent with the background of the victim.

INVESTIGATIVE IMPLICATIONS

Parallel with the incidence of rape being far more extensive than reported in official statistics is the fact that the large majority of rapists are never apprehended. In 2007, there were 90,427 incidents of rape reported to law enforcement that resulted in only 23,307 arrests (FBI, 2008). Victimization data show a higher number of rapes and sexual assaults—191,670 (Catalano, 2005), which means that potentially more than half of rapes and sexual assaults go unreported (and therefore unpunished) to law enforcement (Fisher, Daigle, Cullen, & Turner, 2003). Clearly the vast majority of rapists are never brought to justice as FBI clearance rates for rape averages about 50% per year.

Clearly, victims will be best helped when the investigator is able to provide culturally sensitive care. Cultural sensitivity would include behaviors that are open to diversity among individuals. It is important for one to recognize that there is no standard cookbook approach. There can be much diversity among members of the same ethnic or racial background. Assessment or intake tools can incorporate questions that uncover the cultural significance of events for clients. By asking victims about the meaning this event may hold for their family, church, or social group, the investigator gains insight into the perspective of the survivor and will be able to implement a culturally sensitive plan of action.

UPDATED DISCLOSURE FINDINGS

Carretta et al. (2015) examined 242 female participants aged 18–64 who had reported a completed rape with the past 5 years. Significant differences were found between those with first time disclosure versus those reporting having previously disclosed. A subset analysis of those having experienced one or more occurrences of unwanted sexual assault while involved with the military yielded results highlighting the differences between male and female assault and disclosure. Almost three-quarters (72.7%) of the males used this anonymous survey to report their unwanted sexual experience for the first time versus 36.7% of females (almost twice the percentage of male vs. female) (Burgess et al., 2016). Further, although rates of reporting are low in general relative to rape, reporting of military sexual assault experiences are even lower. None of the 11 males reported being raped to authorities and only 7 (14.3%) of the 49 females reported the sexual assault incident.

SUMMARY

Impact on the victim from even a single incident of sexual assault is profound. Although experiences may be perceived as different based on the specific circumstances surrounding the attack(s), the negative sequelae is present and may appear as physical, emotional, and/or psychological manifestations. Culture and the current political climate in a region continue to play a role in rape and the subsequent trauma globally, and successful prosecution remains an ongoing problem in both developing and industrialized nations. Additionally, disclosure remains elusive in large part due to fear and shame and blame being directed toward the victim. Victimization in the military remains an ever-present phenomenon. Further research devoted to enabling disclosure, changing cultural acceptance of rape as a means for control and dominance, and more effective resources to facilitate prosecution of perpetrators is critical and warranted.

REFERENCES

Abbey, A., Zawacki, T., Buck, P. O., Clinton, A. M., and McAuslan, P. 2006. Alcohol and sexual assault, http://pubs.niaaa.nih.gov/publications/arh25–1/43–51.htm.

Amar, A. F. 2007a. Dating violence: Comparing victims who are also perpetrators with victims who are not. *Journal of Forensic Nursing*, 3(1): 35–41.

Amar, A. F. 2007b. Understanding the veil: Nonstranger sexual assault in the Muslim community. *Journal of Forensic Nursing*, 3(3): 134–136.

American Psychiatric Association. 2013. *Diagnostic and statistical manual of mental disorders*, fifth edition. Washington, DC: Author.

Anders, C. J. 2016. From "Irritable heart" to "Shellshock": How post-traumatic stress became a disease, August 5, 2016. Retrieved from http://io9.gizmodo.com/5898560/from-irritable-heart-to-shellshock-how-post-traumatic-stress-became-a-disease.

Bennice, J. A., Resick, P. A., Mechanic, M., and Astin, M. 2003. The relative effects of intimate partner physical and sexual violence on post-traumatic stress disorder symptomatology. *Violence and Victims*, 18: 94–97.

Bohn, D. K., and Holz, K. A. 1996. Sequelae of abuse. *Journal of Nurse Midwifery*, 41(6): 442–455.

Breslau, N. 2002a. Epidemiologic studies of trauma, post-traumatic stress disorder, and other psychiatric disorders. *Canadian Journal of Psychiatry*, 47(10): 923–929.

Breslau, N. 2002b. Gender differences in trauma and posttraumatic stress disorder. *The Journal of Gender-Specific Medicine*, 5(1): 34–40.

Burgess, A. W., and Holmstrom, L. L. 1974. Rape trauma syndrome. *American Journal of Psychiatry*, 131: 981–986.

Burgess, A. W., Carretta, C., and Lee, W. 2016. Online reporting of military sexual trauma. *Military Medicine*, 181(4): 350–355.

Burgess, A. W., Dowdell, E. B., and Brown, K. 2000. The elderly rape victim: Stereotypes, perpetrators, and implications for practice. *Journal of Emergency Nursing*, 26(5): 516–518.

Campbell, J. C. 2002. Health consequences of intimate partner violence. *The Lancet*, 359: 1331–1336.

Campbell, J. C., and Soeken, K. L. 1999. Forced sex and intimate partner violence: Effects on women's risk and women's health. *Violence Against Women*, 5(9): 1017–1035.

Campbell, R., Lichty, L. F., Sturza, M., and Raja, S. 2006. Gynecological health impact of sexual assault. *Research in Nursing and Health*, 29(5): 399–413.

Cannon, W. B. 1932. *The wisdom of the body*. New York: Norton.

Carretta, C. M., and Burgess, A. W. 2013. Symptom response to a continuum of sexual trauma. *Violence and Victims*, 28(2): 248–258.

Carretta, C. M., Burgess, A. W., and DeMarco, R. F. 2015. To tell or not to tell. *Violence Against Women*, 21(9): 1145–1165.

Catalano, S. M. 2005. *Criminal victimization, 2004*. Washington, DC: United States Department of Justice.

Champion, J. D., Piper, J., Shain, R. N., Perdue, S. T., and Newton, E. R. 2001. Minority women with sexually transmitted diseases: Sexual abuse and risk for pelvic inflammatory disease. *Research in Nursing and Health*, 24(1): 38–43.

Crowell, N. A., and Burgess, A. W. (eds.). 1996. *Understanding violence against women*. Washington, DC: National Academy Press.

Csoboth, C. T., Birkas, E., and Purebl, G. 2005. Living in fear of experiencing physical and sexual abuse is associated with severe depressive symptomatology among young women. *Journal of Women's Health*, 14(5): 441–448.

Daly, R. J. 1983. Samuel Pepys and post-traumatic stress disorder. *British Journal of Psychiatry*, 143: 64–68.

Dangor, Z., Hoff, L. A., and Scott, R. 1998. Woman abuse in South Africa: An exploratory study. *Violence Against Women*, 4(2): 125–152.

Eby, K. K., Campbell, J. C., Sullivan, C. M., and Davidson, W. S. 1995. Health effects of experiences of sexual violence for women with abusive partners. *Health Care for Women International*, 16: 563–576.

Federal Bureau of Investigation. 2008. *Uniform crime reports*. Washington, DC: Federal Bureau of Investigation.

Field, C. A., and Caetano, R. 2005. Longitudinal model predicting mutual partner violence among white, black, and Hispanic couples in the United States general population. *Violence and Victims*, 20(5): 499–511.

Fisher, B. S., Cullen, F. T., and Daigle, L. E. 2005. The discovery of acquaintance rape: The salience of methodological innovation and rigor. *Journal of Interpersonal Violence*, 4: 493–500.

Fisher, B. S., Cullen, F. T., and Turner, M. G. 2000. *The sexual victimization of college women*. Washington, DC: National Institute of Justice.

Fisher, B. S., Daigle, L. E., Cullen, F. T., and Turner, M. 2003. Reporting sexual victimization to the police and others: Results from a national-level study of college women. *Criminal Justice and Behavior*, 31(1), 6–38.

Flack, W. F., Daubman, M. C., Caron, M. L., Asadorian, N. R., Giglotti, S. N., Hall, A. T., et al. 2007. Risk factors and consequences of unwanted sex among university students: Hooking up, alcohol, and stress response. *Journal of Interpersonal Violence*, 22(2): 139–157.

Forster, J. 1969. *The life of Charles Dickens*, 2. London: J. M. Dent and Sons.

Goldstein, J. S. 2001. *War and gender*. Cambridge: Cambridge University Press.

Holmes, M. M., Resnick, H. S., Kilpatrick, D. G., and Best, C. 1996. Rape-related pregnancy: Estimates and descriptive characteristics from a national sample of women. *American Journal of Obstetrics and Gynecology*, 175: 320–325.

Holmes, M. M., Resnick, H. W., and Frampton, D. 1998. Follow-up of sexual assault victims. *American Journal of Obstetrics and Gynecology*, 179: 336–342.

Janet, P. 1889. *L'automatisme psychologique*. Paris: Alcan.

Johnson, I. M., and Sigler, R. T. 2000. Forced sexual intercourse among intimates. *Journal of Family Violence*, 15: 95–108.

Kilpatrick, D. G., Whalley, A., and Edmunds, C. 2002. Sexual assault. In *National victim assistance academy textbook*, ed. A. Seymour, M. Murray, J. Sigmon, M. Hook, C. Edmunds, M. Gaboway, and G. Coleman, chap. 12. Washington, DC: Department of Justice, Office of Victims of Crime.

Koss, M. P. 1993. Detecting the scope of rape: A review of prevalence research methods. *Journal of Interpersonal Violence*, 8: 198–222.

Lathrop, A. 1998. Pregnancy resulting from rape. *Journal of Obstetric, Gynecologic and Neonatal Nursing*, 27(1): 25–31.

Lira, L. R., Koss, M. R., and Russo, N. F. 1999. Mexican American women's definitions of rape and sexual abuse. *Hispanic Journal of Behavioral Sciences*, 21: 236–265.

Martin, S. L., Ray, N., Sotres Alvarez, D., Kupper, L. L., Moracco, K. E., Dickens, P. A., et al. 2006. Physical and sexual assault of women with disabilities. *Violence Against Women*, 12(9): 823–837.

Masho, S. W., Odor, R. K., and Adera, T. 2005. Sexual assault in Virginia: A population-based study. *Women's Health Issues*, 15: 157–166.

McFarlane, J., Campbell, J. C., and Watson, K. 2002. Intimate partner stalking and femicide: Urgent implications for women's safety. *Behavioral Sciences and the Law*, 20: 51–68.

Mullen, B., and O'Connor, T. 2011. Sexual assault response in the military. In *Medical response to adult sexual assault*, ed. L. Ledray, A. W. Burgess, and A. Giardino. St. Louis: STM Learning.

Neville, H. A., and Heppner, M. J. 1999. Contextualizing rape: Reviewing sequelae and proposing culturally inclusive ecological model of sexual assault recovery. *Applied and Preventive Psychology*, 8: 41–62.

Niaz, U. 2003. Violence against women in South Asian countries. *Archives of Women's Mental Health*, 6(3): 173–184.

Palmer, C. M., McNulty, A. M., D'Este, C., and Donovan, B. 2004. Genital injuries in women reporting sexual assault. *Sexual Health*, 1(1): 55–59.

Riggs, N., Houry, D., Long, G., Markovchick, V., and Feldhaus, K. M. 2000. Analysis of 1076 cases of sexual assault. *Annals of Emergency Medicine*, 35(4): 358–362.

Ruch, L. O., and Wang, C.-H. 2006. Validation of the sexual assault symptom scale II (SASSII) using a panel research design. *Journal of Interpersonal Violence*, 21(11): 1440–1461.

Salah, R. 2005. Statement by Rima Salah on Beijing+10, http://www.unicef.org/media/media_25277.html.

Schnurr, P. P., and Green, B. L., (eds.). 2004. *Trauma and health: Physical health consequences of exposure to extreme stress*. Washington, DC: American Psychological Association.

Seyle, H. 1956. *The stress of life*. New York: McGraw-Hill.

Silverman, J. G., Raj, A., Mucci, L. A., and Hathaway, J. E. 2001. Dating violence against adolescent girls and associated substance use, unhealthy weight control, sexual risk behavior, pregnancy, and suicidality. *Journal of American Medical Association*, 286(5): 572–579.

Simmel, G., and Wolff, K. H. 1950. *The sociology of Georg Simmel*. Glencoe, IL: Free Press.

Slashinski, M. J., Coker, A. L., and Davis, K. E. 2003. Physical aggression, forced sex, and stalking victimization by a dating partner: An analysis of the National Violence against Women Survey. *Violence and Victims*, 18(6): 595–617.

Starzynski, L. L., Ullman, S. E., Filipas, H. H., and Townsend, S. M. 2005. Correlates of women's sexual assault disclosure to informal and formal support sources. *Violence*, 20(4): 417–432.

Sugar, N. F., Fine, D. N., and Eckert, L. O. 2004. Physical injury after sexual assault: Findings of a large case series. *American Journal of Obstetrics and Gynecology*, 190(1): 71–76.

Tjaden, P., and Thoennes, N. 1998. *Prevalence, incidence, and consequences of violence against women: Findings from the National Violence against Women Survey*. Washington, DC: National Institute of Justice and the Centers for Disease Control and Prevention.

Tjaden, P., and Thoennes, N. 2000. Prevalence and consequences of male-to-female and female-to-male intimate partner violence as measured by the National Violence against Women Survey. *Violence Against Women*, 6(2): 142–161.

Tjaden, P., and Thoennes, N. 2006. *Extent, nature, and consequences of rape victimization: Findings from the National Violence against Women Survey* (no. NCJ 210346). Washington, DC: National Institute of Justice.

Torres, S., and Han, H. 2000. Psychological distress in non-Hispanic white and Hispanic abused women. *Archives of Psychiatric Nursing*, 14(1): 19–29.

Ullman, S. E., and Filipas, H. H. 2001. Correlates of formal and informal support seeking in sexual assault victims. *Journal of Interpersonal Violence*, 16(10): 1028–1047.

Upchurch, D. M., and Kusunoki, Y. 2004. Associations between forced sex, sexual and protective practices, and sexually transmitted diseases among a national sample of adolescent girls. *Women's Health Issues*, 14(3): 75–84.

van der Kolk, B. A. 1994. The body keeps score: Memory and the evolving psychobiology of post-traumatic stress. *Harvard Review of Psychology*, 1(5): 253–265.

van der Kolk, B. A., and van der Hart, O. 1991. The intrusive past: The flexibility of memory and the engraving of trauma. *American Imago*, 48(4): 425–454.

van der Kolk, B. A., McFarlane, A. C., and Weisaeth, L. (eds.). 1996. *Traumatic stress: The effects of overwhelming experience on mind, body, and society*. New York: Guilford Press.

Wolitzky-Taylor, K. B., Resnick, H. S., McCauley, J. L., Amstadter, A. B., Ruggiero, K. J., and Kilpatrick, D. G. 2011. Reporting rape in a national sample of college women. *Journal of American College Health*, 59(7): 582–587. doi: 10.1080/07448481.2010.515634.

Wordes, M., and Nunez, M. 2002. *Our vulnerable teenagers: Their victimization, its consequences, and directions for prevention and intervention*. Oakland, CA: National Council on Crime and Delinquency.

World Health Organization. 2001. *Putting women first: Ethical and safety considerations for research on domestic violence against women*. Geneva, Switzerland: World Health Organization.

2 Victim Services and SANE/SART Programs

Annie Lewis-O'Connor, Ann Wolbert Burgess, and Carol Anne Harvey Marchetti

CONTENTS

Problems in Reporting 19
Prevalence 21
Underreported Crime 21
Disclosure: To Tell or Not to Tell.. 22
Rape Crisis Centers.. 22
Hospital-Based Victim Care Service: Early Services 23
Rape Crisis Services 25
    The National Sexual Violence Resource Center (NSVRC) 25
The Evolution of SANE and SART 26
    The Antirape Movement and the Development of Rape Crisis Centers 26
    The "Second Assault": Early Treatment of Rape Victims by the System 26
SANE/SART: Past and Present... 27
Structure and Operation of SANE/SART Programs... 28
Backlog of Sexual Assault Kits.. 29
Research on SANE/SART Programs 30
References... 32

Findings from the National Intimate Partner and Sexual Violence Survey (NISVS) indicate that nearly 1 in 5 (18.3%) women and 1 in 71 (1.4%) of men reported experiencing rape at one point in their lives (NISVS, 2010). Rape was defined as an act that includes attempted or completed vaginal, oral, or anal penetration. In the United States, the prevalence of rape is equivalent to one of every six women being raped and 1 of every 33 men. In another survey, findings indicate more than one-third of women in the United States (36% or approximately 42 million women) have experienced rape, physical violence, and/or stalking by an intimate partner at some point in their lifetime (Black et al., 2011). One in three women (33%) have experienced physical violence by an intimate partner and nearly 1 in 10 (9%) has been raped by an intimate partner in her lifetime. Approximately 6%, or almost 7.0 million women in the United States, reported experiencing these forms of intimate partner violence (IPV) in the past year. In the same National Survey, researchers found that nearly one in five women in the United States have been raped in their lifetime (18%) (Black et al., 2011). This translates to almost 22 million women in the United States.

PROBLEMS IN REPORTING

There are problems in determining the statistics in rape. First, the manner in which rape is defined affects incidence and prevalence rates. Incidence, which refers to the number of behaviors of a particular type, may, at present, be more reliable than prevalence, which refers to the proportion of people who engage in a particular behavior.

To count rape and sexual assault (incidence) depends on victim and the police perceptions and interpretations of what occurred. Victims must (1) perceive that a rape has occurred; (2) decide that it was an illegal act; and (3) decide whether to disclose it; the police (or researcher) (4) must decide whether the act meets the definition of an illegal act. For that act to come before a court of law, the prosecutor must decide if the evidence meets the charge. Only if the authorities' classification concurs with that of the victim does the incident become recorded and thus counted.

A second problem in determining the number of sexual assaults is underreporting. Findings from the National Violence Against Women Survey (NVAWS) indicate that only one in five women reported their rape to law enforcement officials (Tjaden & Thoennes, 2006). Guilt, fear of retribution, humiliation, lack of knowledge of and trust in the legal and medical system, and impaired cognitive processing that occurs following intense trauma are some reasons why persons may not report (Burgess, Fehder, & Hartman, 1995). According to the original Holmstrom and Burgess study (1983), in more than half of the cases someone other than the victim was involved in reporting the sexual assault to police. Those statistics have not varied in the last 20 years. A study of nonincarcerated sex offenders found that 126 men admitted they had committed 907 rapes involving 882 different women; the average number of different victims per rapist was seven (Abel et al., 1987).

Contrary to popular belief, rape is not a rare event, but rather affects hundreds of thousands of people (females and males) each year. When compared to other types of serious crimes, rape has a number of unique characteristics. First, as already noted, it is difficult to know how many rapes occur because of the low reporting rate. Second, in contrast to other crimes, there is a subjective element in determination as to whether or not the sexual act occurred against the victim's will. If the victim is of unquestioned chastity and if considerable force was employed by the assailant, then the act is usually considered to be a "real rape." However, if the woman was dating the man or met the man in a bar or over the Internet and said she was forced to have sex with him, some may not perceive the act as rape. Third, rape is the only serious crime in which victims may be held responsible for their own assaults. The belief is still held that women like to be overpowered sexually and that they say "no" when they mean "yes." Rules of evidence accepted in the courtroom may be stringent; for example, signs of resistance or an immediate report is required as proof of nonconsent.

Of the forcible rape cases reported to law enforcement, the clearance rate in 2012 was 40% (FBI, 2012). Clearly, law enforcement needs help to improve its clearance rates. It is understandable that stranger rapes may be difficult to solve but there is also the problem of classification of rape cases in contrast to "unfounded" cases. Philadelphia is a case in point. When DNA from two previously unfounded rape cases in Philadelphia matched the DNA of the rapist–murderer of a University of Pennsylvania graduate student, a reporter for the *Philadelphia Inquirer* began reinterviewing victims who had been tossed in the "unfounded" category. The series of articles pressured the Philadelphia police department to set up a special committee of victim advocates and women attorneys to help review its unfounded cases (called "inactive" by that time).

The past three decades have witnessed significant reform in sexual assault law and the protection of women. Reforms that occurred with the implementation of SANE (sexual assault nurse examiner) programs and SART (sexual assault response team; referred to hereafter as SANE and SART) are notable. The SANE is a specially trained, certified, registered nurse who has forensic training and clinical education to help victims of sexual assault. These nurses offer victims compassionate care and are responsible for assessment, collection of evidence that could potentially lead to the arrest, prosecution, and conviction of the assailant, and referrals and follow-up care. SANEs often work as part of a SART—a coordinated, multidisciplinary community effort that includes law enforcement, detectives, victim advocates, and the SANE (U.S. Department of Justice, 2004). SANE/SART programs provide victims with emotional and mental support but also make the task of evaluating the victim and collecting important evidence as private and sensitive as possible.

PREVALENCE

Prevalence rates reflect the number of individuals who have been raped at any time in their lives. As previously noted, findings from a nationally representative sample of adults indicated that in the U.S. 1 in 5 women, and 1 in 71 men, have reported being raped. Additionally, data from this study indicated that 1 in 20 women and men (5.6% and 5.3%, respectively) have experienced sexual violence other than rape, such as being made to penetrate someone else, sexual coercion, unwanted sexual contact, or noncontact unwanted sexual experiences, in the 12 months prior to the survey (CDC, 2012).

According to CDC (2012), 42.2% of female rape victims were first raped before the age of 18 years; and 29.9% were first raped between the ages of 11–17 years. 12.3% of female and 27.8% of male rape victims were first raped at age 10 years or younger. Findings from a 2011 survey of high school students indicated that 11.8% of girls and 4.5% of boys reported they were forced to have sexual intercourse at some time in their lives (CDC, 2011).

Although sexual assault occurs in all age, race, ethnic, and cultural groups, rape is highest among 20- to 24-year-old black females (Bureau of Justice Statistics, 1995). Females of 16–19 years are the age group next at risk. The national incidence of rape in females 65 years of age and over was 10 per 100,000 in 1990 (FBI, 1993). In the only study found on rape in an institutional setting, Nibert, Cooper, and Crossmaker (1989) reported that of 190 invited to participate in a survey, 58 patients agreed, and 22 reported having been sexually assaulted either by another resident or a staff member while in an institution. Twenty-five percent were over age 50.

UNDERREPORTED CRIME

Sexual abuse is an underreported crime and victims of all ages do not readily identify themselves. The extent of nondisclosure ranges from over 50% (Holmstrom & Burgess, 1983) to as high as 68% (Bureau of Justice Statistics, 1996). Koss (1993), and Acierno, Kilpatrick, and Resnick (1999) have identified several reasons for nondisclosure, including (1) fear of retribution by an offender, especially if the assailant is proximate or known to the victim; (2) fear of stigma attached to being a victim of rape; (3) fear of being blamed; (4) history of negative outcomes following previous disclosure (e.g., court involvement leading to acquittal); (5) lack of encouragement to discuss abuse; and (6) fear of psychological consequences of disclosure (e.g., anxiety or depression upon revisiting the event).

While the barriers to reporting have been identified, there has been little research done on the decision-making process itself from the perspective of individuals who have experienced sexual assault. To understand factors that might influence one's decision about whether or not to file a police report, Marchetti (2012) studied the role of decisional regret in the decision-making process of victims and found that people who reported their assaults to the police experienced significantly less regret about their decision to do so as compared to those who did not decide to report. These findings suggest the importance of providing decisional support (e.g., decision aids) for victims in the acute aftermath of an assault so that they will be better informed, and perhaps feel more empowered to follow through with reporting, which often requires a great deal of courage on behalf of the victims.

According to the FBI (2012), an estimated 84,767 forcible rapes were reported to law enforcement in 2012. This estimate was 5% lower than in 2009 and 10.3 and 6.7% lower than the 2006 and 2001 estimates, respectively. Among adult women surveyed by the CDC in 2010, approximately 27% of American Indian/Alaska Natives, 22% of non-Hispanic whites, 15% of Hispanics, and 35.5% of women of multiple races experienced an attempted or completed rape during their lives (CDC, 2012).

Victims of sexual abuse suffer in silence, actively avoid recalling their trauma, seek help reluctantly, and do not volunteer information about their traumatic experience (McFarlane, 1989).

Because most rape cases go unreported (Crowell & Burgess, 1996), surveys indicate that only a minority of victims who sustain rape-related mental or physical problems obtain effective treatment (Tjaden & Thoennes, 2006; Kilpatrick, 2000). Of those sexually assaulted in 1995, only 32% reported the incident (Bureau of Justice Statistics, 1996). In the Holmstrom and Burgess study (1983), in more than half of the 146 cases, someone other than the victim was involved in reporting the rape to police.

DISCLOSURE: TO TELL OR NOT TO TELL

The underreporting of rape, as previously discussed, is well known, however there is less information on women who fail to disclose to anyone. In a subsample from an anonymous online study, Carretta, Burgess, and DeMarco (2016) reported findings from 242 participants ranged from 18 to 56 years in age with a median age of 27 years. This online study suggests that 24% of 242 women who were nondisclosing compared to those who had disclosed were significantly less likely to seek treatment for emotional injuries. Also, almost two-thirds of nondisclosing women believed the abuse was their fault versus 39.1% of women with prior disclosure. Of clinical interest is that regardless of disclosure pattern, there was no significant difference in reports of depression, anxiety or post-traumatic stress disorder (PTSD) and the majority of respondents endorsed support for online counseling over telephone or individual contact (Carretta et al., 2016).

There is no doubt among victims, victim advocates, forensic nurses, and prosecutors that these programs have been instrumental in assisting victims through the traumatizing experience of rape. This chapter reviews the history of the rape crisis centers and describes SANE/SART services for rape victims.

RAPE CRISIS CENTERS

Rape crisis centers have been providing services for victims for more than 30 years (Koss & Harvey, 1991; Smith, 2004; Heldman & Brown, 2014). This systematized response evolved when rape victims could not expect that family, friends, or medical and legal systems would either understand the nature of their trauma or respond supportively. The grassroots movement took on the tasks of ensuring that victims had access to informed and sympathetic advocate–counselors to assist with the emotional consequences of rape and to deal with the appropriate systems. These centers also considered community education, system reform, and empowerment of women and victims to be central to their mission.

The history of victim care services (VCS) in general and the antirape movement in particular began just 30 years ago. Largen (1985) credits two forces for finally bringing the problem of rape to the attention of the citizens of the United States in the late 1960s. First, primary credit is given to the women's movement for initiating consciousness-raising groups and then "speak-outs," where women began saying publicly what they had not dared say previously about rape. Second, in response to a rising crime rate and the growing community concern over the problem of rape, Senator Charles Mathias of Maryland introduced a bill in September 1973 to establish the National Center for the Prevention and Control of Rape. The purpose of this bill was to provide a focal point within the National Institute of Mental Health from which a comprehensive national effort would be undertaken to conduct research, develop programs, and provide information leading to aid for the victims and their families, to rehabilitation of the offenders, and ultimately, to the curtailment of rape crimes. The bill was passed by overwhelming majority in the 93rd Congress, vetoed by President Ford, and successfully reintroduced. The National Center was established through Public Law 94-63 in July 1975.

Parallel with these political forces were major efforts to organize services for rape victims, including community-based and hospital-based programs during the early 1970s. Although most of the pioneer services were in the form of grassroots self-help programs, now widely known as rape crisis centers, nurses practicing in hospital emergency departments began to develop programs to provide rape counseling services. Boston City Hospital, Boston's Beth Israel Hospital, and Santa Monica Hospital were among the first hospital-based programs; they represent the roots of forensic nursing programs (Lynch, 1993).

HOSPITAL-BASED VICTIM CARE SERVICE: EARLY SERVICES

In 1972, a victim-counseling program was developed as a nurse-managed service at the Boston City Hospital by Burgess and Holmstrom (1974). The counseling approach developed in the early years of this program expanded in the mid-1980s into a five-phase VCS coordinated by advanced practice psychiatric nurses (Minden, 1989). These six phases include various health care providers and networks in communities throughout a state and are suggested for hospital-based programs:

Phase 1: Standards are set and providers are trained in victim care and coordinated with other programs in the city and state.

Phase 2: Acute intervention takes place, with the victim entering the emergency department as well as any other patient unit in the hospital system.

Phase 3: Masters-level-prepared psychiatric nurses or social workers provide crisis intervention follow-up of the victim.

Phase 4: Education regarding sexually transmitted disease, including HIV, is provided according to the age and verbal requests of the victim.

Phase 5: Ongoing therapy is provided through referral to psychiatric clinicians.

Phase 6: Evaluation and research relevant to sexual victimization are undertaken.

The VCS was organized around seven fundamental assumptions:

1. There is a continuum of sexual victimization. Although states and jurisdictions legally define rape differently, three criteria are generally present: (a) sexual penetration of the victim's vagina, mouth, or rectum (b) that occurs without the individual's consent and (c) that involves the use of force or threat of force.

   Sexual assault refers to a wider range of forced or pressured sexual contact, specifically, child sexual assault, incest, acquaintance rape, and marital rape. Furthermore, there are situations involving relationships of unequal power in which the person in authority violates the normal bounds of the relationship and abuses and sexually pressures or forces the subordinate. Such abusive relationships include husband/wife, therapist/patient, parent/child, teacher/student, and employer/employee.

   A basic premise of the VCS is that a patient does not need to meet any stringent legal criteria for rape in order to be considered sexually victimized. The legal system bears the burden of determining the validity of a given charge of rape, whereas the primary responsibility of the VCS is to care for the patient reporting sexual victimization.

2. Sexual victimization is not a rare event. Rape is a serious public health problem. In 1997, there were 96,122 reported forcible rapes. An estimated 70 of every 100,000 females in the country were reported rape victims in 1997, a decrease of 1% from 1996 and 13% from 1993. A 1997 National Crime Victimization Survey, which includes both reported and unreported crimes, found that despite a decline of 7% in the nation's crime rate in 1997, rates of rape and sexual assault did not decline (Kilpatrick, 2000).

3. Responses to sexual assault victims have frequently been based on myths and stereotypes. The stereotype that rape victims are somehow responsible for their victimization is grounded in the belief that women have rape fantasies and that it is acceptable for men to fulfill such fantasies. This belief is also noted in the attitudes that women who dress

provocatively, stay out late, or frequent unsafe areas get what they deserve. Although engaging in certain behaviors may increase one's risk of victimization, the VCS maintains that it is the offender who is responsible for the victimization.

Other myths include that rape is a crime that is prone to false complaints, rape only happens to other people, and rape occurs in dark alleys at the hands of strangers. To the contrary, studies suggest that victims of rape are disinclined to make complaints under current laws and that those who do frequently refuse to continue their testimony because of the manner in which they are treated. Also, contrary to popular belief, acquaintance rape or assault by someone known to the victim is a more frequent occurrence than stranger rape and often happens in the victim's home or another familiar place.

Furthermore, sexual assault and abuse cross all boundaries of class and culture. The fact that victims can be of either sex helps to negate the myth that women are naturally better equipped than men to care for sexual assault victims. The clinician, whether male or female, must be accepting of the patient. A female clinician caring for a female victim might defend against her own feelings of vulnerability by rejecting the patient. In contrast, that same patient might benefit from interaction with a male clinician who acts in a caring manner. Attitude rather than gender determines a clinician's ability to provide victim care (Minden, 1989).

4. Rape or sexual assault represents a trauma or crisis that results in a disruption of the victim's physical, emotional, and social lifestyle. Individuals who have been raped usually describe it as an extremely traumatic event in their lives. Whether an individual is able to cope with the trauma depends on a number of factors, including the nature of the assault, the presence of other stressors, the patient's precrisis functioning and coping skills, and the available support system. The clinician who can communicate a sense of optimism for recovery may help nullify the chronic negative effects of sexual assault.

Rape trauma, a clinical term, describes a clustering of biopsychosocial and behavioral symptoms exhibited in varying degrees by a victim following a rape. Most victims of forcible rape develop a pattern of moderate-to-severe symptoms described as rape trauma syndrome; a minority of victims report no or minimal symptoms. Rape trauma is an acute reaction to an externally imposed situational crisis. The trauma of the victim results from the person's being confronted with a life-threatening and highly stressful situation. The crisis that results when a person is raped is in the service of self-preservation. The victim's reactions to the impending threat to his or her life are the nucleus around which such an adaptive pattern may be noted. For many rape victims, responses during the rape and after the rape correspond to the critical symptoms of PTSD.

5. Rape trauma is a traumatic stressor. Crisis intervention encourages a positive resolution of the victimization experience. Patterns of coping after the assault can be adaptive or maladaptive. The purpose of crisis intervention is to direct the victim into therapeutic coping patterns rather than defensive positions.

The forte of the VCS is crisis intervention; the emphasis is on moving the patient from being a victim to being a survivor. A salient feature of victimization for the patient is a loss of control. Emergency department clinicians can easily mirror the patient's crisis and may also experience feelings of being overwhelmed by the trauma. Consequently, the VCS implements a very structured process for providing victim care, which has helped to reestablish a sense of control for the clinician who can then put energies into stabilizing the patient.

Two phases of care are provided to the rape victim (Minden, 1989). The first phase includes implementation of the sexual assault protocol described in Chapter 14. The second phase is victim follow-up by telephone over a 3- to 4-day period when a counseling referral to facilitate the recovery of the victim from the acute phase is discussed.

6. An interdisciplinary approach to victim care is required. Rape is a complex, multifaceted problem that no one individual or group can resolve alone. Indeed, dealing with sexual victimization requires the collaborative and cooperative efforts of a network of services. Thus, a multidisciplinary team approach helps to meet the diverse needs of the victim and also provides the caregivers with a support system for dealing with the stress of victimization. The VCS provides continuous victim care training for various community agencies and joins with other programs in offering workshops to enhance community awareness of sexual victimization (Minden, 1989).

7. Victim care providers experience "compassion fatigue"—a term coined by trauma expert Charles Figley that describes how working with victims can take a psychological toll on the providers of care. Clinicians working in emergency departments of large city hospitals have very direct and frequent exposure to trauma. Ever-escalating economic constraints and patient acuity present care providers with increasing challenges that are physically, intellectually, and emotionally stressful.

In an effort to address the obstacles that victims of sexual assault face after the emergency room, Dr. Annie Lewis-O'Connor founded and serves as the Director of the C.A.R.E Clinic at Brigham and Women's Hospital in Boston (C.A.R.E—Coordinated Approach to Recovery and Empowerment). This clinic, founded in 2012 addresses access and coordination of services using a trauma-informed model of care. Lewis-O'Connor and Chadwick (2015) concluded that victims of sexual assault faced a myriad of challenges posttreatment in the emergency department and many of the issues were related to the health delivery model, siloed care, and the lack of trauma-sensitive services.

RAPE CRISIS SERVICES

Rape crisis services have come to be standard fare in many communities in the United States. Most such services consist of 24-h crisis lines offering information and support, advocacy in the form of information about the medical and legal systems, accompaniment to medical and legal appointments or court appearances, and supportive post-rape counseling. The counseling has often been offered as a group treatment. In many cases, trained volunteers have delivered the services, but increasingly mental health professionals supervise or carry out the counseling.

THE NATIONAL SEXUAL VIOLENCE RESOURCE CENTER (NSVRC)

The NSVRC, developed by the Pennsylvania Coalition against Rape and funded by the Centers for Disease Control and Prevention in 1999, is the nucleus of a national movement to prevent sexual violence and to sustain a national momentum that influences practice, research, policy, and ultimately, public attitudes and beliefs. The broad goals of the NSVRC are to (1) strengthen the support system serving sexual assault survivors by providing competent leadership, resources, and information to develop capacities of national sexual assault organizations, state sexual assault coalitions, community-based programs, and allied professionals; (2) provide accurate and comprehensive information and technical assistance in supporting effective intervention in the prevention of sexual violence; (3) identify emerging policy issues and research needs to support the development of policy and practice leading to the prevention of sexual violence; and (4) develop the organizational structure and technological capacity supporting the development and implementation of NSVRC activities.

The NSVRC is housed in Enola, Pennsylvania, and provides information and resources, technical assistance, and access to research through its toll-free number and email address. Organizational partners who collaborate with the NSVRC include (1) the University of Pennsylvania as the research partner; (2) the Violence against Women Prevention Resource Center; (3) the VAWnet/National Resources Center; (4) the National Alliance of Sexual Assault Coalitions; and (5) the National Coalition against Sexual Assault.

THE EVOLUTION OF SANE AND SART

THE ANTIRAPE MOVEMENT AND THE DEVELOPMENT OF RAPE CRISIS CENTERS

In the early 1970s, when police departments and rape crisis centers first began to address the crime of rape, little was known about rape victims or sex offenders. Feminist groups had just begun to raise the issue of rape, and in 1971 the New York Speak-Out on Rape had been held, drawing widespread attention to rape. Contemporary feminists who raised the issue early were Susan Griffin (1971) in her now classic article on rape as the "all-American" crime and Germaine Greer (1973) in her essay on "grand rapes" (legalistically defined) and "petty rapes" (everyday sexual rip-offs). Susan Brownmiller (1975) wrote the history of rape and urged people to deny its future. The general public was not particularly concerned about rape victims; very few academic publications or special services existed, funding agencies did not see the topic as important, and health policy was almost nonexistent.

By 1972, the antirape movement began to attract women from all walks of life and political persuasions. Various strategies began to emerge, particularly the self-help program now widely known as the rape crisis center. One of the first such centers was founded in Berkeley in early 1972, known as Bay Area Women against Rape. Within months of the opening of the Berkeley center, similar centers were established in Ann Arbor, Michigan; Washington, DC; and Philadelphia, Pennsylvania. Concurrently, hospital-based rape counseling services began in Boston and in Minneapolis. Soon, centers replicated and services flourished. Although volunteer ranks tended to include a large number of university students and instructors, they also included homemakers and working women. The volunteer makeup usually reflected every age, race, socioeconomic class, sexual preference, and level of political consciousness. Volunteers were, however, exclusively women. Among the women, the most common denominators were commitments to aiding victims and to bringing about social change (Largen, 1985).

THE "SECOND ASSAULT": EARLY TREATMENT OF RAPE VICTIMS BY THE SYSTEM

The rape crisis centers provided victims with the support and counseling that enabled them to move through the traumatizing experience of rape both mentally and emotionally. However, rape survivors would often experience "victim-blaming treatment from system personnel" that would often worsen the victim's physical and mental distress (Campbell, Wasco, Ahrens, Sefl, & Barnes, 2001). While there has been advancement in care and treatment, there is still room for a more reliable response to victims. Additionally, the physical ordeal of the medical examination and subsequent investigation could often be a humiliating and dehumanizing experience for the victim. These post-assault experiences became known as the "second assault" of the victim. Trauma-informed care offers the ideal response to victims of sexual assault (Elliott, Bjelajac, Fallot, Markoff, & Reed, 2005).

Rape victims would often go through a series of uncomfortable experiences after their victimization that would constitute a second assault. First, rape victims were traditionally seen in the emergency room by male physicians and generalist nurses, who often lacked the time and experience to do a thorough examination of the victim that would assist law enforcement and prosecutors (Girardin, 2005). Rape victims were not a high priority for emergency care, and even when medical needs were satisfied, their emotional needs were not. Prior to the SANE programs, medical staffs had an image of the "real" rape victim and much energy went into determining the "legitimacy" of the rape case (i.e., if the victim was really raped). Rape victims often felt depersonalized, lost, and neglected.

Second, the environment of the emergency department and needs of the victim were often at odds. Many victims complained about the long wait, having to wait alone, a lack of privacy, and not being informed of examination results. Rape victims were not a priority with emergency department physicians. Physicians were reluctant to do the rape examination because they lacked experience and training in forensic evidence collection and because they would be vulnerable to being sub-poenaed and required to testify (Bahm, 2001). Physicians were able to examine the victim's body for bruises and prepare slides to look for sperm. However, they were often unaware of the need to collect evidence from clothing, carefully folding clothes to prevent dried stains from brushing off, giving the victim a comb to gather pubic hairs that may have been left by an assailant, or clipping the victim's fingernails to provide skin scrapings of the assailant. There was also a lack of continu-ity of care. Medical departments did not communicate with each other, so victims returning for follow-up care found it difficult to be asked again by new people why they needed medical attention.

Finally, documentation collected on the victim would often include damning information such as prior sexual experience or phrases that included judgmental statements about the victim. Ultimately, victims were left on their own to cope financially, legally, and emotionally with the aftermath of the crime (Holmstrom & Burgess, 1983; U.S. Department of Justice, Office of Violence against Women, 2013).

SANE/SART: PAST AND PRESENT

It was against this backdrop of problems that communities throughout the United States were prompted to involve nurses in the care of the sexual assault victim (Lang, 1999; Ledray, 1999). Nurses, medical professionals, counselors, and advocates working with rape victims agreed that services provided to sexual assault victims in the emergency room were inadequate when compared with the standard of care given to other patients (Ledray, 2001). Thus, SANE programs and SARTs emerged in the 1970s with the first SANE in Tennessee. SANE programs were created whereby specially trained forensic nurses provided 24-h coverage as first-response care to sexual assault vic-tims in emergency rooms and nonhospital settings (Campbell, 2004). According to the International Association of Forensic Nurses, in 1991 there were only 20 SANE programs in the U.S., today there are over 700 (http://forensicnurses.org/?page=a5).

Nurses have always cared for patients who were victims of violence. However, forensic nursing is now recognized as a specialty area of contemporary nursing practice (Taylor, 1998; Winfrey & Smith, 1999; Doyle, 2001). Forensic nursing history has been traced to the eighteenth century, when midwives were called into court to testify on issues pertaining to virginity, pregnancy, and rape (Lynch, 2006). Clinical forensic nursing practice focuses on the collection of evidence from living patients who have been victims of crimes or traumatic injuries. The forensic and clinical training SANEs receive allows them to "relieve emergency departments of a group of patients who typically have nonurgent physical needs but extremely urgent needs for evidence collection, crisis interven-tion, and emotional care" (Girardin, 2005).

Today, SANE programs have grown in number and many are still reaching maturity. Ciancone, Wilson, Collette, and Gerson (2000) conducted a survey of SANE programs in the United States. Of the 58 programs that responded, 55% had been in existence for less than 5 years and 16% had been in exis-tence for more than 10 years. Campbell, Bybee, Ford, and Patterson (2005) surveyed SANE programs and reported on the rapid growth of programs; 58% had emerged within the past 5 years. Trends noted included newer programs created through a joint task force or through collaboration with other commu-nity groups; more diverse funding available, as opposed to using hospital funds; and significantly larger programs with more staff and serving more patients, which reflected organizational growth.

The SANE soon became an integral part of a team of primary and secondary responders known as a SART. As previously mentioned, the SART includes law enforcement, detectives, victim advo-cates, and health care providers. The main goal of a SART is to assist the sexual assault victim through the criminal justice process. The second goal is to increase the odds of successful pros-ecution by enhancing evidence collection and facilitating communication between all parties in the process. The third goal is to help victims recover from and cope with their experience through counseling and support (Girardin, 2005; Wilson & Klein, 2005).

Nationally, the SANE/SART model has grown exponentially. Although virtually all these programs were developed to facilitate standard comprehensive and expert care of sexual assault survivors, the literature clearly shows that policies and procedures do vary from program to program.

STRUCTURE AND OPERATION OF SANE/SART PROGRAMS

SANE programs operate out of a variety of locations including hospitals and community-based facilities. They also vary in terms of their community relationships, structure, services offered, and development. Ciancone et al. (2000) found that the median number of patients seen annually by SANE programs was 95. Approximately 75% of the programs were affiliated with hospitals, police departments, or rape crisis centers. More than half of the exams were conducted in a medical clinic, office, or hospital setting. Ninety percent offered prophylaxis and treatment for sexually transmitted infections (STIs); however, STI cultures, HIV testing, and screening for illegal drugs and alcohol were selectively performed based on whether patients had evidence of active disease, requested the test, or had high-risk exposures. The authors suggested that best-practice protocols be designed to eliminate the inconsistencies among programs and that further research be conducted, particularly the collection of outcome measures in order to define the impact of the programs (Ciancone et al., 2000).

Campbell et al. (2005) conducted a national study of the organizational components of SANE programs that examined four areas: (1) history of the program; (2) current structure, function, and operations; (3) program goals and desired outcomes; and (4) community relationships. A summary of the history and development included how the program began (by a planning committee or task force); why the program was created (need for better care for victims, better evidence collection, reduce waiting time); and funding of program (hospital funds, state grant, private donations, local government grant). A summary of the SANE programs' structures included staffing, location for conducting exams, program setting, and payment for services. A summary of SANE programs' goals and outcomes included primary program goals (provide quality care, improve evidence collection, meet patient's emotional needs, empower survivors; prompt reporting to police). Good outcomes in a case were described as "patient is not blamed or made to feel it was her fault," "patient educated about resources," "good quality medical care," "evidence collected correctly/professionally," and "case is prosecuted and victim ready to talk with a counselor" (Campbell et al., 2005). The last organizational category was community relationships. The quality of community relationships included rape crisis centers, police/law enforcement, prosecutor's office, hospitals, and (for nonhospital-based programs) quality of relationships with other staff in the hospital emergency department and hospital administrators (Campbell et al., 2005).

The SANE programs promote a philosophy of care that is evidence based and consists of the following tasks:

1. Initial medical evaluation: This is not a routine physical exam. The emergency physician will typically take vital signs of the victim; however, the physician is asked not to treat injuries until the SANE documents injuries with pictures and collects evidence. The victim is advised of this procedure and must sign a consent form (Ledray, 2001).
2. Evidentiary exam: The SANE is responsible for conducting the evidentiary examination and ensures that the victim's dignity is protected and that the victim is not retraumatized by the exam. Victims are a part of the decision process throughout the evidence collection phase. Most protocols suggest the examination be completed within 72 h of the sexual assault. However, some research indicates that evidence may be available beyond the 72-h time period. There is significant variation in how evidence is collected. However, all evidentiary exams include the following (Ledray, 2001):
   a. written consent from the victim, documentation of assault history
   b. forms of violence used and where

    c. medical information of the victim including pregnancy status

    d. a physical examination for trauma, genital and nongenital

    e. collecting the victim's clothing and packaging according to state policy

    f. specimen collections from the body surfaces including skin, hair, and nails

    g. collection of biological evidence from the body and orifices

    h. blood drawn and urine specimen for drug testing

    i. DNA screen

    j. prophylactic treatment of STIs or culturing

3. Maintaining chain of evidence and evidence integrity: The SANE is responsible for ensuring complete documentation, with signatures and the disposition of evidence. Additionally, the SANE is also responsible for identifying, collecting, and preserving evidence and for securing evidence in a designated area free of contaminants (Evans, 2003).

4. Crisis intervention and counseling: This includes a mental health assessment and referral for follow-up counseling. This is usually the primary role of the rape crisis center advocate. However, the SANE also provides crisis intervention and ensures that follow-up counseling services are available (Ledray, 2001).

In addition, SANE programs utilize specialized forensic equipment such as a colposcope, which is a noninvasive, lighted, and magnifying instrument for examining the perineum and anogenital area for the detection of small lacerations and bruises (Woodling & Heger, 1986). Other equipment may include a camera attached to the colposcope, and some use toluidine blue dye for the detection of microlacerations and abrasions. SANEs also document bruises and injuries using photography. Today, many are using digital cameras. SANEs are also trained in identifying and documenting patterned injuries, treatment of injuries, maintaining chain of evidence, and providing expert witness testimony (Ledray, 1999).

Building on the success of the SANE model, many communities have established a SART, which is a coordinated community approach to deal with the multiple needs of rape survivors and to prosecute offenders. Under this approach, SANEs work in a team with police and sheriffs, prosecutors, rape crisis advocates or counselors, and emergency department medical personnel to better collect evidence and provide services to victims. Some variations exist with the structure of SART programs. For instance, some programs are hospital based and others consist of medical teams that contract with police or sheriffs' departments (Lewis, DiNitto, Nelson, Just, & Ruggard, 2003). In addition, some states have SART programs that do not have a formal SANE component. For example, Rhode Island relies on medical personnel who are not SANEs to collect forensic evidence as part of their SART (Wilson & Klein, 2005).

BACKLOG OF SEXUAL ASSAULT KITS

There have been great strides made to improve the proper collection of physical and biological evidence among sexual assault victims. Such evidence can be used to reconstruct the crime and establish the identity of the assailant, particularly in cases where a DNA match is found. Hospital clinicians who treat individuals who have been assaulted use a sexual assault kit (SAK), and follow strict and consistent protocols to maintain the integrity of the evidence. The kits include a number of carefully designed forms that guide the exam, and call for information such as patient consent; a narrative and structured account of the assault (e.g., time, location, injuries sustained, number of assailants, etc.); documentation of injuries and other findings on body maps and line item questions; and an accounting of the evidence that was collected during the examination (e.g., swabs, clothing, photographs, etc.). While the protocols for evidence collection have improved greatly, problems regarding the management and storage of the SAKs persist. For example, the number of untested kits from the Los Angeles Sheriff's and Police Departments reached a staggering count of 10,895 in the fall of 2008 (Peterson, Johnson, Herz, Graziano, & Oehler, 2012). To address this serious problem the National Institute of Justice funded the "Sexual Assault Kit Backlog Project" at California State University, Los Angeles (CSULA).

The following is a summary of the principal policy recommendations that stemmed from the research report (Peterson et al., 2012, p. vi):

1. The forensic testing of ALL backlogged sexual assault kits is not recommended. Before testing, the goals of agencies must be clearly defined, the investigation status of cases determined, and agencies become familiar with the likely short- and long-term benefits of such testing. For future testing, unsolved stranger cases should be the primary focus.
2. Advisory committees, composed of law enforcement, medical and forensic representatives should collaborate to establish criteria for future SAK testing. Agencies should commit resources to share and compile data at key decision points in the investigation and prosecution process and work toward the development of consolidated databases and models to better predict successful sexual assault case outcomes and the role of scientific evidence.
3. Crime laboratories are in need of various types of investigative and medical information in order to begin their analyses of sexual assault kit evidence. Laboratories should routinely receive and review investigator case files, medical victim examination reports, and Combined DNA Index System (CODIS) status information before commencing their examination procedures. Also: (a) Post-coital interval (PCI) is a key factor in predicting hits and is unknown (25%+) in an unacceptably high percentage of cases. (b) Data from the sexual assault victim examination reports (areas penetrated, possible ejaculation, use of condom, etc.) yield results useful to criminalists examining sexual assault evidence in the forensic laboratory. (c) Samples from very young victims yield valuable information on biological secretions left on regions of the body that can help inform analytical procedures.
4. All victims, young and old, should report sexual assaults as quickly as possible and undergo sexual assault examinations; this is critically important in the successful recovery of evidence and in deciding if laboratory testing should be undertaken.
5. The long-term effects of SAK testing are also reliant on more detailed information being available on CODIS hits that differentiate true cold hits from "conviction match" hits that occur where the offender's profile is "reidentified" in the immediate case.
6. A range of quantitative and qualitative data is needed from investigators, hospitals, crime laboratories and prosecutors for inclusion in such databases. In particular, better information is needed on the sizable percentage of non-stranger cases (involving intimates, family members, dating, work and/or casual relationships), scientific results, and the role played by scientific evidence in the outcome of these cases.
7. Better published research will result from improved report keeping and comprehensive databases. The quantitative data would collect basic discrete factors on every sexual assault case, its investigation, analysis of sexual assault kit evidence: prosecution, adjudication, and sentencing. Qualitative data would include such factors as the persuasiveness of various factors that influenced arrest, charging, plea negotiation, trial verdict (including interviews with jurors after verdict), and sentencing outcomes.

RESEARCH ON SANE/SART PROGRAMS

The U.S. Department of Justice, Office for Victims of Crimes (2001), reported that SANE programs have made a profound difference in the quality of care provided to sexual assault victims by offering prompt, compassionate, and comprehensive forensic evidence collection. Campbell, Patterson, and Lichty (2005) examined the effectiveness of SANE programs across five areas: (1) promoting the psychological recovery of survivors; (2) providing comprehensive and consistent post-rape medical care (e.g., emergency contraception, STD prophylaxis); (3) documenting the forensic evidence of the crime completely and accurately; (4) improving the prosecution of sexual assault cases by providing better forensics and expert testimony; and (5) creating community change by bringing multiple service providers together to provide comprehensive care to rape survivors. Campbell et al. (2005) found that SANE programs are effective across these areas; however, the authors note that most research on SANE/SART programs has not included "adequate methodological controls" to establish empirical evidence attesting to the effectiveness of such programs.

Early studies of SANE/SART programs were descriptive case studies that did not use control samples of non-SANE/SART cases. For example, Solola, Scott, Severs, and Howell (1983) studied the management of rape cases by the SANE program in Memphis and reported that more than 90% of the victims elected to file a police report of the sexual assault. However, in 38% of the cases, prosecution was not possible because the assailant was unknown. Arrest and successful prosecution was possible in 61.4% of the cases with identified suspects or in only about a quarter of all rape cases. Solola observed increases in the number of guilty pleas in cases with SANE intervention.

In 2006, researchers found that SANE/SART interventions were a valuable tool in the criminal justice system's ability to respond to adult female sexual assault cases. Of particular note are the following: SANE/SART interventions are effective tools in collecting and preserving valuable evidence for prosecution, including DNA evidence. SANE/SART interventions significantly increased the likelihood that charges were filed in sexual assault cases (Nugent-Borakove et al., 2006).

Consistently research supports that SANE/SART programs: enhance the quality of health care for women who have been sexually assaulted, improve the quality of forensic evidence, increase law enforcement's ability to collect information, file charges and refer to prosecution, and increase prosecution rates over time (Crandall & Helitzer, 2003; Campbell et al., 2005).

Several researchers have explored the possible reasons for the increase in conviction rates that may be associated with SANE/SART model. The World Health Organization (2002) reported that a study in Canada found that documentation by trained forensic or other medical providers can increase the likelihood that a perpetrator will be arrested, charged, and convicted. In addition, Ledray (1999), Lenehan (1991), and Little (2001) reported that relevant consistent documentation and evidence collection contributed to an increase in convictions. There is also evidence indicating that when a SANE intervenes there is a higher rate of victim participation in the criminal justice system (Ledray & Summelink, 1996; Ledray, 2001). Researchers have further demonstrated that evidence collection is more accurate when collected by a SANE (Ledray, 2001; Crandall & Helitzer, 2003; Sievers, Murphey, & Miller, 2003). Amey and Bishai (2002) studied the quality of medical care of rape victims, and Crandall and Helitzer (2003) reported on the impact of SANE programs in New Jersey. The latter also found that in Albuquerque, New Mexico, the SANE program established in 1996 improved patient care, improved the job quality of care providers, and increased the number of charges brought against rapists and the number of entered guilty pleas. However, the impact of SANE programs on judicial processes is not always immediate. Wilson and Klein (2005) found in Rhode Island that the impact of the SART program on judicial processes as applied to sexual assault cases was negligible. They attribute the findings to the fact that the Rhode Island program is still maturing. However, the program was found to have immediate and positive results for victims.

The research on SANE/SART programs and forensic research in the area of rape and sexual assault have also focused on forensic markers of injury to rape victims (Burgess, Hanrahan, & Baker, 2005). The early research (outside of descriptive reporting of injuries) has been on the use of the colposcope. Slaughter and Brown (1992) reported finding via colposcope that 87% of rape victims they examined ($n = 131$) had identifiable injury. Slaughter, Brown, Crowley, and Peck (1997) reported findings on 311 women and children and compared them with 75 controls. They found positive anogenital findings in 68% as compared with 11% in the control group having consensual sex ($n = 75$). However, the study included several methodological issues, including the fact that the time from rape to examination varied with the rape victims (up to 72 h after assault), while the controls were examined within 24 h following intercourse.

Sommers, Fisher, and Karjane (2005) analyzed the role of colposcopy in the forensic examination of adolescent and adult women and noted that identifying an injury pattern to predict rape remains problematic. Patel, Courtney, and Forster (1993) warned that if colposcopy was required to support a claim of rape, there was the risk that courts would doubt a woman's history if injury was absent. Injury has been noted to play a role in the reporting of rapes. Bachman (1993) found that the level of injury sustained in a rape increased the likelihood of the rape's being reported to police. Finally, the issue of injury has been studied following consensual sex or tampon use. Fraser et al. (1999) reported on an international sample of 107 women, aged 18–35, followed over a 6-month period to look for changes in vaginal and cervical appearance. Colposcopy noted 56 alterations during 314 inspections with the most common lesions being petechiae (30 of 134), erythema (9 of 314), abrasions (5 of 134), and edema (4 of 314). The incidence of these conditions was highest when the inspections followed intercourse in the previous 24 h or after tampon use. Two primary issues are critical in rape cases: (1) identification of the assailant and (2) establishment of consent (or lack thereof). The issue of identification is being addressed by rape kit DNA evidence. The issue of nonconsent is being addressed by research on differentiating injuries based on visual inspection, contrast media, or colposcopy. One such study is underway by Sommers, Schafer, Zink, and Weybright (2005).

The literature clearly shows how SANE/SART programs have been instrumental in helping rape survivors. These programs provide the emotional and mental support to empower victims while also helping victims navigate the criminal justice process. The next level of evaluation is to review empirical evidence that attests to the efficacy of SANE/SART programs and their impact on judicial processes.

REFERENCES

Abel, G., Becker, J., Mittleman, M, Cunningham-Rathner, J., Rouleau, J., and Murphy, W. 1987. Self-reported sex crimes by nonparaphiliacs. *Journal of Interpersonal Violence,* 2(1): 3–25.

Acierno, R., Kilpatrick, D. G., and Resnick, H. S. 1999. Posttraumatic stress disorder: Prevalence, risk factors and comorbidity relative to criminal victimization. In *Posttraumatic stress disorder: A comprehensive approach to research and treatment,* eds. P. Saigh and D. Bremne, 44–68. New York: Allyn & Bacon.

Amey, A., and Bishai, D. 2002. Measuring the quality of medical care for women who experience sexual assault with data from the National Hospital Ambulatory Medical Care Survey. *Annals of Emergency Medicine,* 39(6): 631–638.

Bachman, R. 1993. Predicting the reporting of rape victimization: Have rape reforms made a difference? *Criminal Justice and Behaviour,* 20(3): 254–270.

Bahm, T. 2001. *Winning sexual assault cases with sexual assault examiners.* Alexandria, VA: American Prosecutors Research Institute.

Black, M., Basile, K., Breiding, M., Smith, S. G., Walters, M. L., Merrick, M. T., Chen, J., and Stevens, M. J. 2011. The National Intimate Partner and Sexual Violence Survey (NISVS): 2010 Summary Report. Atlanta, GA.

Brownmiller, S. 1975. *Against our will: Men, women and rape.* New York: Simon & Schuster.

Bureau of Justice Statistics. 1995. *National crime victimization survey.* Washington, DC: Department of Justice.

Bureau of Justice Statistics. 1996. *National crime victimization survey.* Washington, DC: Department of Justice.

Burgess, A. W., and Holmstrom, L. L. 1974. Rape trauma syndrome. *American Journal of Psychiatry,* 131: 981–986.

Burgess, A. W., Fehder, W. P., and Hartman, C. R. 1995. Delayed reporting of the rape victim. *Journal of Psychosocial Nursing and Mental Health Services,* 33(9): 21–29.

Burgess, A. W., Hanrahan, N. P., and Baker, T. 2005. Forensic markers in elder sexual abuse cases. *Clinics of Geriatric Medicine,* 21(2): 399–412.

Campbell, R. 2004. Sexual assault nurse examiner programs: Evidence of psychological and legal effectiveness. National Electronic Network on Violence against Women Applied Research Forum, VAWNet document: http://www.vawnet.org/SexualViolence/Research/VAWnetDocuments/AR_Sane.pdf.

Campbell, R., Bybee, D., Ford, K., and Patterson, D. 2005. Systems Change Analysis of SANE Programs: Identifying the Mediating Mechanisms of Criminal Justice System Impact. U.S. Department of Justice. Document no. 226497.

Campbell, R., Patterson, D., and Lichty, L. F. 2005. The effectiveness of sexual assault nurse examiner (SANE) programs: A review of psychological, medical, legal, and community outcomes. *Trauma Violence & Abuse,* 6(4): 313–329.

Campbell, R., Wasco, S., Ahrens, C., Sefl, T., and Barnes, H. 2001. Preventing the "second rape": Rape survivors' experiences with community service providers. *Journal of Interpersonal Violence*, 16(12): 1239–1260.

Carretta, C., Burgess, A. W., and DeMarco, R. 2016. Rape: To tell or not to tell. *Violence Against Women*, 21(9): 1145–1165.

Centers for Disease Control and Prevention (CDC). 1991–2011. *High school youth risk behavior survey data.* Available at http://apps.nccd.cdc.gov/youthonline. Accessed on 8/24/2012.

Centers for Disease Control and Prevention (CDC). 2012. *Sexual violence facts at a glance.* Available at https://www.cdc.gov/violenceprevention/pdf/sv-datasheet-a.pdf.

Ciancone, A. C., Wilson, C., Collette, R., and Gerson, L. W. 2000. Sexual assault nurse examiner programs in the United States. *Annals of Emergency Medicine*, 35(4): 353–357.

Crandall, C., and Helitzer, D. 2003. An impact evaluation of a sexual assault nurse examiner (SANE) program. National Institute of Justice. From http://ncjrs.org/pdffiles1/nij/grants/203276.pdf.

Crowell, N. A., and Burgess, A. W. 1996. *Understanding Violence against Women.* Washington, DC: National Academy Press.

Doyle, J. 2001. Forensic nursing: A review of the literature. *Australian Journal of Advanced Nursing*, 18(3): 32–39.

Elliott, D. E., Bjelajac, P., Fallot, R. D., Markoff, L. S., and Reed, B. G. 2005. Trauma-informed or trauma-denied: Principles and implementation of trauma-informed services for women. *Journal of Community Psychology*, 33(4): 461–477.

Evans, M. M. 2003. *Maintaining the chain of custody: Evidence handling in forensic cases.* Washington, DC: AORN.

Federal Bureau of Investigation. Crime in the United States 1993. Washington, DC.

Federal Bureau of Investigation. Crime in the United States 2012. Washington, DC.

Fraser, I. S., Lahteenmaki, P., Elomaa, K., Lacarra, M., Mishell, D. R., Alvarez, F., Brache, V., Weisberg, E., Hickey, M., Vallentine, P., and Nash, H. A. 1999. Variations in vaginal epithelial surface appearance determined by colposcopic inspection in healthy, sexually active women. *Human Reproduction*, 14: 1974–1978.

Girardin, B. 2005. The sexual assault nurse examiner: A win–win solution. *Topics in Emergency Medicine*, 27(2): 124–131.

Greer, G. 1973. Seduction is a four-letter word. *Playboy*, 20(January): 80–82

Griffin, S. 1971. Rape: The all-American crime. *Ramparts*, 10: 26–35.

Heldman, C., and Brown, B. 2014. A brief history of sexual assault activism in the U.S. *Ms Magazine.*

Holmstrom, L. L., and Burgess, A. W. 1983. *The victim of rape: Institutional reactions.* New Brunswick, NJ: Transaction Books.

Kilpatrick, D. G. 2000. *Rape and sexual assault.* Charleston: National Violence Against Women Prevention Research Center, Medical University of South Carolina.

Koss, M. P. 1993. Detecting the scope of rape: A review of prevalence research methods. *Journal of Interpersonal Violence*, 8: 198–222.

Koss, M. P., and Harvey, M. R. 1991. *The rape victim: Clinical and community interventions.* Newbury Park, CA: Sage.

Lang, K. 1999. *Sexual assault nurse examiner resource guide for Michigan Coalition against Domestic and Sexual Violence.*

Largen, M. A. 1985. The anti-rape movement: Past and present. In *Rape and sexual assault*, ed. A. W. Burgess, 1–13. New York: Garland Press.

Ledray, L. 1999. *Sexual assault nurse examiner (SANE) development and operations guide.* Washington, DC: Office for Victims of Crime, U.S. Department of Justice.

Ledray, L. 2001. Evidence collection and care of sexual assault survivors. Violence against Women online resources. From http://www.vaw.umn.edu.

Ledray, L., and Summelink, K. 1996. *Service utilization among sexual assault clients.* Minnesota Sexual Assault Resource Service. Unpublished data.

Lenehan, G. 1991. Editorial: Sexual assault nurse examiner: A SANE way to care for rape victims. *Journal of Emergency Nursing*, 17: 1–2.

Lewis, C., DiNitto, D., Nelson, T., Just, M., and Ruggard, J. 2003. Evaluation of rape protocol: A five year follow-up with nurse managers. *Journal of the American Academy of Nurse Practitioners*, 15(1): 20–25.

Lewis-O'Connor, A., and Chadwick, M. 2015. Voice of the patient: Informing research, policy and practice on violence against women. *Journal of Forensic Nursing*, 11(4): 188–197.

Little, K. 2001. *Sexual assault nurse examiner (SANE) programs: Improving the community response to sexual assault victims.* Washington, DC: Office for Victims of Crime of the Office of Justice Programs of the U.S. Department of Justice.

Lynch, V. A. 1993. Forensic nursing: Diversity in education and practice. *Journal of Psychosocial Nursing,* 31(11): 7–14.

Lynch, V. A. 2006. *Forensic nursing.* Philadelphia: Elsevier.

Marchetti, C. A. 2012. Regret and police reporting among individuals who have experienced sexual assault. *Journal of the American Psychiatric Nurses Association,* 18(1): 32–39. doi: 10.1177/1078390311431889.

McFarlane, A. C. 1989. The aetiology of post-traumatic morbidity: Predisposing, precipitating and perpetuating factors. *British Journal of Psychiatry,* 154: 221–228.

Minden, P. B. 1989. The victim care services: A program for victims of sexual assault. *Archives of Psychosocial Nursing,* 3(1): 41–46.

National Intimate Partner and Sexual Violence Survey (NISVS). 2010. General Population Survey Raw Data. ICPSR34305-v1. Ann Arbor, MI: Inter-university Consortium for Political and Social Research [distributor], 2016-06-09. http://doi.org/10.3886/ICPSR34305.v1.

Nibert, D., Cooper, S., and Crossmaker, M. 1989. Assaults against residents of psychiatric institutions. *Journal of Interpersonal Violence,* 4: 342–349.

Nugent-Borakove, E., Fanflik, P., Troutman, D., Johnson, N., Burgess, A., and Lewis-O'Connor, A. 2006. Testing the efficacy of SANE/SART programs: Do they make a difference in sexual assault arrest & prosecution outcomes? Funded: U.S. Department of Justice. APRI and Boston College. Document No: 214252.

Patel, H. C., Courtney, G. M., and Forster, G. E. 1993. Colposcopy and rape. *American Journal of Obstetrics and Gynecology,* 168: 1334–1445.

Peterson J., Johnson D., Herz D., Graziano L., and Oehler T. 2012. *Sexual assault kit backlog study: Final report.* Washington, DC: National Institute of Justice.

Sievers, V., Murphy, S., and Miller, J. 2003. Sexual assault evidence collection more accurate when completed by sexual assault nurse examiners: Colorado's experience. *Journal of Emergency Nursing,* 29: 511–514.

Slaughter, L., and Brown, C. R. V. 1992. Colposcopy to establish physical finding in rape victims. *American Journal of Obstetrics and Gynecology,* 166: 83–86.

Slaughter, L., Brown, C. R. V., Crowley, S., and Peck, R. 1997. Patterns of genital injury in female sexual assault victims. *American Journal of Obstetrics and Gynecology,* 175: 609–616.

Smith, M. D. 2004. *Encyclopedia of rape.* Westport, CT: Greenwood Press.

Solola, S., Scott, C., Severs, S., and Howell, J. 1983. Rape: Management in an institutional setting. *Obstetrics and Gynecology,* 61: 373–378.

Sommers, M. S., Fisher, B. S., and Karjane, H. M. 2005. Using colposcopy in the rape exam: Health care, forensic, and criminal justice issues. *Journal of Forensic Nursing,* 1(1): 28–34.

Sommers, M. S., Schafer, J., Zink, T., and Weybright, D. 2005. R01NR05352 as described in the computer retrieval of information of scientific protocols at http://crisp.cit.nih.gov/crisp_query.generate_screen.

Taylor, R. 1998. Forensic nursing: Standards for new specialty. *American Journal of Nursing,* 98: 2.

Tjaden, P., and Thoennes, N. 2006. *Extent, nature, and consequences of rape victimization: Findings from the National Violence against Women Survey* (no. NCJ 210346). Washington, DC: National Institute of Justice.

U.S. Department of Justice, Office for Victims of Crime. April 2001. *Sexual assault nurse examiner (SANE) programs: Improving the community response to sexual assault victims* (NCJ 1863366) Washington, DC: U.S. Department of Justice, http://ojp.usdoj.gov/ovc/publications/bulletins/sane_4_2001/welcome.html.

U.S. Department of Justice, Office of Violence against Women. September 2004. *A national protocol for sexual assault medical forensic examinations: Adults/adolescents.* (NCJ 206554) Washington, DC: U.S. Department of Justice, http://www.ncjrs.org/pdffiles1/ovw/206554.pdf.

U.S. Department of Justice, Office of Violence against Women. April 2013. A *national protocol for sexual assault medical forensic examinations: Adults/adolescents.* (NCJ 228119). Washington, DC: U.S. Department of Justice, https://www.ncjrs.gov/pdffiles1/ovw/241903.pdf.

Wilson, D., and Klein, A. 2005. *An evaluation of the Rhode Island Sexual Assault Response Team (SART).* Rockville, MD: National Criminal Justice Research Service, U.S. Department of Justice.

Winfrey, M. E., and Smith, A. R. 1999. The suspiciousness factor: Critical care nursing and forensics. *Critical Care Nursing Quarterly,* 22(1): 1.

Woodling, B. A., and Heger, A. 1986. The use of the colposcope in the diagnosis of sexual abuse in the pediatric age group. *Child Abuse and Neglect,* 10(1): 111–114.

World Health Organization. 2002. *First world report on violence and health,* 166.

3 Youth, Social Media, and Internet Crime

Elizabeth Burgess Dowdell

CONTENTS

Introduction 35
Child Development and Risky Internet Behaviors 36
Social Networking Sites 37
Romantic Relationships and the Internet 38
Risk Assessment 39
Internet Safety 39
Social Media and Cyberbullying 41
Reporting Internet-Related Crime 42
References 43

INTRODUCTION

Technology is changing the way generations communicate, learn, work, spend leisure time, and access information. The last 20 years have been witness to an explosion in new technology that is now available in handheld data devices that not only communicate with letters and text but also with pictures, videos, and sound. Social media and the realities of individuals having a cyber life are best viewed through the behaviors of children and adolescents for whom these activities have become culturally engrained. As technology has increased in power and shrunk in size, access to instant communication, knowledge, photos, news, and other types of media is changing how children and adolescents are defining their experiences as well as themselves. In fact, Internet use among children and adolescents has been shown to be three times greater than that of television and nine times greater than that of radio (Lenhart, Madden, Macgill, & Smith, 2008). Advances in mobile technologies such as cellphones and mobile networks have enabled electronic communications between connected users, that is largely unimpeded by time and space as users can transmit data instantly, 24 h a day, 7 days a week, and from almost any location. This has had vast implications on the amount of time that youth are able to spend online. According to the Pew Research Center's 2015 report, 92% of teenagers in the United States aged 13–17 years old go online daily and 24% report being almost constantly on the Internet (Madden, 2011; Lenhart, Anderson & Smith, 2015). However, mobile connectivity has also extended online activities beyond the traditional boundaries of the home where Internet use was once limited to desktop computers. As such, the vast majority of online activities engaged in by youth have become less amenable to parental supervision and parents are less able to determine whether their children are being exposed to risky or inappropriate behaviors and content in the online world.

Increased risk behaviors in childhood should be seen within the context of child development and the individual's specific age group. For example, adolescents compared to younger children have different levels of risky Internet use, as well as health risk behaviors such as tobacco use, alcohol use, and weapon carrying all of which can have a lasting impact on both short- and long-term development. The presence of one risk behavior has been shown to correlate with the initiation of additional risk-taking and/or violent acts. If Internet risk behaviors follow the same path as health risk behaviors in that they increase as a child ages, then adolescents accessing the Internet, whether through social media, online games, email, blogging, instant messaging (IM), texting, sharing photos, videos, or creating blogs, and webpages that contain personal information, make themselves vulnerable.

The world at large has benefitted enormously from the Internet; however, it is becoming increasingly evident that there is a dark side to the Internet. The technology that permits the virtual instant transfer of information to the entire developed, and most of the underdeveloped world, is the same technology that can be harnessed as a powerful tool for criminally motivated individuals. Among the many areas of Internet-based criminal activity, the alarming rise in Internet-transmitted child pornography is of global importance. Additionally, there is growing apprehension about the potential for self-exploitation, cyber bullying, harassment, access to pornography, online predators, sexual solicitation, identity theft, and cyberstalking.

When discussing Internet crimes against children, much of the focus of law enforcement, safety programs, and the public has been on identifying and apprehending the offenders. However, a new category consisting of individuals victimized online has emerged. Online victimization often results in offline consequences, specifically sexual victimization, exploitation, and fraud. There are many professionals and providers who play a pivotal role in providing screening and clinical intervention services to victimized and exploited individuals across the lifespan. An understanding of the methods used by sex offenders and schemers to exploit and lure children in the context of the Internet is essential for families, law enforcement personnel, nurses, and other health care providers.

CHILD DEVELOPMENT AND RISKY INTERNET BEHAVIORS

The early years of a child's life are very important for his or her health and development. Healthy development, which includes physical, emotional, behavioral, and educational, means that children are able to grow up where their social, emotional, and educational needs are met. Violence and risk-taking behavior can be a frequent part of a child's growth and development and typically increases as the individual ages. Historically, risky behaviors were seen in the health arena such as smoking cigarettes, alcohol, and drug use as well as sexual experimentation. The contemporary health care setting now also sees risk-taking behaviors manifested in the online arena as a result of the increased presence of the Internet in daily life. National studies have found that the majority of today's youth are using the Internet as a venue for social interaction, idea sharing, artistic creations, photography, school work, as well as online journaling or blogging (Issac, Cusimano, Sherman, & Chipman, 2004; Dombrowski, Gischlar, & Durst, 2007; Lenhart et al., 2008; Madden, 2011). Using the Internet also means that they are at risk for being exposed to a variety of sexual and violent material, financial scams, cyberbullying, harassment, and for meeting dangerous people or predators (Issac et al., 2004; Dombrowski et al., 2007; Mitchell, Wolak, & Finkelhor, 2007; Ybarra, Diener-West, & Leaf, 2007; Dowdell, 2011; Dowdell, Burgess, & Flores, 2011; Lenhart, 2014; Office of Juvenile Justice Delinquency Prevention [OJJDP], 2014). Such risk is evidenced by reports made by children and adolescents disclosing exposure to undesired sexual material, explicit pictures, online harassment, and aggressive solicitation (Wolak, Mitchell, & Finkelhor, 2006). Individual online risky behavior can be inclusive of more than one behavior. Internet risk behaviors that have been found to cluster together include sharing of personal information (e.g., name of school, email address, picture of self); corresponding online with an unknown person or later meeting the person offline; engaging in online-initiated harassment (e.g., malicious or offensive jokes); visiting online-initiated sex sites; and overriding Internet filters or blocks (Issac et al., 2004; Dombrowski et al., 2007; Mitchell et al., 2007; Lenhart et al., 2008; Mitchell, Wolak, & Finkelhor, 2008; Lenhart, 2014).

Not surprisingly there are differences regarding online behavior based on age or grade with most differences related to access to the Internet as well as level of parental or caregiver monitoring. For example, the majority of American homes (82.5%) with school-age children report having broadband access which is 9 percentage points higher than the average for all households (Horrigan, 2015). Mobile access to the Internet is becoming more common for many children and adolescents who use their smartphone or other handheld devices. On average, 60% of families reported giving their child his or her first cell phone between the ages of 10 and 11 years while 20% reported giving their child a cell phone at age 8–9 years old (Wartella, Rideout, Lauricella, & Connell, 2013). The majority of teens (74%) between the ages of 12–17 years report that they access the Internet on their cell phones, tablets, and other mobile devices at least occasionally (Madden, Lenhart, Duggan, Cortesi, & Gasser, 2013). Older adolescent girls (55%) who own smartphones use the Internet most often from these phones and 34% of adolescent girls aged 14–17 years report that they mostly go online using their cell phone, compared with 24% of teen boys aged 14–17 years (Madden et al., 2013). Looking-up information and accessing social networking sites are common Internet behaviors.

SOCIAL NETWORKING SITES

The mid-1970s witnessed individual computers being linked electronically to form the basis of computer mediated scientific collaboration, social interaction, and networking. By 2010 there had been an explosion of social networking sites serving a wide variety of interests and individuals. Indeed, social networks created a public service that encouraged relationships between people and the content they shared. Not surprisingly, children and adolescents have been using social networking sites in large numbers. In one study the majority (88%) of the 2,077 high school students surveyed reported using social networking sites. Girls reported using social network sites more often than did boys (91.1% vs. 84.1%). However, more girls (81.4%) than boys (61.6%) reported using a privacy setting on their social network accounts that made their pages available only to those they had "friended" on the site (Dowdell et al., 2011). The same study reported that college age students are also using social networking sites with 91.4% being routinely online, with Facebook the most popular site. Female college students reported visiting a greater variety of websites (15) than did their male counterparts (3) (Dowdell et al., 2011). Sex offenders (Internet offenders who self-reported only an Internet-related sexual offense, such as possessing or transmitting child pornography or soliciting a minor over the Internet, men with a sexual offense that was not-Internet related, including child molesters, rapists, and generic offenders with no known offenses against children) have also reported social networking site usage. In this group, the most popular site among those who reported using a social networking site was Myspace followed by Facebook. Also, the majority of offenders in this study reported disguising their identities when online in teen or child chat-rooms, there are no findings reported to know if this also applies to their social network profile (Dowdell et al., 2011).

That adolescent and college age students have been found to have a higher variety of social networking websites than the offender group (including those who lived in the community and may have had unrestricted Internet access depending upon their probation restrictions) may be reflective of their developmental level where the milestone is experimentation in order to define self, develop autonomy, and fit in with their peers (Dowdell et al., 2011). That the adult offenders are also using social networking sites supports studies in the published literature that indicate social networks have significant adult use (Lenhart et al., 2008; Madden, Lenhart, Duggan, et al., 2013; Lenhart, 2014; OJJDP, 2014).

As more children and adolescents gain access to the Internet through mobile devices, such as smartphones, tablets, and other handheld data devices, social media sites, such as Facebook, Twitter, Snapchat, tumblr, Instagram, online blogs, and other sites have seen a dramatic increase in use. These social media sites allow users to join or create networks based on similar interests or behaviors. Facebook, for example, is a website that allows users to generate a profile containing self-description, demographic information, personal likes, hobbies and affiliations. It allows users to interact through viewing profiles, writing posts, sharing pictures, sending private messages, and online chatting. Not surprisingly, children and adolescents can and do share a wide range of information about themselves on social media sites because the sites themselves are designed to encourage the sharing of information and the expansion of networks. A 2013 survey of 802 adolescents (Madden et al., 2013) reported that:

- Adolescents of all ages are sharing more information about themselves on social media sites than they did in the past.
- Social media sites that encourage photo sharing (e.g., Snapchat, Instagram, etc.) are growing rapidly in terms of adolescent users.
- Teen Twitter use has grown significantly: 24% of online teens use Twitter, up from 16% in 2011.
- The typical (median) adolescent Facebook user has 300 friends, while the typical teen Twitter user has 79 followers.
- Focus group discussions with adolescents show that they have waning enthusiasm for Facebook, disliking the increasing adult presence, people sharing excessively, and stressful "drama," but they keep using it because participation is an important part of overall teenage socializing.
- Sixty percent of teen Facebook users keep their profiles private, and most report high levels of confidence in their ability to manage their settings. Adolescents take other steps to shape their reputation, manage their networks, and mask information they don't want others to know; 74% of teen social media users have deleted people from their network or friends list.
- Teen social media users do not express a high level of concern about third-party access to their data; just 9% say they are "very" concerned.
- On Facebook, increasing network size goes hand in hand with network variety, information sharing, and personal information management.
- In broad, measures of online experience, teens are considerably more likely to report positive experiences than negative ones. For instance, 52% of online teens say they have had an experience online that made them feel good about themselves.

ROMANTIC RELATIONSHIPS AND THE INTERNET

Online relationships are increasing in the adolescent population (Lenhart et al., 2015), and while many can be rewarding others can be dangerous. Many adolescents choose to enter into a casual online friendship or romantic relationship because the Internet provides easy access to individuals different from their families, schools, and communities. It is not uncommon for children and adolescents to turn to the Internet in order to find some sort of support or friend system. Youth that turn to online relationships for support, affirmation, and affection may do so because of feelings of isolation from their families or peers.

Self-exploitation, specifically the creating and distributing of explicit or inappropriate pictures of oneself or peers is an emerging high-risk Internet behavior that can have long-term implications. The practice of "sexting" refers to "sexual communications with content that includes both pictures and text messages, sent using cell phones and other electronic media" (Wolak & Finkelhor, 2011). This practice can also include children and teens in the acts of undressing each other, touching each other, or having sex.

Sexting images can also be posted on social networking websites where they can be downloaded and shared. The potential consequences of such exposure are far ranging and can include legal charges of child pornography and indecent exposure as well as the potential for leaked images to be used by others in an attempt to blackmail or intentionally humiliate. In addition, the photos can end up in the hands of child predators and can be circulated in private forums. The social implications of sexting can be just as devastating for teens when photos are viewed by members of a school team, school, or community. Once something is posted to the Internet, it never goes away; therefore, humiliation and emotional consequences of sexting can be long-term in nature.

For many individuals sexting is part of flirting, playing games, expressing interest in a potential partner, or trying to gain attention from a potential partner. When adolescents were asked about online relationships and romance (Lenhart et al., 2015) the following was reported:

- Fifty-five percent of all teens ages 13–17 have flirted or talked to someone in person to let them know they are interested.
- Fifty percent of teens have let someone know they were interested in them romantically by friending them on Facebook or another social media site.
- Forty-seven percent of them have expressed their attraction by liking, commenting or otherwise interacting with that person on social media.
- Forty-six percent have shared something funny or interesting with their romantic interest online.
- Thirty-one percent have sent them flirtatious messages.
- Eleven percent have made them a music playlist.
- Ten percent have sent flirty or sexy pictures or videos of themselves.
- Seven percent have made a video for them.

RISK ASSESSMENT

Cases that deal with children or adolescents should always include some level of an electronic assessment that screens for individuals who are at risk for injury, are actively risk taking, or complicit in risk. Each case should evaluate the child or adolescent individually assessing age, developmental level, cognitive level, number of data devices (mobile and home), access to Internet, patterns of Internet use, areas of vulnerability, and what that online life or relationship(s) meant to the child or adolescent. Interprofessional teams can be developed to work cases that involve children and adolescents' online behaviors as well as promoting Internet safety and education. The task, however, is to define the Internet in much the same way as other clearly identified domains of potential risk.

INTERNET SAFETY

Law enforcement as well as other professionals can and do provide education about Internet safety behaviors across schools and communities. Educational programs about safe Internet behaviors and risky behaviors in conjunction with resources available to contact for assistance must target parents, health care providers, educators, and other professionals who are in contact with an adolescent age group. Education targeting adolescents about not sharing a friend or family member's Internet or personal contact information must also be included in prevention education. Reinforcing the positive adolescent behavior of sharing online experiences with their parents, educators, or clinicians about online experiences that are both good and bad should be encouraged. Families or individuals who have had negative online experiences, must be encouraged by nurses and other professionals to report inappropriate or dangerous online behaviors to their local police agencies and to the National Center for Missing and Exploited Children (NCMEC) which coordinates the national cyber-tipline. At the NCMEC website there are online links to organizations that have established Internet safety programs that have been used throughout the United States. These programs have used a variety of techniques to educate children and adolescents about Internet safety, such as online learning modules, curriculum-based programs, online games, virtual training, online or web-based workshops for adults/parents, with some programs beginning to employ the strategy of peer-to-peer models to promote Internet safety.

Parents can be encouraged to surf the web with their child routinely as it provides an excellent opportunity for quality time in addition to gaining a better understanding of what the child is being exposed to online. Additionally, spending time online with children gives parents the opportunity to be the "teachers." Even though the Internet can be entertaining and educational, we do not want children to become isolated from their real-life peers. Computers should be located in a public space, such as a living room, recreation room, classroom, or library. In addition, it is beneficial to establish house rules or a contract with children for online safety. Young children should not have online profiles and early adolescents should be given guidance on what and where to post their profile. An online profile is a list of personal information that Internet service providers let you post online. This information allows other users to know more about you, such as your name, age, sex, address, hobbies, and interests. Although children may think having a profile is fun, there are some serious considerations that must be made. Online profiles can provide a "shopping list" of information for sexual predators and can be more harmful than helpful. Knowledge of the types of Internet services children use allows providers to assess risk and to devise individual care plans of education for children, parents, and professionals who work with children.

When talking to children or an adolescent about their online life, questions should focus on risky online and offline behaviors. Online risks to children must be discussed in an open forum. Parents are more often concerned about these issues than children. Children, especially adolescents, often believe or feel that exploitation and crime do not happen to them—but rather happen to "other kids." Online risks to children are a public health concern, and thus a risk assessment screening should be conducted with parents and children. Questions that can provide insight into the child's online behaviors and practices include some of the following:

1. Does the child surf the Internet alone?
2. Does the child go online daily? If so, does he or she spend more than 2 h per day online?
3. Does the child have a cell phone that has Internet access?
4. What type of device is used to access the Internet?
5. What types of Internet services does the child use (i.e., chat rooms, IM, email)?
6. Do the parents have a set of "house rules" regarding Internet use?
7. Do the parents have the child's password(s) for email, cell phone, social networking sites, webpages, blogs, etc.?
8. Does the child have an "online profile"? Where is this profile posted? Has the parent seen the profile?
9. What has the child shared about themselves online; where are they sharing this information (e.g., on a blog, a personal web site, their social network profile)?
10. What sites are being visited by the child routinely?
11. Who are they communicating with online?
12. What do they know about the individual(s) they are chatting with online; and how did they "meet" the individual(s)?
13. What types of websites does the child access (i.e., health information, support groups, hobbies, gaming, music)?

Answers to these questions will indicate whether the child or adolescent is talking with strangers and/or participating in other risky online behaviors. Internet safety interventions should be tailored to fit the child or adolescent's stage of development as well as online behavior(s).

Legal cases involving children or adolescents must also include an assessment of their online life and how it might impact the case. For example, a recent case in New Hampshire illustrates the complexities involved with adolescents and their behaviors on the Internet.

CASE NO. 1

In August 2015, a decision was reached in a trial at one of the nation's most exclusive boarding schools. The case was about an intimate encounter between a 15-year-old girl (freshman) and an 18-year-old (senior) acquaintance, and whether she consented as it escalated. She says he raped her; he maintains that isn't possible, because they didn't have sex. They agree that, in the days before he graduated in June 2014, the senior sent an email to the girl inviting her to join him for a "Senior Salute"—an apparently long-standing ritual where by older students try to hook up with younger girls before they graduate. After some initial reluctance, the girl agreed to meet the senior. The senior sent cordial emails and text messages to the freshman and after the encounter they continued to communicate using emails and texts. In some of those communications as well as those sent to friends confusion and uncertainty can be seen with the freshman saying in court, "I didn't want to come off as an inexperienced little girl," she said. "I didn't want him to laugh at me. I didn't want to offend him" (Bidgood, 2015).

Online communications between adolescents before or after an event can be damaging to the legal case but should be considered using the lens of child development. Children, adolescents, and young adults do not use the Internet in the same ways that parents or adults do. For the young, the Internet has become the main means of communication, of testing behaviors, of evaluating and determining self-esteem or a sense of belonging.

SOCIAL MEDIA AND CYBERBULLYING

Common characterizations of Internet offenders who sexually exploit often comprise of adult offenders attempting to communicate with, make contact with, or solicit sex from minors for the purposes of sexual gratification. While these behaviors are often facilitated through different forms of social media where children are likely to congregate, there are a host of other ways in which youth can be sexually exploited online. Cyberbullying involving sexual exploitation, for example, has become an increasingly prevalent and complex issue facing young people and several publicized cases have evoked responses from law enforcement as well as legislative bodies. These stories have all shared some commonalities and many have culminated in tragic losses of life. For example, in 2008 Jessica Logan committed suicide a few months after a nude cellphone photo had been widely circulated by an aggrieved ex-boyfriend. Her mother lamented that her daughter's suicide was a result of unbearable harassment from peers such as calling her vulgar names and throwing objects at her. In another case in British Columbia in 2012, Amanda Todd hanged herself after a stranger had convinced her to show her breasts on camera and subsequently circulated the image on the Internet, using it as a Facebook profile picture, and repeatedly stalking her as she relocated to different schools. The individual also blackmailed her on multiple occasions, threatening to circulate the photo to her friends if she did not "put on a show."

The above two cases show that the victims experienced significant bullying, harassment, and social ostracism for many months after having their photos circulated amongst their peers. Thus, interventions should address initial acts of nonconsensual distribution of explicit images as well as the potential for continuing harassment from other parties. Furthermore, interventions should be organized around a collaborative effort between professionals, school administrators, and family members to mitigate the potential harms, stigma, and psychological distresses associated with cases of cyberbullying that are shown to affect the normal functioning of a young victim. When cyberbullying cannot be resolved through informal mediation or when acts are serious or criminal in nature, law enforcement personnel must be equipped to identify offenders promptly. Although there are various mediums through which cyberbullying can be facilitated (e.g., text message, social media, webpage forums, email, etc.), most leave behind digital fingerprints that can enable investigators to trace incriminating evidence back to the offender. Therefore, preserving evidence by taking screen captures, printing chat logs, and recording dates and times of the messages or posts may help investigators discern whether a criminal act has indeed taken place, obtain a warrant, and possibly approach the mobile or Internet service provider for further information on the suspect. If a suspect has already been identified, a search warrant may be required by law enforcement personnel to initiate the process of examining electronic devices used by the alleged offender in the commission of the criminal act. To preserve the integrity of any digital evidence, law enforcement agencies must ensure that personnel are well trained in the extraction and examination of such evidence (see Fact Sheet, 2014).

REPORTING INTERNET-RELATED CRIME

Internet-related crime, like any other crime, should be reported to appropriate law enforcement investigative authorities at the local, state, federal, or international levels, depending on the scope of the crime. The primary federal law enforcement agencies that investigate domestic crime on the Internet include the Federal Bureau of Investigation (FBI), the United States Secret Service, the United States Immigration and Customs Enforcement (ICE), the United States Postal Inspection

TABLE 3.1
Crime as Corresponds with Appropriate Federal Agency for Reporting

Type of Crime	Appropriate Federal Investigative Law Enforcement Agencies
Computer intrusion (i.e., hacking)	• FBI local office • U.S. Secret Service • Internet Crime Complaint Center
Password trafficking	• FBI local office • U.S. Secret Service • Internet Crime Complaint Center
Counterfeiting of currency	• U.S. Secret Service
Child pornography or exploitation	• FBI local office • If imported, U.S. Immigration and Customs Enforcement • Internet Crime Complaint Center • ICAC office in state
Child exploitation and Internet fraud matters that have a mail nexus	• U.S. Postal Inspection Service • Internet Crime Complaint Center
Internet Crimes Against Children (ICAC)	• For information by state www.icactaskforce.org
Internet fraud and SPAM	• FBI local office • U.S. Secret Service • Federal Trade Commission (online complaint) • If securities fraud or investment-related SPAM emails, Securities and Exchange Commission (online complaint) • Internet Crime Complaint Center
Internet harassment	• FBI local office • ICAC office in state
Internet bomb threats	• FBI local office • ATF local office
Trafficking in explosive or incendiary devices or firearms over the Internet	• FBI local office • ATF local office

Service, and the Bureau of Alcohol, Tobacco and Firearms (ATF). Federal crime may be reported to the local office, each of these agencies has offices located in every state.

Additionally, the Internet Crimes Against Children Task Force Program (ICAC program) helps state and local law enforcement agencies develop an effective response to technology-facilitated child sexual exploitation and Internet crimes against children. This response encompasses forensic and investigative components, training and technical assistance, victim services, and community education. The program was developed in response to the increasing number of children and teenagers using the Internet, the proliferation of child sexual abuse images available electronically, and heightened online activity by predators seeking unsupervised contact with potential underage victims. The ICAC program is a national network of 61 coordinated task forces representing over 3,500 federal, state, and local law enforcement and prosecutorial agencies. To determine some of the federal investigative law enforcement agencies that may be appropriate for reporting certain kinds of crime, please refer to Table 3.1 (Department of Justice, 2015).

REFERENCES

Bidgood, J. 2015. Owen Labrie of St. Paul's School is found not guilty of main rape charge. *The New York Times,* August 28, 2015. Retrieved from http://www.nytimes.com/2015/08/29/us/st-pauls-school-rape-trial-owen-labrie.html?_r=0

Department of Justice. 2015. Cybercrime reporting resources. Available at: http://www.justice.gov/criminal-ccips/reporting-computer-internet-related-or-intellectual-property-crime

Dombrowski, S. C., Gischlar K., L., and Durst, T. 2007. Safeguarding young people from cyber pornography and cyber sexual predation: A major dilemma of the Internet. *Child Abuse Review,* 16(3): 153–170.

Dowdell, E. B. 2011. Middle school students and risky internet behaviors: Communication with online strangers and offline contact. *CIN: Computers, Informatics, Nursing,* 29(6): 352–359.

Dowdell, E. B., Burgess, A. W., and Flores, J. R. 2011. Original research: Online social networking patterns among adolescents, young adults, and sexual offenders. *American Journal of Nursing,* 111(7): 28–36.

Fact Sheet. 2014. Preparing and responding to cyberbullying: Tips for law enforcement. Joint fact sheet by the IACP, OJJDP, and NCMEC. Retrieved from www.iacp.org/Portals/0/documents/pdfs/IACP_NCMEC_OJJDP_CyberbullyingTipCardforLawEnforcement.pdf

Horrigan, J. B. 2015. The numbers behind the broadband 'homework gap'. Pew/Internet & American Life Project. Retrieved from http://www.pewinternet.org/fact-sheets/mobile-technology-fact-sheet/

Issac, D., Cusimano, M. D., Sherman, A., and Chipman, M. 2004. Child safety education and the world wide web: An evaluation of the content and quality of online resources. *Injury Prevention,* 10(1): 59–61.

Lenhart, A. 2014. Cyberbullying and online teens. Pew/Internet & American Life Project. Retrieved from http://www.pewinternet.org/fact-sheets/mobile-technology-fact-sheet/

Lenhart, A., Anderson, M., and Smith, A. 2015. Teens, technology and romantic relationships. Pew/Internet & American Life Project. Retrieved from http://www.pewinternet.org/2015/10/01/teens-technology-and-romantic-relationships/

Lenhart, A., Madden, M., Macgill, A. R., and Smith, A. 2008. Teens and social media: The use of social media gains a greater foothold in teen life as they embrace the conversational nature of interactive online media. Pew/Internet & American Life Project. Retrieved from http://www.pewInternet.org

Madden, M. 2011. Teens, social network sites & mobile phones: What the research is telling us (Slides). Pew/Internet & American Life Project. Retrieved from http://www.pewinternet.org/2011/12/05/teens-social-network-sites-mobile-phones-what-the-research-is-telling-us-slides/

Madden, M., Lenhart, A., Duggan, M., Cortesi, S., and Gasser, U. 2013. Teens and technology. Pew/Internet & American Life Project. Retrieved from http://www.pewinternet.org/files/old-media/Files/Reports/2013/PIP_TeensandTechnology2013.pdf

Madden, M., Lenhart, A., Cortesi, S., Gasser, U., Duggan, M., Smith, A., et al. 2013. Teens, social media, and privacy. Pew/Internet & American Life Project. Retrieved from http://www.pewinternet.org/2013/05/21/teens-social-media-and-privacy/

Mitchell, K. J., Wolak, J., and Finkelhor, D. 2007. Trends in youth reports of sexual solicitations, harassment and unwanted exposure to pornography on the Internet. *Journal of Adolescent Health,* 40(2): 116–126.

Mitchell, K. J., Wolak, J., and Finkelhor, D. 2008. Are blogs putting youth at risk for online sexual solicitation or harassment? *Child Abuse Neglect,* 32(2): 277–294.

Office of Juvenile Justice Delinquency Prevention (OJJDP). 2014. Internet crimes against children task force information. Retrieved from http://www.ojjdp.gov/programs/progsummary.asp?pi=3

Wartella, E., Rideout, V., Lauricella, A., and Connell, S. 2013. Parenting in the age of digital technology: A national survey. Report of the Center on Media and Human Development. Northwestern University, School of Communication.

Wolak, J., and Finkelhor, D. 2011. Sexting: A typology. University of New Hampshire. Retrieved from http://www.unh.edu/ccrc/pdf/CV231_Sexting%20Typology%20Bulletin_4–6–11_revised.pdf

Wolak, J., Mitchell, K. J., and Finkelhor, D. 2006. Escaping or connecting? Characteristics of youth who form close online relationships. *Journal of Adolescence*, 26(1): 105–119.

Ybarra, M. L., Diener-West, M., and Leaf, P. J. 2007. Examining the overlap in Internet harassment and school bullying: Implications for school intervention. *Journal of Adolescent Health*, 41(6 Suppl 1): S42–S50.

4 Elder Sexual Abuse Victims

Ann Wolbert Burgess

CONTENTS

Introduction 45
Scope of the Problem 46
Literature on Elder Sexual Abuse 46
Barriers in Investigating Elder Sexual Abuse Cases 47
    Intentional versus Unintentional Injury 47
    Older Adult Victim Unable to Communicate 49
    Signs and Symptoms of Abuse 49
    Inadequate Evidentiary Examination 49
    Resident-on-Resident Sexual Abuse 49
    Elder Sexual Abuse in Nursing Homes 50
Selecting Victims 52
Type of Crime 52
Early Recognition and Detection 53
Interviewing Elder Victims of Sexual Abuse 53
Forensic Services 54
Types of Interventions 55
    Individual Counseling 55
    Group Counseling 56
    Music Therapy 56
Living Situations of Elderly Victims 56
    Independent Living 56
    Assisted Living 57
    Nursing Home 58
Intervention for Family Members of Sexually Abused Elders 58
Prevention of Elder Sexual Abuse 59
Suggested Approaches to Elder Victims in Nursing Homes 61
    Crisis Intervention 61
    Nursing Home Staff 61
References 62

INTRODUCTION

Investigation and prosecution of an elder sexual crime present unique challenges to victims, the providers, and the criminal justice system. Medical, legal, and humanitarian costs of such crimes are immeasurable. It has been anecdotally reported that victims often had serious complications or even died from being sexually assaulted, perhaps even more so than a younger cohort. It is believed that older adult sexual assault crimes result in an increased need for more costly health care such as in a nursing home or hospital. Certainly, the personal suffering of the victims and their families must be considered along with a higher cost burden.

When criminal conduct occurs, prompt detection, documentation, and referral are critical to permit effective development of cases. After an occurrence of the crime, all necessary elements must be proved beyond a reasonable doubt. Also, the perpetrator must be identified beyond a reasonable doubt. Finally, the competency of the victim to provide evidence must be determined. These issues are very important with the older adult victim who has physical or mental impairment. A reliable and valid national source of data about the sexual abuse of elders is essential to set standards from which prosecutors can base assumptions to secure the prosecution of offenders.

Understanding how intentional sexual injuries are inflicted on older adults is a growing concern as the population over age 65 increases. This chapter contributes critical information to guide the identification of physical and psychological markers of elder sexual abuse to be integrated by law enforcement and providers. It reviews the scope of the problem, identifies issues that were derived from a study of elder victims of sexual abuse, outlines interviewing techniques with seniors, and suggests interventions for victimized elders.

SCOPE OF THE PROBLEM

The definition of elder sexual abuse includes cases of persons aged 60 and older where there is a physical sexual relationship without the elder's informed consent and including sexual assaults by strangers. A physical sexual relationship refers not only to intercourse but also to other forms of intimate sexual contact, such as touching the genital area or breasts when not associated with a defined nursing care plan.

LITERATURE ON ELDER SEXUAL ABUSE

Crimes against the elderly are of concern to law enforcement (Safarik, Jarvis, & Nussbaum, 2000) as well as health practitioners. Although official statistics are elusive, population data show that an increasing number of the baby boom generation will be aging into the elderly population in the first part of the 21st century. Coupled with the fact that people are living longer, it stands to reason that the risk of violent victimization to the elderly is likely to increase. In addition, over 50% of people older than 65 are women (U.S. Bureau of the Census, 2014). Thus, this information suggests that examination of any factors related to crimes against the elderly that may assist health practitioners for case identification (Burgess, Dowdell, & Prentky, 2000) and law enforcement in rapidly identifying and apprehending responsible offenders and protecting potential elderly victims has merit (Safarik et al., 2000).

There are no reliable estimates of the incidence or prevalence of elder sexual abuse in the community or in facilities (Lachs, Williams, O'Brien, Pillemer, & Charlson, 1998); however, for over 30 years statistics have been reported on sexual abuse of older individuals (Lachs & Pillemar, 1995). Statistics from early studies on sexual assault victims seen in hospital emergency rooms and rape crisis centers were reviewed. MacDonald (1971) reported that 7% of 200 sexual assault victims in Denver were aged 50 and older. Amir (1971) reported that 3.6% of rape victims in Philadelphia were over age 50. Fletcher (1977) found that 5.2% of victims referred to a Syracuse rape crisis center were over 55 years of age. Victims over 61 years composed 2.1% of the 1162 cases seen during the first 19 months of operation of the Miami rape crisis center (Hicks, 1976) and 5.8% were age 41–60. Cartwright and Moore (1989) found that 2.7% of sexual assault victims treated at an inner city hospital were 60 years and older, and a Texas study found that 2.2% of the reported sexual assault victims were women over 50 (Ramin, Satin, Stone, & Wendel, 1992).

Data from cases reported to Adult Protective Services (APS) were another source of information about elder abuse. In 1991, Ramsey-Klawsnik surveyed APS case workers in Massachusetts and identified 28 cases of women believed to have been sexually assaulted in their home, primarily by family members including adult sons and husbands. In a similar study drawing on Ramsey-Klawsnik's work, Holt (1993) reported 90 suspected elder sexual assault victims in England, 86% of whom were female.

The majority was over the age of 85, had dementia, and was frail. Most abuse occurred in the elder's domicile and 90% of the offenders were males upon whom the victim was dependent.

Nursing homes are not immune from elder sexual abuse as both staff and other residents have been identified as perpetrators. Teaster, Roberto, Duke, and Kim (2000) reported 42 Virginia APS cases of sexual abuse in both domestic and institutional settings. They found that 75% of the identified offenders were residents in the same nursing home as the victims. Facility staff members were also identified as offenders. In a study of 20 cases of 18 women and two men referred for civil litigation, Burgess et al. (2000) identified three methods of reporting an assault: informing a family member, sexual abuse that was witnessed, and clues detected by staff or family. In 10 cases, sexual assault examinations were not conducted due to delayed reporting, elder resistance, difficulty communicating with the elder, and difficulty obtaining accurate information. Of the 10 cases that had an examination, six revealed positive evidence. Elder response was identified in terms of expressions of fear and/or avoidance of male staff, change in behavior to withdrawal or lying in a fetal position, and development of new behaviors. All but three perpetrators were identified. Nursing home victims generally had documented symptoms of compounded and silent rape trauma (Burgess & Holmstrom, 1974).

In a study of forensic markers in 125 elder female sexual abuse cases, Burgess, Hanrahan, and Baker (2005) reported that the offender's hand was the primary mechanism of physical injury to the nongenital area of the elder's body and the offender's hands, fingers, mouth, penis, or foreign object were cause of injury to the genital area. Over half of the elderly victims had at least one part of their body injured and nearly half had signs of vaginal injury. Of the 46 cases with forensic results from a rape examination, 35% had positive evidence for the presence of sperm in the vagina, anus, or mouth.

How does the forensic marker (FM) study compare with two national surveys of violence against women (see Table 4.1)? The National Women's Study (NWS) is a longitudinal survey with a probability sample of 4009 American women of which 549 were 55 years or older. The purpose of the NWS was to identify risk factors for rape, physical assault, and post-traumatic stress disorder (PTSD). The National Crime Victimization Study (NCVS) data from 1992 to 2002 were used to study female sexual assault victims over 55 ($n = 8642$, weighted) using the National Archive of Criminal Justice online access forum. The NCVS is the most commonly referenced database on the prevalence of rates and types of violent crime in the United States. The FM study ($n = 125$) had an older sample and higher percentages in terms of recorded intentional injury, forced sex acts, use of weapons, perpetrator known to victim, rape reported to authority, and prosecution success. While the average age of subjects in the FM was slightly older than that in the other studies, basic demographic information is comparable with the NWS and NCVS. The most important observation is the lack of detailed data available at the national level on the sexual victimization of elders. While these differences may be due to sampling bias in the FM study and/or the undersampling of the NCVS and NWS, there is an obvious need to expand the national database to include details of forced intentional sexual injury of elders.

Forensic evidence was lacking in the FM study for several reasons. Some jurisdictions did not process rape kits because a suspect was not identified, standard protocol for the collection of forensic evidence was ignored, or state-of-the-art forensic equipment was not used in the forensic examination. In many cases, no pharyngeal or anal tests were performed, vaginal tests were performed in only about one in four victims, and testing for sexually transmitted disease was rarely performed.

BARRIERS IN INVESTIGATING ELDER SEXUAL ABUSE CASES

INTENTIONAL VERSUS UNINTENTIONAL INJURY

Assessing injury in the older adult as intentional or unintentional is the first step in the critical assessment of allegations. Often the events are not witnessed and accidental explanations are offered. The

TABLE 4.1

Comparison of Studies of Older Women Sexually Victimized

	Forensic Markers Study[a]	NCVS 1992–2002 Rape Victims >60 Years Old[b]	The National Women's Study (15)[c]
	n = 125	n = 8642	n = 549
Victims			
Mean/SD age	78.4	72.2	67
%Female	100	74.6	100
%Caucasians	83.1	73.0	83
%Black	11.9	12.3	8.5
Setting			
%Domestic	42.5	40	ND
%Institutional	38	ND	ND
%Other	19.5	ND	ND
Perpetrators % male	92.4	100	ND
Forced vaginal rape	78	ND	5.3
Forced oral rape	13.4	ND	0.5
Forced anal rape	23.9	ND	0.2
Forced digital rape	11.6	ND	2.2
Physical assault with weapon	15.7	0	3.5
Physical assault without a weapon	84.3	100	2.6
Perpetrator known to the victim	58.3	52.3	9.1
Rape reported to authorities	96.7	44	9.1
Charges made	55.2	50	ND

[a] Forensic Marker Study based on contributed cases by experts.

[b] National Crime Victimization Study (NCVS) is a weighted sample from 1992 to 2002 of women 60 years and older who were sexually abused or assaulted.

[c] The National Women's Study (NSW) is a subgroup of 549 women over 55 from the larger sample of 4009.

ND, no data.

scenario is further complicated when there is more than one caregiver spanning the period that injuries might have occurred. Additionally, there can be conflicting opinions between various health care specialties regarding the nature of the injury. All of these factors combined make the detection and substantiation of elder sexual abuse extremely difficult.

Nursing homes do not promptly report allegations of sexual or physical abuse, which results in delays in the investigation (Burgess et al., 2000). Often, evidence has been compromised and investigations delayed, which results in a reduced likelihood of a successful prosecution (U.S. General Accounting Office [USGAO] 2002). Reasons for untimely reporting of allegations include (1) residents may fear retribution if they report the abuse, (2) family members are troubled with having to find a new place because the nursing home may ask the resident to leave, (3) staff do not report abuse promptly for fear of losing their jobs or recrimination from coworkers and management, and (4) nursing homes want to avoid negative publicity and sanctions from the state.

Older Adult Victim Unable to Communicate

There are situations in which sexual injury is suspected but there is no outcry, witness, or forensic evidence to make a legal determination. However, in equivocal cases, measures should be taken to provide safety for the elder until a determination can be made as to whether (or not) abuse occurred.

Signs and Symptoms of Abuse

As previously noted, the elderly may bruise easily and physical signs are misinterpreted as the consequence of aging. Similarly, emotional symptoms of anxiety and depression with accompanying feelings of fear and confusion are not uncommon complaints of the elderly. The cause of the distress may not be known and the elder is treated for the symptom. A sexual assault, either acute or chronic, may be missed.

Inadequate Evidentiary Examination

Elder victims of sexual assault are less likely to have a complete sexual assault examination, including the collection of an evidence kit, an internal exam, and tests for sexually transmitted diseases. Part of the difficulty may be in the examination of the elder or because there is delayed reporting of the abuse.

Resident-on-Resident Sexual Abuse

The issue of elder sexual activity is sometimes addressed in policy manuals of nursing homes with a section on the sexual rights of the elderly. There is an attitude that sexual activity should even be encouraged among elderly residents. However, the part about consent between the two elders is less clear. In fact, sexual harassment, fondling, and even intercourse are often viewed as "no big deal" and certainly not harmful to the elder. In some nursing homes, nursing home staff are said to ignore the pleas for help by resident females. The cases in this category all involved elderly women who tried to reject the sexual advances of elderly men who, in most cases, preyed on many elderly victims. There was no history of a developing relationship, but rather a predatory style to the act.

CASE NO. 1

Fingerprints lifted from a vase led police to a 47-year-old convicted sex offender who was subsequently arrested and charged in 2004 with sexually abusing two women in their beds at a New York medical center after delivering flowers for an Upper East Side florist. The man entered the room of the first patient, a 58-year-old woman recovering from surgery, lifted her gown and fled when she woke up. The man then entered a second room, where he pulled down the diaper of a 93-year-old patient and got in bed with her. A hospital nurse spotted the man atop the patient and he fled. After the incidents, the police tracked the man through fingerprints left on the vase he brought to the room of the first patient. The man was working as a fill-in deliveryman and was living at a church shelter for the homeless. Five years previously, the man had been convicted of first-degree sexual abuse after a similar incident at another medical center in the area. He had completed the parole supervision period from the first sentence on August 1, 2000—about 1 year before this attack of August 18, 2001. For the first attack, he had been sentenced to serve 0–4 years and was released to parole on April 3, 2000, with only about 4 months of maximum parole supervision (expiring August 1, 2000). Hence, he was free (not under parole supervision) for about a year prior to the August 18, 2001 attacks on two patients. All victims of this rapist suffered significant distress both at the time of the assault and afterwards.

This case illustrates several facts about sexual abuse of the elderly: (1) the elderly are targeted as victims, (2) the location for an assault can be in a populated area, (3) the offender can be a repeat rapist, and (4) the assault is traumatic and the recovery is difficult for the senior.

Although sexual abuse is well established as a major social and health problem with significant physical and psychological consequences for its victims under age 60, the literature has neglected addressing the impact of sexual abuse on persons over age 60. While prevention programs are making a difference in child sexual abuse, there is no prototype in the elder sexual abuse arena for several reasons:

1. Anecdotal and research data are scarce as to the efficacy of treatment programs in the area of elder sexual abuse.
2. There is a history of discrimination against the elderly as well as misperceptions and stereotypes against older adults that has put elders at an increased risk for sexual assault.
3. Barriers to effective health care interventions include delayed reporting of the sexual abuse that results in failure to obtain a timely forensic evidentiary examination and treatment for injuries and infection.
4. There are few resources available for educating seniors and others about the prevention of sexual abuse.
5. There is little information on the motivation of offenders who sexually assault the elderly to provide direction for early detection to reduce offending behavior.

The goal of the next section is to provide investigators with ideas, practices, and solutions to the issues presented when helping older rape victims. The issues with seniors are quite varied and include helping persons with cognitive and physical disabilities and elders who have specific belief systems about sex and sexual violence in general.

ELDER SEXUAL ABUSE IN NURSING HOMES

Despite the considerable attention given to the diversity and ubiquity of sexual assault, it is all the more noteworthy that one of the most vulnerable groups of victims, the residents of nursing homes [estimated by Gabrel (2000) to be 1.5 million persons in 1997], remains in obscurity. Although the reasons for our failure to tackle forthrightly the problem of elder and nursing home resident sexual abuse are unclear, we can certainly posit two explanations: (1) the incomprehensibility and hence rejection of claims of sexual assault of nursing home residents, and, perhaps most importantly, (2) ageism—generalized, negative attitudes, if not outright hostility, toward older and cognitively impaired people (Butler & Lewis, 1973).

All other vulnerable target populations for sexual assault—children, adolescents, the developmentally delayed, and patients with physical and/or mental impairments—have been the subjects of varying degrees of clinical and empirical scrutiny. As with the elderly, when any member of these populations resides in an institutional setting, the risk for abuse increases simply as a function of the dependence on staff for safety, protection, and care.

While no data are available on institutional elder abuse, there are a few descriptive studies of rape in the elderly (Tyra, 1993). Ramsey-Klawsnik (1991) surveyed social workers to study suspected elder sexual abuse cases and identified 28 cases of women assaulted in the home primarily by family members (predominantly sons and husbands). In a study of 760 inner-city hospital victims, 2.7% of the sexually assaulted victims were 60 years or older (Cartwright & Moore, 1989). In a Texas study, 2.2% (*n* = 109) of the reported sexual assault victims over a 5-year period involved women over age 50 (Ramin et al., 1992).

The few studies on elderly rape victims are equivocal regarding injury. Genital trauma, evident even without colposcopy, is more evident in the postmenopausal sexually assaulted woman than it is in her younger counterpart (Cartwright, 1987). However, as with those 65 or younger, rape may occur without obvious injury (Cartwright & Moore, 1989; Tyra, 1993). Medical and forensic records between 1986 and 1991 from 129 women aged 50 years or older and 129 women from a comparison group aged 14–49 were reviewed. Trauma, in general, occurred in 67% of the older group and 71% of the younger group. Genital trauma was more common in the older than the younger group (43 vs. 18%). In contrast, extragenital trauma was more common in younger victims (66 vs. 49%). Forensic findings were similar in both groups; however, in the older group motile spermatozoa were seen only in those examined within 6 h of the assault (Ramin et al., 1992).

While considerable research has been conducted on memory and trauma in adults and children, only a few case reports have dealt with the elderly victim (McCartney & Severson, 1997). In elder sexual abuse cases, the question is raised as to whether the person can truly remember a sexual assault. McCartney and Severson (1997) remind us that the emotional meaning of an experience may be retained when the cognitive meaning is not present. Their case report indicates that an elder, despite cognitive impairments, can develop neurochemical and physiological symptoms of hyperarousal and PTSD. More importantly, they stress that without proper diagnosis there cannot be proper treatment. Sexual trauma and dementia comprise an area of ongoing research (Burgess & Phillips, 2006).

A pilot study of 20 sexually abused nursing home residents identified barriers to effective health care interventions (Burgess et al., 2000). First, delayed reporting of the sexual abuse resulted in failure to obtain a timely medical evidentiary examination, delayed treatment for injuries and infection, and an absence of medical or psychological follow-up care. Second, there was difficulty in performing an evidentiary rape examination due to leg contractures and cognition/memory problems. Indeed, in a number of the victims, fetal position and muscular rigidity made examination impossible. Third, there was evidence of wide variation in sexual assault evidentiary examination, such as lack of colposcope photographs for evidence. Fourth, the offenders who were arrested were either employees of the nursing homes or residents and, without prompt victim identification, were suspected to have abused more than one victim (Burgess et al., 2000).

The 20 predominantly elderly victims (18 women and 2 men) presented with rape-related trauma symptoms (urinary tract infections, nightmares, repeated reference to the event), general symptoms of traumatic stress (e.g., fear, confusion, hypersomnia, lack of appetite, withdrawal), and an exacerbation of symptoms related to their primary diagnoses. Preliminary findings suggested that the presence of a preexisting cognitive deficit such as dementia markedly delayed information processing, impaired communication, and compounded the trauma of the sexual assault. These victims simply were not equipped—physically, constitutionally, or psychologically—to defend against and cope with the proximal effects of assault. Perhaps the single most profound result of the sexual assaults against these victims was that 11 of the 20 victims died within 12 months of the assault.

Over the past decades our awareness of the magnitude and the impact of sexual victimization has increased considerably. Sexual abuse has become an acute problem, manifested in ever-increasing costs to society as well as to its victims. The costs incurred by society include medical and psychological services to aid victim recovery, the apprehension and disposition of offenders, and the invisible climate of fear that makes safety of paramount consideration in scheduling normal daily activities. In addition to the monetary costs associated with sexual abuse (Prentky & Burgess, 1990), the impact of such abuse on the victim has been well documented (Crowell & Burgess, 1996).

The Albert Lea Nursing Home case in Minnesota illustrates the vulnerability of elders and delayed reporting of over 6 months. Beginning in May 2008, the Minnesota Department of Health (MDH) investigated allegations that 15 residents of Good Samaritan Society—Albert Lea were being physically and mentally abused by five nursing assistants. As a result of this investigation, the MDH determined that verbal, sexual, and emotional abuse did occur at Good Samaritan Society— Albert Lea (Stahl, 2014).

Behavioral changes (trauma-related symptoms) noted after disclosure in the Albert Lea elders include

- Offering guarded responses when asked about the abuse;
- Displaying fear or strong ambivalence towards the offender(s);
- Protest behaviors/resistance to personal care;
- Inappropriate boundaries and behaviors;
- Increased anxiety or agitation during cares;
- Exacerbation of symptoms related to primary diagnoses;
- Appetite changes, sleep disturbances (e.g., inverted sleep patterns, hypersomnolence);
- Reenactment behaviors;
- Sexualized behaviors;
- New onset of behaviors; and/or
- Other clinical and behavioral changes (e.g., decreased participation in activities, yelling, crying, deterioration in physical condition).

SELECTING VICTIMS

Good Samaritan employees selected a vulnerable elder whom they knew had cognitive deficits. According to the MDH, the aides "would pull the curtain enough so when they heard a door open, they could stop" their attacks on the patients. Similarly police reports document that the perpetrators "would go into the residents' rooms and shut the door. They would then pull the curtain so that if anyone walked into the room, the curtain would protect them from anyone seeing them holding the residents down, covering residents' mouths, pinching their breasts, applying pressure on their peri-area or doing whatever other inappropriate action was involved." The perpetrators "knew not to leave marks and would only pinch or apply enough pressure to elicit a scream or a yelp of pain and not enough to leave a bruise." The perpetrators targeted residents who had Alzheimer's to such a degree that they either wouldn't be able to report or remember the abuse.

TYPE OF CRIME

The Crime Classification Manual (Douglas, Burgess, Burgess, & Ressler, 2013) defines the type of sexual assault perpetrated as Subordinate Abuse, 313.02. The defining characteristics state the relationship between victim and offender is one of subordination and status imbalance. One person has power and authority over another, in this case by occupation, services required, physical and cognitive status. The offender uses the relationship status to take advantage of the victim.

In this case, the perpetrators were able to take advantage of the elders because of their dementia and used their employee status to gain access to them. The perpetrators targeted residents who had dementia to such a degree that they either would not be able to report or remember the abuse. When talking about their abusive actions, the perpetrators made comments such as: "It's not like they can complain about it" and "It doesn't matter because they don't know what's going on."

The sexual and physical assaults of 15 residents in an Albert Lea nursing home in 2008 outraged Minnesotans, led to the criminal convictions of two nurse aides and prompted a change in state law. Victims and their family members sought justice by filing lawsuits against the nursing assistants, the home, and its owner. Yet by October 2011, all of the civil cases in Minnesota had been dismissed because the victims had died.

State lawmakers considered changing Minnesota's Survival Law, which requires that a personal injury case be dropped if the victim dies of unrelated causes. Advocates for the change say Minnesota is one of only four states with such a requirement, and they point to the Albert Lea case as the prime example of what's wrong with the law. A bill to eliminate the Survival Law was defeated in 2011 during the last day of session in a tie vote in the Senate, after the Minnesota Insurance Federation and Minnesota Hospital Association lobbied against it (Stahl, 2014).

EARLY RECOGNITION AND DETECTION

Early recognition and detection of abuse and reporting of cases means knowing the physical and behavioral indicators of sexual abuse in the elderly and being able to ask the right questions of the elder and to report all suspected cases to the proper agency (e.g., law enforcement, protective services, and/or hospital for forensic services). Two major barriers that mitigate against reporting elder sexual abuse include the victim's reluctance to report and disbelief in elder sexual abuse. In the case of victim reluctance, the senior may be frightened or embarrassed to report or the offender may be a domestic partner, a situation often noted in domestic violence cases. In such situations, the elder may fear being sent to a nursing home and losing his or her independence and/or financial base from the partner. In such a case, a plan needs to be worked out with the elder that will not jeopardize home security by identifying the resources and social support available to help the elder remain in the home. This may require talking with law enforcement and/or the prosecutor regarding charges that can be brought against the offending partner.

The second barrier in reporting elder sexual abuse is that of disbelief. Caregivers, staff, and family may believe the elder is fantasizing or in a cognitive disorganized state or making up a story. As with all ages of victims, staff need to take seriously all reports of sexual abuse. It will be up to experts in the area of elder sexual abuse to determine the credibility of the allegation and up to the prosecutor as to the viability of the case in the criminal justice system. Even if the prosecutor does not find adequate evidence to make the case, the elder should be respected and receive brief therapy services.

INTERVIEWING ELDER VICTIMS OF SEXUAL ABUSE

The following therapeutic tasks are important to develop trust with the elder in order to do an accurate assessment of the complaint of sexual abuse:

1. Tell the senior what to expect. Talk slowly and clearly. Advise victims they will be going to a hospital for an examination for the collection of evidence.
2. Assess the victim's sensory system. Can she or he hear and see people? A quiet and well-lighted area should be used and the investigator or staff person's face should be well in line of vision of the elder. If there are sensory problems, learn how the elder adjusts to the deficit by asking him or her or the family or caregivers.
3. Observe the victim's demeanor. Is she or he quiet, crying, angry, or in distress? Ask how the victim is feeling and if he or she has any questions about what is going to happen. Allow adequate time for the elder to express his or her emotions.
   a. *Signs of physical trauma* include observable objective evidence of injury such as bruises, abrasions, lacerations, and/or bleeding. The elder and accompanying family members need to be told that a comprehensive physical assessment will be conducted by the forensic examiner observing injury to the elder's general body condition and a separate genital examination will be conducted. Evidence of intentional injury is sought by asking the question as to how the injury occurred. Accidental injury needs to be ruled out. For example, nursing home staff have described genital bleeding as the result of "rough peri-care." This may or may not be accidental and needs further investigation.
   b. *Symptoms of physical trauma* include an indication of trauma provided by the elder. For example, the elder may say she was slapped or held by her throat but no observable injury can be noted. The symptom would be noted as part of the forensic record.

c. *Signs of emotional trauma* include observable signs such as crying, rocking, hands shaking, flushed appearance, signs of perspiration. Elders may try to hide their feelings by being very quiet, guarded, or controlled in their demeanor.

d. *Symptoms of emotional trauma* include reports by the elder of what was done to him or her. The record might state that the assailant covered the victim's eyes, held a knife to his or her throat, or pinned the elder to the floor. One victim said that she feared the assailant would try to smother her with pillows that were on her bed.

CASE NO. 2

The sister of a 72-year-old resident was outraged when she learned the administrator had not told her of her sister's two separate complaints of rape. She watched her sister deteriorate after the assaults. The sister began using a walker, developed burning on urination, exhibited anxiety, and was hospitalized for fever secondary to pneumonia. One month later she evidenced a diminished level of consciousness and alertness and was transferred to a hospital and diagnosed with urosepsis. Her condition continued to deteriorate when she returned to the nursing home until she was no longer independent, ambulatory, or able to wheel herself. Her sister took her into her home. After moving into her sister's home, the victim feared that the offender would come to the house and asked her sister to tell him that she lived elsewhere. Despite diagnoses of coronary arteriosclerosis, senile dementia, and mental retardation, the sister gave a consistent account of the rape.

CASE NO. 3

A male resident whose assault was observed by staff refused to remove his clothes at night, instead wearing two and three layers of clothing. The resident persistently would ask to go home and on at least three occasions escaped from the nursing home. Over time, the resident became reclusive, verbally aggressive, and told family members not to visit.

CASE NO. 4

A 73-year-old man acted ashamed and embarrassed, cried at night, said it hurt between his legs, and that he wanted to talk to a judge. He would resist going with staff for his bath, jumped when someone came into the room, and showed rapid mental deterioration.

FORENSIC SERVICES

The reporting of a suspected case of recent elder sexual abuse requires that forensic evidence be collected. The goal of the forensic examination is the systematic and comprehensive collection of evidence from the victim that has been transferred from the perpetrator. It is conducted in a psychologically supportive manner by explaining and requesting consent for each step in the process. Often a family member will be with the elder to help in this process, especially if it is a nursing home case. Photographs will need to be taken; clothing worn during the assault will be collected and slow, careful examination of the victim's body for any transfer of evidence will be conducted.

Saliva and semen will be of prime importance. Hairs and fabrics must be collected and placed on paper for folding. Fingernail scrapings and hairs may be collected. Evidence will be collected from body orifices. The use of a high-intensity light or colposcope will be used and photographs taken. A standard rape kit will be used and all evidence will be air dried and submitted to a police crime laboratory for analysis.

Evidence collection may be different in the elderly than in the adult victim. Assistance may be required for supporting the elder's legs during the inspection. Legs that are contracted from muscle atrophy require gentle pressure for abduction from assistants. Severe contractures may require the legs being held upwards toward the ceiling in order to accomplish external visualization. The fragility of skin and the lack of estrogenized vaginal tissues require very careful handling of the elder's body. Also, a small pediatric speculum is recommended for the internal examination.

TYPES OF INTERVENTIONS

INDIVIDUAL COUNSELING

Law enforcement needs to have a list of counselors who have experience with elderly victims for purposes of referral. The impact of a sexual assault on an elder includes considering the advanced age, general health status, and the diminished cognitive processing. The latter explains why behavioral symptoms may be delayed and prolonged in the elderly. The following behavioral signs and symptoms have been documented in elders in terms of rape trauma syndrome and post-trauma symptoms. Investigators need to remember that some of the symptoms are muted in the elderly due to their declining ability to report problems.

Victimized elders have been noted to exhibit rape-related trauma symptoms of becoming fearful of the location of the rape (e.g., bathrooms, showers), becoming fearful of males and male caregivers if assaulted in a nursing home, experiencing flashbacks (e.g., there is a boy in the closet), and being easily startled (e.g., hyperarousal symptoms). They also will exhibit general symptoms of traumatic stress (e.g., fear, confusion, hypersomnia, lack of appetite, withdrawal) and an exacerbation of symptoms related to existing physical and prior mental conditions. Elders with the presence of a preexisting cognitive deficit, such as a dementia, may have delay in information processing and impaired communication that potentially compound the trauma of the sexual assault. The vulnerability of an elder due to physical and emotional fragility places victims at unusually high risk for severe traumatic reactions to assault. Elder victims simply are not equipped physically, constitutionally, or psychologically to defend against and cope with the proximal effects of sexual assault. One 87-year-old nursing home resident with severe dementia, raped by an attendant, cried constantly for weeks following the assault. Only her daughter's presence helped to relieve the sobbing.

Rape trauma syndrome, which includes both acute and long-term symptom responses to traumatic sexual assault, has two distinct variations: compounded rape trauma and silent rape trauma. In compounded rape trauma, victims have a past and/or current history of psychiatric, psychosocial problems that compound the effects of the sexual assault. In silent rape trauma, expression of assault-related symptomatology is muted, undetected, or absent. Elder sexual abuse victims are subject to both compounded and silent rape trauma. A 77-year-old victim of the Belmont Shore, California, rapist, who was a cancer survivor with a colostomy bag, testified that she was sleeping in her easy chair when she awoke suddenly to someone grabbing the crown of her head. She thought it might be an animal and tried to squirm around only to note the hand got tighter. He led her into the bedroom and raped her and told her to relax and enjoy it. The victim testified that the rapist spoke kindly, asked her about her life, offered her a glass of water at one point, and tucked her in before he left. Two weeks later the rapist returned and raped her in her bed. He had disconnected her motion-detecting lights as well as her phone lines. The victim did not report the first rape due to fear and shame, but did report the second rape. The jury acquitted the defendant for the first assault, claiming no DNA, but convicted for the second rape where there was DNA to match to the rapist. This serial offender was charged and convicted of the rape of 14 women, ages 39–77, over a 5-year period.

Group Counseling

As with younger victims of sexual assault, the agency should have a list of counselors skilled in conducting group work with victims. Elder victims living in the community often join groups with younger victims. The deciding factor is the choice of the elder and whether or not he or she wishes to join.

Music Therapy

Advocates visiting elder victims in an institution can use the technique of music therapy. It requires having a tape recorder and tape of music selected by the elder. The goal of the therapy is to help the victim learn to reduce the anxiety experienced during the assault and in the activation of rape trauma aftermath symptoms.

LIVING SITUATIONS OF ELDERLY VICTIMS

Independent Living

Seniors living independently include those living with their families and/or partners as well as those living alone. If the senior who is raped is alert and verbal, and has minimal memory deficits, the clinician generally follows the same protocols for support services as those for adult victims in general. That is, the clinician meets with the senior, assesses social network support, and provides crisis counseling. The following cases are examples of victims in independent living situations.

CASE NO. 5

A 68-year-old woman was raped and robbed of $80 by an intruder who kicked down her door. The offender managed to get into the apartment building lobby and past a locked front door. The woman had just returned home and left the apartment door ajar. The man walked up to the woman's apartment and asked if he could use her phone. The woman answered that he could not and shut the door but he kicked open the door, pulled out a knife, and ordered her not to scream. An hour later the woman's husband returned home, found his wife in shock, and called 911. The husband's support and the encouragement provided by the therapist and prosecutor enabled the victim to testify in court and help to win a conviction.

CASE NO. 6

In another case, a 73-year-old woman's door window was broken early one morning and when she opened her door, a 25-year-old man jumped inside, grabbed her, covered her mouth, and forced her to promise not to call the police. They spoke different languages, but after they both calmed down, she showed him family pictures, they shared stories, and she offered him food.

The intruder fell asleep, awoke, and went to the bathroom, got undressed, exposed himself to her, and then fell back asleep. The woman barricaded herself in her bathroom with a telephone and called her daughter who called the police. Police found the man's clothing strewn around the house; he wore sweat pants with a condom in his pocket but claimed he was intending to steal jewelry. He had worked at the woman's home as a gardener. He was charged with two counts of residential burglary, one count of home imprisonment of an elder, and one count of elder abuse. One of the two burglary charges arose from another woman, a 78-year-old, who contacted authorities after learning of the incident, saying this man also landscaped her yard earlier that month and when he used the bathroom exposed himself to her.

A jury found the intruder guilty and he was sentenced to 11.3 years in state prison. The charges included elder abuse, which in California statutorily includes stranger victimization of an elder (where the perpetrator reasonably should have known the victim's age).

It was very important in this case that no one (professional or friend) questioned the victim's interactions with the perpetrator. While some individuals unfamiliar with victimizations might find the interactions paradoxical (and wonder why the victim did not fight off the offender), clearly victims of sexual abuse utilize individualized methodologies to cope with criminal violence such as being imprisoned in one's own home with an exhibitionist.

In cases of elderly victims, professionals may also sometimes view elders as weak, helpless or powerless, and incapable of defending themselves from harm. Instead, professionals need to be impressed with some of the creative coping strategies used by elders, other than physically based strategies, when faced with a frightening situation. Clearly, the victim needs to feel that those around him or her see the actions as appropriate, thus reducing the chances that the victim will doubt or question himself or herself.

Assisted Living

An elder living in assisted living generally infers there is a protected environment that has safety features in place. That is, different shifts of staff check on residents over 24-h periods, and meals and cleaning services are often provided.

When an elder is sexually assaulted in a perceived safe environment, such as assisted living or an institution, it causes additional trauma because staff have been trusted and there is a breach in safety and security. Very often, the family feels guilty for not keeping the elder at home. The intervention for the elder needs to focus on verbal and nonverbal signs of stress, behavioral disorganization, aggression, functional ability, and health status. The traumatized elder needs careful observation and a good description of pre-assault behavior from family and staff members for a baseline against which to assess changes.

CASE NO. 7

A 41-year-old man entered the unsecured door of an assisted living facility and raped an 83-year-old woman in her room. The woman reported she was awakened to the man being in her room and that he stated, "Don't scream or I am going to kill you." She further stated that he held her down and assaulted her, taunting her and ordering her to use profanity. She refused. After the assault, the man ran into a facility employee and asked her to help him find a friend who he said worked at the facility. He then put his hand over her mouth and wrestled her to the ground, grabbing her checkbook. He escaped and the employee called 911. The police arrived at 2:45 a.m. and found the perpetrator a few blocks away. When shown videos of himself at the facility, he admitted he entered the premises to seek to sexually assault someone. The son reported that his mother's personality changed after the attack. She moved closer to him but remained withdrawn and reclusive, the opposite of her pre-assault lifestyle.

NURSING HOME

Three common nursing home sexual abuse victim profiles include (1) physically disabled older resident, (2) cognitively impaired resident, and (3) physically impaired younger resident. The physically disabled older resident has no cognitive or mental impairment but requires assistance with mobility. The assistance may be short term, such as needing rehabilitation following surgery, or long term as in residents with complications from a stroke. The cognitively impaired resident has a primary diagnosis of Alzheimer's disease or other dementia and the physically impaired younger resident may have a physical impairment due to a chronic neuromuscular disorder, such as multiple sclerosis or amyotrophic lateral sclerosis (also known as ALS or Lou Gehrig's disease), or an impairment as a result of trauma from a motor vehicle accident or gunshot wound.

Nursing homes are, for the residents, precisely that—a home in which the staff function as the residents' caregivers (in both a literal and figurative sense). The nursing home and its staff are perceived as "safe" and violations represent a more profound betrayal of trust than violations committed outside the sanctity of the nursing home.

The sexual victimization of older adults in nursing homes is under-recognized and underreported. Even when an incident is identified, reporting is delayed and treatment and post-rape services are often inadequate (USGAO, 2002). Furthermore, prosecution of these crimes is fraught with problems related to poor-quality evidence because of delays in reporting. Older adults residing in nursing homes often require assistance with basic activities of daily living such as bathing, dressing, and feeding because of physical and cognitive impairments. These disabilities make an individual dependent upon others and an easy target for a sexual predator (Burgess et al., 2000).

There are approximately 17,000 nursing homes in the nation with 1.5 million older adult residents (USGAO, 2002). In a study of 5297 nursing homes in Pennsylvania, New Jersey, and New York, a quarter of these nursing homes had serious complaints alleging situations that harmed residents or placed them at risk of death or serious injury (USGAO). Concerns about the quality of care have mostly been focused on malnutrition, dehydration, and other forms of neglect. However, there is mounting concern about physical violence—particularly sexual abuse—by those who have been entrusted with their care (Burgess et al., 2000).

In a pilot study of 20 elderly women in nursing homes, the single most profound result of the sexual assaults against these victims was that 11 of the 20 victims died within 12 months of the assault (Burgess et al., 2000). Because more than half of these victims were ages 80–96 at the time of the assault, it obviously cannot be asserted that death was a distal effect of the assault. Although it is not possible to determine in each case whether the assault accelerated death, the fact that more than half of the victims died—not from the assault itself but within months of the assault—is clearly noteworthy, if not alarming.

INTERVENTION FOR FAMILY MEMBERS OF SEXUALLY ABUSED ELDERS

Family members need help when an elder is sexually abused, whether it happens when the elder is living alone, in assisted living, or in a nursing home. The following case relates to the opening case.

CASE NO. 8

When a Queens, New York, woman read about a man assaulting two elderly patients in their hospital beds, she reported it was like reliving her own nightmare. She told a friend she thought it was the same man who assaulted her mother, then 79, in her bed at a New York medical center. The man had been taken into the hospital as a patient and admitted to the narcotics unit. Somehow he escaped from his bed and was lost for nearly an hour before hospital officials found him, dressed in scrubs in her mother's room. When her mother attempted to resist his attempts to abuse her, he slapped her face. The woman was quoted in the newspaper as saying, "Maybe when you are younger, you are more resilient, but my mother was never the same after that. She had nightmares three times a week until she died." The woman said her mother was subjected to over a dozen interviews with police, district attorneys, and hospital staff after the assault. The daughter wondered if it hastened her developing senility. She added, "I live with the guilt because I put her in the hospital originally." She also bemoaned the lack of support groups and organizations to address the problem.

It is common for family members to feel guilty when an elder is sexually abused. They often feel responsible for decisions made for the elder, especially if she or he is in a nursing home. The clinician can explore with the family member the decision for the living situation of the elder, whether it is independent, assisted, or dependent living. Sometimes family members feel doubly guilty that the elder is in a nursing home and then the elder is raped. The exploration of this guilt in terms of realistic parameters is best accomplished in a support group setting and is an important part of counseling. There are care provider support groups for people who have to make a decision to put a family member into a nursing home.

CASE NO. 9

In the following case, a husband of 44 years made the difficult decision to place his 64-year-old wife in a nursing home, as he was unable to care for her due to a developing dementia and her increasing agitation. Three months after her admission, the husband received a telephone call from a discharged employee stating her conscience was bothering her knowing that information was being withheld from him. The former employee went on to relate that the wife had been sexually assaulted by another nursing home resident. When the husband inquired about the incident, the executive director told him that patients are allowed to hug, kiss, and fondle each other, even to the point of sex. When the husband talked directly to the care manager, he learned that his wife and the male resident were both found nude in bed and the male was penetrating his wife. The husband argued it was rape (not consensual sex) given the fact that his wife could not dress or undress herself and could not get into bed by herself. The husband immediately removed his wife from the nursing home and contacted the state ombudsman's office and police to report the rape. Unfortunately, the case lacked forensic evidence and witnesses for a criminal case, but a civil suit was pursued and a settlement reached against the nursing home.

Outreach by an investigator would be critical to recommend intervention both for the wife in the new nursing home and a family member support group for the husband. There was no service available in his state and arrangements were made for him to talk by telephone to another family member of a resident-on-resident nursing home sexual abuse case.

PREVENTION OF ELDER SEXUAL ABUSE

Prevention programs of elder sexual abuse are aimed at public education to help people understand what elder sexual abuse is and how it can be prevented. The programs focus on educating seniors, front line workers, and the public about situations and behaviors indicative of abuse. Case examples from news media provide talking points for discussion. The following case illustrates police working with rape crisis staff to educate seniors.

CASE NO. 10

In a Georgia case, a man cut the back porch screen of a home and attacked an 80-year-old woman. The woman told police a man with a cloth over his head ripped off her pajamas and raped her. He then took her nightclothes and bed sheets with him. The victim took a shower after the man left. The police had little to work with on this case and thus the news media account published the following:

If you are raped, rape crisis organizations urge you not to take a shower or bathe before you are examined. You may have valuable evidence on you. Don't touch the crime scene if possible. The rapist may have touched a surface and police could get a fingerprint. Save all your clothing from the crime and give them to the police. Document any injury you have either by photograph or by showing it to investigators. All of these things will help investigators trying to solve the crime.

Prevention programs for elders living independently in the community, in assisted living facilities, or in nursing homes need to be part of all sexual violence community education programs. The program would include the traditional public education to teach elder safety as well as media ads to raise awareness and to increase reporting of abuse.

The senior safety education component requires an understanding of the level of the elder's independent functioning and the social network support. In addition, there should be emphasis on a safety checklist specifically designed for seniors. It is stressed that prevention is by safety awareness and not by unreasonable fear of attack.

For seniors living alone in a neighborhood, the safety questions are as follows: Does the senior have some connection with neighbors or family? Is there an alert button? Does someone check on him or her each day? Does he or she have good safety locks? Are the outside areas well-lighted so that an attacker cannot hide in the yard or bushes? Are ground-level windows secure and routinely examined? Are workmen or handymen known to family or neighbors? For suspected domestic violence cases, elders should be asked if they have been slapped, hit, or beaten in the last 6 months.

Two case examples illustrate elders living independently who were raped and the relationship of the offenders to them.

VICTIM OF A STRANGER

In Texas, a 95-year-old great-grandmother was trimming grass near some railroad tracks outside her home when she was pushed down by a stranger and raped. Her grandson discovered her after the security company telephoned him that his grandmother's alert button had discharged and she was not responding to her telephone. In this case, the elder's alert button saved her life even though it took many hours for her to be found.

Sometimes the offender is a family member in a domestic rape as in the following case.

DOMESTIC VIOLENCE VICTIM

In Florida, a 94-year-old widow called police to report that her 42-year-old grandson (who lived with his wife in his grandmother's home) had raped her. Police found the elder bleeding and badly bruised. The grandson was found drunk and asleep in the grandmother's bed. Forensic evidence linked him to the crime. Subsequently, the victim's health deteriorated. She became wheelchair bound, required oxygen, and was admitted to a nursing home 3 months after the attack.

SUGGESTED APPROACHES TO ELDER VICTIMS IN NURSING HOMES

CRISIS INTERVENTION

Intervention services are much more difficult to provide for the physically handicapped and/or cognitively compromised patient. The critical first step to a traumatized elder in a nursing home is to try to establish contact and trust using a soothing approach and voice.

Talking therapy is usually not the treatment of choice. Expressive therapies, including music therapy and drawing, may be more useful to calm a frightened and anxious elderly resident. The elder's favorite music tapes played on a cassette can be soothing and calming during a 30-min session with an elder victim. Just sitting quietly with the elder shows safety, compassion, and concern.

Do not avoid expressing that you know something happened to the elder. Even if the victim has serious cognitive deficits, such as through a stroke, do not assume that he or she does not understand. Staff sometimes fail to try to understand the avenues of communication in people with cognitive problems because they assume the elder does not understand.

Develop a system of communication whereby the elder can answer "yes" or "no." Once established, one can try to work with the victim. Use comforting measures such as positioning pillows and adjusting covers. Talk in a soft, soothing voice but be sure the elder can hear. Avoidance of what happened is not a comfort. It is not necessary to dwell on it but do address it. Suggestions are to say, "I know something happened to you and that you were hurt on your body. Can you show me or tell me about it?" It is critical to emphasize the person who hurt the victim has been taken away and that he or she is now safe. The sensory link is important to establish. One might say, "I want to try to understand and talk with you the best way you can. Squeeze my hand if you understand. Nod or blink your eyes to let me know you understand."

Consistency of visits is important. Try to schedule the visit to the nursing home at a consistent time each visit. Short, frequent visits are most therapeutic. Try to visit when the elder is not receiving nursing or other services. Avoid nap times. If no one is available on staff to visit a victim in a nursing home, refer to a visiting nurse association, which can provide a geropsychiatric nurse specialist for consultation and guidance.

Elder victims may have preexisting areas of weakness or vulnerability, primarily physical and cognitive, which serve to complicate or mute the assault symptom presentation. Observe behavior carefully for symptoms of trauma.

NURSING HOME STAFF

A thorough physical, cognitive, and psychosocial assessment should be completed by professional staff at the time of admission to the nursing home. These assessments provide nursing staff and other caregivers with a baseline from which to judge behavioral changes. They need training to detect noteworthy changes in baseline behavior in victims who are likely to exhibit symptoms in a muted or "silent" fashion.

All nursing home personnel should be trained rigorously to identify signs and symptoms of assault-related trauma and to be vigilant about suspicious, pre-assault behaviors, including the same grooming and manipulation observed with most sex offenders. Nursing home staff need to be sensitized to the gravity of the assaults on residents. Stereotypes exist, from cynical disbelief that anyone would sexually assault an elderly individual to what can be described as a perverse sense of amusement.

In conclusion, the elderly victim of sexual violence represents a vulnerable and poorly under-stood population of victims. Elders may be sexually assaulted in their homes or the community, in an assisted living facility, or in a nursing home environment. Offenders can be strangers, domestic partners, family members, another nursing home resident, or a caregiver.

As with all victims, the primary goal of prevention and intervention is safety for the senior. Special adjustments need to be made for the interview and forensic examination process due to the elder's physical and emotional health status. Trauma symptoms will be filtered through any cogni-tive deficits that are present and adjustments need to be made for any short-term memory issues.

The prosecution of offenders of elderly victims is critical to decreasing abuse to additional vic-tims. Law enforcement, sexual assault nurse examiners, medical and mental health staff, social service providers, and prosecutors all need to work together as a team. Most importantly, agencies need to add elder sexual abuse to their community education programs, train their staff in detecting and reporting elder sexual abuse, and recruit staff who will provide crisis intervention services to traumatized elderly victims.

REFERENCES

Amir, M. 1971. *Patterns in forcible rape.* Chicago: University of Chicago Press.

Burgess, A. W., Dowdell, E. B., and Prentky, R. A. 2000. Sexual abuse of nursing home residents. *Journal of Psychosocial Nursing,* 38(6): 10–18.

Burgess, A. W., Hanrahan, N. P., and Baker, T. 2005. Forensic markers in female sexual abuse cases. *Clinics of Geriatric Medicine,* 21(2): 399–412.

Burgess, A. W., and Holmstrom, L. L. 1974. Rape trauma syndrome. *American Journal of Psychiatry,* 131: 981–986.

Burgess, A. W., and Phillips, S. L. 2006. Sexual abuse, trauma and dementia in the elderly. *Victims & Offenders,* 1(2): 193–225.

Butler, R. N., and Lewis, M. I. 1973. *Aging and mental health: Positive psychosocial approaches.* St. Louis, MO: Mosby.

Cartwright, P. S. 1987. Factors that correlate with injury sustained by survivors of sexual assault. *Obstetrics and Gynecology,* 70(1): 44–46.

Cartwright, P. S., and Moore, R. A. 1989. The elderly victim of rape. *Southern Medical Journal,* 82: 988–989.

Crowell, N., and Burgess, A. W. 1996. *Understanding violence against women.* Washington, DC: The National Academies Press.

Douglas, J. E., Burgess, A. W., Burgess, A. G., and Ressler, R. K. 2013. *Crime classification manual.* Hoboken, NJ: John Wiley & Sons.

Fletcher, P. 1977. *Criminal victimization of elderly women: A look at sexual assault.* Syracuse, NY: Rape Crisis Center of Syracuse.

Gabrel, C. S. 2000. Characteristics of elderly nursing home current residents and discharges: Data from the 1997 National Nursing Home Survey. Vital and Health Statistics of the Centers for Disease Control and Prevention, National Center for Health Statistics, no. 312.

Hicks, D. 1976. Medical treatment for the victim: The development of a rape treatment center. In M. Walker and S. Brodsky (eds.) *Sexual assault.* Lexington, MA: Lexington Books, 53–59.

Holt, M. G. 1993. Elder sexual abuse in Britain: Preliminary findings. *Journal of Elder Abuse & Neglect,* 5(2): 63–71.

Lachs, M. S., Williams, C. S., O'Brien, S., Pillemer, K. A., and Charlson, M. E. 1998. The mortality of elder mistreatment. *Journal of the American Medical Association,* 280(5): 428–432.

Lachs, M. S., and Pillemar, K. 1995. Current concepts: Abuse and neglect of elderly persons. *New England Journal of Medicine,* 332(7): 437–443.

MacDonald, J. 1971. *Rape: Offenders and their victims.* Springfield, IL: CC Thomas Co.

McCartney, J. R., and Severson, K. 1997. Sexual violence, post-traumatic stress disorder and dementia. *Journal of the American Geriatric Society,* 45: 77–79.

Prentky, R., and Burgess, A. W. 1990. Rehabilitation of child molesters: a cost-benefit analysis. *American Journal of Orthopsychiatry,* 60(1): 108–117.

Ramin, S. M., Satin, A. J., Stone, I. C., and Wendel, G. D. 1992. Sexual assault in postmenopausal women. *Obstetrics & Gynecology,* 80: 860–864.

Ramsey-Klawsnik, H. 1991. Elder sexual abuse: Preliminary findings. *Journal of Elder Abuse and Neglect*, 3(3): 73–90.

Safarik, M. E., Jarvis, J. P., and Nussbaum, K. E. 2000. Elderly female serial sexual homicide: A limited empirical test of criminal investigative analysis. *Homicide Studies*, 4: 294–307.

Stahl, B. 2014. In Minnesota, abuse lawsuits die with their victims. MN Star Tribune, p. 1. Retrieved from http://www.startribune.com/in-minnesota-personal-injury-abuse-lawsuits-die-with-the-victims/241031031/

Teaster, P. B., Roberto, K. A., Duke, J. O., and Kim, M. 2000. Sexual abuse of older adults: Preliminary findings of cases in Virginia. *Journal of Elder Abuse & Neglect*, 12(3/4): 1–17.

Tyra, P. A. 1993. Helping elderly women survive rape using a crisis framework. *Journal of Psychosocial Nursing*, 34(12): 20–25.

U.S. Bureau of the Census. 2014. Department of Commerce, Washington, DC.

U.S. General Accounting Office (USGAO). 2002. Nursing homes: Complaint investigation processes often inadequate to protect residents (No. 6AO/HEHS-99–80). Washington, DC: Health Education and Human Services.

Section II

Investigation

5 The Relevance of Fantasy in Serial Sexual Crimes Investigation

Robert R. Hazelwood and Janet I. Warren

CONTENTS

Introduction 68
The Human Sex Drive 68
Sex Is a Sensory Act 68
The Paraphilias 69
Fantasy in Sexual Crimes 69
Inanimate Objects 70
    Dolls 70
    Photographs/Magazine Pictures 71
    Pornographic Videos 71
    Clothing 71
Consenting Partners 72
    Prostitutes 72
    Girlfriends or Spouses as Partners 72
Self-Composition 72
Investigative Significance of Fantasy 73
    Fantasy and Intelligence 73
    Fantasy Is Always Perfect 73
    Fantasy Enactment with Wives and/or Girlfriends 74
    Fantasy and the Linking of Cases 74
    Fantasy and Search Warrants 75
    Fantasy and Prosecutive Strategy 76
Summary 76
References 76

CASE NO. 1

A 24-year-old housewife was kidnapped from her home and murdered. At the time of her death, she was four months pregnant. A search of her residence revealed that all of her panties and the bottom half of her bathing suit had been taken. Her badly decomposed body was discovered 2 days later and an autopsy revealed that she had died from paper towels being lodged in her throat. There were no other signs of physical trauma.

Four months later, a woman was abducted and raped. During the assault, the offender forced her to model several sets of teddies. He forced her to ask him to make love to her and, prior to releasing her, he requested a date and obtained her phone number. Two days later, he was observed leaving a Christmas tree on her porch. He was arrested and convicted for the abduction–murder as well as the abduction–rape.

A search of his home uncovered several hundred pieces of lingerie, over two thousand 3 × 5 cards containing information on women whose photographs and personal information appeared in soft pornographic magazines, a spiral notebook with cross-indexed information from the 3 × 5 cards, newspaper articles about women, lingerie catalogs, and the bottom half of the murder victim's bathing suit. His wife advised that the man utilized the materials for masturbatory acts. The subject manifested several paraphilias during this and other crimes. They included fetishism, voyeurism, exhibitionism, and telephone scatology.

INTRODUCTION

Sexuality represents one of the more complex aspects of human experience. It integrates the cognitive, emotional, sensual, and behavioral elements of the individual into a uniquely personal pattern of experience that derives from both internal fantasy and external behavior. While usually a private aspect of a person's life, it becomes relevant to law enforcement once the element of coercion or exploitation is introduced into it.

Theorists (Prentky, Knight, & Rosenberg, 1988) classify the underlying motivation for sexual assault into three main categories: aggression, sex, and power. These primary motivations are frequently expressed in complex sexual fantasies that often begin to develop shortly after puberty. Through a gradual process of enactment, they also become the template for many offenders' patterns of serial sexual offending. They serve a complex organizing function in the behavior of the offender and frequently determine the choice of his verbal interactions with his victim, his preferred sexual acts, and his overall ritualistic (see Chapter 6) patterns of behavior.

The criminal investigator and others involved in the identification, prosecution, and treatment of the offender can learn to make use of these fantasy-driven behaviors within a sexual offense. Through a detailed review of the verbal, sexual, and physical behavior of the offender, the underlying fantasy behavior can be deduced and the motivational themes formulated (see Chapter 7). This information can subsequently be used to identify sexual assaults perpetrated by the same offender (see Chapter 10), determine future patterns of victim selection, and help to predict the scenario of future crimes.

THE HUMAN SEX DRIVE

There are three principal components of the human sexual drive: (1) the biological, (2) the physiological, and (3) the psychosexual. Humans share the biological component with other forms of mammalian life. It constitutes the natural or instinctual urge to engage in sexual activities with others. This instinctual component influences the basic orientation of the sexual impulse but has little influence on the individual form through which it is expressed. As such, it has limited relevance to sexual crimes investigation. The physiological component is activated when the body begins to respond to stimuli in a sexual manner. This response pattern may vary in intensity and be interrupted by a variety of sexual dysfunctions that are physiological in nature. Such information may provide rudimentary information about an offender in unique cases. The psychosexual element constitutes the most variable and individualistic aspect of the human sexual experience. It integrates the highly specific cognitive, sensory, and behavioral stimuli that are arousing to an individual and reflects his or her unique pattern of experience and development. This psychosexual aspect of the sexual experience, in its almost unending variability, provides the criminal investigator and others with the richest source of information about an offender and with the "flavor" of the specific individual he is seeking.

SEX IS A SENSORY ACT

All human beings employ their available senses to enhance their sexual arousal. A thorough review of the ways that the various senses are manipulated in a sexual assault will ensure that a comprehensive assessment of the psychosexual component of the offender's sexual arousal pattern has been captured from the victim.

Sight has been identified as the primary component of the male's sexual response. As indicated in Case no. 1, the offender had his victim model lingerie that he had purchased as props for his fantasy. Without these visual stimuli, he tended to have difficulty becoming sexually aroused. Touch, another important sense related to sexual arousal, similarly manifested itself in the offender's fondling of his victim and in his autoerotic, masturbatory activities with several hundred pieces of lingerie. The offender's request that the victim verbalize a desire to make love to him reflects a use of auditory stimuli to enhance arousal while his post-offense delivery of a Christmas tree behaviorally demonstrates the reciprocity that lay at the core of his sexual fantasy. These fantasy-derived behaviors were consistent across the sexual assaults and murder perpetrated by this particular offender and, as indicated, were instrumental in linking the two offenses to him.

THE PARAPHILIAS

Paraphilia is a term used by the mental health profession to describe what is more commonly called sexual deviation. The *Diagnostic and Statistical Manual of Mental Disorders*, fifth edition (DSM 5) defines paraphilia as referring to a persistent, intense, atypical sexual arousal pattern, independent of whether it causes any distress or impairment which, by itself, would not be considered disordered.

Paraphilic behavior is fantasy driven and is commonly exhibited during sexual crimes. The sexual deviations recognized by the *Diagnostic and Statistical Manual*, fifth edition, include exhibitionism, fetishism, frotteurism, pedophilia, sexual masochism, sexual sadism, transvestic fetishism, and voyeurism. Abel, Becker, Cunningham-Rathner, Mittleman, and Rouleau (1988) have documented that individuals tend to suffer from multiple paraphilias and that individuals identified as having one paraphilia generally suffered from one or more additional forms of sexual deviation. As indicated in Case no. 1, the offender demonstrated multiple paraphilias, including exhibitionism, fetishism, and voyeurism. It is important for investigators to remain aware of this clustering of paraphilic behavior as it argues against one-dimensional descriptions of particular offenders (e.g., "he's just an exhibitionist") and helps to avoid the premature exclusion of offenders from other types of unsolved sexual crimes.

Paraphilic patterns of behavior have been found to remain highly consistent over time. Research suggests that some types of paraphilic behavior can be altered through comprehensive treatment (exhibitionism, for example), while the more aggressive forms of sexual offending (sexual sadism) are unlikely to be changed regardless of the types and length of treatments offered. This stability is demonstrated repeatedly in cases involving the release of a sexual offender from prison who, within months of his release, perpetrates another paraphilic-motivated crime. In such cases, it is assumed that the deviant sexual fantasy has been maintained through masturbatory reinforcement and motivates behavior as soon as external constraints are removed.

The dynamics of these sexual fantasies, their possible paraphilic underpinnings, and their behavioral enactments provide the criminal investigator and others with information that can be used to direct the investigation, prosecution, and treatment of a sexual offender. Contrary to popular belief, there are no obvious demographic characteristics that identify an individual as a sexual criminal. Indeed, the serial sexual criminal is most often found to be like the guy next door (Hazelwood & Warren, 1989). Understanding the role of motivationally driven fantasy and its interaction with the human sexual drive will provide the investigator better insight into the criminal sexual behavior with which he is confronted.

FANTASY IN SEXUAL CRIMES

It is important to note that, for most individuals, fantasy is sufficient to satisfy psychosexual desires and, regardless of its nature, there is no impulse to enact it in reality. For others, fantasy is not satisfactory and there appears to be a progressive desire to transform the fantasy into actual behavior. MacCullough, Snowden, Wood, and Mills (1983) studied 16 sexually sadistic offenders and found that their core sexual fantasy made its appearance around the age of 16 years but took a number of years to be encapsulated into the criminal behavior that led to their arrest. They found that, in the interval between the appearance and enactment of the fantasy, the offender engaged in gradual and partial reenactments of the fantasy (e.g., buying rope, following a woman home) and used these behavioral tryouts as stimuli to enhance his masturbatory activity.

CASE NO. 2

A 22-year-old man abducted a coworker, tortured and raped her. He killed her by taping her nose and mouth and then watched her as she slowly asphyxiated. Twenty-three months later, he abducted, tortured, and raped a second woman, strangling her with his hands as he looked into her eyes. This man had modified his vehicle and constructed a torture platform for use in his crimes. His criminal behavior demonstrated much more criminal sophistication than would be expected in such a young offender. Investigation determined that he had begun discussing his fantasy of capture, torture, rape, and murder with others when he was only 14! From 14 until 22, he developed materials for the crimes, followed women, became familiar with the roads in his county, and modified his vehicles for criminal use.

Researchers have suggested that various factors play a role in the materialization and acting out of deviant sexual fantasy among sexual offenders including personal histories of early traumatic experiences, social isolation, sexual dysfunction, but also cognitive and emotional factors as well (Maniglio, 2010). Sexual fantasizing may have various functions for the offender as well that may include sexual stimulation, selecting specific targets, planning of the offense, mood regulation, or may serve as a coping mechanism for feelings of inadequacy (Gee, Ward, & Eccleston, 2003; Carabellese, Maniglio, Greco, & Catanesi, 2011). It has also been suggested that the content of sexual fantasy can be classified into several subcategories including demographic characteristics of the victim(s), behavioral characteristics of the sexual offense, relational context between offender and victim, situational characteristics such as time and place, and self-perceptual aspects of how the individual envisions himself in the fantasy (Gee, Devilly, & Ward, 2004). Each of these dimensions are potentially revealing to investigators when attempting to draw links between the crime and aspects of the offender's fantasy. Furthermore, certain props or objects may serve to stimulate or facilitate sexual fantasies and may be particularly important sources of corroborating evidence. These may include dolls, images, pornography, and clothing.

INANIMATE OBJECTS

The use of nonliving objects for sexual fantasy play-acting is not uncommon. Such items are passive and nonthreatening, and pose the least likelihood of criminal actions against the individual. In the experience of the authors, dolls, photographs, and clothing are the most common inanimate materials utilized by sexual criminals in lending a sense of reality to their fantasies.

DOLLS

The authors have seen numerous crimes in which female dolls are, in some way, involved. While such cases are frequently the subject of ridicule, it is to be remembered that such behavior is a reflection of the offender's motivationally driven fantasies. In cases observed by the authors, dolls have been subjected to burning, slashing, stabbing, binding, amputation, piercing, and a variety of other, equally bizarre acts.

CASE NO. 3

A doll was found suspended outside a hospital operating room. Its arms had been removed and an opening had been cut between the doll's legs and hair was glued around the orifice. A pencil protruded from the opening between the legs and burn marks were evident over the entire surface of the doll. Sutures closed the eyes and mouth. It was determined that a medical intern was responsible for this aberrant behavior.

PHOTOGRAPHS/MAGAZINE PICTURES

Another common means of acting out such fantasies is to alter photographs or pictures taken from pornographic and non-pornographic magazines. Such alterations include drawings (sexual bondage, mutilation, knives, guns, wounds, blood), cut and paste (replacement of faces or sexual parts), or the placement of favorite pictures in photo albums.

CASE NO. 4

A professionally employed individual died during dangerous autoerotic activities. A search of his office filing cabinets revealed over 100 bondage magazines. Without exception, each page had been altered by drawings or cutting and pasting. He had taken such care that the alterations were all but imperceptible to the naked eye. The modification of such a large amount of material required an inordinate amount of time and effort and was significant in determining the importance he attached to such activity.

PORNOGRAPHIC VIDEOS

Several researchers have demonstrated that a large number of sexual offenders have reported being influenced by pornography to sexually offend (Marshall, 1988; Kingston, Fedoroff, Firestone, Curry, & Bradford, 2008; Williams, Cooper, Howell, Yuille, & Paulhus, 2009). Maniglio (2010) explains that sadistic fantasies in sexual murderers, for example, are often positively reinforced during masturbatory activities. Such offenders may become preoccupied with particular types of pornographic video footage that depict violent, degrading, and aggressive acts against women. In some cases, pornographic videos may help stimulate general rather than offense-specific fantasies that desensitize individuals to deviant, violent, and/or aggressive behaviors and thus may have a disinhibitory effect on sexual offending (Gee et al., 2004). This is not to say that deviant or nondeviant consumption of pornographic material leads to increased sexual offending behavior as there is little evidence to support this claim. However, among a select group of sexual offenders, pornographic material, especially of a violent and aggressive form, may be of investigative significance if supportive of behaviors exhibited during the offense.

CLOTHING

Female clothing, particularly lingerie, is a favorite object for acting out a variety of fantasies. One of the most common activities is the slashing or removal of those portions of clothing that normally cover the sexual parts of the body. Such activities are typically classified as nuisance sexual offenses and officers have repeatedly advised the authors that teenagers are most frequently responsible for such acts. Age does not excuse such behavior and recognizing that sexual behavior is predicated on fantasy should alert authorities to the need for expeditious identification and mental health intervention.

CONSENTING PARTNERS

PROSTITUTES

Any experienced sexual crimes investigator can testify to the value of speaking with prostitutes when investigating a series of ritualistically violent crimes. Prostitutes earn money by being available to anyone for a variety of sexual behaviors. With prostitutes, men can act out their sexual fantasies without fear of rejection or ridicule.

CASE NO. 5

A professionally employed white male was convicted for the murder of a prostitute. He had bound her wrists behind her back and placed her in a bathtub of water where he had intercourse with her. At the moment of ejaculation, he held her head under the water and she drowned. Investigation revealed that he had previously hired several other women for the same activity.

GIRLFRIENDS OR SPOUSES AS PARTNERS

Stereotypically, it had been assumed that perpetrators of sexual crimes either did not have consensual sexual relationships or, if they did, that the more destructive aspects of their sexuality were kept divorced from them. Recent research (Warren & Hazelwood, 2002), however, has determined that many sexual offenders are, in fact, involved in ongoing sexual relationships and that they often act out their fantasies within this context.

SELF-COMPOSITION

Some individuals choreograph their fantasies using themselves as both the subject and object of the behavior. One offender, who tortured and murdered a number of women, audiotaped in detail his descriptions of what he would do to his victims and what he would have them say and do to him. At the end of the tape, he verbalized in a falsetto voice the script he was planning to have his victims repeat to him. His remarks involved statements such as "bite my titties…" and "fuck me in the ass"—verbal behavior he subsequently forced each of his victims to repeat. Other, more dangerous autoerotic activities also often contain a ritualized enactment of fantasy.

CASE NO. 6

A white male was found dead, hanging from a beam in the basement of his house. He was wearing his wife's sweater turned inside out, his wife's shorts turned inside out, and he had placed her panties over his head and face. The belt from her bathrobe was wrapped tightly around his testicles. A video camera had been positioned in such a way as to record his activities. The videotape showed him accidentally dying from asphyxiation. A search of the area around the body turned up a number of sketches that portrayed sadomasochistic scenes—the hangings of a male and female—and the written script of a woman undergoing a military execution by hanging.

Investigation of autoerotic fatalities has frequently revealed transvestic behavior associated with ritualized hanging (Hazelwood, Dietz, & Burgess, 1983). The process of the man presenting himself dressed as a woman so as to elicit arousal from himself (he undoubtedly planned on later watching the video) seems to represent the inversion that lies at the core of this complex form of enactment.

INVESTIGATIVE SIGNIFICANCE OF FANTASY

Over the years, the authors have consulted and conducted research on violent sexual crimes. They have also testified as expert witnesses in such crimes. This experience has led to a great appreciation for the value of understanding the significant role that fantasy plays in sexual crimes. The remainder of this chapter will focus on the practical investigative value such an understanding can provide.

FANTASY AND INTELLIGENCE

Fantasy is essentially a play that is acted out in the mind of a person. This play requires a set, script, actors, a director, and in some cases, a recording device. Occasionally, costumes and/or other props may be involved (see Case no. 5). This ability to fantasize is dependent upon the intelligence of the individual. Continuity of thought is needed when developing a fantasy involving multiple partners or a complex scenario, and continuity of thought requires a degree of intelligence. A person having less than average intelligence has a less complicated internal world and less ability to carry out complex criminal scenarios (see Chapter 5). Based upon this association, the investigator can assume that the more complex the crime is, the more intelligent is the offender.

CASE NO. 7

A female realtor was found hanging by her neck in the attic of a newly built and very expensive home. She had been stabbed twice in the chest. Investigation determined that she had received a call from a man claiming to be a physician who was interested in purchasing an existing home which was located on 5–10 acres of land. He advised that he was relocating his family and practice to the area and was on a house-hunting trip. The realtor, thinking of a substantial fee, advised him that she would be happy to show the home. He told her that he had just arrived in town and was staying at an expensive hotel. He requested that she pick him up in front of the hotel. Investigation revealed that he had not checked into the hotel.

This offender was later arrested and found to have committed a series of violent sexual crimes throughout the eastern United States. An examination of the crime revealed a complex scenario designed to entice a selected victim to a remote location for torture and murder. Although the man's formal education was halted after 1 year of college, it became obvious that he was well above average in intelligence.

FANTASY IS ALWAYS PERFECT

A person's sexual fantasies are always perfect. Every actor in the mental image plays his or her role to perfection. Reality, however, is never perfect, and for that reason, it never lives up to the sexual offender's expectations.

CASE NO. 8

Police recovered an audio-tape belonging to a professionally employed male who had died while on a business trip. On the tape, the man described the murder of a teenage couple. He recorded that he had killed the female and then dwelt, at some length, on the rape and murder of the male. He expressed disappointment over the fact that the young man's blood had saturated the bed sheets and mentioned that he should have placed a plastic sheet beneath the victim's body. He also expressed regret at having cut the male's throat and opined that he should have stabbed him in the kidney as he would have lived longer.

The case investigator requested one of the authors (Hazelwood) to listen to the tape and provide an opinion as to whether it was fact or fantasy. The opinion was that the tape was depicting an actual crime. As previously mentioned, fantasy is always perfect and, in this instance, the man was expressing disappointment and regret over things he had done or failed to do in reality.

It has long been recognized that certain sexual offenders record their sexual fantasies and/or their crimes. This is particularly true of the sexual sadist (Dietz, Hazelwood, & Warren, 1990) and the pedophile (Lanning, 1991). There are two widely accepted reasons for the offender doing so: (1) to enable him to relive the crime for masturbatory acts and (2) to allow him to retain souvenirs or trophies of his crimes. The authors concur in both of these reasons, but suggest a third motivation: to use the recordings of past crimes to more perfectly transform fantasy into reality. By recording the crime, the individual can critique his performance and that of his victim, thereby allowing him to correct those imperfections that are invariably present in reality.

CASE NO. 9

A sexually sadistic killer kidnapped a series of young women, and after photographing them during sexual acts, he murdered them. In one series of photographs recovered by the police, a young woman is kneeling on a bed while performing fellatio on the man. At his feet are several photographs of another victim seemingly performing the same act on the same bed while in the same position.

It was the impression of the authors that the offender was using the photographs to more carefully model and inform his preferred fantasy material.

Fantasy Enactment with Wives and/or Girlfriends

Research by Warren and Hazelwood (2002) has focused on the wives and girlfriends of 20 sexual sadists. Through analysis of the sadist's recordings and exhaustive interviews with the former wives and/or girlfriends of these men, it was found that, without exception, they had acted out their cruel and sadistic fantasies on the women.

CASE NO. 10

A sexually sadistic male, responsible for the rape, torture, and murders of ten women and young girls, would ritualistically abuse his wife in a physical, verbal, and sexual manner. He would beat her almost to unconsciousness; refer to her as a slut, whore, cunt, and bitch; force her to verbally degrade herself; and force her to perform analingus, use oversize foreign objects to assault her anally, and force her to engage in sexual acts with others.

Investigators should ensure that efforts are made to locate women who were intimate partners of the men and interview them to determine whether there is a consistent pattern between the offender's criminal and consensual sexual behavior.

Fantasy and the Linking of Cases

In Chapter 10, the authors describe the difference between the modus operandi (MO), ritual, and signature aspects of a sexual crime. Historically, law enforcement has utilized the MO to link a series of crimes. The authors consider the MO but attempt to identify the signature behaviors to link a series of cases.

CASE NO. 11

An 18-year-old male was tried and convicted of the rape–murder of a 17-year-old female. She had been stabbed more than 30 times, her abdomen was slashed and her throat had been cut. She was left in a ditch after having been vaginally, anally, and orally raped. The man had previously been found guilty of exposing himself to college coeds and was known to have made over 100 obscene and threatening phone calls to two women when he was 15 years of age. During that series of calls, he threatened to cut the women's throats, slash and stab them, rape and anally assault them.

The link between the verbalization of the offender's violent sexual fantasies, via the phone calls, 3 years prior to the murder was obvious and one of the authors (Hazelwood) testified to that effect. Unfortunately, the responsible social agency took no action on the phone calls when the then 15-year-old was referred to them. One of the women who had received the phone calls stated that she had personally advised the mother of the young boy that he was "going to rape and kill someone if something isn't done."

Fantasy and Search Warrants

In criminally acting out sexual fantasies, offenders often utilize materials, or props, to create more psychosexually stimulating scenarios for themselves. By observing the physical, verbal, and sexual behavior acted out during a sexual crime, the investigator can determine the type of sexual fantasy being carried out. It is then a simple step to determining what types of materials, if any, the person would have accumulated to complement his fantasies. Upon identification of a person suspected or known to have committed the crime(s), the affidavit supporting any search warrant should list the materials that this type of assessment suggests. For example, in Case no. 1, the offender obviously had a fetish for teddies. It is quite reasonable, therefore, to suspect that he will have a collection of similar materials (lingerie) for his masturbatory fantasies.

CASE NO. 12

A young woman was kidnapped and kept in captivity for an extended period of time. She was physically, emotionally, and sexually tortured during her captivity. Her statement led the police to believe that they were dealing with a sexual sadist and, based upon research conducted by Dietz et al. (1990), a search warrant was prepared. It listed bondage materials, recording devices, burning and pinching devices, violent pornography, and numerous other materials as items to be prioritized in the search. Items in each of these categories were recovered during the search.

A person's accumulation of materials and involvement with activities designed to enhance his sexual fantasies can contribute to a better understanding, by judge and jury, of the importance of such activities to the offender. Again, in Case no. 1, the police investigation determined that the man had invested over $3000 and inestimable time in collecting, cataloging, and preserving lingerie. In Case no. 4, the offender had literally recreated thousands of pictures in over 100 magazines to enhance his deviant fantasies.

FANTASY AND PROSECUTIVE STRATEGY

As noted previously, the authors have testified as expert witnesses in trials of sexual offenders. One of the principal functions of such testimony is to educate the jury, not only about the offense, but also about the role that fantasy and fantasy materials play in violent sexual crimes. It should be noted that it is often necessary to educate the prosecutive team in matters involving criminal sexuality. They, like many investigators and the lay public, are often naive about the complexity of such crimes and the seeming normality of the offenders.

CASE NO. 13

A 36-year-old woman disappeared after a date with her fiancée. Two years later, an ex-girlfriend of the fiancée admitted to police that she had helped him bury the victim's body. The body was recovered and the man was tried and acquitted in state court. During the trial, the former girl-friend testified that he had brought the victim to the girlfriend's home, forced her to disrobe and then raped her vaginally, anally and orally. He also used a dildo on the victim anally and bound her in a variety of positions using precut lengths of rope. The former girlfriend testified that he had taken over 100 photographs during the crime. Over 1 year later, the federal government indicted him for three counts of perjury (lying about his role in the crime). Interviews of the former girlfriend and a former wife of the subject (15 years divorced) revealed that they had been subjected to similar activities by the man. Five days prior to the trial, the aforementioned photographs were located and he pleaded guilty and was sentenced to 8 years in prison for perjury.

The obvious problem, had the federal case gone to trial, was having to prove that the man killed the victim. This would have been necessary to prove that he lied about his involvement in the crime. A prosecutive strategy, suggested by Hazelwood and FBI Agent Steve Mardigian, was to call the former wife and girlfriend to testify about the consistency in the pattern of the man's sexual behavior over a 15-year period of time. In legal terms, this would be described as a pattern of continuing behavior. Had it been necessary, the testimony of Hazelwood, the former girlfriend, and former wife would have educated the jury about the man's long-standing fantasy involving degradation and punishment which was motivated by a deep-seated hatred of women. Similar education and testimony were necessary in other cases set forth in this chapter.

SUMMARY

Individuals involved in the investigation of sexual crimes should learn the importance of the role of fantasy. Fantasy is the link between the underlying motivations for sexual assaults and the behavior exhibited during the crime. Such an understanding can help to determine linkages between offenses perpetrated by a serial offender, identify materials to be sought through search warrants, and provide informed prosecutorial strategies.

REFERENCES

Abel, G., Becker, J., Cunningham-Rathner, J., Mittleman, M., and Rouleau, J. 1988. Multiple paraphilic diagnoses among sex offenders. *Bulletin of the American Academy of Psychiatry and the Law*, 16: 153–168.

Carabellese, F., Maniglio, R., Greco, O., and Catanesi, R. 2011. The role of fantasy in a serial sexual offender: A brief review of the literature and a case report. *Journal of Forensic Sciences*, 56: 256–260.

Dietz, P., Hazelwood, R., and Warren, J. 1990. The sexually sadistic criminal and his offenses. *Bulletin of the American Academy of Psychiatry and the Law*, 18: 163–178.

Gee, D., Devilly, G., and Ward, T. 2004. The content of sexual fantasies for sexual offenders. *Sexual Abuse: A Journal of Research and Treatment*, 16: 315–331.

Gee, D., Ward, T., and Eccleston, L. 2003. The function of sexual fantasies for sexual offenders: A preliminary model. *Behavior Change*, 20: 44–60.

Hazelwood, R., Dietz, P., and Burgess, A. 1983. *Autoerotic fatalities*. Langham, MA: Lexington Books.

Hazelwood, R., and Warren, J. 1989. The serial rapist: His characteristics and victims (part I). *FBI Law Enforcement Bulletin*, January: 11–17.

Kingston, D., Fedoroff, P., Firestone, P., Curry, S., and Bradford, J. 2008. Pornography use and sexual aggression: The impact of frequency and type of pornography use on recidivism among sexual offenders. *Aggressive Behavior*, 34: 341–351.

Lanning, K. 1991. *Child molesters, a typology for law enforcement*, 3rd. ed. Washington, DC: National Center for Missing & Exploited Children.

MacCullough, M., Snowden, P., Wood, J., and Mills, H. 1983. Sadistic fantasy, sadistic behavior and offending. *British Journal of Psychiatry*, 143: 20–29.

Maniglio, R. 2010. The role of deviant sexual fantasy in the epipathogenesis of sexual homicide: A systematic review. *Aggression and Violent Behavior*, 15: 294–302.

Marshall, W. 1988. The use of sexually explicit stimuli by rapists, child molesters, and nonoffenders. *Journal of Sex Research*, 25: 267–288.

Prentky, R., Knight, R., and Rosenberg, R. 1988. Validation analysis on a taxonomic system for rapists: Disconfirmation and reconceptualization. In *Human sexual aggression: Current perspectives*, ed. R. Prentky and V. Quinsey, 21–40. New York: New York Academy of Sciences Annals.

Warren, J., and Hazelwood, R. 2002. Relational patterns associated with sexual sadism: A study of 20 wives and girlfriends. *Journal of Family Violence*, 17(1): 75–89.

Williams, K., Cooper, B., Howell, T., Yuille, J., and Paulhus, D. 2009. Inferring sexually deviant behaviour from corresponding fantasies: The role of personality and pornography consumption. *Criminal Justice and Behaviour*, 36: 198–222.

6 The Behavioral-Oriented Interview of Rape Victims
The Key to Profiling

Robert R. Hazelwood and Ann Wolbert Burgess

CONTENTS

Introduction 80
Motivation 80
Profiling the Unidentified Rapist 81
Questioning for Behavior 82
    Method of Approach 83
        Con 83
        Blitz 83
        Surprise 83
    Offender's Control of the Victim 84
        Mere Presence 84
        Verbal Threats 84
        Presence of a Weapon 84
    Offender's Use of Physical Force 85
        Minimal 85
        Moderate 85
        Excessive 85
        Brutal 85
    Victim Resistance 85
        Passive Resistance 86
        Verbal Resistance 86
        Physical Resistance 86
    Offender's Reaction to Resistance 86
        Cease the Demand 86
        Compromise or Negotiate 86
        Flee 87
        Threaten 87
        Use Force 87
    Sexual Dysfunctions 87
        Erectile Insufficiency 87
        Premature Ejaculation 88
        Retarded Ejaculation 88
        Conditional Insufficiency 88
        Conditional Ejaculation 88
    Indications of Psychopathy 89
    Type and Sequence of Sexual Acts 89
    Verbal Activity 90
    Forced Victim Verbal Activity 91

Sudden Change in Offender's Attitude...91
Criminal Experience...92
    Novice 92
    Experienced 92
Items Taken 92
    Evidentiary 93
    Valuables 93
    Personal 93
Indications That Victim Was Targeted...93
Summary 94
References...94

INTRODUCTION

A police department submitted their report of a rape investigation to Hazelwood and requested that the crime be analyzed and that a profile of the unidentified offender be prepared. A synopsis of that report follows:

Alicia B, a 21-year-old white female, who resided alone, was asleep in her apartment when she was awakened at 2:30 AM by a man who placed his hand over her mouth and held a knife to her throat. The intruder warned her not to scream or physically resist and told her if she complied with his demands, she would not be harmed. He forced her to remove her nightgown, kissed and fondled her, and then raped her vaginally. After warning the victim not to call the police, the man left. Ignoring the rapist's warning, she called the police and reported the crime. She told them that nothing had been stolen and, because a pillowcase was over her head during the assault, she could not provide a physical description of her assailant. The police noted that the rapist was with the victim for approximately 1 h.

Prior to working on the case, Hazelwood requested that the agency reinterview the victim using a set of questions specifically designed to elicit victim-source information of the offender's behavior during the assault. Using the questions, a nine-page single-spaced typewritten statement was taken from the victim. Based on a more complete statement, Hazelwood prepared a profile of the characteristics and traits of the unidentified offender. The man was subsequently arrested and confessed to the assault of Alicia and several other women as well. The terms *investigator*, *interviewer*, and *analyst* will be used interchangeably in this chapter.

MOTIVATION

During the past 30 years, the authors have reviewed thousands of police reports and rape victim statements. While statements have typically contained details of the crime as well as a great deal of information about the offender's physical description, there has often been a marked absence of information suggestive of the motivation underlying the rape. Contrary to popular belief, Groth, Burgess, and Holmstrom (1977) long ago pointed out that rape is a behavior that assaults the sexual parts of the body serving nonsexual needs. Rather than being the dominant motivation for rape, they found that sexuality was most often used to express power and anger. Given that the initial interview with the victim may not provide the depth necessary for a detailed account of the behavioral patterns exhibited during the rape, a more comprehensive interview schedule may be warranted.

Over a period of time, Hazelwood developed a set of questions designed to elicit behavioral aspects of the crime from the victim, to allow the motivation of the crime to be identified and to provide the analyst with sufficient information to arrive at opinions as to the unidentified offender's characteristics and traits. That set of behavioral questions and instructions moves sequentially through the sexual assault capturing the offender's demeanor before, during, and after the rape has occurred. They are listed next and discussed in much greater detail later in this chapter.

1. Describe the manner in which the offender approached and gained control over you.
2. Describe all actions he took to maintain control over you during the assault.
3. Sequentially describe each act of physical force used by the offender.
4. Did you resist the attacker physically, verbally, or passively? If so, describe in sequence each time you resisted.
5. What was the man's reaction to each instance of your resistance?
6. Did the man experience a sexual dysfunction? If so, describe the sexual difficulty he experienced and of what acts, if any, he performed or demanded you perform to overcome the dysfunction?
7. Describe each sexual act the offender engaged in or forced you to participate in and the order in which they occurred. Include kissing and fondling by the criminal.
8. As precisely as possible, describe what he said to you. Include his tone of voice and attitude in your description.
9. If he demanded that you answer questions, repeat phrases, or respond verbally in any manner whatsoever, specifically describe what you were required to say.
10. Did you observe any change in his attitude and, if so, what immediately preceded the change?
11. What, if anything, did he do to protect his identity from you or the police? What actions did he take to preclude being forensically associated with the crime (e.g., condom, forcing you to shower or douche)?
12. Have you carefully inventoried your personal belongings (e.g., jewelry, photographs, undergarments) since the assault? What, if anything, did he take when he left?
13. Prior to or since the assault have you received any calls, emails, or notes from unidentified persons and, if so, please describe as precisely as possible the content of those communications. Have you been the victim of prowlers, window-peepers, a break-in, or an attempted break-in?

In addition to the preceding questions, it is imperative to obtain the offender's physical description, the direction and mode of travel, accent, physical deformities, etc., and attention should be given to these critical details. However, when the *behaviors* of the rapist are not captured, the investigation is incomplete.

PROFILING THE UNIDENTIFIED RAPIST

There are three essential steps in preparing a criminal investigative profile of an unidentified rapist:

1. A comprehensive interview of the victim to document the rapist's behavior
2. A careful analysis of the victim's statements to identify the motive for the crime, and
3. Forming an opinion as to the characteristics and traits of the person responsible for the crime.

Steps 2 and 3 involve the use of analytical logic accompanied by common sense. They are performed by individuals trained in the process of crime behavior analysis. The first step, however, is the most critical of the three and is one that detectives should accomplish with the most care and precision.

Only the victim can provide the information necessary to complete a behavioral analysis of the rape. Therefore, it is essential for the investigator to establish rapport with the victim through a professional and empathetic approach. Showing compassion and allowing victims to exercise choice and control during the interview process is essential during these stages. The latter can be achieved by beginning with open-ended questions pertaining to the victim's needs and well-being as well as determining whether they have the necessary support systems in place (Campbell, Adams, Wasco,

Ahrens, & Sefl, 2009). Such an approach will not only aid the investigation, but it will also assist the victim in overcoming feelings of fear, anger, and guilt, all of which are typically generated by a sexual assault.

Interviewers should project an attitude of confidence and competence and must not allow personal feelings about the crime, the criminal, or the victim to interfere with their objectivity.

To be successful, the analysts must observe the crime not only from the victim's perspective, but from the offender's as well. This better equips them to answer questions such as: What message is being transmitted by the rapist through the assault? Is it that he is angry and wants to punish women for real or perceived wrongs, or that through his control of the victim he has proven that he is powerful? Or is it a combination of power and anger? The following case provides an excellent example of why this type of analytical approach is necessary.

CASE NO. 1

In a large metropolitan area, a series of rapes plagued the community over a period of months. The rapist controlled his victims without resorting to physical violence, even when confronted by resistance.

One evening, a hospital orderly went off duty at midnight and came upon a male beating a nurse in an attempt to subdue and rape her. The orderly went to her aid and fought the attacker, holding him until the police arrived. Predictably, the orderly received much attention from the media and was given a citation for bravery from the city.

Sometime later, the orderly was arrested for an earlier series of rapes. He was asked why he had rescued the nurse when he was guilty of similar crimes. He became indignant and advised the officers that he would never hurt a woman.

It is obvious that the man who rescued the nurse from the physically violent rapist equated "hurt" with physical trauma. He either failed to consider or completely ignored the emotional trauma experienced by his victims.

As suggested, the motive for rape becomes clear only through a careful study of the behavior exhibited during the crime and, once the motive is identified, the trained analyst should be able to provide the police with an accurate description of the offender's characteristics and traits. The basis for this assumption lies in the axiom that behavior reflects personality.

The manner in which an individual behaves within his various environments portrays the type of person he or she is. One of the criminal's environments (typically the only one to which we have immediate access) is his crime. Through the observation of the criminal's behavior, the trained analyst can form opinions about self-esteem, educational level, and interpersonal skills of the unidentified criminal. How is this possible? It is common to review two rape cases from different investigative jurisdictions involving different offenders that exhibit strikingly similar crime behaviors (e.g., control, domination, use of a weapon, etc.). Why? A large part of the answer lies in the statement by Groth et al. (1977) that "rape is in fact serving primarily nonsexual needs." Assuming the accuracy of this statement, the two individuals having similar needs (i.e., power and/or anger) are both meeting those needs through the sexual crime of rape. Therefore, it becomes logical that the behaviors used by each to achieve the meeting of those mutual needs will be similar.

QUESTIONING FOR BEHAVIOR

The interview should be conducted in a probative yet tactful, professional, and sensitive manner. It should be conveyed by the investigators that they are concerned not only with the arrest and conviction of the offender but also with the victim's welfare. She has survived an emotionally and physically threatening situation, and the importance of the investigator's recognition and acknowledgment of this cannot be overemphasized. The victim should be made to understand that obtaining detailed information from her may very well expedite the offender's identification and arrest.

CASE NO. 2

An elderly woman was raped by a stranger and the case was submitted for profiling. The victim declined to provide the police with the necessary behavioral information. Consequently, the statement was found to be substantially lacking in detail and was returned to the investigating police agency with an article authored by Hazelwood, which explained the importance of capturing such information. The victim read the article, expressed an understanding of complete disclosure and provided the police with a detailed description of the attack.

The behavioral-oriented interview is conducted sequentially and in keeping with the unfolding of the crime, beginning with determining the method used by the offender to approach the victim.

METHOD OF APPROACH

When confronted with a task, a person will select a method with which he or she feels most comfortable and most confident. For example, if four people are faced with an examination, one may choose to study alone, one may want to study in a group, a third may choose to study with another person, and one may decide not to study at all. The criminal, when deciding how to approach a victim, will pick a method that he believes is most likely to be successful and is in keeping with his motive. The authors have identified three approaches used by rapists: "con," "blitz," and "surprise."

Con

This method involves approaching the victim openly by using a trick, ruse, or subterfuge. The rapist may offer or request assistance or directions or pretend to be a salesman or even something as seemingly benign as a volunteer church worker. Initially he is pleasant, friendly, and even charming. His goal is to gain the victim's confidence and negate any feelings of danger the victim may have—until he is in a position to overcome any resistance. Frequently, and for different reasons, he may undergo a sudden change of attitude once she is in his control. This attitudinal change may occur because he wants to convince the victim of his seriousness or it may simply be an indication of the anger motivating his attack. Three traits of the rapist suggested by this approach are that the rapist is more likely to be extroverted than introverted, is not intimidated by women, and is confident in his ability to interact with them.

Blitz

The blitz approach is demonstrated when the offender immediately utilizes *injurious* force to subdue his victim. Examples of this approach can involve knocking the victim unconscious or incapacitating her with chloroform. The attack may occur frontally or from the rear, and there is little or no opportunity for the victim to resist physically or verbally. This approach strongly suggests feelings of hostility and anger toward women and may be indicative of the man's interactions with women in noncriminal situations as well (e.g., selfish, one-sided, abusive).

Surprise

The surprise approach involves the sudden capture of a victim with no injurious force. It is common for the rapist to use his surrounding environment to his advantage either through strategic planning or manipulation to encounter the victim within a location under his control (Rossmo, 2000). In such cases, the rapist may wait for the victim in the back seat of her car, step out from behind a wall in a remote location or from the woods, or capture her while she is commuting from one location to another. He typically uses threats and/or the presence of a weapon to subdue his victims. This approach indicates that the victim has been targeted or preselected through surveillance or window-peeping and, while the selection process may occur shortly before the attack, it most often involves long-term surveillance and intelligence gathering.

OFFENDER'S CONTROL OF THE VICTIM

After the man has gained physical control of his victim, his task is to maintain that control. The method of control utilized by the offender is *primarily* dependent on the motivation (i.e., power or anger) for committing the assault. Less frequently, the control may be a reaction to the resistance of the victim. Four control methods have been observed by the authors: mere presence, use of verbal threats, display of a weapon, and physical force.

Mere Presence

Depending on the fear level and passivity of the victim, it is quite possible that the only control needed is the presence of the offender. For a person removed from the assault situation this may be difficult to comprehend; nevertheless, it is frequently the case. Too often investigators, prosecutors, and judges form opinions on a victim's response based entirely on what they *believe* they would have done in a similar situation. They fail to take into account the victim's personality, the time and location of the assault, and the enormous influence of fear. The interviewer must be careful not to convey a similar judgmental attitude toward the victim as this will no doubt inhibit her willingness to cooperate.

CASE NO. 3

The victim, a 21-year-old woman with a learning disability, had parked her car in her apartment complex. As she got out of the car, a van pulled behind her car and the driver pointed a gun at her, but said nothing. She put down her purse and a yogurt cup and said "Please don't hurt me, I'll do anything you say." The man, surprised at this reaction, told her to get into the van. She walked behind the van to the passenger side, opened the sliding door, got into the rear of the van and closed the door. The man then bound the victim, stabbed her in the heart with a screwdriver and drove off the complex. He took the body to an isolated location and committed a sexual assault on the corpse. If the investigators had not factored in her learning disability or learned that the victim's mother was not surprised at her daughter's reaction given her passiveness, they may have been at a loss to explain the victim's reaction to her killer's approach. The killer was later arrested and confessed to the crime.

Verbal Threats

It is realistic to expect some victims to be intimidated and controlled by harsh verbiage or by threats of physical violence. In all such cases, it is critically important for the interviewer to document the precise wording used by the rapist. What an offender says during an assault is an important behavior that provides insight as to the motive for the attack.

Presence of a Weapon

If a weapon is used to control the victim, it is important to determine when during the assault he presented or indicated he had a weapon. Additional questions should include: Did the victim see it? Was it a weapon of choice (brought to the scene) or one of opportunity (obtained at the scene)? Did he threaten the victim with the weapon and, if so, in what manner? Did he put the weapon down?

Did he *intentionally* inflict any physical injury with the weapon? Ullman (2007) suggests that rather than intending to inflict gratuitous injury to the victim, the offender's primary motivation for using a weapon is to inhibit resistance. However, if significant damage from weapon use is sustained by the victim, this detail may be particularly pertinent when investigators are deciding on the motive.

OFFENDER'S USE OF PHYSICAL FORCE

If the offender used physical force, it becomes a key factor in determining his motivation. The amount of physical violence is *primarily* dependent on assault motivation, although victim resistance also may play a role. The specific level of force used when it was employed; whether the force increased, decreased, or stayed the same; and the rapist's attitude prior to, during, or after the force was used must be determined.

Knowing the level of physical force is important to an accurate behavioral analysis of the rape. Consequently, the interviewer should obtain as precise a description of the force as possible. The victim may exaggerate her description of the physical force used by the rapist for several understandable reasons. In those cases in which there is little or no physical force used, she may fear that the authorities will not believe her. The victim may not have physically resisted the attacker and is experiencing guilt and consequently exaggerates the force. If the victim was never struck or spanked as a child and the rapist slapped her, she may truly *believe* that she had been beaten! Still another possible and plausible explanation for exaggeration is if the victim is unable to differentiate between the sexual assault and the physical assault. For all these reasons, the authors have defined four levels of physical force: minimal, moderate, excessive, and brutal. The use of these descriptive levels is to assist the analyst in arriving at an accurate, reliable, and uniform assessment of the force employed.

Minimal

At this level, there is little or no physical violence. While mild slapping may have occurred, it was clearly employed more to intimidate the victim than to punish her and it is not a repetitive behavior. No medical attention for injuries is required. Under these circumstances, the rapist is not likely to be verbally abusive toward the victim.

Moderate

The second level of force involves the victim being slapped or struck repeatedly and in a painful manner. This occurs even in the absence of resistance. Again, however, the victim requires no medical attention for her injuries. In such cases, the rapist typically uses profanity and is otherwise verbally abusive.

Excessive

At this level, the victim is beaten by the rapist and has bruises and lacerations. Medical attention is required and the victim may be hospitalized. The attacker uses profanity and directs degrading and derogatory remarks toward the victim.

Brutal

The victim is subjected to an extreme and severe physical assault that may include intentional torture. The application of this level results in extensive hospitalization and/or death. The verbal behavior of such an attacker reflects a great deal of anger and hostility.

VICTIM RESISTANCE

When ordered to do something, a person has two options: comply or resist. Victim resistance is defined as any action taken that precludes, reduces, or delays the attack. The authors have identified three methods of victim resistance: passive, verbal, and physical resistance. While alert to physical or verbal resistance, some may overlook or disregard an equally important form of resistance: passive resistance.

Passive Resistance

Passive resistance is evidenced when the victim does not physically or verbally protest, but just simply does not comply with the rapist's demands. An example of passive resistance might involve an offender ordering a victim to remove her clothing with the victim not responding in any fashion whatsoever. While she did not resist physically or verbally resist, she also did not comply with his demand, thus affirming her resistance through noncompliance.

Verbal Resistance

Verbal resistance may include screaming, pleading, refusing (e.g., "No, I won't do that"), or even attempting to reason or negotiate with the attacker. Verbal resistance can also be classified as forceful when it involves loud screaming, yelling, or swearing at the offender. By contrast, passive forms of verbal resistance may include pleading or negotiating with the offender and have been shown to have a greater likelihood of rape completion (Ullman, 2007). In addition, a study by Clay-Warner (2002) showed that physical resistance was more effective than verbal resistance in avoiding rape. The reader should note that while crying is a form of verbal behavior, it is not, for the purposes of this chapter, considered to be a form of resistance.

Physical Resistance

Hitting, scratching, kicking, gouging, or even running away by the victim are examples of physical resistance. Investigators should not automatically assume that physical resistance has taken place. Even people who are normally assertive may become passive during a life-threatening situation. When there is a complete lack of resistance, the victim's personality, the type of approach, and other circumstances surrounding the crime should be taken into consideration. Regardless of the reason, the investigator should never project a judgmental attitude towards the victim.

On the other hand, if any form of resistance is evidenced, the offender's reaction to that resistance will be of particular interest to the analyst.

Offender's Reaction to Resistance

People react to stressful situations in a variety of ways and the manner in which an individual reacts can provide useful information about that individual. No reasonably intelligent person would question those victims of rape experience an inordinate amount of stress. Few, however, would consider that committing a rape also creates stress for most attackers. The possibilities of being identified, arrested, injured, ridiculed, or successfully resisted can combine to create a great amount of stress. The question for the analyst then becomes "How does the unidentified rapist cope with stress?" Consequently, it is behaviorally important for the investigator to determine how the rapist reacted to resistance by his victim.

Cases submitted to the authors over the years reveal five reactions exhibited by most rapists when confronted with victim resistance: (1) cease the demand, (2) compromise, (3) flee, (4) use threats, or (5) use physical force.

Cease the Demand

A rapist encountering victim resistance may simply cease his demand for a particular act or behavior and move to another demand or phase of the attack.

Compromise or Negotiate

In other cases, the man will compromise or negotiate by agreeing to a victim's suggestion (e.g., "Let me do this instead") or by giving the victim alternatives to the activity originally demanded (e.g., "All right, do this then").

Flee

Occasionally, a rapist will, upon encountering resistance, simply leave. The first three reactions are particularly interesting from a behavioral perspective. They suggest that the offender was not motivated to injure physically the victim to force compliance.

Threaten

Other rapists may resort to threats if resistance is encountered. If this is the case, the interviewer should try to capture the exact wording used by the rapist in threatening the victim. If, in spite of the threats, the victim continued to resist the attacker, it becomes important to determine what his reaction was to that continued resistance.

Use Force

When physical force is the reaction to victim resistance, the interviewer must determine the specific level of force (i.e., minimal, moderate, excessive, brutal) used by the offender.

Sexual Dysfunctions

The term *sexual dysfunction* may be defined as an "impairment either in the desire for sexual gratification or in the ability to achieve it" (Coleman, Butcher, & Carson, 1984). Groth and Burgess (1977) conducted a definitive study of 170 rapists and determined that 34% of the offender population suffered a sexual dysfunction during the assault. A study on serial rapists by the authors involved the face-to-face interviews of 41 men responsible for 837 rapes and over 400 attempted rapes. Thirty-eight percent of the rapists reported a sexual dysfunction during their first rape, 39% during a middle rape, and 35% experienced a dysfunction during their last rape (Hazelwood, Reboussin, & Warren, 1989). The occurrence of a sexual dysfunction, coupled with a basic understanding of the causes of the various types of male dysfunctions, can provide potentially valuable information to the analyst.

When interviewing the victim, the investigator should be alert to the possibility that she may not volunteer information about rapist dysfunctions. This may be due to the fact that she does not consider the information to be significant, that she is embarrassed by the acts she was forced to engage in to overcome the dysfunction, or that she is totally ignorant of such matters and did not recognize the impairment as a dysfunction. For these reasons, it may be beneficial for the investigator to explain to the victim the sexual dysfunctions that the rapist may have experienced and their significance to the investigation. The following information will assist in such situations.

Erectile Insufficiency

Previously termed *impotence*, this type of dysfunction affects the male's ability to obtain or maintain an erection sufficient for sexual intercourse. Masters and Johnson (1970) classify the two types of erectile insufficiency as "primary" and "secondary." Males experiencing primary insufficiency have *never been able* to maintain an erection sufficient for intravaginal ejaculation. While this type is relatively rare and not a general concern to the investigator, it is discussed in the interest of completeness. In cases of secondary insufficiency, the male is *currently unable* to obtain or maintain an erection. It is this latter form of impotence that is of interest to the interviewer in the context of this chapter.

Groth and Burgess (1977) compared the occurrence of erectile insufficiency among a group of rapists and a group of 448 nonrapist male patients who had been studied by Masters and Johnson. They found that in both groups erectile insufficiency was the dysfunction most commonly experienced. In the 30 years since that comparative study, the authors (through their involvement in thousands of rape cases, interviews of rapists and their victims, and interactions with police, medical, and mental health professionals) have found that erectile insufficiency continues to be the most common sexual dysfunction in stranger-to-stranger rapes. Confirming findings from previous studies,

Jones, Rossman, Wynn, and Ostovar (2010) found an increased incidence of intrarape violence and nongenital injuries inflicted by offenders who experienced erectile impotence during the assault. The significance of these findings speak to the possibility of a distinct group of sexual offenders whose arousal and/or gratification is dependent upon the infliction of pain and suffering to invoke feelings of fear and humiliation (Bownes & O'Gorman, 1991).

Premature Ejaculation

Masters and Johnson (1970) defined *premature ejaculation* as "ejaculation which occurs immediately before or immediately after penetration." Groth and Burgess (1977) found that this dysfunction affected 3% of the rapists in their study comparing rapists with a nonrapist population of 448 men.

Retarded Ejaculation

This dysfunction is evidenced by the male experiencing difficulty, or even failure, in his attempts to ejaculate. It is important to note that the individual *is not* controlling his ejaculation and thereby intentionally prolonging the sexual encounter, but rather is unable to ejaculate and consequently denied gratification. Groth and Burgess (1977) reported that only 15% of the rapists in their study suffered this dysfunction. Masters and Johnson found it so rare among their patients that they did not rank it. In a study of 30 sexual sadists, Dietz, Hazelwood, and Warren (1990) found that retarded ejaculation was a commonly observed dysfunction in the crimes of the men. During face-to-face interviews of 20 former wives and girlfriends of sexually sadistic men, retarded ejaculation was also found to be a common dysfunction (Hazelwood, Warren, & Dietz, 1993; Warren & Hazelwood, 2002). As Groth (1979) noted, "When the possibility of retarded ejaculation is not taken into account, the victim's version of such multiple and extended assaults may be greeted with doubts and skepticism."

Conditional Insufficiency

Groth and Burgess (1977) identified a fourth form of sexual dysfunction, which they termed *conditional insufficiency*. In such cases, the rapist is unable to become erect until there is forced oral and manual stimulation by the victim. More recently, the serial rape data collected by the authors and others suggest that rapist-forced methods of resolving the dysfunction may not be limited to forced oral and manual stimulation, but may include *any* act or behavior demanded by the offender to resolve the issue. Such demands may include anal sex, analingus, or having the victim verbalize particular words or even dress in certain clothing such as lingerie or high heels.

Conditional Ejaculation

The final type of dysfunction observed by the authors is one for which there has been no research and that is not, to the authors' knowledge, reported elsewhere in the literature. The rapist experiencing conditional ejaculation has no difficulty in obtaining or maintaining an erection, but can only ejaculate after certain conditions have been met. Most often, the conditions involve particular sexual acts and/or paraphilic behavior.

CASE NO. 4

A 33-year-old woman was abducted from her home at approximately 1:30 AM. She was taken to an abandoned farmhouse where she was forced to "model" lingerie which the offender had brought with him. She reported that he was unable to obtain an erection unless she wore a bra, panties, garter belt and hose and he was unable to ejaculate unless she verbalized as though she were consenting and desirous of the sexual activity he was performing. The fact that he had a fetish for lingerie and a fantasy of a consenting sexual partner became obvious.

CASE NO. 5

Two men abducted a young girl and took turns sexually assaulting her, tape recording the activities. One of the offenders forced the girl to masturbate him, instructing her that she was not to release his penis and that she was to understand that having him "cum" was the most important thing in the world for her to do. A period of time goes by and he cannot ejaculate. He then says, "Maybe a pair of pliers will help." He applies the pliers to her body causing her to scream and "beg" him to ejaculate which he does almost immediately.

In Case no. 4, the offender forces the victim to "model" clothing and verbalize in a manner to meet the demands of his fantasy. In Case no. 5, the victim is forced to masturbate the rapist while being tortured before the rapist can ejaculate.

INDICATIONS OF PSYCHOPATHY

It has been long recognized that psychopathy is one of the most salient predictors of violent offending including rape- and sex-related crimes (Hare, 2003). Psychopaths often display very distinct personality traits that set them apart from other types of offenders. These include a constellation of traits including impulsivity, callous lack of empathy, egocentrism, lack of remorse, deceitfulness that are likely to have manifested early in the offender's life (Skrovan, Huss, & Scalora, 2010). For the criminal profiler, a combination of these behaviors may become particularly evident from interviews with the victim and may be helpful in drawing links to behavioral characteristics evidenced in other similar crimes or to personality traits of a suspect in question. Often, retribution or revenge serves as the underlying motive and aspects of the rape frequently display signs of premeditation. However, other researchers have noted the existence of a specific category of sexual psychopaths who are primarily motivated by thrill-seeking, rather than by anger (Porter et al., 2000). Despite these slight differences, investigators should be cued to consider psychopathy when, upon commission of the rape, the offender's behavior is particularly instrumental, deceptive, and devoid of any empathy or remorse.

TYPE AND SEQUENCE OF SEXUAL ACTS

Holmstrom and Burgess (1980) suggest that "documenting the kinds of sex acts that occur during a rape helps us to more clearly understand rape." Ascertaining not only the kind of sex act, but also the sequence of the acts is extremely helpful in determining the motivation underlying a rape. Obtaining this type of information may prove to be difficult because of the emotional trauma suffered by the victim and her understandable reluctance to discuss certain aspects of the crime. Fear, shame, and humiliation are commonly experienced emotions with victims and can inhibit the divulging of information. Most often, the well-trained and experienced investigator can overcome such reluctance through a professional, patient, and empathetic approach.

While it is common for interviewers to ask about vaginal, oral, or anal acts, it is less common for them to ask questions pertaining to kissing, fondling, the use of foreign objects, digital manipulation of the vagina or anus, and fetishistic, voyeuristic, or exhibitionistic acts by the offender. In a sample of 115 adult, teenage, and child rape victims, Holmstrom and Burgess (1980) reported vaginal sex as the most frequent act, but they also reported 18 other sexual behaviors. In a study of former wives and girlfriends of sexual sadists involving face-to-face interviews, Warren and Hazelwood (2002) found 26 additional sexual behaviors (e.g., fetishism, transvestism, whipping, bondage, hanging, sex with others).

CASE NO. 6

During the interview of a serial killer's wife, Hazelwood asked her to provide the types of sexual activities in which she was compelled to participate. She advised that vaginal, anal, and oral sex was a welcome relief from what was more frequently forced upon her. She reported that she was forced to have sex with male and female strangers, to wear clothes in public which were overly revealing, to engage in degrading autoerotic sexual acts, and to participate in the production of homemade pornographic videos for use by other men. She provided photographs taken by the offender to document what she reported.

Similarly, forced repetition and the sequence of forced acts are not commonly reported. More likely the report will simply state that "the victim was raped" or "vaginally assaulted" or "raped repeatedly."

Holmstrom and Burgess (1980) wrote that "forced sexual acts may have various and important sociopsychological meanings." By documenting and analyzing the sequence of the assault, it may be possible to determine what fantasy the offender was acting out, whether he was committing the sexual acts to punish or degrade the victim, or whether he was simply engaging in sexual experimentation. For example, an anger-driven motive to punish and degrade is suggested if the victim reports being anally assaulted and then forced to perform fellatio. On the other hand, if the rapist is acting out a power-driven fantasy of having a consenting sexual partner, he may engage in kissing, fondling, and/or cunnilingus prior to a vaginal rape.

Verbal Activity

"The stereotype of the male rapist's attack is that he attains power and control over the victim through strategies based on physical force. Not only does the rapist use physically based strategies, but he also uses a second set of strategies based on language" (Holmstrom & Burgess, 1979).

A rapist unintentionally reveals a great deal about himself and the underlying motivation for the assault through his verbal interaction with the victim. The words he speaks to the victim, his manner and tone, and what, if anything, he demands the victim say to him are critically important to understanding the rapist.

Specificity is critical. A rapist who says, "I'm going to kill you if you don't do what I say," has unquestionably threatened the victim. However, a rapist who says, "Do what I say and I won't hurt you," may be reassuring the victim in an attempt to alleviate her fear of injury and gain her compliance. The offender who says, "I want to make love to you," has used a passive and expressive phrase that indicates he has no intent or desire to physically injure his victim, while the rapist who states, "I'm going to fuck you," has chosen a much more aggressive style of verbiage and has forcefully expressed hostility to the victim.

Compliments, verbal politeness, expressions of concern, apologies, and any discussion of the rapist's personal life (whether fact or fiction) strongly suggest a fantasy of a consensual encounter rather than what it actually is—rape. These verbal expressions, combined with intimate sexual behaviors such as kissing or fondling may reflect the rapist's attempts to form a pseudointimate relationship with the victim (Lundrigan & Mueller-Johnson, 2013).

On the other hand, derogatory, profane, threatening, and/or abusive verbiage is indicative of an anger-motivated attacker having the intent of using sexual behavior to punish, humiliate, and degrade the victim. Such offenders often have an arrest or social agency history of abusive behavior toward women.

When analyzing a victim's statement, it is recommended that the investigator write down an adjective that accurately describes each of the offender's statements. For example, an appropriate adjective for the phrase, "You're a beautiful woman," would be "complimentary." Other examples include

"Shut the fuck up."...Hostile
"Let me know if I'm hurting you."..Concerned
"Where do you work?"..Inquisitive
"I'm married and have kids."..Disclosing
"You didn't deserve this."..Apologetic
"Tell me what you are doing right now."..Descriptive

Utilizing this method will help the analyst to overcome personal feelings about the offender and thus provide better insight into the offender's motivation and personality. For more information on this technique, see the following chapter.

FORCED VICTIM VERBAL ACTIVITY

Sexual activity among four-legged animals is basically a biological function. Humans, however, are also dependent upon psychosexual (mental and emotional aspects of the human sex drive) involvement for arousal and gratification. The mind and the senses combined dictate what is or is not arousing to the individual. Hearing is a very important sexual sense. This is evidenced by the fact that what a person says to his or her partner during sex can either enhance or reduce the enjoyment of both of them. In a rape, the attacker may demand that the victim speak certain words or phrases that enhance the act for him. What, if anything, the victim was *forced* to say provides knowledge about the nonsexual needs the offender is attempting to satisfy through the assault. For example, a rapist who demands the victim use phrases such as "I love you," "I want you to make love to me," or "You're better than my husband" suggests a need for affirmation (power), which may exist because of self-esteem issues. The man who demands that the victim plead, cry, or scream strongly indicates the involvement of sexual sadism (a paraphilic condition in which the person is psychosexually aroused by the suffering of another) and a motive of anger.

SUDDEN CHANGE IN OFFENDER'S ATTITUDE

The victim should be specifically asked whether she observed any change in the attitude of the rapist while he was with her. Did he become angry, contrite, physically abusive, or apologetic? If she reports such a change, the analyst should then inquire as to what immediately preceded the change.

CASE NO. 7

A rapist captured a married couple in their home. After binding the husband, he proceeded to rape the woman in the presence of her husband. During the rape, the husband, who was blindfolded, asked his wife, "Are you okay?" and she replied, "Yes, he is being gentle." The attacker immediately began to attack brutally her breasts and as a result, she later underwent a mastectomy of both breasts.

During an interview of that rapist, Hazelwood asked why his attitude had changed so dramatically and he answered, "Who the fuck is she to tell me I was a gentleman? I proved to her that I was no gentleman." When pressed for further explanation, the rapist stated, "She was trying to take control and I showed her who was in control." This man was motivated by anger (brutality toward the victim's breasts) *and* power ("I showed her who was in control").

A sudden and unexpected behavioral change may occur verbally, sexually, or as in Case no. 7, physically and may indicate that an emotional weakness has been exposed or that the offender has experienced a rush of fear or perceived a threat of some sort. Triggered by acute feelings of social or sexual inadequacy, the rapist may be suddenly motivated to reassert control and dominance in a sexually aggressive manner (Prentky & Knight, 1991). Occurrences that may cause an attitudinal change can include sexual dysfunction, external disruptions (e.g., phone, knock on door), victim resistance, a perception of being ridiculed or scorned, or even the completion of the sexual aspects of the assault.

As previously mentioned, rape may be a stressful event for the offender, so having knowledge of what creates stress for the man is a valuable psychological tool to possess during police interrogations and is equally useful, for different reasons, to the mental health professional.

CRIMINAL EXPERIENCE

In an attempt to determine the criminal experience of the rapist, the investigator would be well advised to question the victim about what actions the offender took to protect his identity, remove physical or trace evidence, and facilitate his escape. The answers to these questions can be a major factor in determining the experience level of the rapist.

As with any criminal activity, the more rapes an offender has committed, the more proficient he *should* become in committing the crime and eluding detection. While most rapists take some precautionary measures (e.g., wearing gloves, telling the victims not to look at them), some men go to extraordinary lengths to protect their identity. It is the latter group that these questions are primarily designed to address. The investigator needs to know if he is confronted with a novice or an experienced rapist, and such a determination is partially based upon the sophistication, or lack thereof, demonstrated by the offender in protecting his identity.

Novice

The novice rapist is not *generally* familiar with modern medical or forensic technology and takes minimal actions for identity protection. It is expected that such a rapist might wear a ski mask or gloves, change the modulation of his voice, affect an accent, apply a blindfold, bind the victim, or order her not to look at him.

Experienced

When confronted with an intelligent and experienced rapist, the investigator will note that the man's modus operandi suggests a knowledge of scientific and technological advances that is beyond that expected of a lay person. Such an offender may order the victim to shower or douche after an assault, order her to drink grapefruit juice after forced fellatio, take cigarette butts containing his saliva or fingerprints, or even place bed sheets upon which the rape occurred in the victim's washing machine. The experienced rapist may also take steps to delay the victim's reporting his crime or to facilitate his escape (e.g., walking through the victim's residence to disable phones or alarm systems or to preparing escape routes for use after the assault).

As in all subjective analysis of criminal behavior, the experience level of the rapist can only be suggested by his actions. The accuracy of the investigator's interpretation of those actions is dependent upon his training and experience.

ITEMS TAKEN

It is well documented that rapists often steal during their crimes and it is expected that the police will record any theft that occurred during the rape. All too often, however, investigators fail to note a theft unless it involves items of value and the victim may not miss items having no intrinsic value (e.g., a photograph, a pair of panties, or an inexpensive earring). For this reason, the victim should be asked to inventory such items.

The analyst of criminal behavior is not only interested in *if* something was taken, but also *why* it was taken. Items taken by sexual offenders are categorized as (1) evidentiary, (2) valuables, and (3) personal (see Chapter 12).

Evidentiary

These are items that may contain physical or trace evidence of the offender. If such materials are taken by the offender, it suggests experience and/or an arrest history for similar offenses.

Valuables

These items have intrinsic value. If they are taken, the analyst should give attention to the type of item involved as this may indicate age and/or maturity of the rapist. For example, a young offender might steal compact discs (CDs), CD changers, or even speakers, whereas more mature offenders would be expected to take money and jewelry, which are more valuable and much easier to dispose of, conceal, and transport.

Personal

Such items generally have no intrinsic value but instead serve the offender in remembering and/or reliving the crime and/or the victim. Personal items may include driver's license, lingerie, photograph, or even an inexpensive piece of jewelry. Such items, if taken, would be classified as *either* "trophies" or "souvenirs," depending on the offender's motive for committing the crime and taking the item. A trophy represents a victory or conquest, whereas a "souvenir" serves to remind a person of a pleasant experience. It has been the author's experience that the offender who takes a personal item as a trophy may dispose of the item after a period of time and those who take items as souvenirs are more likely to retain them for longer periods of time. Investigators should be alert to the fact that the offender may return the personal items to the victim. Those who have taken the item as a trophy return it because they want to continue feelings of power over the victim through frightening her. One who has taken the item as a souvenir returns it to convince the victim that he meant no harm and with the hope of convincing the victim that he is not truly a bad person.

INDICATIONS THAT VICTIM WAS TARGETED

Rapists quite often target or select their victims prior to committing the crime. For example, a series of rapes in which the victims were invariably alone or only with small children who posed no threat, would suggest that the offender knew of the victims' vulnerability because of the gathering of intelligence, most often through window-peeping or surveillance. Another indication of having been targeted is if the victim reports that the offender's verbal behavior suggested personal or intimate knowledge (e.g., where she works, identity of a boyfriend, what kind of car she drives). If he seemed comfortable in moving through her residence, it may be that he entered and became familiar with the residence prior to the attack. For these reasons, the investigator should determine whether the victim had experienced any of the following prior to the assault:

1. Hang-up or wrong number phone calls
2. Residential or automobile break-in
3. Prowlers or "peeping toms"
4. Obscene notes
5. Attempted or successful break-ins or
6. A feeling of being watched or followed within the recent past.

If any of these have occurred, the investigator should document when and where she experienced these events.

Even when investigators are not fully convinced that the rapist had gathered specific intelligence on the victim, other pieces of information may reveal that the particular geographical area in which the assault took place was a 'comfort zone' familiar to the offender (Strangeland, 2005). Such information may lead investigators to consider whether the area could be in close proximity to the offender's home or whether he is likely to revisit the location.

SUMMARY

Rape is a criminal act involving the sexual parts of the body but serving nonsexual needs (i.e., power, anger, or a combination of the two). Capturing and analyzing the offender's behavior increases the possibility of identifying the motive underlying the assault and consequently describing the characteristics and traits of an unidentified rapist. The victim is the only available source of behavioral information, and it is crucial that the investigator establishes rapport through patience, empathy, and professionalism.

When analyzing the offender's behavior, it is imperative that personal feelings about the crime, the criminal, and the victim are isolated and that the crime is viewed from the perspective of the offender.

The crime behavior provides the investigator with information about the unknown man. Consequently, it becomes obvious that interviewing the rape victim using a set of questions specifically designed to elicit behavioral information is a crucial first step in the behavioral analysis of the rape. The questions set forth in this chapter were developed and refined over a period of years and have been found to be of inestimable value in better understanding rape and the men who commit rape.

REFERENCES

Bownes, I. T., and O'Gorman, E. C. 1991. Assailant's sexual dysfunction during rape reported by their victims. *Medicine, Science, and the Law*, 31(4): 322–328.

Campbell, R., Adams, A. E., Wasco, S. M., Ahrens, C. E., and Sefl, T. 2009. Training interviewers for research on sexual violence: A qualitative study of rape survivors' recommendations for interview practice. *Violence Against Women*, 15(5): 595–617.

Clay-Warner, J. 2002. Avoiding rape: The effects of protective actions and situational predictors of self-protective actions. *Violence and Victims*, 17: 691–705.

Coleman, J. C, Butcher, J. N., and Carson, R. C. 1984. *Abnormal psychology and modern life,* 6th ed. Glenview, IL: Scott, Foresman, and Co.

Dietz, P. E., Hazelwood, R. R., and Warren, J. I. 1990. The sexually sadistic criminal and his offenses. *Bulletin of the American Academy of Psychiatry and the Law,* 18(2): 163–178.

Groth, A. N. 1979. *Men who rape.* New York: Plenum Press.

Groth, A. N., and Burgess, A. W. 1977. Sexual dysfunction during rape. *New England Journal of Medicine*, 297(4): 764–766.

Groth, A. N., Burgess, A. W., and Holmstrom, L. L. 1977. Rape, power, anger and sexuality. *American Journal of Psychiatry*, 134: 1239–1243.

Hare, R. 2003. *The Hare psychopathy checklist: Revised 2nd ed.* Toronto: Multi-Health Systems Inc.

Hazelwood, R. R., Reboussin, R., and Warren, J. I. 1989. Serial rape: Correlates of increased aggression and the relationship of offender pleasure to victim resistance. *Journal of Interpersonal Violence*, 4(1): 65–78.

Hazelwood, R. R., Warren, J. I., and Dietz, P. E. 1993. Compliant victims of sexual sadists. *Australian Family Physician*, 22(4): 44–49.

Holmstrom, L. L., and Burgess, A. W. 1979. Rapist's talk: Linguistic strategies to control the victim. *Deviant Behavior*, 1: 101–125.

Holmstrom, L. L., and Burgess, A. W. 1980. Sexual behavior of assailants during rape. *Archives of Sexual Behavior*, 9(5): 427–439.

Jones, J. S., Rossman, L., Wynn, B. N., and Ostovar, H. 2010. Assailant's sexual dysfunction during rape: Prevalence and relationship to genital trauma in female victims. *The Journal of Emergency Medicine*, 38(4): 529–535.

Lundrigan, S., and Mueller-Johnson, K. 2013. Male stranger rape: A behavioral model of victim–offender interaction. *Criminal Justice and Behavior*, 40(7): 763–783.

Masters, W. H., and Johnson, V. K. 1970. *Human sexual inadequacy.* Boston: Little, Brown, & Co.

Porter, S., Fairweather, D., Drugge, J., Herve, H., Birt, A., and Boer, D. 2000. Profiles of psychopathy in incarcerated sexual offenders. *Criminal Justice and Behavior*, 27: 216–233.

Prentky, R. A., and Knight, R. A. 1991. Identifying critical dimensions for discriminating among rapists. *Journal of Consulting and Clinical Psychology*, 59: 643–661.

Rossmo, D. K. 2000. *Geographic profiling.* Boca Raton: CRC Press.

Skrovan, L. C., Huss, M. T., and Scalora, M. J. 2010. Sexual fantasies and sensation seeking among psychopathic sexual offenders. *Psychology, Crime and Law*, 16(7): 617–629.

Strangeland, P. 2005. Catching a serial rapist: Hits and misses in criminal profiling. *Police Practice and Research*, 6(5): 453–469.

Ullman, S. E. 2007. A 10-year update of "review and critique of empirical studies of rape avoidance." *Criminal Justice and Behavior*, 34(3): 411–429.

Warren, J. I., and Hazelwood, R. R. 2002. Relational patterns associated with sexual sadism: A study of 20 wives and girlfriends. *Journal of Family Violence*, 17(1): 75–89.

7 Analyzing the Rape and Profiling the Offender

Robert R. Hazelwood

CONTENTS

Introduction..98
Selfish versus Pseudo-Unselfish Behavior..99
    Pseudo-Unselfish Behavior..99
        Verbal Behavior...100
        Sexual Behavior...101
        Physical Behavior..101
    Selfish Behavior..102
        Verbal Behavior...102
        Sexual Behavior...103
        Physical Behavior..103
Rapist Typologies..103
    Power Reassurance Rapist..104
        General...104
        Purpose of Attack..104
        Style of Attack..104
    Power-Assertive Rapist...105
        General...105
        Purpose of Attack..105
        Style of Attack..106
    Anger Retaliatory Rapist...106
        General...106
        Purpose of Attack..106
        Style of Attack..107
    Anger Excitation Rapist..107
        General...107
        Purpose of Attack..108
        Style of Attack..108
    Opportunistic Rapist...109
        General...109
        Purpose of Attack..109
        Style of Attack..109
    The Gang Rape..109
        General...109
        Purpose of Attack..109
        Style of Attack..110
A Case Study...110
Criminal Investigative Analysis...114
    Victimology...114
        Low Risk..114

Moderate Risk 114
High Risk... 114
Method of Approach 114
Method of Control.. 114
Amount of Force 114
Victim Resistance.. 115
Reaction to Resistance 115
Sexual Dysfunction 115
Type and Sequence of Sexual Acts 115
Offender Verbal Activity 116
Attitudinal Change 116
What Preceded the Attitudinal Change? 117
Precautionary Actions 117
Items Taken 117
Purpose of the Assault.. 117
Offender Profiling 118
The Profile... 118
Personality Characteristics.. 118
Race 119
Age 119
Arrest History... 119
Marital Status 119
Residence... 120
Education.. 120
Military History... 120
Employment 120
Transportation... 120
Appearance and Grooming.. 120
Summary 121
References.. 121

What is to be expected ... is an understanding not merely of the deeds, but also the doers.

Zilboorg

Discovery consists of seeing what everybody has seen and thinking what nobody has thought.

Szent-Gyorgi

INTRODUCTION

Studying violent crime to determine characteristics and traits of unknown offenders is not a new technique (Brussels, 1968). However, it is certainly one that has captured the imagination of the public as demonstrated by such television series as *Profiler*, *Criminal Minds*, and *Law and Order: Criminal Intent*. In addition to the public's attraction to the subject, criminal justice professionals have written extensively on the subject (Canter, 1994; Palermo & Kocsis, 2004; Keppel, 2006; Ainsworth, 2013).

Until the 1970s, such analyses were primarily found in the realm of psychologists and psychiatrists who, while trained in matters of the mind, lacked experience in conducting criminal investigations. As a result, their profiles were couched in terminology largely alien to the intended audience—the criminal investigator and others in the criminal justice system. In the late 1970s, the FBI's Behavioral Science Unit (BSU), made famous by the academy award winning movie,

The Silence of the Lambs, began studying and applying this technique to a variety of violent crimes with great success. Continuing efforts to improve this investigative tool were an ongoing task of the BSU and later the FBI's National Center for the Analysis of Violent Crime (NCAVC). Current and retired NCAVC members, as well as selected city, county, state, and federal law enforcement officers, have carried this task into the twenty-first century.

Previously termed *psychological profiling* and later *criminal personality profiling*, the term *criminal investigative analysis* was coined to differentiate the procedure from that used by mental health professionals. For the purposes of this chapter, the term *profile* is meant to refer to the characteristics and traits of an *unidentified offender* responsible for a crime or series of crimes. The profile is intended to provide the client agency with significant and useful investigative leads.

Any expertise claimed by an individual is nothing more or less than a combination of one's own experience and what one has learned from the experience of others. The material set forth in this chapter is the result of reading; attendance at seminars, lectures, and courses; exchanging data with others in the field; 34 years in law enforcement; and 13 years as a consultant on violent crime. The author recognizes the impossibility of placing human behavior into specific categories that will be applicable to all rape situations. However, it is possible to analyze a particular offender's behavior during an attack or series of attacks and behaviorally describe the responsible person. That description can then be provided in such a way as to allow his family, friends, and acquaintances to recognize him.

The first step in profiling the unidentified rapist is to interview the victim and document the behaviors exhibited by the criminal. Once a detailed statement is obtained (see Chapter 6), the analyst may then proceed to the next step: carefully analyzing the statement to determine the motive for the assault. Objectivity is a necessity in this process, as is the elimination of any personal feelings about the crime, the criminal, or the victim.

The rapist's behavior is easier to assess when viewed from his perspective. Consequently, the analyst must first determine the *rapist's perspective*: not mental health's, not law enforcement's, not society's, and not even the victim's. The following classifications are presented for the sole purpose of helping the analyst to view the crime from the criminal's point of view.

SELFISH VERSUS PSEUDO-UNSELFISH BEHAVIOR

When behaviorally analyzing the rape victim's statement, the first objective is to determine whether the rapist *intended* the assault to be selfish or unselfish in nature. Categorizing a rapist as unselfish may seem contrary to everything the reader knows or believes about sexual assault. The use of the term is not intended to portray the offender in a favorable light. The terms were selected in an attempt to establish a starting point (using common language) for the analyst to begin the necessary isolation of his or her personal feelings about the offender. It would be simple (and maybe natural) to describe the rapist as a "no-good rotten bastard." Doing so might be emotionally satisfying, but not very analytical or professionally helpful. A profile is meant to describe an individual as those who *know him* would describe him. Of the six classifications of rapists described later in this chapter, only one exhibits "pseudo-unselfish" behavior.

Pseudo-Unselfish Behavior

To the average person, the word *unselfish* implies sharing or caring. In the behavioral context of a rape, however, it has an entirely different meaning, but one that is important to understanding the crime. Pseudo-unselfish behavior by the rapist evidences a belief that his exhibited concern for the victim's welfare will win her over and his hope that she will come to believe he is not a bad person. Of course this is ludicrous, but remember that we are attempting to behaviorally view the crime from the perspective of the rapist. For this rapist, it is important that the victim enjoy (or pretend to enjoy) the activity, as this feeds his need for acceptance and power and fulfills his fantasy of the victim's willing participation.

It is important that the reader understand that most pseudo-unselfish rapists will not exhibit all of the verbal, sexual, or physical behavior set forth next, but the majority will engage in sufficient behavior to allow classification.

Verbal Behavior

The unselfish rapist will verbalize in a manner one would expect to find in a consensual relationship, not a rape. He will try to *reassure* the victim that he does not intend to harm her. For example, he may tell her that if she does as he says, he will not hurt her or that he does not want to hurt her. He is frequently *complimentary*, telling her that she is beautiful, she has nice breasts, she must have a lot of boyfriends, or she is so attractive he wonders why she is not married. He may speak in a *self-demeaning* manner, telling her that she would never go out with him or she would not like him if he removed her blindfold so that she could see him. On the other hand, he might verbalize in such a way as to engage in *ego-building*, with demands for her to say that she loves him, wants to go out with him, or wants him to make love to her.

Often, the unselfish rapist will voice *concern* for his victim's welfare or comfort by asking if he is hurting her, warning her to lock her doors and windows, or asking if she is cold or thirsty. He may engage in what appears to be revealing conversation of a personal nature (*disclosing*), such as telling her that he is a college graduate or that he is married and has children. While the criminal investigator is obviously interested in whether such information is true, the analyst is more interested in the fact that he is conversing in such an unnecessary manner. An example of this type of verbiage is found in the following case.

CASE NO. 1

The victim, a 27-year-old white female, reported that her assailant awakened and raped her at approximately 2:00 AM. The sexual attack lasted no more than 10 min. Following the assault, the offender lay down beside her and conversed for approximately 45 min. While asking her questions about her personal life (job, boyfriend, etc.), he was primarily interested in discussing himself and the events of the evening. He stated that he had parked a short distance away, had left his keys in his car, and was concerned about it being stolen. He told her that a friend (Jack) was outside the residence, but that he wouldn't allow him near the victim because he was drunk. He identified himself as "David" and stated that he had never done anything like this before. Prior to leaving, he apologized and asked her not to call the police. After he left, the victim discovered that $400 was missing from her purse.

The victim immediately reported the sexual assault and theft to the police. Two days later, she returned home from work and found an envelope in her mail box. It was addressed to her, but had no stamp or postmark. Inside the envelope, she found the stolen money and an accompanying note which read:

Fran:
I'm just writing to try to express my deepest apology to you for what I put you through. I know an apology doesn't help the way you must feel right now, but I am truly sorry. I found Jack when I left, sitting on the sidewalk in front of your apartment complex. He was still pretty drunk. He took some money from a purse in your kitchen. He's really an alright guy and doesn't usually steal money. I hope this is all of it. I found my car later. Luckily, it wasn't stolen because my keys were still in it. Anyway, I just want you to know that I have never done anything like this before. I wish I could blame this on Jack, but I can't. You're really a sweet person, and you didn't deserve any of this.

You can tell your boyfriend that he's a lucky guy.

Good bye,
David

Typically, the pseudo-unselfish rapist is *nonprofane*. This is not to say that he will not use profanity, but when he does, it is mild in nature and spoken without much conviction. As occurred in the preceding case, he may be *inquisitive*, asking questions about the victim's lifestyle, occupation, social life, plans, or residence. Very often the victim will report that the rapist was *apologetic* and/or asked her forgiveness, saying that she did not deserve this and that he hopes she will eventually forgive him. Several studies have found caring, persuasion, and reassurance to be the most common features of communication patterns among their samples of rapists (McCabe & Wauchope, 2005). These findings lend support to the notion that power reassurance rapists may constitute the most common type of rape offender.

In summary, the pseudo-unselfish rapist's verbal behavior is most often (1) reassuring, (2) complimentary, (3) self-demeaning, (4) ego-building, (5) concerned, (6) personal, (7) nonprofane, (8) inquisitive, and (9) apologetic.

When studying a victim's statement, the analyst should identify all instances in which the victim reported offender verbiage and offender-forced verbal behavior from the victim and place an adjective that describes the comment in the margin of the statement (e.g., "You are beautiful" = *complimentary*). This provides the analyst with a verbal picture of this offender's fantasy.

Sexual Behavior

As we have seen, the pseudo-unselfish rapist attempts to involve the victim verbally in bringing his fantasy to reality. This is equally true in the sexual aspects of the crime. Interestingly, he does not normally force sexual acts when the victim verbally or physically resists him. While this reluctance to use physical force may emanate from a lack of confidence, it is more likely that he is attempting to bring his fantasy of a willing partner to reality, and the use of force would corrupt that fantasy. Should the victim resist, the pseudo-unselfish rapist may cease the demand, attempt to negotiate or compromise, verbally threaten, or leave. Seldom will he resort to *physical* violence.

He often engages in what the author has termed criminal foreplay in an attempt to sexually stimulate the victim. He may fondle or caress her and demand that she kiss him or insert his fingers vaginally. He may perform cunnilingus prior to penetration and he may demand that she put her arms around him or stroke his neck or back as he rapes her.

If he is confronted with an aggressive or resistant victim, he will spend a relatively brief amount of time with her. He is an intelligent offender and can quickly discern whether his victim is intimidated and passive. If that is the case, he may act out all of his sexual fantasies. In such cases, the sexual acts may include a variety of acts such as fellatio, anal sex, and the insertion of foreign objects as well as vaginal rape. Again, he will not carry out these acts in an intentionally painful manner.

It is important to note that the pseudo-unselfish and selfish rapists may actually engage in, or demand, the same sexual acts—the former when there is a lack of resistance and the latter in spite of resistance. If this occurs, the analyst must carefully compare the verbal and physical (injurious force) behaviors, as they are seldom comparable. The sequence of the sexual acts should also be examined to determine if there was an *intent* to sexually degrade the victim. An intent to degrade would involve a sequence of anal, oral, and vaginal rape, whereas the pseudo-unselfish rapist's sequence of such acts is more commonly oral, vaginal, and anal.

Physical Behavior

The amount of physical force used by the pseudo-unselfish rapist is typically at the minimal level. It was pointed out in Chapter 6 that, at this level, force is used more to intimidate than to punish. While mild slapping may occur, the offender does not intend to physically injure the victim. Instead, he most often relies on threats, the *presence* of a weapon, or the fear and passivity of his victim to obtain compliance.

From a *legal* standpoint, the presence or threat of a weapon is very significant and escalates the seriousness of the offense. From a *behavioral* standpoint, however, the fact that a rapist exhibits a weapon, or claims to have one, does not constitute physical force unless he inflicts bodily injury with the weapon. The author is aware of many instances in which an armed assailant put the weapon away after gaining control of the victim, and he is also aware of a few instances in which the rapist actually turned the weapon over to the victim. Interestingly, two of the victims found themselves incapable of using the weapon and returned it to the offender.* They reported that they were afraid of the weapon, thought it might be a trick (e.g., unloaded gun), or were concerned that they might not be able to incapacitate the assailant and that he would then kill them.

SELFISH BEHAVIOR

Whereas the pseudo-unselfish rapist seeks to involve the victim as an active participant and behaviorally indicates some concern for her welfare, no such credit can be given to the selfish rapist. He does not want the victim to be involved in any way except as an object for his use. He uses the victim in much the same way as an actor uses a prop in a play. He is verbally and sexually selfish and physically abusive. During the time he is with a victim, it is obvious that, above all else, it is his pleasure that matters and he exhibits no concern for his victim's comfort, welfare, or feelings.

Verbal Behavior

Verbally, this man will be *offensive*, *abusive*, and *threatening*. He is extremely *profane* throughout the attack and may call the victim *derogatory* terms such as "bitch" or "cunt." He will attempt to *demean* the victim by telling her that she is sexually unattractive or that he is not surprised that she is unmarried. Frequently, this offender will demand that the victim *humiliate* herself verbally (e.g., asking for or describing sexual activities). He will be consistently *threatening* and *demanding* and his verbiage will be *nonpersonal* and *sexual*. In a study by McCabe and Wauchope (2005), verbal analysis of police rape files revealed that 18% of rape incidents involved angry, demeaning, or threatening themes, amounting to the second most common communication pattern after caring, persuasion, and reassurance themes. An example of selfish verbal behavior is set forth in the following case.

CASE NO. 2

A young female was kidnapped by two serial killers who had soundproofed a van to enable them to torture young women. The victim was tortured, raped, and murdered. Her killers made a tape recording of the young victim's torment. The following is a brief segment of that recording:

RAPIST: What are you doing?
VICTIM: Nothing. I'm doing what you told me to do.
RAPIST: What's that?
VICTIM: I'm sucking on it.
RAPIST: On what?
VICTIM: This.
RAPIST: What's this?
VICTIM: Your dick.
RAPIST: You're sucking on my dick?
VICTIM: That's what you told me to do.
RAPIST: Are you doing it?
VICTIM: Yes.
RAPIST: Tell me what you're doing.
VICTIM: I'm sucking on your dick.

---

* Invariably, when I lecture to police audiences on this subject, the attendees express amazement at the fact that the victim would not take advantage of the opportunity and shoot the rapist. This attitude is quickly changed to one of empathy when I inquire as to how many of them have spouses at home who are afraid of their service weapons and demand that it be kept out of sight.

In summary, the "selfish rapist" is verbally (1) offensive, (2) abusive, (3) threatening, (4) profane, (5) demeaning, (6) humiliating, (7) demanding, (8) nonpersonal, and (9) sexual.

Sexual Behavior

Sexually, this offender will force whatever acts he desires. Again, the victim's fear, comfort, reluctance, or feelings are of no significance to him. Physical, verbal, or passive resistance will not deter his sexual domination and punishment of his victim. Seldom will he kiss his victim unless he feels it will further humiliate her and he is unlikely to fondle or caress; he is more likely to slap, twist, or bite the sexual parts of his victim's body. The victim of this rapist may be forced to perform fellatio, analingus, or self-masturbation as he watches.

Physical Behavior

The level of physical violence employed by the selfish rapist may be moderate, excessive, or brutal (see Chapter 6). The amount of force used depends largely on the motive for the attack and is seldom related to the victim's resistance.* Case no. 3 illustrates this point.

CASE NO. 3

A 33-year-old woman and her husband returned home from an evening out and were confronted with a burglar/rapist. After binding the husband, the intruder began sexually assaulting the wife. Up to this point, he had not been physically violent toward her. Her husband asked about her welfare and she stated, "It's OK, he's being gentle." At that point, the rapist began to pummel her breasts and as a result of the beating, the victim underwent a double mastectomy. Later, while interviewing the rapist, the author asked why he had beaten her breasts so severely and he replied, "Who the fuck is she to say I'm being gentle? I wanted her to know who was in charge, and she found out."

RAPIST TYPOLOGIES

Once the rapist has been classified as either selfish or pseudo-unselfish, the offender may be typed and the motive for the assault becomes more apparent. The author has chosen to use the typology of rapists developed by Groth, Burgess, and Holmstrom (1977). Over the years, he has found these types to be accurate in describing the rapists that he has interviewed as well as the style of attacks

---

* What should a woman do if she is confronted by a rapist? My opinion is that law enforcement officers should not provide specific recommendations when answering this question. I am not suggesting this as an "easy out," but rather as a means of dealing realistically with an impossible task. To begin with, the one who is asked this question is immediately confronted with three unknown variables: (1) environment of the attack, (2) type of rapist, and (3) victim personality. While some research has generally shown that active strategies of resistance against rapists may reduce the likelihood of injury or completed sexual assault (Ullman & Knight, 1993), other research has shown quite the opposite outcome when confronted with aggressive rapists (Carter, Prentky, & Burgess, 1995). My advice to an assertive woman confronted with an unselfish-type rapist in a parking lot would be entirely different from the advice I would give to a passive individual who is confronted with a sexual sadist on a little-used roadway after midnight. Lacking the necessary information, one must proceed cautiously when giving advice. If a person following our advice is brutally beaten and requires long-term hospitalization, we or our organizations could be held liable. Case no. 3 illustrates the inability to determine what may or may not diminish the probability of a victim's being injured. I once heard a speaker advise women in the audience to defecate, vomit, or urinate if confronted with a rapist, as this would surely deter him. I would refer the reader to Case no. 9 of this chapter and simply state that the only person such measures would surely deter is the individual who recommended the tactic. I have no hesitation in providing advice on preventive measures or recommending self-defense courses, firearms training, police whistles, or disabling gases where legal. However, as law enforcement officers, we must remember that when we speak in an official capacity, we speak not for ourselves but for our organizations (Hazelwood & Harpold, 1986).

he has observed in more than 4,000 rape cases on which he has consulted. The four major types are (1) power reassurance, (2) power assertive, (3) anger retaliatory, and (4) anger excitation. The author has taken the liberty of modifying the style of attack in each type and adding some general information as well. Briefly addressed are two less frequently observed types: the opportunistic rapist and the gang rape. The reader will note that the terms *pseudo-unselfish* and *selfish* are used in describing the verbal and sexual styles of attack.

A word of caution is necessary at this point. Seldom does a rapist commit a crime in a manner consistent in every detail set forth. It is more common to find that the offender exhibits some behaviors that are consistent with two or even three types of rapists—in other words, a mixture or blending of behaviors. It is at this point that experience and common sense play a dominant role in the analysis. An excellent example of such an offender may be found in Case no. 10.

Power Reassurance Rapist

General

This is a highly ritualistic offender (see Chapter 5). He is driven by the relational component (consensual) of his complex and ritualistic fantasy. It is often the case that this type of offender suffers from low self-esteem and feels inadequate in several facets of his life, driving him to compensate for these feelings of inadequacy through the sexual domination of women. He feels the victim is someone *special*—not because he knows her, but because of his relational fantasy. He has no *intent* to punish or degrade and is the least likely to physically injure his victim. However, his reluctance to hurt his victim should not be mistaken for genuine concern, but rather to serve his need for personal reassurance. One feature that is of particular importance to law enforcement for interrogation purposes and mental health professionals for treatment purposes is that this man dislikes what he is doing and is afraid that he is going to physically hurt a victim.

Purpose of Attack

This type of rapist assaults to reassure himself of his masculinity and sexual adequacy. He obtains power by taking power away from a woman through forced sexual acts. He literally proves himself to himself. While no one would deny that he degrades and emotionally traumatizes his victims, it is important to understand that he has no conscious intent to do so.

Style of Attack

The power reassurance rapist exhibits pseudo-unselfish verbal and sexual behavior and uses minimal to moderate levels of force. In law enforcement circles, he is frequently referred to as the "gentleman rapist."

He must be geographically comfortable in the attack environment. Consequently, he most often attacks victims in their residences, selecting them in advance through surveillance or window-peeping. He gathers intelligence on the women (e.g., what time they arrive home, if they have overnight guests, what time they go to bed) and the environment (e.g., proximity of neighbors, lighting, cameras, security guards). He may target several victims in advance, which explains why, following an unsuccessful attempted rape, a second attack usually occurs on the same evening in the same general locale.

The victim is either alone or with small children, who pose no threat to him. The offender does not knowingly enter a residence in which an older adult, other than the victim, is present. He commits low-risk crimes (i.e., crimes that pose little or no risk to his well-being) and typically does not force entry, preferring to enter through an unlocked window or door. This is not to say that he will not set up the residence for later entry by breaking glass or prying a patio door while the victim is absent. However, he prefers not to force entry if the victim is home as that escalates the possibility of confrontation and physical violence, which, in turn, corrupts his fantasy of a consenting relationship.

He generally attacks during the early morning hours, using the surprise approach and either exhibiting or claiming that he has a weapon. He selects victims within his own age range and forces them to remove their clothing, thus fueling his fantasy of the victim's willingness to be with him. Generally, the duration of the attack is short-lived due in part to his social ineptitude. However, if he encounters a particularly passive victim, he will take advantage of that situation and spend an extended period of time with her, acting out all of his fantasies. If the victim resists, this rapist is most likely to compromise or negotiate with her. If he experiences a sexual dysfunction, it will most likely be erectile insufficiency or premature ejaculation. This man will also engage in multiple paraphilic behaviors during the attack.

Following the assault and consistent with pseudo-unselfish behavior, he may apologize or ask the victim for forgiveness. Occasionally, he will take a personal item (e.g., lingerie, driver's license) as a souvenir. Additionally, he may be convinced that his victim had experienced some enjoyment during the offense, reinforcing his deluded fantasy of a relationship and encouraging subsequent attempts to revisit (not reassault) or contact the victim either by calling or in writing. For this reason, it is recommended that the victim's incoming calls to be monitored for up to 15 days after the assault.

If this type of rapist is unsuccessful in a rape attempt, he will quickly strike again, possibly the same evening. A successful attack will provide him with the desired feelings of power, but these feelings rapidly dissipate and he attacks again. His pattern of attacks will be fairly consistent and will occur within the same general vicinity or in a similar socioeconomic neighborhood. He will continue to attack until he is arrested, moves, or is otherwise stopped.

This rapist may keep records of his attacks. Such record keeping may be as simple as retaining his souvenirs or as complex as the method chosen by the offender in the following case.

CASE NO. 4

A black male raped more than 20 black females within a short period of time. The victims were always alone and were age-mates to the rapist. He never struck his victims but relied instead upon threats or the presence of a weapon. In several instances, upon encountering resistance, he left the scene rather than resort to physical violence to obtain victim compliance. Upon his arrest, the investigators recovered a business ledger containing each of the victims' names, addresses, telephone numbers, and body measurements and a scoring system for the victims' participation in various sexual acts. The ledger also contained similar information on fantasized attacks of movie stars and popular singers.

POWER-ASSERTIVE RAPIST

General

This offender is a low-to-moderately impulsive rapist. As opposed to the power reassurance rapist, fantasy plays a minor role in his crimes. While involved in the rape of strangers, this type of rapist is frequently responsible for date, spousal, or acquaintance rapes as well.

Purpose of Attack

In contrast to the power reassurance rapist, this man does not admit doubts about his masculinity either to himself or others. To the contrary, he is outwardly a man's man and, as he sees it, is simply exercising his prerogative as a male, evidencing a sense of entitlement. He uses rape to express his virility and dominance over women and whether or not he physically injures a victim is of no consequence to him; she is merely an object to be used for his gratification.

Style of Attack

The power-assertive rapist is sexually and verbally selfish in his attacks. He exhibits no empathy toward his victims and is not concerned about their physical or emotional well-being. This type of rapist most often assaults victims of opportunity, using the con approach, and changes demeanor only after the victim is relaxed and at ease. However, his approach is characterized by a general impulsivity and is not likely to have been well planned ahead of time. He uses moderate to excessive levels of force in controlling the victim and generally relies on his fists for weapons. Aggression is often used as a means to secure compliance rather than the infliction of intentional harm and has been observed to escalate in subsequent sexual assaults. However, if harm ensues, he is likely to be indifferent to the victim's experience of injury or pain especially when confronted with resistance. Like the power reassurance rapist, he selects victims who approximate his own age. His rapes are likely to occur at any location that is convenient and safe as he is often geographically mobile. Frequently, he will rip or tear the victim's clothing from her, discarding it and subjecting the victim to repeated sexual assaults. It is not uncommon for this type of rapist to use alcohol or other substances before the assault.

If he experiences a sexual dysfunction, it is most often retarded ejaculation. Paraphilic behavior is absent from his crimes and his pattern of rape is not as consistent as that of the power reassurance rapist because he assaults when he feels like it. The offender presented in Case no. 5 is an excellent example of this type of rapist.

CASE NO. 5

A female motorist was stranded with her disabled car, when a white male stopped and offered assistance. He raised the hood of her car, examined it for a few minutes, and advised her that it would have to be repaired by a mechanic. Because he was well dressed and very polite, she accepted his offer to take her to a nearby service station. Once in the car, they chatted in a friendly manner until she noticed that he had passed two exits. She inquired as to how far the station was, and he displayed a gun and told her to shut up. She screamed, and he struck her twice on the head, causing her to lose consciousness. When she awakened, she discovered her clothes had been torn off and he was raping her. When she pleaded for him not to hurt her, he cursed her, struck her again and told her to keep quiet. During the next 2 h, he raped her three times and forced her to perform fellatio twice. Following the assault, he threw her out of the car, keeping the clothes, and told her, "Show your ass and you may get some help." The victim was treated for severe bruises and lacerations.

ANGER RETALIATORY RAPIST

General

This is also an impulsive offender, who is less common in frequency than the two previous types but is much more physically violent. Fantasy plays less of a role in this offender's attacks than with any of the three other major types of rapists. He overtly hates women and wants to punish and degrade them. His pronounced hostility towards women often originates from profound personal experiences with women in his life and is likely to have experienced physical abuse and family dissolution during childhood (Holmes & Holmes, 2009).

Purpose of Attack

This rapist is strongly identified with anger and retaliation. As Groth et al. (1977) pointed out, the individuals who fall within this category are getting even with women for real or imagined wrongs. They are angry with women and they use sex as an extremely potent weapon to punish them. They intentionally brutalize their victims and when one interviews the victim of such an attack, it becomes clear that anger is the key motivational component that leads to the sexual expression of aggression (Groth, 1983).

Style of Attack

The anger retaliatory rapist is sexually and verbally selfish and uses excessive to brutal levels of force. The analyst should easily recognize that the use of such unnecessary force is the product of intense rage and fulfills an emotional need to attack and punish, if not destroy. The attack often includes highly degrading and humiliating acts and language that are reflective of his crude opinion of women.

The crime itself is not premeditated in the sense that time was committed to planning or to the selection of a victim. The attack is an emotional outburst that is predicated on anger and what consequently results is an unplanned and hastily carried out offense.

This type of rapist uses the blitz approach, subduing the victim with the immediate application of injurious force and thereby denying her any opportunity to defend herself. The sexual assault and the amount of time spent with the victim are relatively brief. The pent-up anger is vented against the female sexually and physically and, following an attack, the anger begins to build again, and another assault occurs when triggered by rage.

The anger retaliatory rapist attacks women who are age-mates or somewhat older than he is, but not elderly. He assaults women who symbolize other women in his life. The symbolism may be the style of dress, grooming, occupation, height, weight, race, or a host of other possibilities.

As with the power-assertive rapist, this man is likely to tear or rip his victim's clothing off, and because his crimes are anger motivated, they are likely to occur at any time and at any place. His victims are opportunistic in that they cross his path at the wrong time and place. He uses weapons of opportunity—most often his fists and feet. If he experiences a sexual dysfunction, it is most likely to be retarded ejaculation and there is very little likelihood of paraphilic involvement in his crimes. The following case is an excellent example of an anger retaliatory rapist.

CASE NO. 6

The victim, a woman in her late forties, was walking toward her car in a parking lot when a man spun her around and struck her repeatedly in the face and stomach with his fist. In a semi-conscious state, the victim was placed in her automobile and driven to an isolated area, where the rapist ordered her to remove her clothing. As she fumbled with the buttons on her blouse, he cursed her and began tearing her clothes off and throwing them out of the car. As she held her arms up in a defensive posture, he continued to beat her severely and to scream obscenities at her. Forcing her into the rear seat of the car, he attempted to rape her but was unable to obtain an erection. Blaming the victim for a lack of sexuality, he decided that alcohol would "help" her and he forced her to consume a large amount from a bottle, causing her to gag. Under his control for more than 2 h, she was repeatedly beaten and otherwise abused. He finally pushed her into a ditch and drove away. Upon being taken to a hospital, she was found to have fractures of facial and other bones, as well as multiple lacerations. She required extended hospitalization and long months of physical and mental health therapy.

ANGER EXCITATION RAPIST

General

This offender is more commonly referred to as a sexual sadist—a person who is psychosexually aroused by the *suffering* of his victims. He is a highly ritualistic rapist and fantasy plays a major role in his crimes. Of most importance to him is the paraphilic component (e.g., sadism, sexual bondage, voyeurism) of his rich and complex fantasy life. His attacks often become more brutal and ritualized to achieve a higher level of arousal with each subsequent victim. He is the most violent of rapists.

Purpose of Attack

This type of rapist is sexually excited by the victim's *response* to the infliction of physical and emotional pain. It is not the pain itself, but the victim's suffering, fear, and submission that is most satisfying as he yearns for total physical and psychological dominance. This is the least frequently observed type of rapist; however, his rarity is more than compensated for by the viciousness of the attack and the trauma suffered by the victim. Depending on the rapist's maturity, experience, and criminal sophistication, no other sexual crime encountered will be as well planned, rehearsed (either literally or in his dark and complex fantasies), and methodically executed as that committed by the anger excitation rapist. Weapons, transportation, travel routes, recording devices, bindings, escape—virtually every phase is preplanned, with one notable exception: The victim is typically a total stranger. While she may meet the demographic criteria established by the man, there is no known association between them.

Style of Attack

The victims of this rapist are typically females of varying ages, demographics, and race, but the reader should be aware that this offender may also sexually assault men or boys; in other words, he is a polymorphous offender (one who is aroused in a variety of ways and experiments sexually). He is sexually and verbally selfish and most often uses an excessive to brutal level of force, resulting in extensive hospitalization or death. This rapist uses a con approach, but once in a position to do so, he quickly subdues his victims, taking them to a preselected location that provides him with the requisite privacy. He keeps his victims for hours to days, psychologically battering and even physically torturing with instruments and devices.

Victims frequently report that the offender cut the clothing from their bodies and that they were forced to participate in sexual bondage, fellatio, painful insertion of foreign objects into their anus or vagina, and anal rape. Multiple paraphilic behaviors are to be expected as well.

The anger excitation rapist is the *most likely* offender to record his activities with the victim. The method of recording is dependent upon the offender's desires, maturity, experience, and economic ability to afford available technology. The author has observed cases in which the rapist recorded his acts with photographs, video camera, tape recorder, calendars, maps, notes, manuscripts, computers, codes, and sketches or drawings.

The sexual acts forced on the victim are varied and experimental in nature, but all are intended to create suffering, humiliation, and degradation for the victim. Interestingly, the sexual sadist tends to remain emotionally detached from his victims and is almost clinical in his instructions to them. One victim said, "He was like a boring school teacher…speaking in a monotone voice and telling me what to do and what to say." Almost invariably, this offender will experience retarded ejaculation.

There is no apparent spatial or geographic pattern to his assaults. However, because of the highly ritualistic behaviors and the multiple paraphilias exhibited in such cases, the investigator should have no difficulty in linking the assaults committed by such offenders (see Chapter 10). Case no. 7 provides the reader with an example of such a rapist.

CASE NO. 7

The victim, a 32-year-old housewife, disappeared from a shopping center after having purchased groceries from a store. She was driving a motor home at the time of her disappearance. Her nude body was found in the motor home 5 days later. She was lying on her back on the sofa with her hands bound behind her. An autopsy indicated that her death was due to the continued ingestion of small amounts of arsenic accompanied by bourbon. She had been raped several times and it was the opinion of those involved with the case that she had been forced to drink the arsenic-spiked bourbon to induce convulsions of the body for the pleasure of the rapist.

OPPORTUNISTIC RAPIST

General

This is an impulsive type of sexual offender (see Chapter 5) but that is not to say he lacks proficiency as a burglar or robber. He simply had not anticipated committing a sexual assault because he was originally at the assault location to commit a robbery or burglary. Consequently, his arrest record will reflect a history of crimes such as breaking and entering, armed robbery, and burglary.

Purpose of Attack

This may be the only type of rapist whose *primary* motive for the rape is truly sexual. The opportunist offender rapes as an afterthought to the commission of another crime. For example, a man intent on burglarizing a residence finds a female alone in the house and impulsively rapes her. The analyst must be careful not to confuse this type of offender with a robber who consistently rapes during his crimes; that individual should be categorized as one of the four major rapists set forth earlier in this chapter.

Style of Attack

As stated, the opportunist is in the midst of committing another crime (burglary, robbery, kidnapping, etc.) when he impulsively decides to sexually assault. He uses a minimal level of force and spends a relatively short period of time with the victim, leaving her bound when he departs. He is sexually and verbally selfish and typically has been drinking or using drugs prior to the crime. An example of this type of rapist is set forth in Case no. 8.

CASE NO. 8

The victim, a 17-year-old, was normally in school at the time that a burglar entered her residence. Surprised to find anyone at home, the criminal bound and blindfolded the young girl, and after advising her that he wouldn't harm her, he began ransacking the home. Finding the father's liquor cabinet, he consumed a large amount of alcohol and began thinking of the attractive female who was in the house. He became intoxicated and attempted to vaginally assault her, but was unable to maintain an erection. He told the crying girl to be quiet, that he hadn't hurt her, and then he left. Upon his arrest, he expressed regret at what happened and said that he had a daughter the same age as the victim. There was no indication that he had ever attempted such an act previously.

THE GANG RAPE

General

This is one of the most frightening situations in which a victim can find herself. In such a case, the victim is attacked by a group of three or more males who are operating with a pack mentality. Studies on gang rape and multiple perpetrator rape have reported higher levels of gratuitous violence and aggression as well as a greater likelihood of weapon use when compared to single perpetrator rapes (Woodhams & Cooke, 2013). In a sample of 223 group rapes, approximately 20% ended in the victim's death (Porter & Alison, 2006).

Purpose of Attack

There is no apparent purpose in such assaults other than that the victim has been identified by the males as being weak, vulnerable, and somehow deserving of attack. Porter and Alison (2006), replicating observations of previous studies, found that group rapes tended to be perpetrated by young males with an average age of twenty-one against victims of a similar age. Most of the males are attempting to prove something to their peers and consequently are physically and/or sexually violent, and the victim is likely to be traumatized for life. This is especially true of young offenders whose desires for group acceptance make them amenable to peer-pressure and influence.

Style of Attack

While the con approach may be used by one gang member to entice the victim to a location where his fellow assailants lie in wait, the more common approach is the blitz approach as described in Case no. 9. This approach is often characterized by impulsivity and relatively little or no planning. In this case, the extent of planning and organization may involve the predetermination of an approach location and the preparation of transportation to bring the victim to a more secluded area that affords prolonged sexual assault. In the gang rapes that the author has consulted on, the assault is totally selfish in nature, and while the level of force varies from minimal to brutal, the vast majority of the crimes result in extensive injury and hospitalization of the victim. In almost all gang rapes, one person emerges as the leader and it is this individual upon whom the analyst should focus by eliciting detailed information from the victim. Not surprisingly, research by Woodhams and Cooke (2013) revealed that leaders displayed the most severe acts of aggression in gang rapes and had the most influence on other co-offenders' participation and conformity in the act. In many instances, there is also a reluctant participant involved in gang rapes. This individual is relatively easy to identify because he physically or verbally indicates to the victim that he is not in favor of the attack. He may argue with the others or even attempt to help her escape. Obviously, this individual is the weak link in the group and if such a person is described by the victim, the analyst should attempt to profile him as well. The following case illustrates such a rape.

CASE NO. 9

A 19-year-old female was abducted from a phone booth as she was hysterically explaining to her parents that a group of four young men were following her in a car and threatening to rape her. Four hours later, she was found and immediately transported to a nearby hospital where she was treated for a fractured jaw, a broken arm, and severe lacerations of the vaginal and rectal regions. She later reported that she had been forcibly taken from the phone booth and placed in the back seat of the car being used by the gang. As a result of her extreme fear, she defecated and one of the youths suggested that she be released, whereupon a second male, who was the obvious leader, negated that suggestion and instead stated that she needed to be taught a lesson. He then twisted her arm so severely that it broke and forced her to orally clean her soiled clothing. The youth who had objected to the rape again objected and was threatened by the leader. Following this, the leader directed the others to have sex with the young girl, and two complied; the third (the reluctant participant) was sexually unable to perform. The leader then anally assaulted the girl and then forced the victim to perform fellatio on him. Following these acts, he vaginally assaulted her. She was later tied to the rear bumper of the assailants' car and dragged over the roadway.

A CASE STUDY

Now that the reader has been familiarized with the pseudo-unselfish and selfish physical, verbal, and sexual behaviors and the various types of rapists have been described, the author will present a case that was submitted to him for analysis. The case is presented as it was received with changes made only to protect the identity of the victim. Following the case report, the reader will find the author's analysis of the crime. Finally, the author's opinion of the criminal's characteristics and traits will be provided. The rapist has since been identified, and the profile was found to be more than 90% accurate.

CASE NO. 10

Victimology: The victim, Mary, is a white female, 24 years of age. She currently lives alone but previously lived with her parents in another part of the state. Mary attended a university and graduated 2 years prior to the offense. She is an active Catholic, attending church regularly and participating in church events. After graduating, she obtained a teaching job in a junior high school. According to Mary, she is popular with the students at the school and attributes her popularity to the fact that she is young, friendly, outgoing, a nice dresser, and "on their level." Mary is friendly with both black and white students and frequently attends their athletic events. She stated that students would visit her classroom during their free time even though she was not their teacher. She drives an older-model subcompact car, made noticeable by multicolored fenders salvaged from other vehicles. Her personal life is fairly routine, but she has a boyfriend who lives a few miles from her residence. She visits the Catholic church almost daily after school. She also attends a Wednesday night "happy hour" at a local bar/restaurant that attracts a respectable clientele. She is active athletically and eats out infrequently. She observes regular sleeping habits and is careful to draw her curtains at night. She knows of no black male fitting the physical description of her assailant.

Attack environment: Mary resides in an apartment complex. The complex is located in a middle-class neighborhood and is in a well-established area of the city. The complex rents to a variety of people, including elderly, singles, and young couples. Mary's apartment is located at the rear of the complex and is one of 20 apartments. Her residence and the two beside hers are secluded and face a heavily wooded area immediately behind the complex. Her apartment is on the ground floor. A person not familiar with the area would be surprised to find the three apartments in the rear of the complex. The windows of the apartment face the wooded area. The management seems sincere in trying to screen all renters and maintain the quiet environment of the complex. This is evidenced by their success in evicting a recent tenant for creating heavy traffic in and out of the complex because of suspected drug dealing.

Assault: On a Thursday evening, Mary went to bed around midnight. The evening was cool and clear, and she left her windows open to circulate the air. She wore a nightgown and panties to bed. Sometime after 2:00 AM, she became aware of the sensation of something tickling her leg. Thinking it was a bug, she tried to brush it off with her hand. When it continued, she tried to brush it again and felt something she believes was a hand. The room was very dark, but she could see enough to determine that a naked black male was beside her bed. When she sat up, he immediately jumped up and pushed her back down on the bed. He put a hand to her throat and told her to be quiet or he would "blow your head off." Mary began asking him to leave, and he put something, which she thought was metal, to her head and told her he had a gun. He told her he had gotten out of prison 2 weeks before and not to make any trouble since he had killed the other girls he had done this with. Mary asked him how he had gotten into the apartment, and he told her he had climbed in the window. He then grabbed the sheet, but Mary kept asking him to leave. He then said he was going to "kill her if she didn't let go of the sheet, because he wasn't in the mood for fooling around." Mary let go of the sheet, and he pulled her panties off. He then told her to spread her legs, but she refused. He again threatened her, and she held her legs up. He began to perform cunnilingus and continued this for approximately 3 min. During this time, Mary tried to talk to him about his statement about just getting out of prison. She told him that she had worked in a prison and that she didn't think that he had just gotten out. He stated that he was in a prison in another state. She asked him to leave several times, but he told her to be quiet and continued to perform cunnilingus. He then inserted his penis in her vagina. Several times when he hurt her, she cried out, and he quickly put a hand to her throat and warned her not to do it again or he would kill her. Mary told him not to hurt her again, and he responded by telling her to take her top (nightgown) off, which she refused to do. He pushed it up and began licking her nipple. During all this time, he was careful not to raise himself above her so that, in the poor light, she might be able to get a better look at him. He "slid" up her body to lick the nipple. At one point, he bit her nipple, causing Mary to cry out. Mary told him he had hurt her, and he said, "I'll show you how I can hurt you," and inserted his penis again. He told her to "shove your ass" while he was inserting his penis, and she responded by telling him that her working was not part of the deal and that she was not enjoying this. He asked if she was only "half a woman" and she said, "Yes, that's right." At one point, he moved his penis to her anus, but she told him he was in the wrong place and he ceased the attempt. Eventually he ejaculated in her vagina and Mary began asking him to leave again.

During the rape, Mary never saw a weapon, but felt a metal object pressed to her head. When he hurt her and she let him know, he would cease the painful activity. He never struck her during the incident and his threats were not made in an angry, but rather in a stern voice. Mary did not think he had trouble in obtaining or maintaining an erection, although he told her that he was having trouble and compared his erection with "the others." He did not ask her to do anything to help him, apart from saying, "Shove your ass," and Mary said that she did not touch him during the entire incident. She did not think that a premature ejaculation occurred, but could not be certain due to her lack of sexual experience. She felt that the actual intercourse lasted approximately 15 min and that he seemed to be in control of his sexual sensations during that time. He did not demand that she talk to him during the assault or that she speak any particular words to him. He was not abusive or profane at any time and, according to Mary, seemed to care about her. His demeanor changed only when he threatened her and then it was a stern tone, something Mary likened to a father correcting a child.

After the rape, he leaned over the bed, closed the open window, and told her to get out of bed. She asked why, but he just repeated the order. She got out of bed, and he directed her to the living room. He told her not to turn on any lights and placed his hand on her shoulder blade and pushed her ahead. In the living room, he made her lie face down on the rug near her sound system. Mary continually asked him if he was going to leave, but he didn't say anything and she did not hear him put his clothes on. He asked her what she was going to do after he left, and she told him she would probably call her parents and cry. He asked her if she was going to call the cops, and she said no. He then asked where the phone was, and she directed him to the kitchen. She could hear him feeling against the wall but he couldn't find the phone. During the time she was on the floor, he continually ordered her to "keep that nose pressed to the floor." When he couldn't find the phone, he told her to show him where it was located. He then told her to go back and lie down. She did, and he ripped the phone out, saying he was sorry that she couldn't call her folks. He had her show him how to unlock the door (deadbolt lock, manually operated) and took her to the bathroom, keeping a hand on her shoulder. In the bathroom, he obtained a towel, telling Mary not to turn on any lights. They returned to the living room, and he made her lie down again. He ripped the towel into strips, possibly using a kitchen knife, and began to tie one strip over her eyes as a blindfold. He tied it too tight and it hurt her, so she asked him to loosen it, and he did. At this point, she noticed that he was wearing gloves similar to those used by doctors, and also work boots. He tied her hands behind her back and tied one of her ankles. Then, with a wet towel, he began wiping her vagina. He asked her if he had gotten all the "semen"; she answered that she didn't know and asked when he was going to leave. He kept asking what her name was during this time, but she wouldn't tell him. He then tied her ankles together and asked her if she had any money. She replied that she only had $1. He turned on the sound system and the announcer said it was 2:50 AM, and he told her to give him $20 or he would take her sound system. Mary told him that she didn't have $20, but that she would write him a check. He found her purse, took a dollar and change, and asked, "Is your name Mary?" She assumed he had found her driver's license. He then told her that he was going to take the sound system, and she told him he was going to look funny carrying it around. He replied, "There are ways." Mary told him that she wanted the cassette tapes. He wanted to know if they were mood music, and she said no, but that they had identification on them that might incriminate him if he took them.

He asked if she had any beer or wine in the refrigerator and she said no, but he went to the refrigerator and found a bottle of wine. She told him it was cooking wine, but he drank it anyway. He then told her that he was going to do it again and that he was going to do an "ass job." She refused, and he said, "Yes we are." She refused again and said it would hurt her too much. He then placed a knife to her throat hard enough to prevent her from speaking and told her he was going to kill her. He told her that he had a knife and was going to slit her throat. She asked him why, and he said that since she didn't want to "make it" with him that there was no point in her living at all. He then asked why he should let her live, and she told him that she needed to love, to love her parents, her husband, her children. He asked if she had a husband or kids and she said no, that she had meant her future husband. He asked if she was afraid, and she said yes. He then told her that they were going to do it again. He directed her onto her back, but it was painful and she kept rolling on her side. He put the knife to her throat and said that he didn't want any fooling around. He asked her which way she wanted it and she told him she didn't want it any way. He pressed the knife to her throat again and asked if she wanted to live, and she replied yes. At this point, he told her that he used to be a good Christian boy with a nine-to-five job until 1 day he came home and found his wife in bed with another guy. From then on, he just went from one girl to another. Mary told him she was sorry. He told her that if she didn't call the cops, he would be back, and she told him that she would call the police. He then told her that, even in the dark, he could tell that she had "nice features" and a "picturesque ass." Mary told him she didn't think he was from prison, and he laughed and said, "No, this is from your own neighborhood." She said she had some black friends and that she didn't know if she could treat them fairly after this. He asked what friends, and she replied that they were black students. He said, "I don't hang around those punks." Mary felt that he was so strong in his denial that it seemed as if he did hang around them. Mary asked why he had picked her, and he replied that he had heard that she was a "classy chick" and that he had seen her around. She said that didn't mean he had to do this to her, and he replied that if he had asked her to screw around, she would have said no. Mary heard him rip some paper and asked him to leave. He replied that he was and slid the knife down her back and between her hands. She asked him to leave a light on, and he said he had. She then heard the door open and close. She began trying to get the blindfold off, and she felt him tapping her on top of the head. He placed the knife inside the blindfold and told her how lucky she was. She heard a big bang, and the music stopped playing. She heard the door slam, waited a few minutes, and then worked the blindfold off. She hopped to the door, locked it, and worked the towel from around her ankles. She opened the door and knocked on a neighbor's apartment door, and help was summoned.

Subsequent examination by a physician revealed a small laceration on her neck and towel burns on her wrists. Police investigation revealed that the rapist had removed a screen covering the point of entry (a window). Mary described the rapist as a medium- to light-skinned black male, 20–30 years old, 5'8" to 5'10" in height. He had spoken in soft to normal tones and seemed to be articulate. He had been very concerned about physical evidence being left at the scene. She didn't think he had worn the gloves during the rape. The knife was a kitchen knife from her residence. The paper she heard being ripped was determined to be newspaper he had used to light a bowl candle, which was still burning. He had also smoked a cigarette and had taken the butt with him. The "bang" she had heard was from a blow to the sound system with what is believed to have been a metal pipe.

CRIMINAL INVESTIGATIVE ANALYSIS

The investigators in this case utilized the questions set forth in Chapter 6 as a guide during the interview with Mary. As the reader will note, a great deal of interaction occurred between Mary and her assailant. The crime is analyzed next and the significance of the exhibited behavior is described in detail.

VICTIMOLOGY

When a case is analyzed for profiling purposes, victimology is extremely important. An absence of pertinent information concerning the victim may preclude an accurate analysis of the crime. Victims of violent crime are categorized as being either low-, moderate-, or high-risk victims.

Low Risk

Victims classified as low risk have personal, professional, and social lives that do not normally expose them to the threat of crime. Almost without exception, such victims are sought out and targeted by the criminal. Mary would be categorized as a low-risk victim. Her assailant obviously targeted her.

Moderate Risk

Moderate-risk victims are those who would normally be considered low risk, but because of employment (working hours, environment, etc.), lifestyle (meeting dates through advertisement or in singles bars, etc.), circumstances (car breaking down at night), or personal habits (shopping at all-night stores) have an elevated risk of becoming a victim.

High Risk

High-risk victims are those whose lifestyles or employment consistently expose them to danger from the criminal element (drug dealing, residential location, sexual promiscuousness, prostitution, etc.). If a victim is categorized as high risk, the probability of profiling her offender is greatly diminished because the number of potential offenders is extremely large.

METHOD OF APPROACH

The rapist in this case utilized the surprise approach. He entered her residence at an hour when he had reason to believe she would be asleep and unprepared for an attack. In the author's opinion, the victim had been targeted in advance, through either surveillance or window-peeping. The isolated location of the apartment allowed the rapist to observe the victim undetected over a period of time. The offender felt sufficiently comfortable in the residence to remove his clothing prior to approaching the victim and he did not inquire as to whether anyone else was in the apartment or was expected to visit—an indication that he was familiar with Mary's routine and was aware that she lived alone.

METHOD OF CONTROL

Although the rapist told Mary that he had a gun, and she felt a metal object (probably a pipe) at her head, he relied primarily on threats to control her. Of particular interest is the fact that even though he threatened physical violence if she did not comply with his demands, he did not carry out those threats. This suggests that the intent or desire to physically punish the victim was absent.

AMOUNT OF FORCE

The rapist had numerous opportunities to rationalize the use of physical force against the victim and yet he never struck her. The force used by the assailant consisted of (1) pushing her down on the bed,

(2) putting his hand to her throat, (3) biting her nipple, (4) tapping her on the head, and (5) inflicting a slight wound to her neck. Behaviorally, it is of interest that when she told him that he hurt her, he would stop. For example, when she complained of the blindfold being too tight, he loosened it.

It is apparent that a battle of wills was taking place and even though the rapist assaulted Mary sexually, he failed to intimidate her emotionally. He was aware of his failure to psychologically control her and, instead of acting out against her in a physical manner, he chose to destroy something belonging to her (the sound system) in a symbolic attack.

Given the circumstances reported, the level of force exhibited in this attack was minimal. Although the victim's neck was slightly injured, it was such a minor wound that she made no mention of it in her statement. Furthermore, she reported that the rapist seemed to care about her welfare.

VICTIM RESISTANCE

There was a great deal of resistance in this case. Mary resisted the offender verbally by consistently rejecting him, questioning his demands, and asking him to leave. She resisted passively by not complying with his order to remove her nightgown, and she resisted him physically by changing her position to avoid intercourse.

REACTION TO RESISTANCE

There is an interesting pattern of offender reaction to victim resistance. The rapist relied primarily on verbal threats to overcome Mary's opposition. At one point, she refused to remove an article of clothing and he did so himself, thereby ceasing the demand. After refusing to comply with the demand to "shove your ass," the victim was asked if she was "half a woman." Again and again, the potential for physical violence was there, and yet was not applied. As previously mentioned, the offender failed to intimidate Mary, and his lack of a reaction involving physical violence supports the opinion that he had neither the desire nor the intent to physically harm the victim.

SEXUAL DYSFUNCTION

Mary was unable to state with certainty whether any dysfunction occurred. She did report that the rapist had no difficulty in obtaining or maintaining an erection, and he ejaculated within an average amount of time. So even though the offender verbally indicated some difficulty, Mary was not aware of any such problem. However, her lack of sexual experience may have been a factor in her assessment regarding dysfunction.

TYPE AND SEQUENCE OF SEXUAL ACTS

The sexual attack included the following acts in the sequence reported by the victim: (1) cunnilingus, (2) digital manipulation of the vagina, (3) vaginal rape, (4) licking of nipple, (5) vaginal rape, (6) attempted anal rape, (7) vaginal rape with ejaculation, (8) threatened anal rape, and (9) attempted vaginal rape.

The acts of cunnilingus and digital manipulation of the vagina preceded the first rape. The activity and sequencing suggest an attempt to stimulate the victim. This behavior is unnecessary in a rape situation, and its presence indicates an attempt to involve, rather than simply use, the victim. (Behaviorally analyze the crime from the offender's perspective, not your own and certainly not the victim's.) Mary told the offender that she was not enjoying the sex, that her "working" was not part of the deal, and that she did not want sex with him. Following the vaginal rape, he attempted to enter her anally and was told by Mary that he was "in the wrong place." Verbally resisted, he stopped the attempt to anally assault her, entered her vaginally, and ejaculated. Even though he ceased his attempt to anally assault her, the desire for this type of sexual act was strong (i.e., he later told her he was going to do an "ass job"). His expressed desire for anal sex, combined with Mary's description of his having a muscular upper torso and his talk of prison, suggests that Mary's attacker had been institutionalized. This will be more fully discussed in the offender profile presented later.

Sexually, the offender exhibits a mixture of selfish and pseudo-unselfish behavior.

Offender Verbal Activity

The victim in this case was intelligent, articulate, and obviously in control of her emotions. She gave a detailed and comprehensive description of the entire episode and provided an abundance of behavioral information from which to draw conclusions. Nowhere is this more evident than in the victim's recollection of what the rapist said and the manner in which he spoke. When analyzing the statement, the author wrote adjectives to describe what the rapist said. As a result, an interesting picture of the offender began to emerge. Let us examine what he said and objectively describe it using adjectives:

1. He threatened to "blow your head off" and stated that he was "going to kill you." The adjective *threatening* is appropriate for these phrases.
2. He told her to "get out of bed," "spread your legs," and "hold your legs up." Either *commanding* or *demanding* describes these phrases.
3. He related that he had just gotten out of prison, that he used to be a good Christian boy, and that he had been a nine-to-five person until he found his wife in bed with another man. The author described this personal information as *disclosing.*
4. He spoke in a *derogatory* manner when he asked if she were "half a woman."
5. He was *nonprofane.* The victim clearly recalled that he had not used profanity during the course of the crime.
6. He was *apologetic* when he told her he was sorry she could not call her folks.
7. He asked her name, if she had any kids, and if she had a husband. This would accurately be described as *inquisitive.*
8. He was *complimentary* when he told her she had nice features and a "picturesque ass."
9. He was *angry* when she would not comply with his demands. In one instance, he told her how he could hurt her.
10. Finally, he was *self-demeaning* when he said she would not have "screwed around" with him if he had asked her.

An analysis of the verbal behavior reveals that the rapist exhibited a mixture of selfish and pseudo-unselfish behavior. This blending of behavior allows us to see him as those who know him see him. This will be discussed in the later profile.

Attitudinal Change

Mary stated that the rapist's attitude changed only when he threatened her. She described the change as being verbal in nature and said he became stern "like a father correcting a child." We see here that the victim is able to differentiate the sexual assault from the offender's attitude, something that many investigators, victims' advocates, and mental health professionals are unable to accomplish. Her description of this change in attitude is helpful and enlightening when one considers that the rapist is in possession of a weapon, is physically larger and stronger than Mary, and has met resistance repeatedly, yet his threatening attitude is described as being "stern." This is certainly not the stereotypic view of a rapist, yet is very typical behavior for one not desiring to physically harm his victim.

WHAT PRECEDED THE ATTITUDINAL CHANGE?

The victim stated that the only time she perceived a change in his attitude was when he threatened her. In each instance, what preceded the change was resistance by Mary. Some rapists will use physical force in such situations, others will compromise or negotiate, and still others will leave; the rapist of Mary chose to threaten. Why? As has been pointed out earlier, the rapist engaged in a battle of wills with Mary and lost. The author believes that this man is used to winning in confrontations with women and this was certainly a situation that should have yielded a submissive woman—but it did not. His frustrations are evident by his continued threats and finally his retaliatory attack on the sound system.

PRECAUTIONARY ACTIONS

This case is replete with actions taken by the offender to protect his identity, facilitate his escape, and deny investigators physical or trace evidence. Such behaviors include: (1) removing his clothing prior to the attack, thereby reducing the possibility of fiber evidence and also ensuring that Mary would be unable to provide police with their description; (2) disabling the phone, which delayed her ability to report the crime; (3) readying his escape route by having the victim show him how to unlock the door; (4) blindfolding the victim prior to turning on a light; (5) binding her ankles and wrists prior to departure; (6) wiping her vaginal area to remove semen; (7) wearing surgical gloves, which he believed would preclude the possibility of fingerprints and yet allow the sense of touch; and (8) taking the cigarette butt with him, thereby denying police the possibility of determining blood type from the saliva residue.

While a few precautionary measures are to be expected in such crimes, the steps taken by Mary's attacker indicate a knowledge of forensic capabilities beyond that expected of an average person. This area is further addressed in the arrest history section of the offender's profile.

ITEMS TAKEN

The rapist told the victim he wanted $20 or he would take her sound system. When advised that she did not have the money, he took a dollar and some change from her purse. These items would be classified as valuables (see Chapter 12), but the amount is ridiculously small. The author is of the opinion that he took this pittance, not out of need, but rather because he *could*! In other words, he was demonstrating power over Mary.

He threatened to take the victim's sound system and she put him down by telling him he would look funny carrying it around. He later destroyed it. The author does not believe that he had any intention of taking the system. His behavior indicates a more sophisticated and experienced criminal, not one who would take such an item. The offender also took his cigarette butt with him. The cigarette would be classified as evidentiary material (see Chapter 12). Nothing of a personal nature was taken.

The victim reported that there were no calls, notes, or break-ins prior to the offense. Follow-up investigation determined that there had been no attempt by the offender to contact the victim after the assault.

PURPOSE OF THE ASSAULT

Most sexual assaults service nonsexual needs (i.e., power, anger, or a combination of the two). The rapist in this instance was attempting to assert his masculinity. That is to say, he was expressing his male dominance over women—a behavior that he believes to be his right. Such rapists tend to be primarily selfish in their attacks. However, in this case, there was a vacillation between selfish and pseudo-unselfish behavior, but the unselfish behavior exhibited by Mary's rapist was simply another means to further exploit her. If he had been successful in having the victim even feign passion or involvement, he would have believed it was due to his ability to arouse, and thereby control, women. This is a characteristic that would also be found in his noncriminal associations with women.

OFFENDER PROFILING

When training law enforcement officers in the art of profiling, one of the most difficult hurdles for them to overcome is their reluctance to put opinions in writing without *hard* evidence to back them up. This is perfectly understandable inasmuch as they have been trained to *never* put their opinions in writing. Another one of their concerns is that they do not want to be wrong in their assessment and this is also quite natural. It must be remembered, however, that there are no absolutes in human behavior and it is indeed rare that a criminal profile will perfectly match an offender. There may even be instances in which the profile is largely inaccurate and even this is to be expected on occasion. It is, after all, a subjective opinion.

Some critics of profiling have stated that if a profile is incorrect, it will mislead investigators or cause them to overlook or disregard viable suspects. The author is unaware of a single instance in which a profile influenced an investigation in such a manner and finds it very difficult to believe that investigators would disregard a viable suspect simply because the suspect's characteristics and traits did not match those provided in a profile.

THE PROFILE

The following profile was based on the preceding analysis and represented the author's opinion as to the characteristics and traits of the individual responsible for the crime against Mary.

PERSONALITY CHARACTERISTICS

As stated, the purpose of the assault was to express and assert masculinity. The rapist is an overly confident male who is dominant in his relationships with women. His vacillation between selfish and pseudo-unselfish behavior during the assault is indicative of how he is perceived by those who know him. He presents different images to different people in his life. Some would describe him as a respectful and pleasant individual and others would say he is often hostile and angry. His fruitless attempts to dominate Mary suggest that he considers himself to be a macho individual who works at projecting this image to those around him.

He is a self-centered person who dislikes criticism of any type, constructive or not. He is a person who demands instant satisfaction of his needs and desires and would be described as one who lives for the present—tomorrow be damned. Because of this characteristic, his actions are often self-defeating and he seldom achieves long-term goals. He lacks a sense of responsibility and projects the blame for failures onto others or circumstances that he claims are beyond his control. The attitudinal changes exhibited during the attack on Mary strongly suggest that he cannot stand defeat and is known as a poor loser. He dislikes authority of any kind and law enforcement officers with whom he has had contact (see "Arrest History") would describe him as being cocky and arrogant to the extent of antagonizing them.

He exudes confidence and considers himself superior to others, yet he associates with individuals whom he considers beneath him intellectually, economically, or otherwise. His choice of associates is based on whether he can control them. These individuals would describe him as being cool, sophisticated, and somewhat aloof. Recalling his behavior with Mary, it is obvious that he reacts negatively when his authority is challenged; consequently, some would describe him as being easily antagonized and short-tempered.

Because of his self-centeredness, few people are allowed to get close to him. While he knows many people, few really know very much about him. Socially, he frequents those areas he considers appropriate to his station in life, primarily well-known and moderately expensive establishments.

He also enjoys singles bars or similar establishments catering to college-age crowds. The reader will recall that he told Mary he had "seen her around" and she is known to frequent locations similar to those described herein.

He is glib and extremely manipulative. He is dominant in his relationships with women; however, if he encounters a woman he cannot dominate, he will relentlessly pursue her. Women who have dated him over a period of time will report that he was initially charming and attentive, but eventually became overly possessive and irrationally jealous, demanding that they account for the time they spent away from him.

Race

As described by the victim, the offender is a black male. While some may think this is an obvious trait, the author has seen numerous rape cases in which the victim was unsure of, or unable to describe, the race of her attacker. A plethora of research, too, has confirmed the unreliability of cross-racial identification and has been disproportionately responsible for numerous wrongful convictions (Johnson, 1984). Additionally, elements of the assault such as lighting, intentional behaviors by the offender to conceal his identity, or use of blindfolds or drugs may alter the victim's ability to properly identify the perpetrator. Thus, a mixture of psychological and situational factors may preclude accurate identification of the offender's race. For example, a black male, interviewed by the author, was responsible for the rape of 62 Caucasian women, and 31 described him as white and 31 described him as black. In such instances, the analyst takes into consideration the racial makeup of the geographic area, victimology, racial slang, and linked attacks in which one or more victims were able to describe the offender's race.

Age

Age is the most difficult characteristic to provide. Its determination is dependent upon a number of factors, including the type of rapist (e.g., the power reassurance rapist will select victims within his own age range), victim's estimate, type of items taken, and the maturity exhibited during the crime.

The offender in this case is between 26 and 30 years of age. Although the victim is an educated and articulate individual, her opinion of the age of the assailant (20–30) is too broad. Mary's attacker is confident of his abilities with women and is a macho type of person; therefore, he would have selected a woman who approximates his own age range. His ego demands that he attack women he considers to be worthy of his time and attention. In the absence of contradictory information, when dealing with this type of rapist, the offender's age range is generally placed 3 or 4 years on either side of the victim's age (i.e., 20–27); however, in this case, an older individual is indicated.

Arrest History

The precautionary actions taken by the rapist demonstrate a high degree of forensic knowledge and criminal sophistication obtained either through study and experience or previous arrests for similar crimes. It is the author's opinion that the rapist has previously been arrested for rape and/or breaking and entering. His desire to assault Mary anally, coupled with a muscular upper torso, suggests that he has also been incarcerated and participated in upper-body exercises.

His lifestyle (see "Residence") and low income (see "Employment") indicate that he is involved in other criminal ventures. For this reason, it is believed he may be involved in the sale of narcotics and has been arrested for such crimes in the past. He is not believed to be an addict because he did not steal or even search for items of value from Mary's residence. In fact, he destroyed a valuable and easily fenced sound system.

Marital Status

As stated, the behaviors exhibited by Mary's rapist reveal that he is a macho male with a dominant attitude toward women. In the author's experience, such rapists typically marry while in their late teens or early 20s, but their relationships with women are relatively short-lived. For these reasons, it is believed that he is either separated or divorced. While living with his wife, the relationship involved a great deal of conflict and friends would have been aware of the marital problems. Although not physically abusive toward his wife, he would have emotionally battered her. An example of such battering would be his leaving her stranded (and humiliated) at a party following an argument.

Residence

The amount of time the rapist spent with Mary provides two especially significant pieces of information: (1) He was familiar with her routine, and (2) he felt comfortable in the sociogeographic environment in which the assault occurred. The intelligence (see "Education") of the rapist is such that he would not assault in an area in which he felt uncomfortable or where he might be recognized by those who know him. He resides in similar property (rental and middle class) in another area of town. He resides with a black female who is faithful to him but whom he regards as just a necessity. The residence is an apartment or town house, is nicely furnished, and includes an array of upscale video and audio equipment. It serves as a gathering point for large numbers of people at various times of the day or night, and this may have caused suspicious neighbors to alert the police.

Education

The offender is educated beyond the high-school level. His verbiage during the assault, combined with Mary's opinions about him and his strong denial of "hanging around those punks" (students) lead to this opinion. It is possible that his education after high school was obtained while he was incarcerated. As a student, he achieved above-average grades and exhibited potential for high academic achievement. Because of his dislike for authority, it is unlikely that he obtained a 4-year degree or utilized his education in long-term employment. Friends and associates consider his intelligence to be well above average and often seek his advice and counsel. He is considered a leader rather than a follower.

Military History

The offender's strong dislike for authority and regimentation diminishes the possibility of his having served in the military. If he did serve, it would have been as a member of the enlisted ranks and the likelihood of his having been honorably discharged is minimal. His desire to project a macho image would indicate service in the ground forces (i.e., Army or Marines).

Employment

If employed, he will be working in a job for which he is overqualified. His work performance reflects an attitudinal problem, and he complains of being bored. His supervisors report frustration with his performance because of his potential for excellence. He is frequently late or absent and takes offense at being corrected on the job. Again, if employed, his job is more for appearances than income as his primary source of income is from the sale of narcotics or from other illegal activities.

Transportation

In keeping with his lifestyle and image, he will operate a two-door vehicle, 2–4 years old. It is flashy, painted to attract attention, and well maintained. He spends a great deal of time in his car and enjoys driving aimlessly for extended periods of time. He is strongly associated with his car, and friends would describe him and his car as inseparable.

Appearance and Grooming

He is a very neat individual whose normal attire is contemporary, with designer jeans at the lower end of his dress style. He takes a great deal of pride in his personal and physical appearance and is critical of those who do not do the same. He exercises regularly and maintains a high level of physical fitness. He demands that the women with whom he associates be equally conscious of their appearance. He has an expensive wardrobe that is beyond his known financial means. He has regular appointments to have his hair styled and is meticulous about body cleanliness, often bathing or changing clothes two to three times a day.

Note: The reader will observe that the profile is presented using "everyday" language and in such a way that those who know the offender would be able to recognize him.

SUMMARY

The first and most important step in profiling an unidentified rapist is to obtain a detailed statement from the victim. The statement is then analyzed to determine the motive for the crime and whether the offender's verbal, sexual, and physical behavior exhibits a selfish or pseudo-unselfish *intent*. Having formed an opinion as to the offender's motive, the author then uses the typology developed by Groth et al. in classifying the rapist involved. Finally, a description of the offender is set forth in a manner that is easily understood by the investigator and enables those who know the responsible criminal to recognize him.

REFERENCES

Ainsworth, P. B. 2013. *Offender profiling and crime analysis.* New York: Routledge.

Brussels, J. A. 1968. *Casebook of a crime psychiatrist.* New York: Bernard Geis Associates.

Canter, D. 1994. *Criminal shadows.* London: Harper-Collins Publishers.

Carter, D. L., Prentky, A., and Burgess, A. W. 1995. Victims: Lessons learned for responses to sexual violence. In R. K. Ressler, A. W. Burgess, and J. E. Douglas (Eds.), *Sexual homicide: Patterns and motives.* Langham, MD: Lexington Books.

Groth, A. N. 1983. Treatment of the sexual offender in a correctional institution. In J. G. Greer, and I. R. Stuart (Eds.), *The sexual aggressor: Current perspectives on treatment.* New York: Van Norstrand Reinhold Company, Inc.

Groth, A. N., Burgess, A. W., and Holmstrom, L. L. 1977. Rape: Power, anger, and sexuality. *American Journal of Psychiatry,* 134(11): 1239–1243.

Hazelwood, R. R., and Harpold, J. 1986. Rape: The dangers of providing confrontational advice. *FBI Law Enforcement Bulletin,* 55(6): 1–5.

Holmes, S. T., and Holmes, R. M. 2009. *Sex crimes: Patterns and behavior.* Thousand Oaks, CA: Sage Publications, Inc.

Johnson, S. L. 1984. Cross-racial identification of errors in criminal cases. *Cornell Law Review,* 69(5): 934–987.

Keppel, R. 2006. *Offender profiling.* Mason, OH: Thomson Publishing.

McCabe, M. P., and Wauchope, M. 2005. Behavioural characteristics of men accused of rape. *Archives of Sexual Behaviour,* 34(2): 241–253.

Palermo, G. B., and Kocsis, R. N. 2004. *Offender profiling.* Springfield, IL: Charles C Thomas.

Porter, L. E., and Alison, L. J. 2006. Examining group rape: A descriptive analysis of offender and victim behavior. *European Journal of Criminology,* 3(3): 357–381.

Ullman, S. E., and Knight, R. A. 1993. The efficacy of women's resistance strategies in rape situations. *Psychology of Women Quarterly,* 17: 23–38.

Woodhams, J., and Cooke, C. 2013. Suspect aggression and victim resistance in multiple perpetrator rapes. *Archives of Sexual Behavior,* 42(8): 1509–1516.

8 Interviewing the Rapist

Michael R. Napier

CONTENTS

Introduction 124
Developing the Interview Plan 124
Traits of Successful Interviewers 125
Question Formulation 126
Tools of the Profession 126
    Eliciting a Narrative 126
    Reading Minds 127
    Planting Ideas 128
    Theme Development 129
    Test of Commitment 130
    Offender-Specific Tactics 130
        The Power Reassurance Rapist 131
        The Power Assertive Rapist 131
        The Anger Retaliatory Rapist 135
        The Anger Excitation Rapist 135
References 136
Further Reading 137

CASE NO. 1

I was awakened by a nudging of my shoulder. The first thing I saw was a knife blade directly in front of my eyes. In the darkness of my bedroom, illuminated only by my alarm clock light, I heard a male voice saying, "Don't make me use this." That was the last time I saw the knife, but I knew he had it.

I could see the outline of his features when he leaned down to speak. He was a white male about my age. He was clean shaven and smelled of an aftershave I did not recognize.

As he placed a pillow case over my head, he referred to me by my name and said, "Doris, do everything I tell you and I won't hurt you. This won't be anything that you haven't done before, and I know you are alone. I am sure you deserved the manager of the month award from the bank."

I tried to get up, but he pushed me down and sat on my chest. He said, "I told you I will hurt you if I have to. Now be nice like you are with your boyfriend. We are going to start with me up your backside." I struggled harder and told him I would not do that because it would be painful. He said, "Okay, okay. But you will go down on me first." As he removed my panties he remarked, "You're looking fine."

He then patted my cheek and rolled over on his back, pushing my face into his crotch. He was semi-limp. He forced me to perform oral sex until he became erect. Then he quickly rolled me back over and briefly penetrated my vagina until he ejaculated. He asked me if I was "satisfied" and said, "That is probably as good as you ever get, right?"

He told me he would know if I called the police, and that he had a secret hiding place from which he would be watching me. He reminded me he knew where I worked, and that I usually came home alone at about 8:30. He said he would come back and get me if I did anything before counting slowly to 100.

INTRODUCTION

The dialogue in Case no. 1 is a rendering of several real-life rape victim statements. It also depicts the core behaviors (verbal, physical, sexual) of rapists; these behaviors are more fully discussed in Chapter 7 and understanding them is essential to comprehending offender motivation and analyzing the crime. Such behaviors are best identified through a behavioral-oriented interview of the victim (see Chapter 6). This type of interview is highly valued by investigators because it provides useful investigative information such as rapist type, his unconsciously disclosed motivation, and the presence or absence of his fantasy acted out via the rape.

A victim's behavior-oriented statement provides a reliable roadmap on how to approach the rapist in an interview and hopefully obtain admissions and/or a confession. Once the victim has been interviewed, the officer is encouraged to closely read and dissect the statement, noting each of the core behaviors mentioned earlier. This rapist was clearly a power reassurance rapist (see Chapter 7) and this type of rapist is responsible for a large percentage of reported and unreported rapes.

DEVELOPING THE INTERVIEW PLAN

The reader is encouraged to again read Case no. 1 and look for the verbal, physical, and sexual behaviors of the rapist. As stated, recognizing and isolating these behaviors will assist in planning an early interview of a rape suspect:

Verbal Behavior	Physical (Injurious) Behavior	Sexual Behavior
"Doris...I won't hurt you."	No injurious force	Wanted anal sex
"Be nice like with your boyfriend."	Nudged her shoulder	Negotiated oral sex
Negotiated sex acts	Pushed her back down	Was semierect
"You're looking fine."	Patted her on her cheek	Became erect after oral sex
"Are you satisfied?"		Vaginal intercourse to ejaculation
"As good as you ever get, right?"		
He knew where she worked		
"Don't make me use this" (knife).		

Conducting an interview of a victim, witness, or suspect is a difficult and complex matter. Several considerations must be dealt with simultaneously to keep the process on the planned course. The interviewer must keep in mind all case data, the cast of characters, the suspect's role in the crime, all appropriate legal considerations, his interview plan, the question just asked, the answer given, his evaluation of the answer just given in the context of the verbal and nonverbal response, and which question to ask next. The logical and well-constructed interview plan aids in simplifying this difficult process.

Every interview should be a planned event. Interviews are built from a carefully laid foundation designed during its planning and Case no. 1 provides the outline of a basic interview plan. The rapist has unwittingly disclosed his motive, fears, concerns, and interview vulnerabilities. He has also revealed a glimpse into his fantasy. Utilizing the described behavior, the detective will have several valid and reliable clues as to how to conduct the interview.

An analysis of Case no. 1 informs the investigator that he is dealing with a power reassurance rapist and he should keep in mind that the characteristics attributed to such offenders in this chapter will not apply to all such rapists. The information recovered from the victim informs the interviewer of several rapist traits, but there are undoubtedly other characteristics that would also apply.

When planning the interview, this information (as with all unproven information) should be presented to a suspect only by reference, using flexible phrasing such as *probably* or *may be*. By doing so the investigator protects his credibility even if the information is found to be incorrect. If proper terminology is used during the interview, even generalized information (based on perceived rapist type) will not negatively impact the interview process. This technique will be further developed in the section on mind reading.

TRAITS OF SUCCESSFUL INTERVIEWERS

Study a truly talented interviewer and you will observe that he or she has a number of highly specialized personal qualities.[*] The first essential trait of an accomplished interviewer is that victims, witnesses, and even suspects must sense that the officer *feels* the words he[†] speaks. The extent to which they are at ease with the officer determines the level of trust they place in him and therefore determines whether they share their secrets. Such trust lays the foundation for obtaining information that the victim, witness, and certainly the suspect may initially be reluctant to provide. It is widely acknowledged that rapport-building between the interviewer and interviewee represents a crucial component of the interview process especially when details of the crime may be sensitive or be associated with embarrassment, shame, and/or stigma (Read, Powell, Kebbell, & Milne, 2009; Walsh & Bull, 2012).

An effective interviewer is an adaptable salesman—one who projects sincerity at every turn of the interview and yet is able to change course many times during the inquiry. It is imperative that victims and witnesses see an empathetic and professional person across the table. With suspects, the interviewer must genuinely project a high degree of neutrality and impartiality prior to any necessary confrontation—all directed toward obtaining an admission and/or confession. Some have argued that the establishment of a supportive and nonjudgmental interview environment may increase the likelihood of admissions (Kebbell, Alison, & Hurren, 2008; Oxburgh & Ost, 2011). Additionally, while suspected sex offenders may be particularly reluctant to confess their involvement in sexual crime due in part to the perceived length and severity of punishment, some offenders may experience significant remorse and have a strong desire to contextualize their offending behavior in their own terms (Read et al., 2009). Suspects who perceive an interviewer or the environment as threatening may be less willing to provide a truthful account of the crime.

As happens in the professional interview setting, the officer may question the credibility of a victim or witness. He may also have suspicions about the guilt of a suspect. The interviewer must guard against leakage of any bias or skepticism until sufficient evidence is identified to justify that position. To allow one's suspicions to become prematurely known by the interviewee will almost certainly lead to antagonism and distrust. When an officer projects accusatory signals, the interviewee is likely to become defensive. In turn, the officer may interpret the subject's defensiveness as

---

[*] Often the line between personal discovery and stimulation from others blurs. With recognition that an original thought is a rarity, I wish to express thanks and gratitude to several sources that impacted my interview philosophy and practices. From my family tutelage, my education, and experiences in the private sector, a wealth of knowledge was garnered regarding dealing with people. I received interview-specific training from the FBI, Reid and Associates, the CIA, the Department of Defense Polygraph Institute, and Avinoam Sapir's Scientific Content Analysis course. I wish to specifically acknowledge Reid and Associates for adapting known psychological principles and existing police investigative knowledge into a highly useful and ethical interview program. Personal conversations with others having similar interests cannot be given enough credit for stimulating my thought process. My affiliation with the FBI's Behavioral Science Unit and the National Center for the Analysis of Violent Crime led to a deep appreciation of interviewing techniques applicable to violent and evil offenders. This education has continued through association with my learned colleagues at the Academy Group, Inc., in Manassas, Virginia.

[†] The male pronoun is used throughout for ease in reading.

an indicator of withheld information or even outright deception. From that point on, the negativity of both the officer and interviewee may spiral, resulting in lost opportunities to gather valuable data, wasted work hours, and lack of progress in solving the case.

Equally devastating is a poor attitude and demeanor, which will in all likelihood stop the flow of information from the subject that could possibly have been used to the investigator's advantage should the interviewee later become the focus of the investigation. This problem most often surfaces in the interview of witnesses, especially if they have the potential of becoming suspects because of their relationship to the victim (parents of a missing child, the significant other of a missing adult).

Another highly valued trait of a successful interviewer is the ability to identify the reasons a suspect is reluctant to take responsibility for his criminal acts. Most often, this can only be accomplished by initially engaging the suspect in a variety of nonthreatening topics apparently having no connection to the criminal act in question.

The interviewer must be able to maintain control over the inquiry and the person being questioned. He must be able to go beyond listening carefully and be adept at evaluating the sentence structure and the words chosen by the other person, as they will assist in revealing the meaning of the provided information. There are many more traits associated with a successful interviewer, but limited space precludes a discussion of each one.

QUESTION FORMULATION

No constitutional mandate exists regarding the style of questions utilized in interviewing a sexually violent suspect. The courts, however, tend to take a dim view of statements elicited by *close-ended* questions that contain crime-specific information such as, "Tell me more about the white man who left the crime scene in the red Ford Thunderbird." If that information was later "parroted" back to the interviewer, it might appear to corroborate a confession. Such contamination usually occurs when close-ended questions are used early in the interview process. Once the contamination error has been made, it cannot be undone. *Open-ended* questions are introduced by phrases such as "Describe for me…," "Tell me about…," or "Explain how…" and guard against contaminating the interview.

The overall goal of an interview is to obtain information. Therefore, it logically follows that the initial questions ideally should be short and the answers long. The recommended approach is to begin the criminal interview with open-ended questions, allowing the subject to answer without interruption. The proficient interviewer trains himself to remain quiet even when he recognizes incorrect or deceptive information is being provided. Once the subject is committed to a version of events, the interviewer should clarify incorrect or confusing information, again using open-ended questions.

If it is necessary to utilize a direct or close-ended question, that tactic should be reserved for the end of the questioning phase. As much as possible, the phrasing of a close-ended question should avoid any crime details not previously furnished by the interview suspect.

The skilled use of open-ended questions is one of the primary tools of the professional interviewer and is one of the best practices for protecting the interview product.

TOOLS OF THE PROFESSION

As a general rule, the interview should be a straightforward process without fancy footwork. Neither the interviewer nor the interview benefits from complicated ploys, intricate props, or elaborate tricks. There is no need for the questioning to become complicated. Such attempts usually fail because they are transparent to the interviewee.

ELICITING A NARRATIVE

An important aspect of the interview process that provides investigators with an opportunity to obtain potentially crucial pieces of informational evidence is the degree to which a suspect is able to articulate his response to allegations of his involvement in the suspected criminal offense (see Read & Powell, 2011). This usually necessitates open-ended questions aimed at encouraging the suspect to give a detailed and largely uninterrupted narrative of events surrounding the crime. The interviewer's role at this point is to carefully listen, lightly steer the suspect through a sequential description of events, and ensure that the suspect does not veer off course. At the conclusion of the narrative, the interviewer can revisit particular parts of the narrative for clarity and elaboration.

READING MINDS

How would you be affected if another person could accurately tell you what you were thinking? What if the topics of your thoughts could impact the quality of your life if they were known to others? For example, what would be the effect if the boss could read your mind and knew your true thoughts about his management style? One of the most powerful interview techniques available is called "reading minds." Of course the term is not meant to be interpreted literally; however, when properly done, the interview subject feels as though the officer *is* reading his mind. Warren Holmes (1995) referred to this tactic as "taking the wind out of their sails." That metaphor is properly understood to mean the person would be "dead in the water" without any wind.

The destruction of the suspect's confidence in his ability to defeat police interview efforts is one of the primary goals of an effective interviewer. If the mind-reading tactic is properly presented, the suspect will feel the interviewer is taking a walk through his psyche by telling him what he has thought, is now thinking, how he viewed the victim, and even the cause of his behavior. This technique also creates a bond between the interviewer and the suspect. The suspect comes to believe the interviewer knows him intimately and therefore can be trusted with his deeply held secrets. To accomplish this with a sexually violent suspect, there are five rules to be followed:

1. The interviewer's terminology must be somewhat vague and qualified. He must avoid concrete statements such as "I believe that you sat around and in your daydreams planned this rape from start to finish." A more appropriate statement would be "Tom, in all my 20 years of talking with people in your situation, nearly everyone has said that these thoughts just came to them over and over until they formed what appeared to be a good plan." This allows the suspect to hear and interpret the words as he wants. If any statement is too rigid or even a little off the mark, the suspect will hold on to the discrepancy no matter how small and the interviewer will be discredited. From then on, what he says will lack validity. An example of proper wording for Case no. 1 would be: "Tom, in looking at this case one detective concluded that you had no intent to harm Doris..." or "You put the knife down and this was possibly done because you didn't want to use it to harm her." These statements are ambiguous and also illustrate the "good cop–bad cop" technique. They allow the officer to make some points while providing for the possibility of error.
2. Closely aligned to the first rule is the nearly universal principle that criminal interviewers should scrupulously avoid using harsh or highly charged terminology, particularly with "inadequate" personalities such as the power reassurance rapist. This concept generally holds true for other criminals as well. Terms such as *rape, strangulation, jail time*, and *brutal* serve to remind a suspect of penalties if he cooperates with the investigator. Conversely, when the officer refers to "that thing that happened last Thursday in the park," the suspect will clearly know the incident for which he is being questioned.
3. The item or thought being dangled in front of the suspect should not be offered in a blunt manner, but instead, it should be made as the culmination of a few lead-in remarks. For example, "Tom, I have an important thought on this case. It is important and affects you because...." This allows the officer to get the suspect's attention, and it also allows the suspect to track the question's impact and relationship to himself. It is recommended that the

interviewer subtly present his expertise and reputation when beginning his mind-reading statement. Power and status are added to his message when he begins in a manner such as "I have been in this business for 25 years and have been involved in several hundred cases similar to this one. I always try to talk with the men after they make their statements to learn what was really on their mind. One of the things that I have heard time and time again in these situations is that they never had a thought of hurting the woman. In fact, they went out of their way to avoid doing anything that might hurt her. When they tell me that, I always mention it in my report because I believe they deserve credit for having concern for the lady and being a man about it."

4. The mind-reading technique is more powerful when the subject recognizes his own traits and characteristics during the interviewer's recitation. Avoid making statements such as "You are a person who prefers the hours of darkness because you are shy." It is more powerful when the suspect makes that discovery for himself.

5. The interviewer should not mention the suspect's name when reciting what he knows about criminal behavior or criminal mentality.

CASE NO. 2

A known rapist was accused of assaulting a young woman and was the suspect in another case with sexual overtones. The author requested state investigators to interview two prior victims of the suspect using the "behavior-oriented interview" approach. As a result, the similarities in modus operandi and ritual became strikingly clear even though the rapes were more than 10 years apart.

During the suspect interview, the author used the technique of building up the questions to assure the suspect's attention. He then began a recitation of things he had learned from other suspects when in similar situations. The true source of this knowledge was information from the rapist's previous victims that had not been discussed. The offender's name was never associated with the list of *things learned* from those years of working countless cases *like this one.*

Expecting a reaction, close attention was paid to the suspect's demeanor when the lessons learned were being discussed. Like a textbook response, the impact was clear as his face slowly drained of its color. It was obvious the technique had worked to perfection, weakening his confidence to the point that he believed the author truly understood him and knew his secrets. A confession followed a short time later.

PLANTING IDEAS

Using a similar presentation format, the interviewer may provide investigative concepts for the offender to consider, so he may personally determine if they pose a threat to his being identified or linked to a crime. For example, it may become necessary to interview a suspect early in an investigation armed only with circumstantial evidence. This calls for great care because any allegation of guilt, unsupported by evidence, may doom the interview. If the unsupported allegation reduces the subject's respect for the officer, it may also damage any chance for rapport in future contacts—even those in which there may be evidence supporting the offender's guilt.

Rather than alleging irrefutable guilt, the interviewer can speak to the suspect in terms of what evidence is *likely to be developed.* It has been the author's experience that a suspect will visualize how each piece of *possible evidence* would be a threat to his well-being. This technique has been especially effective with suspects having a criminal past.

CASE NO. 3

A 20-year-old female college student mysteriously disappeared from a birthday party with her coworkers. One coworker was a paroled rapist and he disappeared as well. This became a high-profile case and was featured on "America's Most Wanted" television show. When the parolee saw his picture on the television show, he immediately turned himself in and was returned to the location of the abduction. There was no firm evidence linking the missing young woman to the convicted rapist and they were not known to associate with each other.

State authorities requested the author to develop an interview plan for confronting this suspect. The plan had back-up contingencies in the event he refused to participate in an interview. After he was provided his Miranda rights, he was asked if the victim had ever been in his truck. He stated she had never been in his truck and that he would not talk about the victim or the investigation; however, he did not invoke his Miranda rights. The suspect was then, per the interview plan, given the option of returning to his cell or having some time outside where he could smoke and have a soft drink. As anticipated, he chose to remain out of the cell, likely realizing he was going to spend many years behind bars.

Over the course of the next hour or so the investigators remained with the suspect and casually spoke of various ways *this case could unfold, including various types of evidence that might be recovered and could incriminate the suspect.* There was conversation about the amount of blood required for DNA testing, what it would mean if a single strand of the victim's hair was found in his recovered truck, and how crime scene processing worked. The second phase of the interview plan had two tactics. The first was to introduce the good cop–bad cop scenario, using the local prosecutor as the foil. The second tactic was to discuss the role the victim's mother played in using the media to demand the recovery of her daughter. Eventually, the convicted rapist said he wanted to return to his cell and the interview ceased.

Upon contact 2 days later, the offender was pumped up and could not wait to state he wanted to confess. This author's assessment of why the rapist was willing and almost eager to confess was his recognition of various "threats" he found in the investigator's description of how evidence would be collected and used against him. Critical to his decision to confess and lead the investigative team to the victim's body was his self-chosen belief that her mother would be so relieved and thankful for him returning the victim's body that she would speak in his favor at sentencing.

THEME DEVELOPMENT

The absolute heart of effective suspect interviewing is the extensive use of themes that are repeated many times over the course of the same interview, principally in the confrontation and reasoning phases. Themes have a variety of sources and the most effective themes contain examples of human behavior that can be recognized by nearly everyone. The story of the pebble in the shoe is a good example of a highly recognizable story. As the story goes, the longer the person walked, the larger the pebble felt until the pebble was removed from the shoe. Upon examination, the pebble was recognized for what it was, something very small. The interviewer may adapt the tale using the pebble to represent the offender's fear of his situation while pointing out that when examined, with help from the officer, that fear is placed into the proper context of being a manageable problem. The officer is then in a position to offer appealing solutions to the problem.

As an interviewing technique, themes are most often combined with other themes containing similar ideas. The themes may appeal to the suspect for any number of reasons, but largely because they treat the suspect as a vulnerable human being with problems that can be resolved with help from the interviewer. Themes also contain the same excuses the suspect used to justify his criminal deeds to himself. These "sales pitches" will often alleviate the suspect's feelings of guilt. Themes address moral quandaries, not legal guilt and responsibility. Most often themes make use of the psychological processes of rationalization, projection, and minimization (RPM), which are loosely defined next.

When *rationalizing*, the suspect mentally reviews his actions and alters them, usually by leaving out or downplaying his worst acts, and removes himself as the cause of the criminal acts. In rationalizing, the person creates a scenario that excuses his behavior.

Projection is the act of removing blame from the suspect and shifting the responsibility to others. The suspect decides that he would not have acted as he did except for the behaviors of others.

Sometimes the rape suspect will diminish his culpability using soft words as substitutes for more accurate descriptions of his behavior, thus making his role in the criminal act less repugnant. For example, one rapist used the phrase "when we were together," rather than "when I raped her." This is called *minimization*.

RPMs, like themes, are repeated over and over and are used in combination with each other. The aim of RPMs is to make it as easy as possible for a rape suspect to admit to a lessened level of guilt; by doing so, he agrees to some degree of participation in the crime and contact with the victim. His admission has altered the situation morally, but not legally. It is recommended that if an admission is obtained, a brief written statement be taken.

After obtaining the admission, it is the duty of the officer to recommence the interview after taking a short mental break. It is at this time that the interviewer points out all the inconsistencies and errors in the suspect's statement and how the criminal offense could not have occurred as he described. The interviewer then moves the offender to a more accurate position in keeping with the evidence and victim's statements.

Test of Commitment

Avinoam Sapir (1999) has developed a test of commitment for suspects who are thought to be lying in their statements. It is an accepted principle in interviewing that liars lack commitment to their statements. To test a suspect's commitment to his version of events, it is recommended that the interviewer allow the subject to tell his story to the point that he establishes a firm position regarding the allegations.

Once the interviewer has obtained a seemingly firm version of events, he should use the technique of building up a question to obtain the suspect's attention and ask if he should believe him (i.e., "Should I believe the story you have told me?"). If the question is followed by a long pause before the suspect answers or if he states anything other than a definitive "yes" (or an equivalent statement), he has likely lied, or omitted information, in some part of his statement.

To confirm his belief in the suspect's deception or omissions, the officer may follow up by asking, "Can you give me one reason why I should believe your story?" As previously, listen for a longer than necessary pause. A truthful person does not require time to consider this question because he knows he told the truth. Therefore, his answer should be readily forthcoming and closely resemble something like "Because I told you the truth."

Offender-Specific Tactics

When planning the interview strategy, the traits and vulnerabilities of the suspect must be taken into account. As part of the interview plan, the interviewer should document the use of all *sensitive* techniques (e.g., interview strategies suggesting the victim is at fault or that the offender was entitled to attack), ensuring that their use is placed in perspective. Such tactics should be noted in the investigative file in advance of the interview and explained as a technique to obtain a confession. The officer should clearly state that such techniques do not indicate any responsibility on the victim's part or that the rape is justified in any way. The offender bears complete responsibility for his criminal acts.

It is much more effective to tailor the interview approach to fit a specific type of sexual offender rather than trying to use one approach for all sex offenders. To assist in that process the traits of four rapist types (see Chapter 7) are examined and suggested interview strategies are provided.

The Power Reassurance Rapist

The power reassurance rapist is most likely a serial rapist and in the author's experience accounts for more victims than any other rapist type. Therefore, it is recommended that the investigator make the sexual assault having the strongest evidence the sole focus of the initial interview. Once the offender has confessed to one rape, the interviewer can turn to the offender's other cases for resolution.

This type of rapist selects victims through surveillance and is a cautious rapist who must be geographically comfortable within the attack environment. Consequently, it is inadvisable to bluff him about the environment of the rape and its surrounding area. He will likely know the area much better than the investigator does.

The interviewer should keep in mind that the motive driving this rapist is the reassurance of his masculinity. Typically, he is inadequate and has a low opinion of his personal qualities. As a rapist, he seeks power over a female and fulfills a need to *have a sexual relationship with a woman*. His many inadequacies will be evident to the interviewer and it would be counterproductive to remind him (in any way) of his shortfalls as a man, or as a person. Additional specific suggestions are contained in Table 8.1.

It must be noted that this type of rapist shares several personality traits with individuals who give false confessions to escape police attention and pressure (see Chapter 13). By way of example, both have inadequate personality features such as personally devaluing himself; withdrawing from others, including those who could bolster him by providing a support mechanism; lacking those qualities that allow him to assert himself and reduce the impact of stressful situations such as intense police questioning; and internalizing regret or guilt for all the rapes he has committed (even if they are not the subject of the current questioning). Consequently, unless there is firm evidence linking a particular person with the crime or crimes, the interviewer must exercise greater caution than normal. This is necessary because while the interview subject may possess the characteristics associated with a power reassurance rapist and may even give a confession, he may not be responsible for the crimes.

The Power Assertive Rapist

The power assertive rapist is the most likely to enter the police interview room as a suspect. He is verbally, physically, and sexually aggressive with the victim and, as mentioned elsewhere, this rapist is confident of his sexual prowess. Unlike the power reassurance rapist, this man has no doubts about his masculinity. In his assaults, he is asserting his masculinity because he believes that as a man he is entitled to do so. This man views himself as a role model of manhood and virility, and others who know him superficially would agree with that assessment.

He acts impulsively and may have met the victim the same day of the sexual assault. For this reason, some power assertive rapists are also date or acquaintance rapists. However, this type is also frequently observed in stranger-to-stranger offenses. In either case, once he has captured the victim, he employs a moderate or higher level of violence (see Chapter 6) and sexually treats the victim as an object to be used.

In date or acquaintance rape situations, the initial goal of the interviewer is to obtain the offender's agreement that a sexual encounter with the victim occurred. The interview should then proceed by allowing the physical evidence of torn clothing and physical injuries to tell the story of nonconsent and rape.

In Table 8.2, a differentiation is made between the date or acquaintance rapist and the stranger rapist. If the information is applicable to the date/acquaintance rape and stranger rape, the term *both* will be utilized.

TABLE 8.1

Power Reassurance Rapist Interview Techniques

Trait	Technique	Examples
Low self-esteem Unsure of manhood Ashamed of his crime	Build rapport sufficient for suspect to function given his low-self-esteem by pacing the interview.	At outset, refer to him as Mister (Smith) Ask him before using his first name. Use examples of good or decent things he has done, even if exaggeration is required.
No intent to physically harm Does not consider the rape as harm. This is likely the strongest trait benefiting the interviewer.	Mind reading, minimization	Build up his self-esteem. He likely made diligent efforts to not harm the victim. Give him credit for purposefully not hurting the victim. Compliment him on how he had control over the victim and did not do other acts, as some rapists have done. Assure him that sooner or later he will encounter a situation that goes bad and he will hurt or kill a victim. Read his mind by telling him "horror" stories of victims being seriously hurt or murdered.
Brings and considers the weapon as control technique.	Minimization, mind reading, projection	Repeat his belief that he would never have used the weapon, would have left before using the weapon. Only had it to maintain control and keep her from hurting him.
Security conscious, planner, surveillance Average or better intelligence	Building his confidence.	Because he is a loner and maybe socially awkward, do not assume he is mentally challenged or slow.
Poor interpersonal skills	Rapport building. A relaxed, friendly, slow start to the interview. Likely suspicious, on guard for insincerity. Don't expect lengthy verbal exchanges.	Conduct lengthy discussion of the circumstances of his daily life, how he spends his time, who he knows, etc. When introducing subject of interview use soft terms such as "the thing that happened last Tuesday," vs. the rape.
Sexual incompetence	Minimization	Do not mention any sexual dysfunctions, need for masturbation, etc.
Rich fantasy life, preselects victims	Rationalization, minimization, mind reading	After denial, describe how most people in his position have *intrusive thoughts* which cause them to act. They almost always are drawn to a particular woman because of her personal qualities, the type he desires in all his relationships.

(Continued)

TABLE 8.1 (*Continued*)

Power Reassurance Rapist Interview Techniques

Trait	Technique	Examples
Young adult victims Same age range of offender.	Rationalization, minimization, mind reading	Deal with the assault by it has grown out of proportion in offender's mind. Remind him he did not assault an elderly grandmother or a small child, and nothing happened that she had not done before. Combine with other examples of offender behavior that minimize his acts.
"Unselfish or gentlemanly qualities" Low force level Did not verbally abuse her, or use vulgar language Did not physically abuse her Normal sex Desires to please her	Planting seeds, mind reading, minimization, projection, good cop, bad cop.	State he treated her gently, as a lady, wife, like her boyfriend or lover would. Went out of his way to do so. Didn't even call her names, except as a compliment. Only *pressure* applied was because of the way she acted. He even involved her in the type of sex she likes, just wanted to make her happy. Interviewer is aware the prosecutor/supervisor believes he did terrible things, but interviewer has seen all the facts and understands all the efforts suspect made to be nice and treat the victim well Likely, he even stopped some acts when the victim asked him to stop (negotiated with victim).
Minimal force level used	Mind reading, minimization, projection	In interviewer's vast experience, has been told of suspects' real concerns and how he did everything possible not to harm the victim, as long as she did not harm him.
Fantasizes as consenting contact	Minimization, projection, mind reading	This woman is the kind who suspect would like to have met some other way, in another situation. She really liked him, even took off her own clothes, and made no real objections.
	Closers Hard evidence DNA Video from area	If the "hit with evidence" approach is used early, this type of rapist may withdraw from the interview and be unwilling to discuss other crimes. Save these "blunt" tactics as a last resort.

TABLE 8.2

Power Assertive Rapist Interview Techniques

Trait	Techniques	Examples
Has high opinion of himself	Officer subtly controls the interview Begin by directing suspect to particular chair. Rapist believes he is smarter than the officer. Interview should be arranged without an ending time constraint.	Both: If caught in lie(s), do not initially challenge him Collect all lies and misstatements Confront him with them collectively so they will take on the "*feel* of evidence."
Enjoys deferential treatment he receives from other males.	Impress him with competency and authority of interviewing officer.	Both: Upon arrival, acknowledge his presence, but make him wait several minutes before he is taken to interview room. Once the interview has begun, have a planned interruption causing a delay in the process. Another officer, within the hearing of suspect praises the interviewing officer.
Sense of entitlement The right of a male	Minimize crime and project blame onto victim	Both: Indicate officer is dealing with still *another* female complaint.
Views women as objects, inferior	Projection, minimization, mind reading, build-up questions and officer's experience, plant seeds, good cop/bad cop	Date/acquaintance: Encourage him to adopt minimized version of event. She did not know what she wanted, first she was attracted to him because…, encouraged him, then she cooled down, men can't change that fast. Was not suspect's fault she drank so much and was out of control. Stranger: Likely she is making claim because of need to explain what happened to her boyfriend.
Acts impulsively	Minimization	Date/acquaintance: He is smart enough to stay away from this kind in the future. She rushed him and encouraged him and he did not think about how she would handle the situation.
Rapist has sense of entitlement	Minimization, projection, reading minds	Both: Indicate another team is reviewing victim's statement for errors, lies. Her story is likely not a true reflection of actual events. Date/acquaintance: She came on to him or agreed to sex then changed her mind A man can't turn his sex drive on and off at the drop of hat.
Man's man	Rationalization	Date/Acquaintance: He acted as any real man would with an aggressive, suggestive woman.

(Continued)

TABLE 8.2 (*Continued*)
Power Assertive Rapist Interview Techniques

Trait	Techniques	Examples
Physical violence	Projection	Both: Blame victim for any injuries. State she likely became aggressive and attacked him, and he only defended himself.
		Date/acquaintance: Nothing would have happened if she had only been in control of herself. Would likely have been worse if he was not a gentleman and a man able to control her.
	Closers	Indicator of lying: agrees to do it *sometime*.
	Request he undergo polygraph examination	If lying, he will make excuses why he cannot be polygraphed or hypnotized.
	If he agrees, quickly ask how he will do when asked questions specific to victim statement	
Useful with any rapist type.	Test of commitment	

The Anger Retaliatory Rapist

This offender is angry at women for real and imagined wrongs and wants to punish and degrade them. Those who know him understand he has a violent temper and that he hates women, blaming them for all his troubles and failures. His attacks are impulsive and essentially dependent on when he becomes emotionally overloaded; he may attack at any time and at any place. He selects victims of opportunity who happen to cross his path and the fact that they are women is certainly sufficient criteria for this angry offender.

Circumstantial evidence of his propensity to rage against women generally will be available from associates and coworkers. Because this man typically has a diverse arrest history, he is street wise and therefore the overall strategy of an interview is simply to place him near or with the victim at the time of the assault.

The main tools available to the officer are minimization of his acts and projecting responsibility for the event onto the woman. It is possible that a workable theme would be that with today's attitudes, women have it so easy and get jobs that men need to support their families, just because they are women. If the man is receptive, the officer can explain that the best way for him to handle this is to get his opinion of women on the record.

The Anger Excitation Rapist

This rapist is more commonly referred to as a sexual sadist. Of all the rapists, this man will be best prepared to deal with a police interview. It is probable that he will not consent to an interview but will claim his Fifth Amendment rights and demand an attorney, possibly by name. However, the detective should be prepared for him to agree to an interview—the criminal's purpose being not to provide information, but rather to obtain information. He considers himself superior to the police and will use the interview setting to explore the evidence against him.

Do not allow the focus of the inquiry to become diffused by accusing him of multiple assaults. When the subject is believed to be responsible for multiple crimes, it is recommended that the crime with the best evidence be the focus of the interview. Questions should be phrased in a manner that does not provide information to the offender. Questions of this type are discussed in the section on question formulation.

Such offenders are typically narcissistic and the officer's status must be projected as detective or higher, thus playing to the criminal's perceived superiority. His narcissism also creates an inability to withstand criticism, and the officer may subtly criticize an aspect of the crime through questions such as, "The victim said that she fought you in every room of her apartment. Why weren't you able to control her?"

He may be lured into bragging about his cleverness and cunning. However, if this does happen, it will only be after he is convinced that that there is substantial evidence against him.

CASE NO. 4

The serial killer—self-named BTK for bind, torture, and kill—was an infamous sexually sadistic offender in the Midwest. He escaped detection and apprehension for over three decades. Fortunately for society, his narcissism created an inner need for recognition of his perceived brilliance. It also created a need to engage the police and further demonstrate his criminal mastery, and this led to his downfall.

When BTK, aka Dennis Rader, was arrested, he was confronted by his nemesis, Lt. Kenny Landwehr, commander of the Homicide Unit, Wichita, Kansas, Police Department. Lt. Landwehr and FBI Agent Robert Morton showed Rader a computer disc he had mailed to the police and explained the process that had been used to identify him as BTK.

At one point, he was asked to provide the date of a message he had mailed to the media and the police. Landwehr and Morton knew that if Rader provided the date, it would help confirm that he was BTK. As his hand hovered over a calendar, Rader asked if they had DNA evidence to prove he was BTK and it was explained that he had been linked to the crimes by DNA. Rader then said, "I am BTK." This response by BTK epitomizes the sexual sadist's need to be convinced by evidence that he has been caught and his criminal career is at an end.

REFERENCES

Holmes, W. D. 1995. Interrogation. *Polygraph*, 24(4): 252.

Kebbell, M., Alison, L., and Hurren, E. 2008. Sex offenders' perceptions of the effectiveness and fairness of humanity, dominance, and displaying an understanding of cognitive distortions in police interviews: A vignette study. *Psychology, Crime & Law*, 14(5): 435–449.

Oxburgh, G., and Ost, J. 2011. The use and efficacy of empathy in police interviews with suspects of sexual offences. *Journal of Investigative Psychology and Offender Profiling*, 8(2): 178–188.

Read, J. M., Powell, M. B., Kebbell, M. R., and Milne, R. 2009. Investigative interviewing of suspected sex offenders: A review of what constitutes best practice. *International Journal of Police Science & Management* 11(4): 442–459.

Read, J. M., and Powell, M. B. 2011. Investigative interviewing of child sex offender suspects: Strategies to assist the application of a narrative framework. *Journal of Investigative Psychology and Offender Profiling*, 8: 163–177.

Sapir, A. 1999. The L.S.I. Course on Scientific Content Analysis (SCAN).

Walsh, D., and Bull, R. 2012. Examining rapport in investigative interviews with suspects: Does its building and maintenance work? *Journal of Police and Criminal Psychology*, 27(1): 73–84.

FURTHER READING

Depue, R. L., and Depue, J. M. 1999. To dream, perchance to kill. *Security Management*, 43(6), June.

Gudjonsson, G. 1993. *The psychology of interrogations, confessions, and testimony.* Chichester, UK: John Wiley & Sons.

Hazelwood, R. R., and Burgess, A. W. 2001. *Practical aspects of rape investigation.* Boca Raton, FL: CRC Press.

Hazelwood, R. R., and Michaud, S. G. 2001. *Dark dreams.* New York: St. Martin's Press.

Hazelwood, R. R., and Napier, M. R. 2004. Crime scene staging and its detection. *International Journal of Offender Therapy and Comparative Criminology.* Thousand Oaks, CA: Sage Publications.

Hess, J. E. 1997. *Interviewing and interrogation for law enforcement.* Cincinnati, OH: Anderson Publishing.

Inabu, F. E., Reid, J. E., Buckley, J. P., and Jayne, B. C. 2004. *Criminal interrogation and confession*s, 4th ed. Gaithersburg, MD: Aspen Publishers, Inc.

Jayne, B. C., and Buckley, J. P. 1998. Interrogation alert! Will your next confession be suppressed? *The Investigator*, Winter, special edition. Chicago, IL: John E. Reid and Assoc., Inc.

Michaud, S. G., and Hazelwood, R. R. 1998. *The evil men do.* New York: St. Martin's Press.

Napier, M. R., and Adams, S. H. 1998. Magic words to obtain confessions. *FBI Law Enforcement Bulletin*, 67(10): 11–15.

Napier, M. R., and Baker, K. P. 2002. Criminal personality profiling. In S. H. James and J. J. Nordby (Eds.), *Forensic science: An introduction to scientific and investigative techniques,* Boca Raton, FL: CRC Press.

Rabon, D. 2003. *Investigative discourse analysis.* Durham, NC: Carolina Academic Press.

Shuy, R. W. 1998. *The language of confession, interrogation, and deception.* Thousand Oaks, CA: Sage Publications, Inc.

Vessel, D. 1998. Conducting successful interrogations. *FBI Law Enforcement Bulletin*, 67(10): 1–6.

Wichita, Kansas, Police Department. 2006. Video of Dennis Rader interview.

Yeschke, C. L. 1997. *The art of investigative interviewing.* Boston, MA: Butterworth–Heinmann.

Zulawski, D. E., and Wicklander, D. E. 2002. *Practical aspects of interview and interrogation,* 2nd ed. Boca Raton, FL: CRC Press.

9 Collateral Materials in Sexual Crimes

Robert R. Hazelwood and Kenneth V. Lanning

CONTENTS

Introduction 139
Traditional Evidence in Sexual Crimes 139
    Forensic Evidence 139
    Circumstantial Evidence 140
    Eyewitness Evidence 140
    Direct Evidence 140
Evidence in the Online Age 140
Collateral Materials 141
    Types of Collateral Materials 142
        Erotica 142
        Educational 143
        Introspective 143
        Intelligence 144
Summary 147
References 148

INTRODUCTION

Over the years, the authors have assisted investigators in better understanding the significance of materials seized from sexual offenders. Some materials, such as items taken from rape victims, are routinely seized by the police when found in the possession of the offender. However, it is common to learn that the significance of these and other items is not recognized by investigators, prosecutors, or mental health professionals. Seemingly innocuous items such as newspaper articles that are apparently unrelated to the crime, books, and real estate listings may play an important role in a greater understanding of the sexual offender and his criminal behavior.

TRADITIONAL EVIDENCE IN SEXUAL CRIMES

Those who have participated in investigating or prosecuting a sexual criminal know that various types of evidence play critical roles in successfully concluding a case. It is therefore helpful to identify and define the types of evidence that may be encountered in such investigations.

FORENSIC EVIDENCE

Forensic evidence may be defined as physical or trace evidence that can be scientifically matched with a known individual or item. Such evidence includes fingerprints, footprints, body fluids, hairs, and fibers. Through DNA extraction and analysis, forensic specialists are increasingly capable of making a suggestion of guilt or innocence from minute samples of evidence. Forensic evidence, if properly obtained and examined, can be powerful and reliable evidence in any type of crime.

CIRCUMSTANTIAL EVIDENCE

This category of evidence, sometimes referred to as indirect evidence, may be defined as facts or circumstances that tend to implicate a person or persons in a crime. Circumstantial evidence does not directly establish guilt, but can lead to a reasonable inference of guilt based on a series of facts or circumstances. Examples of such evidence might include the fact that a suspect owns a vehicle similar to one reported being in the vicinity of the crime at the time it occurred or a suspect who is known to have made a threat against the victim or to have engaged in similar patterns of behavior observed in the crime under investigation and had the means, opportunity, and motive to commit the crime. Although usually not sufficient to obtain a conviction, if observed in sufficient quantity, circumstantial evidence can constitute a powerful case against an individual.

EYEWITNESS EVIDENCE

Such evidence may include one or more individuals claiming to have witnessed the crime during its commission or to have seen the suspect in the vicinity of the crime. Although believed by many to be the best evidence, its reliability has historically been challenged on the grounds that memory recall and perception can be affected by various psychological factors such as stress, suggestion, the presence of a weapon, and cross-race bias. Practitioners are encouraged to be mindful of these influences as well as procedures in criminal investigation that can distort eyewitness testimony.

DIRECT EVIDENCE

This category of evidence may be defined as tangible items that directly implicate an individual in a crime. Most commonly, such materials include items *used in the crime* (e.g., handcuffs, gloves, mask) or items *taken from a victim or scene of a crime* ("fruits of the crime") and found either in the possession of a suspect or in a location under his control (e.g., home, storage area, car).

Items taken during a sexual crime have previously been classified by Hazelwood (1983):

Personal: Items that belong to the victim and are generally of no intrinsic value (e.g., driver's license, photograph, lingerie). Such items serve to refresh the offender's recollection of the crime and are used in his fantasized reenactments of the offense. Behaviorally, such items are referred to as either "trophies" or "souvenirs." Such items may or may not be retained by a sexual offender.

Evidentiary: Items taken that, if discovered by the police, could be used to implicate the offender in the crime. Such items may include sheets containing seminal fluids, items with fingerprints on them or even a partially smoked cigarette. The offender is not likely to retain such items, but that possibility cannot be ruled out.

Valuables: Items that have an intrinsic value and are taken during the commission of a crime. Generally, the purpose of taking items of value is financial gain. As with evidentiary materials, these items are not likely to be retained by the sexual offender unless he has a personal need for them (e.g., television, CD player).

EVIDENCE IN THE ONLINE AGE

The rise of the Internet and the associated capabilities of media transfer have established new domains in which sex offenders can accumulate and exchange both sexually explicit and nonexplicit materials. While legislative changes and law enforcement agencies have become increasingly acclimated to various forms of sexual offending (especially against children) that can occur and originate online, privacy advocates have fiercely opposed several contentious surveillance practices premised on the interdiction of illegal pornographic material. Consequently, law enforcement officials are consistently faced with a range of theoretical and pragmatic challenges in approaching investigation. In particular, we address these challenges as they pertain to crimes related to sexual acts with minors as well as with sexual offending involving adult victims.

First, law enforcement agencies are tasked with deciding whether to dedicate resources to the proactive policing of the digital world for the preemption of potential sex crimes. Over the years, various initiatives such as the Internet Crimes Against Children (ICAC) Task Force Program have provided support to state and local law enforcement agencies to facilitate responses to the sharing of child pornography, grooming and solicitation of minors, and other forms of behavior that can lead to contact offending. Individual agencies debating whether to include these preemptive forms of policing in their mandate must consider complex issues such as whether a causal relationship between pornography (especially violent subtypes) and rape exists (Goldsmith & Easteal, 1993; Ferguson & Hartley, 2009) and whether such approaches to law enforcement have a net-widening effect, catching those whose pornography viewing habits don't always translate into action (see Long, Alison, & McManus, 2012). Additionally, law enforcement officials who engage in both proactive and reactive investigations must be familiar with privacy law and the limitations of practice that derive from Fourth Amendment protections and other privacy legislation (see Guzzy, 2012). Consulting with legal experts can ensure that investigators have legal authority for seizure of evidence and that said evidence will be admissible in court.

Second, law enforcement agencies also encounter practical issues related to evidence acquisition and analysis. Processes for handling digital evidence should not deviate from general forensic and procedural principles. Successful investigation and subsequent prosecution of cases involving child pornography and solicitation of minors are often contingent on an agency's technological and staffing competencies and their ability to collect and analyze evidence with care and sophistication. Computer hardware and software must be up to date and configured appropriately to permit officers to apply investigatory techniques, store evidence, and conduct analysis. Personnel must be adequately trained in digital evidence collection, online investigation, covert investigation techniques, and monitoring of chat rooms and other forms of communication used to lure minors. Agencies must also retain computer forensic experts who are well-versed in retrieving information from hard drives that have been wiped or encrypted as well as from digital fingerprints (e.g., search histories, cookies, communication logs) in order to gather collateral evidence supportive of prosecution (Novotny, Meehan, Schulte, & Manes, 2002). Investigators should be cognizant of the continually expanding storage capabilities of computers and mobile devices as well as the novel methods of concealing large quantities of data that would otherwise be noticeably present in the offender's home in its physical form. While by no means exhaustive, this summary outlines some of the broad evidentiary considerations relevant to the investigation of rape and other sex offenses in an increasingly digitized world.

COLLATERAL MATERIALS

Prior to beginning a discussion of collateral materials, one should be aware that in the early 1980s, coauthor Lanning noted that preferential sex offenders were very likely to collect theme pornography and other paraphernalia related to their sexual interests. Focusing on child molesters, he began referring to the paraphernalia they possessed as *child erotica*. He defined *child erotica* as "any material relating to children that serves a sexual purpose for a given individual." *Child erotica* is a broader, more encompassing, and more subjective term than child pornography. Lanning intended that this term include such items as fantasy writings, letters, diaries, books, sexual aids, souvenirs, toys, costumes, drawings, and nonsexually explicit visual images. He noted that this type of material might also be referred to as *pedophile paraphernalia*. These materials are usually not illegal to possess or distribute.

Because of the diversity of material that could be considered *child erotica*, there was no way to develop a comprehensive itemization. Consequently, Lanning divided such materials into categories defined by the material's nature or type (i.e., published, unpublished, pictures, souvenirs, trophies, and miscellaneous). However, many investigators began using the term *child erotica* to exclusively describe visual images of naked children that were not considered to be pornographic. Additionally, for many professionals, the term *erotica* implies that the materials were used only for sexual purposes.

Later, coauthor Hazelwood applied the same concept to sexual offenders who acted out against adults and termed the materials found in their possession *collateral evidence*. Instead of dividing the materials into categories according to nature or type as Lanning had done, Hazelwood divided the materials according to purpose or use. The authors agreed that the term *collateral evidence* was a better one and the two approaches were subsequently reconciled for this chapter. Coauthor Lanning did the same in the 2010 edition of his publication, *Child Molesters: A Behavioral Analysis*.

Merriam-Webster (2015) defines the term *collateral* as secondary or subordinate. For the purpose of this chapter, *collateral materials* will be defined as items that inform authorities as to an individual's sexual preferences, interests, or sexual hobbies. It can be valuable as evidence of intent and/or as a source of intelligence. The finding of collateral materials may also influence bail, a guilty plea, and the sentence eventually imposed on the offender.

Collateral materials may include materials with an obvious sexual bent or they may seem benign in nature. Items categorized as collateral may, on occasion, also be classified as *direct* or *circumstantial* evidence. For example, lingerie taken from a rape victim may be sexually arousing to the offender (see "Erotica" section) and may simultaneously be used to link him to the crime (i.e., direct evidence).

The authors have identified four categories of collateral material: *erotica* (material that serves to sexually stimulate); *educational* (material providing knowledge about criminal endeavors, the investigative process, the judicial system, or mental health); *introspective* (material providing the criminal with insight into his sexual and/or behavior disorders); and *intelligence* (materials gathered by the offender that provide him with information about future crimes or information gathered about the offender by the investigator from third parties). The experienced investigator will not be surprised to learn that some materials may be categorized as more than one type of collateral material. For example, a partially clothed and bound female depicted on the cover of a detective magazine may be sexually arousing (erotica) and an article pertaining to a sexual crime in the magazine may also provide information useful to the criminal in circumventing crime detection techniques (educational). These four categories of collateral material are elaborated in more detail below.

TYPES OF COLLATERAL MATERIALS

Erotica

Erotica is defined as any material that serves a sexual purpose for a particular person. When attempting to identify erotica, one should not apply one's own preference for sexual stimuli, but instead remain objective. For example, the average person is not sexually aroused by a length of rope, but for a person with a fetish for rope, such materials can be extremely stimulating. Material suspected of being erotica must be viewed and evaluated in the context in which it is found. The investigator must use good judgment and common sense. For example, in a child molestation case, the subject's possession of an album filled with pictures of the suspect's own fully dressed children probably has no significance. However, his possession of 15 photo albums of fully dressed children who are not related to him may be very significant. The presence of his own child's underwear may not be significant, whereas a suitcase containing other children's underwear would be quite significant. For a more complete discussion of collateral material as it pertains to child-related offenses, the reader is referred to Lanning's work entitled *Child Molesters: A Behavioral Analysis* (2010).

In determining whether a certain item should be classified as erotica, the investigator should consider whether:

- It behaviorally relates to the crime under investigation or to possible paraphilias not evidenced in the crime;
- There is an abnormal amount of the material present and it serves no practical purpose (e.g., multiple sets of handcuffs);
- The material was hidden; and
- The subject has a large financial investment in the material (e.g., $500 worth of pornography).

Common forms of erotica include fetish items; literature, and visual images, either sexually explicit or nonexplicit in nature, that relate to demographically preferred victims; sexual paraphernalia such as inflatable dolls, vibrators, and dildos; fantasy recordings including writings, sketches, drawings, and audio/videotapes/DVDs; records of crimes;[*] plans for future crimes; crime paraphernalia;[†] abused dolls (bound, burned, gagged, punctured, dissected, painted); mutilated or altered pictures of people or animals; media accounts of sexual crimes; advertisements (for clothing, lingerie, adult movies, police paraphernalia); weapons collections; and personal items taken from known victims.[‡]

Educational

This type of collateral material is defined as items that provide the subject with knowledge enhancing his ability to commit a sexual or nonsexual crime, circumvent or thwart law enforcement and/or crime prevention efforts, or manipulate the judicial or mental health process.

Contrary to popular belief, serial sexual offenders do not necessarily have less than average intelligence. Research (Hazelwood & Warren, 1989) refutes this belief and documents the fact that serial rapists generally have better than average intelligence.

Intelligent criminals often attempt to learn as much as possible about the type of crime they are committing and resort to literature sources one would not normally associate with such individuals. Ted Bundy, in an interview with FBI Special Agent William Hagmaier immediately prior to his execution, was questioned about the influence of pornography in his life. Bundy asked Hagmaier if he had read the article entitled "Detective Magazines: Pornography for Sexual Sadists" (Dietz, Harry, & Hazelwood, 1986). Hagmaier advised that he had not and Bundy advised him to do so as it was very accurate.[§] Edward Kemper, an infamous serial killer, was reported to have memorized the Minnesota Multiphasic Inventory. When coauthor Hazelwood was attempting to introduce himself to a convict responsible for more than 60 sexually sadistic rapes, the man said, "I know who you are. When I was raping, I did a literature search on you. I've read everything you've written."

Educational materials commonly observed by the authors in such cases include fictional and nonfictional crime books; newspaper articles reporting sexual and nonsexual crimes; law enforcement and mental health journal articles; textbooks on psychology and/or criminal justice; published court decisions; detective magazines; crime prevention materials; audio/videotaped programs featuring experts on sexual crimes; Internet articles and media; and even movies such as *Murder by the Numbers*.

Introspective

Collateral material falling within this category is defined as materials that provide the offender with information or understanding about his sexual or personality disorders, behaviors, or interests. In conducting research on serial rapists, sexual sadists, and pedophiles, the authors were surprised at

---

[*] Records of crime would also be classified as direct evidence.
[†] Also direct evidence.
[‡] Also direct evidence.
[§] Personal conversation with Mr. Hagmaier, 1987.

the attempts of the men to gain insight into and/or rationalize their deviant sexuality. For example, many pedophiles spend a substantial portion of their lives attempting to convince themselves that their behaviors are not abnormal, but are merely deemed socially unacceptable or politically incorrect at the time. Other offenders may be troubled by what society defines as atypical or abnormal sexual behaviors and turn to publications, college courses, seminars, and in some cases, counseling for answers. Still others recognize that their preferences and behaviors are not normal and are attempting to better understand and thus cope with their deviancy. Such actions do not minimize their responsibility for criminal behavior, but are useful information for sexual crimes investigators, particularly in developing interview strategies.

Introspective materials observed by the authors in sexual crimes include books and other publications on psychopathology; video/audiotapes/DVDs of experts addressing the subject; self-help books; surveys in sexually oriented magazines; and newspaper, magazine, and journal articles on sexual offender research.

Intelligence

This type of collateral material is defined as (1) information or items obtained by the offender in the planning of future crimes, and/or (2) information gathered by law enforcement from third-party sources about the offender. Examples of intelligence are:

1. Materials possessed by the offender that indicate he has planned and collected information for the commission of future crimes. Such materials may include license plate numbers; telephone numbers, email or residential addresses of potential victims; commercial or hand-drawn maps with notations or routes of travel; notes concerning the movements or schedules of another person; surveillance photographs of people or locations; written scripts for victims; and lists of materials that will be needed for the commission of a specific crime.
2. Information obtained from interviews of current or former sexual partners of the subject. This may include spouses, lovers, or prostitutes. Hazelwood, Warren, and Dietz (1993) and Warren and Hazelwood (2002) have reported on the value of conducting such interviews. In sexual crimes, the investigator is specifically interested in obtaining facts and knowledge concerning the subject's sexual fantasies, behavioral preferences, habits, and dysfunctions. Also of interest are locations where he may have hidden additional materials, what stressors were present in his life at the time of the crimes, and whether he sexually behaved with the interviewee in a manner consistent with his criminal sexual behaviors.

CASE STUDY

Coauthor Hazelwood consulted on the following case and subsequently testified at the subject's murder trial. The facts of the case, the items seized from the subject, and the discussion provide classification of the materials as either *erotica*, *educational*, *introspective*, or *intelligence*.

The victim, a pregnant 24-year-old housewife, was abducted from her rural home. She was discovered missing when her husband returned from work and found his 22-month-old infant on the floor of their home. There was no evidence of forced entry and no signs that a struggle had taken place. Missing was the victim's car, a quilt, a telephone with a 20-foot cord, the bottom half of a swimming suit belonging to the victim, and every pair of her panties.

The victim's car was found the following morning about 1/2 mile from the residence. Two days later, her decomposing body was discovered 8 miles from the point of abduction. She was dressed in the same clothing she had been wearing when her husband last saw her and there was no indication that the clothing had been disturbed. The autopsy revealed no evidence of sexual assault and the cause of death was determined to have been aspiration due to two paper towels lodged in her throat. It was the opinion of the investigators that the offender had not intentionally killed the woman.

Within 4 months, a 37-year-old man was identified as the person responsible for the crime. He was an unemployed well digger who had recently been fired. One year prior to the crime, he had drilled a well on the victim's property. He was married, had two children, and resided in a single-family residence in an adjacent county.

The man had served time in prison for burglary and had been released approximately 3 years prior to the homicide. He was a high school graduate and of average intelligence. Investigation determined that the subject had committed a variety of crimes over a 9-month period of time before and after the homicide. The following is a sequential listing of those crimes:

March:	Harassing phone call to a woman
May:	Exposed genitals to a woman
June:	Obscene phone call to a woman
August:	Theft of woman's purse from a car
August:	Kidnap and murder (current case)
November:	Fondling and battery of a woman
November:	Impersonation of a police officer and attempted abduction of a woman
November:	Theft of woman's purse from a car
December:	Theft of property from a business site
December:	Kidnap and rape of a 27-year-old woman

The abducted rape victim was taken from her home, raped at an abandoned farmhouse, driven to a second abandoned farmhouse and forced to model a variety of lingerie, raped a second time, and then driven back to her neighborhood and released.

During a search of the killer's residence, the police seized a large volume of materials, which included collateral and direct evidence. The following is a listing of those materials:

1. More than 2,500 index cards containing information on women who had appeared either nude or in lingerie in *Gallery* or *Que* magazines. On each card, he had written a woman's first name, age, marital status, occupation, hobbies, the initials GND ("Girl Next Door" section of *Gallery*) or FNL ("Friends and Lovers" section of *Que*), and the month and year of the issue in which the photograph and demographic data appeared. In the upper right-hand corner of each card was a numerical rating (0–10) of the woman.

2. A spiral notebook containing information identical to that found on the aforementioned index cards.

3. Hundreds of articles of clothing, including panties, bras, nightgowns, swimsuits, slips, mesh tops, wraparounds, nightshirts, camisoles, and teddies. This apparel, purchased from a mail order firm specializing in such items, was estimated to be valued at $3,000. Several of the items had been placed in plastic bags and identified to allow cross-indexing to the index cards and the spiral notebook.

   Discussion: Items in 1, 2, and 3 would correctly be classified as *erotica*. The subject's purpose in having this information was to allow him to have sex (masturbatory fantasy) with any of the women, whenever he chose. The amount of time and money he spent purchasing, indexing, and maintaining this collection is indicative of the importance he attached to the material. It is also quite obvious that the man had a lingerie fetish: The murder victim's panties and bottom half of her bathing suit were taken and the kidnap–rape victim was forced to model teddies.

4. Over 100 *Gallery* and *Que* magazines.

   Discussion: These magazines would be classified as *erotica*. They dated to within 1 month of his release from prison on burglary charges; this would indicate his preoccupation with such material existed long before his known sexual crimes. Worth noting is the fact that he was particularly attracted to women who were not professional models (GND and FNL). In the authors' opinion, such women were complementary to his fantasies in that he could mentally relate more closely to such women. It is also to be appreciated that he invested over $250 in the magazines even though he was financially stressed.

5. Handwritten notes detailing specific items of lingerie and their cost if ordered from the mail order firm. The amount of the anticipated purchases would have totaled over $7,000.

    Discussion: These notes are *erotica.* Whether he purchased the items is not as significant as the paraphilic preoccupation to possess them.

6. A library book entitled *Rape: The Bait and the Trap* and a newspaper article on law enforcement tips to avoid sexual assault.

    Discussion: Both of these items would be classified as *educational* materials. They provide information on the crime of rape and what techniques the experts recommend to thwart it. The book would also be considered *introspective* in that it contains information on the underlying motivations of rape.

7. Numerous newspaper articles relating to the unexplained disappearances of women and runaway teenage females. These articles included photographs, descriptive data, and investigative methodology. The police determined that the subject was not involved in any of the disappearances.

    Discussion: These items would be classified as *erotica* and *educational* materials. They depicted visual images of the missing women and teenagers and lent reality to masturbatory fantasies. They also gave an indication of the media coverage and police procedures in such cases.

8. Three newspaper articles pertaining to the disappearance, discovery, and autopsy of the murder victim. These articles were hidden in a paper bag behind a basement wall in the offender's home. None of the other materials were hidden.

    Discussion: These media accounts of the crime would be considered *educational* materials in that they allow the man to track the investigation. Recognizing that some types of sexual killers use media accounts to relive the crime for masturbatory purposes, it might seem logical to also categorize the articles as *erotica.* However, it should be remembered that the offender did not *intend* for the victim to die and subsequently released another kidnap victim. Therefore, it is unlikely that he would use such materials for masturbatory behavior. This material would be considered *circumstantial* evidence in that the articles were hidden and related to the crime for which the man was a suspect. All other recovered materials were easily found.

9. Several newspaper articles dealing with noncriminal activities. They included the grand opening of a new drug store with an accompanying photograph of female employees with their names underlined; wedding announcements with photographs of the bride-to-be; the announcement of a surprise lingerie shower (he had underlined the word lingerie); and a photograph of an English model in a bikini swimming suit.

    Discussion: All of these items would be classified as *erotica.* Excepting the model's photograph, the items would also be classified as *intelligence* gathered by the offender for a potential victim pool. He underlined the names of the drug store employees, had a photograph and identifying data on the bride-to-be in the wedding announcement, and knew the identity of the guest of honor at the lingerie shower.

10. Several driver's licenses, license plate numbers, credit cards, and telephone numbers belonging to women.

    Discussion: The driver's licenses and credit cards would be direct evidence as they are proof of their theft and therefore directly link him to crimes. The driver's licenses, license plate, and telephone numbers would be categorized as *intelligence*—information he had gathered on potential victims.

11. The quilt taken from the murder victim's home and the bottom half of the victim's bathing suit. Because of the voluminous amount of lingerie present in the offender's home, the victim's panties could not be positively identified.

    Discussion: The quilt would be categorized as *direct* evidence. The bathing suit bottom would be labeled *direct* evidence as well as *erotica*. While it is possible that the quilt also served to sexually excite the man, there is nothing to indicate that he had a fetish for such material and therefore that assumption cannot be made. It is more likely that the quilt was used to cover the victim as he carried her from her residence.

12. A hand-drawn map depicting the route to a 27-year-old woman's residence. Notations on the map set forth details on her breast size, age of children, and type of car she owned. The investigators followed the map to her home and determined that the man had dug a well on her farm property about 1 year earlier.

    Discussion: The map and notations would be categorized as both *intelligence* and *erotica*. It was learned that the killer had visited her farm on the pretext of checking the functioning of the well. When her husband unexpectedly drove up, the man hurriedly left the farm property.

As previously mentioned, there are two types of *intelligence*: information gathered by the offender in preparing for future crimes and/or victims and information gathered from third parties about the offender. The wife of the subject was interviewed extensively and provided the following *intelligence:*

She said that she was well aware of her husband's preoccupation with female attire, particularly lingerie. He had often purchased teddies and nightgowns for her to wear and he would become sexually aroused when she wore the items. He was a chronic masturbator and would do so openly at all times of the day. He would ejaculate into condoms and leave them lying about their home. When she confronted him with this behavior, he denied the condoms were his and accused her of having affairs.

His extensive collection of lingerie led her to believe that he was having affairs and she began denying him sexual relations for fear of contracting AIDS. She also began refusing to wear lingerie for his pleasure.

She provided information that evidenced he was experiencing several stressors (financial, marital, health, occupational, and sexual) at the time that the known criminal behavior began.

The value of such first-hand information cannot be overestimated. In the instant case, it confirmed one of the subject's paraphilias (fetishism), identified various stressors in his life, and revealed a dysfunctional marriage.

SUMMARY

The authors have assisted investigators and prosecutors in better understanding the significance of materials found in the possession of sexual offenders. In addition to forensic, eyewitness, circumstantial, and direct evidence, investigators should also be cognizant of *collateral materials*.

Collateral materials can include newspaper articles, literature, viewing materials, advertisements, personal notes, fantasy recordings, sexual paraphernalia, collections, and information obtained from consenting and/or paid partners.

Collateral material can augment scientific and other factual evidence in the investigation of sexual crimes. It is helpful in the prosecution of such crimes through the utilization of expert testimony in educating judges and juries as to the significance of the items.

REFERENCES

Dietz, P. E., Harry, B., and Hazelwood, R. R. 1986. Detective magazines: Pornography for the sexual sadist? *Journal of Forensic Sciences*, 31(1), 197–211.

Ferguson, C. J., and Hartley, R. D. 2009. The pleasure is momentary... the expanse damnable? The influence of pornography on rape and sexual assault. *Aggression and Violent Behavior*, 14, 323–329.

Goldsmith, M., and Easteal, P. W. 1993. Sexual offenders and pornography: A causal connection? *Without consent: Confronting adult sexual violence*. Canberra: Australian Institute of Technology, 193–203.

Guzzy, S. 2012. Digital searches and the Fourth Amendment: The interplay between the plain view doctrine and search-protocol warrant restrictions. *American Criminal Law Review*, 49(1), 301–335.

Hazelwood, R. R. 1983. The behavior-oriented interview of rape victims: The key to profiling. *FBI Law Enforcement Bulletin*, September, 7–12.

Hazelwood, R. R., and Warren, J. I. 1989. The serial rapist: His characteristics and victims. *FBI Law Enforcement Bulletin*, February, 14–22.

Hazelwood, R. R., Warren, J. I., and Dietz, P. E. 1993. Compliant victims of sexual sadists. *Australian Family Physician*, 22(4), 3–7.

Lanning, K. V. 2010. *Child molesters: A behavioral analysis*, 5th ed. Alexandria, VA: National Center for Missing & Exploited Children.

Long, M. T., Alison, L. A., and McManus, M. A. 2012. Child pornography and likelihood of contact abuse: A comparison between contact child sexual offenders and noncontact offenders. *Sexual Abuse: A Journal of Research and Treatment*, 25(4), 370–395.

Merriam-Webster. 2015. Definition of collateral. August 2016, Retrieved from www.merriam-webster.com/dictionary/collateral.

Novotny, J. M., Meehan, A., Schulte, D., and Manes, G. W. 2002. Evidence acquisition tools for cyber sex crimes investigation. *SPIE Proceedings*, 4708(1), 53–60.

Warren, J. I., and Hazelwood, R. R. 2002. Relational patterns associated with sexual sadism: A study of 20 wives and girlfriends. *Journal of Family Violence*, 17(1), 107–122.

10 Linkage Analysis
MO, Ritual, and Signature in Serial Sexual Crimes

Robert R. Hazelwood and Janet I. Warren

CONTENTS

Introduction 149
Modus Operandi 150
    Ritualistic Behaviors in Sexual Crimes 151
    Observations Regarding MO and Ritual 151
The Signature in Sexual Crimes 152
A Case Example 152
The Linkage Analysis 154
    The Analysis in the Sanchez and Johnson Cases 154
        The Motive 154
        The Modus Operandi (MO) 155
        The Ritual 155
        The Signature 156
    Dissimilar Features of the Crimes 156
Computerized Linkage Systems 156
Features Other than MO or Ritual 157
Conclusions 157
References 157

INTRODUCTION

Growing awareness of the serial nature of a significant proportion of sexual crimes has motivated scientific and behavioral efforts to determine ways of linking crimes perpetrated by a single offender. Increasingly, DNA analysis allows investigators and prosecutors not only to scientifically determine the identity of the perpetrator in a single case of sexual assault, but also to ascribe responsibility to the offender, in some instances for cases that have occurred over long-time intervals and geographically distinct locales. However, the availability of DNA evidence is only beginning to be consistently and readily obtainable. In a significant proportion of sexual crimes, no DNA evidence is left at the scene or what is available for analysis is insufficient to allow for a definitive identification.

In such cases, behavioral analyses can be used to explore the likelihood that a series of crimes has been perpetrated by the same offender. Based upon an assessment of the modus operandi (MO) and the ritual, unique combinations of behavior, hereafter referred to as the "signature," may be identified to inform the investigation and expert witness testimony at trial. This process of behavioral assessment, referred to as "linkage analysis," involves five assessment procedures: (1) gathering detailed, varied, and multisourced documentation; (2) reviewing the documentation and identifying significant features of each crime individually across the series; (3) classifying the significant features of the crime as either MO and/or ritualistic constructs; (4) comparing the combination of

MO and ritualistic features across the crimes to determine if a signature exists; and (5) compiling a written analysis that details the conclusions derived from the available information.

To demonstrate these principles and the process used in reaching a conclusion, the behavior of one particular offender across two assaults will be presented in some detail. Intrinsic to this kind of analysis is familiarity with various aspects of crime scene analysis and experience either evaluating or investigating a significant number of serial sexual crimes.

MODUS OPERANDI

Law enforcement has historically linked crimes through behaviors of the offender and other elements of the crimes, referring somewhat generically to these dynamics as the "MO," or modus operandi, used or demonstrated by a particular criminal. Within the context of criminal investigative analysis, the MO can be conceptualized as the various behaviors that are requisite for a particular offender to successfully accomplish a crime. As such, it encompasses all behaviors initiated by the offender to procure a victim and complete the criminal acts without being identified. The MO can be quite simple or very complex, with the various degrees of sophistication reflecting the experience, motivation, and intelligence of the offender. Douglas and Munn (1992) observed that the MO is dynamic and malleable and evolves as the offender gains both experience and confidence in his or her patterns of criminal offending.

In serial sexual crimes, the MO evolves quite rapidly over time and can present significant changes in a period of only weeks or months. This evolution manifests itself as a result of experience, the natural process of maturation, and the education, criminal or otherwise, of the offender. For example, an 18-year-old rapist who failed to use a condom and ejaculated vaginally was later convicted because of DNA evidence recovered from the victim. He served 7 years and was released. Within a matter of months, he raped again, only this time he wore a condom. The same 18-year-old rapist stole two 4-foot speakers, a collection of CDs, and a CD player from his first victim. In the offenses subsequent to his release from prison, he stole only money and jewelry from his rape victims. Another offender reported studying the professional literature on his crime of choice as well as popular magazines that discuss in detail the crime scene behavior of infamous offenders. When he was later interviewed as part of a federally funded research grant, he met the interviewer saying, "I know who you are. When I was raping, I did a literature search on rape and I've read everything you've ever written."

Forces outside the offender can also impinge on the manner in which the crime is implemented. The unavailability of a victim, the behavioral response of the victim, the interruption of an offense by another person—all represent circumstances that can change aspects of the MO. One behavioral analyst was approached by a detective asking for guidance regarding a series of rapes. He indicated that the offender had raped 16 women and had been labeled the First-Floor Rapist. When the analyst asked about a 17th report that he found in the stack of documents, the detective asserted that the 17th offense must have been perpetrated by another offender as it had occurred on the second floor of an apartment building. The faulty assessment of the detective failed to capture the life contingencies that can impact the criminal behavior of an offender. He had obviously not considered the possibility that the offender was unable to find a victim or to locate an unlocked window on the ground floor that particular evening and was therefore required to execute entry into a second floor apartment to carry out his criminal intent.

However, not all features of the MO are subject to change. If a certain behavior has worked well for an offender and has not resulted in any unwanted outcomes, it is likely to be observed in future crimes of the same offender. As each behavior is executed over a number of situations, the criminal becomes more familiar with a particular series of behaviors and, therefore, more able to anticipate the outcomes of them. As with many other aspects of human behavior, this routinized aspect of the crime scene behavior affords the offender a sense of familiarity and control, which allows him to focus more intently on the sexualized or aggressive motive for the crime.

RITUALISTIC BEHAVIORS IN SEXUAL CRIMES

The ritualistic aspects of a sexual crime emanate from the internal psychology of a particular offender as opposed to the situational demands of committing a crime. These behaviors derive from the motivation for the crime and the sexual fantasy that expresses it. They are symbolic, as opposed to functional; as such, they are highly individualized and reflect the aspects of the crime scene that are *unnecessary* to the accomplishment of the crime, but *pivotal* in expressing the primary motivation or purpose of the criminal act itself. Geberth (1996) has linked this fantasy-based element of a sexual crime to the unique psychodynamics of the individual responsible for enacting these impulses through the criminal behavior.

The ritualistic aspects of a crime can also change over a series of offenses, either due to the refinement and more complete reflection of their underlying intent or fantasy substrate or through the addition of unexpectedly arousing aspects of a prior offense. This is suspected in cases of serial rape in which the offender escalates the degree of physical force, uses increasingly intricate bindings, and introduces distinctive verbal exchanges over a series of assaults. While earlier research suggests that 75% of serial rapists do not escalate in the degree of physical violence they inflict over time, 25% do escalate. Apparently some find that more severe degrees of violence or dominance enhance their arousal (Warren et al., 1999). In other instances, bindings that began as a way of restraining the victim can be seen to develop into a very intricate process both in terms of the materials used and the manner in which the victim is restrained. For example, one serial rapist engaged in sexual bondage with all 55 of his victims in 12 states. In his first few rapes, he bound his victims using their clothing. Over time, he began using medical tape, precut lengths of rope that he brought to the crimes, and eventually handcuffs. In a different series of sexual murders, statements demanded of the victims became an increasingly central and salient aspect of the crime, with specific and repetitive statements by the victim being scripted by the offender.

OBSERVATIONS REGARDING MO AND RITUAL

In assessing the MO and ritualistic aspects of a crime, certain additional themes or observations emerge from the application of this type of analysis:

1. It is not uncommon for a crime scene analyst to identify more elements of the MO than of the ritual. This is not unexpected as the MO may include time, day, and location of the crime; the weapon used; sex and age of victim; the offender's mode of travel; and any number of other variables. The ritual, on the other hand, is much more narrowly focused, comprising those acts specifically designed to complement the motivation for the crime and to meet the psychosexual needs of the offender.

2. All aspects of the ritual may not be present in every crime (Douglas & Munn, 1992). The *time* available, *mood* of the offender, and *external circumstances*, such as a roommate coming home, may all prevent the full repertoire of desired behaviors from being enacted. Each of these factors can result in the ritualistic aspects of the crime being diluted, modified, or interrupted depending on the internal state of the offender and the contingencies of a particular crime.

3. Some features of the crime may serve as part of the ritual and not be recognized as such by the analyst. For example, the manner used by an offender to approach his victim would most often be viewed as part of the MO. However, one serial killer who focused only on middle-class female victims for rape and murder used guile to convince the women to accompany him. After his capture, he reported that he obtained an inordinate sense of power from his ability to convince middle-class and intelligent women to go with him, a total stranger, without having to resort to physical violence.

4. Some elements of the crime may function as both MO and ritual. In one particular series, a serial rapist captured numerous adult male and female couples at gunpoint in their homes and forced the wives to tie their husbands' hands and feet with shoelaces. Such behavior would correctly be categorized as MO as it helped to ensure success by allowing the perpetrator to control both adults simultaneously and to use one to immobilize the other. However, having the wife neutralize the male "protector" also served as a ritualistic feature of the crime in that it psychosexually excited the perpetrator.

5. There may be instances in which one or more ritualistic aspects of the crime remain known only to the offender (Douglas & Munn, 1992). One serial killer recorded his daily fantasies about capturing a particular type of woman for sexual assault. He remained very focused on victim demographics such as body style, color and length of hair, and breast size. Such features obviously played an important psychosexual role in the offender's crimes, but were only recognized as being part of his ritual after the discovery of his records.

6. When an "impulsive" sexual offender (Hazelwood & Warren, 2001) is involved, the crime may be devoid of ritualistic behaviors. Such criminals act out with little or no planning. Fantasy plays a very small role in their crimes and the involvement of paraphilic or other ritualistic behavior is seldom observed with this type of offender. However, as with all human behavior, criminal or otherwise, there will be exceptions. The reader will note such an exception in the discussion of the Sanchez and Johnson cases that follows.

THE SIGNATURE IN SEXUAL CRIMES

Douglas and Munn (1992) described the signature as the "calling card" of an offender. In the current context, this term is used to describe a unique combination of behaviors that emerges across two or more offenses. It is a pattern that may include aspects of both the MO and the ritual. Recognition of this unique signature aspect of a crime most commonly occurs when crime analysts and/or investigators are attempting to link two or more crimes that have occurred in either close physical or temporal proximity or times or locations that are highly divergent.

Occasionally, the signature is presented in the courtroom by qualified experts to enhance legal arguments that a series of crimes, separated often by time and distance, were committed by the same offender. This type of testimony was allowed in a California case in which one of the authors was allowed to testify that the same person was responsible for a series of six rapes (*California v. Kenneth Bogard*, 1996). In New Jersey, the Supreme Court reviewed a similar type of testimony and allowed the expert to testify regarding similarities across a series of offenses, but did not allow the expert to offer an opinion as to whether the crimes had been perpetrated by the same person (*State of New Jersey v. Steven Fortin*, 2000). In a somewhat different context, testimony regarding a review of the signature aspects of two crimes was offered by the prosecution at a hearing to determine if two murders would be joined for prosecution (*South Dakota v. Robert Anderson*, 1998). Similar to the qualification of all expert witnesses, the analyst offering this testimony must be qualified through education and experience, with the final decision regarding the reliability and probative value of the testimony being determined initially by the judge and eventually by the jury.

A CASE EXAMPLE

At 12:50 a.m. on November 12, 1994, Margarete Sanchez, a 25-year-old Hispanic woman, was found dead inside one of four large concrete sewer pipes lying on the ground between a footpath and a well-traveled, six-lane highway. Ms. Sanchez left her boyfriend, Fernando Gonzalez, and her four children in a motel room at about 11 p.m. to walk to the convenience store a few blocks away. When she did not return, Mr. Gonzalez sent some teenagers to look for her and when they returned without having found her, he set out along the path to look for her. As he approached the four concrete pipes, he noticed foodstuffs lying on the path. When he bent down to examine the materials, he saw

Ms. Sanchez's body in one of the pipes and cried out. Tory Smith, who had been working on his car under a streetlight on a nearby street, came over and together they removed her body from the pipe. She wore a striped T-shirt, but was braless and nude from the waist down. Smith draped his T-shirt over the lower portion of Ms. Sanchez's body.

A woman who lived directly across the street from the crime scene told the police that she and a male friend were returning to her residence at about 11:30 p.m. when she saw a light-skinned male leave the area of the concrete pipes. Another witness who was driving on the six-lane highway reported that at about 11:30 p.m., he observed two people by the pipes and they appeared to be waving their arms. He told the police that one of them was taller than the other and the shorter person had bushy hair (as did Ms. Sanchez). The police found a convenience store receipt at the scene that was dated and time-stamped at 11:29 p.m. A cheese-steak sandwich was among the items on the receipt, but it was not found at the scene.

One hundred and fifty feet from the body, the police found Ms. Sanchez's shorts and panties hanging from a bush. The panties were inside the shorts and the right rear pocket was pulled out. A short distance from the shorts, a partially eaten cheese-steak sandwich was found on a stone wall. The police determined that an inexpensive necklace had also been taken from Ms. Sanchez.

She had been brutally beaten in the upper part of her face and this resulted in severe bruising. Fists were believed to be responsible for the blunt force trauma to Ms. Sanchez's face. Her nose was broken and her hyoid bone was fractured. Death was attributed to manual strangulation from the front. Although there was no evidence of recent ejaculation, there were spermatozoa present in the vagina. Mr. Gonzalez advised that he last had vaginal sex with Ms. Sanchez the night before her death and had last had anal sex with the victim 1–2 weeks before her death. It was the medical examiner's opinion that the presence of the spermatozoa was not associated with her murder.

Ms. Sanchez's anus had been torn and the body had not reacted to the tearing, indicating that she had died before the healing process could begin. The anal injuries were attributed to a violent penetration either with fingers or penis. Furthermore, Ms. Sanchez had been bitten at least twice on her chin and again on the outer aspect of her left breast.

The crime remained unsolved until the following year. The following April at about 8:45 p.m., Samantha Johnson (pseudonym), an off-duty female police officer, was driving her marked police cruiser to her home. She was traveling southbound on an interstate highway and observed a compact car parked in a northerly direction in the southbound breakdown lane. She parked her cruiser in front of the smaller car and both Ms. Johnson and the male driver got out of their cars, meeting between them. She identified herself as a police officer and the man acknowledged her status and gave her his driver's permit. Smelling alcohol, Officer Johnson gave him a Breathalyzer test. The man tested positive for intoxication and she took him to her car and called for another officer to take the man to jail. The officer advised that because of other duties he could not assist her for at least 40 min. The man had been cooperative, so she told the other officer that she would wait for him.

Within 30 min the man began trying to convince Officer Johnson to let him go and "everything would be okay." She later testified that he had remained calm during their conversation, but that suddenly "he went bonkers." She recalled him hitting her with his fists and then she lost consciousness. She awakened to find him attempting to strangle her from the front and she pried one of his fingers back and then lost consciousness a second time. After again regaining consciousness, she found herself nude from the waist down and in the passenger seat with the man driving her cruiser at a high rate of speed. Her kidnapper had driven away with her when the second officer arrived to take custody of the man. She opened the door and hung on as the man shouted for her to "jump, bitch." She reported that he pushed her as she jumped from the car while it was traveling between 65 and 75 mph. Amazingly, she survived.

Officer Johnson had been beaten in the upper part of her face and this resulted in severe bruising around her eyes. She had also suffered a broken nose. She had been bitten on the chin and also on the outer aspect of her left breast. Her lower garments had been removed and even though her shirt was in place, her bra had been ripped off her body. The would-be killer had also inflicted severe vaginal and anal injuries on Officer Johnson.

THE LINKAGE ANALYSIS

As summarized earlier, five steps characterize the linkage analysis:

1. *Gathering the necessary documentation*: In a series of *rape cases*, this phase of the assessment focuses on the victim's statement, police and medical reports, a commercial map depicting the significant locations associated with each of the crimes, and the distances between the points. Significant locations include points of confrontation, assault, and release of the victim. In *homicide cases*, necessary documentation would include police and autopsy/toxicology reports, crime scene, and autopsy photographs, and if all crimes occurred within a particular city, a commercial map depicting the abduction and murder sites if known, the body disposal sites, and the distances between each of the various locations.

2. *Reviewing the documentation and identifying the significant crime features*: This phase of the assessment allows the analyst not only to capture the significant features of each crime, but also to become intimately familiar with each offense in the series. It also provides a readily available source for accessing crime behavior without having to repeatedly search through volumes of data.

3. *Analyzing the crimes and recording all MO and/or ritualistic features*: At this stage, the analyst conducts an in-depth study of the significant crime features and identifies those behaviors that are MO and those that are ritualistic in nature.

4. *Determining if a signature exists across the crimes*: The analyst seeks to determine whether a unique combination of behaviors (i.e., a signature) exists across the series of crimes.

5. *Preparing the opinion*: The opinion is provided in a written report that, at a minimum, should include a listing of the materials reviewed, any site visitations, a listing of those crime features that make up the MO, those crime features that compose the ritual, and the unique combination of behaviors identified as the signature. The analyst must also be prepared to discuss any dissimilarities noted across the series of crimes under consideration and why they have no impact on the written opinion.

The person who attempted to murder Officer Johnson was arrested and convicted of numerous felony offenses. He was then extradited to the state in which Margarete Sanchez was murdered and stood trial for that homicide. While the analyst was not allowed to testify that the same person was responsible for both crimes, he was allowed to testify as to the MO, the ritual, and the similarities he had identified across both crimes.

THE ANALYSIS IN THE SANCHEZ AND JOHNSON CASES

The analyst was requested to prepare a report with two opinions: (1) identify the primary motive for the attacks and (2) determine if a signature existed across the crimes.

The Motive

It was the analyst's opinion that anger was the primary motive underlying both crimes and that this anger had been acted out in a sexually violent manner. It was believed that the taking of the necklace from Ms. Sanchez was of secondary importance to the offender. This opinion derived from the following: (1) both victims were brutally beaten, with the amount of force being much greater than that needed to subdue the victims for either robbery or sexual assault; (2) both victims were manually strangled (manual strangulation is a more personal method of killing than is strangulation with a ligature); and (3) both victims had injurious anal penetration, a form of sexual assault closely associated with anger-motivated sexual crimes. The analyst later learned that an informant had been told by the offender that he used his fingers to grasp the victim's vagina and anus to drag the woman from one location to another.

The Modus Operandi (MO)

The analysis of the crimes determined that the following features shown in Table 10.1 formed the MO in the murder of Sanchez and the attempted murder of Officer Johnson.

The Ritual

Table 10.2 illustrates the features that were determined to form the ritual present in both cases. It is noted that these features complement the primary motivation of anger and also serve to psychosexually arouse the offender.

TABLE 10.1

The Modus Operandi in the Cases of Margarete Sanchez and Samantha Johnson

Margarete Sanchez (1994)	Samantha Johnson (1995)
High-risk crime	High-risk crime
Impulsively committed crime	Impulsively committed crime
Female victim	Female victim
Similar age (25 years old)	Similar age (34 years old)
Victim of opportunity	Victim of opportunity
Alone at time of crime	Alone at time of crime
Heavily traveled road	Heavily traveled road
Occurred during darkness	Occurred during darkness
Blunt force (fists)	Blunt force (fists)
No weapon used	No weapon used
Trauma to upper face	Trauma to upper face
Nude from waist down	Nude from waist down
Shorts and panties intertwined	Pants and panties intertwined
Shirt left on, breasts free	Shirt left on, breasts free
No (fresh) seminal fluids on/in victim	No seminal fluids on/in victim

TABLE 10.2

Ritual Elements and Features in the Cases of Margarete Sanchez and Samantha Johnson

Margarete Sanchez	Samantha Johnson
Brutal facial beating	Brutal facial beating
Manual strangulation from the front	Manual strangulation from the front
Injurious anal penetration	Injurious anal penetration
Bite to chin	Bite to chin
Bite to outer aspect of left breast	Bite to outer aspect of left breast

TABLE 10.3
Dissimilar Features of the Two Crimes

Margarete Sanchez	Samantha Johnson
Hispanic	White
Murdered	Attempted murder
Sandwich/shorts/necklace taken	Vehicle taken
Found in concrete pipe	Found on highway
Fractured hyoid bone	N/A
Victim walked to site	Victim drove to site
11:30 p.m.	8:45 p.m.
Occurred on Monday	Occurred on Thursday–Friday
5′4″ tall	5′9″ tall
120 pounds	140 pounds
Different state	Different state

The Signature

The opinion was formed that a signature did exist across the two crimes. In this case, the signature involved both MO and ritualistic features. While each element of the killer's MO had been individually observed in other crimes, the analyst (despite involvement in several thousand sexual crime investigations) had never encountered all of the features in any other single crime. Nor had he seen the combination of ritualistic features in any single previous crime. This co-occurrence of both the functional aspects of the MO and the more symbolic and ritualistic aspects of the crime created the signature of this particular offender.

DISSIMILAR FEATURES OF THE CRIMES

As mentioned, it is important that the analyst also note any dissimilarities in the crimes under consideration and be prepared to discuss why they do not impact negatively on the signature opinion. The following features of the two crimes, illustrated in Table 10.3, were found to be dissimilar.

Of the 11 features noted, 8 of them (race, height, weight, time, day, state, mode of travel, and disposal site) can be attributed to the crimes being impulsively committed against victims of opportunity. As to the remaining three elements (fractured hyoid bone, murder, and theft of a personal item), they certainly pose no threat to the signature opinion. Although Ms. Sanchez was murdered and her hyoid bone was fractured, from the testimony of Officer Johnson, there was no question that the killer was intent on killing her via manual strangulation. Had the second officer not arrived when he did and had Officer Johnson not succeeded in escaping, it is probable that she would also have been manually strangled to death and demonstrated a fractured hyoid bone. It is also probable that this same interruption deterred a theft from the personal effects of Officer Johnson.

COMPUTERIZED LINKAGE SYSTEMS

There has been increasing empirical support for the use of behavioral case linkage (see Woodhams, Hollin, & Bull, 2007). Available research supports behavioral consistency across offenses of one offender and interindividual variability (i.e., allowing for offences perpetrated by different offenders to be distinguished from each other). The development of crime databases have allowed for computerized linkage systems such as ViCAP and ViCLAS to show distinct patterns of similarities in behavioral characteristics of offenses such as common MO, rituals, and signatures (Bennell, Snook, Macdonald, House, & Taylor, 2012). However, Woodhams et al. (2007) suggest that while computer-assisted behavioral linkage has the potential to yield predictions of offence commonalities, the "clinical" expertise of the investigator is crucial to contextualize the behaviors exhibited during the crime. The authors use the example of computer-assisted linkage which may identify repeated punching of the victims' faces as common to two instances of rape, but without any further consideration of the context of the physical assaults. The investigator's expertise, on the other hand, would allow a more vigilant distinction between repeated punching as a means to gain control of the resisting victim and the infliction of excessive physical trauma as an expression of anger and aggression.

FEATURES OTHER THAN MO OR RITUAL

There will invariably be features of a sexual crime that cannot be accurately described as being part of either the MO or ritual and that may not be fully understood by the analyst. In this case, the taking of Ms. Sanchez's shorts with panties intertwined, the taking of the cheese-steak sandwich, and the partial eating of the sandwich cannot be appropriately labeled as MO or ritualistic. Because the pocket of the shorts was turned inside out, it is probable that the killer took Ms. Sanchez's shorts as he searched for money and/or possibly drugs, and he took the cheese-steak sandwich and partially consumed it *after the killing.*

As with almost every sexual crime, there are also elements in these murders that may never be satisfactorily explained. Ms. Sanchez's location in the concrete pipe is puzzling. It is reasonable to conclude that the killer moved her into the pipe so that he could carry out his crime without being observed or to delay her discovery; if so, that act becomes part of his MO. However, if she crawled into the pipe in an unsuccessful attempt to get away from her killer, then it is not related to the offender's choice of behavior.

CONCLUSIONS

The serial nature of a significant proportion of sexual crimes has motivated efforts to determine ways of linking crimes committed by a single offender. In such cases, behavioral analysis can be used to explore the likelihood that a series of crimes was committed by the same person. An assessment of the MO and the ritual demonstrated during sexual crimes can result in the identification of a unique combination of behaviors or "signature." The signature is viewed as a highly individualized combination of habitual aspects of offending behavior combined with the fantasy and motive for a particular series of crimes perpetrated by a single offender. It is assumed that the combination of behaviors observed in the signature of a crime series is so distinct as to inform not only the investigation of multiple sexual crimes but also aspects of court decision making regarding specific offenders. Within the investigative context, this type of analysis not only can assist the investigative team in organizing their information and networking with other police jurisdictions, but also can help with crime prevention efforts by identifying the possible time and location of potential future crimes perpetrated by the same offender. When offered in the legal arena, it can provide a framework for helping to inform judges and juries as to the various behavioral components of serial sexual crimes and the uniqueness of a particular combination observed across a series of offenses. As a form of crime scene behavioral assessment, linkage analysis offers the experienced investigator or evaluator a framework for distilling a large amount of crime scene information into a succinct comparative framework that can inform efforts to identify the offender and potentially link offenses within the legal arena.

REFERENCES

Bennell, C., Snook, B., Macdonald, S., House, J. C., and Taylor, P. J. 2012. Computerized linkage systems: A critical review and research agenda. *Criminal Justice and Behavior*, 39(5): 620–634.
California v. Kenneth Bogard. 1996, February. California Supreme Court hearing in San Diego, CA.

Douglas, J. E., and Munn, C. 1992. Violent crime scene analysis: Modus operandi, signature, and staging. *FBI Law Enforcement Bulletin*, February: 16–20.

Geberth, V. J. 1996. *Practical homicide investigation*, 3rd ed. Boca Raton, FL: CRC Press.

Hazelwood, R. R., and Warren, J. 2001. The sexually violent offender: Impulsive or ritualistic? In R. R. Hazelwood and A. W. Burgess (Eds.), *Practical aspects of rape investigation: A multidisciplinary approach*, 3rd ed., 97–113, Boca Raton, FL: CRC Press.

South Dakota v. Robert L. Anderson. McCook County Court (April 9, 1998). Hearing.

State of New Jersey v. Fortin. 2000. 745 A.2d 509, NJ.

Warren, J., Reboussin, R., Hazelwood, R., Gibbs, N., Trombetta, S., and Cummings, A. 1999. Crime scene analysis and the escalation of violence in serial rape. *Forensic Science International*, 100: 37–56.

Woodhams, J., Hollin, C. R., and Bull, R. 2007. The psychology of linking crimes: A review of the evidence. *Legal and Criminological Psychology*, 12: 233–249.

11 False Rape Allegations

Robert R. Hazelwood and Ann Wolbert Burgess

CONTENTS

Introduction 159
Definition 160
Potential Consequences of a False Allegation 160
    Imprisonment of an Innocent Person 160
    Impact on Legitimate Victims of Rape 161
    Emotional Problems in Need of Attention 162
    Problems Confronting the Investigator 162
Classification of Unfounded Rape Cases 163
    Sex-Stress Situations 163
    False Rape Allegation 165
    Delusional Rape Allegation 167
Who Makes a False Allegation? 167
Motives for False Rape Allegations 168
    Attention/Sympathy 168
    Anger/Revenge 168
    Alibi 169
False Allegations and the Adaptation Continuum 169
    Munchausen Syndrome 169
    Mental States 169
    Factitious Disorders and Malingering 171
    Factors Consistent with False Allegations 171
        Initial Complaint 171
        Assailants 172
        Sexual Assault 172
        Evidence 172
        Injuries 172
        Personality and Lifestyle Considerations 173
        Other 173
Investigatory Considerations 174
    Second Opinion 174
Summary 175
Acknowledgments 175
References 175

INTRODUCTION

Compared to other types of serious crimes, rape has a number of unique characteristics. First, because of the low reporting rate for this crime, it is difficult to know how frequently rape occurs. Accurate estimates of the incidence and prevalence of rape are not readily available, as it is believed that the majority of victims do not report to the police, receive medical attention from hospitals, or seek help from service agencies such as rape crisis centers (Kilpatrick, Best, & Veronen, 1985; Wolitzky-Taylor et al., 2011; Kruttschnitt, Kalsbeek, & House, 2014). Second, it is still believed by many that women like to be overpowered sexually and that when they say "no" they really mean "yes." Third, rape and abuse are predominantly perpetrated by the male segment of the population and selectively borne by the female segment of the population. Fourth, rape instills fear in victims and serves to limit their freedom by placing constraints on their activities (Riger & Gordon, 1988). Finally, unlike other crimes, there is still considerable variation in what constitutes a "real" rape. Depending on the jurisdiction, law enforcement agents and child protective service workers may use the terms *unfounded* when there is insufficient evidence to support the complaint and *false allegation* to dismiss the complaint of a "nonbelievable victim." The purpose of this chapter is to unravel the complexities of false allegations of rape including why it occurs and its implications on victims, investigators, and justice.

DEFINITION

In order to properly conceptualize false allegation of rape and obtain consistent prevalence estimates, it is crucial to provide a clear working definition. Katz and Mazur (1979) defined *false report* as a "deliberate lie by the alleged victim accusing a man of a rape that did not occur. It may also be a fantasy report that the female believes is true" (p. 207). These authors also write that wide discrepancies in the reported frequency of false allegation are due to differences in definitions and criteria, and due to the source of the judgments in these situations.

McDowell and Hibler, in the first edition of *Practical Aspects of Rape Investigation: A Multidisciplinary Approach* (1987), presented a sensitive treatment of the issue of false allegation, which included the role of defense mechanisms, secondary gain, and other psychological aspects. They asserted that investigators can make sense of these false claims once they discover the purpose served for the victim by such an allegation. However, a precise definition of the very phenomenon they described was omitted.

McDowell (1990), in another source, again failed to define the concept, but described three conditions used to classify cases as false allegations:

1. Victim recants complaint.
2. Victim fails polygraph.
3. Investigation reveals allegation to be false.

These criteria may be interpreted as being very broad and imprecise, thereby leaving a wide margin for discretionary interpretation and action.

For the purposes of this chapter, *false allegation* is defined as falsely alleging that a sexual assault has occurred against one's person, or the person of another. The alleged assault may be in the form of touching or penetration, or having been forced to touch or penetrate another in a sexual manner. The person making such an allegation is herein referred to as a "pseudovictim." It should also be acknowledged that those who make false allegations are almost exclusively depicted in a negative manner, as having malicious intent or ulterior motives. However, it would be a mistake to allow these normative assumptions to obscure the underlying complexity of false allegations. As discussed later, there are multiple and complex reasons a person may make a false allegation and the pseudovictim may or may not identify a particular person or location.

POTENTIAL CONSEQUENCES OF A FALSE ALLEGATION

IMPRISONMENT OF AN INNOCENT PERSON

Imprisonment of a man falsely accused of rape has been described since Biblical times. Potiphar, an Egyptian captain of Pharaoh's guard, employed Joseph to watch over his household. Potiphar's wife "cast her eyes upon Joseph ... caught him by his garment, saying lie with me." Joseph resisted this temptation but his rejection of her caused her to say that the Hebrew servant came to "mock her," that she lifted up her voice and cried, and that he fled leaving his garment with her. Potiphar imprisoned Joseph for 2 years (Genesis 39).

Although not resulting in imprisonment, a more contemporary, and nationally infamous, false allegation case occurred in the 1980s in Duchess County, New York. Tawana Brawley, a 15-year-old black female was reported missing and not found until a period of 4 days had passed. She was observed in the back yard of a townhouse, which had been previously occupied by her family, standing in a green garbage bag and literally hopping around the yard before lying down and pulling the bag over her head. Her hair had been cut short, she had feces smeared on her body, and "KKK" and "nigger" had been printed on her body with a soot-like substance. She refused to speak with police, but, speaking through her aunt and mother, reported that she had been abducted, taken to a wooded area, and repeatedly raped by four to six white men, one of whom had a police-style badge. Reverend Al Sharpton and others became involved and it was alleged that the county police and prosecutor were involved in a cover-up to protect members of the local police force. Consequently, the national news media became involved and then-Governor Cuomo asserted state jurisdiction over the investigation, which resulted in the formation of a combined state and federal task force. One of the authors (Hazelwood) was involved in the case from the very beginning. After an intensive and lengthy criminal and state grand jury investigation lasting more than 7 months, it was concluded that Brawley had falsified the story. Additionally, the grand jury found no evidence of a cover-up by law enforcement officials and recommended that their minutes be released to the public.

A more recent but equally infamous incident involved a black female alleging that she had been assaulted by several white Duke University lacrosse team players. Again the national news media became involved because of inflammatory statements made by the local prosecutor. This matter collapsed from a preponderance of evidence supporting the defense, a lack of evidence supporting the allegation, and numerous conflicting statements given by the alleged victim. The state attorney general intervened and issued a blistering statement concerning the abilities and motivation of the local prosecutor.

IMPACT ON LEGITIMATE VICTIMS OF RAPE

It is generally accepted that today's law enforcement officer is a better educated and more sensitive officer than in the past. This is particularly true of those officers charged with the responsibility of investigating sexual crimes, as is documented by the largest empirical study ever conducted of police attitudes and beliefs about rape (LeDoux & Hazelwood, 1983). Most detectives are alert to any indication of bias or antiquated ideas toward the woman alleging rape, although exceptions do remain. Page (2007) found that more highly educated police officers (any level of college) and those with greater experience in rape investigations were less supportive of rape myths and more likely to hold egalitarian views of women and their experiences with rape.

Many departments require officers assigned to sexual assault investigative duties to attend special courses designed to instill sensitivity and empathy toward women who have been sexually assaulted.

It is also important to consider that false rape allegations can serve to propel myths that have significant impacts on processes of justice. For example, the historical exercise of extensively cross-examining the complainant's sexual history can be seen in part to have emanated from a misconception of the frequency of false rape allegations (Gunby, Carline, & Beynon, 2012). Lisak, Gardinier, Nicksa, and Cote (2010) claim that there is considerable evidence of the pervasiveness of rape myths that continue to affect how rape victims and their cases are perceived by police and investigators. As a result, these beliefs may contribute to underreporting if victims have increasing doubts as to whether investigators will take their claims seriously or will be overly suspicious about the validity of their claims.

EMOTIONAL PROBLEMS IN NEED OF ATTENTION

On occasion, those who make false allegations have legitimate problems worthy of attention in their own right. However, if their complaints are accepted at face value, the underlying problem will go untreated and may surface at a later date. When rape complaints are determined to be false, investigators would be wise to seek the assistance of mental health professionals qualified to identify underlying problems.

PROBLEMS CONFRONTING THE INVESTIGATOR

False allegations can result in a variety of problems and most experienced investigators have taken false crime reports of one type or another. Needless to say, one should always be sensitive to the possibility of a false report. Surprisingly, even though the phenomenon of the false rape report is well recognized, there has been a lack of careful research into the problem and little is published on the topic. O'Neal, Spohn, Tellis, and White (2014) affirm that theoretical and empirical research on motivations for false allegations of rape has been scarce. Studies describing false allegation in child sexual abuse are uniform in reporting the sparse literature in the area (Rosenfeld, Nadelson, & Krieger, 1979; Benedek & Schetky, 1984; Green, 1986). These same authors concurred that when child custody is a prominent issue, the frequency of the occurrence of false allegation rises dramatically. Vindictiveness and psychological dysfunction on the part of the parents may underlie such complaints.

Investigators often experience a difficult task of balancing credibility and suspicion. Lefer (1992) highlights how sometimes this balance is disturbed. She asserts, "It is as though the victim is the one on trial; every gesture, ... word can be held against her" (Lefer, 1992). Further, Lefer asserts that when there is any inconsistency in the report, validity of the entire allegation comes into question. She raises the issue of emotionality by writing that "women who are unemotional may be conveying that they were not disturbed by the 'alleged' event, hence, the absence of harm. Women who are overwrought come across as emotionally unstable, and thus not credible."

Investigators may suspect a false allegation when the victim repeatedly changes his or her accounts of the assault. This was one of the issues in the Duke University lacrosse team case. Given research that demonstrated the potential of traumatic events to impair memory (Byrne, Hyman, & Scott, 2001), care must be taken to distinguish a true changing of the story from a legitimate recollection of additional data. In both true and false claims, new information and more detail may be added in subsequent interviews. The false claimant wishes to "shore up" the allegation to make it more believable, while the genuine victim (as composure and equilibrium are regained) may remember more detail and descriptive data in the days following the assault. This situation places investigators in a very delicate position: Worst-case scenarios are that the pseudovictim successfully manipulates the system for personal gain or that the legitimate victim is further traumatized by aggressive attempts on the part of investigators to elicit the ultimate "truth."

Related to this same discussion is the distinction one must make between deliberate deceit and an honest mistake. The person making a false allegation may offer data that differ from the original report to further deceive and mislead the authorities. In the initial stages of an investigation, a legitimate rape victim, because of stress and psychic pain, may provide incorrect information related to an altered ability to accurately process information. Investigators should be vigilant about inaccuracies or ambiguities regarding factual elements of the case, but acknowledge that some degree of inconsistency can be expected in an investigation. The mere presence of a factual discrepancy should not automatically lead the investigator to declare the allegation to be false, but consider that confusion, impaired memory, or other events may be at play (Saunders, 2012). Also, previous research has pointed out that rape victims may omit certain details of the rape that they perceive would percolate suspicion or undermine the veracity of their claim (Kelly, 2010).

To some investigators, omissions of pertinent details may appear as willful attempts of deceit, such as when victims overlook the use of illicit substances before or during their victimization (Hunt & Bull, 2012; Saunders, 2012). That said, investigators should avoid making rash determinations of invalidity on the basis of inconsistencies or omissions in verbal testimonies without referring to other elements of the case.

When a rape or, for that matter, any crime occurs, there must be three elements: perpetrator or perpetrators, act or acts, and a setting or set of conditions. One can make a false allegation with reference to any or all of these elements. In the following section, we address some of the problems related to the classification of false accounts of rape used in law enforcement.

CLASSIFICATION OF UNFOUNDED RAPE CASES

Prosecutors and investigators find the term *false allegation* of little utility unless the complainant in some way says that the account is untrue. It is more common to use general terms such as *unfounded*, *refusal to prosecute*, and the like. These categories allow law enforcement to close cases without arriving at conclusions. Cases of false allegation are frequently included in these categories. Some jurisdictions may routinely relegate a large percentage of rape complaints to this disposition simply as a means of closing an investigation when it becomes difficult. However, the classification may conflate cases where there is a lack of corroborating evidence or a refusal of the victim to go further in the investigation or prosecution with what we have outlined as false allegation of rape (Marshall & Alison, 2006). It may also occur that a case may be considered "baseless" and, thus, classified as unfounded if the complainant's account does not meet the investigators' interpretations of rape. Because of these reasons, rates of false allegation may have been inflated and misrepresented. For example, it may be reported that false allegations of rape occur at the rate of 30%, when what is really meant is that 30% of cases have been classified as "unfounded."

The following section sets forth common reasons for a rape complaint being "unfounded" and recommends more accurate categories. Police consideration of using such categories would greatly assist in differentiating between "unfounded" cases of sexual assault and truly false allegations of sexual assault. It would also help determine whether national statistics on clearance compiled by the FBI are accurate.

SEX-STRESS SITUATIONS

Sex-stress situations are cases in which a male and female initially agreed to have sexual relations but then something "went wrong." Sometimes this may involve strong feelings of guilt or remorse about a previous sexual encounter and the subsequent accusation of rape. In other cases, there may be a legal confusion regarding consent under a state of intoxication from alcohol or drugs (O'Neal et al., 2014). It is also common for a third party to become aware of the situation in which sexual intercourse has occurred and define it as rape or convince the female to allege rape seeing it as a way out of some dilemma.

It is particularly important for nursing, rape crisis, and mental health professionals to understand sex-stress cases (Carretta & Burgess, 2013). First, they greatly influence how the system deals with rape. Staff members tend to become obsessed with trying to determine if the situation is a rape case and, consequently, a tremendous amount of energy goes into "diagnosing" rather than helping the victim. Second, these females are victims in their own right and have many emotional concerns over what has been an upsetting experience.

The two main types of sex-stress cases are (1) mutual agreement and (2) financial gain. In a typical mutual agreement case, both parties agree to have sex but then one person wishes to deny the act or suddenly becomes repulsed by their own behavior. The following case illustrates a situation where there is a reported set of circumstances, a reported act, but no actual offender.

CASE NO. 1

Roberta, a 27-year-old female civilian employee of a state police department, made a report of rape. She disclosed the alleged rape to a male coworker, telling a very detailed and complex story. She reported that when she was walking to her car from a disco club, a police sergeant known to her jumped out from behind a car and grabbed her from behind. He forced her into a van and ripped her clothes off. When she refused to spread her legs he cut her thighs repeatedly (all cuts were superficial and within the reach of the victim). He also slashed at her breasts. As she gave this account, she showed her coworker the injuries. She also had reported that the assailant succeeded in having vaginal sexual intercourse with her.

A formal complaint was made to Internal Affairs, which initiated a full investigation and the officer in question was suspended from duty. After the initial disclosure to the coworker, Roberta became markedly uncooperative and resistant to investigative efforts. She refused to submit material evidence and refused the polygraph. Eventually she did turn in her dress which was liberally stained with semen.

The investigating police officer sought consultation regarding the possibility of this being a false rape allegation for two reasons. First, the alleged assailant cooperated fully with the investigating officer, refused the opportunity to retain an attorney, and readily agreed to forensic evaluation and a polygraph examination (which he passed). Second, concurrent to this complaint was a highly publicized case involving another police officer who was convicted of raping a woman he stopped for a motor violation. Consultation supported the investigating officer's suspicions and suggestions for proactive interviewing techniques were made.

Roberta, on reinterview, admitted to having made a false allegation. She admitted to repeated and consensual sexual intercourse with a male, previously unknown to her, whom she had picked up at a disco. When she awoke the next morning she found she had overslept, was late for work, and felt "dirty." Consequently, she inflicted the mutilating injuries and fabricated her story. The falsely accused officer had shown considerable interest in Roberta at work and was therefore believed to be a viable suspect. While no charges were brought against Roberta, she was referred for counseling and remained in therapy for an extensive period of time.

A second example of a sex-stress case involves a situation where a parent suspects sex has occurred, perceives some danger to the daughter's reputation, and assumes responsibility in the matter. Another similar scenario involves the teenager reporting the sex to the parent as rape in order to receive pregnancy prevention advice. The following is such a case where the circumstances and perpetrator were falsely reported, but the act was true.

CASE NO. 2

Samantha was a pretty 15-year-old girl who arrived home well past her curfew on a Friday night. She tearfully and reluctantly told her parents that she had gone to the skating rink with her friends and at closing time, she and her friends left the building with the intention of walking home. According to Samantha, a young man who worked at the rink offered to drive her home. She accepted his offer and went willingly with him to his car and, instead of taking her home, he drove to a deserted area and forced her to have intercourse with him. The parents immediately contacted the police who took a statement and transported Samantha and her parents to the regional rape crisis center where a nurse was summoned. She completed the necessary examination and evidence collection without incident.

The case was evaluated as being a possible sex-stress situation and a female supervising officer conducted a second interview. Samantha retracted her allegation, stating that she had consensual sex with her boyfriend and was consequently late arriving home. Because of her fear of punishment, she created the fictional scenario.

As mentioned, some sex-stress cases involve a monetary situation. It is not uncommon for sex workers to encounter a situation in which the customer does not live up to the agreed verbal contract. The client may not pay for services obtained or he may even rob the woman. In such cases, it is not uncommon for prostitutes to allege rape and turn to the police, who are rightfully expected to conduct a professional investigation and see that the victim is taken to the hospital for medical attention.

FALSE RAPE ALLEGATION

In false rape allegations, *generally* all three components of the allegation are false (i.e., the act, the perpetrator, and the circumstances). These are situations where the pseudovictim is motivated to deceive by exaggerated psychological needs for attention, to avoid unwanted consequences, to cover up for inappropriate behavior, or for financial motives. The pseudovictim has a conscious understanding that the complaint is false. The following case represents a false allegation of rape motivated by a desire to avoid unwanted circumstances.

CASE NO. 3

Melissa, a 17-year-old student, reported that she had "skipped" an entire day of classes with some fellow students. The group went to an abandoned house where they danced and consumed beer. Walking home, she sat down on a park bench to rest and a large male came up behind her, held a knife to her throat and took her into nearby woods. She began to struggle and he superficially cut (scratched) her three times on either side of her neck. He forced her to undress and vaginally raped her twice, failing to ejaculate on both occasions.

Following the second rape, he allegedly cut the words "Mike's Girl" into her abdomen. The rapist then forced her to consume a large quantity of vodka, explaining that no one would believe the story of a drunk.

No supporting medical or trace evidence of the rape was present and the words cut into her abdomen had been overwritten. Experienced detectives interviewed Melissa and she admitted that she had contrived the story to avoid punishment for skipping school. She explained that she had cut the words into her stomach while looking in a mirror.

The motive of financial gain was responsible for the false allegations presented in Case nos. 5 and 6.

CASE NO. 4

Dorina, a single mother who lived in public housing, brought her two young girls to the rape crisis center for evaluation following allegations of child molestation. No evidence to support the allegation was found in either child. The child advocate informed her that under provisions of "victim's compensation," victims of violent crime may apply to the state for compensation in amounts up to $3,000. The only requirement is that a police report be filed. Dorina filed a police report and was awarded $2,000 for each child.

Approximately 6 months later, and after making a police report, Dorina again appeared at the center stating that two unknown males had broken into her home, raped her, and left. She was unable to provide a useful description and no injury or evidence was present. She was again advised of the availability of victim's compensation and she made application and was compensated in the amount of $3,000.

Eighteen months later Dorina once again reported a rape to the police. She was transported to the rape crisis center where she was again evaluated. As before, she was unable to adequately describe her assailant and again neither trauma nor evidence was found. Under the provisions of the victim's city compensation program, compensation can only be awarded one time per individual. Several months after the alleged second assault against herself, Dorina brought suit against the city public housing authority, seeking punitive damages in the amount of $150,000. Her claim was that both criminal assaults occurred because of a faulty lock on the door to her public housing and she claimed that she made a formal report requesting appropriate repair of the lock. No record of such a report was ever found and it was determined that all of the allegations made by Dorina had been false and were financially motivated.

CASE NO. 5

Micaela, a teenage single mother, was brought to the rape crisis center by a police officer. She claimed to have been abducted from the street in her neighborhood by an unknown assailant who dragged her into a vacant house and raped her vaginally. It was noted that during her medical examination, she mentioned several times that her food stamps had been stolen from her by the assailant. She seemed more concerned about the missing food stamps than about the rape and was unable to give a meaningful description of the assailant. Although she had reported the alleged crime promptly, there was no medical, physical, or trace evidence to support her allegation.

While Micaela was dressing, the nurse asked the police officer if he knew about the theft of the food stamps and he said that that had been her primary concern since she first had made the complaint. He went on to say that there was a lively black-market in the exchange of food stamps for drugs. The officer explained that lost or stolen public subsidies, such as food stamps, can only be replaced if a police report is made. After several attempts to complete the investigation, the police were of the opinion that it was a false allegation made for the purpose of obtaining additional food stamps.

An exaggerated psychological need for attention was the underlying motive for the false allegation in the following case.

CASE NO. 6

A 31-year-old woman reported that she had been abducted from a mall parking lot by three Hispanic males in a battered pick-up truck. One of the men explained in broken English that they were going to beat her husband for having an affair with his wife. However, they were having trouble finding him and they wanted her help.

Over a period of hours, she intentionally misled the men as to the whereabouts of her husband and eventually they became frustrated and decided to rape her to teach her husband a lesson. The woman reported that her clothes were ripped off her body and each of the men raped her. All withdrew before ejaculating so as to leave no DNA evidence. They then dropped her off and warned her not to report the crime.

There was a lack of medical, trace, or physical evidence to support the allegation of rape and police investigators learned that the "victim's" marriage was experiencing difficulty. The couple had not engaged in sexual relations during the past year and the husband had recently informed his wife of his intent to leave her for another woman. The complainant admitted making up the story so that her husband would realize that she was sexually attractive to other men and that she had "risked her life to protect him."

DELUSIONAL RAPE ALLEGATION

In delusional rape allegations, all three components of an allegation (the act, the offender, and the circumstances) are false. In these situations, the complainant is psychotic and/or delusional. In some cases, this pseudovictim may make several complaints, and not be consciously aware of making multiple complaints because the delusion is a continuous part of her thinking. In speaking with the person, it may become obvious that she is suffering a major mental illness. Even so, it is important to carefully evaluate the complaint because there may be a current or past abuse situation that the person is trying to communicate, as in the following case.

CASE NO. 7

Ann, a 37-year-old homeless woman, was admitted to a large emergency department for the sixth time in a 3-month period. In each instance, she reported she had been sexually assaulted. She had dirt and leaves in her vagina, superficial cuts and scratches on her inner thighs and a vague description of the man who she alleged had raped her. She further advised that the man had been stalking her for a period of time. While waiting to be seen by the nurse, Ann was angry and volatile with severe mood shifts and little control over her anger. When the nurse examiner came into the room, Ann cried and reached for her hand saying she just wanted to talk to someone who understood and cared.

The nurse examiner's assessment was that Ann's reports of rape were a cry for help for childhood sexual abuse and the goal became to get Ann into counseling where, over time, her issues could be discussed (Ledray, 1994).

WHO MAKES A FALSE ALLEGATION?

Although empirical research is limited, there are several studies that have attempted to determine the frequency of false rape allegations and deserve further consideration. Lisak and colleagues (2010) reported over a 10-year period that 5.9% of reported sexual assaults were found to be false. Taken with other findings in the literature, they argue that more accurate estimates of prevalence of false allegations may lie somewhere between 2% and 10%. Other researchers have suggested that false allegations of rape are lower (Kelly, 2010) or are at least consistent with rates of false allegations of other crimes (Rumney, 2006). The disparities between estimates of prevalence have been well documented and, as mentioned previously, can be attributed to wide ranging definitional criteria (Saunders, 2012). Receiving considerably less attention from researchers have been the demographic characteristics that are most commonly associated with persons making false allegations of rape. Acknowledging this scarcity, Hazelwood and Napier (2004) reported on 20 active and retired federal, state, and city law enforcement officers from different regions of the United States (Washington, DC, California, Texas, Nebraska, Virginia, Florida, Iowa, and Washington) and two provinces in Canada who were telephonically surveyed in a structured manner as to their anecdotal experience with staged crimes (false allegation of rape is one type). Each of these officers had served as a crime analyst ("profiler") within his or her department and consequently was much more experienced with violent crime than the average investigator. It is to be noted that this survey was not intended to provide detailed predictive analysis, but to report investigative perceptions. The officers were asked to approximate the number of violent crimes they had been involved with and the number of fatal and nonfatal staged crimes they had encountered over the years. These officers had 560 years of cumulative law enforcement experience and an estimated 33,360 consultations on violent crimes. Of that number, they estimated that 903 had been staged; of the 903 staged crimes, 411 dealt with death scenes and 492 with nonfatal false allegations of sexual assault.

The officers reported that, in their experience, the person typically making the false allegation was female (100%); Caucasian (100%); 15–20 years of age (10%), 31–45 years of age (25%), or 21–30 years of age (65%).

While it is not intended that this information be generalized to the entire population, the findings that the person most often making a false allegation of rape is Caucasian, female, and between 21 and 30 years of age is consistent with the authors' experience and with other studies that have found similar results (see McNamara, McDonald, & Lawrence, 2012). However, it is important to note that there are no educational, occupational, or intellectual boundaries in this arena. The authors are aware of false complaints being lodged by nurses, psychologists, schoolteachers, college students, members of the criminal justice system, and female dancers. Investigators would be wise to disregard any criteria presented to them.

MOTIVES FOR FALSE RAPE ALLEGATIONS

Those who make false allegations may have legitimate problems worthy of attention in their own right. Yet if their false allegations are accepted at face value, rather than as symptoms of psychological needs, the legitimate problems may go untreated and can result in future difficulties. As has been stated, a false allegation, especially when it is based on malice, can result in a grievous injustice. Only by understanding those making false allegations can investigators hope to provide needed assistance for them and protection for everyone else involved.

ATTENTION/SYMPATHY

Persons making false complaints to elicit attention and/or sympathy usually have overwhelming feelings of inadequacy. They desperately *need* attention, usually in the form of concern and support. In their suffering, a claim of rape may seem a likely method to force a favorable response from friends and relatives as well as the authorities. They may have tried lesser methods of getting attention (e.g., pretending to be ill), which failed. Most important is how the complaining person reacts to the concern and support resulting from the allegation. In typical rape situations, even the most compassionate and supportive response cannot fully alleviate the horror experienced by the victims. However, for individuals in need of attention, this solicitude may very well fill their needs.

ANGER/REVENGE

In such cases, the complainant is or was emotionally involved with the person she names as the perpetrator and is motivated by a desire to "get even" for real or imagined wrongs. A typical revenge case may involve retaliation as a responding behavior to rejection. Because the subject is identified, this type of false allegation poses the greatest danger of a miscarriage of justice. In the authors' experience, it is not uncommon for the pseudovictim to withdraw or modify the complaint after the investigation is initiated.

ALIBI

In such situations, the pseudovictim alleges a sexual assault to avoid unwanted consequences (e.g., a teenage girl may allege rape if she stays out overnight without parental permission) or to cover up for inappropriate behavior (e.g., infidelity). As an example, a married woman involved in a sexual affair might allege that she was raped after returning home extremely late in a disheveled state.

FALSE ALLEGATIONS AND THE ADAPTATION CONTINUUM

The creation of a factitious crime to avoid personal responsibility for some act or failure obviously represents an extreme departure from the way mature people normally deal with their problems. The extent to which false claims capitalize on actual events is unknown. However, there appears to be a rough continuum of false reports.

Such claims may involve a slightly distorted report of an actual event to cases in which props (e.g., threatening letters or messages written in the "victim's" blood) were used. In its most extreme manifestation, the report can include bizarre scenarios supported by self-inflicted injuries or even self-mutilation and, while such cases are rare and occur at the far end of the continuum, it is incumbent that medical and mental health professionals, interveners, and criminal investigators understand that they may encounter such situations.

While the pathology involved in self-mutilation to support the false claim of rape is rare, factitious claims of illness or injury on a much lower level are well-recognized phenomena in the medical literature.

MUNCHAUSEN SYNDROME

Severe cases of self-inflicted injuries or illnesses in which medical attention is sought have been termed Munchausen syndrome (Asher, 1951). The name derives from the central figure in a book of tall tales and fabulous adventures who was named after Hieronymous Karl Friederich Freiherr von Munchausen, a retired soldier known for his generosity and graphic conversations that took the form of "serious narration of palpable absurdities." The key to understanding Munchausen syndrome is that the patient is trying to use hospitals and clinicians in the service of pathologic psychological needs under the guise of seeking medical treatment for an ostensibly legitimate illness.

Munchausen syndrome is based on a preoccupation with manipulation. These patients appear to be compulsively driven to make their complaints. As Gawn and Kauffmann (1955) noted, "While he is aware he is acting an illness, he cannot stop the act." Therefore, reports may capitalize on circumstances and occur only occasionally, or they may be a well-developed means of adapting and part of an extensive history. The degree to which Munchausen syndrome patients defend their claims is in direct proportion to their need to be seen as victims. Dramatic, extreme cases are not likely to confess to the hoax, and those who present such cases are prone to become enraged at the suggestion that their illnesses are anything but genuine (Nadelson, 1979; Pandratz, 1981).

MENTAL STATES

In much the same way that Munchausen syndrome patients manipulate hospitals and doctors, a fraudulent claim of rape might be interpreted as a form of manipulation directed at the criminal justice system. This kind of manipulation is conceptually similar to other kinds of behavior (i.e., malingering and self-mutilation) that are well documented as medically achieved coping mechanisms (Ford, 1973). In Munchausen syndrome patients there is also a continuum, ranging from exaggerated claims of infirmity to actual self-induced illness (Grinker, 1961). At the extreme end of this continuum, life-threatening injuries are masqueraded as being legitimately contracted

(Carney, 1980; Carney & Brown, 1983). Even child abuse, disguised as natural illness, is suspected of being an under-recognized means of gaining attention (Vaisrub, 1978; Hodge, Schwartz, Sargent, Bodurtha, & Starr, 1982; Meadow, 1982; Waller, 1983).

Although police officers and investigators are used to seeing people who have been harmed or injured by others, they are less accustomed to seeing those who have harmed themselves. Most such instances involve a suicide or attempted suicide. Since self-inflicted injuries used to support a claim of rape or sexual assault are infrequently seen, it is logical for police to initially accept them at face value. Where self-inflicted injuries are recognized as such and are serious or appear to be very painful, it is understandable that police officers may look upon the "victim" as being psychotic. This is seldom the case. Nevertheless, these individuals are psychiatrically impaired and should be assisted in obtaining professional help. The following case illustrates this phenomenon.

CASE NO. 8

A 25-year-old housewife reported receiving obscene phone calls and threatening letters that were made out of words cut from magazines and newspapers and pasted on a sheet of blank paper. A short time later, she alleged being raped in her apartment by an unidentified intruder who threatened to return and kill her if she reported the rape to police. She had numerous bruises on her face, a bite mark on her left breast, and rope burns on her wrists. During a polygraph examination, she admitted to fabricating the entire series of events. To support her fabricated story, she had run face first into a support post in her basement to inflict the bruises, had bitten her own breast, and had inflicted the rope burns. She told the investigators that her husband did not understand her or pay attention to her anymore and she was testing his love for her.

As one proceeds along the continuum, the amount of violence the pseudovictim claims was used against her can reach fantastic levels and the presenting dynamics of the case can become increasingly extraordinary.

CASE NO. 9

A 31-year-old woman alleged that she had been captured by a man as she entered her car in a parking lot. The man ordered her to undress and forced her to perform fellatio. After he ejaculated, he had her spit the fluids into a plastic bag which he later took with him. He then tied her to her steering wheel, gagged her, and inflicted more than 50 superficial cuts on her body, none of which impacted a sensitive area of her body. The woman admitted that it was a false allegation and asked the investigator for help. He agreed to help her find mental health care. Unfortunately, she committed suicide before being treated. Investigation resulted in a suspicion that the woman suffered borderline personality disorder, a few features of which are suicidal gestures, threats, and mutilating behavior.

Keep in mind, however, that legitimate rapes may also incorporate varying levels of misperception; because of this, every aspect must be scrutinized. Support and assistance for the pseudovictim, when appropriate, can only be given by a careful and objective examination of the information, physical and trace evidence, and victimology. The woman in Case no. 10 was in obvious need of professional help and the officer had taken steps to arrange such help. The self-esteem of the woman in Case no. 9 had been eroded by her husband's inattention. By claiming to be the recipient of obscene phone calls and letters, and by claiming to have been raped, she was effectively making a statement of her perception of worth, both as a person and as a sexually desirable partner. Her willingness to engage in self-injurious behavior to support her false claim underscores the seriousness of her emotional problems.

FACTITIOUS DISORDERS AND MALINGERING

To be considered by investigators is the possibility of factitious disorders. Such disorders involve the feigning, production, or exaggeration of physical and/or psychological symptoms that facilitate the individual's objective of assuming the sick role (Feldman, Ford, & Stone, 1994). Such persons do not seek recognizable external incentives of evading court proceedings or obtaining drugs, as in malingering, but instead assume the "patient" role (APA, 2000). Feldman and colleagues discuss the cases of four women who claimed to have been the victims of rape; the allegations were later proven to be false. They suggest factitious rape may be prompted by a search for nurturance; by dissociation, leading the pseudovictim to believe that trauma earlier in life is ongoing; by a need to be rescued from real, current abuse; and by projections of anger onto specific male targets. Although dramatic, factitious rape is rare, argue the psychiatrists; the thorough investigations of rape claims are advocated even when patients have known histories of deceptive behavior.

FACTORS CONSISTENT WITH FALSE ALLEGATIONS

In the authors' experience, the following features have been found to be consistent with a false allegation. It is imperative that the reader recognize that some of these features will also be found in legitimate allegations of a sexual assault. Consequently, the question often asked is, "When is a false allegation indicated?" The appropriate response is, "Only when your doubts *overwhelm* the evidence supporting the complaint should you begin to consider the possibility of a false allegation."

Initial Complaint

The manner in which a rape allegation comes to the attention of law enforcement authorities is significant. As is common in legitimate complaints, there are frequently delays in making a report and the reports are often made to someone other than the police.

When initially being interviewed, the pseudovictim may attempt to direct the discussion to "safe" areas. Safe areas are characterized by references to force, resistance, injuries, or other terms illustrative of harm whereas "unsafe" areas deal with facts about the crime and/or the offender. In support of this observation, Marshall and Alison (2006) found that false claimants, when reporting their alleged victimization, tended to overemphasize the significance of violent and demeaning behavior and were less likely to report psuedointimate behavior. For example, when asked to describe the assailant (an unsafe area), the pseudovictim may respond, "He was huge and he kept hitting me [force] and I was kicking and screaming [resistance] and look what he did to me [injuries]." The initial report may be either extremely vague or unnecessarily detailed, as in the following case.

CASE NO. 10

One of the authors (Hazelwood) traveled to England to testify in a serial rape case. The series consisted of 17 rapes and the consulting author was asked to review the statements written by the victims. In 16 cases, the victim's statement averaged five to nine pages in length. However, the statement of the 17th victim was 28 pages long.

The rape occurred at 8 p.m., but the statement began with the victim awakening at 6 a.m. By the end of page 12, the "victim" had fixed breakfast, and bagged lunches for her husband and two children, showered and dressed, shared morning tea with a neighbor and watched television. Over the next 8 pages, the woman described cleaning house, having afternoon tea and biscuits, helping her children with their homework, fixing and eating dinner.

In pages 21–26 she described how her husband had stomach illness and asked her to take the family dog for its nightly walk in the park, how she dressed in preparation for the walk in the rain, and strolling through the darkened park as Fido reluctantly looked for a suitable place to do his business. In the last two pages, she wrote of being leapt upon by a "huge swarthy stranger" who knocked her to the ground, ripped her slacks off, tore her knickers from her body, penetrated (no ejaculation), jumped up, and ran away.

Hazelwood and his partner, Judd Ray, met with the investigators and prosecutors on the next day and they were informed that the subject had pleaded guilty to 16 rapes, but stated, "I damn well didn't do the other one." The woman in question later recanted her complaint. The reason that she reported a rape: She was mad at her husband for making her take the dog for its walk in the rain.

Assailants

Typically, pseudovictims report a large and overpowering offender (see Case no. 10) or multiple offenders, such as in the Tawana Brawley or Duke University lacrosse team cases. In stranger-to-stranger false allegations, the offender may be described as a "friend of an unrecalled friend" (e.g., "I believe I met him at a pool party this summer, but I have been to seven or eight pool parties this year"). Interestingly, when describing the style of attacker, pseudovictims do not describe a power reassurance rapist (see Chapter 7).

Sexual Assault

The pseudovictim typically reports only those sexual acts in which she normally engages. For example, a woman who does not engage in anal sex is unlikely to report anal rape.

Evidence

Law enforcement correctly places a premium on the evidence supporting an allegation of rape because it often provides the information necessary for prosecution of a case. An absence of the evidence usually associated with rape is sometimes as revealing in identifying a false allegation, as is its presence in establishing that a rape occurred:

- While the presence or absence of seminal fluids should never be the determining factor in a rape case, ejaculation is most often absent in false allegations.
- The reported crime scene does not support the "victim's" report (e.g., ground cover is not disturbed in wooded area; no signs of a struggle in residence).
- Damage to clothing is inconsistent with location of injuries.
- Confirming forensic reports are absent (e.g., lack of foreign pubic hairs).

Physical evidence can sometimes be ambiguous (i.e., in those cases when determination of consent is complex). In such cases, corroborating evidence is often considered crucial when intercourse has occurred.

Injuries

First, it must be understood that the presence of injuries in false claims is not to be expected. However, when present, the nature of the individual's injuries can provide a great deal of information about what did or did not happen. Men or women who make false rape allegations and support the claim with injuries tend to present a surprisingly uniform pattern of wounds and behavior:

- Pseudovictims are seemingly indifferent to their injuries.
- Injuries were made with fingernails or instruments commonly used by the "victim" (e.g., fingernail file, scissors).

- Injuries do not impact sensitive areas of the body (e.g., nipples, vaginal lips, scrotum).
- The "victim" reports that the injuries occurred while attempting to defend herself, yet the location of the injuries is inconsistent with defense wounds.
- When sharp or pointed weapons are used, the resulting wounds are cuts and not stabs.
- When cuts are inflicted, there may be "hesitation" wounding present.

The areas of the body that are attacked are also of investigative interest. Those portions of the body not normally covered by clothing (i.e., wrists, hands, neck, face) are impacted by superficial injuries, whereas those areas of the body normally covered by clothing (i.e., chest, abdominal region) are likely to be impacted by more serious injuries.

The investigator may occasionally encounter "sensational" injuries (i.e., designed to capture the imagination of the investigator or medical authorities) as in the following case.

CASE NO. 11

A single woman returned home late one evening and reported that upon entering her residence, she was struck in the face, dragged to her bedroom and forced to undress. She alleged that the assailant raped her repeatedly and continued to slap her in the face as he verbally assaulted her with demeaning and profane slang. He remained throughout the night and after raping her a final time the next morning, he forced her outside and into the woods surrounding her home. He then inserted a tree branch into her vagina so deeply that it had to be surgically removed.

Personality and Lifestyle Considerations

In false rape allegations, extensive and important victimology is often available. In general, such information suggests that the pseudovictim has experienced numerous personal problems and that her ability to cope is seriously impaired. For example, the investigator may find that the rape follows one or more escalating incidents revealing difficulties in her relationships. Obtaining answers to the following questions will be useful in arriving at an objective opinion as to the legitimacy of the complaint:

- Does the person have a history of mental or emotional problems (particularly referencing self-injurious behavior, with hysterical or borderline features)?
- Has she previously reported assault or rape with similar circumstances?
- Did her allegation follow a similar recently publicized crime (suggesting modeling, in which the similarity to the publicized crime offers credibility)?
- Does the complainant have an extensive record of medical care for dramatic illnesses or injuries (see Munchausen syndrome)?
- Do friends or associates report postassaultive behavior of the complainant that is inconsistent with her allegation?
- Did she recently have any negative experiences that could create stress (e.g., breakup of a relationship, failing grades) or any positive experiences that could create stress (e.g., impending graduation, job promotion)?

Other

Over the years, criminal investigators, medical and mental health professionals, and rape crisis counselors have advised the authors of behaviors they have come to associate with false allegations of sexual assault. These behaviors are set forth here, but again, it is to be noted that the presence of such behaviors does not "prove" that an allegation is false:

- Displaying an *abnormal* amount of dissatisfaction with the efforts of the investigator or helping professional;
- Continual recall of additional information such as, "Oh, did I tell you that I was receiving obscene phone calls 2 months ago?" or "Are you interested in an attempted break-in of my apartment a month before the attack?";
- Lack of interest when police develop a suspect;
- Symmetrical injuries (e.g., three "cuts" each on the thighs);
- Claiming that the right questions are not being asked of her;
- Old clothes worn when clothing is ripped or torn; and/or
- Asking for clothing to be returned.

INVESTIGATORY CONSIDERATIONS

SECOND OPINION

When a false claim of rape is suspected and there are serious questions concerning the truth of the report, a critical issue arises: A confrontation has to take place and if the doubts are incorrect, the victim's trauma may be greatly compounded. Such a confrontation almost always destroys any relationship that may have developed between the victim and the confronting interviewer. One method of handling this challenge to the complainant's credibility without sacrificing the primary investigator's rapport with the individual is to introduce a second party who can act as a buffer. The primary investigator needs to maintain a nonjudgmental, supportive, and sympathetic relationship with her and it is counterproductive for him or her to voice any doubts as to the veracity of her report.

It is recommended that unresolved inconsistencies, conflicts, or the lack of supporting data be pointed out by a supervisor (or a coworker playing the role of a supervisor), thereby maintaining the vital relationship between the complainant and the primary investigator. The second investigator should conduct an additional and confrontational interview of the individual.

The style of confrontation should be empathetic and supportive since false allegations are usually attempts to protect self-esteem and harsh challenges may increase the individual's defensiveness. It is often effective to present doubts in such a way that it is clear those doubts are based upon information provided by the individual herself (e.g., "You reported that you were raped in the woods over a 3-h period and we examined your clothes carefully, but could not find any evidence of grass, twigs, leaves, or stains on them"). This decreases interpersonal conflict while conveying the impression that investigators have been thorough and objective. It also allows for adjusting investigative hypotheses and gives the person an opportunity to provide additional information without having to place herself in a psychologically threatening position.

The reaction of factitious victims to this approach varies. At the low end of the adaptive continuum, there is usually an emotional confession, mixed with despair and relief. The amount of energy required to maintain her story is exhausting and this becomes a time for her to cooperate and to seek solace. Exaggerators and malingerers often provide great detail as to how and why they masqueraded as a rape victim. For those who adhere to their statements in the face of overwhelming contradictory evidence, it may be advantageous to request they take a polygraph examination.

At the extreme end of the adaptation continuum, the complainant's distortions are internalized. For her own well-being, she needs to believe what she is saying because she is unconsciously terrified of losing control. Consequently, no matter how the confrontation is handled, her denial is intensified. Predictably, she reacts with outrage. If the family is advised of the findings, they may be of great assistance in her eventual recovery. Unfortunately, because of the disordered lives of pseudovictims, they are often estranged from their families.

SUMMARY

False allegation is a term frequently used and heard in discussions of interpersonal crime. Though simple on the surface, this concept becomes vague and complex under scrutiny. This chapter explored the concept of false allegation in the context of rape, which usually occurs in isolated places where there is no one to support or refute an individual's claims.

False allegations of rape sometimes are not recognized by investigators and are infrequently addressed in the literature. The reason for this is obvious; these are acts that are designed to appear plausible. The key to understanding fabricated complaints of rape lies in determining how a false allegation helps the complainant manipulate, control, or mentally recoup her self-esteem. Therefore, it is the context in which the allegation occurs that provides the framework for understanding the dynamics of the problem.

A final word of caution: Even those individuals who are emotionally prone to make a false allegation can be raped. Basic principles of police professionalism require that officers who investigate rape remain objective and compassionate. If they do not, the veracity of the allegation may never be known and the victim—for she is a victim in either case—may never receive the help and support she needs.

ACKNOWLEDGMENTS

The authors thank the following for contributing case examples: Margaret Aiken; Eddie Grant; David Muram, M.D.; Robin Jones; Patricia Speck; and Nola Mendenhall.

REFERENCES

American Psychiatric Association (APA). 2000. *Diagnostic and statistical manual*, 4th ed., text rev., Washington, DC: American Psychiatric Press.

Asher, R. 1951. Munchausen syndrome. *Lancet*, 34: 339–341.

Benedek, E., and Schetky, D. 1984, October. Allegations of sexual abuse in child custody cases. Paper presented at the annual meeting of the American Academy of Psychiatry and the Law, Nassau, Bahamas.

Byrne, C. A., Hyman, I. A., and Scott, K. L. 2001. Comparisons of memories for traumatic events and other experiences. *Applied Cognitive Psychology*, 15: S119–S133.

Carney, M. W. P. 1980. Artifactual illnesses to attract medical attention. *British Journal of Psychiatry*, 136: 542–547.

Carney, M. W. P., and Brown, J. P. 1983. Clinical features and motives among 42 artifactual illness patients. *British Journal of Psychology*, 56: 57–66.

Carretta, C., and Burgess, A. W. 2013. Symptom responses to a continuum of sexual trauma. *Violence and Victims*, 28(2): 248–258.

Feldman, M. D., Ford, C. V., and Stone, T. 1994. Deceiving others/deceiving oneself: Four cases. *Southern Medical Journal*, 87(7): 736–738.

Ford, C. V. 1973. The Munchausen syndrome: A report of four new cases and a review of psychodynamic considerations. *Psychiatric Medicine*, 4(1): 31–45.

Gawn, R. A., and Kauffmann, E. A. 1955. Munchausen syndrome. *British Medical Journal*, 2: 1068.

Green, A. 1986. True and false allegations of sexual abuse in child custody disputes. *Journal of the American Academy of Child Psychiatry*, 25(4): 449–456.

Grinker, R. R. 1961. Imposture as a form of mastery. *Archives of General Psychiatry*, 5: 53–56.

Gunby, C., Carline, A., and Beynon, C. 2012. Regretting it after? Focus group perspectives on alcohol consumption, nonconsensual sex and false allegations. *Social & Legal Studies*, 22(1): 87–106.

Hazelwood, R. R., and Napier, M. R. 2004. Crime scene staging and its detection. *International Journal of Offender Therapy and Comparative Criminology*, 48(6): 744–759.

Hodge, D., Schwartz, W., Sargent, J., Bodurtha, J., and Starr, S. 1982. The bacteriologically battered body: Another case of Munchausen by proxy. *Annals of Emergency Medicine*, 4: 205–207.

Hunt, L., and Bull, R. 2012. Differentiating genuine and false rape allegations: A model to aid rape investigations. *Psychiatry, Psychology and Law*, 19(5): 682–691.

Katz, S., and Mazur, M. 1979. *Understanding the rape victim*. New York: John Wiley & Sons.

Kelly, L. 2010. The (in)credible words of women: False allegations in European rape research. *Violence Against Women*, 16(12): 1345–1355.

Kilpatrick, D. G., Best, C. L., and Veronen, L. J. 1985. Factors predicting psychological distress among rape victims. In Charles Figley (Ed.), *Post-traumatic therapy and victims of violence*, 113–141. New York: Brunnmer/Mazel.

Kruttschnitt, C., Kalsbeek, W. D., and House, C. S. 2014. Estimating the Incidence of Rape and Sexual Assault. Committee on National Statistics, Division of Behavioral and Social Sciences and Education. Washington, DC: The National Academies Press.

LeDoux, J., and Hazelwood, R. R. 1983. Police attitudes and beliefs toward rape. *Journal of Police Science and Administration*, 13(3): 77–89.

Ledray, L. E. 1994. Rape or self-injury? *Journal of Emergency Nursing*, 20(2): 88–90.

Lefer, H. 1992. Women and the truth: Who says we're lying? *Elle*, 6: 194–200.

Lisak, D., Gardinier, L., Nicksa, S. C., and Cote, A. M. 2010. False allegations of sexual assault: An analysis of ten years of reported cases. *Violence Against Women*, 16(12): 1318–1334.

Marshall, B. C., and Alison, L. J. 2006. Structural behavioural analysis as a basis for discriminating between genuine and simulated rape allegations. *Journal of Investigative Psychology and Offender Profiling*, 3(1): 21–34.

McDowell, C. 1990. False allegations and fuzzy data: A new look at crime analysis. *Police Chief*, 57(November): 44–45.

McDowell, C., and Hibler, N. 1987. False allegations. In *Practical aspects of rape investigation: A multidisciplinary approach*, ed. R. R. Hazelwood and A. W. Burgess, 275–299. New York: Elsevier.

McNamara, J. J., McDonald, S., and Lawrence, J. M. 2012. Characteristics of false allegation adult crimes. *Journal of Forensic Sciences*, 57(3): 643–646.

Meadow, R. 1982. Munchausen syndrome by proxy. *Archives of Diseases of Childhood*, 57: 92–98.

Nadelson, T. 1979. The Munchausen spectrum: Borderline character features. *General Hospital Psychiatry*, 1(1): 11–17.

O'Neal, E. N., Spohn, C., Tellis, K., and White, C. 2014. The truth behind the lies: The complex motivations for false allegations of sexual assault. *Women & Criminal Justice*, 24(4): 324–340.

Page, A. D. 2007. Behind the blue line: Investigating police officers' attitudes toward rape. *Journal of Police and Criminal Psychology*, 22(1): 22–32.

Pandratz, L. 1981. A review of the Munchausen syndrome. *Clinical Psychology Review*, 1: 63–78.

Riger, S., and Gordon, M. T. 1988. The impact of crime on urban women. In *Rape and sexual assault II*, ed. A. W. Burgess. New York: Garland.

Rosenfeld, A., Nadelson, C., and Krieger, M. 1979. Fantasy and reality in patient's reports of incest. *Journal of Clinical Psychiatry*, 14: 159–164.

Rumney, P. 2006. False allegations of rape. *Cambridge Law Journal*, 65(1): 128–158.

Saunders, C. L. 2012. The truth, the half-truth, and nothing like the truth: Reconceptualizing false allegations of rape. *British Journal of Criminology*, 52(6): 1152–1171.

Vaisrub, S. 1978. Baron Munchausen and the abused child. *Journal of the American Medical Association*, 239(8): 752.

Waller, D. A. 1983. Obstacles to the treatment of Munchausen by proxy syndrome. *Journal of the American Academy of Child Psychiatry*, 22(1): 80–85.

Wolitzky-Taylor, K. B., Resnick, H. S., McCauley, J. L., Amstadter, A. B., Kilpatrick, D. G., and Ruggiero, K. J. 2011. Is reporting of rape on the rise? A comparison of women with reported versus unreported rape experiences in the National Women's Study-Replication. *Journal of Interpersonal Violence*, 26: 807–832.

12 Interrogation and False Confessions in Rape Cases

Richard A. Leo

CONTENTS

Introduction..177
Pre-Interrogation Investigation 178
The Police Interrogation 179
    Step 1: Shifting the Suspect from Confident to Hopeless...179
    Step 2: Offering the Suspect Inducements to Confess...180
Risk Factors for False Confession 180
    Situational Risk Factors 180
    Individual Risk Factors 181
The Problem of Contamination...182
The Different Types of False Confession..182
    Voluntary False Confessions 182
    Compliant False Confession (Stress-Compliant and Coerced-Compliant)............................182
    Persuaded False Confessions (Coerced-Persuaded and Noncoerced-Persuaded)...................183
The Consequences of False Confessions 183
Conclusion 184
References..184

INTRODUCTION

At the end of 2015, the National Registry of Exonerations at the University of Michigan had logged 1705 post-conviction DNA and non-DNA exonerations since 1989 (National Registry of Exonerations, 2015). Approximately 13% ($N = 217$) of these wrongful convictions were due to false confessions, and virtually all of these have occurred in either homicide or rape cases. Many more false confessions occur in cases that do not go to trial or result in acquittal (Gould, Carrano, Leo, & Hail-Jares, 2014; Drizin & Leo, 2004), and most false confessions are simply never discovered (Leo, 2008). In a recent survey, police investigators in America estimated that 5% of the suspects they interrogated falsely confessed (Kassin et al., 2007). Although researchers have documented hundreds of proven false confessions in recent decades, these cases are universally believed to be the tip of a much larger problem (Kassin et al., 2010).

Researchers and practitioners alike have long wondered why the innocent might confess to serious crimes, especially ones that carry lengthy prison sentences or life imprisonment (Leo, 2008). For more than a century—but especially in the last three decades—social science researchers have undertaken various types of empirical studies (field, observational, laboratory, documentary) to advance scientific knowledge about how interrogation procedures influence suspects' perceptions, overcome a suspect's denials, and elicit the decision to confess (Kassin et al., 2010). Although there now exists a substantial empirical body of research explaining why the innocent sometimes falsely confess when interrogated, this phenomenon remains poorly understood and counterintuitive, as numerous recent survey studies have shown (Chojnacki, Cicchini, & White, 2008; Henkel, Coffman, & Dailey, 2008; Leo & Liu, 2009; Costanzo, Shaked-Schroer, & Vinson, 2010; Blandon-Gitlin, Sperry, & Leo, 2011).

Most people continue to believe in what the author calls the *Myth of Psychological Interrogation*—that an innocent person will not falsely confess unless he is physically tortured or mentally ill (Leo, 2001). However, confessions by the innocent continue to occur with troubling frequency (Leo, 2008), and most documented ones are from cognitively and intellectually normal individuals (Leo & Ofshe, 1998; Drizin & Leo, 2004). False confessions still lead to erroneous convictions of the innocent (National Registry of Exonerations, 2015), and thus continue to pose a serious problem for the American criminal justice system in general and law enforcement in particular (Garrett, 2011).

The central issue for researchers and practitioners is no longer whether false confessions exist, but why they occur and what can be done to prevent them.

No responsible scholar or practitioner suggests that the police knowingly seek to obtain false confessions from the innocent or that prosecutors knowingly seek to convict the innocent. Indeed, there is little evidence that intentional abuses of power currently occur with significant frequency. Rather, false confessions now occur primarily due to a lack of proper training, poor investigative practices, and the use of scientifically invalidated and/or high-risk interrogation techniques and strategies. American police do not always receiving training on how to avoid eliciting false confessions, which interrogation methods and individual characteristics increase the risk of eliciting false confessions and why, or how to recognize different types of false confessions and their distinguishing characteristics. This chapter briefly describes the psychological process of interrogation and explains why false confessions, like truthful ones, can be understandable responses to certain interrogative procedures and strategies.

PRE-INTERROGATION INVESTIGATION

Police investigators do not choose to interrogate individuals randomly. Rather, they typically first investigate a case before deciding whether to interrogate. Reid and Associates, the creators and trainers of the dominant police interrogation approach in the United States, instruct detectives to investigate thoroughly before interrogating (Inbau, Reid, Buckley, & Jayne, 2013). In other words, police investigators should have solid evidence before placing a suspect in an interrogation, a psychological process of pressure and persuasion that once started, according to the Reid Method of interrogation, seeks to validate the investigators belief in the suspect's guilt (Leo, 2008). Whether to interrogate is therefore a critical decision point in the investigative process, and a mistake at this early stage may be the first error that contributes to a false confession (Leo & Drizin, 2010).

Sometimes well-meaning police investigators mistakenly conclude based on poor decision criteria that an innocent person is likely guilty, and, as a result, commence an accusatory interrogation. Empirical studies have shown that such mistaken judgments may result from poor police training that is not consistent with the findings of scientific research or best practice standards. For example, Reid and Associates trains investigators to engage in behavioral analysis—that is, to evaluate a suspect's body language and demeanor to determine whether a suspect is likely lying (and thus likely guilty) or telling the truth (and thus likely innocent)—during pre-interrogation interviewing in order to decide whether to place the suspect in an interrogation (Inbau et al., 2013). Detectives are taught, for example, that subjects who avert their gaze, slouch, shift their body posture, touch their nose, adjust or clean their glasses, chew their fingernails, or stroke the back of the head are likely to be lying and thus likely guilty. Suspects who are guarded, uncooperative and offer broad denials and qualified responses are also believed to be deceptive and therefore guilty.

Although police trainers usually mention that no single nonverbal or verbal behavior is, by itself, indicative of lying or truth telling, they nevertheless teach detectives that they can reliably infer whether a subject is deceptive if they know how to interpret his or her body language, mannerisms, gestures, and styles of speech (Inbau et al., 2013). Yet empirical studies have shown that police investigators, like lay people, cannot reliably distinguish truth tellers from liars based on their analysis of someone's demeanor and body language at levels much greater than chance (Ekman & O'Sullivan, 1991; Bond & DePaulo, 2006), and that the method of behavior analysis taught by Reid and Associates appears to lower pre-interrogation judgment accuracy, while increasing investigators' self-confidence in their assessments (Kassin & Fong, 1999; Vrij, Mann, & Fisher, 2006). This research shows that speculative judgments about a suspect's likely guilt or innocence based on a subjective assessment of his or her demeanor is a poor substitute for an analysis of real evidence on which to base the decision to interrogate.

THE POLICE INTERROGATION

After identifying a suspect, investigators often meet with that person to elicit information. The detective(s) may intend the meeting to be an investigative interview, or that it be the first step of an adversarial interrogation. The initial use of an interview format allows the investigator to better develop rapport, to lead the suspect to believe that he is helping authorities solve the crime (Leo, 1996), and to perceive that the questioning is nonthreatening (Leo & White, 1999). If the detective(s) decides to move from an interview to an interrogation, the elicitation of a Miranda waiver typically signals the transition (Leo, 2008). Empirical studies show that 80–90% or more of suspects typically waive their Miranda rights (Thomas & Leo, 2012).

Modern interrogation techniques and strategies are designed to break through the resistance of a rational person who knows he is guilty, convince him to stop denying his culpability, and persuade him to confess (Ofshe & Leo, 1997; Inbau et al., 2013). Investigators elicit the decision to confess by influencing the suspect's perception of (a) the nature and gravity of his immediate situation, (b) his available choices or alternatives, and (c) the consequences of each of these choices (Ofshe & Leo, 1997). Detectives seek to persuade the suspect that he has few options but to confess and that the act of admitting his knowledge and/or involvement in the crime is the most sensible course of action in his situation.

STEP 1: SHIFTING THE SUSPECT FROM CONFIDENT TO HOPELESS

From a psychological perspective, American police interrogation is essentially a two-step process (Ofshe & Leo, 1997). The goal of the first step is to cause the suspect to perceive that he has been caught; that his guilt can be objectively and conclusively demonstrated to any reasonable person; and that there is no way out of this predicament.

Presuming the suspect is guilty, the investigator is likely to rely on several well-known interrogation techniques to successfully communicate that the suspect has been caught, that no one will believe his denials, and that the case evidence objectively establishes his guilt. The interrogator may repeatedly accuse the suspect of having committed the crime, express unwavering confidence in the suspect's guilt, and seek to reverse a suspect's denials by either cutting them off or challenging them as implausible, illogical, or contradicted either by the detective's superior knowledge and experience or the existing case evidence (Leo, 2008). These techniques may lead a suspect to believe that he has the burden of proving his innocence.

The most effective technique used to convince the suspect that it is futile to deny his guilt is to confront him with what appears to be objective and irrefutable evidence of his guilt. Empirical studies have shown police interrogators often tell criminal suspects that the evidence establishes their guilt (Leo, 1996; Feld, 2013): if police possess real evidence, researchers call this a true evidence ploy. If police are making up, lying about, or exaggerating nonexistent evidence, researchers call this a false evidence ploy (Ofshe & Leo, 1997). Police investigators may, for example, tell a suspect that physical or trace evidence, eyewitnesses, or even polygraph results show the suspect participated in or committed the crime when in fact such evidence may not exist. The purpose of doing so is to convince the suspect that his guilt will be established beyond any reasonable doubt and thus that his best option is stop denying and start confessing.

STEP 2: OFFERING THE SUSPECT INDUCEMENTS TO CONFESS

In the second step of interrogation, the detective seeks to persuade the suspect that the benefits of agreeing with the investigators assertions clearly outweigh the costs of continuing to deny culpability, and thus the only way to improve his situation is by admitting guilt (Ofshe & Leo, 1997). To accomplish this, the officer may present the suspect with incentives or inducements that communicate that he might receive some personal, moral, legal, or other benefit if he confesses to the crime.

These inducements can be arrayed along a continuum and for analytical purposes have been classified into three categories: low-end, systemic, and high-end inducements (Ofshe & Leo, 1997). Low-end inducements refer to self-image, interpersonal and/or moral appeals that suggest the suspect will feel better or improve his social standing if he stops denying and starts confessing. Systemic inducements are intended to focus the suspect's attention on the discretionary ability of criminal justice officials to positively influence the processing and/or outcome of his case if he accepts responsibility, cooperates with authorities, and admits guilt. An investigator uses high-end inducements if he implicitly or explicitly suggests that the suspect will receive less punishment, a lower prison sentence, or prosecutorial or judicial leniency if he confesses and/or more severe treatment by the criminal justice system if he does not confess (Ofshe & Leo, 1997).

Through this two-step psychological process of interrogation, the investigator's goal is to move the suspect from denial to admission by motivating him to perceive that—given the nature of his situation, the limited choices available to him, and the consequences of each choice—it is futile to continue to deny the crime and the only way to improve his situation is by confessing. As Kassin has recently observed: "As to why anyone would confess to police, research on human decision-making has shown that people make choices that they think will maximize their well-being given the constraints they face.... In this context it is easy to appreciate the power of a psychological approach to interrogation—which is explicitly designed to increase the anxiety associated with denial and to decrease the anxiety associated with confession, thereby making it easier for the rational suspect to make the decision to confess" (Kassin, 2015: 33). Recent experimental research has shown that suspects often tend to make admissions in order to avoid the negative short-term consequences of continued denial even if it increases the negative long-term consequences of confession (Madon, Guyll, Scherr, Greathouse, & Wells, 2012; Madon, Yang, Smalarz, Guyll, & Scherr, 2013).

RISK FACTORS FOR FALSE CONFESSION

Social scientists have extensively studied and identified factors that elevate or increase the risk of eliciting false confessions (Kassin et al., 2010). Factors associated with the techniques, methods, strategies, and/or environment of interrogation are referred to as *situational* risk factors. Factors associated with an individual's personality traits and characteristics are referred to as *dispositional* or *personal* risk factors.

SITUATIONAL RISK FACTORS

1. *Lengthy Interrogation*. Lengthy interrogation/custody is a *situational* risk factor for making or agreeing to a false confession during police interrogation (Kassin et al., 2010). Empirical studies indicate that the overwhelming majority of routine custodial interrogations last less than 1 h (Leo, 1996; Feld, 2013), whereas the combined time period of custody and interrogation in most interrogations leading to a false confession is more than 6 h (Drizin & Leo, 2004). The Reid and Associates' police interrogation training manual specifically recommends that police interrogate for no longer than four (4) hours absent "exceptional situations" and that "most cases require considerably fewer than four hours" (Inbau et al., 2013: 597). Lengthy detention and interrogation is a significant risk factor for false confessions because the longer an interrogation lasts, the more likely the suspect is

to become fatigued and depleted of the physical and psychological resources necessary to resist the pressures and stresses of accusatory interrogation (Davis & Leo, 2012). Lengthy interrogation can also lead to sleep deprivation, which heightens interrogative suggestibility (Blagrove, 1996; Harrison & Horne, 2000).

2. *False Evidence.* Social science research has shown that false evidence ploys are virtually always present in interrogations leading to false confession, and are substantially likely to increase the risk of eliciting false confessions from innocent suspects (Kassin et al., 2010). Most suspects do not know that police detectives can legally lie by pretending to have incriminating evidence that does not exist. The use of false evidence ploys can lead a suspect to perceive that he is trapped, that there is no way out of his situation because the alleged evidence against him assures he will be convicted, and thus that he has little choice but negotiate the best available outcome to mitigate his eventual punishment. As substantial basic and applied psychological research has shown (Loftus, 2005; Kassin et al., 2010), the use of false evidence ploys are effective at eliciting compliance (Leo, 2008), confusing some suspects into believing that such evidence really does exist (Ofshe & Leo, 1997), causing some suspects to doubt themselves, and even causing some suspects to develop false beliefs and/or memories of committing crimes (Leo, 2008; Wright, Wade, & Watson 2013; Shaw & Porter, 2015).

3. *Minimization.* Sometimes investigators portray the offense in a way that minimizes its moral, psychological and/or legal seriousness, thus lowering the perceived cost of confessing by communicating that the consequences of confessing will not be that serious (Leo, 2008). Interrogation techniques and strategies that minimize the legal seriousness of the crime, in particular, are associated with and known to increase the risk of eliciting false confessions (Kassin et al., 2010). Such minimization strategies can imply leniency, reduced punishment, or even no punishment at all if the suspect perceives that there is no consequence to confessing (i.e., either that the act to which the suspect is confessing is not a crime or that it carries little or no penalty) (Kassin & McNall, 1991). Conversely, interrogation techniques and strategies that exaggerate the legal seriousness of the crime— that is, suggest that the suspect will face a bad or perhaps the worst possible outcome if he or she does not make or agree to an incriminating statement—are also associated with and known to increase the risk of eliciting false confessions (Kassin et al., 2010). Such interrogation strategies can imply harsher treatment, confinement, punishment, sentencing and/or other negative outcomes if the suspect fails to comply and confess (Ofshe & Leo, 1997).

4. *Threats and Promises.* The use of implied and/or explicit promises of leniency, immunity and/or a tangible benefit, as well as the use of implied and/or explicit threats of harm, significantly increases the risk of eliciting a false confession (Kassin et al., 2010). Indeed, as empirical social science research has repeatedly demonstrated, promises of leniency—like threats of harm or harsher punishment and whether explicit or implicit—are widely associated with police-induced false confession in the modern era and are believed to be among the leading causes (Drizin & Leo, 2004). Like other *high-end* inducements, promises and threats contribute to creating a sense of despair and hopelessness in a suspect's perceptions of his available options during interrogation (Ofshe & Leo, 1997).

Individual Risk Factors

While the use of high-risk interrogation techniques are often the primary cause of false confessions, certain types or groups of individuals are far more vulnerable to the pressures of interrogation, having their will overborne and/or making a false confession. This includes individuals who are mentally ill, and therefore may confess falsely because they are easily confused, disoriented, delusional, or experiencing a nonrational emotional or mental state. This also includes juveniles and individuals with a low IQ or low-level cognitive functioning, who may be more vulnerable to interrogators because of their inability to understand the nature or gravity of their situation, their inability to foresee the consequences of their actions, their inability to cope with stressful situations and/or their eagerness to please others, especially authority figures. Juveniles may also be more easily intimidated than adults and may lack the maturity, knowledge, or sense of authority needed to resist simple police pressures and manipulations. Finally, this also includes individuals who, by their nature and personality, are naive, excessively trusting of authority, highly suggestible and/or highly compliant and who are therefore predisposed to believe that they have no choice but to comply with the demands of authorities or who simply lack the psychological resources to resist the escalating pressures of accusatorial interrogation (Kassin et al., 2010).

THE PROBLEM OF CONTAMINATION

Contamination is the leakage or disclosure to a suspect of nonpublic case facts that are not likely guessed by chance (Ofshe & Leo, 1997). A suspect's knowledge of unique case facts may be contaminated by third parties such as the media, witnesses to a crime, or by investigators. Researchers have found that contamination by police regularly occurs in false confession cases. In a study of the first two-hundred and fifty (250) post-conviction DNA exonerations of innocent prisoners in the American criminal justice system, Garrett (2011) found that contamination was present in 95% of the false confession cases in this data set. In a recent follow-up study, Garrett found that 91% of the more recent DNA exonerated false confessions were contaminated (Garrett, 2015). Police interrogation training manuals universally instruct police not to provide suspects with crime facts that are likely to be known only by the true perpetrator and the police (Inbau et al., 2013). The problem with contaminated confessions is that they contain detailed case facts that create the misleading appearance of corroboration to third parties and increase the risk that a false confession will be treated as true one and thus lead to an erroneous prosecution and wrongful conviction.

THE DIFFERENT TYPES OF FALSE CONFESSION

Kassin and Wrightsman (1985) first identified three conceptually distinct types of false confession—voluntary, coerced-compliant and coerced-internalized. Kassin and Wrightsman's typology or classification scheme offers a useful conceptual framework for better understanding confessions (Gudjonsson, 2003). Synthesizing the existing research literature, Ofshe and Leo (1997) have extended and modified Kassin and Wrightsman's initial typology.

Voluntary False Confessions

A voluntary false confession is offered either in the absence of police interrogation or in response to minimal police pressure. Individuals volunteer false confessions in the absence of police questioning for a variety of reasons—a morbid desire for notoriety, the need to atone for real or imagined acts (Gudjonsson, 2003), a need for attention or fame, the desire to protect or assist the actual offender, an inability to distinguish between fantasy and reality, or a pathological need for acceptance of self-punishment (Kassin et al., 2010). High-profile crimes such as the Lindbergh kidnapping in the 1930s, the Black Dahlia murder in the 1940s, or the JonBenet Ramsay and Nicole Brown Simpson murders in the 1990s may attract hundreds of voluntary false confessions (Gudjonsson, 2003).

Compliant False Confession (Stress-Compliant and Coerced-Compliant)

A compliant false confession is given when the pressure, stress and/or coercion of custodial questioning overwhelms the suspect and he comes to believe that the only way to end the experience is by confessing (Ofshe & Leo, 1997). There are three potential sources of stress during the interrogation; the environment, the detective's interpersonal style, and the techniques and strategies used during the process. During interrogations, detectives commonly (and legally) structure the environment to induce stress. They place the suspect in an unfamiliar setting, they separate him from others, and they control the pace, length, and intensity of the questioning. The officer's interpersonal style may be one that is alternately confrontational, demanding, and insistent. Finally, the techniques and strategies of the questioning officers may be designed to induce anxiety by attacking the suspect's self-confidence and appearing not to listen when he claims his innocence. Even though the suspect knows he is innocent, he may make a false confession because the prospect of continued interrogation is intolerable. If the officer suspects that the person making the confession is doing so simply to end the interrogation, he should attempt to obtain crime information from the individual that will corroborate the confession absent any contamination. Such information should be known only to the police and true offender (Leo, Drizin, Neufeld, & Taslitz, 2013). Officers should be aware of the legal ramifications of engaging in verbal and nonverbal behavior that threatens the well-being of a suspect and should avoid engaging in such activities. Furthermore, officers should make no promises that they are not legally empowered to make.

PERSUADED FALSE CONFESSIONS (COERCED-PERSUADED AND NONCOERCED-PERSUADED)

Persuaded false confessions occur when an innocent suspect comes to doubt the reliability of his memory and becomes temporarily persuaded that it is more likely than not that he committed the crime, despite having no memory of doing so. In rare cases, a persuaded false confessor may develop actual false memories of having committed the crime (Wells & Leo, 2008). The suspect usually comes to believe that he probably did or could have committed the crime, or logically must have committed have done so in light of what he has been told, and he "confesses" in hypothetical, tentative, or speculative language that he could have, he probable did, or must have, or he may have committed the crime. The language he uses to confess reflects his uncertain belief state and lack of personal knowledge about the crime facts (Ofshe & Leo, 1997).

Persuaded false confessions occur in part when investigators refuse to accept the suspect's report of having no memory of committing the crime. Reid and Associates emphatically admonishes police interrogators never to tell a suspect who states that he cannot remember committing the crime that he did so (Inbau et al., 2013). When it appears that such a confession is being made, the investigator should be careful to avoid providing the suspect with case details or answering the suspect's questions about the crime. The investigator should also determine whether the information provided by the suspect could have been obtained from other police officers, the media, or the community.

THE CONSEQUENCES OF FALSE CONFESSIONS

While it is not presently possible to provide a valid quantitative estimate of the incidence or prevalence of false confessions (Leo & Ofshe, 1998), it is well established that false confessions occur with troubling frequency and sometimes lead to the wrongful conviction of the innocent. A person who confesses is likely to be treated more harshly by those within the criminal justice system. An officer who obtains a confession is inclined to consider the case solved. Prosecutors tend to make the confession the centerpiece of their cases and are less likely to initiate or accept plea bargains (Leo & Ofshe, 1998). The defendants may have more difficulty in obtaining bail, and defense attorneys are more likely to pressure their clients to plead guilty because the risk of conviction is greatly increased. Even the triers of fact may become biased in favor of conviction when confession is involved. For all these reasons it is imperative that police and prosecutors do their best to catch false confessions prior to trial.

CONCLUSION

False confessions can be prevented, and it is imperative that all reasonable steps be taken to ensure that they do not occur. One of the most important procedural safeguards to reduce the possibility of false confessions is a comprehensive training program for law enforcement officers who will conduct interrogations.

As a minimum, investigators should be trained in the following four areas:

1. The existence, variety, causes, and psychology of false confessions—if investigators are taught the logic, principles, and effects of psychological interrogation methods, they will not only become more knowledgeable about false confessions but they will also be more effective in obtaining truthful ones.
2. The indicia of reliable and unreliable statements and how to distinguish between them—it has long been a generally accepted principle in law enforcement that valid confessions are supported by logic and evidence. The proper way to assess the reliability of a confession is by analyzing the suspect's post-admission narrative (detailed discussion of the crime after an admission has been given) against the underlying crime facts to determine whether it reveals guilty knowledge and is, in fact, corroborated by existing evidence (Leo et al., 2013).
3. Officers cannot reliably intuit whether a suspect is innocent or guilty based on their uncorroborated suspicions—police must base their opinions about an individual's guilt on much more reliable and conclusive evidence and should ensure that they have done all within their power to corroborate the confession. True confessions most often provide information that leads to corroborating evidence, whereas false confessions, absent contamination, by their nature cannot do so.
4. Investigators must be trained to avoid inadvertent contamination or feeding of nonpublic case facts to suspects during interrogation.

Professional investigators are aware that false confessions sometimes happen, and that confessions must always be independently verified and corroborated. A confession that cannot withstand objective evaluation should not be accepted.

REFERENCES

Blagrove, M. 1996. Effects of length of sleep deprivation on interrogative suggestibility. *Journal of Experimental Psychology: Applied*, 2, 48–59.

Blandon-Gitlin, I., Sperry, K., and Leo, R. A. 2011. Jurors believe interrogation tactics are not likely to elicit false confessions: Will expert witness testimony inform them otherwise? *Psychology, Crime and Law*, 17, 239–260.

Bond, C., and DePaulo, B. 2006. Accuracy of deception judgments. *Personality & Social Psychology Review*, 10, 214–234.

Chojnacki, D., Cicchini, M., and White, L. 2008. An empirical basis for the admission of expert testimony on false confessions. *Arizona State Law Journal*, 40, 1–45.

Costanzo, M., Shaked-Schroer, N., and Vinson, K. V. 2010. Juror beliefs about police interrogation, false confession and expert testimony. *The Journal of Legal Empirical Studies*, 7, 231–247.

Davis, D., and Leo, R. A. 2012. Interrogation related regulatory decline: Ego-depletion, failures of self-regulation and the decision to confess. *Psychology, Public Policy and Law*, 18, 673–704.

Drizin, S., and Leo, R. A. 2004. The problem of false confessions in the post-DNA world. *North Carolina Law Review*, 82, 891–1007.

Ekman, P., and O'Sullivan, M. 1991. Who can catch a liar? *American Psychologist*, 46, 913–920.

Feld, B. 2013. *Kids, cops and confessions: Inside the interrogation room*. New York: New York University Press.

Garrett, B. 2011. *Convicting the innocent*. Cambridge, MA: Harvard University Press.

Garrett, B. 2015. Contaminated confessions revisited. *Virginia Law Review*, 101, 395–454.

Gould, J., Carrano, J., Leo, R. A., and Hail-Jares, K. 2014. Predicting erroneous convictions. *Iowa Law Review*, 99, 471–522.

Gudjonsson, G. H. 2003. *The psychology of interrogations and confessions: A handbook*. New York: Wiley.

Harrison, Y., and Horne, J. 2000. The impact of sleep deprivation on decision making: A review. *Journal of Experimental Psychology: Applied*, 6, 236–249.

Henkel, L., Coffman, K., and Dailey, E. 2008. A survey of people's attitudes and beliefs about false confessions. *Behavioral Sciences and the Law*, 26, 555–584.

Inbau, F., Reid, J., Buckley, J., and Jayne, B. 2013. *Criminal interrogation and confessions*, 5th ed. Burlington, MA: Jones & Bartlett Learning.

Kassin, S. 1997. The psychology of confession evidence. *American Psychologist*, 52, 221–233.

Kassin, S. 2015. The social psychology of false confessions. *Social Issues and Policy Review*, 9(1), 25–51.

Kassin, S., and Wrightsman, L. 1985. Confession evidence. In S. Kassin and L. Wrightsman (Eds.), *The psychology of evidence and trial procedure*, 67–94. Beverly Hills: Sage Publications.

Kassin, S., and McNall, K. 1991. Police interrogation and confessions: Communicating promises and threats by pragmatic implication. *Law and Human Behavior*, 15, 233–251.

Kassin, S., and Fong, C. T. 1999. "I'm innocent!" Effects of training on judgments of truth and deception in the interrogation room. *Law and Human Behavior*, 23, 499–516.

Kassin, S., Leo, R., Meissner, C., Richman, K., Colwell, L., Leach, A., et al. 2007. Police interviewing and interrogation: A self-report survey of police practices and beliefs. *Law and Human Behavior*, 31, 381–400.

Kassin, S., Drizin, S., Grisso, T., Gudjonsson, G., Leo, Richard A., and Redlich, A. 2010. Police-induced confessions: Risk factors and recommendations. *Law and Human Behavior*, 34, 3–38.

Leo, R. A. 1996. Inside the interrogation room. *Journal of Criminal Law and Criminology*, 86, 266–303.

Leo, R. A. 2001. False confessions: Causes, consequences, and solutions. In S. D. Westervelt and J. A. Humphrey (Eds.), *Wrongly convicted: Perspectives on failed justice*, 36–54. Newark: Rutgers University Press.

Leo, R. A. 2008. *Police interrogation and American justice*. Cambridge, MA: Harvard University Press.

Leo, R. A. and Ofshe, R. 1998. The consequences of false confessions: Deprivations of liberty and miscarriages of justice in the age of psychological interrogation. *Journal of Criminal Law and Criminology*, 88, 429–496.

Leo, R. A., and White, W. S. 1999. Adapting to *Miranda*: Modern interrogators' strategies for dealing with the obstacles posed by *Miranda*. *Minnesota Law Review*, 84, 397–472.

Leo, R. A., and Liu, B. 2009. What do potential jurors know about police interrogation and false confessions? *Behavioral Sciences and the Law*, 27, 381–399.

Leo, R. A., and Drizin, S. 2010. The three errors: Pathways to false confession and wrongful conviction. In D. Lassiter and C. Meissner (Eds.). *Police interrogations and false confessions: Current research, practice, and policy recommendations*, 9–30. Washington, DC: American Psychological Association.

Leo, R. A., Drizin, S., Neufeld, P., and Taslitz, A. 2013. Promoting accuracy in the use of confession evidence: An argument for pre-trial reliability assessments to prevent wrongful convictions. *Temple Law Review*, 85, 759–838.

Loftus, E. 2005. Planting misinformation in the human mind: A 30 year investigation of the malleability of memory. *Learning & Memory*, 12, 361–366.

Madon, S., Guyll, M., Scherr, K. C., Greathouse, S., and Wells, G. L. 2012. Temporal discounting: The differential effect of proximal and distal consequences on confession decisions. *Law and Human Behavior*, 36, 13–20.

Madon, S., Yang, Y., Smalarz, L., Guyll, M., and Scherr, K. C. 2013. How factors present during the immediate interrogation situation produce short-sighted confession decisions. *Law and Human Behavior*, 37, 60–74.

National Registry of Exonerations. 2015. See http://www.law.umich.edu/special/exoneration/Pages/about.aspx (Last accessed November 28, 2015).

Ofshe, R., and Leo, R. A. 1997. The decision to confess falsely: Rational choice and irrational action. *Denver University Law Review*, 74, 979–1122.

Shaw, J., and Porter, S. 2015. Constructing rich false memories. *Psychological Science*. January 14, 2015, 1–11.

Thomas, G. C. III, and Leo, R. A. 2012. *Confessions of guilt: From torture to Miranda and beyond*. New York: Oxford University Press.

Vrij, A., Mann, S., and Fisher, R. 2006. An empirical test of the behavioral analysis interview. *Law and Human Behavior*, 30(3), 329–345.

Wells, T., and Leo, R. A. 2008. *The wrong guys: Murder, false confessions, and the Norfolk Four*. New York: The New Press.

Wright, D., Wade, K., and Watson, D. 2013. Delay and déjà vu: Timing and repetition increase the power of false evidence. *Psychonomic Bulletin Review*, 20, 812–818.

13 Rape Escalating to Homicide

Robert R. Hazelwood and Janet I. Warren

CONTENTS

Introduction 187
Primary Motivational Themes 188
    Acting Out a Homicidal Fantasy 188
    The Unintentional Murder of a Rape Victim 189
    An Impulsive Reaction to Victim Resistance 190
    Seeking a Psychosexual Plateau 190
    Witness Elimination 192
    Drug Intoxication 193
    Monotony and Boredom 194
Conclusions 195
References 196

INTRODUCTION

The genesis of this chapter can be traced to two of our earlier research projects which examined the dynamics of serial rape and the escalation of violence among these offenders. The first study involved men who were documented to have raped 10 or more women, the majority (85%) of whom were strangers to them (Hazelwood & Warren, 1990). One of these men had raped more than 60 women, and in 18 of these assaults, he hung, strangled, or drowned the victims almost to the point of death. However, in each of these instances, he interrupted his attack prior to the death of the victim and rendered medical assistance to the woman. He then called 911 and reported the victim's location and the need for assistance. During the interview, he proudly told the lead author "I never lost a victim." When asked why he didn't kill a victim, he firmly said "I didn't want to," and refused to elaborate further. This man, who was a medical professional, reported that he most enjoyed working in emergency rooms because, "[t]hat's where you get to play God."

This rapist was one of 41 men interviewed who collectively raped 837 women and were known to have engaged in over 400 attempted rapes that were not completed for a variety of reasons. Further analyses of these same data found that the majority of the rapists in the study did not escalate in the physical violence or force that they used with each victim, staying at the same or similar levels of blunt force during their first, middle and last sexual assaults (Warren, Reboussin, & Hazelwood, 1989). However, within this group, ten men (24%) escalated in physical violence over the course of their criminal offending, with two (5%) ultimately murdering at least one of their victims. The offenders who increased in their use of blunt force were found to be different from the non-escalating rapists in their total number of assaults, the number of days between rapes, the degree of victim resistance experienced, and the presence of sadistic acts during their last assault.

Ten years later, we conducted a second study of serial rapists, this research involving 108 serial rapists who had offended against 565 women. Based upon the blind coding of crime scene behavior manifested during each assault, we again found that 25% of the sample escalated in the amount of physical violence used over the course of their offending, while the majority of the offenders remained consistent in most aspects of their crime scene behavior (Warren et al., 1999). When these two groups of rapists were compared on 58 behavioral scales describing their verbal, physical, and sexual behavior during each assault, 15 of the scales were significantly different between the two groups at the time of their first assault. Specifically, the escalating rapists conveyed more personal information about themselves to the victim, tended to make more excuses, expressed more hostility in general—particularly toward women, manifested an interest in verbal scripting—especially to compliment the rapist, used more blunt force, inflicted more injuries on the victim, used more force than necessary to complete the rape, perpetrated assaults that lasted longer and involved more planning, behaved in ways that appeared to be designed to humiliate the victim, demonstrated a preference for penetration with a foreign object, expressed more profanity, and were more specific in their victim selection. When we examined behavior over all of the rapes, we also found that those rapists who increased in the blunt force used against their victims were characterized by more total rapes committed, displayed a trend toward raping older women, and had less serious and less extensive criminal histories at the time of their arrests.

When these two studies were considered together, the data and the interviews contained within them led us to be interested in the reasons for the escalation in violence associated with serial rape, and more specifically why some rapists escalate to murder while the large majority of them do not—regardless of how often they offend aggressively against women. In exploring this question, we reflected on our joint experience in conducting research, providing case consultations, and being required to provide courtroom testimony in cases of rape and homicide. Based upon these experiences, we identified seven reasons that we believe might help to explain the trajectory from sexual assault to murder, each of which will be presented to the reader with accompanying case histories. As these derive primarily from our case experience, it is important to emphasize that they are not empirical findings but rather hypothesis-generating ideas that will warrant further investigation and study.

PRIMARY MOTIVATIONAL THEMES

Acting Out a Homicidal Fantasy

The first reason for rape escalating to homicide is that the offender is literally acting out a fantasy of murder (Hazelwood & Warren, 1990). This is, in all likelihood, the least common reason for such a dramatic escalation of violence but one that exists as portrayed in Case no. 1 summarized below. It is important to note that while rape or other forms of sexual assault may accompany the murder these sexual acts are auxiliary to the core purpose of the crime, with the central intent being to murder a generic or specific victim.

CASE NO. 1

At 17 years of age, JR was arrested for luring a 17-year-old red-haired girl into his home and attempting to strangle her. It is reported that for this behavior, he was warned about his actions, directed to obtain counseling, and was released. Two weeks later, his stepfather gave the police pictures of women upon which JR had superimposed images of nooses positioned around their necks. Three years later when JR was 20 years of age, a red-haired girl spurned his advances and he ran his vehicle into her car. At 22 years of age, he persuaded another red-haired girl to come into his home and released her only after she began to scream. One year later he was arrested, tried, and convicted of having murdered 17-year-old GW by hanging. GW was the red-haired daughter of a police detective. Investigation revealed that JR had convinced GW to pose for him in a "fake hanging" scenario as he took photographs of her wearing clothes he had purchased for the occasion. Police later found fantasy scripts involving sexual violence and thousands of composite images of violent sexual assaults he had created of women and girls taken from social media sites. One of his fantasy scripts was titled "[GW]'s Surprise" in which he wrote about her body dancing as she was hung to death. He also had 72 videos, some which depicted women being sexually assaulted postmortem.

What triggers the homicidal behavior? No one knows for sure, but Robert Prentky wrote "the research on sexual homicide indicates that the offenders will behaviorally try out parts of the fantasy before they commit murder. The acting out of the fantasy usually intensifies it" (Prentky et al., 1989). Reid Meloy has written "There are likely multiple reasons, some internal and some external, but an important behavioral one is the fact that over time the intensity of a sexually violent fantasy lessens while at the same time, the fantasy disinhibits the tendency to act it out in real life" (Meloy, 1992; Meloy, draft opinion, 1998; Meloy, 2000).

THE UNINTENTIONAL MURDER OF A RAPE VICTIM

Frequently, the death of a rape victim is an unintentional consequence of the crime and sometimes can be a result of an unforeseen error or misjudgment made during the commission of the sexual assault. In such cases, the primary and intended goal of the offense was the sexual assault of the victim. The following case (discussed in greater detail in Chapter 21) conveys the unexpected consequence of a sexual assault that ends in murder.

CASE NO. 2

JRW kidnapped pregnant 29-year-old NG from her rural home shortly after her husband left for work. There was no sign of a struggle at the scene and this was attributed to the fact that her infant child was present, a factor that might have diminished the forcefulness of her resistance to avoid bringing harm to her child. The victim's body was found at an illegal trash dump and the forensic examination determined that she had choked to death on paper towels lodged in her throat. Her clothing had not been disturbed and there was no evidence of further trauma to her body. The crime scene investigation determined that after being abducted, NG was placed in the trunk of her car and transported a short distance to the location where JRW had parked his truck. A roll of paper towels was found in the trunk of the victim's car and when JRW attempted to move the victim from the trunk, it is believed that NG began screaming and JRW put the paper towels in her mouth to muffle the screams. JRW next placed NG in his truck and drove to an unknown location where he intended to rape the victim. Upon arrival at that location, he discovered she had died of asphyxiation, leading him to dispose of her body in the trash dump that was near-by.

Three months after the death of NG, JRW kidnapped a second young mother from her residence, placed her in his truck and drove her to a deserted farmhouse. He brought items of lingerie to the crime and forced the woman to "model" the clothing for him as he became aroused. He kept her for several hours as he kissed, fondled, and vaginally raped the victim repeatedly. She complained about being thirsty and cold and JRW gave her a blanket and left the scene of the crime after carefully binding the victim. He left and returned with soft drinks for the victim and then drove the victim to a location proximate to her home, asking her for a date before releasing her from his vehicle. Within days of her abduction and shortly before Christmas, JRW brought a six-foot blue spruce Christmas tree to her home, placing it on her porch. This act was observed by her father who recorded the license plate number of JRW's truck as it drove away, leading to his arrest and eventual conviction for the prior murder of NG.

Hazelwood testified for the prosecution in the guilt phase of JRW's trial explaining the significance of the collateral materials (Hazelwood & Lanning, 2009) recovered from his residence and he was found guilty of murdering NG. Hazelwood later testified for the defense in the sentence phase, describing the manner in which he interacted with the rape victim and opining that JRW was a Power-Reassurance rapist (see Chapter 7), who had a fantasy of a consenting relationship and had not intended to kill NG. JRW was sentenced to death and his sentence is currently under appeal.

An Impulsive Reaction to Victim Resistance

The escalation to homicide may simply be the offender's spontaneous response to a victim's resistance. In the author's experience, the rapist is most likely an anger-motivated offender with a volatile temperament (see Chapter 7). Again, the offender's intended goal in assaulting the victim is rape and not homicide.

CASE NO. 3

A 24-year-old white female was found dead from multiple stab wounds in her first-floor apartment where she resided alone. She was 5′9″ and weighed 165 pounds, and her parents reported that she would have "fought to the death" to defend her virginity. She had defense wounds on both hands and her right thigh and six stab wounds to her chest, two of which penetrated her lungs, resulting in her death. She was lying on her back, nude from the waist down. Blood spatter evidenced that the physical assault and knife attack occurred in the kitchen and that once subdued, she had been dragged into the carpeted living room where she was violently raped, and a large amount of seminal fluid deposited. The murder weapon was a large kitchen knife which belonged to the victim and which the killer had "hidden" beneath a chair cushion adjacent to the apartment door.

A behavioral reconstruction of the crime suggested that the victim was using the knife to prepare a meal and was surprised by the offender after he entered her apartment through an unlocked window. She physically fought him and was struck by the intruder three to four times in the face. The offender picked up the knife and the victim grabbed the blade as he was attempting to stab her, thus sustaining the defensive wounds to her hands. She went to the floor and kicked at the man and he stabbed her thigh and then her chest. Eventually she succumbed to her wounds and was dragged to the living room. Medical examination determined that the victim was a virgin until the rape and that she would have lived approximately 40 min after the chest wounds were inflicted. The significance of this information was that the killer violently raped his victim as she was drowning in her own blood.

The perpetrator of this crime was identified and linked to several other rapes of women living alone in apartments in the same general region of the city. In each case, the victim was subdued by several blows to the face and the rape followed with no further physical trauma inflicted on the victim. In this case, the victim refused to yield to her attacker and was murdered.

This case presents a compelling example of a rapist who killed and not a killer who raped. This man impulsively murdered when confronted by vigorous resistance but was not deterred from his primary goal of rape.

Seeking a Psychosexual Plateau

Paraphilic disorders often co-occur (Abel et al., 1987), and singularly and in combination can play a dominant role in the sexual fantasy of a rapist, prompting different types of sexual crimes over the course of the individual's criminal offending (Abel, Becker, Cunningham-Rathner, Mittelman, & Rouleau, 1988). In the following case, the evolution of these different paraphilically motivated crimes occurred over 2 years, eventually culminating in the murder and necrophilic assault of his last victim. In this case, videos were made by the perpetrator of two of his homicides; these videos were transcribed and supplemented with the perpetrator's own description of the physical and sexual behaviors that were occurring (Gibb, 2011).

It is our impression that these materials along with evidentiary facts revealed during investigation of the case provide a clear illustration of what we refer to as the psychosexual plateau of a particular repeat sexual offender. We use this phrase in an attempt to describe evolving behaviors between subsequent offences that can be understood as attempts by an offender to capture and reenact their core sexual or masturbatory fantasy. It is likely that escalation in violence over a series of sexual assaults is associated with gradual reduction in inhibitions, allowing the offender to carry out the more brutal aspects of this core fantasy. Attendant behaviors are influenced by the desire to construct the perfect combination of experiences and imagery that compel a powerful sexual release through orgasm. This process was illustrated carefully by the perpetrator in Case no. 4 and detailed in an assortment of writings, CDs, and DVDs.

CASE NO. 4

RW was a Colonel in the Canadian Air Force, having served for 23 years, and having been promoted to Commander of a large Air Force base when he was arrested for murder. All of his known crimes occurred over a 2-year period when he was in his mid-40s, and after his arrest, he provided law enforcement with detailed confessions of his rape and murder offenses, corroborated by CDs and DVDs.

From 2007 to 2009, RW was responsible for more than 86 sexually related crimes, these falling within what appears to be three distinct crime categories, each reflecting an escalation of crime scene behavior both in terms of the complexity of the crime behavior and the harm inflicted upon a victim. The first set of crimes (window-peeping and 82 home invasions) have been referred to as "nuisance offenses," despite their role in bringing RW closer to his rape and murder victims. After breaking and entering vacant homes, RW tended to enact his interest in cross-dressing using articles of pre-teen, teen, and adult female clothing. He photographed himself in these lingerie items while located in the residences, made videos of the interior of the homes, and created films of photographs of the various family members who resided in each home. During this series of crimes, RW engaged in voyeurism, breaking and entering, cross-dressing, photographing, and the theft of lingerie. While undoubtedly exciting to RW, he apparently discovered that these actions did not afford him what he envisioned being his own unique psychosexual plateau.

The second set of offenses involved the sexual assault of two women, both of whom he found sleeping in their own homes. The first assault occurred on September 17, 2009. He captured a sleeping 20-year-old woman at knifepoint, forced her to "model" lingerie, engaged in sexual bondage with her, kissed and fondled her, took photos, and made videos of her actions. He did not rape her but left her nude and bound to a chair, assuring her as he left that he would not place any of the images of her on the Internet. Two weeks later, on September 30, 2009, RW captured a sleeping 47-year-old woman by striking her with a flashlight. He again engaged in sexual bondage, cut her T-shirt and bra off with a knife, kissed and fondled her, took photographs, made videos, and left her bound nude. These offenses involved intimate interactions with real victims but did not culminate in orgasm and did not apparently constitute the psychosexual plateau that he continued to seek.

Days prior to the third group of crimes, RW entered and familiarized himself with his first murder victim's residence. She was a 38-year-old member of the Canadian Air Force who served on the same base that RW commanded and who had once served as a flight attendant on a flight he piloted. On November 24, 2009, he entered her home and she confronted him in the basement of the residence. He severely beat her with a flashlight, resulting in a heavy loss of blood. He then moved her to her bedroom where he stripped and bound her. From the prosecutor's transcripts of the video, it is known that he whispered in her ear, "[d]o you want to die?" He repeatedly raped the woman, vaginally and anally, before suffocating her and later performing sexual acts on her dead body. He took photographs and made videos of the assault and positioned and photographed the body of the dead women before he left her residence.

A linear tracing of RW's sexually oriented behaviors up to this point in time would include voyeurism, breaking and entering, cross-dressing, lingerie thefts, capturing victims, sexual bondage, photographing and making of videos, fondling and digitally assaulting, vaginal rape, anal assault, homicide, and necrophilia. Despite the increasing expanse of these behaviors and their ultimate harm of the victims, RW apparently did not experience full sexual satisfaction and found himself motivated to move further.

RW's final victim was a 27-year-old woman he had observed on his travel route home from his Air Force base. He captured her as she slept in her home on January 28, 2010. She was killed on January 29, 17 h after her capture. The killing occurred in a second home belonging to RW and his wife. In the intervening hours, the young woman was vaginally, anally, and orally raped by RW. He photographed and made a video DVD of the extensive assault. During the encounter, RW inspected the private areas of the victim's body, positioning her in a variety of positions, photographing, and making videos as he examined her. At one point, while forcing her to perform fellatio, he placed two ligatures around her neck, and asked if she knew their purpose (no), he told her they were there in case he felt something he "didn't like." At one point, he cross-dressed in her lingerie as he assaulted her. The woman remained totally compliant over the 17 h she was held captive by RW, but, using a ligature, he strangled her from the rear. While in prison, he wrote to this victim's mother and told her that her daughter was "a very nice person."

It is unclear how RW's behavior might have escalated had he not been captured. His behavior, however, reflects the evolving interplay of different paraphilic interests and the choice to escalate from sexual assault to murder. In both instances, actual sexual penetration of his victims occurred only in instances in which the victim was ultimately murdered. Across the two murders, he added cross-dressing and ligature strangulation to his panoply of paraphilic sexual interests and in so doing inverted his gender identity while conducting a detailed inspection of the female body. It seems likely that his orgasm was not linked specifically to the murder of his victim. Our prior research on sexually sadistic murderers has indicated that sexually sadistic murderers prefer a face-to-face positioning vis-à-vis their murder victim (Warren, Hazelwood, & Dietz, 1996).

WITNESS ELIMINATION

Rapists in this category execute their crime with the expectation that it will culminate in murder, not because of a conscious sexual interest in murder, but rather as their preferred means of avoiding detection and apprehension by law enforcement. The following case provides an example of this category, and is of historical interest in crime scene analyses, as the offender is believed to be the first serial killer to have taken and developed photographs of his three murder victims (a fourth victim was rescued). The information in Case no. 5 was taken from police reports and mental health records.

CASE NO. 5

HG was born on December 8, 1927, to a very strict father and an indulgent mother who owned a stationery store in the Bronx, New York City. His mother reported that when HG was 3 or 4 years of age, she observed him wrapping a string around his penis, closing the loose end in a drawer, and leaning or pulling back. When he was 12 years old, he habitually masturbated, and on one occasion his mother found him suspended from a rope around his neck and masturbating. His father told him that his facial blemishes were the result of his masturbation, and if he continued, he would lose blood and go crazy.

As a teenager, HG began "snatching" purses from women and throwing them back to the victims. He also engaged in window-peeping and entering the residences of women. While a teenager, he kidnapped women off the street and took the victims to isolated areas where he would bind, and fondle, but not rape, the women. After serving time in prison, he moved to Los Angeles where he hired a 19-year-old model to pose for sexual bondage photographs, telling the woman that they were for the front covers of detective magazines. He eventually drove her to the nearby desert where he strangled and buried her.

His second murder victim was a woman he met through a "lonely hearts" club. He again drove her to the desert where he took a series of bondage photographs of the victim before he strangled her to death. His final murder victim was a prostitute whom he "hired" to pose for bondage photographs and once again, he took her to the desert where she was strangled and buried.

A fourth woman was also kidnapped and taken to the desert, but she fought him for control of his gun and a passing motorcycle officer rescued her and arrested HG. There is no evidence that he ever dated a woman and all known interactions with women involved criminal acts ranging from "prowling" and purse snatching to kidnapping and murder.

When arrested, HG immediately confessed and told investigators that he raped the women and killed them to ensure there would be no witnesses and he would not be returned to prison. A search of his residence resulted in the recovery of the photographs he had taken of the victims prior to their murders. Also recovered were a large number of "detective" magazines (Dietz, Harry, & Hazelwood, 1986) with their covers depicting distressed women in bondage poses. He explained that he was not aroused by the nudity of the women but rather by the photographs which appeared designed to convey their helplessness at the hands of a man.

DRUG INTOXICATION

Offenders in this category tend to decide to rape a woman, and because of the ingestion of drugs or alcohol, find themselves losing control of the situation, at times leading to a frenzied response that can conclude in the unplanned death of the victim. The following case illustrates this category of crime and involves a killing by an offender who had no previous violent criminal history.

CASE NO. 6

A 38-year-old construction worker with an arrest history of burglary, grand larceny, and resisting arrest, but no history of sexual assault, was introduced by a mutual friend to his 19-year-old victim days before her death. After becoming high on drugs, he went to the victim's apartment to obtain the phone number of the mutual friend. The attractive woman, dressed in a nightgown and robe, answered the door and gave him the number. Based upon this encounter, he decided to "have sex" with the woman. He returned unarmed to the apartment, and after telling her that the number she had given him was incorrect, she invited him in while she checked the number. A physically violent confrontation occurred and blood spatter evidence indicated that they had fought in the kitchen, living room, and bedroom of the small apartment. He used at least seven different weapons in the victim's murder, stabbing her with a butcher knife and at least two paring knifes, hitting her multiple times with a large heavy wooden table lamp, strangling her with the lamp's electrical cord, and hitting her with a hot iron, essentially branding her face. Finally, he put a cloth in her mouth. In his confession, he stated that she wouldn't stop breathing so he stomped her chest with his feet. When found by a coworker, she was lying on the living room floor with her robe ripped open, her legs spread, her torn panties hanging on one leg, her nightgown pulled above her breasts, and the cloth in her mouth.

The perpetrator made no effort to sanitize the crime scene but he took her camera, and on the same day, he unsuccessfully attempted to pawn it at two businesses located near the victim's residence. He also took her car and was captured 6 days later in an adjacent state while driving the vehicle. Beneath the front seat of the car was a bent paring knife with the victim's blood on it.

This case suggests that there was little prior planning of a forced sexual encounter and that the disinhibiting effects of the drugs both prompted the forced sexual interactions and the frenzied manner in which the woman was murdered. It appears likely that had the perpetrator not ingested drugs, he would have reached a different decision about how to express his sexual attraction to his victim and might have found an alternative resolution to his sexual arousal.

MONOTONY AND BOREDOM

The individuals represented in this category are sexual sadists who have been found to keep their victims in captivity for days to years. In these instances, the perpetrator subjects the victim to a wide variety of sexual behaviors over time and gradually begins to experience the sexual interactions as repetitive and monotonous. There is no deepening of the relationship in these circumstances and it is possible that familiarity with the victim also begins to distort and undermine the experience of terror and dominance that is central to the arousal of the sadist. When the victim begins to lose their appeal for these various reasons, this type of offender tends to murder their victims and dispose of their bodies as a "house cleaning" function that will allow them to move on to their next victim. Such an ending becomes almost inevitable as there is no other way to end the relationship given the exposure that the victim has had to the perpetrator and the inevitability of the victim reporting them to the police should they gain their freedom. In this type of instance, the murder is not a part of the sexual act but rather the avenue for new sexual explorations and experiences.

CASE NO. 7

PB committed a series of physically violent, but non-homicidal rapes (i.e., broken arm while committing anal rape) in Canada, and prior to apprehension, acquired a nickname in the media. He was simultaneously engaging in a progression of deviant behavior with his girlfriend, KH, who eventually became his wife. He forced her to wear her 15-year-old sister's clothing, to respond to the sister's name during sex, to verbally demean herself, to drink his urine, and to solicit and have sex with prostitutes. Eventually, the couple became involved in the rape and murder of her sister. The young girl's death was listed as an accidental death due to alcohol intoxication. She vomited while lying on her stomach as PB anally raped her. The couple dressed her and notified the parents. Medical personnel were called but when they arrived at the location of the assault they were unable to revive her.

Following the death of this young woman, PB kidnapped a 14-year-old girl and held her in captivity for a 2- to 3-day period. During this time, he and his wife repeatedly raped her vaginally, anally, and orally. Tiring of this victim, PB strangled her to death using a ligature. His wife then participated in the abduction, sexual assault, and murder of a second 15-year-old victim. During this time, PB was becoming progressively more physically violent with his wife. His wife's mother unexpectedly visited their home and found that her daughter had been severely beaten. She transported her to a hospital where she met with police and eventually assisted them by providing testimony against her husband. She also assisted the police in locating the video that had been made documenting the murders.

Much less frequently, the sexually sadistic offender's victims are rescued or released by their captors. This process is described in the book, *The Perfect Victim* (McGuire & Norton, 1988), which describes the 7-year captivity of a sex slave who spent almost every night sleeping in a box beneath the bed of the couple who were holding her captive.

CASE NO. 8

CH had a long standing fantasy of possessing a female sexual slave. When 18 years of age, he met a 14-year-old girl who had never been on a date or been kissed by a boy. They married when she was 15 years old and he shortly thereafter began to introduce her to bondage and other sexual acts totally alien to the young girl. Within a short period of time, she became a "compliant victim" (see Chapter 23), and he became comfortable telling her of his wish to find and keep in captivity a sex slave. Based upon her acquiescence, he kidnapped a 15-year-old girl and brought her to their residence, where he tortured and raped her in the presence of his teenage wife. Wanting to keep her as a slave, but realizing that the walls of their duplex apartment would not sufficiently muffle her screams, he took her into the bathroom and attempted to remove her "voice box." Unable to staunch the flow of blood, the young woman died and the couple disposed of her body.

The young wife continued to be subjected to her husband's increasingly painful sexual demands. He told her that if he had a sexual slave, he could act out his fantasies with the other women, saving his wife from the sexual demands he was making on her. Eventually, the young woman agreed that her husband could have a sex slave if he agreed to her having a child. Together, they kidnapped a 21-year-old woman who was hitchhiking. She was immediately bound and her head was encased in a "head box" that precluded her hearing and screaming. She was taken to their single-family residence where she was tortured, raped, and placed into a coffin-like box which fit beneath the couple's bed.

This woman was kept in captivity for 7 years and was gradually allowed more freedom (i.e., working in the backyard, babysitting their child, obtaining employment at a local motel, and attending church). She was even taken for a weekend visit with her parents whom she hadn't seen or corresponded with for 6 years. Following the visit, she left with CH and was returned to captivity. After church one Sunday, the woman confided to her pastor of her state of captivity and he immediately notified the police who rescued her from the home.

It was this case that prompted our interest not only in compliant victims but also the wives of sex offenders. Women in both of these positions come to play an essential and contributory role in the continuation of the violence and their own subjugation to degradation and humiliation.

CONCLUSIONS

We would like to underscore that our identification of motivations that we believe prompt the escalation of rape into murder are relevant only to the small minority of sexual assaults that become lethal (Dietz, Hazelwood, & Warren, 1990). By far, the majority of rapes remain terrifying experiences which end with the victim alive, although physically and emotionally injured. Clearly, one component of the rape that magnifies the fear and horror is the loss of all control and the inability to anticipate how the assault is going to end.

We anticipate that our observations will assist law enforcement in determining, based upon the crime scene information, whether the murder is the intent of the crime or an unexpected consequence of a rape. We have observed a tendency to quickly interpret any sexual murder in terms of the sexually sadistic intent of the perpetrator, a potentially premature conclusion that can lead investigators to anticipate the wrong type of offender and to initiate a search for evidence that is unlikely to exist. Our various motivations are designed to separate rape from murder and to create an analytic space in which the evidence can be used to reconstruct the motivation underlying the sexual assault and to more accurately anticipate the future intent and behavior of a yet to be apprehended perpetrator.

We anticipate that our development of the concept of a psychosexual plateau will be of use to law enforcement when they are trying to assess the patterning within a particular series of crimes. It will help to guide the assessment of whether a particular offender has identified their preferred form of sexual offending or has not yet reached their core masturbatory fantasy, suggesting that their crime behavior can be expected to continue to evolve potentially involving increasingly violent and lethal behavior. It is our impression that this escalation is often, if not always, associated with the comingling of paraphilic disorders with the presence of sadistic and necrophilia interests being found in the most prolific and deadly of sexual offenders.

Our experience also suggests that the means by which a woman is murdered can be used in some instances to infer the motivation for the murder that has occurred. Our prior research has demonstrated that sexual sadists prefer to murder their victims through strangulation with the face of the women being positioned in such a way that they can see and register the terror and horror the woman is experiencing as she dies. This type of intimate dominance and ultimate control is not present in other instances of sexual murder, in which there are high levels of blunt force injury and evidence of frenzied interactions between the victim and the perpetrator. As observed in prior research (Ressler & Burgess, 1985), highly disorganized crime scenes can be indicative of serious mental illness of the perpetrator, particularly when there are bizarre ritualistic aspects of the crime scene and the absence of semen in any part of the woman's body.

In closing, we would like to emphasize that these observations derive from case experience and do not reflect the results of quantitative research. Of course, it is unlikely that these ideas will ever be subject to full empirical analyses given the complexity of obtaining a cooperative sample of forthcoming rapists and sexual murderers who are available for in-depth study. We do hope, however, to begin the discussion of the differences between rape and sexual murder, with this distinction being relevant not only to law enforcement but also to victims and those who are responsible to responding to them.

REFERENCES

Abel, G. G., Becker, J. V., Cunningham-Rathner, J., Mittelman, M., and Rouleau, J.-L. 1988. Multiple diagnoses among sex offenders. *Bulletin of the American Academy of Psychiatry and the Law*, 16, 153–168.

Abel, G. G., Becker, J. V., Mittelman, M. S., Cunningham-Rathner, J., Rouleau, J.-L., and Murphy, W. D. 1987. Self-reported sex crimes of nonincarcerated paraphiliacs. *Journal of Interpersonal Violence*, 2(1), 3–25.

Dietz, P. E., Harry, B., and Hazelwood, R. R. 1986. Detective magazines: Pornography for the sexual sadist? *Journal of Forensic Sciences*, 31(1), 197–211. doi: 10.1520/JFS11872J.

Dietz, P. E., Hazelwood, R. R., and Warren, J. 1990. The sexual sadistic criminal and his offenses. *Bulletin of the American Academy of Psychiatry and the Law*, 18, 163–178.

Gibb, D. A. 2011. *Camouflaged killer: The shocking double life of Colonel Russell Williams*. New York: Berkley Books.

Hazelwood, R. R., and Lanning, K. V. 2009. Collateral materials in sexual crimes. In R. R. Hazelwood, and A. W. Burgess (Eds.), *Practical aspects of rape investigation: A multidisciplinary approach*, 4th ed., 201–210. Baton Rouge, FL: CRC Press.

Hazelwood, R. R., and Warren, J. I. 1990. Criminal behavior of the serial rapist. *FBI Law Enforcement Bulletin*, 59, 11–16.

McGuire, C., and Norton, C. 1988. *Perfect victim: The true story of "the girl in the box" by the D.A. who prosecuted her captor*. New York: Dell Publishing.

Meloy, J. R. 1992. *Violent attachments*. Northvale, NJ: Jason Aronson, Inc.

Meloy, J. R. 1998. Unpublished draft opinion, June 22.

Meloy, J. R. 2000. The nature and dynamics of sexual homicide: An integrative review. *Aggression and Violent Behavior*, 5, 1–22. doi: 10.1016/S1359-1789(99)00006-3.

Prentky, R. A., Burgess, A. W., Rokous, F., Lee, A., Hartman, C., Ressler, R., and Douglas, J. 1989. The presumptive role of fantasy in serial sexual homicide. *American Journal of Psychiatry*, 146, 887–891.

Ressler, R. K., and Burgess, A. W. 1985. Crime scene and profile characteristics of organized and disorganized murders. *FBI Law Enforcement Bulletin*, 54(8), 18–25.

Warren, J., Hazelwood, R., and Dietz, P. E. 1996. The sexually sadistic serial murderer. *Journal of Forensic Sciences*, 41, 970–974.

Warren, J., Reboussin, R., and Hazelwood, R. R. 1989. Serial rape: Correlates of increased aggression and the relationship of Offender pleasure to victim resistance. *Journal of Interpersonal Violence*, 4(1), 65–78.

Warren, J. I., Reboussin, R., Hazelwood, R. R., Gibbs, N. A., Trumbetta, S. L., and Cummings, A. 1999. Crime scene analysis and the escalation of violence in serial rape. *Forensic Science International*, 100, 37–56. doi: 10.1016/S0379-0738(98)00158-3.

14 Cold Case Investigation

R. Stephen Mardigian and Roger L. Depue

CONTENTS

Definitions 200
Resource Limitations 200
Solvability Factors 200
The Four Levels of Prioritization 201
   Pitfalls and Lessons Learned 201
The Multi-Agency Team Approach 202
Case Reactivation Concerns 203
Case Reorganization Issues 203
Review Original Case File 203
Crime Reconstruction 204
Investigative Plan 204
Interviews of Nonfamilial Persons 205
Nontraditional Investigative Techniques 206
Suspect Interview/Interrogation 206
Technology Support 207
Summary and Conclusion 207
References 208

There was a time in the not too distant past when homicide and rape cases were initially investigated vigorously using whatever state-of-the-art techniques existed at the time until all logical leads were exhausted. The cases were then slowly relegated to the "pending inactive" file where they sat until, and unless, new information of value came to the attention of investigators. As time passed, if no new information was forthcoming and the press of new business demanded the attention of investigators and police administrators, the unsolved cases often sank into obscurity and only remained in the minds of the veteran investigators of the department. With the advent of new scientific technology and sophisticated investigative techniques, investigators started to reopen those "old dog" cases and began to gain some measure of success at applying the recent advances to the "cold" unsolved cases. Consequently, as more and more cases were solved, there was renewed interest in dedicating manpower and other resources to the cases that had been previously considered old and cold. Eventually, increased success in the reinvestigations caused the emergence of the "Cold Case Squad" in large police departments across the country. Reinvestigations became a realistic second chance for justice and closure. What follows is a description and explanation of the highly sophisticated functions of these squads and some guidelines and suggestions about how to organize and manage a highly efficient Cold Case Squad. (For the purposes of this chapter, the term "cold case" will refer to an unsolved *death* investigation unless otherwise specified.)

DEFINITIONS

This chapter begins by providing the reader with definitions of law enforcement terms to be used.

* *Cold case* is a term used to identify an unsolved crime that has been extant for a period of time with all logical leads having been covered and solvability is considered unlikely or very questionable. Cold cases are typically assigned low priority by investigating agencies.
* *Viable cold case* is used to describe a cold case with the potential to benefit from reinvestigation.
* *Cold case squad* is a team responsible for examining cold cases to determine their viability and for initiating reinvestigation when appropriate.
* *Cold Case Analysis Program (CCAP)* is a systematic process designed to examine cold cases in the most efficient and productive manner possible.

RESOURCE LIMITATIONS

In most law enforcement agencies there are competing priorities and limited time and resource resources. Available manpower and equipment needs, budgetary constraints, and caseload assignments significantly impact a department's ability to address overall responsibilities. Cold cases generally draw upon those allocated resources producing a strain on the available assets for new business. It is therefore difficult for many departments to authorize spending and allotted resources on cold cases. New cases necessarily take priority over cold cases which have no apparent information of value. It is therefore advantageous to apply available time and manpower toward the solution of new cases where evidence is fresh, witnesses are identified, contact of persons of interest and suspects is possible, and citizen concern and media interest is intense. Because the approximate number of new cases is estimated based on the volume of cases experienced in previous years, budgetary, equipment, and personnel support is projected and subsequently allocated to deal with these new cases. Cold cases generally draw upon those same resources unavoidably producing a strain on the department's ability to meet the investigative demand placed on it. It may become difficult, if not impractical, for many departments to authorize spending and other valuable resources on cold cases.

SOLVABILITY FACTORS

A successful CCAP program depends on assessing the solvability factors of any cold case. One must ask and answer the question: "Which cases have greater potential for successful investigation and prosecution?" Establishing a screening process is critical to the selection of cases that are acceptable for investigation. Any cold case under consideration for reinvestigation review should have identifiable attributes that make it a potentially successful case for solvability. Some questions that need to be addressed are: Does the case have sufficient investigative information to allow for new analysis and interpretation? Is there a "known perpetrator"? Is there a person or persons investigators believe are responsible for the crime, but do not have sufficient evidence to prove their theory? Are there other viable suspects or persons of interest? Is there a body (corpus delicti), or evidence indicating there was a victim, that had been disposed of in a manner that the body will never be recovered? Was an autopsy performed and was a cause of death established? How much physical evidence exists and were proper crime scene procedures followed? When crime scene evidence is recorded and preserved properly, the case can be reexamined again and again. Are there existing written laboratory and/or photographic records? Are there witnesses available for reinterview? Was there a known or suspected motive? Is there information (intelligence data) in the file concerning a relative or friend of the victim and was suspected to have been involved in the crime? Will new technologies apply to the case? Depending on the answers to these questions, a prioritization of cases for potential reinvestigation can be made.

THE FOUR LEVELS OF PRIORITIZATION

Not all unsolved cold cases will benefit from a reinvestigation. In fact, there are some cases which should not be considered for re-evaluation. Criteria that have the potential to maximize chances for successful reinvestigation and prosecution are offered below:

Level one is when a suspect is known and there is physical evidence available that can be used to identify that person as the perpetrator. Sometimes new technology may be applied to the case. For example, DNA from sperm that has been properly collected and preserved from a raped or murdered victim, can now be compared to that suspect to determine the likelihood of guilt or innocence.

The second level of cold case prioritization is when there is an unknown subject, but physical evidence exists that can be analyzed by new technology. When suspects or persons of interest are developed, that evidence can be used to compare with the individual(s) and used to eliminate or confirm crime involvement. The third level of prioritization is when there is an unknown subject and there is no physical evidence for comparative use, but new witness intelligence provides material information. As an example, someone may be identified, or voluntarily comes forward, who provides guilty knowledge of a crime to another person who in turn informs the authorities about the contact as in Case no. 1.

CASE NO. 1

In one case which remained unsolved for 21 years, a teenage associate of the young female sexual homicide victim bragged to a school friend that he had killed a young girl in his neighborhood. This conversation took place 2 years after the crime. The discovery of this conversation occurred during investigative reinterviews of all friends and associates of the victim and suspects. After 19 years, the school friend to whom the admission had been made, no longer felt allegiance to the fellow student and told investigators of the incriminating conversation. This information was successfully utilized during an interview of the new suspect, who was then 36 years of age, resulting in the successful prosecution and conviction of the killer.

The fourth and lowest level of prioritization for cold case re-evaluation occurs when there is no known suspect or the victim cannot be identified or located, and there are no witnesses and little or no evidence, which can be used to identify a perpetrator. For example, the bones of an unidentified deceased victim are found and no other evidence or witnesses exist.

PITFALLS AND LESSONS LEARNED

- Which cold cases are selected for reinvestigation are directly correlated with which ones have the best chance for successful resolution and prosecution. Accordingly, it becomes imperative to take full advantage of available resources through establishing a definitive prioritization system (such as above) for case selection that maximizes chances for positive resolution.
- It is imperative that reexamined cold cases are evaluated under the umbrella of an investigative effort and not as a critique. When conducting the review, investigators should avoid using potentially critical remarks about the initial investigative efforts such as, *"I don't understand why they did or did not do…,"* *"Why wasn't this done?"* or *"Why was it done this way?"* Such comments are often viewed as being accusatory or unfair criticism of the prior investigative effort and the previous investigator(s). Remember, the reexamination may benefit greatly from the assistance of the initial investigator.

- Early involvement and support from the prosecuting attorney is an essential element to successful resolution.
- Supportive management and commitment from leadership are "keys" to success.
- Avoid overloading cold case investigators. Considerable time and energy will be expended reevaluating an unsolved cold case, locating and reviewing files, reexamining physical evidence, and locating witnesses. Investigators should not be unduly burdened by also being assigned new cases.
- Impartiality is an essential aspect of unsolved case re-evaluations. Case theories will develop in situations which may have undergone extensive investigation. These theories sometimes become the basis upon which factual evidence is later developed or corroborated through active investigation. While all theories should be considered in any reinvestigative effort, these ideas should not exclude other possibilities.
- Reinvestigations can be extremely time-consuming. Prior investigative efforts requires close scrutiny before decisions are made as to what should be redone.
- Many things may have changed since the initial investigation. Examples of such changes include the original crime scene setting, topography, and overall geography. Each area must be considered in relationship to the current environment. Societal mobility may also make locating significant witnesses or suspects a difficult endeavor.

THE MULTI-AGENCY TEAM APPROACH

Police agencies frequently find themselves having to reduce the amount of investigative activity which can be directed toward unsolved cold cases due to budget, manpower, technical, and other resource restrictions. These constraints, however, may be offset through implementation of a Multi-Agency Team Approach, which allow resources and financial costs to be shared between contributing agencies.

A Multi-Agency Team may be comprised of individuals having special knowledge and skill sets. Original case investigators, when available, should be invited to join the team. In this day and age there are investigators who specialize in cold case investigation and again, where available, their participation should be solicited. The team selection process should begin with an emphasis on identifying highly experienced homicide investigators who have developed interview and interrogation talents, are skilled in crime scene reconstruction and forensic evidence, and who have knowledge and experience with courtroom procedures and providing testimony. Investigators from jurisdictions where the crime(s) were committed are assets to such task forces. Federal law enforcement personnel may provide resources not otherwise available and often can assist with timely coverage of out-of-state leads. Laboratory technicians and scientists should assist with the reanalysis and re-evaluation of physical evidence. It is essential to have the local prosecutor on board because it makes no sense to reinvestigate a cold case if prosecution will be declined.

When choosing individuals to reinvestigate cold cases, the desired qualities should include:

1. Honed interpersonal skills
2. Good listeners
3. Demonstrated patience
4. Experience in managing "sources of information"
5. Known for "Street smarts"
6. Common sense
7. Creative and innovative problem solving abilities.

Quite often, these types of officers are recognized as the best investigators and therefore are already overassigned. Moreover, departments intent on participating in a Multi-Agency Task Force should first consider the level of commitment and support they are willing to invest in the group and to the individuals and an understanding that the team will need adequate time and opportunity to achieve success.

CASE REACTIVATION CONCERNS

One of the first steps in working unsolved cold cases and/or the development of a Multi-Agency Task Force is to gauge the level of interest and potential commitment that might be received from the law enforcement community, the prosecutor's office, and the media. The higher the level of interest by each of these entities, the more they will support the team. Steps should be taken to assess the level of interest by contacting individuals who have a professional as well as a personal interest in solving the case(s). Examples might include: investigators who previously worked the case, current police administrators, prosecutors who were or potentially would be involved in the case(s), and even reporters who have knowledge of the case.

Securing support from departmental leaders at the outset is imperative in that they likely will be influenced by ongoing responsibilities and present priorities and cold case investigators will often have to compete for resources and funding.

Prosecuting attorneys who are enthusiastic and committed to solving the case(s) can provide valuable advice on various legal issues that are bound to come up as the reinvestigation progresses. Such issues may include recent case law and court decisions, retroactive legislation, rules of evidence at the time the crime was committed, statute of limitations, prior invocation of rights by a suspect, privileged communications, and prior investigative steps taken which may taint a new investigation. It is noted that the FBI has agents who are trained legal advisors and who work as teammates with investigators in the preparation of federal cases. It is suggested that a similar arrangement be applied at the local or state levels, especially when Multi-Agency Task Forces have been established to address cold cases.

The media is often willing to accept an interesting cold case for publicity and this can become a valuable asset to a renewed investigative effort. Care should be taken when soliciting media input that such coverage facilitates rather than interferes with the investigation.

CASE REORGANIZATION ISSUES

Dormant cold cases should be updated and reorganized for the renewed investigative effort. Crime scene materials must be gathered and assembled in a logical manner. Significant persons (i.e., witnesses, suspects, persons of interest) who were involved in the case should be identified and their prior statements assembled in a logical manner. All evidential material, including crime scene and autopsy photographs, must be categorized into a coherent order. Cases with extensive amounts of data should be computerized to facilitate retrieval during the reinvestigation. Legal issues and opinions must be identified and all investigative leads previously covered must be reexamined for their value. A systematic and phased investigative plan of action may then be put into place.

REVIEW ORIGINAL CASE FILE

While maintaining objectivity, team members should thoroughly evaluate all theories that evolved during the initial investigation, and attempt to assess how or if those concepts were adequately verified or confirmed. As the team examines the case file, it should determine the original investigative focus. It will also be necessary to identify leads that may have gone unrecognized or been overlooked. Previous interviews must be reviewed with the understanding that new interviews may be necessary to address issues not resolved as well as any inconsistencies. Essential material covered during the prior interviews should, if necessary, be covered again for clarification and/or elaboration. At this juncture the team might explore having the prior investigation submitted for an interpretation by behavioral specialists (i.e., from the FBI's National Center for the Analysis of Violent Crime at Quantico, VA). Such an analysis could potentially shed light on investigative approaches or crime motivations not previously considered.

Questions arising from the file review must be put into an investigative and/or interview plan oriented toward getting definitive answers. It is noted that unsolved cold cases seldom have adequate information regarding the victim's habits and lifestyle. Consequently, a comprehensive plan must be put in place to learn everything possible about the victim(s). A list of all past and/or potential witnesses and suspects should be made and their reinterviews prioritized. Investigators should keep in mind the possible linkage to other cases and consider their submission to the FBI Violent Criminal Apprehension Program (VICAP).

While examining the original case file, it would be wise to update any original visual aids or to develop new ones. For instance, detailed maps which plot out significant crime scene areas are useful tools that provide investigators with insight and perspectives of what the environment was like at the time the crime was committed. Any renewed investigative endeavor can, where available, also be supported with crime scene sketches and charts, preferably drawn to scale. Timelines can also be useful implements for depicting significant events and locations related to the victim's or suspect's activities.

As part of the case review, detailed interviews of the originally assigned investigators, medical examiners, and crime scene technicians should also be conducted. These interviews can be extremely beneficial as new investigators prepare to reexamine a cold case. It is essential that the interview approach of these professionals be tactful, nonjudgmental, and use open-ended questions, avoiding any suggestion of reproach or displeasure for things that were done or not done in the past.

CRIME RECONSTRUCTION

When all information has been collected, the team is ready to reconstruct the crime. Materials such as crime scene and autopsy photos, sketches, diagrams, visitation of the crime scene when possible, investigative and laboratory reports, case notes, and interviews are presented to team members who then begin brainstorming. This is the theory development and testing phase. It follows the Criminal Investigative Analysis (CIA) model; *WHAT* happened? A narrative about what took place is begun. Then the question of *HOW* the crime scene came to be like it was when found is discussed. (The crime must be explained in a step-by-step manner with explanations of what the offender and victim sequentially did until the team is led to an understanding of how the circumstances of the crime scene came to be as they were found.) Now the team is ready to begin speculating about *WHY* it happened. This is the formulation of potential motive(s) for the commission of the crime. Once those motive(s) are identified, then the team can begin to speculate about *WHO* (the type of person(s) likely to have behaved in the fashion revealed in the crime scene. At this point the team begins to formulate the profile or characteristics and traits of the unknown offender(s). Upon completion of this step it is an appropriate time to begin constructing the investigative plan.

INVESTIGATIVE PLAN

Because time has passed since the commission of the crime, individuals with knowledge of the crime who previously were reluctant to talk or get involved may now be more approachable (see Case no. 1). With the passage of time, the memories of persons associated with the crime may move away from honoring and praising of the victim and others and toward a more realistic portrayal of them. These memories may reveal more accurate information than that obtained in the original investigation. Questions regarding feelings or "hunches" about who may have committed the crime are appropriate during reinvestigations of unsolved cold cases.

The initial investigative phase should begin with a revisit to the victim's family. The family members can be told that there is renewed interest in looking at the case and that a team is approaching the case with a new perspective. Explain to them that new techniques and technologies have been developed that could benefit a reinvestigation. Explain that a thorough examination of the victim's life usually brings about additional information that may come from the reinterview of family members, friends, and acquaintances. Caution should be taken when interacting with family, especially if their involvement has not been removed from suspicion.

The hopes and expectations of the family members must not be unrealistically heightened. This is particularly true if the initial investigation was very thorough and there is no apparent room for improvement. Cold cases will be very difficult to solve when the original investigation accomplished everything that could reasonably have been done.

INTERVIEWS OF NONFAMILIAL PERSONS

Start with peripheral witnesses and associates first. These interviews may bring about new information resulting from changing relationships and associations. It is important to realize that this interview group may include (and alert) the suspect(s) and they may prepare themselves for accusation or leave the area to avoid being contacted. The person(s) having the least personal relationship with the victim should be the first interviewed and then gradually move toward those with closer relationships with the victim. Following these interviews of closer associates, consider additional contacts with them as they may also be worthwhile.

CASE NO. 2

Investigative interest was renewed on a 21-year-old unsolved case which involved the brutal decapitation of a 9-year-old female victim. A more recent murder of another young female had occurred in the same general area causing renewed interest and examination of the older case for possible similarities. While the more recent homicide was solved and found to have no connection to the older case, the investigators became intrigued with a particular suspect in the older unresolved case. A peripheral interview of a former religious leader and family associate of the suspect resulted in significant new information. The former pastor acknowledged that he had seen the replica metal sheriff's badge, which had been found beneath the child's body, inside the suspect's residence prior to the murder. This new information caused a new and intensive investigative effort which included coordination and support from the local prosecutor's office. A well-planned reinterview of the suspect resulted in his being charged, arrested, and prosecuted for the crime.

As seen in the following case, investigators should also be alert to the possibility that potential suspects may do something suspicious immediately following the interview.

CASE NO. 3

In a 10-year-old murder case, during the reinterview of a former coworker of the female murder victim, investigators noted inconsistencies with his original statement from years before. Originally he spoke of the victim in highly complimentary terms. In the current statement, he alleged that she used drugs and slept with her boss. This difference caused investigators to take a more serious look at him as a potential suspect. Investigators monitored his behavior while increasing the scope of their investigation and determined that following the reinterview the coworker left a note for his current girlfriend informing her that he would be "leaving the area for a while" and he prepared to flee to California. Subsequent investigation revealed him to be the killer.

Remember that change in relationships over time is the investigator's ally. These interviews may include current and former friendships, coworkers, neighbors, sexual partners, relatives, room-mates, cell-mates, among many other possibilities.

CASE NO. 4

During the reinterview of a murdered woman's fiancé 15 years after her stabbing death at her place of employment, the man made statements such as "I don't care to get involved" and "I already told the police everything I know." When it was pointed out to him that he had been engaged to marry the victim and knew her better than anyone else, and could tell investigators about her habits and lifestyle, he reluctantly agreed to talk to them "for a few minutes." His reluctance caused investigators to take a closer look at the fiancé. Reexamining the case file and evidence reports, investigators theorized that the killer may have cut himself while plunging the knife into the victim because there was no hand guard on the murder weapon (butcher knife left at the scene). The investigators speculated that the killer's hand could have slipped down the wet wooden handle of the knife onto the blade thereby lacerating his hand. A laboratory technician opened the knife handle and found blood inside the handle. A DNA test of the blood inside the knife handle was compared to the fiancé's DNA obtained from cigarette butts found in the trash. A positive match was made providing the evidence needed for the prosecution and conviction of the fiancé.

NONTRADITIONAL INVESTIGATIVE TECHNIQUES

When contemplating the approach to a suspect or person of interest, nontraditional techniques should be considered. For example, pretending to conduct a marketing survey may be appropriate to make an initial contact with a person allowing investigators to obtain information such as employment, occupation, age, education, training, religious affiliation, marital status, organizational memberships, vehicle ownership, assets, health and physical condition, interests, and associates. Community policing contacts also afford opportunities to gain information in an unobtrusive way.

Ambient camera placement may be of use to determine the activities and routine of a suspect or a person of interest. These camera surveillance devices can be set up around the person's residence, place of employment or amusement. Some cameras may already be in place and their tapes can be reviewed for information of value (banks, ATMs, retail businesses, hotels, apartment houses, service stations, public spaces, parking lots, busy intersections, traffic control devices).

As noted in Case no. 4, obtaining a DNA sample may be of value. Anything that may have come into contact with bodily fluids can be examined for DNA traces such as saliva contact with discarded bottles and cans, cigarette butts (as in Case no. 4), envelope and stamps, blood specimens from bandages, semen on bedding, clothing, and hair follicles. A ruse may also be used in this regard (i.e., furnishing the suspect a return envelope, the flap of which must be licked).

Crime scene investigators should be trained and encouraged to think in a futuristic sense during the collection and preservation of evidence. There may be "potential evidence" collected during a crime scene investigation. What is potential evidence? Imagine that investigators realize a crime scene may contain bacteria or odors that, in the future, can be analyzed and linked to specific individuals. Scientists know that persons carry unique collections of bacteria on their bodies that can be attributed to individuals and that each person possesses an individual odor. This fact is already exemplified by the use of dogs to track suspects. Crime scene investigative techniques may soon be developed to capture a sample of bacteria or an air sample at the crime scene and stored in some pristine way until forensic science developed the means for comparison of the samples and suspects (*Between Good and Evil*, Depue & Schindehette, 2005).

SUSPECT INTERVIEW/INTERROGATION

Planning the interview is critical. If not the most frequent mistake made in this area, the failure to plan the interview tailored to the personality of the subject is certainly one of the most common mistakes. As much information as possible must be obtained about the suspect or person of interest *prior to the interview.* A valuable tool for this purpose is the Indirect Personality Assessment (Ault & Hazelwood, 1995). This tool allows the investigator to assess the subject's strengths and weaknesses that may be exploited during the interview. An Indirect Personality Assessment generally includes elements such as overall personality and lifestyle information, interests, habits, likes, dislikes, strengths, weaknesses, educational level, skills, substance use and abuse, values, support system, and relationships.

Planning the interview also includes where and when the interview should take place and the environment. These decisions depend largely on information obtained from the Indirect Personality Assessment. For example, some interviews are best conducted at night in the police environment while others may be best conducted in a neutral setting during the daytime.

Props may be useful during the interview. Recognizing that care must be taken not to divulge "Hold Back Information" (known only to the offender and the police), potential "props" included in this category are such items as photographs of the victim or crime scene, evidentiary items related to the crime, maps and diagrams, investigative files, filing cabinets and binders, visual aids created for the investigation and courtroom, and news media coverage of the crime.

TECHNOLOGY SUPPORT

Computer data systems are available for use such as the Combined DNA Index System (CODIS) which enables federal, state, and local crime laboratories to exchange and compare DNA profiles electronically; the FBI's National DNA Index System (NDIS) which enables laboratories participating in CODIS to exchange and compare DNA profiles on a national level; the Automated Fingerprint Identification System (AFIS) is a biometric identification methodology to obtain, score, and analyze fingerprint data and; the FBI's Integrated Automated Fingerprint Identification System (IAFIS) which is being developed to provide identification services nationally to law enforcement and other organizations where criminal background histories are a critical factor in consideration for employment. In addition to fingerprint identification systems, there is an Automated Palm Identification System (APIS) to match and compare palm prints. Other helpful systems are the Cyanocrylate Latent Fingerprint Development System (also called the super-glue system) that involves lifting prints from surfaces previously considered impossible such as leather and cloth. Then there are lasers that allow for enhanced ability to detect latent prints, and Alternate Light Sources (ALS) that allow for viewing evidence that cannot be seen with the naked eye. Some items are treated with chemical dyes and stains which require the use of forensic lights for viewing evidence.

Forensic examination of trace materials has been greatly enhanced over the years. The search for, and identification of materials such as human hairs, animal hairs, textile fibers and fabrics, ropes, feathers, and kinds of wood fiber, which could not have been found in the past, are now being identified because of modern technological advances. Cases are being proven by advanced examinations of geological materials and soil types. These are just a few of the examples of advancements in forensic science that can aid in the reexamination of cold cases.

SUMMARY AND CONCLUSION

In these days of limited resources, cold case investigations must compete with other pressing needs of the police department. Therefore, it must be ascertained early whether or not there are sufficient resources and support for establishing a cold case operation. However, police administrators need to be aware that recent advances in scientific examination of evidence and CIA have resulted in a great deal of success in the reinvestigation of cold cases. A successful plan should begin with the support of department administration, prosecutor's office, and the media. If the resources and support are present, then a plan for a cold case squad is feasible. In establishing a cold case operation, it is important to determine the "solvability factors" of the cold cases within the department. Do these cases possess the critical elements (potential suspects, witnesses, evidence, and records) necessary to make success likely? A prioritization of unsolved cases is necessary and the cases most likely to benefit from reinvestigation should be considered first. The reinvestigation process should be careful not to become a hard critique of the initial efforts to solve the case. The Multi-Agency Team Approach is a valuable concept to share the cost and talents of several departments. Following the careful assembly of the team and the selection of the cases with the highest level of solvability, it is necessary to thoroughly review each case. When a case is selected, identify the specific resources available and employ the latest scientific and analytical techniques. If specific resources are indicated but not available, the assistance of outside agencies and laboratories may be necessary. Begin the crime reconstruction by using the systematic CIA method. Reconstruction of the crime is necessary to identify the behaviors exhibited by the victim and the perpetrator and will usually lead to the most likely motive(s) for the commission of the crime. A behavioral profile of the unknown perpetrator can often be formulated. New leads are acquired by conducting interviews and reinterviews of all available persons associated with the case. Investigators need to expand on previous interviews by encouraging interviewees to speak freely about past relationships and old allegiances and to speculate about their own theories concerning suspects and events. Once a suspect(s) is identified, as much information as possible should be collected prior to the interviews. The Indirect Personality Assessment is a valuable instrument for this purpose. Throughout the reinvestigation, new methods of scientific examination and technical support should be considered such as fingerprint identification, DNA comparison, scientific examination of trace materials, as well as those on the periphery of discovery (individual bacteria and odor). As new information is obtained and processed, progress will be made toward answering the questions necessary to move the reinvestigation forward toward success.

Cold Case Investigation and imaginative crime scene analysis techniques hold great promise for discovering additional information, evidence, and suspect identification. These advances can make the difference between placing the file back in the "pending inactive" file cabinet and securing a successful arrest, prosecution, and conviction. It is gratifying for the investigators to bring closure to an unsolved cold case and a measure of justice to victims and their loved ones.

REFERENCES

Ault, R. L. Jr., and Hazelwood, R. R. 1995. *Indirect personality assessment in practical aspects of rape investigation: A multidisciplinary approach.* 2nd ed. New York: CRC Press, Inc., 12, 205–218.

California Department of Justice. 2002. *Cold case investigation manual.*

Commonwealth of Virginia Department of State Police. 2003. Internal documents, cold case investigations.

Depue, R. L., and Schindehette, S. 2005. *Between good and evil.* New York: Warner Books, 293–294.

Depue, R. L. 2014. Criminal investigative analysis. In Weisburd & Bruinsma (Eds). *Encyclopedia of criminology and criminal justice.* Berlin: Heidelberg.

Minnesota Department of Public Safety, Bureau of Criminal Apprehension, Unsolved Homicide Unit Guidelines. 2002. Management and investigation of unresolved homicides.

Texas Rangers, Department of Public Safety, Unsolved Crimes Investigation Team Guidelines. 2003. Investigation of unsolved homicides/major crimes.

The Academy Group, Inc. 2002. Internal documents, cold case analysis program.

Turner, R., and Kosa, R. July 2003. *Cold case squads: Leaving no stone unturned.* United States Department of Justice, Bureau of Justice Assistance Bulletin, www.ojp.usdoj.gov/BJA.

Section III

Forensics and Court

15 Physical Evidence in Sexual Assault Investigations

Tara Crider

CONTENTS

Introduction 212
Types of Evidence 212
Identifying Physical Evidence 213
    Observation and Perception 214
    Principle Theory of Exchange 214
    Evidence Recovery 215
    Lighting Techniques—Oblique, UV, and ALS 215
    Evidence Comparison 216
    Contamination 217
    Safety Precautions 218
General Crime Scene Approach 218
Initial Phase 218
    Crime Scene Integrity 219
    Interviews 219
    Authority to Search 220
    Preliminary Scene Survey 220
    Documentation 220
    Overall Photography 221
    Rough Sketch 221
Collection Phase 222
    Mid-Range and Close-Up Photography 222
    Measurements 222
    Collection 223
    Packaging 223
Final Phase 223
Physical Evidence Commonly Identified in Sexual Assault Investigations 224
Biological Evidence 224
    Nuclear DNA 224
    Polymerase Chain Reaction (PCR) 225
    CODIS 225
    DNA Preservation 225
    Mitochondrial and Y-Chromosome DNA 225
    Other Advancements in DNA Analysis 226
    Locating Biological Evidence 226
    Collecting Biological Evidence 227
    Packaging Biological Evidence 228
Blood 228
Semen 229
Vaginal Secretions 230

Saliva..230
    Bite Marks...230
    Cigarette Butts..231
    Chewing Gum 231
    Drink Ware 231
    Other Sources...231
Wearer DNA...231
Touch DNA 232
Urine and Feces...232
Hair and Fiber Evidence 232
    Locating Hair and Fiber Evidence 233
    Collecting Hair and Fiber Evidence...233
    Packaging Hair and Fiber Evidence 236
Physical Evidence Recovery Kit..236
    Known DNA Sample..236
    Known Hair Samples 237
    Swabs 237
    Oral Rinse...237
    Fingernail Scrapings...237
    Clothing..237
    Other Elimination Samples 238
Other Types of Physical Evidence 238
    Clothing and Bedding 238
    Condoms and Condom Wrappers 238
Drug Facilitated Sexual Assaults 238
Summary..239
Acknowledgments..239
Further Reading 239

INTRODUCTION

Forensic science and crime scene investigation (CSI) have become popular fields of study over the course of the last 15 years. This may be due to advances in the field; however, it is also likely attributed to the popularity of this genre on television to include shows such as *CSI: Crime Scene Investigation* and the numerous spin-offs since its inception. The public believes they have a general understanding of forensics and thus have grown to expect, or even demand, the recovery of physical evidence in all cases. This phenomenon is known as the CSI effect. The CSI effect can have a direct impact on how a jury reviews presented evidence and assess the facts of a case during trial. With forensic science in the forefront, succinctly explaining the lack of physical evidence at a crime scene has become just as important as understanding why physical evidence was located, and the value of both scenarios to the investigation. The objective of this chapter is to focus on how to *identify* evidence at a crime scene, specifically a sexual assault incident, and to then properly *document*, *collect*, and *preserve* this evidence. The primary responsibility of a crime scene investigator is to retain the integrity of the crime scene as a whole and any evidence located at the crime scene. Without following appropriate procedures the scene could be compromised and the evidence could be unrecognized, lost, destroyed, or altered in a way that makes it useless to the investigation.

TYPES OF EVIDENCE

There are many types of evidence that one may encounter during the course of an investigation. Evidence can range from witness statements to charts used for courtroom testimony to actual physical evidence such as a firearm recovered at the crime scene. Although any one of these types of evidence may be important to an investigation, the most relevant type of evidence in sexual assault cases is usually physical evidence, which will be the focus of this chapter. Physical evidence is sometimes referred to as "real evidence," and is defined as any tangible object which has an actual role in the investigation. Physical evidence can be broken down into a variety of categories which include but are not limited to the following: controlled substances, digital media, firearms and tool marks, biological fluids and stains, impressions, fingerprints, questioned documents, and trace evidence.

The intent of this chapter is not to provide an all-inclusive list of physical evidence found at a crime scene—this could be anything! Rather, the goal is to provide information about common types of evidence found in sexual assault cases. Although this chapter will focus on physical evidence, as an investigator, one should never discount the value of other types of evidence in sexual assault cases. Witness statements are often times very powerful and considered a key piece of evidence in an investigation and during courtroom testimony. Investigators should be encouraged to educate themselves in the identification and recovery of all types of evidence and all arenas of forensic science. The beginning sections of this chapter will review physical evidence and CSI in a general sense, as most practices applied to physical evidence can translate to any type of crime, including sexual assaults. As the chapter proceeds, a more thorough examination of evidence specifically found in sexual assault cases will be discussed.

IDENTIFYING PHYSICAL EVIDENCE

One of the first documented cases using physical evidence and forensic science to assist in an investigation dates back to 13th-century China. The investigator of this case determined the murder weapon to be a sickle by testing various types of blades on animal remains. The investigator then asked all the farmers of the town to gather in one place and bring their sickles. Flies were attracted to the smell of blood on the sickle that had been used as the murder weapon. When confronted, the subject confessed to the murder.

Typically, the source of physical evidence will come from one of three locations: the crime scene, the victim, or the suspect. This is known as the CSI triangle (Figure 15.1), and the investigator's goal is to link a suspect to a victim, a victim to a crime scene, or a crime scene to a suspect using physical evidence. In the case of the farmer and sickle, the investigator was able to use the sickle to link the suspect to the victim.

Putting the CSI triangle into practice isn't the only benefit to examining physical evidence. Physical evidence can also be integral in establishing an element of the crime. This can be especially critical in sexual assault cases. The investigator must be able to prove that the events did, in fact, occur. Physical evidence can also prove or disprove an alibi, support or refute witness statements, and provide information about or confirm the identity of a suspect.

Although the heading to this section of the chapter is Identifying Physical Evidence, that is somewhat misleading. For many types of physical evidence, the true identity of the item needs to be confirmed by a forensic scientist. In respect to this section and the crime scene investigator, identifying physical evidence is simply referring to locating evidence at a crime scene or on the

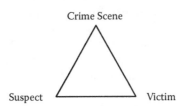

FIGURE 15.1   The crime scene triangle.

person, either a victim or suspect. Once located, the crime scene investigator may submit the item to a forensic laboratory and request that a forensic scientist conduct a variety of examinations in order to positively identify an item. For example, an investigator locates blue smearing on the clothing of a victim in a hit-and-run incident. The investigator should simply refer to this piece of evidence as a blue smear, and not assume or document that it is paint transfer until a forensic scientist is able to examine this smear in closer detail. The trace evidence examiner will use a microscope and other physical and chemical tests to determine the color, shape, and other properties of the blue smear to determine if it is in fact vehicle paint. Furthermore, he or she may be able to determine if it is, or is not, similar to or consistent with the paint from a suspect vehicle. The crime scene investigator may have located the item of evidence, but the forensic scientist has identified the item of evidence. Another example would be red staining on the wall of a homicide scene. The crime scene investigator certainly needs the skill set necessary to locate that red stain and identify it as physical evidence, however the serologist or DNA examiner will analyze the red stain to confirm its identity as blood.

OBSERVATION AND PERCEPTION

Two key skill sets necessary for locating physical evidence at a crime scene include observation and perception. Observation is using one's five senses to accurately document their surroundings. Perception is using an individual's background, experience, training, and education to interpret those observations. A good investigator needs to utilize both of these skills to identify evidence at a crime scene. For example, a crime scene investigator may identify a red stain on the wall in the shape of a hand. He or she is able to make general observations about the item's color and shape, while an investigator with bloodstain pattern training may use his or her education to make additional conclusions about the red stain, such as identifying it as a swipe, wipe, or other type of transfer.

PRINCIPLE THEORY OF EXCHANGE

So, how does physical evidence get left at a crime scene, on a victim, or on a suspect? This transfer of physical evidence is based on a principle known as Locard's Theory of Exchange. Edward Locard studied medicine and law in France in the 1800s and 1900s. He started the first police laboratory in 1910 and is often considered the founding father of forensic science. His principle is the driving force behind the transfer of physical evidence. Locard's Theory of Exchange states that an exchange takes place when two things come into contact with one another; "Every contact leaves a trace." When a person enters a room, they will leave a piece of themselves behind in that room and will take a piece of that room away with them. When two people come into contact with one another, they will both leave a piece of themselves on the other person. This theory is directly related to, and should better help you understand, the CSI triangle.

There are several different types of transfer that can occur in any given situation. Primary or direct transfer is evidence that is exchanged directly from one source to another source. For example, hair from the suspect is found in the victim's bed where a sexual assault occurred. Another example would be a fiber from the victim's pillowcase that is found on the suspect. Secondary or indirect transfer is evidence that is exchanged from one source to another, with one or more intermediate sources in between. For example, hair from the suspect's dog is located in the victim's bed where a sexual assault occurred. This dog hair originated from the dog, which was then transferred to the suspect, and then eventually recovered from the victim's bed. Another example would be a fiber from the victim's pillowcase is found inside of the suspect's vehicle. The fiber originated from the pillow case, was transferred to the suspect during the crime, and then deposited inside the suspect's vehicle at a later time.

Based on Locard's Theory of Exchange, evidence is always present at a crime scene—or at least was present at one point in time. The major factor in determining how long evidence will remain in any one location is persistence. Some items are naturally more fragile than others. For example, at an outdoor crime scene, a strand of hair left by the suspect may be blown away prior to the investigator's arrival; whereas a gun left at that same scene will likely not blow away. The gun will persist for a longer period of time. Some items of evidence may be intentionally or unintentionally obliterated. The suspect may intentionally wipe away fingerprints left on the front door of the victim's home or the first responding officer to the scene may accidentally step on a shoeprint left by the suspect on the vinyl flooring. Evidence will persist, or remain, in its original location until it is further transferred, lost, degraded, changed, or collected as evidence.

EVIDENCE RECOVERY

The inability to persist is just one reason an investigator may fail to recover an item of evidence, but there are additional variables to consider as to why this may occur. In some instances, the crime scene investigator simply fails to recognize the item as being evidence. There is an important point to make here about the necessity for communication between the crime scene investigator and the detectives assigned to the case. If the detectives learn an important piece of information about the incident while conducting interviews or canvassing the neighborhood, this information must be relayed to the crime scene investigator as soon as possible. For example, during an interview of a female victim, she may state that the suspect used a paper towel to clean himself after a sexual assault. The suspect then threw the paper towel away in the trash can before leaving the scene. If the crime scene investigator is not aware of this information, they may observe the paper towel in the trash can, but perceive that it is just trash and not a potential item of evidence. Conversely, if the crime scene investigator locates an item of evidence that provides a probable immediate lead in the case, this information must be relayed to the detectives. For example, a baseball hat bearing the name of a local university sports team with a jersey number stitched onto the back of the hat was recovered at the point of entry to a burglary scene. This information provides an immediate investigative lead for the detectives, and must be provided to them as soon as possible. Communication between both parties is paramount in executing the most effective and efficient overall investigation.

Another variable to consider when exploring why investigators may not recover physical evidence at a crime scene is lack of observation. The evidence may be present, and may be recognized and valued as evidence, but if the investigator fails to notice it, then it cannot be documented, collected, and preserved. Evidence is typically not observed either due to its small size and lack of distribution, or because the investigator was disorganized and careless during the crime scene search. The best way to eliminate the chance of overlooking evidence is to use a systematic approach to the crime scene search method. If the crime scene is processed in an organized and logical fashion, the investigator will reduce the likelihood of inadvertently destroying or altogether missing vital pieces of evidence. This systematic approach to CSI will be visited in great detail later on in this chapter. A second method for ensuring small evidence or evidence lacking in number is not missed during an investigation is to utilize an assortment of lighting techniques to enhance the scene and its attributes.

LIGHTING TECHNIQUES—OBLIQUE, UV, AND ALS

Through the use of different lighting techniques, investigators can aid themselves in observing otherwise invisible evidence. By placing a beam of light at a very narrow angle, almost parallel, to the surface that is being searched, the light will cast shadows across items that may not have been visible to the naked eye. This lighting technique is called oblique light and is one of the crime scene investigator's best friends. For example, oblique lighting across the threshold of a door that has been identified as the suspect's point of entry may reveal a hair that would have been missed if the oblique light had not been utilized. In addition, oblique lighting across the floor of a home may reveal shoeprints created in dust that would not have been visible with existing lighting conditions.

Other types of lighting sources that can assist in locating evidence include ultraviolet (UV) light and an alternate light source (ALS). The visible spectrum of light, that which the human eye can see, is between 400 and 700 nm and represents the colors red through violet. UV light is between 180 and 400 nm. UV light can be useful in checking for bloodstains at a crime scene. Bloodstains absorb all light and turn black under a UV light. UV lighting can also be useful in identifying other biological stains, but this light source can also be dangerous. An investigator must use precautions when utilizing this type of equipment. UV light can cause sunburn, even to the human eyes, so protective goggles must be worn at all times. UV light can also be damaging to DNA if the exposure time is too long. When using UV light to search for blood or other biological stains, it is important to limit the amount of time the stain or fluid is exposed to the UV light. Alternatively, an ALS can also enhance biological stains or other physical evidence without as many possible damaging effects. An ALS is an instrument that allows a specific wavelength of light to be emitted through a band filter. This narrow wavelength of light is then passed onto the evidence and then through a barrier filter (i.e., goggles). What remains is an area that fluoresces. Many items including biological evidence, fibers, and inks have an inherent fluorescent property, or a glow, when viewed under an ALS. With a specific wavelength setting and the appropriate use of a filter, evidence that was once invisible to the naked eye may become apparent. Research suggests that the most effective wavelength range in assisting with crime scene processing is the blue-green range, between 410 and 530 nm. Certain ALS manufactures have a Crime Scene Search setting on the ALS. The specific nanometer used for this setting is not released by the manufacturer, but is commonly referred to as "blue light." A typical blue light source and the use of an orange barrier filter will cause a majority of biological fluids, fibers, and hairs to fluoresce.

Evidence Comparison

Evidence where the originating source is unknown is often considered and referred to as a "questioned sample." These questioned samples may be recovered from a crime scene, a victim, or a suspect. A "known sample" is evidence that originated from a known source. The goal is to determine if enough similar characteristics exist between the questioned sample and the known sample for the forensic scientist to conclude that an association exists between the two samples. The degree of association between the questioned and known samples depends on the number of class characteristics and individual characteristics that the two samples share.

Characteristics of physical evidence can either be considered a class characteristic or an individual characteristic. A class characteristic means it could have originated from more than one source. An individual characteristic means that it originated from a single source, to the exclusion of all other sources. Evidence with individual characteristics is unique evidence. For example, a suspect breaks into the victim's home via a basement bedroom window and leaves a shoe print in the mud next to the window well. Class characteristics of this shoe print include the brand, size, and tread pattern shape of the shoe—Nike, size 11, hexagonal pattern. Individual characteristics of this shoe print include the wear pattern or any defects in the tread such as a cut that make that shoe print unique. If a suspect is identified, his or her shoes can be collected and compared to the shoe print impression recovered at the crime scene. If enough detail in the shoe print impression is present, the forensic examiner may be able to identify that the shoe print impression did come from the shoe collected from the suspect to the exclusion of all other shoes. In the example above, the shoe print impression recovered from near the window well is the questioned sample and the suspect's shoe is the known sample.

This comparison between evidence characteristics is done in an effort to establish the source of the evidence. Although individual characteristics are strived for in forensic comparisons, the value of class characteristics should not be discounted. Class characteristics can offer investigative leads or drive the suspect into a confession. Furthermore, if enough items of evidence are present with class characteristics, although circumstantial, this may be enough for a jury to find a defendant guilty. Although physical evidence is often preferred, and as outlined earlier, come to be expected, many solid cases have been and remain made on the heels of a collection of irrefutable circumstantial evidence.

Control samples are another form of known samples and are used to ensure if a test is properly working. For example, when testing an area of carpet that has red staining on it, an investigator can use a presumptive blood test. If the test is positive, this could mean that the stain is blood. It could also mean that something in the carpet is interfering with the test. The presumptive test should also be run on an area of the same type of carpet, but that which does not include any red staining. The test should show a negative result, meaning that the carpet itself is not the reason for the original test to show a positive result. The sample taken of the carpet in a non-red stained area is considered the control sample.

Elimination samples are also considered known samples and are taken from a source which may have had legitimate access to a crime scene or to a person. In the shoe print example above, the investigator should consider taking an elimination shoe print sample from the home owner. The forensic laboratory will be able to eliminate the home owner as the person who left the shoe print impression in the mud. Some of the more common types of elimination samples taken during an investigation include fingerprints and DNA. Elimination samples should be taken from anyone who had lawful access to the crime scene, often including first responding officers.

CONTAMINATION

Being knowledgeable in the principles behind the theory of exchange, it is important for the crime scene investigator to prevent any transfer of items to or from the scene after the crime has been committed. This includes the transfer of material from the crime scene investigator to the crime scene. One precaution that should be taken while processing any crime scene is the use of personal protective equipment (PPE). These measures should, at a minimum, include disposable gloves. Based on the type of scene the investigator is handling, consideration should also be given to the use of hair nets, safety goggles, masks, booties, or full protective coveralls. This author recalls one crime scene investigator who wore sweat bands around his wrists to prevent sweat from dripping down and contaminating his crime scene.

With advances in DNA technology and the sensitivity of touch DNA, investigators could inadvertently transfer their own DNA, or foreign DNA from the outside of their gloves, to the item of evidence. Imagine touching a doorknob to the front door of a home with your gloved hand. Many others have certainly touched this same doorknob prior to your contact, and when it is touched with your gloved hand, their preexisting DNA may be transferred to the outside of your glove. If your same gloved hand is then used to collect an item of evidence, the preexisting DNA from the doorknob that was transferred to the outside of the glove could then be transferred to the item of evidence. This is a classic example of contamination, and every effort should be made to avoid this issue. Another example, which has become an increasing problem in forensic laboratories across the country, is crime scene personnel answering their cell phone with a gloved hand, and then continuing to process the crime scene. Just envision the amount of DNA that exists on a cell phone. Not only do we constantly touch it, but we also speak into it, creating a collection of saliva. In today's society, it is unlikely that an investigator will be able to avoid answering the cell phone during a CSI—everyone wants updates—but if this should occur, it is vital for the investigator to don a fresh pair of gloves before proceeding.

It is also wise to consider using a different crime scene investigator to search the following: the physical location of the crime, the victim, and the suspect. This will prevent any cross-contamination between the scenes. Although preferred, it is often impractical to deploy three crime scene personnel for one incident. If unable to use separate search persons for the scene, victim, and suspect, the investigator should change his or her clothes and PPE prior to addressing a new scene or person.

Care must also be given to the use of equipment and instruments within the crime scene. If possible, disposable instruments are the preferred method of collection for many items, but if the agency is unable to provide disposable instruments, then they should be cleaned with a 10% bleach solution prior to usage at any crime scene.

SAFETY PRECAUTIONS

Law enforcement personnel, to include crime scene investigators, are listed as an occupation at risk for exposure to blood borne pathogens by the Occupational Safety and Health Administration (OSHA). OSHA advocates that employees should treat all human blood and body fluids as if they are infected with disease. The preventive measures to control exposure are called universal precautions, and several are listed below:

- Disposable gloves should be worn, especially if there are cuts, scratches, or breaks in the skin
- Gloves should be changed when torn or punctured
- Appropriate eye protection should be worn to protect against splashes or sprays
- Contaminated sharps should be placed in appropriate closable, leak-proof, puncture-resistant containers
- Containers holding contaminated sharps should be labeled BIOHAZARD
- Eating, drinking, and smoking should be prohibited in areas where blood or other body fluids are present
- Wash hands after removal of gloves and other PPE
- Remove gloves and other PPE in a manner which will not contaminate unprotected skin
- Decontaminate equipment and instruments with a 10% bleach solution.

GENERAL CRIME SCENE APPROACH

CSI can be approached in a variety of ways, and where the investigators have received their training will surely dictate how they execute their crime scene processing method. As mentioned before, a systematic approach to CSI is the best practice in order to identify, document, collect, and preserve evidence. The systematic approach presented below is offered as an example of one way to assure every crime scene is investigated in a detailed and organized manner. By maintaining a degree of flexibility, this model can be applied to almost every type of crime scene, large or small, that one may encounter. It is recommended that all steps be followed unless some extenuating circumstance prevents the investigator from doing so; and in those cases, the investigator should simply document why a step or series of steps was not completed. If the investigator learns to follow this systematic approach to CSI, any type of crime scene can be effectively and efficiently investigated. Furthermore, if a systematic approach is followed, the investigator is more readily able to reconstruct the crime scene should the need arise. Finally, by adopting a detailed, systematic, and organized approach to CSI, it limits the areas for which error could occur and certainly helps in eliminating any potential issues that may arise during a court proceeding.

The systematic approach to CSI can be broken down into three phases: initial phase, collection phase, and final phase. Each of these phases is described in further detail below.

INITIAL PHASE

The job of investigating crime scenes can often be emotional and disturbing, even for the most experienced crime scene investigators. Mental preparation should begin prior to any dispatched call for service, and is just as important as preparing supplies and equipment. Sexual assaults are heinous, often violent crimes against another human being, and can certainly affect the crime scene investigator. It is important to understand how to approach the incident professionally, while also maintaining empathy for the victim. Most agencies also have some level of employee assistance, which can be beneficial if the investigator needs therapy after investigating particularly cruel crimes.

Prior to arriving on scene, the investigators should be prepared for the recovery and collection of any type of evidence they may be faced with addressing. Their vehicles should be well stocked with supplies and working equipment. Furthermore, investigators should always consider their own safety and well-being during the course of the investigation. In dealing with sexual assault cases, biological evidence is a common type of evidence that one encounters. All biological evidence should be considered a biohazard, and the investigator should observe universal precautions.

CRIME SCENE INTEGRITY

Upon arriving at the crime scene, protecting the integrity of the scene should be at the forefront of every crime scene investigator's mind. Typically, the first responding officer will have a perimeter established, but often times it is not large enough. Keep in mind that as the suspect flees the area, he or she will also be leaving potential evidence along the way. A good rule of thumb for the investigator is to double the initial boundaries set by the first officers on scene. This can be accomplished in several ways. One can use physical barriers such as walls to a building or police cars; one can also use police personnel or crime scene banner guard. Once these new boundaries have been established, the investigator can work his or her way from the outside of the perimeter to the inside of the perimeter. This large perimeter can always be reduced as an area of the crime scene is cleared by the investigator, but one can never work from the inside of the scene outward as evidence will surely be lost or destroyed if not properly protected. Also, to maintain scene integrity, the investigator should begin or assign someone to maintain a crime scene log. A crime scene log, or entry/exit log, simply records the names of people who enter the crime scene, the time they enter and the time they leave. It is paramount that only those with a legitimate purpose or need to enter the crime scene be allowed to do so. Remember, Locard's principle applies to everyone, not just suspects. That being said, anyone who enters the crime scene will leave traces of themselves behind, and take traces of the scene away. As discussed above, one can take precautionary measures to assist in preventing this from occurring.

INTERVIEWS

After ensuring the crime scene is secure, the investigator must interview the first responding officer and any other persons that may have entered the crime scene. The first responding officer has the best working knowledge of the case at that point in time, and the crime scene investigator must use his or her knowledge of the incident and the scene to formulate a plan for a systematic approach to the crime scene. Below is a list of five basic questions that should be asked of a first responding officer:

- What did they see?
- Where have they walked?
- What have they touched?
- Did they move anything?
- Did anyone else enter the crime scene?

Asking the officer what they saw inside of the crime scene will help in determining the type of equipment that may be needed. This could range from the officer seeing a specific item of evidence that requires a special collection technique to the need for supplemental lighting inside the crime scene. Asking where the officer walked and what they touched will aid in considering the need to obtain elimination samples. These elimination samples from the first responding officer, medical personnel, witnesses, or anyone else that may have entered the scene without the proper protective equipment will assist the laboratory in determining if the unknown samples collected from the crime scene came from a person with legitimate access to the area or from a potential suspect. Asking the officer if he or she moved anything will help the investigator determine if his or her observations of the crime scene are a result of the crime, or from a source of contamination. Determining from the officer if anyone else entered the crime scene will allow the investigator to compile a list of persons from whom it will be necessary to interview and collect elimination samples. Of course there are a plethora of additional questions that should be asked of the initial responding officer and other persons on scene, but these are typically determined on a case-by-case basis.

AUTHORITY TO SEARCH

After a thorough interview of the first responding officer, medical personnel, and any other witnesses is complete, the investigator must take into account the authority that exists to search the crime scene area in question. Sometimes consent is given by a person on scene with legal authority to give consent, other times a search warrant will need to be obtained. The legal aspects concerning searches is beyond the scope of this book; however, it is important to mention as it must be considered prior to the start of any crime scene search.

PRELIMINARY SCENE SURVEY

The investigator should conduct a preliminary scene survey, which includes an initial walk-through of the crime scene. This allows the investigator to assess the scene to determine the extent of the scene, what additional equipment and personnel needs they may have, and to identify evidence. This walk-through should be done via an established working route. One thing to consider when conducting the walk-through and determining the best working route, is the original path taken through the scene by the first responding officer. If possible, use this same pathway to minimize the areas that are disturbed. Also consider the entrance and exit points that the suspect may have used, and avoid using these areas as the same entrance and exit points used by crime scene personnel.

In addition to the points made above, the working route should flow in a logical progression through the scene by addressing each item of evidence as it is reached along the pathway. There should be no need to walk past five pieces of evidence to address an item on the far side of the room. This only lends to the possibility of moving, altering, destroying, or losing evidence along the way. The one exception to addressing evidence as it is located along the working route would be if evidence is deemed perishable or fleeting in nature. All fleeting evidence should be addressed first, so it is not lost prior to collection. This perishability factor should be considered when determining the most logical progression through the crime scene.

While performing the preliminary scene survey, the crime scene investigator will need just a few pieces of equipment to accomplish this task. These few pieces of equipment include gloves, a flashlight, a notebook and writing instrument, and a camera. As discussed earlier in this chapter, oblique lighting is extremely significant and important during the crime scene search. As the investigator makes his or her way through the scene, oblique lighting should be used on all surfaces—floor/ground, walls, furniture, and countertops—to ensure that no evidence is overlooked.

DOCUMENTATION

During the preliminary scene survey, the investigators will begin their note-taking, rough sketch, and overall photography. It is unwise to reenter the crime scene time and time again to take photographs, notes, and sketches. Rather, these three things should be initiated, and done simultaneously, during the first walk-through. At this point in the crime scene search, note-taking should include environmental conditions and evidence considerations. Environmental conditions may include the outdoor weather, the indoor temperature, the condition of doors and windows (open/closed, locked/unlocked), the condition of lights and appliances, any evidence of food preparation, and odors. Evidence considerations are simply a list of things of interest that the investigator observes during his or her initial walk-through. Some of these items may end up being insignificant, and not collected as evidence. Other items may not even be listed in the initial note-taking as evidence because they did not become apparent until later during the crime scene search. The point is to facilitate observations, and get an idea of what can be expected for evidence recovery. Evidence should not be touched or moved at this point in the process, and a more thorough search of the scene will be conducted at a later time. The investigator should only be concerned about documentation and getting a grasp on the nature and complexity of the scene. It is important to note that any documentation of the scene is discoverable in court and should be maintained in a neat, concise, and professional nature at all times. Documentation should be objective and without use of opinion and language that could be damaging to the validity of the evidence and investigation.

Overall Photography

Crime scene photography and crime scene sketching are lengthy and complex topics on their own and are beyond the scope of this book. There are a multitude of textbooks which address these specific topics. Although they are a very important part in properly documenting a crime scene, the specific details of crime scene sketching and photography will not be discussed here; rather a general reference to the type of sketch and the photographs required at each step during the systematic approach to CSI will be mentioned. It is incumbent upon the investigator to become familiar and learned in the techniques necessary to successfully photograph and sketch a crime scene.

At this point in the preliminary scene survey, the investigator should begin his or her overall photography of the crime scene. The first photograph taken should be an establishing photograph which documents the location of the crime scene. This can be a street sign, a home address, or landmark. The list is endless and will vary with each scene. As investigators make their way through the scene, using the working route that they have determined will be the least destructive and most logical progression, they will begin to take overall photographs of the scene. These overall photographs, whether indoors or outdoors need to capture a 360° view of the scene or of each room, and the area encompassed in each subsequent photograph should overlap slightly with that of the previous photograph. A picture speaks a thousand words. This statement is so true, especially when it comes time to describe a crime scene to a judge or jury. The investigator should strive to take photographs that will "paint a picture" of the crime scene and tell the story as if those viewing the pictures were actually present themselves.

Rough Sketch

A rough sketch should be started at this point in the process, and should be updated often as the investigator makes his or her way through the scene. This sketch does not need to be to scale; however, it should be proportional. If the crime scene is indoors, each floor of the building should be sketched, and then a separate in-depth, detailed sketch should be completed for areas of high interest or high activity. For example, a perpetrator enters a home by breaking a basement bedroom window, makes his way through the home to the top floor master bedroom, where the homeowner is killed, and then the suspect leaves through the same basement bedroom window. Each floor of the home will have a floor plan style rough sketch, taking up enough space to roughly fill one sheet of graph paper. Then the investigator must consider which areas within the home are the most important to the case. In this example, the point of entry and exit is the basement bedroom and the homicide occurs in the master bedroom. An in-depth or larger-scale rough sketch of just the basement bedroom and just the master bedroom should be done in supplement to the overall rough sketches of each floor of the home. These in-depth sketches usually consist of just a single room, and will also take up enough space to fill a single sheet of graph paper. One may think that photography and good note-taking is enough to properly document the scene; however, often times a photograph cannot accurately represent the relationship between things in a room. The rough sketch acts to tie the notes and the photographs together, and all three act in concert to provide the best form of documentation for the investigation.

Consideration can also be given to other supplemental types of documentation. Specialized panoramic photography equipment or cameras with panoramic capabilities exist, but should only serve as supplements to traditional crime scene photographs. Videotaping of a crime scene can be very beneficial, especially for use during a jury trial. However, caution should be given to the microphone on the video recorder. The microphone should be turned off if possible or at least ensure that no personnel on scene are speaking while the videotaping is underway.

Upon completion of the preliminary scene survey, the investigator will have accomplished a systematic walk-through of the scene, taken notes regarding environmental conditions and evidence considerations, taken overall photographs, and began a rough sketch of the scene. It is recommended that the crime scene investigator brief the lead detective in the case at this point in time. It has previously been emphasized that communication between the two parties is key in a successful investigation. As investigators get ready to move into the next phase of the systematic approach to CSI, they should consider setting aside an area for their equipment, evidence collection, and trash collection. This area should be close enough for easy access, but should not interfere with the area of the crime scene that will be processed.

COLLECTION PHASE

The investigator's next step will be to develop an evidence collection plan. This plan should be based on the evidence that was noted during the initial phase, its location within the scene, and proximity to the working route. The investigator should, at this point, have taken into consideration any evidence that may be perishable. If deemed to have a high perishable factor, this evidence should be collected first in order to maintain its integrity and assist in preservation. If no evidence is inherently perishable, then the evidence should be collected in order along the working route.

MID-RANGE AND CLOSE-UP PHOTOGRAPHY

The investigator will now reapproach the crime scene, but should do so in a manner to maintain the working route they established in the initial phase. To address the first item of evidence, the investigator will begin with photography of the item. The first photograph taken should be a mid-range photograph. A proper mid-range photograph includes the item of evidence and a fixed object within the scene. This photograph will serve to show the relationship of the item within the scene as a whole. Next, a close-up photograph will be taken of the item as it sits *in situ* within the scene, and then finally another close-up photograph will be taken of the item with the addition of a properly labeled scale. The scale should be labeled with the case number, date, item number, and investigator name. Placing a scale into the photograph serves two purposes. This label is a good form of documentation, and the scale offers an overall measurement of the size of the item.

MEASUREMENTS

Next, the investigator should measure the location of the item within the scene. There are many ways to measure crime scenes, and of course, advancements in technology are continuously making this task easier. No matter the method selected, it should allow for the evidence to be permanently fixed into the scene. The specific location of an item of evidence may be crucial to the investigation, even if not readily apparent at the time. Secondly, it is critical to be able to reconstruct the crime scene at a later date if necessary.

COLLECTION

After the item has been photographed and measured, it should be added to the rough sketch. Then, the investigator should get ready to physically touch and collect the item. Just prior to doing so, he or she should change his or her gloves to a fresh, unused pair to prevent contamination. With a fresh pair of gloves on, the investigator can now pick up the evidence and meticulously examine it for additional forensic value. Careful consideration should be given to how the item is collected. This chapter will go into greater detail as to collection methods later on, specifically for items commonly found at sexual assaults, but as a general rule of thumb, the collector should make contact with the item in a location that is not commonly touched or manipulated. For example, when collecting a glass beer bottle, the middle portion of the bottle is most commonly touched by the person drinking from it, and grasping the bottle near the base where it would be awkward to hold, may be the best place for the investigator to touch for collection and examination purposes. The reason for doing this is to avoid unintentionally wiping away any fingerprints or DNA deposited in these areas that are commonly touched. As investigators examine the evidence, it should be carefully detailed in their notes. The type, size, shape, and color should be noted, as well as any writing or serial numbers located on the item.

Most importantly, the person who physically collects the item should be documented. This information is paramount to maintaining a chain of custody of the item. Every agency should have some form, or method of documentation, to track not only who has had access to the evidence, but also where the evidence has been located. From the crime scene, to the police department, to the crime lab and back; each step needs to be recorded as a part of the chain of custody. The chain of custody is one area that is often challenged by a defense attorney in court. If careful documentation is maintained about who had access to the evidence, beginning with who collected the evidence, and where the evidence has been located since collection, there should be no question as to the integrity of the item during trial.

PACKAGING

After the item is collected and examined, it should be properly packaged for preservation. Some forensic laboratories provide their jurisdictions with a written guide on how to best handle and package evidence. Certain laboratories have policies in place that require an investigator to package an item in a specific way. All types of packaging scenarios cannot be covered, however, greater detail in how to package evidence recovered in sexual assault cases will be discussed later in this chapter.

After addressing the first item of evidence, the above-described steps of the collection phase will begin again for each new item of evidence, and will continue until all items of evidence have been collected and the crime scene has been thoroughly searched. During the collection phase, the crime scene personnel will also search through cabinets, drawers, under beds, and all areas of the scene to ensure no evidence is overlooked. It is a good idea to utilize some sort of physical evidence recovery checklist, or evidence log, as the investigator makes his or her way through the collection phase. As an example, this checklist could include columns for item number, description of item, location the item is found, and who collected the item. Additionally, it is recommended to have check boxes for each item to record if the item has been added to the sketch, measured (with units of measure), and photographed (midrange, close-up without a scale, and close-up with a scale). This form of documentation can only assist in ensuring no steps are missed and an organized, systematic method is maintained throughout the crime scene search.

FINAL PHASE

The final phase of the systematic approach to CSI includes several important tasks. The investigator should process any fixed surfaces in the scene for fingerprints. All bloodstain pattern and trajectory documentation are completed in the final phase. Additional measurements must also be taken to include furniture and overall measurements of the scene. Not every piece of furniture placed on the rough sketch necessarily requires measuring, and just those pieces with some direct importance to the scene or an item of evidence needs to be measured. The investigator should then complete one final search of the scene. It is also recommended that the investigator brings in another person who has not been involved, or at least not directly involved, in the investigation. This final search and the fresh eyes of a new investigator will ensure that no item of evidence is missed.

Finally, the investigator should take another series of overall photographs, known as exit photographs. These pictures will document the condition of the scene as it is left at the completion of the crime scene search. They should also include photographs of any damage done during the entry or search of the crime scene.

PHYSICAL EVIDENCE COMMONLY IDENTIFIED IN SEXUAL ASSAULT INVESTIGATIONS

There are three types of crime scenes that one may typically encounter in a sexual assault investigation, and these include the physical location where the assault took place, the victim, and the suspect. The investigator should treat each of these three scenes separately, and use a detailed, organized, and systematic approach to evidence recovery for each scene. A variety of physical evidence could be located at each of these three scenes, although the recovery method may differ when collecting evidence from a physical location than it would from a person. Although the list is endless for types of evidence one may encounter during a sexual assault investigation, the focus of this chapter is to discuss the most common types and prepare the investigator for the best practices in identifying, collecting, preserving, and documenting this evidence.

BIOLOGICAL EVIDENCE

Biological evidence is probably the most common type of physical evidence at a sexual assault crime scene, and is often the most probative type of physical evidence one can recover. Biological evidence is a source of DNA which although technically a class characteristic (identical twins have the same DNA, so it cannot be attributed to a single source) still offers impressive statistical analysis to assist in the identification of a person. Biological evidence can include semen, vaginal secretions, blood, skin cells in the form of saliva, perspiration and urine, tissue, hair, bone, and teeth. There are general practices for locating and collecting biological evidence at a crime scene, but some specific types of biological evidence have special techniques that will be addressed separately. In order to appreciate the value of biological evidence, a review of DNA must first be visited.

Nuclear DNA

The human body is made up of trillions of cells which all have different functions. Some cells enable you to see or hear, while others produce insulin or enzymes to help digest food. Deoxyribonucleic acid, or DNA, is located within the nucleus of many of these cells and is responsible for instructing them what to do and how to function. DNA is composed of two strands called chromosomes that are twisted together in a double helix format. Specific locations along the chromosomes called loci (locus, singular) are the location where genes, or alleles, are located. Most people have the same genes—it is what makes us human, have two arms and ten fingers, know how to talk, and how to think. However, there are a small set of genes that makes everyone different and unique. This small set of genes is what a DNA analyst targets in an effort to identify an individual.

Human DNA contains 23 pairs of chromosomes, for a total of 46 chromosomes. During fertilization, the mother contributes one chromosome and the father contributes one chromosome to each of these pairs. Because the order in which these genes can be organized on a chromosome is endless, variation exits in each child born. The only exception to this is identical twins since they are the result of fertilization of only one egg, which later splits into two identical embryos. These two embryos will have the same DNA. Simply stated, no two people are exactly alike and no two people will have the same DNA profile, except in the instance of identical twins. This is very valuable evidence when it comes to identifying an individual.

POLYMERASE CHAIN REACTION (PCR)

Regardless of the actual size of the sample taken, DNA collected in a forensic investigation is initially too small for any analysis, and needs to be properly prepared before it can be analyzed. The forensic DNA examiner must first extract or separate the DNA fragments from the material in which it is contained, whether this is a swab or a piece of fabric. The cell membrane is then broken and the DNA is released. Polymerase Chain Reaction, or PCR, is used to read the genes on the chromosome and amplify the genetic material. PCR makes millions of copies of specific regions of DNA, enough so that it can be analyzed and a DNA profile can be created by the examiner. This profile is unique to each individual and can be compared to profiles that are developed from known samples submitted by the suspect or victim.

CODIS

If a suspect has not been identified in an investigation, the unknown suspect profile developed from the sample collected at the crime scene or from the victim can be entered into a DNA databank known as CODIS, or Combined DNA Index System. CODIS is a nationwide databank that contains unknown DNA profiles from unsolved cases and known samples from offenders. Each state maintains a list of offense types for which a sample of DNA is required to be taken from the convicted person and entered into the CODIS databank.

DNA PRESERVATION

There are factors, of course, that affect the quality and integrity of the DNA, which can ultimately determine if a profile can be developed. Environmental conditions present at the crime scene, or the manner in which the DNA sample is preserved may all contribute to the quality of DNA the forensic scientist has at the time of analysis. Water, heat, humidity, and UV light from the sun or investigative light sources can degrade DNA, and certain enzymes act as DNA inhibitors. If the sample is wet and stored in an un-breathable container, putrefaction may occur, bacteria may flourish, or mold may grow on the sample, rendering it useless. DNA samples exposed to any of these factors may exhibit partial profiles, a result of the loss of alleles at a given loci, known as drop-outs.

MITOCHONDRIAL AND Y-CHROMOSOME DNA

Modern techniques and major advancements in technology allow for some degraded biological evidence to be tested for DNA. Mitochondrial DNA (mtDNA) is a small, circular set of genes located outside of the nucleus of the cell. In contrast to nuclear DNA which is inherited from both sets of parents, mtDNA is inherited only from the mother. mtDNA is beneficial to the forensic scientist because a higher number of copies, more than a thousand, exist in the cell as compared to nuclear DNA. Thus, mtDNA is typically a better sample to use when dealing with degraded or low-level samples of DNA. Since mtDNA is inherited from the mother, no variation exists, and all individuals in the same maternal lineage will have the same mtDNA profile. For example, if a family includes a father, mother, daughter and son, then both the daughter and son will inherit the mtDNA from their mother. The mother, daughter and son will all have the same mtDNA profile. This results in mtDNA being much less discriminatory than nuclear DNA. mtDNA analysis is most often used in the identification of human remains. Bone and teeth can be difficult sources for obtaining a nuclear DNA profile, so mtDNA may be used as a secondary means to make an identification. mtDNA is also used in the analysis of DNA from hair samples. Nuclear DNA only exists in the soft tissue surrounding the root of the hair, but mtDNA exists in the shaft area of the hair. If a crime scene investigator locates a strand of hair where the root is no longer attached, mtDNA may provide a profile that can assist in identifying the suspect. Typically, hair will only contain tissue around the root when it is forcefully pulled, and not when it is shed naturally or cut from the body.

Y-chromosome DNA analysis looks specifically at 17 areas on the Y (male) chromosome. The Y-chromosome is DNA that is inherited only from the father, and thus all males in the same paternal lineage will have the same Y-chromosome profile. Using the same example as above, if a family includes a father, mother, daughter and son, then only the son will inherit the Y-chromosome profile from his father. Just like mtDNA, this results in Y-chromosome DNA being much less discriminatory than nuclear DNA. The primary advantage of Y-chromosome DNA testing is its use in sexual assault cases. Certain samples, such as fingernail scrapings or biological fluids with no or low sperm count, prove challenging for the DNA analyst to separate the male and female cells. By specifically targeting the Y-chromosome DNA, or ignoring all female DNA, the forensic scientist may be able to isolate and focus only on the male DNA present.

OTHER ADVANCEMENTS IN DNA ANALYSIS

Most forensic laboratories currently use a DNA analysis system called PowerPlex16 (PP16). PP16 looks at a total of 16 loci on the human chromosome. One of the challenges that DNA analysts face is the ability to recover a full profile, or all 16 loci, from degraded or inhibited DNA samples. Vast improvements in technology have allowed the generation of smaller amplification areas, thus increasing the probability of obtaining a full profile from a degraded sample. One such method is the use of mini-STR (Standard Tandem Repeat), which uses a different type of chemistry than PP16, and may be able to overcome the possible degradation and/or inhibition issues present in a sample.

Another method at the forefront of DNA research is PowerPlex Fusion DNA analysis. PowerPlex Fusion can be used for any type of DNA sample, to include degraded or low level samples. PowerPlex Fusion looks at a total of 24 loci, so 8 more loci than PP16. This increases the chance of being able to make an identification if one, or more, allele(s) exhibit dropout, and it is much more discriminatory than PP16. Additionally, PowerPlex Fusion looks at two Y-Chromosome loci to improve interpretation of mixture profiles.

There are also computerized DNA interpretation systems that use advanced statistical analysis in an effort to estimate a possible genetic profile in complex, DNA mixture profiles. This is particularly useful in sexual assault cases where the victim previously had consensual intercourse with one individual and then was sexually assaulted by another individual, or the assault was perpetrated by multiple individuals. The developed DNA profile may consist of a mixture of three, or more, persons. These computerized DNA systems can estimate how probable a certain individual may have or may not have contributed to that DNA mixture profile.

LOCATING BIOLOGICAL EVIDENCE

In searching for biological evidence at a crime scene, the investigator should start by conducting a general, visual search with the naked eye. As previously discussed, evidence is apparent just by simple observation and perception techniques. However, there are times that biological evidence will not be readily apparent, and the investigator must utilize other techniques to locate this type of evidence. Through the use of an ALS, investigators may increase their chances of locating this type of evidence. This is especially helpful when the exact location of the crime scene is unknown.

In using normal, white light, all the colors of the light spectrum are reflected. An ALS allows the investigator to specify a specific wavelength in the light spectrum to exit the instrument. Many biological fluids have an inherent fluorescent property which means they will absorb light at a given wavelength and convert it into light of a longer wavelength and intensity. If the investigator uses a barrier filter, often in the form of goggles, to block out any remaining visible light, the result will be the item of interest fluorescing, and thus becoming visible to the investigator.

Most biological evidence will fluoresce between 415 and 535 nm. At these specific wavelengths, the investigator will need to use either a yellow or an orange barrier filter for visibility. If the investigator does not deploy an ALS during the course of the crime scene search, he or she may vastly limit the ability to identify and recover the evidence that is located within the scene.

COLLECTING BIOLOGICAL EVIDENCE

Biological stains can be easily degraded or destroyed and the investigator must take precautions to ensure the integrity of the stain is maintained. Some factors that affect the condition of a biological stain include moisture, heat, humidity, and sunlight. If the biological evidence is exposed to any of these conditions, it must be considered perishable and should be one of the first items addressed in the collection phase.

There are three methods that are recommended for collecting wet or dry biological evidence:

1. Collect the entire item that the stain is present upon
2. Cut the stain from the item
3. Swab the stain

If practical and efficient, it is best practice to always collect the entire item that the stain is present upon. For example, biological staining on a shirt from a sexual assault victim can easily be documented and collected. It is not too cumbersome to package and can be easily transported from the scene to the laboratory. However, a stain observed on a bulky comforter may be too difficult to package and transport from the scene to the police department or forensic laboratory. In the case of a bulky comforter or perhaps a stain observed on the carpet, the investigator may consider cutting out an area from the comforter or carpet which includes the stain; however, good judgment must prevail, and it may not always be wise to cut and destroy items that belong to a victim who has already experienced a traumatizing event. The investigator must also weigh the potential for evidence to be recovered at the forensic laboratory from other areas of the comforter that may not have been readily apparent at the crime scene.

In most cases, it is reasonable, efficient, and effective to swab the stain as a method of collection. When swabbing an area of suspected wet biological fluid, the investigator should concentrate as much of the stain as possible in one location of the swab. It may feel natural to want to twirl the swab in the fluid; however, it is better practice to rub the swab back and forth along one single edge of the swab. This allows the stain to concentrate in one area and maximize the chance for recovery by the forensic laboratory. The swabbing technique for a dry biological stain differs slightly than when addressing a wet biological stain. Since the stain is dry, it must be reconstituted in order for it to absorb onto the absorbing material of the swab. A common method for accomplishing this task is to place two drops of distilled water onto the absorbing material of the swab, then rub the swab back and forth through the questioned stain in order to concentrate the sample on one side of the swab. Two drops of distilled water are recommended as it has been shown to be the least amount needed for reconstitution, but will also limit the degree to which it dilutes the sample.

If the biological stain is wet, it should be recovered immediately and transported to a location where it can be properly air dried. There are many commercial grade drying cabinets or hoods available that can facilitate the drying of wet evidence, or an agency can simply designate a secured area for the specific purpose of air drying wet biological materials. One practice that is recommended for wet stains on fabric, especially clothing or bedding, is to place paper between the layers of fabric so that the stain does not soak from one area of fabric to another area of fabric. The location of the stain may play an important role in the investigation, and its original location should be preserved. The protection of fabric layers should be done on scene, and the paper should remain between the layers in question as it is drying. If the investigator's agency does not have the ability to air dry evidence, it should be transported to the forensic laboratory immediately to allow the scientists to address the evidence.

If the biological stain is dry, the investigator can consider scraping the stain using a clean, new scalpel blade. Great caution should be taken when using this method as tiny particles of the biological evidence will become airborne and could present a biohazardous condition. If the item that the stain is present upon cannot be collected or cut out, it is generally advised that the stain be swabbed as the preferred collection method.

As a reminder, the best practice is to collect the entire item which the stain is located upon, cut out the stained area from an item, and finally to swab the questioned area. Many factors play a role in making the determination as to which recovery method is best. An investigator must balance the need for maximizing the collection and integrity of the sample with efficiency and reality of the recovery method, as well as ensuring his or her safety is maintained and taking into consideration the level of his or her training.

PACKAGING BIOLOGICAL EVIDENCE

Once dry, or if the item was already dry, it should be packaged in a breathable, paper container such as a manila envelope, paper bag or cardboard box. Examples of packaging material that should not be utilized for this type of evidence include plastic evidence bags, biohazard bags, or garbage bags. The packaging material cannot be air tight as the container may retain moisture and cause mold to grow on the evidence. The forensic laboratory used by this author tells many stories of opening up evidence packages only to find that the item is covered in mold and rendered utterly useless to the case. Often times a need arises for the use of primary and secondary containers. For example, many agencies use swab boxes as a primary container for packaging of their swabs. Swab boxes are commercially available and have holes on the sides to facilitate drying. These swab boxes need to be placed into a secondary container in order to maintain the integrity of the evidence. All biological evidence that is to be submitted to the forensic laboratory for analysis should be in a package that can be fully sealed with packing tape or evidence tape. All openings of the package should be sealed with this tape to prevent the escape of evidence and the introduction of an outside material to the evidence within the package. It is then recommended that all seals be initialed by the investigator. This is one way to ensure that the evidence has not been tampered with and to maintain the chain of custody.

BLOOD

In addition to searching for blood with the naked eye and the use of an ALS, there are other methods for detecting blood at a crime scene that may prove to be useful. Some of these methods are considered presumptive tests for blood, meaning they require additional testing by the laboratory before they can be confirmed as blood. Some common examples of presumptive blood tests include phenolphthalein and immunoassay testing. A sample of suspected blood can be collected onto the tip of a swab, and then a drop of phenolphthalein added to the same area on the swab. It is important to note that the swab used for the presumptive test is not the same swab that should be sent to the laboratory as the evaluative sample. An additional swab of the same stain should be collected and untreated to be submitted to the forensic laboratory.

Alternatively, the suspected blood sample can be added to a packet that contains a series of vials to include phenolphthalein, which are broken in a sequential manner. Phenolphthalein will react with the hemoglobin in blood and cause a color change reaction. If the swab or the liquid in the packet of vials turns pink, it is a positive reaction indicating the presence of blood. Immunoassay testing uses a collection tube to recover a sample of the suspected blood stain. Once the suspected blood is on the collection tube it is placed into a solution, or transport medium. This mixture is then added to a test bar via a dropper. Human hemoglobin in blood will react to the reagent and cause a red colored stripe to show on the test bar, which is a positive reaction for the indication of human blood. This is a similar concept to a home pregnancy test. Both phenolphthalein and immunoassay testing can cause false positives, meaning a positive result may be obtained for items that are not truly human blood. If a positive result is obtained using a presumptive blood test, the stain in question must then be collected and sent to the forensic laboratory for confirmation. If the questioned stain is too small for both a presumptive test and subsequent collection of the stain for laboratory analysis, then the presumptive test should be avoided and the whole sample collected for laboratory analysis.

Luminol is another chemical test that can be used to detect blood. Luminol differs from the presumptive blood tests above because it is used to locate latent blood, meaning blood that is not visible to the naked eye. Using Luminol for latent blood detection typically occurs in the final phase of the systematic approach to CSI as it is destructive in nature. Luminol is a molecule in powder form that is premixed into two solutions and placed into a spray bottle. Prior to use inside of the crime scene, the solution should be tested on a known blood sample, which is usually provided by the company from which the Luminol was purchased. The Luminol solution should also be tested on a control area, which should be the same medium from which you are testing for blood, but in a non-affected area. A positive result with the known blood sample and a negative result with the control sample should be noted and documented. The solution is then sprayed over suspected bloodstained areas, in a misting like application, and approximately one foot away from the surface medium. In darkness, Luminol will react with the hemoglobin in blood and cause a chemiluminescence, or a bright blue-colored glow. Luminol is very sensitive, and will react with minute traces of blood; however it is not very specific and can cause many false positives to include bleach and other cleaning materials.

Again, Luminol is not a presumptive test for blood, rather it used to detect blood that is invisible or diluted, or blood that has been cleaned up or obliterated. Luminol is not destructive to DNA; however, it can dilute the sample to a point where DNA can no longer be recovered. It should be sprayed sparingly, and only used to detect and photograph the stain prior to collection. If a positive reaction is obtained using Luminol, those areas should then be collected for further analysis by the forensic laboratory.

Prior to any bloodstain collection, the investigator should give consideration to any possible patterns that may be visible in the staining. If patterns are visible, then additional documentation must precede any collection. Bloodstain pattern documentation can be complicated and takes specialized training, which will not be addressed in this book. It is only important to recognize that much information can be obtained from the pattern of bloodstains, and it should be documented appropriately so it can be analyzed by an expert at a later date.

If there does not appear to be a pattern in the bloodstain, a representative sample of the red stains should be collected. For example, if a suspected blood trail is observed leaving the scene of the crime, the first and last drops of blood should be collected as well as drops in between. The number of drops collected in between is determined on a case-by-case basis, but should be a good representation of the trail—for example, collect a new blood drop every 10 feet.

SEMEN

Semen stains are a common biological fluid associated with sexual assaults, and often the most valuable evidence in making a case against a suspect, corroborating a victim's statement or suspect's actions, or even refuting a suspect's statement. When discussing semen stains, it is important to first address some terminology. Sperm, short for spermatozoa refers to male reproductive cells, which can only be viewed with the assistance of a microscope. Semen, also known as seminal fluid, is a thick, white, organic fluid that may contain spermatozoa.

Semen stains can be seen with a general visual exam or with the use of an ALS. However, the ability to detect semen stains is dependent on the fluid and the fabric. The fabric itself may have fluorescent properties and wash out the seminal stain when viewed with an ALS, or the stain may not be concentrated enough for the reaction to cause fluorescence. Flat and dark or plain fabrics are typically better for visualizing a semen stain. Examples include underpants, t-shirts, nylons, and toilet paper. Soft or fuzzy and light or patterned fabrics are typically more difficult to visualize a semen stain. Examples include sweatpants, terrycloth, and bath towels. Also, just because it fluoresces does not mean it is semen. False positives can occur, and there are several presumptive tests that the laboratory can conduct in order to confirm the identity of the stain as semen.

One presumptive test for semen is the acid phosphatase (AP) test. AP is a naturally occurring enzyme in the prostate gland, and is present in large amounts in seminal fluid. AP is also present in vaginal fluid, although in much less quantity and this is why the AP test is only a presumptive test for semen. If the AP test produces a positive result, the forensic scientist will then examine the stain under a microscope and identify spermatozoa. Underneath the microscope, the scientist can determine if the sperm cells have an intact tail and head. Tails are very fragile and may even fall off during preparation for the microscope slide treatment. If tails are present, this likely indicates that sexual intercourse occurred within the last 24 h.

There are also reasons the laboratory may obtain a negative AP test. One reason is because the biological stain submitted to the laboratory is not semen. A second reason that the laboratory may obtain a negative AP test is because seminal fluid is present in the stain, but not sperm cells. If the AP test is negative, the forensic scientist will then conduct a p30 test which is used only in the absence of sperm cells. Reasons for low or no sperm cells in the seminal fluid can be the result of a vasectomy, or due to age, disease, or other circumstances. The older the person, the less sperm present in his seminal fluid. Diseases that can contribute to low or no sperm count include diabetes, alcoholism, cancer, and certain types of infections. Frequent ejaculation can also lead to a low sperm cell count.

VAGINAL SECRETIONS

There are no presumptive tests for vaginal secretions, but if a suspected vaginal secretion stain is observed it should still be collected. This is especially true if the victim's statements need to be corroborated or if the suspected vaginal secretion stain is located on the suspect or the suspect's clothing. The forensic laboratory can conduct a DNA analysis on the stain in an effort to develop a DNA profile and determine the source or contributor of the stain.

Often times the sample collected at the crime scene is a mixture of sperm cells and vaginal cells. Sperm cells are relatively hardy, so during the denaturing process, the vaginal cells will burst and can be separated from the sperm fraction. If those are the only two contributors in the sample, the separation of sperm and vaginal cells allows for the DNA analyst to obtain a single source profile.

SALIVA

Bite Marks

Biting may be associated with sexual assaults and care should be given to examining the victim for any signs of bite marks. If observed, the victim should be instructed not to touch or wash the area unless washing is required for immediate medical treatment. The victim's safety and health should be paramount to the recovery of forensic evidence. Bite marks provide the possibility of two forensic examinations. A forensic odontologist can compare the teeth impressions in the skin to a mold of the suspect's teeth and can identify individual characteristics in the teeth which may lead to the positive identification of a suspect. Secondly, saliva can be recovered from bite marks. The investigator must take care in preserving both the impressions from the teeth and the deposited saliva. The bite mark should be properly photographed, both without and with a scale. Then a swab should be moistened using two drops of distilled water. The swab should be rubbed in areas surrounding the impression, both inside and outside of the teeth marks, but not in the impression itself. Once the swabs have been collected for the saliva content, a mold can be taken of the teeth impressions. A material such as Mikrosil or ReproCAST, both of which are available commercially, can be used to make this mold. Mikrosil and ReproCAST are casting materials that consist of a silicone and a hardening material that are deposited onto the impression and allowed to dry. Once dry, it can be removed, and a cast of the impression will be left. The cast should be packaged in a rigid container to prevent the addition of erroneous markings to the impression in question.

CIGARETTE BUTTS

Cigarette butts should be collected with a gloved hand or disposable, one-time use tweezers. They can then be placed into a paper evidence fold or glassine envelope. Paper evidence folds will be discussed in greater detail in the hair and fiber section. Glassine envelopes are made of a material similar to wax paper, and are commercially available for purchase.

CHEWING GUM

Chewing gum should be collected using a gloved hand. Using tweezers to collect chewing gum is not advised as there may be impression evidence in the gum that could be obliterated with the pressure of a tweezers pinch. The chewing gum should be placed into a glassine envelope. Paper products should be avoided to prevent the gum from sticking to the paper, and create difficulty in recovery at the forensic laboratory.

DRINK WARE

Bottles, glasses, and cups can be processed in the field for saliva and fingerprint recovery, or they can be collected in a manner to preserve both and sent to the laboratory for recovery. If it is to be processed in the field, the rim of the drink ware should be swabbed using a swab moistened with two drops of distilled water. The remainder of the item can be processed for fingerprints. If the item is to be collected and sent to the laboratory for processing, it should be collected using a gloved hand. Keep in mind that the area to touch when picking up the item should be an area that is not generally touched during normal handling of the item. The item can then be placed into a rigid container and should be secured to prevent it from moving and possibly obliterating any fingerprints on the item. A less likely, but interesting piece of potential evidence that could also be found on drink ware are lip prints identified by chelioscopy, a forensic technique that deals with the identification of humans based upon lip trace, prints, and impressions.

OTHER SOURCES

Saliva can be found on anything that has been spit, chewed, or sucked upon, and this chapter cannot review all potential sources. However, some other common sources of saliva to consider are food, envelopes, or stamps.

WEARER DNA

Items of clothing can also contain DNA which is referred to as wearer DNA. Clothing items, hats, or eyeglasses discarded by the suspect should be collected as evidence and submitted to the laboratory for DNA analysis. See the clothing and bedding section below for additional instructions on how to collect and preserve these types of evidence.

TOUCH DNA

Our DNA is deposited in various locations and on a variety of things all the time. Every time we touch something, skin cells are sloughed off and deposited on the surface of the item touched. The ability of the laboratory to obtain a DNA profile from a touch DNA sample depends on a variety of factors. Some of these factors include how long the object was touched, how it was touched, and with how much force it was touched. The longer an item is touched, the more skin cells will be transferred onto the object. If the object is squeezed, for example, it will contain more skin cells than if it was simply brushed against. Touch DNA is a very challenging source of DNA as it often produces low-level and mixture samples. The item for which the touch DNA sample is collected from must be taken into consideration. For example, when investigating a bank robbery, the suspect is seen touching the doorknob when exiting the bank. Consider how many other people have touched that exact doorknob throughout the course of the day. In all likelihood, the DNA analyst will develop a mixture of DNA belonging to any number of persons, and will be unable to separate the profiles and identify the suspect. However, the potential value of touch DNA should not be ignored.

This author's agency has had multiple success stories to include several homicides solved from touch DNA results. One such case involved a gentleman who was found stabbed to death in the middle of the road. Investigators on scene noted that his pockets appeared disturbed, and suspected that the perpetrator may have killed the victim during the course of a robbery. Swabs of the victim's interior pockets were collected as well as swabs of the wrist and elbow areas of the victim's sweatshirt. Investigators theorized that a struggle may have ensued between the suspect and victim, and identified the wrist and elbow areas on the sweatshirt were areas that the suspect would have likely touched during the scuffle. The two touch DNA samples were analyzed and a DNA profile was developed by the forensic laboratory. This DNA profile was entered into CODIS and a "hit" was made to an existing profile in the databank. The suspect was identified, charged with homicide, and found guilty in a court of law.

Touch DNA samples are challenging for the laboratory to analyze because they often contain levels of DNA that are too low for analysis or they contain complex mixture samples, as in the bank robbery example described above. There are many factors that play a role in determining whether a touch DNA sample will be good enough to develop a profile, but this evidence should never be discounted. Especially with the advent of newer and more advanced DNA technology, the probability of obtaining a DNA profile from a touch DNA sample is becoming more and more likely.

URINE AND FECES

Urine and feces may also contain DNA evidence; however they are typically not a good source of DNA. Urine and feces contain skin cells sloughed off from the body as they pass through the system. If urine or feces is located in a toilet, the water in the toilet bowl dilutes the sample and further reduces the chance of obtaining a DNA profile. If the urine is a dried stain, the item containing the stain should be submitted, or the stain should be swabbed. Urine in liquid form and all fecal matter should be submitted to the forensic laboratory immediately. If immediate submission is not possible, the samples should be refrigerated and submitted to the laboratory within 1 week of collection.

HAIR AND FIBER EVIDENCE

Sexual assaults are typically a violent and close encounter between the victim and suspect, and many things can be transferred between the two during this contact. Trace evidence is considered to be anything microscopic in nature, but two of the most common types of trace evidence recovered in sexual assault investigations are hairs and fibers. Hair continuously falls from our bodies, and we are constantly in contact with textiles such as clothing, bedding, and carpet. In the field, the investigator is unable to scientifically confirm if the item is actually a hair or a fiber, so it is often simply termed "hair or fiber" for the purposes of documentation and report. Once a forensic examination in the laboratory can be conducted, then the item can be classified, and specified as either a hair or a fiber.

Hair can then be further classified as animal or human and may contain nuclear or mtDNA that can be used to identify a suspect. Certain laboratories will also examine hair to determine the location of the body that the hair originated from, the racial origin of the hair, and other characteristics such as bleaching or dying. These additional hair examinations pose a challenge to the laboratory, especially in determining race. Many people are from a mixed racial background, so the traditional characteristics of hair seen in a given race, are not as clearly defined as in the past.

Fiber examinations include determining or comparing physical, chemical, and optical properties. The color, shape, diameter, fluorescence, and solubility are just a few of the many tests that a forensic scientist can employ. The actual identity of a fiber may not help the investigation very much; however comparisons between known and unknown fiber samples are usually very helpful in linking points on the CSI triangle.

LOCATING HAIR AND FIBER EVIDENCE

In searching for trace evidence at a crime scene, just like when searching for biological evidence, the investigator should start by conducting a general, visual search with the naked eye. This should be followed with a search of the same area utilizing an oblique lighting source. Using oblique light can produce shadows off items of evidence that assist in making them visible. This is the most practiced technique used in searching for hairs and fibers. After using oblique lighting, the investigator should consider using an ALS to further increase the chances of locating evidence. Most hair and fiber evidence will fluoresce between 415 and 515 nm and require either a yellow or an orange barrier filter for visibility.

COLLECTING HAIR AND FIBER EVIDENCE

Hair and fiber evidence is by nature very transient and should be collected immediately upon observation for fear of inadvertently losing the evidence. If the hair or fiber appears secured to an item, such as bedding or clothing, then the entire item should be collected and sent to the laboratory for a forensic scientist to retrieve. If possible, wrap the item in paper in an effort to collect any debris or trace evidence that may fall or become dislodged from the item during transport.

If the hair or fiber is very loosely attached to an item, or is on an item that cannot be easily collected, then the investigator must collect each individual hair or fiber observed. There are several methods for which this can be accomplished. A gloved hand or a pair of disposable, one-time use tweezers can be used to grasp and place the hair or fiber evidence into a paper evidence fold. A paper evidence fold can be made in the field, and is an excellent way to securely collect and preserve many types of trace evidence. Figure 15.2 provides instructions for how to create a paper evidence fold. Another collection method is to use the sticky side of low-tack tape such as post-it notes. Do not use packing tape, duct tape, or other tapes considered high-tack, as the forensic scientist will be unable to retrieve the trace evidence from the tape for analysis. If using a post-it note for collection, the note can be folded in half to secure the trace evidence, and then placed into a paper evidence fold for collection.

Another method for collecting hairs and fibers that is often referenced in training material is to vacuum an area of interest. Although this method may have been popular in the past, most forensic laboratories no longer recommend this technique because not only are the items of interest collected, but all of the debris in that area is collected, and this proves very difficult for the laboratory to separate. If the investigator has a large area of interest to collect hairs, fibers, or other trace evidence, it is recommended to break the area up into grids and use post-it notes to collect the top layer of trace evidence from each grid.

Paper Evidence Fold Instructions

Step One: Place the trace evidence in the center of a clean, unused sheet of paper.

Step Two: Fold the sheet of paper into thirds.

Step Three: Fold the thirds in half.

FIGURE 15.2 Instructions for how to create a paper evidence fold.

(*Continued*)

Step Four: Fold the paper into thirds again, but in the opposite direction as done in Step Two.

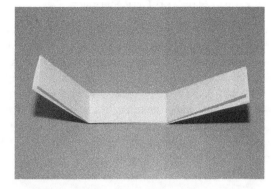

Step Five: Fold one edge into a point.

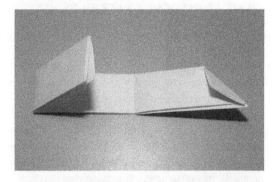

Step Six: Insert the pointed end into the outermost opening of the opposite end.

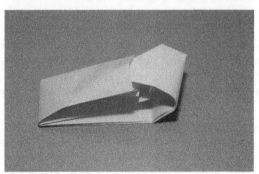

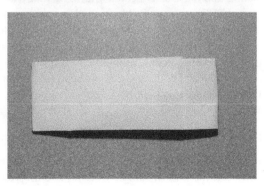

FIGURE 15.2 (CONTINUED) Instructions for how to create a paper evidence fold.

PACKAGING HAIR AND FIBER EVIDENCE

Wrapping items in paper or placing hairs and fibers into a paper evidence fold is only considered the primary packaging container. This wrapped item must then be placed into a manila envelope, paper bag, or box. If the item is to be examined for DNA evidence, all openings must be sealed to prevent the escape of any evidence or the introduction of anything to the evidence.

Do not package trace evidence such as hairs and fibers into plastic. Plastic bags create static electricity and when the forensic scientist opens the item to retrieve the trace evidence, it may unintentionally fly out of the plastic due to the electric charge and be unrecoverable. Do not package trace evidence loosely in an envelope or paper bag as it may inadvertently leak from the packaging material and be lost indefinitely.

PHYSICAL EVIDENCE RECOVERY KIT

Remember that one of the main goals of collecting physical evidence in any criminal investigation is to be able to link the victim, the suspect, and the crime scene. Physical evidence also plays a role in showing that a crime did in fact occur, or in the case of sexual assaults, that sexual contact occurred between the victim and the suspect. In order to accomplish this, the laboratory will examine questioned evidence recovered from the victim, the suspect, and the scene to known samples taken from the victim and the suspect. Physical Evidence Recovery Kits, or PERKs, have been created to assist in maximizing the recovery of forensic evidence from victims and suspects. In some jurisdictions, PERKs are provided by forensic laboratories or local hospitals; in other jurisdictions the kits must be purchased commercially. The contents of a typical PERK are outlined below and can easily be constructed. It is wise that several of these kits be kept on hand for immediate use in sexual assault cases.

The victim PERK is designed for victims that are either male or female, and can be used on victims of any age (children or adults). The victim PERK can be used regardless of the type of sexual assault—vaginal, anal, sodomy, fellatio, or digital penetration. Although the victim PERK can also be used for fondling-only cases, it is not specifically designed for this type of case. The victim PERK is designed for use within 72 h of the assault. Studies have shown that semen will typically exist in the vaginal vault for 72 h; however, many forensic laboratories will still accept PERKs for analysis even if they were collected more than 72 h after the assault.

Suspect PERKs are similar to victim PERKs and should be utilized if a suspect is identified and detained within 24 h of the assault. The evidence contained on a suspect is often very transient in nature, and must be collected within this narrow time frame. The contents described below for a typical PERK are applicable for both a victim and suspect PERK.

Many jurisdictions now have Sexual Assault Nurse Examiners, or SANEs, who are specifically trained in collecting evidence in a PERK. Using a SANE for the collection of a PERK is recommended because not only do they have specialized training in the effective and appropriate collection of evidence in these types of cases, they are also trained in providing specific, quality care for victims of sexual assault.

KNOWN DNA SAMPLE

Known DNA samples are an important piece of evidence in sexual assault cases. The laboratory will need the known sample to eliminate the victim's DNA profile from any questioned samples recovered, and will use the suspect's known DNA sample, if available, for comparison. There are typically two ways in which the investigator can collect a known DNA sample from the victim—blood or buccal. The PERK includes a bloodstain card, which requires a medical professional for collection. A good alternative to the bloodstain card for the known DNA sample is to take a buccal swab from the inner cheek. This is done by rotating two swabs, simultaneously, inside of the subject's inner cheek, and having the individual saturate the swabs with saliva. Buccal swabs are less invasive than taking a blood sample, do not require a trained medical professional, and reduce the risk of being exposed to blood borne pathogens.

Although a buccal sample is usually the preferred method of obtaining a known DNA sample, the investigator should not collect a buccal sample from the victim if fellatio occurred during the assault. In cases of suspected fellatio, an oral rinse sample should be collected from the victim, and the known DNA sample from the victim should be taken via the bloodstain card.

KNOWN HAIR SAMPLES

The known hair samples include collection from both head hairs and pubic hairs. At least 25 hairs should be pulled (not cut) from the head of the victim and the suspect. These head hairs should be a representative sample of the area, color, and length of hairs observed throughout the head. The comb provided in the PERK should then be used to comb the pubic hairs. This is done over a clean paper evidence fold to collect any debris that may fall out. The comb can also be collected in the paper evidence fold. At least 25 hairs should then be cut, not pulled, from the pubic area.

SWABS

The swabs contained within the PERK are to be used for a variety of locations and their collection is dependent upon the type of case being investigated. The swabs are typically used for the vaginal, anal, scrotal, and penile areas. The investigator should also consider taking swabs of the suspect's fingers in digital penetration cases. This is beneficial because the suspect's DNA will typically be overpowered in the vaginal vault and no suspect profile will be developed, but the laboratory may be able to identify the victim's DNA from the suspect finger swabs.

ORAL RINSE

As mentioned above, an oral rinse collection can be beneficial in cases where suspected fellatio has occurred. Saline solution is used to irrigate the victim's mouth in an attempt to recover semen.

FINGERNAIL SCRAPINGS

Wooden scraping devices are included in the PERK to collect any debris deposited underneath the subject's fingernails. The scrapings are typically taken from each hand separately and should be done over a clean paper evidence fold. The wooden scraping device should then be collected in the paper evidence fold as well. An alternative to fingernail scrapings is to cut the fingernails, but a clean, new nail clipper should be used for each hand. If the subject's fingernails are too short for cutting or scraping, consider swabbing the fingers by moistening a swab with two drops of distilled water.

CLOTHING

The subject should be instructed to stand over a large piece of paper intended to catch any debris that may fall to the ground as they disrobe. This piece of paper can then be collected and included in the PERK. Each item of clothing should be packaged separately and sealed in a paper bag. These bags are typically too large to be included inside of the PERK.

Most PERKs are designed to be sealed on site by the SANE and then provided to the investigator for transportation to the forensic laboratory. These kits no longer require refrigeration as they had in the past. The only exception to this rule is if liquid or wet samples are collected, to include a soaked tampon or sanitary napkin. If liquid or wet samples are collected as a part of the PERK, they must be transported to the laboratory immediately or temporarily refrigerated and transported to the forensic laboratory within 1 week of collection.

OTHER ELIMINATION SAMPLES

Consideration should be given to obtaining other, necessary, elimination DNA samples in the investigation. If other persons had a legitimate reason to have come into contact with the victim, whether physical or sexual in nature, a known sample of their DNA should be collected as well. A common example of this scenario is when the victim had consensual intercourse with an individual prior to the sexual assault.

OTHER TYPES OF PHYSICAL EVIDENCE

CLOTHING AND BEDDING

Clothing and bedding may often contain biological stains, hairs, and fibers or wearer DNA, as addressed above in the previous sections. However, as a general rule if the clothing or bedding has any staining, paper should be placed between the layers of the fabric to prevent the transfer of the stain to other layers. Also, as a general rule, clothing and bedding should be collected in paper in an effort to capture any trace evidence that may become dislodged during transportation. This paper can be constructed into a large paper evidence fold to ensure that all evidence is secured within the fold, and then the paper evidence fold can be placed into a secondary packaging material such as a manila envelope, paper bag, or cardboard box.

CONDOMS AND CONDOM WRAPPERS

Used and unused condoms can be found discarded at the scene and certainly may provide valuable information. Unused condoms should be collected using a gloved hand or disposable, one-time use tweezers and then air dried prior to packaging in paper. A used condom contains important DNA information on both the interior and exterior of the condom. Presumably, the suspect's DNA would be on the interior of the condom and the victim's DNA would be located on the exterior of the condom. Both areas need to be carefully preserved with every effort made to prevent mixing of the two samples. The very top of the condom can be tied shut with string, and then suspended inside of a clean, unused ice cream container or cardboard box. This should be done in such a fashion to prevent the exterior of the condom from touching the sides of the packaging container. The used condom could also be placed into a plastic Tupperware container by closing the lid over the very top of the condom. Used condoms may never fully air dry, and should be submitted to the forensic laboratory immediately. If immediate submission is not possible, the used condom should be refrigerated and transported to the laboratory within 1 week of collection. Certain condom manufacturers use unique combinations of powders, spermicides, and lubricants. These trace materials may be found inside of the victim and could assist in determining the type of condom used during the sexual assault.

Condom wrappers may also contain valuable forensic evidence such as fingerprints or touch DNA. The investigator must also consider that the suspect may have ripped the wrapper open with his teeth and thus deposited saliva on the wrapper. Additionally, a condom wrapper may have originated from a strip of adjoined condom wrappers, and when torn from that strip leave a unique pattern called a fracture. The fracture on the condom wrapper found at the crime scene may be matched to the fracture from the originating strip. This is called a fracture match analysis and is considered an individual characteristic with positive identification.

DRUG FACILITATED SEXUAL ASSAULTS

Drug Facilitated Sexual Assaults (DFSAs), also known as date rape, involves the unlawful seduction of a victim and incapacitation with the use of a drug. Alcohol is the number one drug used in DFSAs, but some other common date rape drugs include Rohypnol, GHB, and Ketamine.

Rohypnol (flunitrazepam), or "roofies," are tasteless, odorless and can easily dissolve in liquid. Rohypnol may be detected in urine for approximately 5 days after ingestion. GHB (gamma-hydroxybutyrate) is clear, odorless, and tastes somewhat salty. GHB may only be detected in the body for approximately 12 h. Ketamine is a clear liquid or a white powder and is legally used for sedation of large animals at veterinary clinics. Ketamine metabolites may be detected in urine for approximately 7 days.

Some commonly observed symptoms when a date rape drug was used include sedation, muscle relaxation, reduced inhibitions, amnesia, and poor judgment. If a DFSA is suspected, the victim's blood and/or urine can be collected and subsequently analyzed by a forensic toxicologist. Drugs will typically be found in higher concentrations in the blood than in the urine; however drugs will also generally dissipate much faster in the blood than in the urine. Most PERKs contain vacutainer tubes that can be used to collect a blood sample or plastic cups that can be used to collect a urine sample. If a blood or urine sample is collected, it must be submitted to the laboratory immediately, or refrigerated and transported to the laboratory within 1 week of collection.

Detecting drugs in the blood or urine of the victim is challenging due to the short half-life of these commonly used drugs seen in DFSAs. Crime scene investigators should consider looking for additional evidence at the scene of the sexual assault which may indicate that a drug had been used. For example, trace amounts of the suspected drug may be located in drink ware, or bottles of the drug may be located in the suspect's medicine cabinet. Unfortunately, proving drug consumption in DFSA cases often times depends upon the investigation and witness statements, and not physical evidence.

SUMMARY

A thorough understating of evidence identification, collection, preservation, and documentation is paramount in a successful CSI. This chapter strives to provide information on a systematic approach to CSI and direction in addressing the most common types of physical evidence in sexual assault investigations. All crime scenes are unique and one may encounter any number of varying types of evidence. Challenges, such as difficult or unusual types of evidence, may be presented at the crime scene. However, if the investigator remains organized and systematic, they will ensure that no evidence is overlooked or mishandled.

There are many resources available for reference in the field, such as evidence handling guides, and most forensic laboratories work closely with local law enforcement and are available to answer questions or offer suggestions on best practices. Each laboratory is different, and it is important to recognize the capabilities and requirements of the forensic laboratory in your jurisdiction.

One of the most common questions asked by crime scene personnel is whether or not to collect an item at a crime scene. This author preaches and follows the following motto:

"It is better to collect it and not need it, than to not collect it and wish you had."

ACKNOWLEDGMENTS

This author would like to express sincere appreciation to Adam Crider, Kimberly Hamby, Ariel Kendall, and Brianna Miller for their assistance, time, and dedication in the preparation of this chapter.

FURTHER READING

Bevel, T., and R. M. Gardner. 2008. *Bloodstain pattern analysis with an introduction to crime scene reconstruction*, 3rd ed. Boca Raton, FL: CRC Press.

FBI Laboratory Services, and U.S. Department of Justice. 2011. *FBI handbook of forensic services.* Washington, DC: Federal Bureau of Investigations. www.fbi.gov/progams/lab/handbook/intro.htm

Fisher, B. A., and D. R. Fisher. 2012. *Techniques of crime scene investigation*, 8th ed. Boca Raton, FL: CRC Press.

Gardner, R. M. 2011. *Practical crime scene processing and investigation*, 2nd ed. Boca Raton, FL: CRC Press.

Robinson, E. M. 2010. *Crime scene photography*, 2nd ed. Waltham, MA: Academic Press.

Saferstein, R. 2014. *Criminalistics: An introduction to forensic science*, 11th ed. Upper Saddle River, NJ: Prentice-Hall.

Virginia Department of Forensic Science. 2015. *Evidence handling and laboratory capabilities guide.* Richmond, VA: Virginia Department of Forensic Science. www.dfs.virginia.gov/documentation-publications/evidence-handling-and-laboratory-capabilities-guide/

16 Medical Evaluation of Sexually Abused Children

Andi Taroli

CONTENTS

Multidisciplinary Investigations..242
The Pediatrician's Role..242
The Scope of the Problem..243
"Children Are Not Little Adults"..244
    The Pediatrician's Mantra...244
The Medical History...245
    The Patient's History (Interview)..245
    General Principles for Interviewing Children..245
        Setting...246
        Timing..246
        Questions..247
        Number of Interviews...247
        Pertinent Medical Content...247
    Past Medical History, Family and Social History, and System Review.......................248
The Physical Examination..248
    Colposcopy...249
    Examination Positions...250
    The Hymen—Myths and Truths...250
    Examination Findings...251
        Acute Injury...251
        Chronic Examination Findings...252
    Why Are Positive Physical Findings Uncommon?..252
    "Penetration, However Slight"..253
    Evidence for Absence (of Physical Findings)...258
    The Written Report...261
Forensic Evidence Collection...261
    Where the Evidence Is (And Where It's Not)...261
Sexually Transmitted Infections (STIs)...262
False Allegations of Sexual Abuse in Children...262
Sequelae..265
References...266
Further Reading...267

"Primum Non Nocere"

Investigation of child sexual exploitation requires specialized skills and training, which includes a basic understanding of the medical assessment of child victims. The information in this chapter is a foundation for that expertise—investigators are encouraged to utilize the references and resources provided at the end of the chapter for further study.

MULTIDISCIPLINARY INVESTIGATIONS

"A long pull, and a strong pull, and a pull all together."

Charles Dickens—*David Copperfield*

There is perhaps no greater need for communication and cooperation than in child sexual abuse investigations. No one (except the sex offender) benefits from a clumsy, disjointed process that re-traumatizes child victims and creates roadblocks to investigation and successful prosecution.

Cases involving child victims are unique in that both law enforcement and child protection workers must both investigate and reach conclusions about the validity of allegations, though usually to a different burden of proof. Multiple interviews, repeated examinations, misunderstandings, and frustration were the norm when two separate investigations occurred, often leading the victim to recant, become uncooperative, or appear to give inconsistent statements as a stressful, lengthy process took a heavy toll on the child and family.

In 1985 the first Child Advocacy Center (CAC) firmly established the concept of a multidisciplinary team (MDT), consisting of law enforcement, social services, prosecutors, victim services, and medical and mental health professionals, located in a supportive, nonthreatening setting for the child victim, and conducive to cooperation between the investigative agencies. Cooperative investigation will

- Reduce trauma to an already victimized child,
- Enhance the quality of the investigation,
- Promote accountability, and
- Increase the appropriate utilization of community resources.

Since 1985, the number of MDTs and CACs has increased almost exponentially: as of 2015, 777 such centers recognized by the National Children's Alliance (the accrediting body for CACs) exist in the U.S., and MDT investigation is now standard practice in the field.

THE PEDIATRICIAN'S ROLE

pe·di·a·tri·cian (noun) [peèdee ə trish 'n] *a doctor who specializes in the care and development of children and in the prevention and treatment of children's diseases*

The pediatrician plays an integral role in the assessment of child sexual abuse, as well as its recognition, prevention, and treatment. Pediatric specialists in child maltreatment are doctors first and foremost, whose primary goal is to promote the health, safety, and well-being of their young patients. An expert in child sexual abuse must have adequate education, training, and sufficient experience (some say over at least 1,000 examinations) in order to prevent misdiagnosis and potential miscarriage of justice. Experienced examiners are more consistent and objective in their diagnoses, and less influenced by the presenting history of allegations. Peer review is essential for newly trained examiners, who should routinely review cases with other experts either in person or by utilizing electronic HIPAA compliant, peer-review imaging software. Keeping in mind the enormous personal, financial, and societal costs of misdiagnosis, the forensic pediatricians must:

- Keep impeccable records and understand the importance of documentation,
- Understand proper evidence collection techniques,
- Provide records for documenting a chain of custody for evidence obtained, and
- Prepare and provide court testimony.

The child abuse expert's role at trial is to educate the judge or jury, explaining in understandable terms how the evaluation was done, the details of the examination findings and their significance, and to give an expert opinion (the diagnosis).

Child abuse pediatrics is now a distinct subspecialty with its own certification administered by the American Board of Pediatrics, with 324 pediatricians attaining such certification in the U.S. by December 2013. Forensic pediatrics encompasses a rapidly expanding body of clinical knowledge and research; the specialist must understand the usefulness *and limitations* of the medical contribution to the investigation. In addition, the International Association of Forensic Nurses has established guidelines for sexual assault nurse examiners in pediatrics (SANE-P) to establish consistent education and training in the collection of evidence for child victims.

Clinicians in any field arrive at a diagnosis by relying on a detailed assessment of: (1) the patient's complaint; (2) the past medical, family, and social histories; (3) the medical examination; and (4) diagnostic testing. Pediatricians often rely heavily on information presented by caregivers (information which may or may not be true). The ultimate diagnosis will also be affected by variations in child development, the range of normal child sexual behavior, the home environment, cultural factors, and most importantly, the pediatrician's knowledge of the psychosocial dynamics of child sexual exploitation (AAP Guidelines, 1999).

It is well documented that child sexual abuse and other adverse experiences commonly occur together (Bowen, 2000; Dong et al., 2004). There is strong evidence that child sexual abuse, physical abuse, neglect, parental substance abuse, domestic violence, and crime in the home are interrelated, underscoring the need for a comprehensive pediatric evaluation in these cases—not simply a detailed look at the genitals (AAP Guidelines, 1999; Dong, Anda, Dube, Giles, & Felitti, 2003).

Although many physicians may be called upon to evaluate a child alleged to be sexually abused, many are not adequately prepared to do so. In one survey of pediatricians, 53% of respondents felt their training in abuse was inadequate, and did not feel confident doing sexual abuse examinations (even though half of those were currently performing them) (Arnold, Spiro, Nichols, & King, 2005). A similar Canadian survey also showed that pediatricians felt child protection is a neglected area of pediatric training (Ward et al., 2004). Disturbing results of a national survey of U.S. pediatric chief residents revealed that a third of them could not identify the urethra or the hymen on photos of prepubertal female genitalia. It is incumbent upon every physician caring for children to know their limitations, to be aware of community resources, and to make appropriate referrals to one of a growing number of pediatricians with special expertise in evaluating and treating sexually abused children.

THE SCOPE OF THE PROBLEM

Current knowledge indicates that about 1 in 4 girls and 1 in 6 boys will become victims of sexual abuse before they turn 18. According to the FBI's National Incidence-Based Reporting System (NIBRS) data (1991–2012), nearly 70% of all sexual assaults reported to law enforcement involve children under 18: 34% of all victims are less than 12, and kids under 6 years old make up 14% (Figure 16.1). The same data shows us that of offenders who victimize children 6 years old or younger, 40% are themselves juveniles. These youngest children are also most likely to be sexually abused by family members, with strangers accounting for only a small fraction of offenders against children.

Establishing accurate estimates of the occurrence of child sexual exploitation is complicated, however, by

- A lack of uniformity in crime reporting,
- Victims who never report their abuse,
- Established cases of abuse with no identified perpetrator, and
- Cases declined for prosecution, often because of the young age of the victim.

It is also difficult to compare studies of incidence and prevalence, mainly due to variation in study design: definitions of abuse (e.g., contact vs. noncontact), sample characteristics (e.g., nonuniform

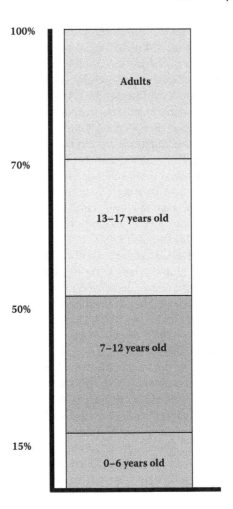

FIGURE 16.1   Age distribution of all victims of sexual assaults reported to law enforcement (NIBRS data).

age groups), and sampling techniques (random vs. probability). Crimes against children often escape detection by the criminal justice system; this statement is not only generally accepted, but is also supported by the reports of both offenders and victims (Prentky, Knight, & Lee, 1997). Further evidence for the reliability of this statement comes from retrospective surveys: representative samples of adults in the general population provide fairly consistent prevalence data—25% of women and 16% of men report being sexually abused as children (Felitti, Anda, Nordenberg, & Williamson, 1998). One study indicates that about a third of adult women sexually abused as children never told anyone about their victimization prior to the research interview (Smith et al., 2000).

"CHILDREN ARE NOT LITTLE ADULTS"

THE PEDIATRICIAN'S MANTRA

The evaluation of child victims differs significantly from that of adults in almost every aspect:

- The child's ability to describe what happened may be minimal to nonexistent.
- Disclosures may be delayed weeks, months, or years after the abuse occurred.
- Sexual contact involving bodily injury is uncommon.
- Physical evidence and examination findings are unusual.

- Healed anogenital injuries may be obscured by physical maturation and hormonal changes.
- Sexually transmitted infections are detected less frequently, especially in the youngest victims (Beck-Sague & Soloman, 1998; Stevens-Simon, Nelligan, Breese, Jenny, & Douglas, 2000; Ingram, Miller, Schoenbach, Everett, & Ingram, 2001; Kelly & Koh, 2006; Ramos, Lukefahr, Morrow, Stanberry, & Rosenthal, 2006).
- Family members or caregivers may be unsupportive or actively interfere with the disclosure and assessment.
- Allegations may surface in the context of visitation or custody disputes.

THE MEDICAL HISTORY

THE PATIENT'S HISTORY (INTERVIEW)

Physicians rely on a detailed history of the presenting problem to make a diagnosis—every medical student learns that arriving at the correct diagnosis almost always comes from the history alone. Child sexual abuse is no exception. It is imperative, then, to optimize every aspect of the child's history, or interview, in order to obtain the maximum information with the least trauma and distress to the child.

In the U.S., variation exists in who takes the lead in obtaining the child's history or interview. The task may fall to Child Protective Services, police, specialized interviewers, physicians, or some combination of these. In most situations, statements made to a physician will fall under the hearsay exception (when the history is obtained for the purpose of diagnosis and treatment), allowing the physician to testify to those statements. Many MDTs and CACs utilize forensic interviewers, who are specially trained in objective, fact-finding interviews. Forensic interviewers may also gather medical history, as well as information needed by law enforcement and child protection—again, to reduce stress on the child victim by decreasing the number of people with whom they must share details of traumatic experiences. An in-depth discussion of forensic interviewing is beyond the scope of this chapter, however, it is imperative for anyone conducting child abuse investigations that they thoroughly understand how to conduct a "minimal facts" interview, and have an appreciation for the methods utilized in conducting a forensically defensible investigative interview. For a concise summary of the basic tenets of forensic interviewing, please refer to the guidelines set forth by the American Professional Society on the Abuse of Children (APSAC), Cornerhouse, or the National Institute of Child Health and Human Development (NICHD) protocol.

GENERAL PRINCIPLES FOR INTERVIEWING CHILDREN

Children's language capabilities and linguistic styles vary considerably; unless you are aware of these potential barriers to good communication, and practice overcoming them, the information you gather may be sparse and seemingly contradictory. *Problematic interviews are most often the result of poor interviewer technique.* The interviewer should not lead the child or suggest information, and above all, not add to the child's distress. Other factors affecting the quality of the disclosure and a child's willingness to talk include

- The age of the child,
- The intrusiveness of the sexual contact,
- The relationship with the offender,
- Support of the non-offending parent, and
- An intentional versus "accidental" (discovered inadvertently) disclosure.

For example, a child assaulted once by an unfamiliar acquaintance is more likely to make a disclosure than the child who is chronically molested by an alcoholic father that terrorizes the family with unpredictable violence.

FIGURE 16.2 The interview room should be comfortable, be suitable for different age groups, and have few distractions.

Setting

In order to maximize the child's comfort and improve memory retrieval, the setting for the child's interview should be relaxed, friendly, and supportive. Hectic emergency departments, with their buzzers, alarms, and interruptions, are frightening places. So are police stations, as children may assume they were brought there because *they* are in trouble. This is typical when children come from families that consider law enforcement "the enemy." CACs provide a neutral, comfortable setting, with child-friendly interview rooms and minimal distractions. Most often, these interview rooms are equipped with closed circuit viewing and recording capabilities (Figure 16.2).

If a medical examination will accompany the interview, apprehension about getting shots or other fears should be allayed. Speak to the child alone, away from the non-offending parent or other caregivers. Children are often afraid, embarrassed, and reluctant to discuss details of their abuse in front of people who are emotionally involved with the perpetrator, especially when it comes to the more intrusive aspects of the abuse. Investigators should try *not* to interview children in their homes—it is essential that the setting be emotionally neutral, a place where they can feel safe and reasonably secure that the perpetrator won't show up unexpectedly.

Timing

Once the child's safety has been assured, the examination and interview can be scheduled for a time when the child will be most cooperative—it's unreasonable to expect a tired, hungry child to give a detailed, reliable history. Scheduled examinations are appropriate for most child sexual abuse evaluations, as disclosures are commonly delayed. The history and examination may need to be performed immediately for acute assaults (generally, less than 72 h prior), if there is a complaint of anogenital pain or bleeding, or if there is risk of continued exposure to the alleged perpetrator. Immediate evaluation of acute assaults allows for the administration of prophylactic antibiotic treatment in cases of genital contact or exposure to body fluids, and offers the opportunity to collect forensic evidence.

Questions

The first and most important rule when talking to children about sexual abuse is to avoid suggestive and leading questions. Use open ended questions as much as possible (e.g., "and then what happened?"), and focused, multiple choice type questions as little as possible (e.g., "did it happen at night, during the day, after school, or some other time?"). Direct questions and those that can be answered with a "yes" or "no" should be used sparingly, if at all. To avoid asking "how many times" something happened (very difficult for children to answer), ask the child to describe distinct, specific episodes of the abuse. *Only those individuals trained in interviewing children should utilize dolls, drawings, or other objects to obtain information* (APSAC Guidelines, 1995, 2002). If not recorded, the information obtained should be documented in exquisite detail, as should any statements made spontaneously by the child during the performance of the physical examination.

A word of caution: history taking should be just that—finding out what happened, where, when, how—and not an opportunity for therapy or counseling. The sole purpose of taking the history is to obtain an objective account of events, signs, and symptoms; if a determination of abuse has been made, the child should be referred to an appropriate mental health professional.

Similarly, the interviewer should remember to keep their expressions and responses neutral. Displaying shock or embarrassment may cause the child to minimize, "forget," or shut down completely. Praise for answering questions, or threats to provoke disclosure are both ill-advised and forensically disastrous. The interviewer must be unbiased, and willing to entertain the "null hypothesis," that is, that no abuse occurred.

Number of Interviews

Reducing the stress of repeated interviews has been a focal point of the MDT and CAC approach to child sexual abuse assessment. At any age, divulging embarrassing details of sexual abuse to one person is difficult; extending that level of trust to multiple strangers on multiple occasions becomes a cruel punishment for the disclosing child. There are other advantages to minimizing the number of interviews conducted: apparent inconsistencies in the allegations are reduced, (usually caused by differences in interviewer technique and use of language), as is the potential for a "tainted" or contaminated history. These problems are best avoided by using a single, unbiased interviewer for repeat or extended interviews.

Pertinent Medical Content

Providing medical care for children who have been sexually abused involves gathering enough information to formulate a differential diagnosis (a list of all *reasonably* possible diagnoses), narrowing the possibilities, and coming to a conclusion "within a reasonable degree of medical certainty." The physician would be remiss if he or she were unaware of information which, on the surface, seems unrelated to medical care. Elements of the child's history, such as a description of the perpetrator's appearance, locations where the abuse occurred, or other reports of collateral evidence provide insight into the veracity of the child's statements. These details also assist in assuring the child's safety and potential for future contact with the perpetrator. Similarly, one must assess other factors observed during the child's history, such as level of spontaneity when answering questions, guardedness, or appearing "rehearsed." All these pieces are important parts of the diagnostic puzzle. (For an in depth discussion of this topic, please refer to the chapter on Collateral Materials.)

In addition to the details of the abuse scenario, the medically focused history should include

- The extent of the sexual contact,
- Perception of pain or discomfort,
- Occurrence of injury or bleeding
- Exposure to body fluids.

Some knowledge of the alleged perpetrator may help to determine the child victim's risk of exposure to sexually transmitted disease—for example, an adult male perpetrator with history of incarceration poses a much greater risk than an inexperienced 12-year-old boy.

Girls should be asked when their last menstrual period began, and their age at menarche (initial onset of menses), since pregnancy may even occur during a girl's first menstrual cycle. All children should be asked about the possibility of other perpetrators or incidents of sexual abuse they may have experienced. Sexually active victims should be questioned about any recent consensual sexual contact and use of condoms.

Past Medical History, Family and Social History, and System Review

Physical or behavioral indicators supporting a diagnosis of child sexual abuse can often be found when an experienced clinician elicits a detailed medical history from the accompanying parent or caregiver. Conditions or complaints may be discovered which had been mistakenly attributed to other causes prior to the disclosure of sexual abuse. Patients may have had previous medical attention for symptoms of urinary tract infections, vaginal discharge or bleeding, or anogenital discomfort. A history of enuresis (bedwetting), urinary frequency or urgency, and dysuria (pain with urination) may be due to irritation resulting from genital contact. It is also important to ascertain whether the child has had any previous history of anogenital injury or surgery, as any abnormalities found on examination will be interpreted with this in mind.

Behavioral changes resulting from sexual abuse are most often nonspecific reactions that can occur in response to many other types of traumatic experiences, such as divorce, domestic violence, or death of a loved one. Depression, anxiety, anger, poor self-esteem, sleep or appetite disturbance, and declining school performance are commonly seen. Behavior that is more specific for abuse includes sexual acting out that is intrusive or developmentally inappropriate. Clearly, children of any age who try to insert things into another person's genitals or anus, or try to put their mouths on other people's genitals are distinctly out of the range of normal sexual behaviors. Self-destructive behaviors, such as substance abuse, cutting, running away, and risky sexual behaviors may also be seen, especially in older children and teens.

The pediatric assessment should also include an inquiry into the living arrangement and social circumstances of the child's home. Studies have clearly demonstrated that exposure to abuse, neglect, or household dysfunction has a high degree of co-occurrence with other types of maltreatment and other adverse childhood experiences. Identification of other harmful exposures is crucial for intervention and treatment. These adverse experiences—abuse (physical, sexual, or emotional), neglect, witnessing domestic violence, and exposures to substance abuse, mental illness, or criminal activity in the home—have significant, cumulative effects on the child's future health and well-being (Felitti et al., 1998).

THE PHYSICAL EXAMINATION

This section will focus mainly on the examination of the prepubertal child, since the examination of adolescents is similar to that of the adult, and is discussed in detail elsewhere in this text.

Ideally, and for several reasons, the child victim should not undergo more than one examination when allegations of sexual abuse arise:

- Like repeated interviews, repeated examinations are unduly stressful for the child, particularly when the examiner is not comfortable or skilled in performing them.
- Repeated examinations focus undue attention on the child's genitals, instead of on the crucial aspect of the investigation—the history.
- The initial contact with a medical provider (often the local Emergency Dept.) may be viewed as the examination performed for the purpose of diagnosis and treatment; subsequent

examinations (by pediatric specialists) might be seen as purely "investigative." Statements made to the initial physician, then, would be exempt from the medical hearsay exception, but subsequent conversations may not, and the specialist's findings will be regarded with suspicion.

Child victims should be referred to the most experienced medical professional available for an examination. In addition to those reasons outlined earlier in this chapter, a specially trained pediatrician is more likely to be aware of all the normal variations that can be seen on genital exam. Lack of familiarity with normal variants can result in a belief that there is "evidence" when there is none, can damage the credibility of your case if the physician is shown to be incorrect, or could result in wrongful prosecution. The examiner also needs to be familiar with an array of diseases, infections, and conditions occurring in children that are often mistaken for abuse: strep infection, Crohn's disease, hemangiomas, lichen sclerosus, and urethral prolapse are just a few.

A head-to-toe physical examination should always be performed to detect any associated findings of abuse or neglect. A complete examination also has therapeutic value, offering both patient and family reassurance of the child's health and normalcy. Any signs of trauma (bruises, bite marks) should be photographed and/or documented in drawings. Particular attention should be paid to abrasions, petechiae (pinpoint hemorrhages), or bruises that correlate with the victim's description of events. Examples include

- Fingertip bruises on the thighs or buttocks,
- Petechiae on the palate (roof of mouth) from forced fellatio
- Ligature marks.

COLPOSCOPY

Many, if not most, clinicians who routinely perform sexual abuse examinations for children utilize a colposcope to aid in the visualization of genital structures, to document any positive findings, and to assist in peer review. The colposcope is basically a magnifying video camera, providing video or still images (Figure 16.3). Images captured during the examination are officially part of the medical record.

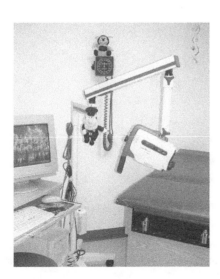
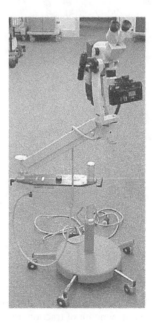

FIGURE 16.3 Examples of colposcopes (Welch Allyn on left; Zeiss on right).

EXAMINATION POSITIONS

The drawings shown here demonstrate the different positions utilized for adequate examination of the genitalia (Figure 16.4a,b). The pediatrician can amuse the child and decrease fears by playing with the imaging system, allowing the child to see their own wiggling fingers or toes magnified on the computer screen. A supportive parent or caregiver should be present for all sexual abuse examinations. When approached in a caring and gentle fashion, children usually have no problems during the genital examination. The process should be explained to them ahead of time to minimize their apprehension. In the *prepubertal* child, the examination is primarily conducted by external inspection of the genital structures; a speculum is never used in a conscious child as it would cause severe pain. The labia are separated and pulled out and down for maximal visualization. If it is necessary to explore the vagina, the patient must be taken to the operating suite for an examination under anesthesia. Once puberty has begun, however, various methods can be utilized to examine the edges of the hymen: large-diameter cotton swabs, Foley balloon catheters, or a small speculum to assess the vaginal walls for trauma.

THE HYMEN—MYTHS AND TRUTHS

Male and female investigators alike are often mistaken about what can and cannot be discovered by the examination. Myths and misconceptions abound, and any discussion of examination findings is useless until these are cleared up:

- Every normal female has a hymen.
- It is not an impenetrable membrane—it does not break, rupture, burst, pop, or provide proof of virtue (or lack thereof).
- From birth, the hymen has an opening in it. The hymenal membrane has a sort of donut shaped appearance—only very rarely is a female infant born without any opening in her hymen.

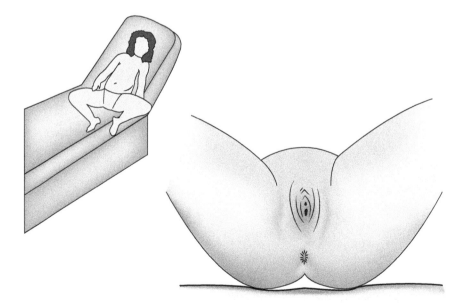

FIGURE 16.4a Examination position: frog-leg supine position. The child is lying on her back, feet together, knees parted. The labia are pulled out and down for maximal visualization. Appearance of structures may vary depending on the amount of traction used.

FIGURE 16.4b   Examination position: knee–chest prone position. The examiner's thumbs push the labia up and outward, while gravity causes the hymen to drop down for a better view of the entire width of the inferior portion.

- The hymen is an *internal* structure—it is recessed in between the labia majora and labia minora, at the very entrance to the vagina. It is NOT injured or affected by horseback riding, gymnastics, bicycling, or like activities.
- Being an internal structure, there is no "casual" way to come in contact with the hymen (no matter what perpetrators may try to tell you), just like there's no casual way to come in contact with someone's tonsils.
- Measuring the opening in the hymen cannot distinguish between abused or non-abused girls (Ingram, Everett, & Ingram, 2001; Berenson et al., 2002).

EXAMINATION FINDINGS (FIGURE 16.5)

Acute Injury

Examination of the male genitalia is a lot more straightforward than that of the prepubertal female (for obvious reasons), so the majority of this section is devoted to the evaluation of girls.

Contact with the internal genitalia (in between the labia) may cause a range of findings, from mild erythema (redness) and slight swelling, to abrasions, petechiae, or lacerations and contusions. The friction and pressure during sexual contact causes irritation and inflammation. Because the area in between the labia includes the urethra (the outlet for urine), symptoms of sexual abuse sometimes includes dysuria (pain with urination), day or nighttime wetting, and frequent urination. Children may report vaginal pain or discomfort, with or without bleeding.

Lacerations or tears of the hymen may extend partially through the membrane, or completely transect it through to its base, where the hymen inserts on the vaginal wall. Anal trauma may

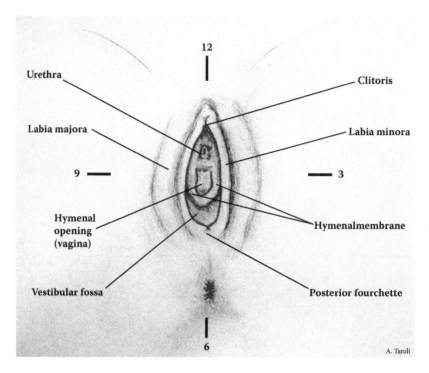

FIGURE 16.5   Prepubertal genital anatomy, with clock-face descriptive anatomy.

include minor fissures (superficial tears), abrasions, bruising, or severe lacerations. Rectal bleeding may occur at the time of the abuse, or later, with passage of feces.

Chronic Examination Findings

The examination of a sexually abused child is most often normal—that is, without any physical findings to "confirm" the abuse. The more superficial the injuries sustained, the more quickly and completely they heal. Larger, deeper wounds are more likely to leave some physical abnormality as they heal. When physical findings *are* present, they are usually found in the inferior portion of the hymen (between the 4 and 8 o'clock positions). In the past, a variety of what we now know to be normal variants were considered to be indicative of healed penetrating injuries. Research over the years has shown that very few examination findings can be considered "proof" of sexual abuse. Residual findings from previous hymenal injury ranges from a normal appearing hymen to deep notches or clefts, or complete transections (healed lacerations) through to the base of the hymen between the 4 and 8 o'clock positions, leaving little or no hymenal tissue at that point. There may be wide areas in which the hymen appears to be "missing" in the inferior portion of the membrane, scars of the posterior fourchette or vestibular fossa, or perianal scars. All of these findings must be confirmed by different examination positions and examination techniques. (For a complete discussion of the significance of various physical findings, refer to Adams et al., 2015.)

WHY ARE POSITIVE PHYSICAL FINDINGS UNCOMMON?

Absence of evidence is not evidence of absence

Steven Jay Gould

The hymen is a ring of tissue surrounding the entrance to the vagina. It often has a donut-shaped or crescent-shaped appearance, and to document examination findings, clinicians use a clock-face reference to describe location (Figure 16.5). Before puberty, that is, before onset of estrogen production, the hymen and surrounding tissues are thin and vascular, giving an extremely reddened appearance which is frequently mistaken by parents as being abnormal.

The hymen is made up of tissue called mucosa—like the mucosa inside the mouth, minor injuries to the mucous membranes of the vagina and hymen heal very rapidly and very completely, usually without leaving any residual sign that injury has occurred. (Think about what happens when you bite the inside of your cheek.) With superficial abrasions and lacerations, the epithelium regenerates by about 48–72 h, and by 5–7 days, evidence of that injury may be completely absent. The likelihood of residual physical findings increases with more extensive injury. Deeper wounds heal by repair, with formation of granulation tissue and wound retraction. New vascular connective tissue develops in the first few days after injury, and matures over several months, changing in color from red to pink to pale.

Injuries to the anus and surrounding tissue heal in a similar fashion. Significant lacerations may distort surrounding structures as they heal, but often do not; some scars may be difficult to differentiate from normal skin tags or variations in perianal skin.

When puberty begins and estrogen levels increase, the hymen responds by becoming thicker, redundant, less vascular, and markedly elastic. After all, the body is preparing for the time when not just a penis, but a baby, will be passing through the vagina. Contrary to popular myth, a significant percentage of mature females have no bleeding after their first sexual intercourse. Any positive findings from injuries occurring prior to puberty may be obliterated or obscured as the child matures, further complicating the medical assessment. Figures 16.6–16.18 demonstrate a few of the features discussed here, and Figure 16.19 gives some insight into their significance.

"PENETRATION, HOWEVER SLIGHT"

An adult's perception of what constitutes "penetration" is formed by experience: something passing through the hymen and into the vagina, or into the anal canal. It is important to remember that most young children will not understand the word "penetration;" if you ask them if something went

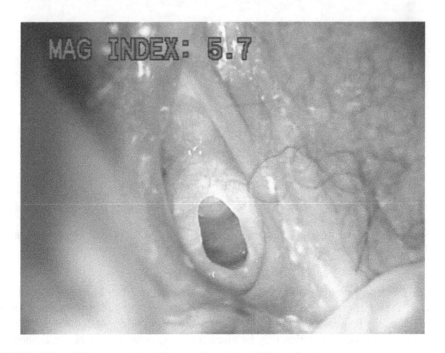

FIGURE 16.6 Normal hymen, early puberty, and annular configuration.

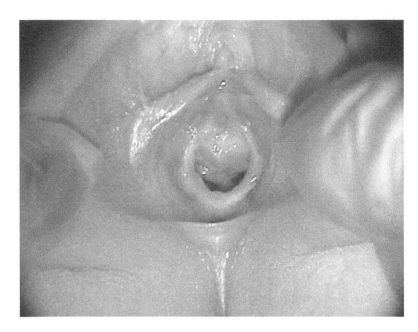

FIGURE 16.7 Normal prepubertal hymen with scalloped edges as seen in the frog–leg supine examination position.

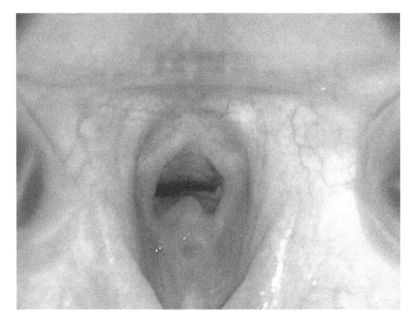

FIGURE 16.8 Same patient as in Figure 16.7, shown in knee–chest prone position. Gravity aids the hymenal membrane to drop downward, better delineating the width and edges of the membrane.

"in" their private part or vagina, their idea of what constitutes "in" may be different than yours. To children who have no frame of reference for the behavior, anything that puts pressure on the genitals or parts the labia may be perceived to be "in," even if the object does not contact the hymen or go into the vagina. A similar description may be given for the sensation of an object pushed between the buttocks and against the anus, but not passing into the rectum. This knowledge helps parents

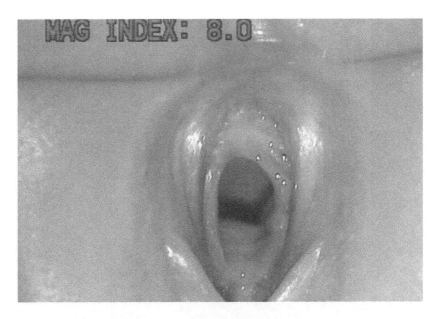

FIGURE 16.9   Normal prepubertal hymen, crescentic, knee–chest prone position.

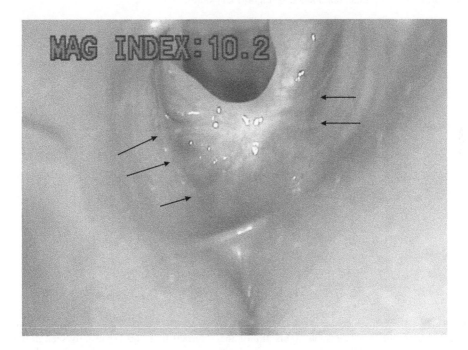

FIGURE 16.10   Normal prepubertal crescentic hymen, with prominent vestibular bands.

and investigators understand why there is no physical injury when the child insists there was "penetration." For legal purposes however, what qualifies as penetration is the slightest contact with the anal or genital orifice: in essence, any contact parting the labia majora, or in between the buttocks, against the anus.

Another important reason for the lack of physical findings in sexually abused children is the type of sexual acts committed by perpetrators: fellatio, cunnilingus, fondling, masturbation, and "vulvar

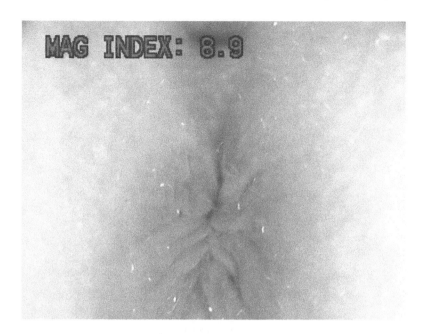

FIGURE 16.11 Symmetrical anal folds (rugae); normal examination.

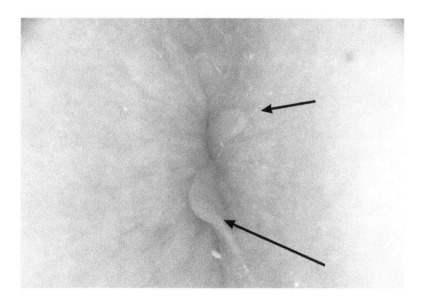

FIGURE 16.12 Hypertrophied perianal skin folds at the 2 and 5 o'clock positions, in a young boy disclosing a history of recurrent anal penetration by his grandfather. Normal skin tags are usually seen in the 12 and 6 o'clock positions; tags off the midline may be more likely to represent scars from old, healed trauma, but this is still an indeterminate finding.

(or labial) coitus"—in which the penis is pressed and rubbed against the genitalia, in between the legs. The buttocks may be used in a similar fashion. Friction and rubbing of body parts may produce only some redness and mild swelling, which disappears quickly. In addition, perpetrators frequently use some type of lubrication (saliva, KY jelly, lotions, etc.) to decrease the likelihood of injury. Remember, decreasing the likelihood of pain and injury decreases the perpetrator's likelihood of being discovered.

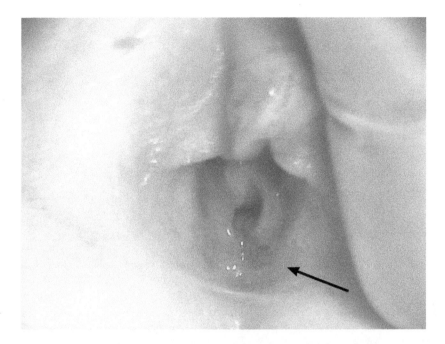

FIGURE 16.13 Eight-year-old girl with history of vaginal, anal, and oral penetration 8 h prior to exam. Semen was recovered from the child's underwear. There is an acute laceration of the hymen at the 5 o'clock position, with surrounding contusion.

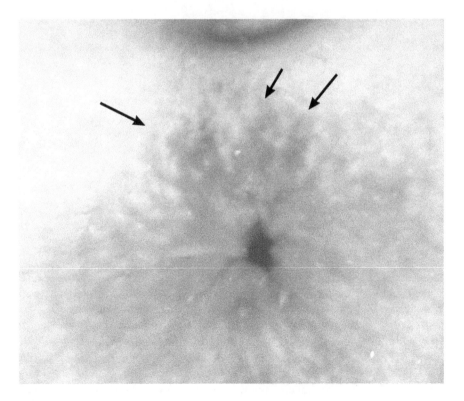

FIGURE 16.14 Same patient as in Figure 16.13: acute anal abrasions and superficial lacerations (arrows), and contusions surrounding the anus.

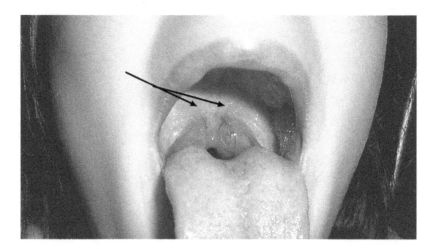

FIGURE 16.15   Same patient as in Figures 16.13 and 16.14: petechiae and erythema of the posterior palate and pharynx after forced fellatio. This child also had abrasions and bruises on her back and buttocks resulting from the assault.

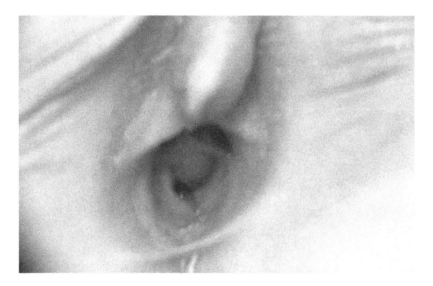

FIGURE 16.16   Same patient as in Figure 16.13, 2 weeks later. The complete transection of the hymen is healing but still visible.

EVIDENCE FOR ABSENCE (OF PHYSICAL FINDINGS)

It's hard for most people to imagine that small children are not seriously injured by sexual contact, but research has demonstrated the infrequency with which sexually abused children have abnormalities on examination. In 2000, Berenson et al. reported on a comparison of large groups of abused and non-abused girls between 3 and 8 years old. The results demonstrated that the genital examination of the abused girls did not differ significantly from the non-abused group. Another study (Heger, Ticson, Velasquez, & Bernier, 2002) reported on medical findings of almost 2,400 children who were specifically referred for evaluation of sexual abuse. Overall, examinations were normal in 96.3% of cases. When prepubertal children with significant injury due to sexual abuse were followed to healing with photocolposcopy (some requiring surgical repair), most anogenital trauma healed quickly, and most often without residual physical findings (Heppenstall-Heger et al., 2003).

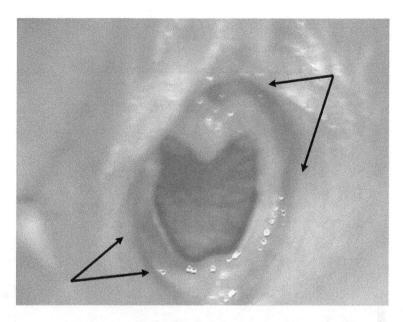

FIGURE 16.17 Contusions and petechiae of the hymen between the 1 and 3 o'clock positions, and between 7 and 9 o'clock in a 5-year-old who disclosed digital penetration and fondling 1–2 days prior to exam.

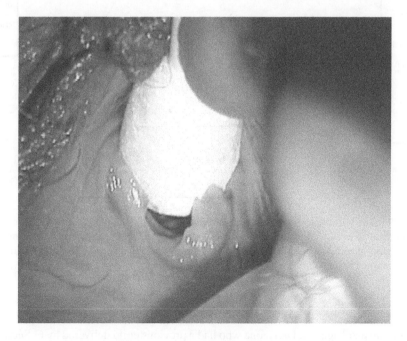

FIGURE 16.18 Wide section of absent hymen in an adolescent, demonstrated with the assistance of a large-diameter cotton swab.

Studies of adolescent girls are also impressive: in 2004 Adams et al. described the examinations of 27 teenaged girls who admitted to a past history of penile/vaginal intercourse—52% of those had no findings suggestive of past penetration. When 36 teens who had become pregnant as a result of sexual assault were examined (Kellogg, Menard, & Santos, 2004), only 2 of these had definitive hymenal evidence of penetrating genital trauma. Strikingly, these two did *not* include one girl that

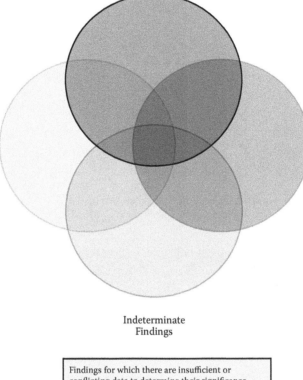

Structures seen in newborns or observed often in
nonabused children; examples include
irregularities of the hymenal edges, skin tags,
smooth areas of perianal skin

Normal Anatomic
Variants

Diagnostic of
Trauma and/or
Sexual Abuse

Highly
suggestive of
abuse even
without a
disclosure.
Examples:
acute
lacerations and
contusions to
anus or
genitalia, healed
complete
transections of
the hymen,
presence of
sexually
transmitted
disease

Other Medical
Conditions

Examples:
skin
infections,
rashes, labial
adhesions,
nonspecific
vaginal
discharge,
lichen
sclerosus

Indeterminate
Findings

Findings for which there are insufficient or
conflicting data to determine their significance.
Examples: deep hymenal notches, areas
of hymen </= 1 mm width, genital warts (without
other indicators of abuse), anal dilatation > 2 cm

FIGURE 16.19   The Venn diagram reminds us of the many possible combinations of findings that can be seen in children being evaluated for sexual abuse. The history given by the child remains the most important aspect of the assessment. Aside from pregnancy or recovery of semen from the child's body, the history will often determine the relevance of physical findings. (From Adams, J. A., *The APSAC Advisor*, Summer, 9–12, 2005.)

had a previous miscarriage and D&C, one who had a previous child delivered by C-Section, and one who had an abortion a few months prior to examination. So, it is abundantly clear: "normal" does not mean "nothing happened."

This information is of paramount importance; professionals from medicine, child protection, law enforcement, and prosecution need to be very comfortable in the knowledge that even with allegations of digital or penile penetration, physical findings are *not* expected. Investigators will then be able to focus on the child's history. These concepts must also be communicated effectively to judge and jury, so that the child's story will not be discounted as inaccurate.

THE WRITTEN REPORT

The words and phrases used in composing the medical report will be scrutinized by everyone involved in the investigative and legal aspects of child sexual abuse cases. The medical diagnosis is formulated by combining information from the past history, the child's statements, physical examination, and diagnostic studies. The opinion is given to a reasonable degree of medical certainty, which is no different than a diagnosis offered in any other field of medicine. Clinicians should not use vague, abbreviated diagnostic terms, such as "findings consistent with abuse." The documentation should provide a concise summary of all the pertinent information utilized in coming to a conclusion. The child's statements, symptoms related to sexual abuse, physical findings, and results of diagnostic studies should all be explained as to their relevance—how they each support or discount the likelihood of sexual abuse. This practice not only provides insight into that patient's medical assessment, but also serves to inform and educate anyone who reads the report. The diagnostic process is complex, and the physician's report should reflect that.

FORENSIC EVIDENCE COLLECTION

There are some essential differences between forensic evidence collection in child sexual abuse cases and adult sexual assault. For example, issues of evidence environment and the presence of transfer evidence assume much different significance—abuse most commonly occurs in a child's own home; mingling of victim and perpetrator's trace evidence would be expected. Since child sexual abuse is usually nonviolent, blood stains are rare. During contact, ejaculation is usually external, disappearing quickly as the child is bathed and clothing is laundered. Forensic specimens are unlikely to be recovered from any source when the child's disclosure comes long after the last episode of sexual contact. For prepubertal children, DNA evidence is likely only if the assault occurred within 24 h.

However, even in cases where the initial complaint is of fondling within that time period, an urgent examination may also be indicated, since it is not uncommon for a child to disclose more intrusive events during a detailed interview. At least one study has shown several children with positive forensic evidence which was not anticipated by the initial history (Christian et al., 2000). Conversely, the presence of positive physical findings on examination of the genitalia does not predict recovery of DNA. The presence or absence of genital examination findings should not be used as a basis for collecting forensic evidence from the body.

In adults and adolescents, the window of opportunity for collecting vaginal swabs after ejaculation can be up to 96 to 120 h when utilizing DNA amplification techniques, methods that enable detection of minute amounts of DNA; the vaginal pH and cervical mucous promote survival of sperm, and sperm have been documented to persist in the vaginal and cervical canal for almost a week. With young child sexual abuse victims, however, ejaculation usually does not occur internally, and the vaginal environment in the prepubertal girl is not favorable to the survival of sperm.

WHERE THE EVIDENCE IS (AND WHERE IT'S NOT)

The 72-h time frame recommended for evidence collection became standard practice based on adult studies done before development of newer DNA detection methods. Several recent studies, however, make a good case for modifying not only the timing of performing rape kits, but also what kind of specimens should be obtained in the *prepubertal* child:

- A retrospective study of 273 children under 10 years old evaluated for acute sexual assault demonstrated that over 90% of positive forensic findings (of any type) were obtained within 24 h of the assault; after 24 h, virtually all forensic evidence was recovered from clothes or linens. No swabs from the child's body were positive for blood or semen after 13 h post assault (Christian et al., 2000).

- Another retrospective study involved 122 children under 13 seen within 24 h of sexual assault. Semen or sperm was only detected on body swabs from those 10-year-old and over or on clothing or other objects (Palusci, Cox, Shatz, & Schultze, 2006).
- In 2006 Young et al. published retrospective data on children seen within 72 h of sexual assault. None of the 49 children under 12 years had positive forensic evidence from body sites; the three positive samples in that group were all from underwear. In contrast, 13 of 31 adolescents had positive tests, all from body sites (in eight of these cases, clothing was positive as well). All positive rape kits were from children (older and younger groups) presenting within 24 h of the assault.

These studies, though not utilizing newer DNA detection methods, strongly suggest that:

1. Forensic evidence is unlikely to be found on the prepubertal child's body more than 24 h after sexual contact.
2. Semen or sperm is more likely to be identified on the body of an older, female child who has not bathed since the sexual contact.
3. The highest yield for positive forensic evidence is on clothing, linens, or other objects.

These studies also provide support for the clinical assumptions that

- A child's history of pain is associated with an increased likelihood of genital injury and positive forensic evidence,
- A history of bleeding is associated with genital injury and positive forensic evidence.

SEXUALLY TRANSMITTED INFECTIONS (STIs)

The occurrence of STIs and the yield from cultures obtained from prepubertal children without symptoms is low. Obtaining internal cultures from young children can be quite uncomfortable both physically and psychologically. The decision of whether to perform cultures on a sexually abused child should be made on a case-by-case basis, dependent on several factors: the likelihood of exposure to body fluids, the local incidence of STIs, presence of symptoms in the child, and the perpetrator's risk level of having STIs. The CDC and Adams et al. (2015) offer guidelines for the evaluation of STIs in sexually abused children.

In general, the detection of STIs in children (beyond the neonatal period) should suggest the occurrence of sexual abuse. This has exceptions, however, depending on which infection is present.

- Infection with gonorrhea, syphilis, HIV, Chlamydia, and Trichomonas in children indicates that the child has been sexually abused.
- Infections that *may support*, but do not confirm, sexual transmission include
  - Genital warts (HPV) (especially in children greater than 5 years old),
  - Anogenital herpes (HSV type I or II), if accompanied by disclosure of abuse or other indicators.

The recommended timing of initial sexual assault examination for child victims is exhibited in Table 16.1.

FALSE ALLEGATIONS OF SEXUAL ABUSE IN CHILDREN

This section will deal with false or mistaken allegations of sexual abuse of young children, which differ considerably from false accusations presented by an adolescent or adult. (Refer to Chapter 11.)

TABLE 16.1

Recommended Timing of Initial Sexual Assault Examination for Child Victims

Urgency	Timeframe for Behaviors and/or Symptoms Exhibited

Immediate	• Medical, psychological, or safety concerns (e.g., pain, bleeding, suicidal ideation, commercial sexual exploitation)
	• Assault requiring forensic evidence collection
	   • Occurring within 24 h for prepubertal child
	   • Occurring within 72 h for older children, adults
	• Need for emergency contraception
	• Need for post-exposure prophylaxis for STIs, including HIV

Urgent	• Assault within 2 weeks without emergency medical needs identified
Nonurgent	• Child disclosures with allegation of assault more than 2 weeks prior, without any emergency medical needs identified • Sexualized behavior • Family concerns of child sexual abuse
Follow-up	• Examination findings need clarification or documentation of resolution/healing • Need for further STI testing/treatment • Confirmation of examination findings by an inexperienced examiner

Source: Adams, J. A. et al. *Journal of Pediatric & Adolescent Gynecology*, 2015.

The complexities involved in sexual abuse allegations concerning very young children stem in part from having not one, but multiple complainants: (1) the child, (2) the parent or caregiver, and (3) the "interveners"—therapists, interviewers, family, friends. Each has information and an opinion to offer, and possibly a special interest in the outcome of the investigation.

Cases where child sexual abuse is alleged, but eventually disproved, usually fall into one of a few categories. (N.B.: this does not include "unfounded" cases, in which there was not enough evidence to *either* prove or disprove the allegations.)

- Fabricated allegations by a parent or caregiver with an agenda.
- Embellished reports of normal or borderline child behavior or physical signs/symptoms, either by a caregiver with an agenda, or a caregiver who is preoccupied with sexual abuse.
- Misinterpretation of events, behaviors by the child or alleged perpetrator.
- The victim blames someone (*anyone*) else rather than the true perpetrator, usually out of fear or a strong emotional bond with the perpetrator.

"A liar should have a good memory."

Quintilian (A.D. c. 35–A.D. c. 95)

It is rare that very young children intentionally lie about being sexually abused. A child's ability to lie about something they have no direct experience with is virtually nonexistent. In reality, more children lie about *not* being abused (Oates et al., 2000; Malloy, Lyon, & Quas, 2007). Children may withhold certain pieces of information about sexual acts that particularly disgust or embarrass them. Very often, a child will tell someone just enough to get an adult to intervene and stop the abuse. When they feel safe, they may then want to suppress the magnitude of their trauma, and deny the true extent of the abuse. When young children do lie about sexual abuse, they usually do so to please a parent or adult, acting under the influence of their parents, or much less commonly, to seek attention or express anger.

Keep in mind, however, that it is much easier for a child to lie when asked "yes" or "no" questions. Children, like adults, are also much more likely to lie when they think they are going to get in trouble or need to save face. It is also true that young children who are "coached" provide significantly less detail when asked follow-up questions. It will be difficult, if not impossible, for a young child to invent the sensations, surroundings, and details for events they have not experienced.

More often than not, the child who appears to be lying will in fact simply be inaccurate in his report:

- His memory may be distorted by the emotional and psychological trauma of the abuse. The child who dissociates during sexual abuse will have limited ability to recount what happened (Everson, 1997).
- Part of the child's statement may be influenced by age-appropriate fears ("the monster from my closet came into my bed") or the need to maintain a sense of control and self-esteem ("then I stabbed him and he ran away!") (Everson, 1997).
- The child is confused by the perpetrator's intentional misrepresentations or deceptions. ("We're just playing a game, right?"; "That's not blood, that's just red marker on my finger.")
- Memory distortion may result from medications or drugs given to the child by the perpetrator.
- The child's history has been affected by exposure to family conversation about the abuse and/or perpetrator. This is especially evident when children adopt adult-type language to describe the abuse. ("Uncle John fondled me and molested me.")
- The child's history may have been tainted or contaminated by suggestions, assumptions, or misconceptions of "interveners," that is, therapists, interviewers, physicians, and family members. This speaks to the recommendation that children have as few interviews as possible, by the least number of well-trained interviewers as possible.
- If the victim has strong emotional ties to the perpetrator, or feels threatened, the child may attribute the abuse to a "safer" target, such as a distant relative, teacher, or neighbor.

Like adults, children will alter the facts of a story to make themselves look better. They may embellish the story out of fear they won't be believed if the abuse isn't "severe" enough, or conversely they may significantly minimize the abuse out of embarrassment, fear, or love for the perpetrator.

Sexual abuse allegations concerning a child at the center of a custody dispute is one of the prickliest situations encountered by those who assess child sexual abuse. The sources of vexation include

1. The involved child is usually very young, pre-verbal, or young enough to be suggestible.
2. The usual lack of any physical findings or forensic evidence in all child sexual abuse cases.
3. These cases require an extraordinary number of man-hours by professionals from medicine, law enforcement, social services, child protection, mental health, prosecution, and victims' services, sometimes from multiple jurisdictions.
4. The bias inherent in stories presented by each side of the family.
5. The bitter, hostile atmosphere between parents.

False allegations account for only a small portion of cases when families are engaged in child custody disputes (Gunter et al., 2000). The prime focus in investigating these cases should be the child's disclosure: a meticulous accounting of every aspect of the disclosure provides invaluable insight into the sincerity of the parent's concern. Factors to consider:

- To whom did the child disclose? Disclosure to an objective third party (teacher, nurse) inspires confidence in the report; disclosure to a parent may cause some doubt.
- What triggered the disclosure? Complaints of pain when bathing or with urination may trigger a disclosure, or if a child is questioned about sexually acting out. Statements made "out of the blue" may be more suspect.

- What exactly did the parent ask? Be specific. ("What happened to your peepee?" is very different from "Daddy hurt your peepee, didn't he?")
- When did the first disclosure occur? Was it the day before a custody hearing?
- How did the disclosure come to attention of authorities? Trace the disclosure in time from initial statement to your involvement.
- How many people have talked to the child—and who are they? Family and friends will have a different impact on a child than a teacher or daycare provider.
- What exactly did each person say to the child? What are the potential sources of a tainted or contaminated history?

Even the most skeptical investigator must recognize, however, that a valid allegation may arise once the child is out of the abusive environment and feels safe, or if the child fears they will be returned to an abusive parent.

SEQUELAE

"What's done to children, they will do to society."

Karl A. Menninger, American psychiatrist (1893–1990)

Child sexual abuse has an impact on individuals for a lifetime and on society for generations. Experiencing sexual abuse in childhood has been associated with

- Post-traumatic stress disorder
- Attention deficit disorder
- Depression, anxiety
- Substance abuse
- Risky sexual behaviors, sexually transmitted diseases
- Unintended pregnancy, male involvement in teen pregnancy
- Increased risk of adult sexual assault

Co-occurring adverse childhood experiences such as household dysfunction, substance abuse, domestic violence, and criminal activity in the home all contribute to the long-term influence on children's lives in a cumulative manner (Felitti et al., 1998; Hillis, Anda, Felitti, Nordenberg, & Marchbanks, 2000; Shipman, Zeman, Penza, & Champion, 2000; Weinstein, Staffelbach, & Biaggio, 2000; Dong et al., 2003).

Investigators working in the field long enough often encounter the same families repeatedly through the years. The study of the intergenerational cycle of abuse is still in its relative infancy, considering that child sexual abuse was not accepted as a problem by society until the 1970s. About half of women whose children are victimized were sexually abused themselves, a result of several risk factors such as maternal relationship difficulties, psychological problems, and substance abuse, all of which may interfere with a mother's ability to recognize risk and protect her children (Smith, Davis, & Fricker-Elhai, 2004). Maternal resilience (effective efforts at recovery from their own abuse) is associated with protection from the intergenerational passage of child sexual abuse (Leifer, Kilbane, T., & Kalick, 2004).

Every child who has been sexually abused should be referred for a competent psychological evaluation. Resilience and recovery from trauma has been shown to be associated with the ability to accurately remember and verbalize negative past experiences. This knowledge should be shared with families early on: it is not uncommon for parents to assume that very young children will simply forget about the abuse, or believe that it is best to "move on" and not talk about it. Therapy should also include an assessment of the family dynamics and level of support. It has consistently been shown that adjustment of sexually abused children is associated with parental support (Elliott & Carnes, 2001). The possibility that other children in the home have been abused must also be explored. The victim and family will need guidance and support throughout the long and frustrating process of criminal prosecution.

REFERENCES

Adams, J. A., Kellogg, N. D., Farst, K. J., Harper, N. S., Palusci, V. J., Frasier, L. D., et al. 2015. Updated guidelines for the medical assessment and care of children who may have been sexually abused. *Journal of Pediatric & Adolescent Gynecology.* doi: 10.1016/jpag.2015.01.007.

Adams, J. A., Botash, A. S., and Kellogg, N. 2004. Differences in hymenal morphology between adolescent girls with and without a history of consensual sexual intercourse. *Archives Pediatrics & Adolescent Medicine,* 158: 280–285.

American Academy of Pediatrics (AAP); Kairys, S. W., Alexander, R. C., Block. R. W., Everett V. D., Hymel, K. P., and Johnson, C. F. 1999. Committee on child abuse and neglect, guidelines for the evaluation of sexual abuse of children: Subject review. *Pediatrics,* 103: 186–191.

American Professional Society on the Abuse of Children. 1995. *Practice guidelines: Use of anatomical dolls in child sexual abuse assessments.* APSAC, Chicago, IL.

American Professional Society on the Abuse of Children. 2002. *Practice guidelines: Investigative interviewing in cases of alleged child abuse.* APSAC, Chicago, IL.

Arnold, D. H., Spiro, D. M., Nichols, M. H., and King, W. D. 2005. Availability and perceived competence of pediatricians to serve as child protection team medical consultants: A survey of practicing pediatricians. *The Southern Medical Journal,* 98: 423–428.

Beck-Sague, C., and Solomon, F. 1998. Sexually transmitted diseases in abused children and adolescents and adult victims of rape: Review of selected literature. *Clinical Infectious Diseases,* 28 (Suppl 1): S74–S83.

Berenson, A. B., Chacko, M. R., Wiemann, C. M., Mishaw, C. O., Friedrich, W. N., and Grady, J. J. 2000. A case-control study of anatomic changes resulting from sexual abuse. *American Journal of Obstetrics and Gynecology,* 182: 820–834.

Berenson, A. B., Chacko, M. R., Wiemann C. M., Mishaw, C. O., Friedrich, W. N., and Grady, J. J. 2002. Use of hymenal measurements in the diagnosis of previous penetration. *Pediatrics,* 109: 228–235.

Bowen, K. 2000. Child abuse and domestic violence in families of children seen for suspected sexual abuse. *Clinical Pediatrics,* 39: 33–40.

Christian, C. W., Lavelle, J. M., DeJong, A. R., Loiselle, J., Brenner, L., and Joffe, M. 2000. Forensic evidence findings in prepubertal victims of sexual assault. *Pediatrics,* 106: 100–104.

Dong, M. M., Anda, R. F., Dube, S. R., Giles, W. H., and Felitti, V. J. 2003. The relationship of exposure to childhood sexual abuse to other forms of abuse, neglect, and household dysfunction during childhood. *Child Abuse & Neglect,* 27: 625–639.

Dong, M., Anda, R. F., Felitti, V. J., Dube, S. R., Williamson, D. F., Thompson, T. J., et al. 2004. The Interrelatedness of multiple forms of childhood abuse, neglect, and household dysfunction. *Child Abuse & Neglect,* 28: 771–784.

Elliott, A. N., and Carnes, C. N. 2001. Reactions of nonoffending parents to the sexual abuse of their child: A review of the literature. *Child Maltreatment,* 6: 314–331.

Everson, M. D. 1997. Understanding bizarre, improbable, and fantastic elements in children's accounts of abuse. *Child Maltreatment,* 2: 134–149.

Felitti, V. J., Anda, R. F., Nordenberg, D., and Williamson, D. F. 1998. The relationship of adult health status to childhood abuse and household dysfunction. *American Journal of Preventive Medicine,* 14: 245–258.

Gunter, M., du Bois, R., Eichner, E., Rocker, D., Boos, R., Klosinski, G., et al. 2000. Allegations of sexual abuse in child custody disputes. *Medical Law,* 19(4): 815–825.

Heger, A., Ticson, L., Velasquez, O., and Bernier, R. 2002. Children referred for possible sexual abuse: Medical findings in 2384 children. *Child Abuse & Neglect,* 26: 645–659.

Heppenstall-Heger, A., McConnell, G., Ticson, L., Guerra, L., Lister, J., and Zaragoza, T. 2003. Healing patterns in anogenital injuries: A longitudinal study of injuries associated with sexual abuse, accidental injuries, or genital surgery in the preadolescent child. *Pediatrics,* 112: 829–837.

Hillis, S. D., Anda, R. F., Felitti, V. J., Nordenberg, D., and Marchbanks, P. A. 2000. Adverse childhood experiences and sexually transmitted diseases in men and women: A retrospective study. *Pediatrics,* 106: e11.

Ingram, D. M., Everett, V. D., and Ingram, D. L. 2001. The relationship between the transverse hymenal diameter by the separation technique and other possible markers of sexual abuse. *Child Abuse & Neglect*, 25: 1109–1120.

Ingram, D. M., Miller, W. C., Schoenbach, V. J., Everett, V. D., and Ingram, D. L. 2001. Risk assessment for gonococcal and chlamydial infections in young children undergoing evaluation for sexual abuse. *Pediatrics*, 107(5): e73.

Kellogg, N. D., Menard, S. W., and Santos, A. 2004. Genital anatomy in pregnant adolescents: "normal" does not mean "nothing happened." *Pediatrics*, 113: e67–e69.

Kelly, P., and Koh, J. 2006. Sexually transmitted infections in alleged sexual abuse of children and adolescents. *Journal of Paediatrics and Child Health*, 42: 434–440.

Leifer, M., Kilbane, T., and Kalick, S. 2004. Vulnerability or resilience to intergenerational sexual abuse: The role of maternal factors. *Child Maltreatment*, 9: 78–91.

Malloy, L., Lyon, T., and Quas, J. 2007. Filial dependency and recantations of child sexual abuse allegations. *Journal of the American Academy of Child Adolescent Psychiatry*, 46: 162–170.

Oates, R. K., Jones, D. P., Denson, D., Sirotnak, A., Gary, N., and Krugman, R. D. 2000. Erroneous concerns about child sexual abuse. *Child Abuse Neglect*, 24: 149–157.

Palusci, V. J., Cox, E. O., Shatz, E. M., and Schultze, J. M. 2006. Urgent medical assessment after child sexual abuse. *Child Abuse & Neglect*, 30: 367–380.

Prentky, R. A., Knight, R. A., and Lee, A. F. S. 1997. *Child sexual molestation: Research issues*. U.S. Department of Justice, Office of Justice Programs, National Institute of Justice Research Report, Washington, DC.

Ramos, S., Lukefahr, J. L., Morrow, R. A., Stanberry, L. R., and Rosenthal, S. L. 2006. Prevalence of herpes simplex virus types 1 & 2 among children and adolescents attending a sexual abuse clinic. *Pediatric Infectious Disease Journal*, 25: 902–905.

Shipman, K., Zeman, J., Penza, S., and Champion, K. 2000. Emotion management skills in sexually maltreated and nonmaltreated girls: A developmental psychopathology perspective. *Development and Psychopathology*, 12: 47–62.

Smith, D. W., Davis, J. L., and Fricker-Elhai, A. E. 2004. Cognitions about risk in women with abuse histories. *Child Maltreatment*, 9: 292–303.

Smith, D. W., Letourneau, E. J., Saunders, B. E., Kilpatrick, D. G., Resnick, H. S., and Best, C. L. 2000. Delay in disclosure of childhood rape: Results from a national survey. *Child Abuse & Neglect*, 24: 273–287.

Stevens-Simon, C., Nelligan, D., Breese, P., Jenny, C., and Douglas, J. M. 2000. The prevalence of genital human papillomavirus infections in abused and nonabused preadolescent girls. *Pediatrics*, 106: 645–649.

Ward, M. G., Bennett, S., Plint, A. C., King, W. J., Jabbour, M., and Gaboury, I. 2004. Child protection: A neglected area of pediatric residency training. *Child Abuse & Neglect*, 28: 1113–1122.

Weinstein, D., Staffelbach, D., and Biaggio, M. 2000. Attention-deficit hyperactivity disorder and posttraumatic stress disorder: Differential diagnosis in childhood sexual abuse. *Clinical Psychology Review*, 20: 359–378.

FURTHER READING

Finkelhor, D., and Ormrod, R. 2001. *Offenders incarcerated for crimes against juveniles bulletin*. US Department of Justice, Office of Justice Programs, Office of Juvenile Justice and Delinquency Prevention, Washington, DC.

Finkelhor, D., Ormrod, R., Turner, H., and Hamby, S. L. 2005. The victimization of children and youth: A comprehensive, national survey. *Child Maltreatment*, 10: 5–25.

Giardino, A. P., Finkel, M. A., Giardino, E. R., Seidl, T., and Ludwig, S. 1992. *A practical guide to the evaluation of sexual abuse in the prepubertal child*. Sage Publications, Newbury Park, CA.

Jones, L. M., Cross, T., Walsh, W. A., and Simone, M. 2005. Criminal investigations of child abuse—The research behind "best practices". *Trauma, Violence, & Abuse*, 6: 254–268.

Julich, S. 2005. Stockholm syndrome and child sexual abuse. *Journal of Child Sexual Abuse*, 14: 107–129.

Makoroff, K. L., Brauley, J. L., Brandner, A. M., Myers, P. A., and Shapiro, R. A. 2002. Genital examinations for alleged sexual abuse of prepubertal girls: Findings by pediatric emergency medicine physicians compared with child abuse trained physicians. *Child Abuse & Neglect*, 26: 1235–1242.

McCann, J., and Voris, J. 1993. Perianal injuries resulting from sexual abuse: A longitudinal study. *Pediatrics*, 91: 390–397.

MMWR. *Sexually transmitted disease treatment guidelines*, 2006. Department of Health and Human Services, Centers for Disease Control and Prevention, 55 (RR-11).

Poole, D. A., and Lamb, M. E. 1998. *Investigative interviews of children*. American Psychological Association, Washington, DC.

Quas, J. A., Davis, E. L., Goodman, G. S., and Myers, J. E. B. 2007. Repeated questions, deception, and children's true and false reports of body touch. *Child Maltreatment*, 12: 60–67.

Reece, R. M., and Ludwig, S. 2001. *Child abuse—Medical diagnosis and management*, 2nd ed. Lippincott Williams & Wilkins, Philadelphia, PA.

Santucci, K. A., Nelson, D. G., McQuillen, K. K., Duffy, S. J., and Linakis, J. G. 1999. Wood's lamp utility in the identification of semen. *Pediatrics*, 104: 1342–1344.

Smith, D. W., Witte, T. H., and Fricker-Elhai, A. E. 2006. Service outcomes in physical and sexual abuse cases: A comparison of child advocacy center-based and standard services. *Child Maltreatment*, 11: 354–360.

Sexual Assault of Young Children as Reported to Law Enforcement: Victim, Incidence, and Offender Characteristics. July 1, 2000. www.bjs.gov/index.cfm?ty=pbdetail&iid=1147 U.S. Department of Justice, Office of Justice Programs, Office of Juvenile Justice and Delinquency Prevention.

Young, K. L., Jones, J. G., Worthington, T., Simpson, P., and Casey, P. H. 2006. Forensic laboratory evidence in sexually abused children and adolescents. *Archives of Pediatrics & Adolescent Medicine*, 160: 585–588.

17 Injury and Forensic Examination of the Victim

Kathleen P. Brown and Marilyn S. Sommers

CONTENTS

Introduction 269
Genital Injury Overview 270
Genital Injury Prevalence 270
    Injury Prevalence with Visual Inspection 270
    Injury Prevalence with Staining Techniques 271
    Injury Prevalence with Colposcopy Technique 271
    Location of Genital Injury 272
    Comparison of Genital Injury Prevalence Following Consensual Sexual Intercourse 272
Genital Injury Type 273
Role of Genital Injury in Criminal Justice Proceedings 273
The Forensic Examination 274
    Team Approach to Forensic Services 274
Access to the Sexual Assault Response Team 275
Role of the Forensic Examiner 275
Consent 276
History 276
Forensic Examination 276
    Clothing 277
    Detection of Bodily Injury 277
    Collection of Forensic Evidence 278
    Examination of Genitalia 279
    Rectal Examination 280
Proper Handling (Management) of Evidence 280
Chain of Custody 281
Documentation 281
Drug and Alcohol Testing 281
Therapy and Prophylaxis 282
Conclusion 282
Practice Points 283
References 283

INTRODUCTION

Survivors of sexual assault require comprehensive, efficient, and sensitive care as soon as possible after the assault. Survivors have physical and emotional sequelae after sexual assault that must be addressed. This chapter reviews the literature on genital injury prevalence, location of genital injury, injury in consensual intercourse, documentation, common definition of genital injury pattern, skin color, and best practice. In addition, this chapter outlines the forensic examination, and treatment as well as collection of evidence from a victim of sexual assault. Examination after sexual assault is needed for early intervention, and treatment of physical injuries and for the purpose of collection of transferred forensic evidence from the victim's body. Specialized training in the forensic examination is advised for physicians and sexual assault nurse examiners.

GENITAL INJURY OVERVIEW

Detection and management of genital injury is important from both a health care and a criminal justice standpoint. While complications from genital injury are relatively uncommon, injuries need to be identified and treated so that discomfort and the risk of infection and scarring are minimized. Genital injury also plays a significant role at multiple decision-making points during criminal justice proceedings, such as the decisions to report, file, prosecute, and convict (Sommers, Fisher, & Karjane, 2005). Documentation of genital injury is a critical component of the forensic examination, especially given that an important reason for not reporting to the police is the "lack of proof that an incident happened" (Fisher, Cullen, & Turner, 2000). Forensic evidence documenting injury following sexual assault can be used as one of the constellation of factors of evidence to enhance the government's case in allegations of sexual assault. It also assists the jury or judge in making an informed decision to convict or not.

Genital injury can be described in multiple dimensions. Genital injury prevalence is defined as the proportion of women with an occurrence of injury as calculated from injury frequency. Genital injury frequency is defined as the number of injuries counted by an examiner during each aspect of the examination: visual inspection, colposcopy, and toluidine blue (or other contrast media) application. In females, genital injury is often described by three locations: external (labia majora, labia minora, periurethral area, perineum, and posterior fourchette), internal (fossa navicularis, hymen, vagina, and cervix), and anal (anus and rectum; Sommers et al., 2006). Genital injury severity is defined as the area and degree of injury. Finally, genital injury types are described as tears, ecchymoses, abrasions, redness, and swelling, or TEARS (Slaughter, Brown, Crowley, & Peck, 1997; Sommers, Schafer, Zink, Hutson, & Hillard, 2001; Sommers, 2007).

GENITAL INJURY PREVALENCE

Genital injury prevalence is calculated by using the frequency of genital injury in a given population. Following sexual assault, the prevalence of genital injury varies by examination type and ranges from 5% on direct visualization (Massey, Garcia, & Emich, 1971) to 87% with colposcopic technique (Slaughter & Brown, 1992). Commonly, three strategies are used for genital examination: (1) direct visualization; (2) staining techniques (or contrast media) such as Gentian violet, Lugol's solution, toluidine blue, or fluorescein, which are applied topically to accentuate and demarcate injuries and make them more visible to the eye; and (3) colposcopy, the use of a magnifying instrument, or colposcope, that generally has some type of image capture (photograph, digital image, etc.). A new possibility introduced by researchers from Finland is ultraviolet (UV) light (Erkkila, Rainio, Huhtala, Salonen, & Karhunen, 2014).

INJURY PREVALENCE WITH VISUAL INSPECTION

Between 1970 and 1995, investigators using direct visualization during the sexual assault examination in large sample populations (>100) found a genital injury prevalence of less than 40% in series composed of women, adolescents, and children (Massey et al., 1971; Hayman, Lanza, Fuentes, & Algor, 1972; Everett & Jimerson, 1977; Cartwright, 1986; Goodyear-Smith, 1989). In an early report on sexual assault victims, Massey et al. studied 480 females and found detectable gynecologic injuries in only 5.2% of the sample. Other investigators reported injury prevalence of 20–40%, and most injuries were relatively minor. For example, in 1223 women and children, only 20 victims had severe vaginal and vaginoperineal lacerations, whereas 199 had minor genital injuries (Hayman et al., 1972). Cartwright reported similar findings in 440 females: an adjusted frequency rate of 0.2% for genital injury requiring treatment and 16.1% with no treatment needed.

Investigators often reported differences in injury prevalence in children as compared to adults, but others reported differences in prevalence based on injury severity. In a study of women and children after sexual assault (N = 190), Goodyear-Smith (1989) found that 19.5% of children and 40% of adults had genital trauma (bruising, inflammation, tenderness, abrasions, or lacerations), and 3.5% of children and 6% of adults had anal injury. Everett and Jimerson (1977) studied 117 women and children who had a sexual assault examination and reported that 19% had minor genital injuries (lacerations and abrasions) and 7% had major vaginal or perineal lacerations.

More recently, authors have reported higher injury prevalence with visual inspection: between 50 and 60% in a sample of women (N = 1076) seen in an emergency department (Riggs, Houry, Long, Markovchick, & Feldhaus, 2000) and in 801 sexual assault survivors (Gray-Eurom, Seaberg, & Wears, 2002). Some authors, however, continue to report lower prevalence depending on injury classification (Sugar, Fine, & Eckert, 2004; Maguire, Goodall, & Moore, 2009). Because one study had lack of control over the examination and very little detail on injury classification, it was not included in this review (Crane, 2006).

INJURY PREVALENCE WITH STAINING TECHNIQUES

Toluidine blue was first described as a mechanism to highlight cervical neoplasms (Richart, 1963), but it is also used to identify injury during the forensic examination because it adheres to areas of abraded skin and microlacerations (Crowley, 1999). Several investigators using small sample sizes (N = 24–44) found an injury prevalence of 40–58% when using toluidine blue after sexual assault (Lauber & Souma, 1982; McCauley, Guzinski, Welch, Gorman, & Osmers, 1987). Lauber and Souma, however, defined injury as laceration only. In an investigation that changed clinical practice, Jones, Dunnuck, Rossman, Wynn, and Nelson-Horan (2004) found that when using toluidine blue before and after a standard forensic examination, 1 of 27 female patients demonstrated a new genital injury from speculum insertion. This study not only caused a change in sexual assault examination protocols in North America but also suggested that a factor existed in the studies cited previously that may have confounded their results.

INJURY PREVALENCE WITH COLPOSCOPY TECHNIQUE

The first description of a forensic examination using a colposcope in adults following sexual assault appeared in 1981 (Teixeira, 1981). With a colposcope, Teixeira was able to identify 11.8% more cases of sexual assault in 500 females than were found by conventional examination. Other investigators replicated his findings that colposcopic technique was better than direct visualization and toluidine blue contrast to detect injury in children (Muram & Elias, 1989; Woodling & Heger, 1986). In a small sample (N = 17), investigators found that the colposcope documented trauma in 9 of 17 cases (53%) whereas gross visualization documented trauma in only 1 case (6%).

Colposcopic technique is generally associated with documentation of a higher injury prevalence than other techniques, particularly when combined with staining techniques. For example, examiners using colposcopy technique and staining found an injury prevalence of 83% in adolescents and 64% in women (N = 209; Jones, Rossman, Wynn, Dunnuck, & Schwartz, 2003). Sachs and Chu (2002) reported an injury prevalence of 81% in 209 sexual assault survivors while Slaughter and Brown (1992) found a genital injury prevalence of 87% in 131 sexual assault survivors. This same research team later found genital injury in 68% of the victims reporting sexual assault (Slaughter et al., 1997).

A 2013 meta-analysis of published studies on injury data following sexual assault was unable to draw firm conclusions about the precise prevalence of genital injury due to heterogeneity of research methodology (Kennedy, 2013). The 26 included studies, published between 1972 and 2011, reported a very wide range in the prevalence of genital injury after sexual assault, from 5% to 87% of cases, with a median of 29.3% and a mean of 34.8%. Despite the primary conclusion being that this data could not be relied upon, the author was however able to robustly conclude that, "injury is absolutely not a necessary outcome of sexual violence."

LOCATION OF GENITAL INJURY

The most common location for genital injury in young adult and adult females is the posterior fourchette, a tense band of tissue that connects the two labia minora. Other common locations in female children and adults are the labia minora (two thin inner folds of skin within the vestibule of the vulva), hymen (thin membrane composed of connective tissue that overlies the vaginal opening), and fossa navicularis (shallow depression located on the lower portion of the vestibule and inferior to the vaginal opening; Lauber & Souma, 1982; Slaughter & Brown, 1992; Slaughter et al., 1997; Grossin et al., 2003; Jones et al., 2003). While prevalence by location varies somewhat among studies, Slaughter et al. (1997) found that, of injured females, 70% had a posterior fourchette injury, 53% a labia minora injury, 29% a hymen injury, and 25% injury at the fossa navicularis. Jones et al. (2003) reported similar findings in women and girls (N = 766); 78% had injuries at one of the four locations mentioned earlier, although women experienced less injury to the hymen and greater injury to the perianal area as compared with girls.

In a study using a different classification system, Grossin et al. (2003) found that in 161 female sexual assault victims examined within 72 h of the assault, 20% had vulvovaginal injuries (injuries of the external female genitalia, including the labia, clitoris, and vaginal opening and vaginal injuries), 11% had hymeneal injuries, and 7% had anal injuries. In contrast, adult sexual assault victims in Nigeria had a low detection of genital injury, with only 14 of 171 adult victims having documented injury to the vulva, 18 with vaginal injury, and 10 with injuries of the hymen (Olusanya, Ogbemi, Unuigbe, & Oronsaye, 1986). These findings were replicated in a small series of victims in Northern England (Bowyer & Dalton, 1997).

In summary, the majority of evidence in large series of sexual assault cases indicates that the posterior fourchette and labia minora are the most common locations of genital injury in adult females, although not all studies have similar findings with regard to location of genital injury. A cohort study compared macroscopic genital injury prevalence in 500 women alleging penile–vaginal rape with that in 68 women who had recently had consensual sex. Lacerations (mostly of the posterior fourchette) followed by abrasions (mostly of posterior parts of the labia) were the most common types of injury, and both were significantly more common in cases than controls (McLean, Roberts, White, & Paul, 2011).

COMPARISON OF GENITAL INJURY PREVALENCE FOLLOWING CONSENSUAL SEXUAL INTERCOURSE

Investigators and clinicians who study genital injury following sexual assault have also been interested in injury prevalence in the consensual sexual intercourse population. Investigators studying a small series of women with vaginal injuries combined a sample of women who were sexually assaulted (N = 7) with women who had consensual coital injuries (N = 24). The most common presenting sign in these two groups was vaginal bleeding (Wilson & Swartz, 1972). In two review articles, the authors noted that minor trauma to the vagina commonly accompanied vaginal intercourse (Elam & Ray, 1986; Geist, 1988). They also noted that vaginal intercourse was often accompanied by tears in the lower part of the hymen and posterior fourchette and that the most common injuries during a female's first intercourse were hymenal lacerations and tears. A prospective study with a small sample (N = 18) demonstrated that following consensual intercourse, 61.1% of the cases had positive findings with colposcopy and contrast dye. Injuries included increased vascularity of the vagina, vascular enlargement (telangiectasia), broken capillaries, and microabrasions (Norvell, Benrubi, & Thompson, 1984).

With several exceptions, injury prevalence following consensual sexual intercourse is generally reported at approximately 10%. In a study of 48 women who had voluntary sexual intercourse within 48 h of the exam, investigators found a 10% injury rate (McCauley et al., 1987). All participants with injuries gave a history of dry or painful intercourse. This proportion of injury is similar to those found by other investigators in the consensual sex population (Lauber & Souma, 1982; Slaughter et al., 1997). Fraser et al. (1999) followed 107 sexually active women, aged 18–35 years, over a 6-month period. They investigated changes in vaginal and cervical appearance. In 3.5% of the inspections, they reported a total of 11 abnormalities: three ulcerations, two ecchymoses, five abrasions, and one tear. The prevalence of injury was highest when examinations occurred after intercourse in the previous 24 h or following tampon use.

In the Slaughter et al. (1997) study, injured controls ($N = 8$) had trauma limited to a single site as compared with their nonconsensual counterparts. Four participants experienced ecchymosis and four a single tear or abrasion. Five of the injuries were on the posterior fourchette and three on the hymen. In a more recent study, the investigators reported that 30.4% of consensual participants ($N = 46$) and a surprisingly low 32.1% of nonconsensual participants ($N = 56$) had genital injury (Anderson, McClain, & Riviello, 2006). These study findings raise interesting questions about the low injury prevalence in the consensual population reported previously.

Astrup, Ravn, Thomsen, and Lauritsen (2013) found that the most common genital abnormality in both consensual and nonconsensual groups was a single laceration at the 6 o'clock position, but that any other positive findings were more common in the nonconsensual group. The conclusion was that nonconsensual intercourse was associated with larger lesions and more extensive genital injury than consensual intercourse, although the small sample size (39 cases and 98 controls) and the presence of uncontrollable variables in the control group make it difficult to draw firm conclusions.

Further work is needed with methodologically rigorous studies to determine injury prevalence following consensual sexual intercourse, and how injuries that occur during consensual sex compare to the injuries that occur during sexual assault.

GENITAL INJURY TYPE

Genital injury types are described as TEARS (Slaughter et al., 1997; Sommers et al., 2001):

- Tears are defined as any breaks in tissue integrity including fissures, cracks, lacerations, cuts, gashes, or rips.
- Ecchymoses are defined as skin or mucous membrane discolorations, known as "bruising" or "black and blue" areas due to the damage of small blood vessels beneath the skin or mucous membrane surface.
- Abrasions are defined as skin excoriations caused by the removal of the epidermal layer and with a defined edge.
- Redness is erythematous skin that is abnormally inflamed due to irritation or injury without a defined edge or border.
- Swelling is edematous or transient engorgement of tissues (Sommers, 2007).

Other less widely used injury classification systems exist as well. One group of investigators proposed an injury typology that included nonperforating soft-tissue injury, lacerations, or current bleeding (Biggs, Stermac, & Divinsky, 1998). The TEARS classification, however, is the most commonly used and at this point is the classification most likely to provide comparable data across studies and clinical practice.

ROLE OF GENITAL INJURY IN CRIMINAL JUSTICE PROCEEDINGS

In recent years the role of nongenital and genital injuries in criminal justice proceedings has become clearer, but the role of genital injury alone is less clear. Two studies using a retrospective review of medical records in the 1970s and 1980s found no correlation between judicial outcome and the severity of all injuries (genital and nongenital; Tintinalli & Hoelzer, 1985; Penttila & Karhumen, 1990). Penttila and Karhumen, however, reported that in cases when the defendant was imprisoned, there were significantly more victims with severe injuries than in other categories of criminal justice outcomes. Several limitations are apparent in these two studies. The examination protocols were most likely visual inspection only, reducing the likelihood that all injuries were detected. In addition, while injury frequency was calculated separately for genital and nongenital injury, injury prevalence was determined on the basis of any injury type. The definitions of severe or major injury were questionable. Severe injuries were defined as skeletal fractures or trauma that required major operative repair in one study and numerous bruising, scratches, abrasions, and lacerations in the other study. Thus, one study excluded any genital injury from the severe category (Tintinalli & Hoelzer, 1985) while the other had a very broad definition of major injury that included minor conditions such as scratches (Penttila & Karhumen, 1990).

Other studies did not differentiate between genital and nongenital injuries, making generalizations difficult. McGregor, Le, Marion, and Wiebe (1999) developed a clinical injury scoring system by using practitioners' ratings and a statistical scoring strategy. The score had a range of 0 (no injury) to 3 (severe injury) and a combined multirater kappa score of 0.87. Both genital and nongenital injuries were included in the scoring, and only nongenital injuries fit the criteria for "severe." The investigators also found that the odds ratio (OR) for filing charges associated with moderate or severe injury was 3.33 (95% confidence interval [CI] 1.06–10.42), but genital injury alone was not associated with the filing of charges. In a replication study ($N = 462$), the investigators found an association for injury severity and filing of charges in the following categories: mild injury (OR = 2.85, 95% CI = 1.09–7.45), moderate injury (OR = 4.00, 95% CI = 1.63–9.84), and severe injury (OR = 12.29, 95% CI = 3.04–49.65). Severe injury was the only variable associated with conviction. Genital injury alone was not associated with either filing of charges or conviction (McGregor, Du Mont, & Myhr, 2002).

Rambow and colleagues reported on 182 sexual assault cases, 53 of which had the potential for successful prosecution (a victim willing to testify and an identified assailant). They found that 34% of these cases resulted in a successful prosecution, and evidence of genital or nongenital injury was significantly associated with a successful legal outcome (Rambow, Adkinson, Frost, & Peterson, 1992). In perhaps the most rigorous protocol of all of these studies, investigators used a population-based, retrospective review of forensic evidence in 801 forensic examinations (Gray-Eurom et al., 2002). All examiners used a standard protocol, underwent initial training, and maintained monthly peer review during the study period. They found injury in 57% of the forensic examinations. Survivors > 18 years of age (OR = 2.23, 95% CI = 1.2–4.16), the presence of trauma (OR = 1.93, 95% CI = 1.08–3.43), and weapon use by the assailant (OR = 2.00, 95% CI 1.05–3.81) were all significantly associated with successful prosecution. No attempt was made to differentiate between genital and nongenital injury or to grade injury severity.

At this time the role of genital injury in the filing of charges and conviction has yet to be fully understood. No investigators using state-of-the-art examination techniques, rigorous research methods, and a valid and reliable classification system for genital injury severity have studied the criminal justice outcomes following sexual assault. Until rigorous studies are available to guide forensic and criminal justice practices, the literature supports detailed documentation of genital and nongenital injuries to be used as evidence in court proceedings.

All research in this area has been plagued with multiple uncontrollable variables which make reliable conclusions virtually impossible. Just about the only conclusion which can be made with confidence is that both consenting and non-consenting sexual contact may or may not result in genital injury. The question of consent remains for the jury to decide.

THE FORENSIC EXAMINATION

TEAM APPROACH TO FORENSIC SERVICES

Sexual Assault Response Teams (SARTs) are collaborative groups that bring together multidisciplinary sexual assault stakeholders (e.g., police, prosecutors, medical/forensic examiners, rape crisis advocates) to improve the community response to sexual assault (Greeson & Campbell, 2015). SARTs are increasingly popular and are recommended for adoption by national agencies (Department of Justice, 2013; National Sexual Violence Resource Center [NSVRC], 2011). SARTs were developed to address problems associated with the community response to sexual assault (Zajac, 2006).

The role of rape care advocacy in the period immediately after assault is to provide emotional support via accompaniment during interview and examination. Law enforcement is responsible for conducting an interview and beginning an investigative process. Prosecutors and the police crime laboratory provide guidelines for the collection of evidence. The police crime laboratory analyzes any evidence collected related to the crime of sexual assault. A trained nurse or physician conducts the examination, and collects evidence from the victim's body. A physician and or an advanced practice nurse provides medical prophylaxis and treatment. Law enforcement, rape care advocacy, nurses, and physicians must be available to victims 24 h a day, 7 days per week.

Greeson and Campbell (2013) reported a high degree of cross-systemic coordination found in SARTs. Their study found that, in most communities, survivor contact with the legal system regularly results in referrals to advocacy and medical/forensic services and consultation between the legal system and medical/forensic examiners is also common.

ACCESS TO THE SEXUAL ASSAULT RESPONSE TEAM

Victims of rape or sexual assault can report the crime in a number of ways. The victim may call 911 giving her or him access to police. The victim may call a rape crisis hot line, or the victim may appear in the emergency room of a hospital or an outpatient center accompanied by a family member or friend. Many victims do not report this crime fearing "revictimization" by the legal system or the health care system or both. Many victims are fearful of not being believed by police or health care providers. Many victims also fear retaliation by the offender if they report the crime. Some victims according to Patterson, Greeson, and Campbell (2009), indicated that they did not report the assault because they were not sure that what happened constituted a rape or that they were deserving of post-assault assistance.

Only a minority of rapes are ever reported to the police. Wolitzky-Taylor et al. (2011) analyzed data from the National Women's Study-Replication (NWS-R) and found that 15.8% of women's only, or most recent, rape experiences were reported to the police, a rate that is similar to those found in other national surveys (Bachman, 1998; Chen & Ullman, 2014). This low reporting rate is especially troubling, given that formal reporting is the only means through which prosecution of perpetrators can occur, leaving the vast majority of perpetrators going undetected.

It is important for team members to recognize victims' hesitancy to report. Creation of easy access to the team and appropriate, consistent, and caring initial responses to contact is crucial to victim reporting.

ROLE OF THE FORENSIC EXAMINER

A registered nurse or a physician who has been trained to provide comprehensive and competent care to sexual assault survivors in the immediate aftermath of an assault is an important member of the sexual assault response team. This person's specialized training includes interview skills, assessment for injury skills, and knowledge about collection of forensic evidence and therapies for prevention of sexually transmitted infections (STIs) and pregnancy. Forensic examiners must have photography skills and must be prepared to testify in a court of law.

A format for interview by the forensic examiner should be designed and approved by all members of the sexual assault response team. Interviews by law enforcement and interviews by forensic examiners do not have the same focus. Law enforcement interviews begin the investigative process. Forensic examiner interviews are for purposes of diagnosis and treatment. Similar to any medical or nursing interview, interview questions are designed to guide examination. Interview prior to examination cannot always be accomplished, but is very desirable.

CONSENT

Consent from the victim must be obtained before examination and treatment. In a true medical emergency, consent is assumed and medical personnel proceed. When the survivor is able to consent, permission must be obtained for examination, for reporting the crime to law enforcement, and for taking photographs.

Each state defines age for consent, what qualifies as emancipation, and exceptions for consent in minors without parental permission in areas such as the treatment of STIs or treatment of pregnancy. Forensic examiners must explore the law describing consent in the state in which they practice.

Consent to report to law enforcement is vital to investigation. Victims may refuse reporting to law enforcement. If the victim/survivor chooses not to consent to report, examination and treatment are provided, but forensic evidence is not collected.

Photographs are an important component of evidence collection. Permission to photograph must be obtained prior to taking pictures with a camera or via a colposcope.

HISTORY

Medical/nursing history should be obtained prior to physical examination and treatment whenever possible. History includes chronic diseases, medications, allergies (particularly to medication), and immunizations received. For female victims, information on last menstrual period should be requested, as should method of birth control.

For female victims, history of last consensual intercourse must be obtained. Police crime laboratory analysis requires this information. Analysis of evidence submitted and results uploaded in law enforcement databases requires the knowledge that secretions from recent consensual sex may be incorporated into the specimen post assault submitted for evidence.

History of events that occurred after the assault should be obtained. These include bathing or showering, changing clothes, douching, gargling, urinating or having a bowel movement, and eating or drinking.

FORENSIC EXAMINATION

The word rape is originally derived from the Latin verb rapere: to seize or take by force, and until relatively recent history, most definitions of rape have referred to an act of forced vaginal intercourse perpetrated through actual or threat of physical violence, associated with a presumption of resistance on the part of the victim. Gladly, many modern legal definitions have now replaced the "use of force" with a "lack of consent" as rape's defining feature; as opposed to "free agreement," which requires active participation. This change is recognized by the legal profession as having facilitated a seismic change in how the crime of rape is conceptualized and prosecuted, and it is hoped that societal attitudes will also adapt to incorporate a basic awareness that the use of force is not a necessary precondition for intercourse to take place without consent, and that physical resistance is not a universal response by victims of rape. The popular image of rape as a violent event in which injury is necessarily incurred is promoted by the fact that these are the typical types of rape which make the news headlines, and it is felt that some victims who do not sustain injury may sadly be less inclined to report the crime due to a perception that they may not be believed when they can see no physical evidence to support what happened (Walker, 2015).

In order to discover evidence, the body of the victim is carefully inspected by the examiner for any possible transfer of evidence from the crime scene to the victim or from the suspect to the victim. Evidence collected is called trace evidence meaning it is small compared with other evidence submitted to police crime laboratories. The body is systematically inspected for injury and presence of trace evidence. Any organized method of inspection is acceptable. The most common organizational method is head and neck, chest and abdomen, arms, back, and legs. Pelvic examination and inspection of the rectum and buttocks end the examination. All injury is described and photographed. All trace evidence is collected and packaged in a systematic fashion after it has been dried. Evidence can be lifted with gloved hands, scraped with a glass slide, reconstituted with moistened cotton swabs or pieces of gauze, or picked up with forceps with plastic covers to protect the tips.

Examinations are recommended for individuals who experience sexual assault, regardless of their intent to report to local police. This examination ensures the patient's medical needs are met and evidence collection and documentation of the event can be preserved for possible future prosecution.

A national survey on forensic analysts' perspectives showed that sexual assault nurses are highly respected and valued for the quality of their evidence collection (Campbell, Greeson, Fehler-Cabral, and Kennedy, 2015).

CLOTHING

The clothing worn during the assault is a possible source of DNA evidence. Clothing is placed within paper bags and submitted for analysis to the police crime laboratory. If the clothing worn during the assault is not the clothing the victim wears to the examination, the clothing she or he is currently wearing should be submitted and law enforcement will request that the clothing worn during the assault also be submitted to the police crime laboratory. The victim places items of clothing in paper bags with each piece of clothing placed in a separate paper bag to prevent cross contamination. Items of clothing usually sent for evidence collection are shirt, pants or skirt, and underwear. Coats and shoes are usually not submitted unless there is evidence present on them. The purpose for sending clothing is to allow the police crime laboratory to inspect each piece for transfer of evidence from the crime scene or from the suspect to the clothing. The item most frequently found to contain transfer from the suspect to the victim's clothing is women's underwear (Ledray, 1992). If the victim changed underwear before arriving in the emergency department, it is important that the underwear worn during and/or right after the attack be found and delivered to the police laboratory.

Each item of clothing must be dry prior to being sent to the lab. At times, when an item of clothing is soaked in blood, drying must occur in the police evidence room. If this is the case, the item is placed by the examiner within a biohazard bag for protection of the law enforcement officer. The wet item is then given to the law enforcement officer for his or her care. The officer will take responsibility for freezing the item, drying it, or taking it directly to the crime laboratory. If the clothing is dry after forensic examination, the paper bags are sealed with evidence tape, identified, and passed to law enforcement. Law enforcement may choose to examine the clothing for rips, tears, and stains prior to sealing the paper bags. If this occurs, the officer should wear gloves. If the victim is unable to undress herself or himself, the examiner should wear gloves while the clothing is removed. If clothing must be cut in order to be removed, cutting should not occur through rips or tears or stains.

DETECTION OF BODILY INJURY

The victim/survivor is inspected for signs of injury on the body. Inspection should occur with good light sources. High-intensity lights and a Wood's lamp are commonly utilized. Inspection should be done slowly and carefully with the history of the event in mind throughout. Bruising should be noted. Any soft-tissue injury, laceration, contusion, redness, or swelling should be noted, photographed, described in the record, and drawn on a body map contained within the record. Any areas of pain or tenderness should also be noted.

Photographs should be taken of each injury. At least one orienting photo should be taken that clearly reveals the body part containing the injury. At least one close-up photo should be taken of each injury. One photo should be taken of each injury with a scale, and one photo should be taken of each injury without a scale.

Inspection for injuries obtained during the assault is important for treatment and may be vital to investigation. Inspection most commonly begins with the head and neck area. Lacerations, abrasions, scratches, and bruises of the head and neck area are noted and photographed. The eyes are carefully inspected for petechiae and retinal hemorrhage. The nose and the ears are inspected with an otoscope for bleeding, swelling, or bruising. Behind the ears must be inspected for signs of bruising. Mouth and lips are inspected for injury. Early bruising and petechiae have been observed in victims of oral sexual assault in the mouth and throat area (Maida, 2010). Any indication of early bruising of the neck should be noted and photographed.

The entire body is inspected for bruising, scratches, lacerations, abrasions, and edema. The breasts should be carefully inspected for saliva, bruising, scratching, and swelling. The inner thighs of the survivor should be carefully inspected for scratching and bruising. The inner thighs are also a common place for the discovery of semen. A Wood's lamp may assist in this discovery. Also, abrasions on the back are commonly discovered after sexual assault (Maida, 2010).

One hundred and sixty-two victims consented to body examination and 153 to genital examination in a study by Maguire et al. (2009). Nongenital (body) injuries, mainly minor, were observed in 61.1% (99/162). There were 652 injuries, (55.7%) bruises, (40.5%) abrasions, 25 (3.8%) lacerations, the remaining 11 (1.6%) included deliberate self-harm, burns, and bites. These were found on the legs (47.5%), arms (27.5%), body (19.5%), and head and neck (5.5%). Twelve had more than 15 injuries (range 16–40). The younger age group, under 20 years, had less body injury than older women (44% vs. 55%, OR = 1.69, 95% CI = 0.89–3.20, $p < 0.10$) and three of the seven women over 50 years had body injury. Complainants reporting alcohol consumption prior to assault had more body injuries (72% vs. 43%, OR = 3.33, 95% CI = 1.67–6.66, $p < 0.001$).

One hundred and thirty-seven women (85.1%) were examined within 72 h by Maguire, and they had a much higher rate of body injury (66% vs. 33%, OR = 4.0, 95% CI = 1.59–10.04, $p < 0.01$). Assaults occurring outdoors resulted in a greater frequency of documented injury (79% vs. 52%, OR = 3.45, 995% CI = 1.59–7.47, $p < 0.01$) (Maguire et al., 2009).

COLLECTION OF FORENSIC EVIDENCE

Forensic evidence is collected from the survivor's body. Her or his body is inspected for transferred blood, semen, and saliva. The history of the event guides the examination for evidence. A Wood's lamp can be helpful in finding semen and saliva. Dried blood found on the survivor's body may be scraped off with the side of a glass slide onto a piece of paper. The paper is folded druggist style and placed within an envelope. If dried blood cannot be scraped off the body, it can be lifted with cotton swabs slightly moistened with sterile water. These swabs are then dried at room temperature and packaged in an envelope.

The purpose for searching the body carefully for transferred cells is identification of the person being accused via DNA.

A buccal swabbing is taken from the survivor. These samples become the known or reference source of DNA in the investigation. The oral cavity is swabbed with cotton swabs with the area around the gums and teeth as the area of concentration. These specimens are analyzed for DNA from the suspect.

DNA can be found in any human tissue or body fluid containing cells. The new methods for analyzing DNA require minimal amounts of substance. Careful searching of the body can reveal important forensic evidence that can be analyzed for the presence of DNA. DNA can be retrieved from samples of blood, flesh, seminal fluid, vaginal fluid, saliva, hair with roots, perspiration stains, and dandruff in sufficient sample.

EXAMINATION OF GENITALIA

Examination of genitalia and rectal examination conclude the examination. The female victim should be appropriately draped and reclining on a gynecology table for this examination. A male victim can be examined on an examination table and should also be draped appropriately.

Inspection begins the genital examination. Colposcopy assists in the detection of injury. If a colposcope is not available, a digital camera can be utilized. The examiner carefully inspects the external genitalia using the colposcope or digital camera to detect any injury. Common injuries found on external genitalia include tears, ecchymosis, abrasions, redness, and swelling. Photographs are taken via the colposcope or camera. Inspection of external genitalia and orienting photographs, if they are to be taken, are done before evidence is collected. The photographs will then demonstrate the appearance of the genitalia prior to collection of evidence. The number of photographs taken is a decision made by the team. A common approach is one or two "orienting" photographs of external genitalia that include the entire area followed by photographs centering on any injured area in the external genitalia. Each area of injury in addition to being photographed should be described in the record and drawn on a body map within the record. Colposcopic photography of genital lesions in adult rape victims is a very important form of documentation allowing for supervision, teaching, and second opinions in an ethically difficult setting. The interpretation of colposcopic photographs is not necessarily straightforward. Interobserver agreement is not perfect, and interpretations should be peer checked. When colposcopic photography is used for documentation in a court of law, the expert should be aware of possible variations and limitations in the interpretation of the photographs.

Agreement with the findings of the nurse examiners was 80% when evaluating tears/abrasion in the posterior fourchette, but lower when evaluating other entities (Astrup, Thomsen, Lauritsen, & Ravn, 2012).

The external genitalia may be swabbed for semen. Swabbing can be done with moistened cotton swabs or with moistened 2×2 gauze. If the victim is a male, the penis and scrotum may be swabbed. Careful attention during swabbing must be paid to the multiple folds in the scrotum. It is not recommended that the examiner place any swabs into a male victim's urethra. This procedure is painful and will not produce transfer evidence.

Positions required for good visualization are lithotomy with legs in stirrups, and the knee–chest position. Firm, but gentle traction of the labia is required for visualization of the hymenal tissue. The colposcope can aid in identification of the tissue.

Toluidine blue dye is an acidophilic, metachromatic, nucleic stain. It was first described in 1963 by Richart as a method of highlighting cervical neoplasms. Since then, it has been used as part of the examination of the complainant of sexual violence. It stains the nuclei of damaged epithelial cells, helping distinguish acute injuries or breaks in the skin from noninjured areas. The surface layer of nontraumatized vulvar skin contains no nuclei. Trauma exposes deeper layers of the epidermis where squamae are nucleated and undergoing maturation. Note that toluidine blue is spermicidal and therefore could interfere with other forensic tests. Positive stain results may also have causes other than trauma (e.g., any inflammatory cause as well as benign or malignant vulvovaginal disease).

If toluidine blue dye is applied in female victims, it should be placed on external genitalia at sites of injury prior to insertion of the speculum. After initial photographs, the dye is applied to areas of injury using a swab or swabs. Excess dye is then dabbed away with a baby wipe. Photographs of any injury are then retaken with the dye in place.

A perhaps surprising result in Astrup et al. (2012) is that pictures taken after using toluidine blue dye are not interpreted more precisely than those without the dye.

Internal genitalia in the female victim are inspected secondarily. Speculum insertion is required for internal inspection. Orienting photographs of the vaginal walls and cervix should be taken. One or two "orienting" or overall photographs will demonstrate the appearance of internal genitalia prior to collection of evidence. Photographs of any areas of injury are then taken. Each injury should be photographed as well as described in the report and drawn on a body map within the record.

Vaginal swabbing is done after inspection. The vagina is swabbed with cotton applicators. One applicator can be inserted into the cervix. Other swabs are utilized to absorb any secretions visualized in the vagina. The swabs must stay in place for a few minutes for purposes of absorption. Any secretions noted on the speculum when it is withdrawn from the vagina can also be swabbed. Secretions on the bottom blade of the speculum are derived from surface area underneath the cervix. Swabbing the speculum allows for collection of secretions from this area.

According to Maguire et al. (2009), of 153 patients who consented to genital examination, injury was documented in 60 (39%) women, 32 were less than 20 years (27% vs. 33%, OR = 1.73, 95% CI = 0.90–3.33, $p < 0.1$). One hundred and eleven genital injuries were recorded. These incorporated 35 tears or lacerations of the hymen, 25 at the anus; abrasions (31) were mainly on the fossa navicularis, posterior fourchette, and labia minora, and bruises (15), mainly around the anus. Women examined within 72 h of the assault had significantly more injury than those examined after 72 h (40% vs. 7%, OR = 3.70, 95% CI = 1.05–13.09, $p < 0.05$). Virgins had significantly more genital injury compared with previously sexually active women (60% vs. 33%, OR = 3.03, 95% CI = 1.45–6.33, $p < 0.01$). Strangers assaulted 37% (16/43) of reported virgins and almost half of women with previous sexual experience. Genital injury was associated with acquaintance assault (48% vs. 29%, OR = 2.33, 95% CI = 1.19–4.57, $p < 0.05$) but was less prevalent in women using oral or injected contraception (28% vs. 45%, OR = 2.04, 95% CI = 0.92–4.57, $p < 0.10$). There was no statistically significant association with genital injury and assault occurring outdoors, alcohol consumed prior to incident, parity and antidepressant use (Maguire et al., 2009).

RECTAL EXAMINATION

Rectal examination is performed after genital inspection and collection of evidence. Anoscopy is performed if the interview denotes known or suspected sodomy and the patient consents to the procedure. Swabs for forensic evidence can be collected via the anoscope. The rectum is inspected in both the lithotomy and side lying position in all cases of sexual assault. The rectum is carefully inspected using gentle but firm traction. Tears, bruising have been noted after rectal assault (Geist, 1988). The rectum is inspected utilizing the colposcope or digital camera. Any injuries are photographed via the colposcope or camera. Toluidine blue dye may be used to enhance visualization of perianal injuries. Swabs from the rectum are obtained prior to application of dye.

The buttocks should be inspected before completion of the examination. Evidence in the form of semen or saliva should be collected from the buttocks if present. Elam and Ray (1986) in their interesting review of sexually related trauma, subdivide anorectal trauma into five types: traumatic proctitis, nonperforating mucosal lacerations, disruptions of the anal sphincter, retained foreign bodies, and transmural perforation of the rectosigmoid colon. Diagnosis of transanal rectal injuries may be delayed due to late presentation. Sexual assault should be suspected if rectal injuries are diagnosed (Elam & Ray, 1986).

PROPER HANDLING (MANAGEMENT) OF EVIDENCE

The common methods for drying swabs: in a drying box, in individual test tubes clearly identified in a test tube rack, or pushed through an upside down Styrofoam cup. Swabs must be kept separate from each other to prevent transfer of evidence during the drying process. The source of the swabs must not be confused during the drying process.

Any and all evidence collected must be labeled properly. Swabs must be placed in envelopes clearly marked "vaginal," "oral," or "rectal." Each piece of evidence must be marked on the container (indirect marking) with description, name, number or other designation, person who recovered the evidence, and date. An evidence log should be part of the permanent record. Each piece of evidence collected should be marked on the evidence log.

A common way to organize the collection of evidence is via an "evidence collection kit." For profit companies manufacture evidence collection kits. Each kit organizes the collection process slightly differently. Both the forensic examiner and the police officer should sign the evidence log and the sexual assault evidence collection kit if one is utilized. The kit is sealed with evidence tape by the examiner.

Any evidence collected during examination is turned over to law enforcement. If the victim brings evidence to the examination that cannot be contained within an evidence collection kit, it is given to law enforcement. For example, if the victim brings a condom utilized during the assault to the examination, the condom is placed in a biohazard bag and given to law enforcement. Menstrual pads and tampons collected as evidence are also packaged separately from the kit and given to law enforcement. Clothing collected during the examination is given to the officer via sealed paper bags.

CHAIN OF CUSTODY

Chain of custody for evidence must be maintained throughout the examination. The purpose of chain of custody is to demonstrate that the evidence was never left unattended, thus leaving open the possibility for tampering. Evidence must be in the control of the forensic examiner or the law enforcement officer at all times or it must be under lock and key with minimal availability to the key. The evidence log indicating what was collected (clothing, condom, tampon) and the kit should be signed and dated by both the officer and the examiner. Evidence must be collected properly, stored properly (no higher than 70°F), and transported properly via the law enforcement officer, and documented as to its collection and transfer. Each sexual assault response team must develop procedures to ensure chain of custody for all pieces of evidence. Without meticulous procedure and documentation of procedure related to chain of custody, evidence may not be considered in a court of law.

DOCUMENTATION

Concise and well-organized documentation is important in sexual assault cases. A clear and easy to use charting system is important for consistency in charting among the examiners and for clarity in the prosecutor's office. Photographs should be submitted to law enforcement. A photography log should be included in the record. In this log, each picture taken, colposcopic pictures included, should be listed with a number and description of what has been photographed. Body maps and maps of genitalia on which to draw injuries are recommended. At times, drawings become necessary in a court of law. The TEARS acronym can be utilized in the recording of injury to genitalia. The image of a clock face is frequently used as a method of identifying location of genital injury.

Documentation should be nonjudgmental and draw few conclusions. Documentation should be legible and clear. Forensic examiners typically conclude documentation with a statement indicating consistency or inconsistency of physical findings with history from the victim.

DRUG AND ALCOHOL TESTING

The decision to provide blood or urine for toxicological screening is made by the forensic examiner. The examiner may recommend screening based upon the interview of the victim and/or the neurological evaluation of the victim. If toxicology screening is to be obtained, a specimen or specimens should be collected and submitted to law enforcement under guidelines for chain of custody. The specimen should be collected per police crime laboratory regulations in a timely manner. Clinical toxicology (of an additional specimen) can be performed in the hospital laboratory for quick results as needed.

THERAPY AND PROPHYLAXIS

Medical therapy is implemented as required. Suture of lacerations, treatment of fractures, and other medical therapies are a priority and are implemented prior to evidence collection.

Prophylactic treatment for STIs and prevention of pregnancy should be addressed in every case of female sexual assault. Male survivors of sexual assault require prophylaxis for STIs. The Centers for Disease Control (CDC) publishes a protocol for prevention of STIs after sexual assault that is updated at intervals (CDC Sexually transmitted diseases treatment guidelines, 2010). Risks for HIV prophylaxis and treatment are discussed in the CDC document. Cultures are generally not taken in the immediate aftermath of sexual assault. Treatment is the current recommendation with cultures obtained at follow-up visits. Protocol for treatment of STIs is followed according to the CDC-published standard with deviations for age, weight, allergies, or pregnancy implemented throughout the guidelines

Prevention of pregnancy is offered to all female victims of sexual assault. Prevention of pregnancy is achieved via emergency contraception. An existing pregnancy may be ruled out via a pregnancy test prior to administration of emergency contraception.

Plans for completion of STI treatment should be included in written discharge instructions. Discharge instructions should also contain information about follow-up visits, 24-hour help lines, and how to contact rape care advocacy centers.

CONCLUSION

Women and men, young and old, deserve compassionate, complete, comprehensive care as soon as possible after sexual assault. The development of highly specialized teams containing members from law enforcement, health care, and rape care advocacy helps ensure that all victims of sexual assault receive an integrated, concise, and timely response to sex-related crimes. Forensic examiners ensure the collection of evidence that enhances investigation of sexual assault and helps to ensure the safety of victim/survivors.

Objective forensic evidence may influence victim/survivors to report their experiences to police, encourage police to file a complaint, and persuade prosecutors to file rape charges and pursue a conviction (Sommers et al., 2005).

Additional work is needed, however, to understand the multiple dimensions of the pattern of genital injuries after rape and sexual assault. By expanding the definition of pattern of genital injury to a multidimensional model, including genital injury prevalence, frequency, location, severity, and type, scientists may be able to further explicate the differences between injury patterns in the consensual and nonconsensual populations. Measurement strategies with validity and reliability testing are not yet available for all the dimensions of genital injury pattern, but with further scientific work, the use of a comprehensive model of injury pattern will inform the health care science in critical ways and will provide representative evidence in criminal justice proceedings.

Findings in Sommers et al.'s (2006) study are intriguing and open new avenues for research. Two ready explanations are available to explain findings that white and black women have a statistically significant difference in injury prevalence. Differences in skin pigmentation may alter the ability of the examiners to observe injury regardless of the technique employed, although white and black individuals have a continuum of skin color that is not bound by race and has a wide variation. Sommers's findings suggest that individuals with darker skin may be at a disadvantage for injury identification with the current examination strategies (direct visualization, contrast media, colposcopy). On the other hand, works studying women after vaginal deliveries indicates that women with dark skin may have a protective factor against injury that is not present in lighter skin, although bias may have confounded the results of those investigations (Howard, Davies, DeLancey, & Small, 2000; Robinson, Norwitz, Cohen, McElrath, & Lieberman, 1999). Although skin color is a socially charged issue, it is critical that further exploration occurs across the continuum of skin pigments to ensure that those with darker skin color are not placed at a disadvantage during the forensic examination. With advanced measurement strategies that reflect a multidimensional definition of bodily injury and genital injury patterns, health care and criminal justice practices will have a stronger scientific basis for decision making and the most rigorous techniques can be employed to benefit all sexual assault victims.

As the legal definition of rape moves from the "use of force" to "lack of consent" as rape's defining feature, forensic examiners are partially responsible for destroying myths surrounding sexual assault.

In conclusion consider the following "practice points" provided by White (2013).

PRACTICE POINTS

1. It is not the norm for victims of rape or sexual abuse to have body injuries or genital injuries.
2. The clinician examining the victim undertakes a therapeutic as well as a forensic role.
3. Care should be taken to give back power and control to the victim and not further "objectify" him or her.
4. When genital injuries in the female are sustained, they tend to be minor and at the posterior part of the vulva.
5. The clinician must consider differential diagnoses objectively, based on the history and examination findings.
6. Reporting rates are low for female victims of sexual violence and possibly even lower for male victims. Victims may present to clinicians with a variety of signs and symptoms, but no direct disclosure.

REFERENCES

Anderson, S., McClain, N., and Riviello, R. J. 2006. Genital findings of women after consensual and nonconsensual intercourse. *Journal of Forensic Nursing*, 2(2): 59–65.

Astrup, B., Ravn, P., Thomsen, J. L., and Lauritsen, J. 2013. Patterned genital injury in cases of rape—A case-control study. *Journal of Forensic and Legal Medicine*, 20: 525–529.

Astrup, B. S., Thomsen, J. L., Lauritsen, J., and Ravn P. 2012. Detection of spermatozoa following consensual sexual intercourse. *Forensic Science International*, 221(1–3): 137–141. doi: 10.1016/j.forsciint.2012.04.024.

Bachman, R. 1998. The factors related to rape reporting behavior and arrest: New evidence from the National Crime Victimization Survey. *Criminal Justice and Behavior*, 25: 8–29.

Biggs, M., Stermac, L. E., and Divinsky, M. 1998. Genital injuries following sexual assault of women with and without prior sexual intercourse experience. *Canadian Medical Association Journal*, 159(1): 33–37.

Bowyer, L., and Dalton, M. E. 1997. Female victims of rape and their genital injuries. *British Journal of Obstetrics and Gynaecology*, 104: 617–620.

Campbell, R., Greeson, M., Fehler-Cabral, G., and Kennedy, A. 2015. Pathways to help: Adolescent sexual assault victims' disclosure and help-seeking experiences. *Violence Against Women*, 21: 824–847.

Cartwright, P. S. 1986. Reported sexual assault in Nashville–Davidson County, Tennessee, 1980 to 1982. *American Journal of Obstetrics and Gynecology*, 154(5): 1064–1068.

Centers for Disease Control and Prevention (CDC). 2015. *Sexually transmitted diseases treatment guidelines, 2015*, Vol. 64, No. 3. Morbidity and Mortality Weekly Report, U.S. Department of Health and Human Services. Recommendations and Reports, June 5.

Chen, Y., and Ullman, S. 2014. Women's reporting of physical assaults to police in a national sample: A brief report. *Journal of Aggression, Maltreatment & Trauma*, 23(8): 854–868.

Crane, P. A. 2006. Predictors of injury associated with rape. *Journal of Forensic Nursing*, 2(2): 75–83.

Crowley, S. 1999. *Sexual assault: The medical–legal examination*. Stanford, CT: Appleton and Lange.

Elam, A. L., and Ray, V. G. 1986. Sexually related trauma: A review. *Annals of Emergency Medicine*, 15: 576–584.

Erkkila, M., Rainio, J., Huhtala, H., Salonen, A., and Karhunen, P. 2014. Evaluation of anogenital injuries using white and UV-light among adult volunteers following consensual sexual intercourse. *Forensic Science International*, 242: 293–298.

Everett, R. B., and Jimerson, G. K. 1977. The rape victim: A review of 117 consecutive cases. *Obstetrics and Gynecology*, 50(1): 88–90.

Fisher, B. S., Cullen, F. T., and Turner, M. G. 2000. The sexual victimization of college women. National Institute of Justice Research Report, Washington, DC. http://www.ncjrs.gov/pdffiles1/nij/182369.pdf.

Fraser, I. S., Lahteenmaki, P., Elomaa, K., Lacarra, M., Mishell, D. R., Jr., Alvarez, F., et al. 1999. Variations in vaginal epithelial surface appearance determined by colposcopic inspection in healthy, sexually active women. *Human Reproduction*, 14(8): 1974–1978.

Geist, R. 1988. Sexually related trauma. *Emergency Medicine Clinics of North America*, 6(3): 439–466.

Goodyear-Smith, F. A. 1989. Medical evaluation of sexual assault findings in the Auckland region. *The New Zealand Medical Journal*, 102(876): 493–495.

Gray-Eurom, K., Seaberg, D. C., and Wears, R. L. 2002. The prosecution of sexual assault cases: Correlation with forensic evidence. *Annals of Emergency Medicine*, 39(1): 39–46.

Greeson, M. R., and Campbell, R. 2013. Sexual assault response teams (SARTs): An empirical review of their effectiveness and challenges to successful implementation. *Trauma Violence Abuse*, 14(2): 83–95. doi: 10.1177/1524838012470035.

Greeson, M., and Campbell, R. 2015. Coordinated community efforts to respond to sexual assault: A national study of sexual assault response team implementation. *Journal of Interpersonal Violence*, 30(14): 2470–2487.

Grossin, C., Sibille, I., de la Grandmaison, G., Banasr, A., Brion, F., and Durigon, M. 2003. Analysis of 418 cases of sexual assault. *Forensic Science International*, 131(2003): 125–130.

Hayman, C. R., Lanza, C., Fuentes, R., and Algor, K. 1972. Rape in the District of Columbia. *American Journal of Obstetrics and Gynecology*, 113(1): 91–97.

Howard, D., Davies, P. S., DeLancey, J. O. L., and Small, Y. 2000. Differences in perineal lacerations in black and white primiparas. *Obstetrics and Gynecology*, 96(4): 622–624.

Jones, J. S., Dunnuck, C., Rossman, L., Wynn, B. N., and Nelson-Horan, C. 2004. Significance of toluidine blue positive findings after speculum examination for sexual assault. *The American Journal of Emergency Medicine*, 22(3): 201–203.

Jones, J. S., Rossman, L., Wynn, B. N., Dunnuck, C., and Schwartz, N. 2003. Comparative analysis of adult versus adolescent sexual assault: Epidemiology and patterns of anogenital injury. *Academic Emergency Medicine: Official Journal of the Society for Academic Emergency Medicine*, 10(8): 872–877.

Kennedy, K. 2013. Heterogeneity of existing research relating to sexual violence, sexual assault and rape precludes meta-analysis of injury data. *Journal of Forensic and Legal Medicine*, 20: 447–459.

Lauber, A. A., and Souma, M. L. 1982. Use of toluidine blue for documentation of traumatic intercourse. *Obstetrics and Gynecology*, 60(5): 644–648.

Ledray, L. E. 1992. The sexual assault examination: "Overview and lessons learned in one program." *Journal of Emergency Nursing*, 18(3): 223–232.

Maida, R. 2010. Investigating sexual assault: A community response to victim survival. Office of Justice Assistance, US Department of Justice, Washington, DC.

Maguire, W., Goodall, E., and Moore, T. 2009. Injury in adult female sexual assault complainants and related factors. *European Journal of Obstetrics & Gynecology and Reproductive Biology*, 14(2): 149–153.

Massey, J. B., Garcia, C. R., and Emich, J. P., Jr. 1971. Management of sexually assaulted females. *Obstetrics and Gynecology*, 38(1): 29–36.

McCauley, J., Guzinski, G., Welch, R., Gorman, R., and Osmers, F. 1987. Toluidine blue in the corroboration of rape in the adult victim. *The American Journal of Emergency Medicine*, 5(2): 105–108.

McGregor, M. J., Du Mont, J., and Myhr, T. L. 2002. Sexual assault forensic medical examination: Is evidence related to successful prosecution? *Annals of Emergency Medicine*, 39(6): 639–647.

McGregor, M. J., Le, G., Marion, S. A., and Wiebe, E. 1999. Examination for sexual assault: Is the documentation of physical injury associated with the laying of charges? A retrospective cohort study. *Canadian Medical Association Journal*, 160(11): 1565–1569.

McLean, I., Roberts, S. A., White, C., and Paul, S. 2011. Female genital injuries resulting from consensual and non-consensual vaginal intercourse. *Forensic Science International*, 204: 27–33.

Muram, D., and Elias, S. 1989. Child sexual abuse—Genital tract findings in prepubertal girls. II. Comparison of colposcopic and unaided examinations. *American Journal of Obstetrics and Gynecology*, 160(2): 333–335.

National Sexual Violence Resource Center (NSVRC). 2011. Anti-sexual violence movement, prevention, rape/sexual assault. NSVRC Publications, Newsletters, The Resource.

Norvell, M. K., Benrubi, G. I., and Thompson, R. J. 1984. Investigation of microtrauma after sexual intercourse. *The Journal of Reproductive Medicine*, 29(4): 269–271.

Olusanya, O., Ogbemi, S., Unuigbe, J., and Oronsaye, A. 1986. The pattern of rape in Benin City, Nigeria. *Tropical and Geographical Medicine*, 38(1986): 215–220.

Patterson, D., Greeson, M., and Campbell, R. 2009. Understanding rape survivors' decisions not to seek help from formal social systems. *Health & Social Work*, 34: 127–136. [PubMed: 19425342]

Penttila, A., and Karhumen, P. J. 1990. Medicolegal findings among rape victims. *Medicine and Law*, 9(3): 725–737.

Rambow, B., Adkinson, C., Frost, T. H., and Peterson, G. F. 1992. Female sexual assault: Medical and legal implications. *Annals of Emergency Medicine*, 21(6): 727–731.

Richart, R. M. 1963. A clinical staining test for the in vivo delineation of dysplasia and carcinoma in situ. *American Journal of Obstetrics and Gynecology*, 86(6): 703–712.

Riggs, N., Houry, D., Long, G., Markovchick, V., and Feldhaus, K. M. 2000. Analysis of 1,076 cases of sexual assault. *Annals of Emergency Medicine*, 35(4): 358–362.

Robinson, J. N., Norwitz, E. R., Cohen, A. P., McElrath, T. F., and Lieberman, E. S. 1999. Epidural analgesia and third- or fourth-degree lacerations in nulliparas. *Obstetrics and Gynecology*, 94(2): 259–262.

Sachs, C., and Chu, D. 2002. Predictors of genitorectal injury in female victims of suspected sexual assault. *Academic Emergency Medicine,* 9(2): 146–151.

Slaughter, L., and Brown, C. R. 1992. Colposcopy to establish physical findings in rape victims. *American Journal of Obstetrics and Gynecology*, 166(1 Pt 1): 83–86.

Slaughter, L., Brown, C. R., Crowley, S., and Peck, R. 1997. Patterns of genital injury in female sexual assault victims. *American Journal of Obstetrics and Gynecology*, 176(3): 609–616.

Sommers, M. S. 2007. Defining patterns of genital injury from rape and sexual assault: A review. *Trauma, Violence, and Abuse: A Review Journal*, 8(3): 270–280.

Sommers, M. S., Fisher, B., and Karjane, H. 2005. ED rape exam using colposcopy: Issues in health care, forensics, and criminal justice. *Journal of Forensic Nursing*, 1(1): 19, 28–34.

Sommers, M. S., Schafer, J. C., Zink, T., Hutson, L., and Hillard, P. 2001. Injury patterns in women resulting from sexual assault. *Trauma, Violence, and Abuse: A Review Journal*, 2(3): 240–258.

Sommers, M. S., Zink, T., Baker, R. B., Fargo, J. D., Porter, J., Weybright, D., et al. 2006. Effects of age and ethnicity on physical injury from rape. *Journal of Obstetric, Gynecologic and Neonatal Nursing*, 35(2): 199–207.

Sugar, N. F., Fine, D. N., and Eckert, L. O. 2004. Physical injury after sexual assault: Findings of a large case series. *American Journal of Obstetrics and Gynecology*, 190(1): 71–76.

Teixeira, W. R. 1981. Hymenal colposcopic examination in sexual offenses. *The American Journal of Forensic Medicine and Pathology*, 2(3): 209–215.

Tintinalli, J. E., and Hoelzer, M. 1985. Clinical findings and legal resolution in sexual assault. *Annals of Emergency Medicine*, 14(5): 447–453.

U.S. Department of Justice, Office of Justice Programs, Bureau of Justice Statistics. 2013. *Rape and sexual assault victimization among college-age females, 1995–2013*, Special Report, December 2014, NCJ 248471. Sofi Sinozich, BJS Intern, Lynn Langton, Ph.D., BJS Statistician.

Walker, G. 2015. The (in)significance of genital injury. *Journal of Forensic and Legal Medicine*, 34: 173–178.

White, C. 2013. Genital injuries in adults. *Best Practice & Research Clinical Obstetrics and Gynecology*, 27: 113–130.

Wilson, F., and Swartz, D. 1972. Coital injuries of the vagina. *Obstetrics and Gynecology*, 39(2): 182–184.

Wolitzky-Taylor, K. B., Resnick, H. R., McCauley, J. L., Amstadter, A. B., Kilpatrick, D. G., and Ruggiero, K. J. 2011. Is reporting of rape on the rise? A comparison of women with reported versus unreported rape experiences in the National Women's Study-Replication. *Journal of Interpersonal Violence*, 26: 807–832. [PubMed: 20522886]

Woodling, B. A., and Heger, A. 1986. The use of the colposcope in the diagnosis of sexual abuse in the pediatric age group. *Child Abuse and Neglect*, 10(1): 111–114.

Zajac, J. J. 2006. Report on the national needs assessment of Sexual Assault Response Teams. Document 2004-vf-gx-k007. Enola, PA: National Sexual Violence Resource Center.

18 Prosecuting Rape Cases
Trial Preparation and Trial Tactic Issues

Teresa Scalzo

CONTENTS

Introduction 287
Conducting an Offender-Focused Prosecution 287
Enhancing the Victim's Credibility 289
    Victim Interview 291
    Direct Examination 291
    Expert Testimony Regarding Victim Behavior 293
General Trial Strategies 294
    Preparation 294
    Witness Order 294
    Pretrial Motions 294
    Voir Dire 294
    Opening Statement 295
    Victim Cross-Examination 296
    Medical Testimony 296
    DNA 297
    Toxicologist and/or Pharmacologist 297
    Cross-Examination of the Defendant 298
    Closing Argument 300
    Jury Instructions 300
Additional Trial Strategies 301
Summary 301

INTRODUCTION

Rape cases are typically the most difficult cases to successfully prosecute because jurors' beliefs in common rape myths cause them to question victim credibility, which in turn causes them to question the veracity of the entire case. This chapter discusses techniques that prosecutors can employ both before and during the trial to ensure successful rape prosecutions. First, this chapter will address techniques for conducting offender-focused prosecutions and highlighting defendants' predatory practices. Next, this chapter will offer suggestions for enhancing victims' credibility. Finally, this chapter will propose general trial strategies for presenting the case as persuasively as possible.

CONDUCTING AN OFFENDER-FOCUSED PROSECUTION

Prosecutors generally focus on the offender when prosecuting criminal cases. When prosecuting a rape, however, they tend to focus on the victim and any of the victim's flaws or vulnerabilities. This is especially true in the prosecution of nonstranger rape cases. Rape cases must be tried in the same way that other criminal cases are tried—with a focus on the offender. The facts of some cases will make it easy to use an offender-focused prosecution. Other cases, particularly those in which the defense raises the defense of consent, may be more challenging. An offender-focused prosecution can demonstrate to a jury that the defendant is a predator who engaged in purposeful actions as opposed to a "nice guy" who, through no fault of his own, became caught in a bad predicament (i.e., the rape allegations). When conducting an offender-focused prosecution, prosecutors should construct arguments to focus on the offender's behavior and reveal it as purposeful. In addition, prosecutors should seek to introduce evidence of an offender's other bad acts whenever possible.

A prosecutor should construct arguments that focus the jury's attention on the offender's behavior and highlight any predatory actions. Commonly, prosecutors try rape cases by explaining away flaws in the case and apologizing for the victim's vulnerabilities. It is more effective, however, to show the jury why a predator would target a person with those vulnerabilities. Examples of offender-focused prosecution strategies include the following:

- *The imperfect victim.* Generally, the worse a victim initially appears to be as a witness, the better a target the victim was for the defendant. For example, an offender might select a victim who was voluntarily under the influence of drugs because the offender recognizes that drug users are going to be less credible in the eyes of the police and prosecutors as well as the jury or too high to remember sufficient facts to either identify the offender or testify at trial. Prosecutors should remind the jury that defendants carefully select victims with the intention of not getting caught. As a result, prosecutors should acknowledge a victim's imperfections and point to the evidence that demonstrates that the defendant selected the victim because her imperfections made her the "perfect victim."

- *Cases with minimal force or no traditional weapon.* Many rapists use only the force necessary to overcome the victim's resistance. This may equate to nothing more than lying on top of the victim and pinning her arms down. Further, rapists may gain control of their victims through the use of surprise, deception, manipulation, planning, premeditation, or betrayal of the victim's trust. As a result, prosecutors must investigate the manner in which the rapist gained control over the victim. For example, did the offender lie to the victim by promising her a safe ride home and then drive her to a dark, isolated field where he raped her? Did he trick her by asking to come inside her home to use the bathroom? If so, the prosecutor should explain that this behavior was purposeful and constituted the defendant's weapons. Prosecutors should also argue that the offender preyed upon the victim's surprise, trust, or naiveté. Specifically, the offender counted on the victim being in a vulnerable position caused by his lies and manipulation.

- *Delayed reporting.* Rather than viewing the delayed report as vulnerability on the part of the victim, consider whether the defendant played a role in delaying the report. Interview the victim and ask why she reported the rape when she did. Did the defendant do something as part of his "exit strategy" to keep the victim quiet? Did he threaten her or her family members or friends, either with force or blackmail (by threatening to get her into trouble for any bad decisions she made that he took advantage of)? Did he make her question her own judgment by telling her she had led him on, thereby causing him to rape her? If so, prosecutors should explain the delayed report in terms of the defendant's exit strategy and detail how he effectively silenced the victim. For example, the prosecutor could argue, "He tried to shame her into silence." Prosecutors must not merely point out the defendant's threats; they must label the threats as "the defendant's exit strategy." In addition, in non-stranger rape cases, prosecutors should show the jury any post-rape manipulation where the offender used any of the victim's weaknesses he knew about to silence her.

Next, prosecutors should present evidence of the defendant's other bad acts whenever possible. Many states have some form of Federal Rule of Evidence 404(b) that can be used to introduce other bad acts. All too often, the investigation focuses solely on the current case and does not look for prior rapes or attempted rapes. Frequently, the victim's background is investigated and questioned, but the defendant's background is not. When possible, prosecutors should ask investigators to interview the defendant's friends, prior girlfriends, and others who might know of any prior assaults. Although these individuals may have a motive to lie, they may also be willing to assist or may unknowingly offer some helpful information. If the defendant has any prior cases, review those cases, even if they were dismissed. Further investigation might be warranted. The prosecutor in the current case should also seek out any prosecutors who prosecuted the defendant on prior occasions to gain insights into his personality that may not be apparent from the criminal file. Prosecutors should not focus only on completed rapes; other acts can be used to demonstrate the defendant's pattern of behavior toward women. Significantly, other assaults or behavior that did not result in a completed rape still may support the argument that the offender deceived the victim, manipulated her, or planned and premeditated the rape. In addition to prior cases, look for lawsuits, restraining orders, professional misconduct records, employment records, and military records. Be creative in finding and using other bad acts. Even a simple Internet search may reveal something useful.

The successful use of other bad acts evidence is illustrated by a case in which the defendant sought out overly intoxicated women and lured them to an isolated location. When they were alone, he attempted to kiss and fondle them. The women who were sober enough to fight him off were lucky enough to be left alone. However, the defendant raped the woman who was so intoxicated that she was not able to stop his advances. In this case, the prosecutor was able to successfully argue that the defendant sought out potentially vulnerable victims and took steps to test them and determine whether they were vulnerable enough for him to prey upon. His decision to rape the woman who ultimately became his victim was a conscious choice made only after specifically testing her ability to resist. It was not merely a spontaneous bad decision. In this way, the prosecutor showed that the rape was carefully planned and executed and not just a situation where the victim failed to make clear that she did not consent.

When introducing evidence of other bad acts, make sure to research your jurisdiction's rules of evidence and case law. If notice is required, be sure to file the requisite notice. Even if the law is clear, it is generally best to prepare a legal brief on this issue to present to the judge as the judge may not be as familiar with the specific law or facts as the prosecutor who has spent a great deal of time preparing to present the case. Assist the judge by presenting the necessary arguments for a favorable ruling.

Finally, when selecting a theme for the case, pick one that is offender focused. One example is "a predator picks his prey." Use the theme throughout the case to keep the focus on the offender's choices and behaviors. The jury must be reminded that the defendant's actions were intentional and not merely the result of spontaneously made poor decisions.

ENHANCING THE VICTIM'S CREDIBILITY

Jurors' negative perceptions of victim credibility can be a significant barrier to success in rape cases. Credibility of the victim and provability of the case are inherently intertwined, in large part because rape is a crime of secrecy. There are almost never eyewitnesses to a rape. Moreover, rape cases rarely have physical evidence that conclusively proves that a rape occurred. Prosecutors are left with the victim's word, which means that jurors must find the victim credible before they will convict the defendant. Prosecutors must ensure that the victim testifies in the most convincing manner possible. Pretrial preparation of the victim, therefore, is as important in a rape case as the execution of the direct examination. Further, it is crucial that prosecutors support and protect victims prior to trial to ensure that they are confident and compelling witnesses.

First, a victim must feel supported and protected in order to testify comfortably at the trial. This is critical to the jury's evaluation of the victim's credibility. Prosecutors must establish close relationships with the victim advocates in their communities so that they are able to connect victims with those advocates. Victim advocates can provide support and assistance to victims, including securing any necessary treatment or services. Prosecutors should also allow victim advocates to accompany the victim to any preparatory sessions, interviews, and hearings. In addition, prosecutors should provide a safe and comfortable place for the victim to wait to testify. They should also be certain to ask the victim if she needs any additional support.

Next, prosecutors should protect the victim's privacy and integrity through the preparation and filing of legal motions. It is critical to protect the victim because a victim who feels protected throughout the criminal justice process is less likely to become angry or defensive on the witness stand. When a victim becomes angry or defensive, jurors are likely to believe that she has something to hide, instead of understanding the behavior as a normal human reaction. A number of strategies can be used to protect the victim:

- *Utilize pretrial motions to protect the victim's physical safety and privacy.* The most obvious example of a victim protection motion is a motion to revoke bond. This can be done if the defendant poses a specific threat to the victim—for example, if he contacts or threatens her. In addition, the prosecutor can request a no-contact order to keep the defendant from contacting the victim. Another example is a motion to clear the courtroom of individuals who might threaten or attempt to intimidate the victim. Prosecutors can also request extra deputies for the courtroom or arrange for a deputy or police officer to escort the victim between her car and the courthouse before and after any hearings. The defendant or his friends or family frequently take these opportunities to intimidate the victim. Although you may not always succeed in preventing the intimidation, the victim will see that you are fighting to protect her, which will translate into her increased confidence on the witness stand.

- *Do your best to protect the victim's identity.* If possible, use her initials and date of birth in court documents as opposed to her full name. Work to educate the media about the danger to victims' safety and integrity when their personal or identifying information is revealed. Make specific requests that they not reveal the victim's identity.

- *Oppose frivolous defense motions intended to harass and intimidate the victim.* For example, oppose motions requesting a psychological examination of the victim. Challenge motions asking for the victim's counseling records unless there is some reason to believe that the records would yield exculpatory evidence. These examinations and the exposure of records often fail to yield exculpatory information and can result in embarrassment to the victim. Force the defense to litigate these motions and to demonstrate that they are not frivolous or merely intended to harass the victim. A victim who knows that her private counseling records are going to be released to the defense and possibly revealed at trial may refuse to cooperate with the prosecution in order to protect her privacy.

- *Oppose attempts to pierce the rape shield law and challenge inappropriate defense attempts to dissuade the victim from testifying.* Often, defendants and their attorneys employ tactics designed to dissuade the victim from testifying with the hope that the prosecutor will either not find out or will do nothing. This is demonstrated by a case in which the defense investigator served subpoenas on a rape victim's friends and informed them that they would be called "to testify that the victim slept around" in an effort to intimidate the victim. The testimony was prohibited by the rape shield law, which prevents the introduction of a victim's sexual activity unless it is required by an exception or on constitutional grounds. In such a situation, prosecutors should move to quash the subpoenas and file a motion to exclude the testimony under the rape shield law. If the prosecutor does not have standing to quash the subpoena(s), he or she can advise the victim to seek a civil attorney to quash the subpoena(s). The prosecutor should also inform the victim about rape shield laws and keep her informed about the evidence that will be introduced and excluded at trial. An informed victim will be harder for the defense to intimidate. For many victims, knowledge is power and is sufficient to keep them strong enough to testify.

Victim Interview

Whether or not the prosecutor participates in the initial victim interview, at some point the prosecutor will have to interview the victim in order to prepare for trial. It is important to recognize that the neurobiology of trauma causes victims' memories to be formed differently than memories formed during a nontraumatic event. Brains dominated by stress and fear tend to encode experiences as fragmentary sensations and emotions. Thus rape victims often have a difficult time recounting events in a linear fashion, especially soon after the event. In fact, due to how the brain processes trauma-related information, many victims may seem to be withholding information, lying, or otherwise telling an incredible tale when interviewed with traditional linear questioning tactics. If pushed too hard for details that were never recorded or very difficult to recall, they may try to fill in gaps—not because they are making things up but because they are sincerely trying to do their best to answer inappropriate questions from the interviewer. Or the interviewer may give the message that without a linear and gapless narrative the victim will not be believed or taken seriously. Therefore, the initial interview should be conducted with techniques that are consistent with the impact of trauma on the brain and memory, which will capture the reality of the crime as experienced by the victim, and will give the prosecutor a much better understanding of what happened.

A trauma informed interview should begin with making the victim feel as comfortable as possible, by informing her about what to expect and giving her (appropriate) choices wherever possible. Then the victim should be asked what she is *able* to tell about what she *experienced*. The words "able" and "experience" are critical here, as they let the victim know that you understand she may not be able to remember everything (including things she really wishes she could remember), and that she is only expected to remember what she experienced and what her brain encoded into memory in a traumatized state—not necessarily what "actually happened," in the way a video recording would have captured. Instead of following up with linear questions such as who, what, where, and when after the initial narrative, the prosecutor should ask about the five senses. "What did you hear?" "What did you feel in your body?" "What did you smell?" A person recounting a traumatic experience like sexual assault is more likely to remember sensory and peripheral details. The details that are remembered will not necessarily be in sequential order or a clear linear narrative. Eliciting those experiential details greatly enhances the ability of the listener to understand the assault, by painting a realistic picture of the experience and how it felt for the victim. When a prosecutor uses these sensory and peripheral details at trial, the jury is more likely to understand the experience from the *victim's* perspective, including any counterintuitive behaviors, not the perspective of the perpetrator or their own misunderstandings and biases about how what "real" sexual assaults are like.

Direct Examination

Testifying in court can be a traumatic event for rape victims, who are forced to mentally relive the details of their assaults in front of the defendant and a courtroom of strangers. Consequently, in addition to supporting and protecting victims prior to trial, prosecutors must carefully prepare them to testify. Assuming the prosecutor has conducted a trauma informed interview as discussed above, the prosecutor can use the information gathered during the interview by incorporating sensory and peripheral details into the direct examination. The following suggestions can be used to present the victim's testimony in the most persuasive manner possible:

- *Work with the victim to understand any behavior that the jury may perceive as counterintuitive.* To explain a victim's response to rape to a jury, the prosecutor must first understand it. The open ended questions, including the sensory questions, asked during the victim interview or preparatory sessions, should have given the prosecutor a thorough understanding of what the victim experienced during the rape. This lays the foundation for understanding counterintuitive behaviors. When crafting the direct examination, identify any behaviors that jurors will perceive to be counterintuitive, such as not screaming during the rape, failing to immediately report the rape, or continuing to socialize with the rapist. Work with the victim to identify and understand these behaviors. Remember that it is not uncommon for victims to recognize that something horrible happened to them without labeling it as rape. Often, a victim may not label the traumatic experience as rape until after a discussion with a friend, law enforcement officer, or doctor. If the victim did not immediately label the experience as rape, it was not unreasonable for her to delay in reporting. Moreover, the victim may have engaged in illegal or immoral behavior prior to the rape, causing her to comply with the rapist's demands or delay in reporting.

- *Ask the victim to explain any behavior jurors may have a hard time understanding during direct examination.* For example, in a case of delayed reporting, the prosecutor should ask the victim to explain the time and circumstances of the report. When did the victim report and why? Another example is a victim who was on a date with the offender at the time of the assault and did not report immediately. Later, however, the victim may have gone to the hospital because she thought she had contracted a sexually transmitted infection. Sometimes, those to whom victims first describe their assault will convince them to contact the police. Prosecutors should explain to the jury that the time and circumstances of reporting enhance the victim's credibility.

- *Give the jury a foundation to understand the victim's behavior.* When explaining victim behavior to a jury, a prosecutor must present the jury with enough evidence of the victim's background to enable them to understand that her reaction, while counterintuitive to them, was absolutely natural to her. The prosecutor must personalize the victim in order to give the jury a context in which to evaluate a victim's credibility accurately. Consider the example of a college student who was using cocaine on the night she was raped and who delayed in reporting because she knew she would lose her scholarship if her college found out that she was using cocaine. Before explaining the cocaine use to the jury, explain that the victim was the first in her family to attend college and that, without her scholarship, she would have been unable to afford to continue her schooling. When the jurors appreciate the impact of losing the scholarship, they will be more likely to understand why she did not report the rape and therefore more likely to find her credible.

- *Explain the importance of "little lies" to the victim.* Tell the victim that the most important rule for her to follow in the courtroom is to be truthful. Tell her to be honest about ALL details of the event, even if the details seem insignificant or are embarrassing. Even the most honest of victims may not appreciate the devastating impact of "little lies." For example, an underage victim might not want to admit that she voluntarily drank alcohol with the defendant. Prosecutors must explain to the victim that "little lies" as well as attempts to hide or exaggerate even the smallest of details will be uncovered by the defense on cross-examination. In closing, the defense will use the "little lies" as evidence that she is not credible and therefore cannot be believed about the rape.

- *Instruct the victim on the importance of accuracy.* Prosecutors must ensure that victims use accurate language to describe their assaults. For example, a victim may use the term *ripped* to describe the defendant's action of roughly removing her panties, even when the panties were not torn. The slightest imprecision opens the door for cross-examination and may call the victim's credibility into question. If the victim is not accurate when she testifies, it is the prosecutor's job to clarify her testimony. Ask the victim what she meant when she used the word *ripped*. In the example set forth here, the prosecutor must ensure that the victim articulates that the panties were pulled off roughly but not torn.

- *Explain the importance of remaining calm on the witness stand.* Explain that a victim who becomes angry will be unable to think clearly. In addition, the defense may suggest to the jury that the victim who becomes angry and hostile on the witness stand should have been able to fight off the rapist. This may give credence to the defense allegation that the victim consented.
- *Explain inconsistencies.* In rape cases, the slightest inconsistencies in the victim's statements or testimony may seriously impact the victim's credibility. Prosecutors must review all victim statements, identify any inconsistencies or partial revelations and address them with the victim and other witnesses prior to trial. Explain major inconsistencies in direct examination. Prepare the victim to answer the defense's inevitable questions about the inconsistencies. When the jurors understand that the inconsistencies were not deliberate lies on the part of the victim, they will be more likely to find her credible. Remember to reinforce in closing that it is natural to have some inconsistency in any case. In closing, the prosecutor can tell the jury that if the jurors were interviewed 3 months after the end of the case, there would be 12 versions of what happened during the trial.
- *Demonstrate that the defendant "became a stranger" if he was known to the victim.* In cases where the defendant truly was a stranger, prosecutors can easily rebut any insinuation by the defense that the victim consented. However, in cases where the victim knew the defendant, jurors may have a harder time believing that the defendant raped the victim due to the pervasiveness of the myth that rape is perpetrated by strangers. In a case where the victim knew the defendant prior to the rape, remind the jurors that it was reasonable for her to trust him. Because the victim trusted the defendant, she did not recognize the danger until it was too late. It is critical for prosecutors to demonstrate how the defendant tricked the victim and used her trust to take advantage of her. At trial, first have the victim explain the type of person the defendant appeared to be and explain who he really was. Ask the victim to describe for the jury the moment she realized that she was in danger and that the defendant was going to rape her. Ask her to describe any changes in his demeanor, speech, or behavior. The contrast will show the jurors that although the defendant did not initially fit their stereotype of a "real" rapist, he is, nevertheless, guilty. It is important to demonstrate that the defendant tricked the victim into believing that he was someone who would not hurt her. Argue that the defendant became a stranger to the victim when he raped her.
- *If the consent defense is used, show the jury how the victim said no.* If the victim said no more than once, ask the victim, "After you said no the first time, then what happened?" Emphasize the repeated attempts to say no by incorporating them into the questions. For example, if the victim physically resisted, ask, "After you said no three separate times, then what happened?" In closing, argue that the victim said no three separate times, then after telling him no three times, she showed she meant no by kicking him and pushing him. It must be clear to the jury that it was obvious to the defendant that the victim did not consent.

Expert Testimony Regarding Victim Behavior

In cases in which a victim's counterintuitive behavior might cause the jury to find that she is not credible, consider presenting expert testimony to explain the victim's reactions. An experienced expert can explain behaviors a jury might otherwise not understand. An expert need not be expensive. For example, a community-based victim advocate who has worked with many victims and can articulate the various behaviors victims commonly engage in, including those that the jury is likely to perceive as counterintuitive, would be a qualified witness who might not charge a large fee for testifying. Psychologists, social workers, police officers, FBI experts, and sexual assault forensic examiners are other potential choices for experts who can explain that rape victims behave in any number of ways and that there is not one consistent form of victim behavior.

GENERAL TRIAL STRATEGIES

PREPARATION

Rape cases require more preparation than other types of cases. To the extent possible, the prosecutor should work with investigators as early as possible in the case. As discussed previously, the prosecutor should begin to work with the victim as soon as he or she is able. Interview the victim and prepare her prior to the preliminary hearing or grand jury proceeding. Interview and prepare all other potential witnesses as well. If it is important enough to call a witness in a rape case, it is important to take the time to prepare the witness. When possible, visit the crime scene and examine any physical evidence. During trial, use photos and diagrams to recreate the reality of the crime for the jury. Consider preparing a timeline or creating demonstrative evidence. Review all inconsistencies and be prepared to explain them. Identify any issues in the case that the jury may question and be prepared to address them.

WITNESS ORDER

Witnesses do not necessarily need to be presented in chronological order. If there is a witness who supports the victim's testimony in a way that makes the victim seems more credible, present that witness before the victim. With this approach, when the jury hears the victim's testimony, they will already be inclined to find her credible. For example, consider starting with a witness who saw the victim immediately after the incident in a highly emotional state or a medical witness who treated an injury. When the jury hears the victim's testimony, they will be less inclined to question it because they have already heard the corroborating witness. Again, anything the prosecution can do to strengthen the victim's testimony will enhance the chance of success at trial.

PRETRIAL MOTIONS

In addition to the use of other bad acts, victim protection, and rape shield motions as discussed previously, prosecutors should consider filing a motion *in limine* to limit irrelevant defense evidence about "bad" victim behaviors. For example, if the victim is a drug user but did not use drugs on this occasion, file a motion to preclude any mention of the victim's drug use. If the victim has a criminal record, consider filing a motion to prohibit mentioning her record. Although prosecutors should not apologize for case weaknesses, they should not allow the defense to take advantage of them.

VOIR DIRE

Although voir dire can be used to educate a jury panel, it is unlikely that prosecutors will be able to change long-standing prejudices of jurors who are inclined to believe rape stereotypes and myths. Prosecutors will generally be more successful by eliminating jurors who hold such deep-rooted beliefs that they cannot be fair. By asking questions in voir dire about jurors' preconceived opinions, the prosecutor can try to keep people with such biases off the jury.

In some jurisdictions voir dire is oral, in others it is written, and in still others it is a combination of oral and written. Regardless of the format of voir dire, prosecutors must attempt to educate the jury and screen out jurors who cannot be fair in a rape case. In addition to traditional voir dire questions, prosecutors should address the following areas during voir dire:

- *Identify prior victims, defendants, and their friends and family.* Prosecutors must identify jurors who have either been victimized or accused of rape or who have close friends or family members who have been victims or accused. Tell the jurors to listen to the entire question before responding and then ask: "Is there anyone here who has been either themselves or a close family member been either a victim of or accused of sexual assault?"

When possible, it is best to ask any follow-up questions in a sidebar to prevent embarrassment to the juror and avoid poisoning the panel. Let the jurors know in advance that you will ask the judge to discuss any responses in private at the bench.

- *The need for corroboration.* Members of the public who are unwilling to admit that they believe that women lie about rape will often freely admit that they would hesitate to convict a defendant of rape without some form of corroboration, even though this is not required for a conviction. Therefore, in cases where there are no eyewitnesses or corroborating physical or medical evidence, prosecutors should ask whether jurors would have a difficult time finding the victim credible without any eyewitnesses or corroborating physical or medical evidence. Ask, "If you believe the victim beyond a reasonable doubt, can you convict the defendant?"

- *Lack of significant physical injury.* In cases where there is no significant physical injury, prosecutors should ask whether jurors expect physical injury. Ask if they would have a difficult time finding the victim credible due to the lack of injury.

- *Victim behavior that is not consistent with juror expectations.* In cases where the victim behaved in a way that is counter to jurors' expectations of how a victim should behave, consider asking how the jury expects a victim to behave. For example, if there is a delayed report, ask jurors if they can think of reasons why a rape victim might delay in reporting. In addition, prosecutors should ask whether the jury will wait to hear the victim's reason for reporting when she did before deciding whether the victim is credible. Similarly, prosecutors should ask the jury about any other behaviors that may cause them to question whether the victim is credible.

- *Prior relationship.* If there was a prior relationship between the victim and the defendant, the prosecutor should ask whether this concerns the jury.

- *No weapon.* In cases where no gun, knife, or other traditional weapon was used, the prosecutor should ask whether jurors understand that it is possible that rapists may gain control and overpower their victims without a traditional weapon. The prosecutor can use examples that highlight the way the defendant gained control of the victim. For example, a prosecutor could ask, "Do you believe that it is possible for a defendant to gain control over a victim by using his ability to adversely affect the victim's job?"

- *"Bad" victim behavior.* If there is any "bad" behavior on the part of the victim, such as prostitution, drinking, or using drugs, the prosecutor should ask whether the jury has any biases or preconceived notions. The prosecutor can also ask whether jurors believe that such behavior is a justification for rape.

- *Imperfect victim.* In cases of unsympathetic or imperfect victims, prosecutors should tell the jury that the law does not distinguish between victims. Instead, the jury must consider the law and whether each of the elements of the crime has been met. To decide based upon sympathy for the defendant or prejudice against the victim would violate their oath. Ask if the jury can promise to decide the case based upon the evidence and not whether they like or dislike the victim or defendant. Extract from jurors a promise that they will follow the law whether they agree with it or not.

- *Juror education.* Ask questions to develop the theory of the case. For example, the prosecutor can ask, "Have you ever been betrayed by someone you trusted?" or "Has someone ever taken advantage of your vulnerabilities?"

OPENING STATEMENT

An opening statement is the first opportunity for the prosecutor to fully reveal to the jury the essence of the case. A prosecutor should re-create the reality of the crime by painting a clear image of the facts of the case for the jury. Foremost, be confident in presenting the opening statement. Never apologize to the jury for the lack of evidence. (Juries, unlike judges, are unfamiliar with inadequacies of a case.) Bring out the best points and defuse the worst points of the case. Do not be afraid to address the weaknesses, but de-emphasize them. Ensure that the opening incorporates an offender-focused theme and is presented in a manner that focuses on the offender.

VICTIM CROSS-EXAMINATION

Prepare victims not only for direct examination but also for the harsh reality of cross-examination. In cases where the defense is consent, cross-examination may be particularly aggressive. Victims who are prepared in advance for the challenge of the experience will be better witnesses when they testify. It will also be easier for victims to endure the trial process if they understand that they are not being asked difficult questions because they are a bad person or because they did something wrong. Instead, if they are being cross-examined harshly, it is because the defense attorney is protecting his or her client. An advocate may be extremely helpful to the victim and to the prosecutor by being present during preparation for cross-examination and during the trial itself. It may be helpful to have a colleague practice cross-examining the victim.

Review all areas of the victim's testimony about which it is likely she will become emotionally upset or angry, such as drug or alcohol use or prior admissible sexual contact with the defendant. Advise her that she will be asked for full details about the sexual experience with the defendant. Explain to the victim that if she becomes angry or hostile, the jury is likely to believe she has something to hide. Tell the victim not to be rude or sarcastic in answering the defense attorney's questions, even if the defense attorney is rude or sarcastic to her. In addition:

- Tell the victim that when appropriate, you may object to stop an improper line of questioning and whenever you object, she is to stop answering the question until the judge indicates otherwise.
- Remind the victim to answer only the question that is asked and not to volunteer any additional information.
- Explain to the victim that if she does not understand the question, she should say that she does not understand the question.

MEDICAL TESTIMONY

Many jurors believe that all women who are raped sustain serious physical injuries. They do not understand how a rape can occur without injury. The reality is that very few rape victims sustain any physical injuries other than the rape itself. When a medical examination is done, it is important to present it thoroughly, even if it shows that no injury occurred. If a sexual assault forensic examination was done, do not stipulate to testimony about the exam. Have the nurse or doctor who performed it explain it in as much detail as possible. The procedure is long, invasive, and uncomfortable. Jurors who understand what the victim had to endure in order to prosecute the case will be more likely to find her credible.

In addition to explaining the details of the examination, it is important to present expert testimony explaining any injury or lack thereof. When injury exists, use an expert to explain that the victim's description of how the injury occurred is consistent with the examiner's findings. This explanation of her physical injuries and their consistency with the victim's testimony becomes crucial in arguing to the jury that the victim should be believed.

If there is no injury, use the expert to explain how it is possible that a woman could be raped but have no physical injuries. If the victim has not suffered any trauma to her vaginal area, the defense attorney will try to argue to the jury that the lack of vaginal injury is consistent with the defendant's version of consensual intercourse or no intercourse at all. Typically, the defense will argue, if the victim had been forced, she would have suffered some type of injury to the vagina. To a layperson, this argument is persuasive. However, it is inaccurate. Therefore, in a case without genital trauma, bring in a medical expert to educate the jury on this issue. Have the expert testify that in his or her training, practice, and experience, significant physical injury from a rape is extremely rare. The doctor or sexual assault forensic examiner should explain the female anatomy and how rarely visible bruises or tears are noted even in confirmed sexual assault cases. The expert should conclude with his or her expert medical opinion that the lack of trauma is entirely consistent with the victim's version of events.

DNA

Advances in DNA technology have made it far easier to prove the defendant's identity in rape cases. Often, when the defendant realizes that his identity can be proven, he resorts to the consent defense. In such cases, prosecutors must decide whether to present testimony regarding DNA testing or to rely on the defendant's concession that intercourse occurred. The prosecutor must consider his or her own community's expectations; however, it is generally preferable to present evidence of DNA testing to show that the prosecution was thorough and did everything in its power to investigate the case completely. Be careful not to spend so much time on DNA testimony that the jury might begin to wonder whether there is actually a question as to its soundness.

Do not forget that DNA evidence can do more than prove the defendant's identity. It can reinforce the victim's version of events. If the victim states that the defendant licked her breast and there is DNA evidence to confirm that he did so, present the evidence to the jury. Every piece of the victim's testimony that can be corroborated strengthens the prosecution's case.

If DNA evidence exists in the case, review all lab reports, quality control reports, chain of custody documentation, and all other reports from the lab. Anticipate areas of weakness in your case and work with an expert on how to overcome the challenges.

In cases where there is no DNA evidence, the prosecutor must consider whether to present an expert to discuss how it is possible for intercourse to occur without DNA evidence being left behind. If the defendant opts to use the consent defense, expert testimony may not be necessary. However, if the defense is that the intercourse never occurred, the prosecutor should present expert testimony explaining how the absence of DNA is not inconsistent with the victim's testimony.

TOXICOLOGIST AND/OR PHARMACOLOGIST

In cases of drug or alcohol-facilitated sexual assault (see Chapter 23), the prosecutor must decide whether to use a toxicologist and/or pharmacologist to address challenging issues. It may be necessary to explain that the victim was incapable of consent. In the case of a victim who was unconscious at the time of the rape, a toxicologist and/or pharmacologist can be used to explain that it is possible for a person to remain unconscious throughout the rape, as jurors may have a hard time believing that a victim would remain unconscious for any part of a rape. When choosing an expert, remember that it is possible that the same witness may be qualified to testify on both toxicology and pharmacology, but this should not be assumed.

In cases of drug-facilitated sexual assault where drug testing failed to reveal the presence of a drug, an expert should be used to explain the challenges inherent in detection. Use the expert to explain how long the suspected drug remains in the blood or urine if the testing was done outside that time period. Ask the expert to explain the sensitivity of any equipment that was used in the testing process and the inability to detect drugs under a certain amount. If no drug was found and the victim was drinking alcohol, explain that the amount of alcohol the victim consumed was not sufficient to cause the physical reaction and level of intoxication the victim experienced, thereby supporting the theory that the victim was drugged. Explain that many date rape drugs mimic the impact of alcohol because they, like alcohol, are central nervous system depressants.

Prosecutors may decide to use a toxicologist and/or pharmacologist in rebuttal if any issues arise during the case. This option is particularly useful when the defense alleges that the victim was not unconscious during the rape as she testified, but instead, blacked out due to excessive alcohol consumption and cannot remember the events of the evening. Often, the defense will allege that the victim initiated the intercourse and was an active participant but does not remember because she experienced a blackout. An expert can explain that it does not matter whether the victim was blacked out or passed out. In either state, she was not capable of consenting and would have appeared extremely intoxicated to an observer.

CROSS-EXAMINATION OF THE DEFENDANT

Defendants in sexual assault cases are not easy to cross-examine. They have a substantial interest in lying and may actually believe their own lies. Often, they will minimize and rationalize. In addition, they have generally spent a good deal of time thinking about the case and rehearsing. Most of the challenges inherent in cross-examination of a defendant in a rape case can be overcome by thorough preparation. Do not assume that the defendant will choose not to testify. In every rape case, prepare as though the defendant will testify, even when the defense attorney denies that his or her client will testify. Try to learn as much as possible about the defendant. Obtain any available material, including prior criminal and civil files, prison records, prison visitor logs, military records, work or school records, and health records.

When cross-examining, avoid rehashing the direct examination. Repeating the direct examination is not only boring to the jury, it allows the defendant to emphasize key defense points a second time. Identify a limited number of key points to challenge on cross. Remember that the purpose of cross-examination is to make points that can be used in closing to reinforce the prosecution's case.

Although it is generally best to ask leading questions whenever possible, at times it may be necessary to ask open-ended questions. Prosecutors, unlike defense attorneys, do not always have the luxury of knowing the answer to every question that will be asked. However, be cautious with open-ended questions as they may give the defendant another opportunity to tell his or her story.

Listen carefully as the defendant testifies. Key in on the words he uses. What exactly is he saying? Is he saying "No one saw me there" or "I was never there"? Often, defendants reveal the truth unwittingly. If the defendant says, "No one saw me there," have him repeat that portion of his testimony. Highlight his exact words in closing. Also, be aware of defendants who use legal language that suggests over preparation by the defense attorney. Varying the order of cross may confuse this defendant and shake him from his overly prepared story.

Consensus-based cross-examination may be particularly effective when the defense is consent. In this type of cross-examination, the prosecutor should attempt to get the defendant to agree to as many of the facts of the case as possible. Ideally, the prosecutor will be able to argue in closing "the only fact with which he disagrees is the one that makes him guilty—whether or not she consented." In closing, the prosecutor can use a demonstrative exhibit listing all points of agreement between the defense and prosecution and emphasizing that the only disagreement was whether or not the victim consented, the very point which makes him guilty.

Every case is different and the prosecutor must prepare for each individual case; however, some arguments are fairly common in rape cases. The following is a list of suggested topics for cross-examination:

- For cases where the defendant initially denied having intercourse with the victim and later changed his defense to consent after learning of forensic evidence, focus on the changes in the defendant's statements and what the defendant knew when making each statement. A timeline can be used in closing to reinforce how the defendant changed his story depending on what he thought the prosecution knew.
- For cases where the defendant used force or a weapon, focus on the amount of force or weapon used. It may be effective to ask the defendant very specific details about the attack to show that the defendant enjoyed brutalizing the victim.

- For cases where coercion or a nontraditional method of force was used, focus on the circumstances of gaining control of the victim and taking advantage of the victim's vulnerability.
- If the defendant is an anger retaliatory rapist (see Chapter 7), ask questions about women generally. What was the defendant angry about? What was the relationship with the victim? Why did the defendant choose this victim? Is the victim like the defendant's mother or whomever the defendant is angry at?
- If the defendant is a power assertive rapist, ask questions to show that he believes that he can do whatever he wishes to women because he is entitled.
- If the defendant lied or manipulated the victim, ask questions to highlight the lies and manipulation. Verify that he said or did the things the victim alleges. Ask questions to verify the actions that constituted the defendant's exit strategy.
- When the defendant behaved inconsistently, ask questions to highlight the changes in behavior. Did the defendant act one way before the rape and then change his behavior immediately after? Does the defendant have a girlfriend or wife? Do not attempt to get the defendant to concede that he behaved inconsistently; instead get him to agree to the specific actions. In closing, reiterate the inconsistent actions and argue that the defendant behaved inconsistently because he is guilty.
- Emphasize any behavior that shows consciousness of guilt.
- Focus on tiny details. Often, when a defendant is forced to be specific, lies are exposed.

If the defense is consent, ask the following:
- Did the victim say no? How? When? How many times?
- Did the victim say yes? How? When? How many times?
- The defendant chose the victim. When the defense is consent, the defendant must acknowledge that he wanted to have sex with the victim. If not, how did the sex occur? Many defendants will be hesitant to admit this point, making their story appear less credible.
- What were the defendant's intentions? Did he want to have sex with the victim? If so, what steps did he take in order to have sex with her? If not, was it just an accident?
- Did he want to get the victim alone? If so, what steps did he take to get her alone?
- If the defendant claims that there was a relationship or that he was dating the victim when, in fact, there was no relationship, tie him to details. Ask if there was a relationship. How long was the relationship? When did they meet? Did he know her friends or family? Was he in love with her? How much in love was he? Did he tell anyone about it? Who? When? What?
- If the defendant claims that he knew the victim "wanted him," explore her "desire" and show how ridiculous this is. Ask how he knew she wanted him. How did she communicate her desire? A look? Body language? Words? Do other women want him?
- What behavior does he think constitutes consent? Kissing? Fondling? Drinking? Wearing certain clothing? Going to a bar by herself?

In cases with an imperfect victim, the defendant will often attack the victim in his testimony. The prosecutor must show that the defendant's trashing of the victim is an attempt to deflect from his actions and get the jury to engage in victim blaming. The defendant wants to hide from the jury the fact that he selected the victim and decided to rape her. The prosecutor can refocus the jury on the defendant's intentions and behavior by showing the differences between the time of the rape and now:
- Contrast the romantic descriptions of the encounter versus negative descriptions of the victim. What happened to change things, if not the rape? Corroborate the lack of prerape conflict.
- Did the victim's behavior change after the rape? When did she become imperfect? He liked her enough then to have sex with her; why does he have negative things to say now?

- What motive does she have to lie? If she is normally a liar, why was he with her?

In cases where the defendant committed other illegal acts such as drug use, it may be effective to ask about these acts. However, be cautious when venturing into this area. Know the law and file required notices under the "other acts" rule.

CLOSING ARGUMENT

The closing argument is a very crucial part of a criminal trial. The closing should be at least 90% written (at least in outline form) before the trial begins. The closing is the prosecutor's opportunity to show the jury why he or she has proven all elements of the crimes charged. Apply the facts to the law and explain to the jury why the defendant is guilty. Be deferential to the judge by telling the jury that the judge will instruct them on the law, but you would like to take a few moments to discuss it and how it applies to the facts of the case. If the prosecutor uses language similar to the language used in the jury instruction, the jury will have a better understanding of the case than if they had heard the legal definition only once. Carefully analyze any key issues in the case such as the lack of any requirement that the victim offer physical resistance. Review all corroborative evidence and show the jury that there is more than just the victim's word for them to rely upon. Explain to the jury how the evidence shows that the victim is credible.

In addition, the following suggestions can enhance the prosecution's closing argument:

- Urge the jury to resolve credibility issues in favor of the victim and the government witnesses and give them reasons for doing so.
- Recreate the reality of the crime for the jury. The jury must be able to picture the crime from the victim's perspective in order to understand the horrific nature of the case. Describe the fear that the victim felt. Although a prosecutor cannot ask the jury to put themselves in the victim's shoes, the prosecutor can describe the case in such a way that it is real for the jury.
- In cases of an imperfect victim, tell the jury that a trial is not a popularity contest, but rather a search for the truth. Remind them of their oath to follow the law and not decide the case based upon sympathy or prejudice.
- Stress the testimony of neutral or unbiased witnesses.
- In cases where the defendant testifies, remind the jury that they must evaluate the testimony by the same yardstick that they evaluate the victim's testimony.
- Use the emotional aspects of the rape—that the dignity of the victim has been attacked.
- Remind the jury that it is their solemn oath to obey the law even if they do not agree with or approve of it.
- As always during the course of the trial, be proud to be a prosecutor and be proud to represent the interests of the victim and the community at large. Never apologize for the lack of evidence. If you are confident, then that confidence transcends to the jury.

JURY INSTRUCTIONS

If standard jury instructions are insufficient, prosecutors should consider drafting proposed instructions. Prosecutors must ensure that the jurors understand that a delayed complaint does not mean that the victim is a liar. Draft an instruction that explains to the jury that they must consider the victim's reasons for reporting when she did in evaluating her credibility. Draft an instruction that states that there is no need for corroboration if the jury believes the victim's testimony. Also, draft an instruction that explains that the victim's testimony must be evaluated in the same manner as all other witness testimony. Jurors may mistakenly believe that the victim should be held to a higher standard of credibility.

ADDITIONAL TRIAL STRATEGIES

- Personalize the victim but do not refer to adult victims by their first name. Say "Donna Jones cried for help" or "Miss Jones will tell you."
- Depersonalize the defendant. Refer to the defendant as "the defendant" whenever possible.
- Do not spend the case defending any weaknesses. Answer the defense's most fallacious points, but otherwise spend the case on the offensive showing the strength of the prosecution's case and how the elements have been met.
- During defense arguments, do not be afraid to object. Although most judges will give defense attorneys considerable leeway, do not allow defense attorneys to violate the rules of evidence or prejudice the jury. Do not get carried away and object continuously, but set the tone with appropriate objections.
- Never refer to the victim's version of events as the victim's "story."

SUMMARY

This chapter discussed techniques that prosecutors can employ to ensure success in rape prosecutions. Combine an offender-focused prosecution with techniques for enhancing the victim's credibility to ensure success. Working with the victim prior to trial and filing key pretrial motions are as critical to success as courtroom skill in a rape case.

Section IV

Offender Populations

19 Sexual Victimization of Children

Rape or Molestation

Kenneth V. Lanning

CONTENTS

Introduction 305
Contrasting Factors 308
Conclusions 317
References 317

INTRODUCTION

In 1985 I was an invited presenter at a large anti-pornography conference being held at a major U.S. university. A significant number of the attendees were either conservative Christians or liberal feminists. These distinct groups tended to agree on few social issues other than their strong opposition to pornography but for different reasons and with different definitions of what it was. Pornography was and still is a complex and controversial issue. The focus of my presentation, however, was limited to "Child Pornography." Early on in my presentation, I pointed out that my topic was less contentious because, unlike with adults, children cannot consent to be in pornography and the resulting images are always illegal.

During a break at the end of my presentation, several women approached me. The one arriving first was quick to tell me that she disagreed with my comments concerning consent by adult women. She stated that primarily because of our male-dominated society women are brainwashed and cannot truly make such decisions. I actually enjoy discussing such dissenting opinions. As we engaged in an intense but respectful discussion concerning this, however, a second woman standing nearby was becoming increasingly agitated. She finally interrupted and told the first woman to leave me alone and stop harassing me. She proclaimed that she knew I was right because when she was 12-years-old she had been sexually "molested." With that, the first woman replied that she knew I was wrong because when she was 12-years-old she had been "raped." They then began to engage each other in a heated disagreement. With that, I politely walked away. Ever since I have wondered why, although both women had apparently been sexually victimized at the age of 12, one identified herself as a child who had been *molested* and the other as a female who had been *raped*. Recognizing that not all cases are the same, I suspected this was most likely influenced by the details and dynamics of their individual victimizations. Over the years, I have thought about this incident many times and speculated about what those circumstances might have been. This discussion is rooted in that long ago encounter and supported by my more than 30 years experience and analysis since.

What exactly do the terms *rape* and *molestation* mean and imply? Are there variations in definitions as these terms are commonly used and do they matter? To what extent does the term *rape* apply to the sexual victimization of children? Are there differences between *rape* and child-*molestation* cases? Is a sexually victimized 12-year-old girl the victim of rape or molestation? Does it matter if a child cooperates or complies in the sexual activity? Does a chapter on sexual victimization of children belong in a book on rape investigation?

In 2015 media reports of three cases further illustrate these issues. I do not accept the total accuracy of media accounts of crimes. However, these cases will be briefly discussed here only to stimulate thought and discussion about the confusion created by variations in perceptions, terminology, and definitions of sexual victimization. In addition, the media is how most people get their information and form their opinions concerning criminal sexual activity.

In one case, a female high school teacher pleaded guilty to sexually victimizing three adolescent boys who had been her students. Multiple media accounts concerning this case consistently reported that the sexual activity between the teacher and the boys was clearly not the result of threats or use of force or violence.

The media stories contained statements such as: "Prosecutors say she befriended the boys, allowing them to hang out in her classroom, and the relationship later turned sexual," "One victim testified that the relationship began with kissing between class periods and eventually led to intercourse," "Another said he considered her to be his girlfriend during their yearlong sexual relationship," "The prosecutor acknowledged that the teenage boys were flirtatious with her," "Victim having problems at home would cut class to hang out with her," "Victim had sex with her in a church parking lot, at her home, and at a park over 9 months," "The mother of one of the boys told the judge she believed she was grooming him," "Defense attorney claimed the state failed to establish probable cause to believe that the intercourse that occurred was without consent," "The defense attorney claimed she was relentlessly pursued for months by these young **men** (emphasis added)," and "Judge said you were the adult, you were the teacher, you were the one that could have stopped that from happening."

However, the media also reported the following: "She was charged with rape after police investigated three counts of unlawful sexual activity with a minor," "She pleaded not guilty to felony rape charges in court in a head-turning tight top," "Her lawyer asked a judge to throw out three counts of 1st degree felony rape and one count of 1st degree felony sodomy," "One civil lawsuit was withdrawn after state attorneys said the schools are not responsible for injuries arising from assaults," "She pleaded guilty in exchange for having 11 other charges dropped, including three 1st degree felony rape charges," "She pleaded guilty to three counts of forcible sexual abuse, a 2nd degree felony," "Her attorney said she agreed to the plea deal because she wasn't sure what might happen at trial," and "The severity of the charges stem from the incident involving a teacher and a student."

Whether or not the boys cooperated in or even initiated the sexual activity, they are still victims of a crime. But do terms like *assault*, 1st degree felony *rape*, and 2nd degree felony *forcible sexual abuse* imply that threats or force and violence were used? Although the information provided by the media accounts does not indicate any use of force, the teacher pleaded guilty to forcible sexual abuse. Is the sexual activity considered forced solely because it was between a teacher and students? Was it initially considered *rape* only because intercourse was involved? If the teacher had not pleaded guilty would a jury have expected evidence that she used threats or force? Did the defense attorney deliberately refer to the victims as "young men" to imply their consent should matter? Was the media observation that the teacher was dressed in a "head-turning top" included in the story to help explain and justify the behavior of the adolescent boy victims?

In the second 2015 case, a young man was charged with six sexual assault charges, three of them felonies and put on trial. The charges involved events that took place when the defendant was an 18-year-old senior and the victim was a 15-year-old female freshman at the same high school. The media described it as "the trial of a former student at an elite prep school accused of raping a freshman as part of a tradition called Senior Salute." The victim alleged her sexual assault involved penile and digital penetration and oral sex against her will after she clearly and repeatedly told him "no." The defendant alleged the two did have sexual contact but it consensual and did not involve sexual intercourse.

The jury heard all the evidence and testimony in the case. When the jury's verdict came back it appeared they did not totally believe either the defendant or the victim. They found the defendant not guilty of the aggravated felony charges involving penetration against her will (i.e., rape) but guilty of misdemeanor charges involving penetration knowing she was under the age of 16 and the age difference between them was less than four years. The jury believed that, unlike the defendant alleged, they did have sexual intercourse but that, unlike the victim alleged, sexual activity was not violently forced against her will.

The media reported, "a jury cleared him of rape and convicted him instead of misdemeanor sexual assault for having intercourse and other sexual contact with an underage girl" and "didn't believe the assertions that he and the girl didn't have intercourse but also didn't believe her contention that it was against her will." Interestingly, the jury did find the defendant, who had used an online computer to help arrange the meeting with his high school classmate, guilty of a felony charge of using a computer to seduce, solicit, lure, or entice a *child* to commit a sexual sex assault. The defendant was ultimately sentenced to one year in jail and was ordered to register as a sex offender.

To oversimplify, the jury decided the victim was a child who had been *molested* and not a woman who had been *raped*. Was the 15-year-old girl the victim of sexual violence? Was the online solicitation law intended for situations involving high school classmates using social media to meet? If an 18-year-old high school senior tries and succeeds in nonviolently seducing a 15-year-old freshman at his school into having sex, does that make him a dangerous sex offender? Is he then a child molester, a rapist, or a sexual predator? Is a 15-year-old "underage girl" the same as a child? If the 15-year-old girl was not forced into the sexual activity why did she allege she was when force was not required in order for the activity to be a crime? Is her post-offense behavior in this case consistent with that of many other compliant child victims? How does typical advice to prevent sexual victimization of children (e.g., say no, yell, and tell) apply to this case?

In the third case, two defendants were on trial for the highly publicized aggravated rape and sexual battery of an unconscious 21-year-old woman. State law indicated that sexual battery sometimes was also called "sexual assault" and the media repeatedly referred to this crime as a "sexual assault." As was all the other perspective jurors, a male was specifically asked if he had ever been the "victim of rape or sexual assault" or if anyone he knew had been the "victim of unwanted sexual touching." He answered no and was eventually placed on the jury. After the two defendants were found guilty, it became known that that when he was a 16-year-old boy this male juror had been a "victim of statutory rape." Defense attorneys quickly filed motions for a mistrial. During a hearing on the defense motion, this juror testified that he neither lied nor intentionally misrepresented himself. He answered no because he did not consider himself to be a "victim." He said he was in a consensual relationship with a 23-year-old neighbor. He had engaged in sexual activity with this man over 100 times and even met with the man after charges were filed. He indicated that his parents had pursued the prosecution and he was against it. The defense attorneys did not challenge the nature of his victimization. They did describe him, however, as "deceitful and manipulative" with an agenda and claimed he should have discussed his "rape case" when given the chance. In spite of the juror's explanation, the judge overturned the convictions with the failure to disclose "the truth" resulting in the presumption of jury bias.

I do not know for certain the details of this juror's victimization or if he deliberately lied or intended to mislead the court. From a layperson's perspective, however, his answers could be considered reasonable and accurate. Although still a crime, his sexual victimization was nothing like what allegedly happened to the victim in this case. His victimization was not "unwanted" and did not constitute "rape or sexual assault" as most people understand the terms and as they were being applied to this case. The problem and need for a costly retrial was caused, at least in part, by the use of poorly worded, defined, and understood voir dire questions. So-called "statutory rape" of a child does not require an assault and may be wanted. Many such compliant child victims do not believe they are victims and often disclose their victimization with many seeming and embarrassing contradictions.

The various charges and outcomes in these cases may have been the result of meticulous analysis of the statutes and deliberate legal strategy, but they are certainly poorly understood by the general public and even many professionals.

Although individual cases can always vary, in this chapter common contrasting factors between sexual victimization of adults and children and rape and molestation will be discussed from a criminal justice perspective. Other perspectives will be considered to the extent that they affect the investigative process. The primary focus of this discussion will be on how these contrasting factors are applied to the investigation of sexual victimization of children by adult offenders. For this discussion children will generally be defined as individuals who have not yet reached their 18th birthday. In spite of this common definition, there is not an absolute and instantaneous dividing line between being a child and being an adult. As children move into adolescence, the dynamics of their sexual victimization become closer to those of adults. In fact, depending on the perspective and circumstances, sexually victimized adolescents might be counted as girls who were molested and females who were raped. In addition, little of what is typically advocated about preventing sexual victimization of children (e.g., say no, yell, and tell) seems to apply to the reality of the development and behavior of most adolescent children.

CONTRASTING FACTORS

Important contrasting rape or molestation factors in sexual victimization of children cases that need to be understood and evaluated by investigators include:

1. **Terminology Used**—There can be important distinctions between precise legal definitions of criminal sexual behavior and a wide variety of imprecise lay definitions. These distinctions can affect perceptions and stereotypes concerning the dynamics of cases. A broad range of legal terms (e.g., "contributing to the delinquency of a child," "indecent liberties or lewd conduct," "sodomy," "aggravated sexual battery," "sexual assault" "solicitation") has been used to refer to sex crimes. Those who sexually victimize children have historically been referred to as *molesters* and those who sexually victimize adults as *rapists*. Is it possible to sexually molest an adult and rape a child? Is the choice of the term used determined by a precise legal definition or vague common usage? The term *rape* has historically involved sexual penetration against the will of the victim. As a result, the term *rape*, more than the term *molestation* generally communicates greater involvement of force and violence. Terms like *assault, forcible sexual abuse,* and *sexual violence* have a similar inference.

   The term *molest* has been defined as to bother, interfere with, or annoy. It has, however, increasingly come to convey some type of sexual activity with children. In fact, a current dictionary defines it as "to annoy, interfere with, or meddle with so as to trouble or harm, or with intent to trouble or harm; to make improper advances to, especially of a sexual nature; or to assault or attack (especially a child) sexually" (*Webster's New World College Dictionary,* 2009). Child molestation is also frequently referred to as *child sexual abuse,* especially when the offender is a family member, or *sexual exploitation of children,* especially when the offender is not a family member such as an acquaintance. I prefer the term *sexual victimization of children.*

   The term *molestation* is still fairly common and used by professionals, including law-enforcement officers, and nonprofessionals alike. For some a child molester is a stranger to his victim but not necessarily a father having sex with his daughter. Although the term *rape* has historically been linked more with the sexual victimization of adults, the sexual victimization of children can certainly involve its traditional elements of penetration against the will of the child. For a variety of reasons, the term *rape* is being used less often and the term *sexual assault* more often. The term *sexual assault* can certainly be applied to both sexual victimization of children and adults but seems to be used more often as a replacement for the violence more often associated with *rape.* Some might differentiate between nonviolent child *molesters* who coax or pressure the child into sexual activity and violent child *rapists* who overpower or threaten to harm their child victims. Variations in who is considered a child and the use of terms such as *statuary rape* make the distinction between *molestation* and *rape* even less clear.

To further complicate the issue, the choice of which term to use is often influenced more by emotion and politics than precise definitions. The exact same case involving the sexual victimization of a child could be referred to as "a teacher had a physical relationship with a teenage student," "a pedophile molested a child," or "a predator raped a baby." Whatever terms are used, their definitions must be clearly understood AND consistently communicated.

2. **Relevance of Consent**—Although there can be legal differences involving certain elements of the offenses and their statute of limitations, for criminal justice purposes the fundamental legal difference between the sexual victimization of adults (i.e., *rape*) and children (i.e., *molestation*) is the issue of consent. In cases involving sexual activity between adults, with a few rare exceptions, there must be a lack of consent in order to have a crime. Children are certainly victimized against their will, but with sexual activity between children and adults, there can be a crime even if the child cooperates or "consents." Legal standards of age of consent for different associated activity (e.g., marry, sex acts, child pornography, abduction, etc.) with different individuals (e.g., adult, peer, parent, teacher, coach, etc.) can differ from state to state and under criminal and civil law. For example, in some jurisdictions 16-year-olds may be able to consent to have sex with the man down the street, but not with their father or schoolteacher. There is sometimes inconsistency in how the law evaluates consent when addressing cases involving sexual partners of varying age differences. In order for sexual activity between peers close in age to be a crime likely to be prosecuted, it would usually have to involve lack of consent in some form (Lanning, 2010).

The relevance of consent is by far the most significant and least understood legal difference between *rape* and *molestation*. Whether or not the child resisted, said "No," was overpowered, immediately reported it, or even enjoyed the sexual activity are not necessarily elements in determining if an adult criminally sexually victimized a child. It might affect the seriousness of the crime (i.e., degree of a felony or misdemeanor). Does emphasizing that children have the right to say no, imply that they then also have an obligation to say no or the right to say yes? Even those children who nonviolently initiate and enjoy the sexual activity with an adult can be victims in the eyes of the law. It is the adult who has the legal obligation and maturity to say "No" to such advances.

To assist in helping sexually active adolescents and adults to better understand the issue of consent the focus used to be on the concept of "no means no." Now many focus instead on the concept of "yes means yes." Sex education in some schools is focusing on the concept that sex is consensual only when both partners are sober and clearly state their willingness to participate through affirmative, conscious, and voluntary agreement every step of the way. Although primarily targeted at college students, it is also being communicated to younger teens and children. Some argue that responses such as "maybe," "OK," "sure," and "fine" all mean "no." Such new administrative standards for consent may be implemented at schools and other institutions, but their affect on legal criteria and the reality of dating behavior remains to be seen.

The term *prostitution* refers to a type of sex related criminal activity in which both parties are technically committing the crime. Because this could also be true for children involved in prostitution, it has become increasingly common to refer to this crime as *human trafficking*. This emphasizes that the child has been forced into the activity against their will. Although such cases certainly do exist, it is not always the case. As when applying the term *rape* to the sexual victimization of children the term *human trafficking* seems to imply there must be lack of consent in order for the child to be a real victim. The term *human trafficking* is emotionally appealing for child advocates but it creates perception problems about the nature of all such cases.

Also related in part to the issue of consent is the investigative relevance of sexually explicit visual depictions of victims recovered during an investigation. Adults can consent to be in such images (i.e., pornography) or the images can be taken without their consent. Either way, the resulting depictions could be valuable collateral evidence in a sexual victimization investigation. Because children can never consent, however, sexually explicit images of children are in and of themselves illegal. Such images, therefore, are not only potential collateral evidence, but can also be the basis for separate criminal charges. Child pornography images can also be created and disseminated (i.e., *sexting*) by the children in the images with no adult involvement. Child pornography should be viewed as both a violation of the law and as possible corroboration of child sexual victimization. Mandatory minimum sentences now result in many offenders facing considerably longer sentences for child-pornography violations than they would get if they were convicted of sexually molesting children.

I use the term *compliant child victim* to describe those children who in any way, partially or fully, cooperate in their sexual victimization without the threat or use of force or violence (Lanning & Dietz, 2014). Consent should not be the determining legal issue with child victims even if they are "compliant," but sadly it often is. The age difference between the parties involved in the compliant sexual activity is also a significant factor. Society and even many professionals tell compliant children in so many ways they are not real victims. They are held to the adult standard for sexual victimization instead of the child victim standard. From a legal or criminal justice perspective, *compliant adult victims* are not victims but *compliant child victims* are victims. I do NOT refer to such children as *compliant child not-victims*. I have repeatedly been told that the consent of children to have sex with adults does not matter. Yet, when I discuss cases in which they are compliant many get upset. If it does not matter, why does it matter so much?

In my extensive experience I have regularly seen how indications of compliance or cooperation by the child victim have needlessly swayed the investigation, prosecution, and sentencing of a serious crime. In fact I have repeatedly been asked to provide expert testimony educating the court about the behavior of *compliant child victims*. It is extremely important to recognize that because children might lie about part of their victimization does not mean the entire allegation is necessarily a lie and they are not victims. Such lying is usually the result of shame, guilt, and embarrassment over their socially unacceptable compliance. Child victims should not be held to idealistic and superhuman standards of behavior. Their frequent cooperation in their victimization must be viewed as an understandable human characteristic that should have little or no criminal-justice significance. Based on my experience the lying of child victims who engaged in compliant behavior concerning varying aspects of their victimization is so common it can be corroborative (Lanning, 2010).

Why such compliance by children is so misunderstood and troubling is influenced by factors such as: (1) the historical concept of *rape*, (2) varying definitions and perceptions of who is a child or minor, (3) differences in how children are viewed when victims and when offenders, and (4) unfortunate emotional rhetoric by some child advocates about childhood innocence.

In theory, the law recognizes developmental limitations of minors and affords them special protection. The reality of age of consent is not so simple. Sympathy for victims is inversely proportional to their age. Understanding all this is especially problematic for the public (i.e., potential jurors), professionals (i.e., teachers, physicians, therapists, clergy members), and even the child victims who lack specialized training in criminal law and may not rely on strict legal analysis. Many have also been influenced by the media, professionals, and prevention programs that either state or imply erroneously all child victims are forced or tricked into sexual activity with adults. When an adult and child have sex under unforced circumstances, the adult is always the offender and the child is always the victim.

By definition, sexual activity between adults is not *rape* if both want it. Sexual activity between an adult and a child can be *molestation* and a crime even if the child wants it. The reason we protect children and do not recognize their legal consent to have sex with adults is not because they are innocent, but because they are developmentally immature (e.g., brain development, cognitive decision making, judgment).

3. **Use of Violence**—Related to consent is the use of violence. For some, this violent aspect is so pervasive that they even prefer the term *sexual violence* to terms such as *rape* or *sexual assault*. This seems to be especially true when referring to the sexual victimization of women. There is a federal *Violence Against Women Act of 1994* (VAWA) that has been reauthorized and expanded three times (2000, 2005, and 2013) and now generally lumps together domestic violence, sexual violence, dating violence, and stalking. In spite of the law's name, it is supposed to be gender neutral and is applied to teens. In either case, the law's name and supporters seem to emphasize the *violent* nature of these crimes. This emphasis is more problematic with child victims.

Discussing or referring to the sexual victimization of children under umbrella terms such as *rape* or *sexual violence* can create unrealistic and unnecessary expectations about the nature of the crime. Some children, especially pubescent adolescents, are violently sexually victimized much like adult rape victims. They are accessed and controlled through the threat or use of force or violence. More children, however, are sexually victimized and controlled through the use of nonviolent techniques such as coercion and grooming. Some of the sexual acts engaged in with a child might be considered violent in nature, but violence is not used as the primary access and control mechanism. In essence, if such victims were adults, the sexual activity would not be a crime. When one adult grooms or seduces another adult it is most often referred to as dating.

An acquaintance child molester who uses violence to control victims is more likely to be quickly reported to law enforcement and easily identified. An acquaintance molester who seduces his victims can sometimes go unreported for years if not indefinitely. The repeated use of terms such as *rape* and *sexual violence* when discussing or inquiring about the sexual victimization of children assumes or implies in the minds of many that all real child victims resist sexual advances by adults; are then overpowered by coercion, trickery, threats, weapons, or physical force; and then report it the first chance they can. Offenders with reasonably good interpersonal skills can usually control children without resorting to threats or use of violence.

In the United States during the early 21st century the term most commonly used to refer to any adult who sexually victimizes a child is *predator*. Many child molesters are certainly predatory in their behavior, but the widespread use of this term can be unfortunate and counter-productive. The term has a very negative connotation and conjures up an image of disguised evil and inevitable violence. In my experience the most prolific and persistent child molesters rarely use violence to manipulate and control their victims. Some child molesters are described as "nice guys" not because they successfully disguised their true wickedness but because overall they actually are nice. Some level of violence is almost always present in the sexual victimization of an adult. Violence, as it is traditionally defined, is frequently not present in the sexual victimization of children.

4. **Sexual Motive**—Obvious sexual behaviors (e.g., vaginal or anal intercourse) can be motivated by nonsexual needs (e.g., power and/or anger). It is often said and widely accepted that rape, which has traditionally required sexual penetration, is not a sex crime but a crime of violence. Offenders who rape adults are the sex offenders most likely to exhibit predominately situational motives and behavior patterns (Lanning, 2010). In my opinion, this is the primary reason it is said so often that *rape* is not really about sex. In spite of this common and politically correct view, some rapists are preferential-type sex offenders (Lanning, 2010) and for whom rape *is* primarily about sex.

One hears it less often said, however, that child molesting is not about sex or is not a sex crime. This is most likely due to the fact that more child molesters exhibit preferential patterns of sexual behavior and often do not use physical force or violence to control their victims (Lanning, 2010). Some have argued, however, that even child molestation is not primarily about sex because there is nothing sexually attractive or arousing about very young prepubescent children. Such an argument indicates total ignorance concerning what it means to be a *pedophile*. Because such children do not sexually arouse most people does not mean the offender's behavior is not motivated primarily by sexual gratification.

Sex can also include deviant sexual acts involving behavior such as sadomasochism, bondage, urination, defecation, peeping, and indecent exposure. Seemingly nonsexual behavior can be motivated by sexual needs. Some offenders who are embarrassed or ashamed of such bizarre preferences with adults may act them out with child victims. In addition, because an offender is motivated predominately by deviant sexual needs, does not mean he cannot also be motivated by some nonsexual needs. The sexual victimization of both adults and children can to varying degrees involve both sexual and nonsexual needs.

5. **Sexual Disorder of Offender**—Those who sexually victimize children are more likely to be labeled with a mental health diagnosis (*Diagnostic and Statistical Manual of Mental Disorders*, 5th Edition) such as *pedophilia* or *pedophilic disorder*. Other than occasionally the diagnosis of *sadism* or *antisocial personality disorder* (*psychopathy*), there is currently no consistent and specific mental health or *paraphilic disorder* for those who rape adults. Attempts to directly link a *paraphilia* to the act of rape have so far been rejected for a variety of reasons. As stated, it is even politically correct to say that rape is not about sex and therefore cannot be a *paraphilia* by definition.

Although the *rape* itself may not be related to a specific recognized paraphilic disorder, some rapists are preferential-type sex offenders and will express their sexual preferences (e.g., ritual) during the commission of the rape. On an investigative level the presence of *paraphilias* often means highly repetitive and predictable behavior focused on specific sexual interests that go well beyond a *method of operation* (MO). The concept of MO—a repeated pattern of behavior engaged in by an offender because it works and will help him get away with the crime—is well known to most investigators. An MO is fueled by thought and deliberation. Most offenders change and improve their MO over time and with experience. The repetitive patterns of behavior of sex offenders can and do involve some MO, but are more likely to also involve the less-known concept of sexual *ritual*. Sexual *ritual* is a repeated pattern of behavior engaged in by an offender because of a sexual need; that is, in order to become aroused and/or gratified a person must engage in the act in a certain way (Lanning, 2010).

During criminal prosecution, sex offenders will sometimes produce forensic, mental-health evaluations diagnosing no sexual disorders. The diagnosis of numerous mental disorders such as depression, bipolar disorder, attention-deficit disorder, anxiety disorder, Asperger's disorder, obsessive–compulsive disorder (OCD), personality disorders, and "Internet-addiction syndrome" is often introduced as mitigating circumstances for consideration, especially in the sentencing phase of the case. Mental disorders such as these are rarely the basis for an insanity-type defense.

Because sexual attraction to prepubescent children is harder for people to understand, some might be more inclined to consider the diagnosis of a mental disorder. Most, however, do not care about such a disorder and believe there is no cure for it anyway. If there is a diagnosis of sexual disorders argued in court, it is rarely disorders such as *pedophilic disorder* or *sexual sadism disorder*. Such disorders are more publicized and have significant emotional impact. Arguing to the court that you have them will rarely help an offender.

6. **Victim Access and Number of Incidents**—Other than in date-rape cases, the perpetrator in a rape case is more often a stranger or slight acquaintance that the victim cannot identify by a correct name. Although strangers do sexually victimize children, in about 90% of molestation cases the perpetrator is a family member or acquaintance that the child can usually correctly identify by name. In rape cases, each victim is more likely to be victimized by an offender in one incident during a shorter time frame. In child-molestation cases, each victim is more likely to be victimized by an offender in multiple incidents over an extended period of time. However, as with children sexually victimized by acquaintances, many adults victimized by an acquaintance in a dating situation may be reluctant to disclose due to their feelings of shame, guilt, and embarrassment.

7. **Disclosure and Interviewing Process**—Why child or adult victims do not all promptly disclose their sexual victimization is a complex issue. There is still a stigma attached to being the victim of sexual assault. With cases involving child victims certain dynamics especially applicable to children must be understood. Disclosure issues involving child victims are the primary reason why the statute of limitations for the prosecution of such cases is typically longer or nonexistent.

   Interveners cannot rely on or expect all children to resist and report their sexual victimization. Child victims who are seduced, manipulated, or have engaged in compliant sexual behavior often lie to varying degrees to make their victimization more socially acceptable or please an adult. Such child victims, even after becoming adults, either deny their victimization or disclose it in inaccurate ways because they suffer from varying degrees of shame, guilt, and embarrassment. Failure to immediately report it, initial denials when questioned about it, attempts to describe it in more socially acceptable ways, varying versions of what happened, embarrassment and shame, and reluctance to tell their parents, guardians, or others, and anger over the relationship ending are all consistent with child victims seduced and manipulated by an adult offender. Underlying such behavior is often an effort to meet expectations and the legal requirements of a so-called *rape* case.

   If children in molestation cases do lie, it may be because factors such as shame or embarrassment over the nature of their victimization increase the likelihood they will misrepresent the sexual activity. Investigators must recognize and address these dynamics when interviewing child victims. The standard for adult victims of sex crimes should not be automatically applied to child victims. It makes no sense to ask children to tell parents/ guardians or authority figures only about unwanted sexual contacts. They are children. Sexual activity with adults is a problem whether or not it is wanted. Society in the United States tends to have stereotypical concepts of the innocence of children and malevolence of those who sexually victimize them. Even some trained professionals seem to have an emotional or political need to believe all child victims are forced into unwanted sex by violent predators.

   Both adult and child victims can struggle with and be reluctant to admit having had pleasurable physiological responses to forced or unwanted sexual activity. This problem can be magnified with child victims who were compliant. The idea that some children might enjoy certain sexual activity or behave like human beings and engage in sexual acts as a way of receiving attention, affection, gifts, and money is troubling for society and many investigators. Interveners who excessively or emotionally refer to the child's sexual victimization as *rape* may, for example, influence the child's version of events to conform to that view. In cases involving sexual exploitation by acquaintances the children interviewed have often not previously disclosed their victimization. They are more likely being interviewed only because the victimization was discovered or a suspected or known sex offender had access to them. These types of interviews are extremely difficult and sensitive.

   There are also significant differences between how universities covered by Title IX U.S. Education Amendments of 1972 handle reports of sexual victimization of adult students and how K-12 schools covered by mandatory reporting laws handle reports of sexual vic- timization of child students. Although not always done, schools are generally required to report suspicions of child abuse to the lawful authorities (e.g., law enforcement, child pro- tective services). Under Title IX and U.S. Department of Education guidelines, however, colleges and universities are required to make every effort to comply with victim requests for confidentiality and to conduct their own administrative investigations of reports of *sexual violence*. The university may conduct such concurrent administrative investiga- tions with little deference for any ongoing criminal investigation by police. In addition, the standard of proof is only a preponderance of evidence resulting in potential expulsion. Many larger universities have their own police departments who I assume would conduct more typical criminal justice investigations. Law enforcement must be aware of university policy concerning their implementation of Title IX and how it will affect their awareness of a crime and investigation.

K-12 schools, universities, and most organizations providing offenders with access to victims seem to have a problem properly addressing, and reporting cases of sexual victim- ization primarily due to some combination of ignorance and damage control.

8. **Prevention Approaches**—Prevention strategies for both adults and children will vary depending on whether the offender is a stranger, acquaintance, or family member. Prevention advice can be divided into avoidance and confrontation strategies. For adults much of the potentially effective avoidance advice (e.g., dress, abuse of alcohol or drugs, high-risk behavior and internet activity, etc.) is considered by some to be politically incor- rect and constitutes blaming the victim. Many potential victims believe they should not have to alter their lifestyle and make accommodations in any way. Adults do have the right to make such choices in their lifestyle but if victimized one result might be more difficulty in proving the required lack of consent. It is their decision to make. I believe, however, that advice focusing more on avoidance strategies is the most effective.

Confrontation advice (e.g., use of weapons, defensive tactics, screaming, etc.) is more popular but often ignores the risks of escalating the violence in ways that increase the like- lihood of more serious injury if the techniques fail. Advocates of such tactics frequently discount those risks and do not address important variations in the personalities of the potential victims and offenders and the location of the confrontation that greatly affect the successful implementation of the tactics.

Some of this prevention advice for adults can be adapted in age appropriate ways to children, but certain differences between adult and child victimization must be understood. Adults bear a greater responsibility for preventive measures than children. Adults but not necessarily children should know better. The avoidance choices of children are often lim- ited by their developmental judgment and control by adults. Avoidance strategies for chil- dren are most often discussed in "stranger danger" and online safety programs. Adults who refuse to adjust their lifestyle choices seem to have no problem instructing children to do so. Telling children to "do as I say and not as I do" does not seem to work very well, especially as children get older. Confrontation advice is often too simplistic and unrealistic.

Ignoring the fact that research tells us that 99% of children abducted by a nonfamily member are released relatively unharmed (Hammer, Finkelhor, & Sedlak, 2004), chil- dren are routinely told to scream, struggle, and fight when confronted by a stranger. As with confrontation advice to adults, the increased risks of harm involved in resisting this way are usually not mentioned. Much of the prevention advice targeting children simply ignores their developmental reality. As stated, the primary reason we do not recognize the consent of children is because of their developmental immaturity.

In cases involving offenders who are acquaintances and family members, the most common confrontation advice for children seems to be some version of "say no, yell, and tell" or "recognize, resist, and report." What is usually ignored is the fact that children are human beings and not angels from heaven. Children learn to manipulate their environment to get what they want from birth. Adolescent children are interested in sex and often engage in high-risk behavior without considering or comprehending the consequences. Children are human beings with normal needs, wants, and desires. As human beings and like adults, many children are willing to trade sex, whether or not they fully understand what it is, for the affection and attention of a nice guy or potential boyfriend or girlfriend. Many victims wind up suffering from "say no, yell, and tell" guilt based on what they were told in prevention programs. Again, their consent is not supposed to matter.

Advice to prevent the sexual victimization of children by adult acquaintances is more complex and challenging to implement. How do you warn children about molesters who may be their teacher, coach, clergy member, therapist, or Internet "best friend forever" (bff) and whose only distinguishing characteristics are they will treat the children better than most adults; listen to their problems and concerns; and fill their emotional, physical, and sexual needs? Will families, society, and professionals understand when the victimization is suspected, discovered, or disclosed (Lanning, 2010)?

A great deal of prevention advice simply does not distinguish to which types of sexual victimization it applies. For example the right to say "no" or resist would be applied differently to an unknown individual or stranger, family member, teacher, or coach. The sexual harassment policies of any organization are inadequate to address sexual victimization of children because they have limited application to children. By definition sexual harassment involves UNWANTED sexual advances. When targeted at children, such advances are a problem whether wanted or not.

Adolescents are frequently considered and counted by child advocates as children in order to emphasize the large scope of the child-victimization problem. But then often little or nothing said or done about addressing the problem seems to apply to the reality of adolescent victims. If adolescents are considered child victims of sexual exploitation, then their needs, interests, and desires must be realistically recognized and understood when addressing the problem.

Does an adult bear any responsibility for becoming a victim of rape or domestic violence because he or she didn't follow prevention advice? Does a child bear any responsibility for becoming a victim of sexual molestation because he or she didn't follow prevention advice? When used in prevention programs, the term *predator* will often be inconsistent with the perceptions of potential child victims. Moreover it may incorrectly suggest to staff members, parents, guardians, and program participants that people who are pleasant, kind, and helpful cannot be sex offenders. If the term is used, any discussion should clearly include the possibility such predators may regularly practice their faith, work hard, be kind to neighbors, love animals, and help children.

9. **Evaluating False Allegations**—The issues of both child molestation and violence against women have significant emotional and political perspectives that make objectively dealing with false allegations very sensitive and difficult. Some advocates seem to feel that assessing and evaluating and attempting to corroborate allegations is unnecessary and somehow constitutes revictimization or making them feel threatened or unsafe. Law enforcement investigators can be child or victim advocates in general, but not during their investigation of a specific case. Objectivity with some skepticism is a proper and professional response (Lanning, 1996). It is not the investigator's job to believe but to listen to an alleged victim. Finding corroboration is one of the best things an investigator can do for a victim. The amount of corroborative evidence available might depend on the type of case, sexual activity, and offender(s) involved. Corroboration might be more difficult in an isolated one-on-one case perpetrated by a situational sex offender and easier in a sex-ring case perpetrated by an acquaintance-preferential sex offender (Lanning, 2010). Lack of corroboration when there should be corroboration is significant when evaluating allegations

In a rape case the investigation usually focuses on determining if the alleged single sexual event actually took place and there was lack of consent. As stated, the element of lack of consent is the key investigative difference between sexual victimization of adults and children. It can often be difficult to prove lack of consent beyond a reasonable doubt and alleged victims sometimes furnish inaccurate information about it.

In a child molestation case the investigative focus is usually on evaluating the consistency over time of multiple alleged sexual events. Allegations involving multiple acts, on multiple occasions, over an extended period of time must be evaluated in their totality, consistency, and context. Cases involving long-term sexual contact with child victims who engaged in compliant behavior should not be assessed and evaluated by comparisons to cases involving isolated, forced sexual assaults.

Many indicators suggesting a false allegation in a rape case have little application to the evaluation of most acquaintance child-molestation cases, especially those involving repeated access and prolonged sexual activity. Such child-molestation cases are very hard to classify as either a valid or false allegation. Victim claims may include allegations that appear to be false, but that does not mean the case can be labeled in totality as "a false allegation." I once consulted on a case in which a behavioral analyst improperly attempted to evaluate an allegation of sexual victimization of a child using the criteria for false allegations set forth in a book on rape investigation.

The behavior and reactions of such child victims should not be evaluated for consistency with that of victims who have been forced against their will, but with that of victims who have been manipulated into their victimization. Failure to immediately report it, initial denials when questioned about it, attempts to describe it in more socially acceptable ways, varying versions of what happened, embarrassment and shame, and reluctance to tell their parents/guardians and others, and anger over the relationship ending are all consistent with child victims seduced and manipulated by an adult offender who is an acquaintance. When many of these child victims eventually do disclose their victimization, they are often mad and feel deceived and used when they find out the offender had a new girlfriend or will no longer respond to their contacts. Similar behavior (e.g., denial, lying, changing versions, inconsistencies), however, can be seen in cases involving false allegations. Juries have the right to hear and consider all explanations for such behavior. Making some false allegations does not necessarily mean an entire allegation is false. The court can sometimes be assisted in this evaluation through the use of an education witness who is a true expert in the type of case being adjudicated.

10. **Criminal Investigative Analysis**—Because the offender is frequently a stranger, behavioral analysis of an allegation of rape usually focuses on developing a *profile* or personality description of the unknown perpetrator. In a date-rape case in which the offender's identity is usually known, the behavioral analysis would typically focus on the issue of evidence of lack of consent. Each victim, however, is usually sexually assaulted one time by the offender. Other analysis efforts can involve linking cases together and evaluating if the offender is a serial rapist.

Sexual *ritual* and its resultant behavior are determined by erotic imagery, are fueled by fantasy, and can often be bizarre in nature. Most important to investigators, offenders find it difficult to change and modify *ritual*, even when their experience tells them they should or they suspect law-enforcement scrutiny. The ritual patterns of many sex offenders have far more significance as prior and subsequent like acts than the MO of other types of offenders. Understanding sexual *ritual* is one key to investigating certain sex offenders.

Because the offender is most often a family member or acquaintance, behavioral analysis of an allegation of child molestation usually focuses on evaluating the consistency of the allegations and, if valid, how to prove the case against the offender whom the child victim can name. Especially with acquaintance offenders, each offender can have multiple victims and each victim can be victimized multiple times.

CONCLUSIONS

Some might consider an analysis such as this to be irrelevant nitpicking. However, my more than 40 years experience has repeatedly illustrated to me how varying and inconsistent definitions and stereotypical and inaccurate perceptions can influence how cases are investigated, prosecuted, and decided. Applying adult standards for sexual victimization to children excludes a significant number of child victims. I would like to believe that the best way for professionals to counteract inaccurate and misleading stereotypes concerning the sexual victimization of children is to educate people with accurate and factual information. The well-intentioned but unrealistic idealization of children only makes the problem worse for many child victims. Objective investigation should be about facts not feelings.

Professional fact-finders should understand and use correct, clear, and consistent definitions for their terminology. In many ways, definitions are more important when discussing than investigating cases. Insight and understanding should be communicated during investigations and prosecutions, but especially in interviews with the media and presentations in training and prevention programs. Clear understanding can also affect perceptions concerning who is a victim of a crime and why.

Objective professionals need to use precise language and minimize concepts involving all offenders as *evil predators*, and all children as *innocent victims*. Grooming is an explanation to help understand the reasonable behavior of child victims and not an excuse to help maintain an unreasonable belief in the innocence of children. Generalized statements about all offenders and all victims should be limited. To use an old cliché, "apples should be compared to apples."

To avoid unrealistic and problematic expectations when referring to the sexual victimization of children the term *rape* should be reserved for cases clearly involving sexual penetration and lack of consent and the term *sexual violence* should be reserved for cases clearly involving threats or physical violence to access and control the victim. In an ironic twist, in child victim cases (*molestation*) in which lack of consent is not necessarily required, many want the investigation to confirm it. In adult victim cases (*rape*) in which it is usually required, many want the investigation to ignore it.

REFERENCES

Hammer, H., Finkelhor, D., and Sedlak, A. 2004. *Missing, abducted, runaways, and thrown away children in America*, NISMART-2. Washington, DC: U.S. Department of Justice, Office of Justice Programs, Office of Juvenile Justice and Delinquency Prevention.

Lanning, K. V. 1996. The "witch hunt," the "backlash," and professionalism. *The APSAC Advisor*, 9(4): 8–11.

Lanning, K. V. 2000. Compliant child victim: Confronting an uncomfortable reality. In E. Quayle and M. Taylor (Eds.), *Viewing child pornography on the Internet* (pp. 49–60), Dorset, United Kingdom: Russell House Publishing.

Lanning, K. V. 2010. *Child molesters: A behavioral analysis*, 5th ed. Alexandria, VA: National Center for Missing & Exploited Children.

Lanning, K. V., and Dietz, P. E. 2014. Acquaintance molestation and youth-serving organizations. *The Journal of Interpersonal Violence*, 29(15): 2815–2838.

Webster's New World College Dictionary (2009). New York, NY: Random House.

20 The Sexual Crimes of Juveniles

John A. Hunter

CONTENTS

Introduction...319
Developmental Issues 320
Typology Research...321
    Modus Operandi..322
Violent Juvenile Sex Offenders...323
Investigative Issues..326
    Detection 326
    Guidelines for Interviewing Juvenile Sex Offenders 326
Mental Health Evaluations...327
Disposition Decision Making and Management...328
Effective Community Programming 329
Treatment Focuses 330
Treatment Outcomes 330
Juvenile Sex Offender Registration and Community Notification 333
References...333

INTRODUCTION

Juveniles (typically defined as those under 18) accounted for 14% of the arrests for forcible rape and 18% of the arrests for other sex crimes (excluding prostitution) in the United States in 2012 (UCR, 2012). Consistent with overall trends in youth-perpetrated violence, juvenile sexual crime peaked in the early 1990s and has declined since that time (UCR, 2005). Statistics do show that juvenile arrests for forcible rape have decreased more dramatically than arrests for other sex offenses, and that in recent years there has been an increase in the number of juvenile females who have been arrested and brought before the court for sex crimes (excluding forcible rape; Snyder & Sickmund, 2006). While the arrests of juvenile females for sex crimes has increased since the mid-1990s, it should be kept in perspective that juvenile females account for only about 2% of juvenile arrests for forcible rape and 9% of juvenile arrests for other sex offenses (Snyder & Sickmund, 2006). Hence, data continue to suggest that adolescent males account for the preponderance of cases of juvenile sexual offending.

Public and professional concern about juvenile sexual perpetration rose in the 1990s in response to the referenced rise in juvenile violent crime and retrospective studies suggesting that juvenile sexual offending potentially portended more chronic and insidious patterns of sexual aggression. With regard to the latter, interviews of incarcerated adult sex offenders indicated that 40–50% reported a juvenile onset to their deviant sexual interests and behavior (Marshall, Barbaree, & Eccles, 1991). Furthermore, in many cases such behavior appeared to grow progressively more invasive and serious over time (Abel, Osburn, & Twigg, 1993). While these retrospective studies helped bring needed attention to the problem of juvenile sexual offending, the cited data may have led to an exaggeration of the likelihood that sexual aggression in childhood and adolescence leads to adult offending. At issue are problems associated with retrospective data and sampling biases. As more adolescent sexual offenders were treated and prospectively tracked into adulthood, this impression of the continuity of juvenile and adult sexual offending began to change.

Treatment program outcome data suggest that sexual recidivism rates are relatively low (5–15%) in adolescent males, and that these youths are, in fact, more likely to commit nonsexual than sexual crimes after release from institutional programs (Becker, 1990; Kahn & Chambers, 1991; Caldwell, 2007). However, there is increasing evidence that juvenile sexual offenders are a heterogeneous population with observed differences in patterns of sexual offending (e.g., victim sex and age), underlying determinants of the behavior, amenability to treatment, and risk of sexual and nonsexual recidivism. Thus, some youths appear more difficult to treat and at higher risk to sexually re-offend than others. The differential characteristics of subgroups of these youths and related typology research are reviewed in this chapter.

DEVELOPMENTAL ISSUES

An understanding of juvenile sexual offending necessitates attention to its underlying causes or etiology. One developmental factor that has received considerable professional attention is a preceding history of *child maltreatment—including both sexual and physical abuse.* The incidence of sexual victimization in adolescent male sexual offenders ranges from 40–80% across studied samples (Hunter, Figueredo, Malamuth, & Becker, 2003). Sexual victimization rates appear to be even higher in sexually abusive prepubescent and female youths (Mathews, Hunter, & Vuz, 1997). Hunter and Figueredo (2000) found that sexually abused male children who went on to sexually offend as adolescents could be differentiated from their similarly victimized, but nonoffending counterparts on four variables:

1. They were younger at the time of the initial sexual victimization.
2. They reported a higher number of incidents of abuse.
3. They reported that they waited a longer period of time to report their abuse.
4. Upon reporting, they experienced their families as being less supportive of them.

These results are consistent with the belief that the earlier and more intense the developmental trauma is, the more debilitating its effects are. The findings also point to the importance of familial and social support in coping with and overcoming the effects of trauma.

Consistent with high rates of childhood sexual victimization, approximately two-thirds of adolescent male sexual offenders report a history of physical abuse by a father or stepfather (Hunter et al., 2003). Such reported histories can be linked to higher measured levels of depression and anxiety in adolescent male sex offenders (Hunter et al., 2003). Also prevalent in samples of these youths are reported histories of exposure to violence against females and male-modeled antisocial behavior; a preadolescent onset to pornography and substance use is associated with such exposure. Research suggests that early and prolonged exposure to interpersonal violence is particularly detrimental when it occurs in the absence of counterbalancing prosocial experiences. Many juveniles who engage in delinquency and sexual aggression not only have been exposed to violence, but also have not had close relationships with healthy male and female role models. Thus, they may be more vulnerable to the internalization of antisocial values.

Research suggests that aggressive and delinquent youths often harbor the belief that aggression is an acceptable and effective means of resolving interpersonal conflict and achieving goals (Lochman & Dodge, 1994). Frequently coupled with a belief in the utility of aggression are demonstrated deficits in self-efficacy and social competency (Zigler, Taussig, & Black, 1992). Therefore, these youths not only believe that aggression will lead to interpersonal success, but also perceive themselves as likely to fail if they employ alternative problem-solving strategies. Childhood exposure to violence against females has been linked to lower levels of emotional empathy in adolescent male sexual offenders and exposure to antisocial males to higher reported levels of emergent delinquent behavior during adolescence (Hunter, Figueredo, Malamuth, & Becker, 2007).

While most juveniles who engage in sexual and other forms of delinquency appear to desist from engagement in such behavior as they enter adulthood, in some cases these behavioral patterns may reflect a downward-spiraling developmental trajectory. Studied differences among subgroups of these youths are summarized in the following discussion.

TYPOLOGY RESEARCH

The observed heterogeneity of adolescent male sexual offenders has complicated legal and clinical decision making and led to efforts to develop an empirically sound typology and decision-support tools. The author's initial typology research suggested that a meaningful differentiation could be made between those youths that sexually offend against younger children (5 or more years younger) and those that target peers and adults. In one of the first studies to explore this dichotomy, Hunter, Hazelwood, and Slesinger (2000a) compared 62 offenders against children with 64 offenders of peers and adults. Comparisons were made on victim selection and crime modus operandi using police investigative records.

"Peer/adult" offenders were found to be more likely to have a female victim (93.7 vs. 67.7%) and to have selected a victim who was either a stranger or an acquaintance (84.4 vs. 59.7%). They were also more likely to have committed their offense in a public area (e.g., park; 28.1 vs. <10%) and to have acted in concert with other offenders (28.1 vs. 6.5%). This group of juvenile sex offenders was also more likely to commit the sex crime in association with other criminal activity (23.8 vs. 4.8%) and displayed higher levels of aggression and violence in commission of the offense. In this regard, 27% of the peer/adult offenders displayed moderate or greater physical force during the assault in contrast to 8.3% of the offenders against children. Similarly, 26.2% of the peer/adult offenders used a weapon, in contrast to 16.1% of the offenders of children. Finally, within the small subset of juvenile sex offenders that murdered their victim, 85.7% were offenders of peers and adults.

In a follow-up study of 182 adolescent male sex offenders in institutional treatment programs, Hunter et al. (2003) further researched this dichotomy. As predicted, juveniles that sexually offended against pubescent females employed more force in the commission of their reference sexual offense and were more likely to use a weapon and be under the influence of alcohol or drugs at the time of the offense. They could also be differentiated from offenders of prepubescent children in that they were less likely to be related to their victim and commit the offense in the victim's home or their own residence, as opposed to another setting. These youths were also more likely to have a prior arrest history for a nonsexual crime and, upon personality assessment, demonstrated less anxiety and depression, and fewer pronounced social self-esteem deficits.

In more recent typology research, Hunter and colleagues have explored the presence of three major, prototypic subtypes of adolescent male sexual offenders using Knight and Prentky's (1990; Prentky & Knight, 1991) combined "deductive-rational" and "inductive-empirical" research strategies: using theory and existent research to formulate the prototypic subtypes and then conducting empirical studies to validate and refine them. The three theoretically formulated subtypes are (1) life-course persistent (LCP) youths, (2) adolescent nonparaphilic youths, and (3) early adolescent-onset, paraphilic youths. The first two subtypes were informed by Moffitt's theory of youth-perpetrated delinquency. Specifically, it was hypothesized that LCP youths are those who manifest long-standing patterns of delinquent and aggressive behavior and show evidence of underlying psychopathy in their personality makeup (i.e., superficial relationships, impulsivity, callousness, etc.; Moffitt, Caspi, Dickson, Silva, & Stanton, 1996). In addition to their being relatively psychopathic, it was hypothesized that they tend to aggressively seek dominance interpersonally and manifest specific hostility toward females. The latter construct (i.e., hostile masculinity) has been studied by Malamuth, Linz, Heavey, Barnes, and Acker (1995) as a predictor of sexual aggression in adult males. It involves viewing females in a negative and pejorative manner, including the endorsement of rape myths.

Similar to Moffitt's second subtype of delinquent youths (i.e., adolescent-onset), adolescent-onset, nonparaphilic sexual perpetrators were hypothesized to engage in transient sexual offending—either as a form of adolescent experimentation or in compensation for psychosocial deficits that impair their ability to form and maintain healthy peer relationships. The third group of youths, early adolescent-onset, paraphilic, is believed to represent cases of early-onset pedophilia. As such, they are similar to one of Knight and Prentky's adult child molester subtypes in that they are hypothesized to be primarily motivated in their sexual offending by deviant sexual interests.

Cluster analysis was applied to data from a national sample of 256 adolescent male sexual offenders receiving sex offender treatment in an institutional or community-based setting. Initial results (Hunter, Conaway, Figueredo, Malamuth, & Becker, 2007) suggest the presence of five subgroups of these youths: (1) life-course persistent–antisocial, (2) adolescent-onset–experimenters, (3) socially impaired–anxious and depressed, (4) pedophilic interests/antisocial, and (5) pedophilic interests/nonantisocial. In brief, both the life-course persistent–antisocial and pedophilic interests/nonantisocial subgroups evidence lengthy childhood histories of exposure to violence and an early developmental onset to the viewing of pornography and drug/alcohol use. The primary difference is that the former group appears more inclined to sexually offend against peer and adult females than the latter.

Of the five prototypic subtypes, the life-course persistent–antisocial subgroup has the highest rate of arrests for nonsexual crimes and appears to have the highest reported rate of childhood exposure to violence. Adolescent-onset–experimenters appear less psychosocially and psychosexually disturbed than other subgroups and report less childhood exposure to violence and less preadolescent pornography/substance use than either the life-course persistent–antisocial subgroup or the pedophilic interests/antisocial subgroup. They also appear to have the lowest average number of victims of the five subgroups; however, in their victim choice and adolescent-manifest pattern of alcohol and drug use, they more closely resemble life-course persistent–antisocial youth than either socially impaired–anxious and depressed youth or those in the pedophilic interests/nonantisocial subgroup. The latter two subgroups appear to sexually offend predominantly against children. The author's current research involves the longitudinal tracking of these subgroups through treatment in an effort to further test hypotheses about subgroup differences in treatment amenability and response. These results will be published as new data are gathered and analyzed.

Modus Operandi

Hunter et al. (2000a) examined the modus operandi of juvenile sex offenders, including where the crimes were committed and how the offender gained control over the victim. Juveniles that offended against children most frequently committed their sexual offenses in the victim's residence (63.9%), followed by the perpetrator's residence (when other than the victim's residence; 13.1%). Fewer than 10% committed their offenses in a public area. Most of these juvenile perpetrators approached the victim without explanation or use of threat or force (over 40%), or they used trickery or guile to gain victim compliance (about 25%). Threat to the victim or victim's family was evidenced in only 16% of the cases and physical force or coercion in 12.5%.

Threat, intimidation, and coercion appeared to play a more prominent role in how offenders against children maintained control over the victim and maintained victim silence. Approximately one-third of these adolescents used intimidation and 17.6% used physical force to maintain control; 29% threatened harm to the victim or his family if he revealed the sexual assault. Although the majority of the offenders against children did not display high levels of violence, their sexual assaults were quite invasive. Penis–vaginal rape was reported in 69% of the assaults of female children and penis–anal rape in 46.45% of the assaults of younger males.

Juvenile offenders against peers and adults committed their offenses in both the victim's residence (45.3%) and public areas (28.1%). Most frequently (40.4%), they would lie in wait for the victim and "surprise" him or her. A "blitz" attack, wherein there was the immediate use of injurious force, was evidenced in 12.8% of the cases. Intimidation and force were commonly displayed as means of maintaining control over peer and adult sexual assault victims. Intimidation was used in close to one half of the cases, a weapon in 29.2%, and injurious force (other than with a weapon) in 16.7%. Over one-fourth of these victims were threatened with violence if the assault were to be revealed. The majority of the sexual assaults (63.5%) involved penis–vaginal rape; penis–anal rape was evident in 19% of the cases.

VIOLENT JUVENILE SEX OFFENDERS

While the majority of juvenile sex offenders do not appear to be highly aggressive or violent, a subset of these youths engages in instrumental or gratuitous violence. As previously noted, these youths are more likely to be those who target peers or adults than those who offend against children. However, even within the subpopulation that targets children, there are those youths that seriously injure or kill their victims.

Violence in juveniles has been studied as a function of personality and family characteristics. Youths low in social competency and those viewing aggression as an effective means of achieving interpersonal goals display higher levels of interpersonal violence than other youths. Similarly, those youths with long-standing difficulties with impulse control and affect modulation manifest higher levels of delinquency and aggression throughout childhood and adolescence (Block, 1995; Caspi, Henry, McGee, Moffitt, & Silva, 1995).

A number of violent youths also appear to score high on measures of risk taking and novelty seeking (Sigvardsson, Bohman, & Cloninger, 1987; Krueger et al., 1994). These traits may be related to psychopathy, a strong predictor of violence in adults (Harpur & Hare, 1994). Psychopathic adults have been described as shallow, callous, and lacking in remorse, and they often lead unstable and antisocial lives. Psychopathy may be manifest in childhood and displayed in the form of impulsivity, insensitivity, and problem externalization (Frick, O'Brien, Wootton, & McBurnett, 1994; Lynam, 1998). Finally, a number of family factors have been found to be associated with violence in youth, including parental criminality, harsh parental discipline, and authoritarian child-rearing attitudes (Farrington, 1989).

Aggression in juvenile sex offenders has also been studied in relationship to crime scene characteristics. Hunter et al. (2000a) found that "victim difficulty" better predicted level of violence than indices of "environmental risk" (risk of detection), alcohol/drug use during the crime, or "degree of planning/control." Victim difficulty was computed for analytic purposes to reflect effort required in gaining control over the victim based on the victim's gender, age, and level of resistance to the attack. The product of being a male victim, of an age representing greater physical prowess, and offering greater resistance to the assault predicted higher levels of perpetrator violence. In this study, both child and peer/adult victim resistance tended to result in a response of physical force from the adolescent perpetrator.

Hunter, Hazelwood, and Slesinger (2000b) extensively analyzed seven cases wherein the juvenile perpetrator murdered the victim. A peer/adult offender committed six of these homicides. Only one of these victims (a 9-year-old boy) was a male and none were related to the offender. The scene of the crime varied. Three of the victims were murdered in their homes, one in the home of the perpetrator, one in a convenience store, and two in outdoor locations. Based on review of police interrogation reports, it was concluded that in only two cases did the assailant immediately display violence. In the remaining cases, there was an escalation of violence. The perpetrator used a weapon in six of the seven cases. The weapon was a knife in two cases, a gun in one case, and a blunt object in the remainder. In two cases, it was apparent that the victim had been intentionally tortured. The sexual assault involved penis–vaginal rape in three cases, penetration with a foreign object in two cases, cunnilingus in one case, and apparent penis–anal rape in another. In three of the seven cases, there was evidence suggesting that the victim had been raped postmortem. Three of the victims died of strangulation, two as a result of stabbing, one by gunshot, and one from massive internal bleeding. In two cases, there was evidence of "overkill" (i.e., much more violence than needed to end life).

CASE NO. 1

A 15-year-old Caucasian female was repeatedly bludgeoned with a large rock and assaulted with a wooden stick by a 15-year-old Hispanic male. The victim knew the assailant and had been seen leaving a party with him prior to the offense. According to the offender, he was engaging in consensual sexual intercourse with the victim when he experienced impotence and was subsequently ridiculed by her. The assailant stated, "I went nuts," and described beating the victim with his hands and then a rock. The victim was found with a sharp 11-inch wooden stick penetrating her vagina. The victim had died as a result of multiple cranial and internal injuries, including a perforated bladder. The assailant had no previous sexual or nonsexual arrest record.

CASE NO. 2

A 54-year-old white female was strangled, then raped postmortem by a 15-year-old black male in her home. The assailant was an acquaintance of the victim and lived on the same street. The victim had allowed the adolescent to enter her home after he requested to use her dryer. The youth confessed to having pretended to leave the victim's home, only to hide and attack the victim by surprise. He reportedly strangled her with a telephone cord before raping her and fleeing with about $2.25 in change and the victim's car keys. The youthful murderer was apprehended 4 days later at his high school, where he had been keeping the victim's car.

Among violent juvenile sex offenders are isolated cases of emerging or fully developed sexual sadism. Sexual sadism is a paraphilia that involves sexual excitement and arousal to the psychological or physical pain, suffering, or humiliation of others. It is by nature chronic and persistent. Although seemingly rare, these cases reflect the potential for a pattern of violent and very dangerous sexual offending. The following case is presented to illustrate how sexual sadism can have an early developmental onset and portend a pattern of progressively more serious and violent sexual offending.

CASE NO. 3

"A" was 10 years old when he was first referred for residential treatment by his home state's Department of Social Services. This referral was made with the support of his biological mother and stepfather following revelation that he had vaginally and anally raped his 4-year-old brother and 2-year-old sister. Notably, the younger brother had also been burned with an iron by the perpetrator. The local juvenile court had been notified of the assaults, but had chosen not to become formally involved due to the perpetrator's age and familiarity with the family.

"A"'s initial presentation was unremarkable. Like the majority of pre-pubescent youth engaging in sexual offending, he had a prior history of sexual victimization. He related that the adolescent male son of his babysitter had anally sodomized him when he was approximately 4 years old. This apparently happened on several occasions when he was spending the night at the babysitter's house while his mother was working. "A" related in therapy sessions that he always believed that his mother knew about his victimization but chose to do nothing about it. However, he freely admitted that he did not tell anyone about the abuse until much later and therefore there was no obvious reason why she should have known.

"A" did not seem different than other young children in the residential program and was judged to be responding well to treatment. He was generally compliant with therapeutic directives, was not a major behavior problem, and did reasonably well in school. His parents, although out of state, remained in close contact with "A" and participated in telephonic and "face-to-face" family therapy sessions. He verbalized a strong desire to not repeat his behavior, expressed remorse for the sexual offending, and demonstrated competence in taught self-control skills.

"A" was discharged after approximately 13 months of residential treatment to the custody of his mother. The discharge plan called for him to spend nights with his maternal grandparents to reduce the risk of sexual offending. The grandparents lived in the same neighborhood with the mother and the plan permitted "A" to be able to fully participate in family functions under adult supervision. Arrangements were also made for him to see a juvenile sex offender treatment specialist in a nearby town. However, the mother later admitted that she did not follow through on this recommendation.

"A"'s mother re-contacted the residential treatment center approximately 1 year after his discharge and requested that he be re-hospitalized. She was quite distraught while revealing that "A" had sexually re-offended against his younger sister, and in an even more serious manner than previously. "A" presented for treatment the second time as a more surly, non-remorseful, and less compliant 13-year-old. Several months of intensive clinical work and case investigation were necessary before he revealed the full extent and motivations for his sexual re-offending. "A" eventually revealed that he had deliberately tortured his then 4-year-old sister on numerous occasions by slapping and choking her, vaginally and anally raping her, pouring a caustic cleaning agent into her vagina, and forcing her to eat molded food and drink his urine. He reported that he had deliberately sabotaged the placement at his grandparents by noncompliance with rules so that he would be returned home and have access to his siblings.

"A" reported that his mother, in an attempt to keep him away from the younger children, would lock him in his room at night and have the grandmother stay in the bedroom of the younger siblings. "A" confided that he had stolen his mother's house key when she was away and gone to a local hardware store where he had a duplicate made. At night, while his mother and stepfather were away working, he would crawl out of his bedroom window (his door was locked from the outside) and enter the house through the front door (using his new key). He would then quietly wait until his grandmother fell asleep, whereupon he would enter his sister's bedroom, put his hand over her mouth, and carry her to his room. Once in his room, he would gag her with a "t-shirt" so that her screams could not be heard, begin his nightly ritual of rape, sodomy, and torture. Following his abuse of his sister, he would return her to her bedroom unbeknownst to the still sleeping grandmother. He would then relock his bedroom door, exit the house through the front door, and re-enter the house through his bedroom window. This behavior continued nightly until the younger sister, previously too afraid to report the abuse because she had been threatened with death, finally in desperation confided to her mother what was happening.

"A" eventually revealed in therapy that he was sexually aroused by his sister's screams of pain and terror, and frequently masturbated to these thoughts. He stated that these urges had been present during his first residential stay, but that he had not reported them to his therapist or the staff because he knew that this would prevent him from being returned to his mother and thus the opportunity to reoffend. He stated that he had left the treatment center the first time with every intention of re-offending and had not taken his treatment seriously. He stated that he had targeted his sister because she was younger and less capable of verbalizing the abuse than his brother. He calmly described how he had planned and fully intended to kill his sister and family before being caught. The plan called for him to kill his sister by choking her. He then was going to set the house on fire and crawl out of his bedroom window, making it look like he and the family had perished in the fire.

INVESTIGATIVE ISSUES

Detection

The author's clinical experience and available relevant research suggest that juveniles are often not apprehended and brought to the attention of the police until after they have committed several sexual offenses. There are numerous reasons for this delay in detection. Victims are often young and may not report the offense out of fear, confusion, or embarrassment. Parents of sibling victims may be hesitant to report the crime because of concern as to what may happen to the youthful perpetrator or family if external authorities become involved. Many adult and peer victims do not report their victimizations out of concern about potentially embarrassing and difficult social and legal consequences. Other victims may not know the assailant and can offer police only limited identifying information.

Because of the difficulty in detecting juvenile sexual offending, criminal investigators are likely to encounter juveniles who have been engaging in sexual offending (whether or not the offending is limited to one victim) for some time. This may be even more likely if the offender is intelligent, socially skilled, and from a "protective" family system (Prentky & Knight, 1993). Obtaining a full and accurate report of the youth's history of offending is typically a significant challenge. This may be even more so today than it was 15 years ago, given the more severe legal repercussions that youths potentially face when acknowledging criminal sexual behavior.

Guidelines for Interviewing Juvenile Sex Offenders

The investigator should expect that the juvenile will be resistant to acknowledging his sexual offenses. Aside from fear of legal consequences, many of the youths apprehended for the first time are embarrassed and confused about their sexual offending and its meaning. Even though the problem may have been present for some time, it is unlikely they have previously talked to anyone about it or spent much time attempting to understand it. For those with previous criminal justice experience, they may see acknowledgment of further criminal activity as a guarantee of correctional placement and hence are poorly motivated to cooperate.

It is generally prudent to interview alleged offenders following the interviewing of the victim, the victim's family (in the case of child victims), and the offender's family (when the victim and offender are living within the same family system). Victims, including young children (see Goodman & Saywitz, 1994) and their families, can provide valuable crime information that can subsequently be used in the interrogation of the juvenile perpetrator. The absence of investigator knowledge of crime detail enhances the likelihood that the offender will completely deny the allegations or minimize the seriousness and extent of the sexual offending.

Hunter, Hazelwood, and Slesinger (unpublished data) found that offender and victim reports of juvenile sexual crimes are frequently discrepant. These report discrepancies traverse both the nature of the assault and the modus operandi of the assailant. For example, in nearly 32% of the cases where the victim stated that vaginal intercourse had been attempted or completed, the adolescent perpetrator denied it. In 75% of the cases wherein the victim stated that force was used by the perpetrator, the perpetrator denied it. Similarly, 45% of the juvenile perpetrators denied the use of a weapon when the victim had reported that one had been used. These data illustrate the importance of thorough interviewing of victims and their families in the investigation of juvenile sexual crimes and the filing of charges.

Effective interviewing of juveniles is a skill that requires attention to both *process* and *content* issues. The following guidelines are offered:

- Interviews are more productive when the youth fully understands the nature of the inquiry and how the information that he provides will be used. In particular, to the extent that he sees cooperation with the investigation as helping portray him in a more favorable light and potentially making him eligible for less severe legal dispositions, he will be more likely to cooperate. Therefore, investigators should be as familiar as possible with how juvenile sexual offenders are processed and disposed by the local courts and share this information with the youth and his family. Especially helpful is the sharing of information about the opportunity for motivated youths and supportive families to receive specialized treatment services in lieu of correctional placement.

- Youths need to understand the seriousness of the inquiry, and confrontation may be necessary at times. However, interviews are generally more productive when conducted in a positive and even-handed manner. Investigators should convey an attitude of confidence and the expectation that the youth will cooperate because it is in his best interest to do so.

- Questions should be posed in a straightforward manner, using language that the youth understands. Pedantic, esoteric, and legalistic terminology should be avoided. Such language is not only incomprehensible to most of these youths, but also apt to increase their anxiety and resistance.

- Investigations should include a focus on how and why the victim was *selected*, the method of gaining *access* to the victim, the means by which the perpetrator gained and maintained *control* over the victim, and whether and how he attempted to maintain *victim silence*. Questions should be specifically directed at determining whether intimidation or force was used and whether a weapon was employed.

- In investigating sexual crimes, it is generally wise to first focus on the *behavioral* aspects of the crime. What did the perpetrator say and do and how, in turn, did the victim respond? Secondly, questions can be directed at the *thinking patterns* or *cognitions* of the perpetrator. What was he thinking about before, during, and after the crime? Lastly, questions can be directed at how the perpetrator *felt* (his emotions) before, during, and after the crime. The reverse of this order of questioning may result in social embarrassment and inhibit the youth from further revelations.

- The investigator should attempt to develop a chronological sequencing of the sexual crimes of the youth. How old was the youth when he first began offending? Is there evidence of a consistent pattern to the offending as it relates to victim age, gender, and type of sexual perpetration? Is there evidence of a progression in the nature and seriousness of the offending over time? Particularly important is the determination of whether the behavior has become more violent over time. Also of legal and clinical disposition relevance is whether there is evidence that the sexual perpetrations reflect sexual compulsivity and paraphilic interests.

MENTAL HEALTH EVALUATIONS

Juveniles arrested for sexual crimes are often referred for mental health evaluations. Sometimes these referrals are made prior to adjudication in an attempt to help determine whether the youth is a sex offender or whether the problem is serious enough to warrant formal legal processing. The author cautions against such pre-adjudication mental health evaluations for the following reasons.

Mental health providers, including those with special training and experience in working with juvenile sexual offenders, enter into a realm of clinical and legal complexity when they attempt to conduct pre-adjudication evaluations. As discussed by Hunter and Lexier (1998), youths facing prosecution are placed in a position of double jeopardy when referred for these evaluations. Their conversations with the mental health evaluator are not confidential to the extent that they reveal information about the abuse of children or danger to self or others. If the youth in the course of a mental health evaluation reveals an unknown sexual crime or previously unknown details of sexual crimes of which he has been accused, he could be prosecuted on the basis of the divulged information. On the other hand, if the youth refuses to talk to the clinician about such matters, he may be construed as uncooperative and unmotivated for treatment. In the latter case, the court may use this information in support of the need for prosecution or perceive the youth as a poor candidate for community-based treatment.

Criminal justice professionals should be aware that there are no psychological or psychophysiological tests, including the plethysmograph, that are valid for determining whether an individual (juvenile or adult) is a sex offender or has committed a particular sexual crime. Therefore, mental health evaluators have no other way of determining the guilt of an individual accused of a sexual crime short of that individual's confessing to the crime. The author notes that the polygraph, though not typically considered a "mental health" evaluation tool, also has limitations for this type of inquiry. Aside from the issue of admissibility in court, its reliability and validity are potentially affected by a number of issues, including the subject's age, his mental status, his level of intelligence, and the examiner's level of training and experience in its administration and interpretation.

This author therefore recommends that mental health and other forensic evaluations be conducted after adjudication and before sentencing. Mental health evaluations should be directed at helping determine the *nature of the sexual behavior problem* underlying the sexual crime, the individual's *level of dangerousness* and *risk for re-offending*, his *intervention needs*, and his *amenability to treatment*. This information should be submitted to the court prior to sentencing to aid in disposition decision making.

DISPOSITION DECISION MAKING AND MANAGEMENT

Courts are faced with critical decisions about what to do with convicted juvenile sex offenders. Should they be committed to corrections or placed in a treatment program? Should treatment and management take place at the level of the community or is institutionalization necessary to maintain community safety and adequately address the youth's needs?

These are obviously difficult questions that require careful consideration of statute guidelines and precedents, public opinion and community resources, and a thorough understanding of the youthful offender and his family. It is with regard to the latter that mental health, probation and parole, and social services professionals can make a contribution. Professionals tasked with making recommendations to the court may want to take into consideration the following:

- The *type of offending* the youth has displayed. Juveniles that offend against peers and adults are generally more predatory and violent. Many are not appropriate for community-based care.
- The youth's level of *denial and accountability* regarding his sexual offending. Research (see Hunter & Figueredo, 1999) supports the relevance of these attitudes at the time of clinical assessment. Youths steeped in denial and those blaming the victim or others for the sexual assault generally perform poorly in community-based treatment programs.
- The individual's past *criminal record* for sexual and nonsexual offenses and his sexual offense history. Those youths with more extensive criminal records and offending histories are at higher risk for re-offending. It should be remembered that nonsexual recidivism rates generally exceed sexual recidivism rates for juvenile and adult sex offenders.
- Assessment of the presence of *paraphilic interests and arousal* and *psychopathy*. Deviant sexual arousal and psychopathy are two of the most robust predictors of sexual recidivism in adults. Although more rare in juveniles, their detection should alert the evaluator to an increased risk for program failure and recidivism. Individuals high in sexual deviance and/or psychopathy are generally poor candidates for community-based treatment.
- The extent to which the youth has *multiple psychological problems* and manifests problem behaviors in a variety of environments (e.g., home, school, community). Youths reflecting pervasive problems require more intensive services and supervision.

- The level of *family support* for the youth and his effective management and treatment. The living environment of the youth is very important in shaping his attitudes toward treatment and willingness to comply with legal and therapeutic directives. Successful community-based management requires the cooperation and support of responsible caretakers. Caretakers must perform critical monitoring functions and be willing to work toward necessary systemic change.
- The *identifications and peer affiliations* of the youth. Youths with antisocial and delinquent affiliations are believed to be at higher risk for further criminal behavior.
- The available *community resources*. As discussed in the following section, effective community-based management requires comprehensive programming reflecting well-integrated criminal justice, mental health, and social services management efforts.

EFFECTIVE COMMUNITY PROGRAMMING

The author is of the opinion that the majority of juveniles that offend against children can be safely and effectively managed within the community. However, successful community management depends not only on the careful screening of referred youths, but also on the development of a comprehensive system of care and management.

Programming for juvenile sex offenders should be conceptualized as a community-wide effort. Key stakeholders should have a voice in both the design and implementation of the program. This includes, but is not limited to, the following: the juvenile and adult courts, the prosecutor's office, the public defender's office, the local schools, social services, and public and private mental health service providers. It may also include representatives from victim advocacy groups and parents of victims and offenders. All of these groups need to work together to ensure that the program fully responds to the needs of the community and operates in accordance with community safety standards.

It is particularly important that an effective interface be achieved between the criminal justice and mental health service delivery systems. In order to fully benefit from treatment, the juvenile must be willing to confront his problems and assume responsibility for his past and future behavior. Treatment requires the willingness of the youth to comply with therapeutic directives and sustain therapeutic diligence. Adjudication and ongoing court supervision and monitoring help ensure that the youth remains accountable for his behavior and fully committed to his rehabilitation plan.

One particularly effective strategy for motivating youths to fully avail themselves of the opportunity to receive help for their problems is to adjudicate and sentence them, then suspend the sentence contingent on successful completion of treatment. Under such arrangements, the court assumes a monitoring role and hearings can be scheduled on a regular basis to review the youth's progress in achieving treatment goals. Recalcitrant youths or uncooperative families can be warned of the consequences of noncompliance and probation can be revoked when necessary.

Probation and parole officers provide an important evaluative and supervisory function within the previously described framework. They help assess whether the youth and family are fully complying with therapeutic and court guidelines and whether the intervention plan seems to be working. They serve as an important conduit of information between the court and service providers and can assist in the identification of needed resources for the youth and family.

The author supports *social–ecological* models of intervention for juveniles with sexual behavior problems. These models (see Henggeler, 1999) are premised on the assumption that delinquent behavior is a product of the individual's interaction with the multiple social environments in which he functions, and interventions should therefore be multisystemic in design and focus. Consistent with this model, interventions for juvenile sexual offenders should reflect an understanding of systemic influences (e.g., family, school, peer group) on the likelihood that the youth will sexually re-offend. Therapists working from this model seek to strategically involve a variety of important caretakers of the youth (e.g., parents, extended family members, teachers) in the implementation and evaluation of the treatment plan.

Hunter, Gilbertson, Vedros, and Morton (2004) describe two model community-based treatment programs for juvenile sexual offenders that adhere to the previously outlined principles. The first is operated by Wraparound Milwaukee and the second by the Norfolk, Virginia, juvenile court. The latter program involves an assessment and intervention team that consists of trained probation/parole officers and mental health providers. Each program has broad community support and a high level of interagency cooperation. While both programs have produced low sexual recidivism rates (under 10%) and demonstrated fiscal efficiency, the longer standing Milwaukee program has demonstrated a reduced utilization of corrections and residential placement for adjudicated juvenile sex offenders. Details about these programs can be found in the referenced publication.

TREATMENT FOCUSES

The treatment of juvenile sex offenders should reflect an understanding of skills necessary for maintenance of control over sexual behavior and the formation of healthy interpersonal relationships. Therefore, therapeutic attention to the following is advised:

- The enhancement of *social competencies*. Rehabilitation is dependent on having the skills to form and maintain healthy interpersonal relationships. Most juvenile sex offenders can benefit from social skills and anger management training.
- The fostering of *self-efficacy and self-esteem*. Youths need to believe in their capacity to make positive life changes.
- Improvement of *impulse control and judgment*. Juvenile sex offenders can benefit from interventions designed to help them understand the thoughts, feelings, and events that led up to their sexual offending and how to control urges to act out. Cognitive–behavioral methodologies designed to improve impulse control and judgment can be useful in helping them deal with both sexual and nonsexual (e.g., substance abuse tendencies) impulse control problems.
- *Male mentoring* and the instilling of a healthy sense of masculinity. Mentoring by older, healthier, and successful males is important to the resocialization of juveniles that have engaged in sexual offending.
- Education in *healthy sexuality*.
- *Victim empathy*. Youths need to understand and fully appreciate the impact that their behavior had on the victim and the victim's family.
- *Relapse prevention*. Each youth and his or her caretakers should have a comprehensive and well-conceived plan for preventing future sexual offending.

TREATMENT OUTCOMES

Largely because of a dearth of federal funding, very few randomized clinical studies have been conducted on the treatment of juvenile sex offenders. Extant studies were largely conducted by practitioners of multisystemic therapy (MST; see Borduin & Schaeffer, 2001). However, there are quite a few noncontrolled outcome studies that suggest that the majority of treated juvenile sex offenders do not go on to sexually re-offend or become adult sex offenders. For example, Waite et al. (2005) found that less than 5% of 261 male juvenile sex offenders treated in a state-corrections juvenile sex offender program sexually reoffended over a 2- to 11-year follow-up period. Alexander (1999) reviewed 79 treatment outcome studies and found that the sexual recidivism rate for treated juvenile sex offenders was approximately 7%. Furthermore, there is evidence that treated juvenile sex offenders have lower sexual recidivism rates than those who do not receive treatment. Worling and

Curwen (2000) found that 5.17% of treated versus 17.8% of nontreated youths sexually re-offended over 2–10 years. Walker, McGovern, Poey, and Otis's (2004) meta-analysis supported the effectiveness of treatment for juvenile sex offenders ($r = 0.37$) and suggested that cognitive–behavioral approaches were the most effective form of treatment.

The author has published three studies (Hunter & Santos, 1990; Hunter & Goodwin, 1992; Hunter, Ram, & Ryback, 2008) that suggest that specialized cognitive–behavioral methodologies (e.g., satiation therapy) are effective in reducing paraphilic (i.e., "deviant") sexual interests in adolescent male sex offenders. In the Hunter and Santos study, 20 treated youths achieved a 39.3% reduction in phallometrically measured arousal to male pedophilic cues over a 2-month treatment period and a 33.5% reduction in arousal to female pedophilic cues. In the most recent study (Hunter et al., 2008), a 19-year-old pedophilic youth who participated in satiation therapy (note: this study utilized an "A-B-A-B" quasi-experimental research design) showed significant reduction to self-reported sexual interest in male children over the course of treatment. Whereas arousal to young males was 96%—the magnitude of arousal to same-age males upon treatment inception, it was only 24% at study termination.

The last case example illustrates how even severely sexually disturbed youths, with extensive psychiatric comorbidity and limited intellectual capacity, can benefit from intensive intervention when motivation is sustained.

CASE NO. 4

"E" presented for treatment as a 16-year-old bi-racial male with a history of attempted rape, school failure, and out-of-control behavior within the home. Prior to admission, he had approached a female clerk in a clothing store with a knife and directed her to a back room where he intended to rape her. The assault was prevented by a customer entering the store and calling for help. "E" later confided to his therapist that he frequently fantasized of stalking women and violently raping them. His potential for sexual aggression had been in evidence for approximately 1 year prior to the attempted rape. He had attempted to fondle a female teacher providing him with home-bound instruction and had aggressively grabbed a female technician who had entered his room at the state psychiatric hospital where he initially had been placed for observation.

In addition to having a sexual behavior disorder, "E" was diagnosed in the residential sex offender program as suffering from paranoid schizophrenia, depression, and mild mental retardation. He verbalized feelings that women laughed and made fun of him, and required a very high level of supervision to prevent aggression toward female staff. He was observed as being challenging of male authority as well, and was prone toward physical and verbal outbursts when frustrated. He frequently stated that he felt that his condition was hopeless and that he was destined to sexually reoffend and consequently spend the remainder of his life in prison.

An African-American family had adopted "E" at birth. His adoptive parents divorced when he was approximately 4 years old following a lengthy history of paternal alcoholism and spousal abuse. "E" vividly described numerous incidents when he was a young child where he had witnessed his father verbally abuse and physically beat his mother. He verbalized having wanted to rescue his mother from his father's abuse during these times, but being afraid of incurring his father's wrath and subsequently losing his affection if he attempted to intervene on her behalf.

"E"'s mother stated that he first displayed aggression toward her following an incident wherein he was reprimanded for running about the house in a boisterous and out-of-control fashion. He was wearing his father's denim jacket at the time. When he refused to obey her, she threatened to spank him. At that point, he picked up her broom and threatened to hit her with it.

"E"'s mother stated that he progressively became more difficult to manage in and out of the home as he got older. He reportedly had difficulty making friends as a child and became increasingly socially isolated over time. He ultimately had to be removed from school and placed in "home-bound" instruction after a long history of disobedience and behavioral disruption in the classroom.

While in residential placement, "E" was aggressively treated with a combination of anti-psychotic, anti-depressant, and anti-androgen medications. He also received individual, group, and family therapies. "E" formed a very positive alliance with his male therapist and talked extensively of his uneasiness around females, his underlying sense of inadequacy and hopelessness, and his confused feelings about his father.

An attempt was made to involve his father in "father–son" therapy sessions. Upon arriving for the first such session, the father commented to the therapist (in the presence of his son) that he didn't see how boys in the program could be expected to make any changes in their sexual behavior when they were surrounded by so many scantily clad and sexually tempting females. (It is noted that the females in the program were housed on different units, carefully supervised at all times, and subject to strict dress codes.)

These sessions came to an abrupt halt after "E" unsuccessfully attempted to process with his father how the early childhood witnessing of fights between his mother and father had frightened and confused him. The father immediately stood up, informed "E" that if he wanted to "feel sorry" for anyone that it should be for him, his father, not his mother. He angrily asserted that "E"'s mother was a strong and aggressive person and that she had been the one who had inflicted injury on him, not the other way around. This assertion was made in spite of the fact that the father was approximately 6 feet, 3 inches tall and weighed 250 lbs, the mother was of average height and weight, and there was never the suggestion in "E"'s reports that the mother had ever initiated any of these incidents. Much to the distress of "E" (and the therapist), the father stormed out of the session, never to return. According to "E"'s mother, the father drove to her home to confront her on putting these ideas in his head, and said that he was going to "punish" "E" for telling the therapist about these events by not coming back to see him anymore.

"E" became progressively more attached to his individual therapist over time and began to verbalize that he saw him as a "father" figure. Although he episodically became distraught and pessimistic that he could prevail in learning to control his aggressive sexual urges, aggressive outbursts became less frequent and intense over time. Anti-androgen medication appeared to be helpful in diminishing, and eventually eliminating, fantasies of wanting to attack and rape women. Anti-psychotic medication appeared effective in improving the quality of his thinking and judgment, and anti-depressant medication in helping improve his mood. "E" also responded well to special education and vocational training.

Due to the severity and clinical complexity of his problems, "E" required residential placement over a period of 5 years. The treatment plan included his very slow and progressive re-introduction into therapeutic environments that included females.

Ultimately, he was able to interact with female staff and residents in a variety of therapeutic settings without displays of behavioral aggression or volatility, and go on supervised community and family (with mother) outings. He was also able to form a number of important and "emotionally corrective" relationships with female peers. Prior to discharge, he was placed in a transitional living environment within the residential program (i.e., group home–like setting). Discharge was not effected until he demonstrated behavioral and emotional stability for an extended period of time (24 months).

Discharge planning involved the careful coordination of services with his mother and his home community. He was ultimately placed in a group home for the chronically mentally ill in his home town operated by the publicly funded community services board. During the day, he attended a day treatment program that included ample opportunity for social and recreational and vocational pursuits. He was able to visit with his family on weekends and holidays. A physician administered and monitored his medications and he was provided with supportive counseling. At last contact with his therapist from the residential program, there had been no episodes of sexual aggression in the 2 years since his discharge from residential care.

JUVENILE SEX OFFENDER REGISTRATION AND COMMUNITY NOTIFICATION

Juvenile sex offender registration and community notification laws have been topics of considerable debate and controversy given the highly restrictive sanctions imposed on juvenile registrants and the relatively weak empirical support for the ability of these programs to reduce recidivism rates (Letourneau & Armstrong, 2008; Caldwell & Dickinson, 2009). Because adjudicated juveniles charged with sexual offenses are assumed to be at a greater risk for reoffending than juveniles charged with nonsexual offenses, their inclusion in sex offender registries has become a priority in legislative efforts to reduce sexual violence and improve community safety (Letourneau & Miner, 2005). Since 1996, every state has complied with the federal mandate to create sex offender registration and community notification laws. As part of the Adam Walsh Child Protection and Child Safety Act enacted in 2006, states have been required to expand sex offender registries to include juvenile sex offenders. To date, at least 37 states have mandated the registration of juvenile sex offenders for qualifying offenses.

Some of the major criticisms of the application of these laws to juvenile offenders have included misguided assumptions about rates of juvenile sexual recidivism, overly punitive restrictions on residency and employment, the application that stigmatizing labels may contribute to reoffending and increased risk of depression and suicide, the conflation of juvenile and adult sex offenders in relation to their risk profiles, and a generally weak evidence base for the effectiveness of these interventions. Rather than supporting the taken-for-granted assumption that juvenile sex offenders have a high risk of sexual recidivism, several studies have demonstrated that there are no significant differences in recidivism rates between sexual and nonsexual offending juveniles (Caldwell, 2007; Letourneau & Armstrong, 2008; Stevenson, Smith, & Sekely, 2013), with some researchers suggesting that sexual offending juveniles are actually less likely to sexually recidivate than other juveniles who commit nonsexual offenses (Calleja, 2015). Furthermore, various researchers have reiterated the need to acknowledge subtypes of sex-offending juveniles who have different risk profiles, patterns of offending, and treatment needs as their conflation can result in mismatched rehabilitation and management approaches as well as net-widening effects in which juveniles at low risk for reoffending are subjected to very stringent forms of community supervision (Malin, Saleh, & Grudzinskas, 2014; Calleja, 2015). It is hoped that the typology research presented in this chapter can help law enforcement practitioners and other professionals engage in more comprehensive risk assessment, appreciate the variability in juvenile sexual offending, and craft dispositions accordingly.

REFERENCES

Abel, G. G., Osburn, C. A., and Twigg, D. A. 1993. Sexual assault through the life span: Adult offenders with juvenile histories. In H. E. Barbaree, W. L. Marshall, and S. M. Hudson (Eds.), *The juvenile sex offender*, 104–117. New York: Guilford Press.

Alexander, M. A. 1999. Sexual offender treatment efficacy revisited. *Sexual Abuse: Journal of Research and Treatment*, 11(2): 101–116.

Becker, J. V. 1990. Treating adolescent sexual offenders. *Professional Psychology: Research and Practice*, 21(5): 362–365.

Block, J. 1995. On the relationship between IQ, impulsivity, and delinquency: Remarks on the Lynam, Moffitt, and Stouthamer-Loeber 1993 interpretation. *Journal of Abnormal Psychology*, 104(2): 395–398.

Borduin, C. M., and Schaeffer, C. M. 2001. Multisystemic treatment of juvenile sexual offenders: A progress report. *Journal of Psychology & Human Sexuality*, 13(3–4): 25–42.

Caldwell, M. F. 2007. Sexual offense adjudication and sexual recidivism among juvenile offenders. *Sexual Abuse*, 19: 107–113.

Caldwell, M. F., and Dickinson, B. A. 2009. Sex offender registration and recidivism risk in juvenile sexual offenders. *Behavioral Sciences and the Law*, 27: 941–956.

Calleja, N. G. 2015. Juvenile sex and non-sex offenders: A comparison of recidivism and risk. *Journal of Addictions & Offender Counseling*, 36: 2–12.

Caspi, A., Henry, B., McGee, R. O., Moffitt, T. E., and Silva, P. A. 1995. Temperamental origins of child and adolescent behavior problems: From age three to fifteen. *Child Development*, 66(1): 55–68.

Farrington, D. P. 1989. Early predictors of adolescent aggression and adult violence. *Violence and Victims*, 4(2): 79–100.

Frick, P. J., O'Brien, B. S., Wootton, J. M., and McBurnett, K. 1994. Psychopathy and conduct problems in children. *Journal of Abnormal Psychology*, 102(4): 700–707.

Goodman, G. S., and Saywitz, K. J. 1994. Memories of abuse: Interviewing children when sexual abuse is suspected. *Child and Adolescent Psychiatric Clinics of North America*, 3(4): 645–661.

Harpur, T. J., and Hare, R. D. 1994. Assessment of psychopathy as a function of age. *Journal of Abnormal Psychology*, 103(4): 604–609.

Henggeler, S. W. 1999. Multisystemic therapy: An overview of clinical procedures, outcomes, and policy implications. *Child Psychology and Psychiatry Review*, 4(1): 2–10.

Hunter, J. A., Conaway, M., Figueredo, A. J., Malamuth, N. M., and Becker, J. V. 2007. Prototypic subtypes of adolescent male sexual offenders.

Hunter, J. A., and Figueredo, A. J. 1999. Factors associated with treatment compliance in a population of juvenile sexual offenders. *Sexual Abuse: Journal of Research and Treatment*, 11(1): 49–67.

Hunter, J. A., and Figueredo, A. J. 2000. The influence of personality and history of sexual victimization in the prediction of juvenile perpetrated child molestation. *Behavior Modification*, 24(2): 241–263.

Hunter, J. A., Figueredo, A. J., Malamuth, N. M., and Becker, J. V. 2003. Toward the development of a typology. *Sexual Abuse: A Journal of Research and Treatment*, 15(1): 27–48.

Hunter, J. A., Figueredo, A. J., Malamuth, N., and Becker, J. V. 2007. Emotional empathy as a mediator and moderator of nonsexual delinquency in juvenile sexual offenders. *Journal of Family Violence*, 15(1): 27–48.

Hunter, J. A., Gilbertson, S. A., Vedros, D., and Morton, M. 2004. Strengthening community-based programming for juvenile sex offenders. *Child Maltreatment*, 9(2): 177–189.

Hunter, J. A., and Goodwin, D. W. 1992. The clinical utility of satiation therapy with juvenile sexual offenders: Variations and efficacy. *Annals of Sex Research*, 5(2): 71–80.

Hunter, J. A., Hazelwood, R., and Slesinger, D. 2000a. Juvenile perpetrated sex crimes: Patterns of offending and predictors of violence. *Journal of Family Violence*, 15(1): 81–93.

Hunter, J. A., Hazelwood, R., and Slesinger, D. 2000b. Juvenile sexual homicide. *The FBI Law Enforcement Bulletin*, 69(3): 1–9.

Hunter, J. A., and Lexier, L. J. 1998. Ethical and legal issues in the assessment and treatment of juvenile sex offenders. *Child Maltreatment: Journal of the American Professional Society on the Abuse of Children*, 3(4): 339–348.

Hunter, J. A., Ram, N., and Ryback, R. 2008. Use of satiation therapy in the treatment of adolescent-manifest sexual interest in male children: A single-case, repeated measures design. *Clinical Case Studies*, 7(1): 54–74.

Hunter, J. A., and Santos, D. 1990. The use of specialized cognitive–behavioral therapies in the treatment of juvenile sex offenders. *International Journal of Offender Therapy and Comparative Criminality*, 34: 239–248.

Kahn, T. J., and Chambers, H. J. 1991. Assessing reoffense risk with juvenile sexual offenders. *Child Welfare*, 19: 333–345.

Knight, R. A., and Prentky, R. A. 1990. Classifying sexual offenders: The development and corroboration of taxonomic models. In W. L. Marshall and D. R. Laws et al. (Eds.), *Handbook of sexual assault: Issues, theories, and treatment of the offender,* Vol. xvii, p. 405. New York, NY: Plenum Press.

Krueger, R. F., Schmutte, P. S., Caspi, A., Moffitt, T. E., Campbell, K., and Silva, P. A. 1994. Personality traits are linked to crime among men and women: Evidence from a birth cohort. *Journal of Abnormal Psychology*, 103(2): 328–338.

Letourneau, E. J., and Armstrong, K. S. 2008. Recidivism rates for registered and non-registered juvenile sexual offenders. *Sexual Abuse*, 20: 393–408.

Letourneau, E. J., and Miner, M. H. 2005. Juvenile sex offenders: A case against the legal and clinical status quo. *Sexual Abuse: A Journal of Research and Treatment*, 17(3): 293–312.

Lochman, J. E., and Dodge, K. A. 1994. Social–cognitive processes of severely violent, moderately aggressive, and nonaggressive boys. *Journal of Consulting and Clinical Psychology*, 62(2): 366–374.

Lynam, D. R. 1998. Early identification of the fledgling psychopath: Locating the psychopathic child in the current nomenclature. *Journal of Abnormal Psychology*, 107(4): 566–575.

Malamuth, N., Linz, D., Heavey, C., Barnes, G., and Acker, M. 1995. Using the confluence model of sexual aggression to predict men's conflict with women: A ten year follow-up study. *Journal of Personality and Social Psychology*, 69: 353–369.

Malin, H. M., Saleh, F. M., and Grudzinskas, A. J. 2014. Recent research related to juvenile sex offending: Findings and directions for further research. *Current Psychiatry Reports*, 16(440): 1–7.

Marshall, W. L., Barbaree, H. E., and Eccles, A. 1991. Early onset and deviant sexuality in child molesters. *Journal of Interpersonal Violence*, 6: 323–336.

Mathews, R., Hunter, J. A., and Vuz, J. 1997. Juvenile female sexual offenders: Clinical characteristics and treatment issues. *Sexual Abuse: Journal of Research and Treatment*, 9: 187–199.

Moffitt, E. E., Caspi, A., Dickson, N., Silva, P., and Stanton, W. 1996. Childhood-onset versus adolescent-onset antisocial conduct problems in males. Natural history from ages 3 to 18 years. *Development and Psychopathology*, 8: 399–424.

Prentky, R. A., and Knight, R. A. 1991. Identifying critical dimensions for discriminating among rapists. *Journal of Consulting & Clinical Psychology*, 59(5): 643–661.

Prentky, R. A., and Knight, R. A. 1993. Age of onset of sexual assault: Criminal and life history correlates. In G. C. Hall and R. Hirschman (Eds.), *Sexual aggression: Issues in etiology, assessment, and treatment*, 43–62. Washington, DC: Taylor & Francis.

Sigvardsson, S., Bohman, M., and Cloninger, C. R. 1987. Structure and stability of childhood personality: Prediction of later social adjustment. *Journal of Child Psychology and Psychiatry and Allied Disciplines*, 28(6): 929–946.

Snyder, H. M., and Sickmund, M. 2006. Juvenile offenders and victims: 2006 national report. Washington, DC: U.S. Department of Justice, Office of Justice Programs, Office of Juvenile Justice and Delinquency Prevention.

Stevenson, M. C., Smith, A. C., and Sekely, D. 2013. Attitudes toward juvenile sex offenders: Predictors of support for juvenile sex offender registration: Educated individuals recognize the flaws of juvenile registration. *Journal of Child Sexual Abuse*, 22: 231–254.

UCR. 2005. Uniform Crime Reports, Federal Bureau of Investigation, Washington DC. http://www.fbi.gov/ucr/ucr.htm.

UCR. 2012. Uniform crime reports, Federal Bureau of Investigation, Washington, DC, https://www.fbi.gov/about-us/cjis/ucr/crime-in-the.u.s/2012/crime-in-the.u.s.-2012/tables/38tabledatadecoverviewpdf.

Waite, D., Keller, A., McGarvey, E. L., Wieckowski, E., Pinkerton, R., and Brown, G. L. 2005. Juvenile sex offender re-arrest rates for sexual, violent nonsexual and property crimes: A 10-year follow-up. *Sexual Abuse: Journal of Research and Treatment*, 17(3): 313–331.

Walker, D. F., McGovern, S. K., Poey, E. L., and Otis, K. E. 2004. Treatment effectiveness for male adolescent sexual offenders: A meta-analysis and review. *Journal of Child Sexual Abuse*, 13(3–4): 281–293.

Worling, J. R., and Curwen, T. 2000. Adolescent sexual offender recidivism: Success of specialized treatment and implications for risk prediction. *Child Abuse & Neglect*, 24(7): 965–982.

Zigler, E., Taussig, C., and Black, K. 1992. Early childhood intervention: A promising preventative for juvenile delinquency. *American Psychologist*, 47(8): 997–1006.

21 Female Sex Offenders

Janet I. Warren and David A. McLeod

CONTENTS

Introduction...337
Theoretical Perspectives on Female Sex Offending 337
Prevalence and Patterns...340
Etiologies of Female Sex Offending..342
    Deviant Sexual Arousal...342
    Psychiatric Disorders and Substance Abuse 342
    Cognitive Distortions 344
    Relational Offending...344
    Domination and Control..345
    Romantic Love 345
Empirical Typologies of Female Offenders 346
Investigatory Significance of the Paradigm 348
References...350

INTRODUCTION

The motivational factors that contribute to female sex offending and the crime scene behaviors that define it are clearly distinct from those that characterize sex offending by men. While there is no doubt that sexual crimes by women occur less often, the undisclosed nature of this particular type of criminal behavior has kept it out of the purview of most policy and programming initiatives and until recently has limited the research that has been conducted concerning it. The intimacy with which women provide physical care to children, combined with the pervasive stereotype of men as the more sexually aggressive gender, has surely contributed to this lack of attention to the issue. However, the emergence of sexual registration laws across the country has helped to augment the research into different patterns of female offending. These studies have been enriched by more recent research that seeks to describe the specific offense styles of female sex offenders, to provide ecological theories of the internal and external factors that contribute to offending, and to illustrate the distorted attitudes that appear to be unique characteristics of women who sexually offend against children. Research into child protection service systems, as well as the nature of the child sexual abuse encountered within them, has also begun to provide estimates of the frequency at which women are found to be responsible for the sexual abuse of children within the family and as part of their role as caretakers. The current chapter reviews the data that are available on this topic, and includes a discussion of its investigative significance to law enforcement and child protective service investigators.

THEORETICAL PERSPECTIVES ON FEMALE SEX OFFENDING

Early attempts to scientifically study sexual deviancy were formalized by Krafft-Ebing in his publication of *Psychopathia Sexualis* in 1886. His work represented the first medical text that sought to describe and classify the full range of deviant sexual behavior that had been observed by the medical profession, and it used case studies to introduce various etiological theories of the conditions that were being examined. The majority of his text was devoted to sexually deviant behavior observed in men, although he did reference certain behaviors that he had observed to occur not infrequently among women.

Coining the term *masochism* after the writings of Sacher-Masoch, Krafft-Ebing referred to this behavior as "the association of passively endured cruelty and violence with lust" (p. 27). He observed that cases of this type were recurrent among women, but that cultural customs at the end of the nineteenth century tended to repress their manifestation and reporting. He went on to describe two cases he had experienced directly and one that he had heard about from a physician at the General Hospital of Vienna. He made reference to instances of "periodic insanity," in which female patients experienced a pronounced increase in their sexual feelings and behaviors. A condition he termed *hermaphroditism* or *virginity* involved females who experienced themselves sexually to be male. When reflecting on sexual behavior with children, Krafft-Ebing identified patterns observed in nymphomania and satyriasis in which sexual contact was sought with males of all ages, including children. He presented four cases of pedophilia, all involving men, but mentioned the case of one woman who sent her two daughters away, fearing that she might sexually molest them. He also referenced two case studies from a psychiatric textbook that described two women who became sexually excited by children as young as 5 years of age.

Some years later, Chideckel (1935) completed his work on female sexual perversions, describing from historical accounts and case studies instances of tribadism, masochism, sadism, nymphomania, transvestism, bestiality, and exhibitionism. In his writing, he referred to kleptomania as a form of female sexual perversion and reflected on the mental life of the prostitute, suggesting that her experience of inferiority motivated her wish to remain immersed in the life of the brothel. He used a cross-cultural perspective to develop his thesis that female perversions reflected various forms of mental disease that had been manifest throughout history and could be found in civilizations of all levels of cultural advancement. Around the same time, Wulffen (1934) explored sexual deviance among women, observing that some women were sexual criminals who engaged in exploitative and illegal sexual behavior, including several cases of sexual abuse against children.

The incestuous longings that constitute the oedipal complex of psychoanalytic theory became a central therapeutic construct in the first half of the twentieth century, as Sigmund Freud began to describe the "family romance" that he believed characterized the emotions of all developing children. When first beginning the practice of psychoanalysis, Freud believed the reports of incest that he heard from his patients were true and that the rate of sexual abuse involving children was extraordinarily high. However, as his experience grew, he came to perceive that in many instances what he was hearing was the expression of an unconscious fantasy that expressed the child's eroticized love of the parent. This realization helped to define his description of the unconscious mind and the oedipal complex, two central psychodynamic constructs that continued to influence psychoanalytic treatment and theory for the next 100 years.

Over the ensuing years, concerns began to be expressed by some child advocates who began to assert that this particular component of psychoanalytic theory was prompting therapists to disregard true accounts of sexual abuse and to misinterpret as unconscious fantasies the real sexual crimes that were occurring against children. This controversy continued to plague the field for the next 50 years, and contributed for many years to confusion concerning the acceptance and investigation of allegations of childhood sexual abuse, specifically those that involved female abusers. Fueling this type of controversy were publications such as the one by Rosencrans (1997), who summarized nine cases of grown men who had in fact been sexually abused by their mothers for many years as they were growing up. These men consistently reported telling no one of their ongoing sexual involvement with their mothers, and referred to it as the most hidden aspect of their lives.

In the 1960s, efforts to understand patterns of sexual offending began to move away from psychodynamic explanations of intrapsychic conflict and began to focus on behaviorism and the environmental influences that supported the development of behavioral patterns related to sexual life. These behaviorist conceptualizations of sexual offending were influenced by McGuire, Carlisle, and Young, who in 1965 published the article, "Sexual deviation as condition behavior: A hypothesis". This publication revolutionized thinking about behavioral approaches to sexual deviance, hypothesizing that early accidental or abusive sexual experiences were of central importance because they provided the material that was invariably integrated into an individual's masturbatory fantasies. According to this theoretical perspective, each act of masturbation served to strengthen the habit force of deviant imagery, culminating over time into a paraphilic form of sexual expression. Moreover, if the initial fantasy began to lose its evocative power, it would be restimulated by an increase in its deviant content. McGuire et al. suggested that with the continued conditioning of the deviant masturbatory fantasy, the nondeviant responses of the individual began to decrease in appeal and "simply fade away" over time (Laws & Marshall, 2003, p. 84).

Based upon this description of sexual offending as a distorted manifestation of sexual desire, behavioral treatment programs began to emerge which sought to reduce the deviant sexual fantasy of the offender. These interventions tended to employ phallometric assessments of the deviant sexual fantasy followed by behavioral therapies designed to bring about reduction of deviant sexual arousal. These varied across different treatment programs but over time included reconditioning through thematic shifts, fantasy alternation, directed masturbation, and satiation (Laws & Marshall, 1991). Research on these approaches resulted in contradictory findings concerning the long-term efficacy of these treatments and gradually led to the expansion of these ideas into a cognitive–behavioral approach to understanding and treating sex offenders.

The new cognitive–behavioral approach continued to address the issue of deviant sexual arousal, but recast it as only one part of the larger constellation of experiences that lead to sexual offending. From this broader perspective, this expanded treatment approach began to focus on the social and communication skills that were found to be deficient in many sex offenders (Marshall, 1971; Barlow, 1974), these being attributes that were deemed to be in need of remediation if the individual was to be provided opportunities for developing interest in appropriate sexual acts and partners. Later developments added treatment modules designed to address assertiveness, sexual dysfunction, and gender role behavior, eventually culminating in a relapse prevention framework. This treatment format focused on the individual's specific risk factors for reoffense, including broad lifestyle factors, cognitive distortions, deviant sexual arousal, and deficits in coping skills (Marques, 1984). The relapse prevention program became popular across varied treatment settings but was tested only on men, who constituted nearly 99% of the individuals arrested for sexual crimes and sentenced within the criminal justice system. At the time, no efforts were made to identify the cognitive processes and sexual fantasies that were unique to women who offended sexually.

However in 1984, Finkelhor and Russell began to discuss the specific facets of female sexual offending, with Wolfe (1985) providing illustrative case examples and Cavanaugh-Johnson (1988) describing 13 female offenders aged four to 13 years who were treated in a specific program for abuse-reactive children. These efforts were followed by a summary of 44 treatment programs for female sex offenders (Knopp & Lackey, 1987) and eventually books by Elliott (1994) and Saradjian (1996). These publications confirmed that rates of sexual abuse by female offenders were greater than originally thought, and that their offending behavior and treatment needs were quite different than those of men.

In 1999, Ward and Keenan sought to expand the relapse prevention model of sex offender treatment by identifying certain implicit theories held by male sex offenders who sexually abused children. These theories were presented as reconstructions or mental representations that could be used to explain the cognitive distortions often found with sexual offenders. As such, they appeared to integrate the individual's knowledge, convictions, suppositions, ideas, opinions and desires in such a way that enabled them to offend sexually against children. Ward and Keenan identified five of these implicit theories, including the notion that children were sexual objects characterized by sexual desires and the ability to make sexual choices, that the perpetrator was a special kind of person who was entitled to have their sexual needs met when and with whom they wanted, that the world was a dangerous place and that it was necessary to fight back and achieve dominance and control over others, that the world was essentially uncontrollable and inexorable in its actions and that the offenders has been endowed with deviant preferences that they were unable to suppress or manage, and that sexual activity was predominantly beneficial and unlikely to harm another person. In 2009, Beech,

Parrett, Ward, and Fisher sought to explore these implicit theories and concluded that with the exception of entitlement, female sex offenders shared similar cognitions as their male counterparts.

The most current theoretical perspective concerning female sex offenders tends to focus on their repeated exposure to trauma over various periods of their lives. The effects of trauma on brain development have been well-documented by the adverse childhood experiences study (Felitti et al., 1998; Foege, 1998) which found that adverse life experiences disrupted brain development, leading to impairments in social, emotional, and cognitive functioning. These impairments have been further attributed to many female sex offenders, being viewed as precursors to inadequate emotional regulation, diminishing the ability of the individual to cope with the stress and demands of parenting and resulting in what can manifest as ineffective, neglectful, or even abusive parenting styles. A second pathway of these early traumatic events has been theorized to contribute to distorted concepts of appropriate sexual relationships and an inability to manage appropriate sexual self-regulation (Elliott, Eldridge, Ashfield, & Beech, 2010). Perry (2000) and Cozolino (2010) have also produced an extensive array of studies detailing the developmental disturbances that emerge as a result of exposure to prolonged trauma throughout childhood and adolescence. McLeod, Natale, and Johnson (2015) have applied these findings to female sexual offenders and associate these types of experiences with the problems in attachment and appropriate boundary definitions found commonly among women who sexually offend against children.

These neurodevelopmental pathways have been documented in empirical research, which demonstrates that women who sexually abuse children have often grown up in chaotic families characterized by the presence of various forms of sexual and physical abuse, in many instances perpetrated by multiple offenders (de Young, 1982; Korbin, 1986; Marvasti, 1986; O'Connor, 1987; Cooper & Cormier, 1990; Cooper, Swaminath, Baxter, & Poulin, 1990; Travin, Cullen, & Protter, 1990; Allen, 1991; Sheldrick, 1991; Higgs, Canavan, & Meyer, 1992; Freel, 1995; Hislop, 1999; Miccio-Fonseca, 2000; Nathan & Ward, 2002; Nelson, 2003). When compared to male offenders, the trauma histories of female sex offenders are far more significant and complex (Strickland, 2008). Miccio-Fonseca (2000) assessed the family dynamics of 18 female sex offenders and found that 56% described a family member who had seriously hurt or killed another person, and 50% had a family history characterized by suicidal behavior. Elliott et al. (2010) studied 43 female sex offenders referred for treatment between 1998 and 2007 and found that 42% reported being the victim of childhood sexual abuse, 49% reported having poor attachment to their primary care-giver, 51% reported parental rejection or neglect, and 67% reported some combination of emotional, physical, or sexual abuse.

Comparisons between female and male sex offenders further indicate that female sexual offenders tend to have been abused by a larger number of perpetrators, and to have been abused more frequently by individuals within their family, including siblings. The abuse they experienced was also found to begin at an earlier age and to last for a longer duration of time than the abuse experienced by their male counterparts (Oliver, 2007; Frey, 2010). Hislop (1999) found that the sexual abuse experienced by women who had molested children was generally severe in nature. Of the 43 female sexual offenders in her study, 32 reported a history of childhood sexual abuse beginning, on average, at 7 years of age. The abuse that did occur was also found to continue for an average of 8 years. Fromuth and Conn (1997) surveyed college women and found that 22% acknowledged having had sexual contact with younger children, usually when they were children or adolescents. None of these young women had ever come to the attention of the police or mental health counselors, and yet 77% of these young women reported having been sexually abused prior to their own sexual experiences with children.

PREVALENCE AND PATTERNS

Over the past decades, it has been assumed that only a very small proportion of sexually abusive or aggressive acts occurring each year are perpetrated by women, an assumption that is being challenged by recent research suggesting that the scope and implications of female offending behavior is more significant than previously imagined (Colson, Boyer, Baumstarck, & Loundou, 2013). The available research, however, varies considerably depending on the sources from which the data are collected, and the available studies often contain significant disparities in the details of offending behavior and the offender and victim profiles associated with the crimes.

In 1979, Groth reported on a retrospective study of 348 male sexual offenders. Within this group, he found that 8.3% of the men reported having been sexually abused by a female adult, and 4.3% reported that the perpetrator was a somewhat older, female peer. In their reexamination of data collected as part of the American Humane Association (AHA) (1987) and National Incidence Studies (National Clearinghouse on Child Abuse and Neglect), Finkelhor and Russell (1984) found that 6% of female victims and 14% of male victims were abused by a female adult during childhood.

Risin and Koss (1987) identified 216 college males who reported having been sexually abused in childhood. Almost four-fifths of this sample indicated that they did not tell anyone about the sexual abuse while it was occurring, and over half of these young men reported that their childhood sexual abuse had been perpetrated by a female. Rosencrans (1997) reported on 93 females who had been sexually abused by their mothers as children. As with the men, 95% of the women reported that they had not told anyone about the abuse while it was occurring. Over two-thirds of these women reported being sexually abused by more than one adult, a finding that supported the growing literature documenting revictimization of sexually abused children both prior to and after reaching adulthood.

McLeod (2015) recently conducted a secondary analysis of data from the National Child Abuse Neglect Data System (NCANDS) from 2010, and found 66,765 substantiated child sexual abuse cases, 13,492 or 20.9% of which had a female as the primary perpetrator. Within this sample, the male perpetrators offended against male victims in 19.9% of the substantiated complaints and female victims in 80.5% of the substantiated complaints. In contrast, the female offenders sexually abused male victims in 31.8% of the substantiated complaints and female victims in 68.2% of the substantiated complaints. The male and female perpetrators were both found to have victims ranging in age from newborn to 18 years of age; however, the women had a greater prevalence of abusing younger victims ranging from 5 to 9 years of age. The relationship between the victim and perpetrator also varied based upon the gender of the perpetrator. Perpetrators of child sexual abuse were four and a half times more likely to be female if the perpetrator was the biological parent of the child, and three times more likely to be female if the child was adopted. The perpetrator of the abuse was also more likely to be female if the child was experiencing drug-related problems, had a disability, or had prior reports of having been sexually abused. Perpetrators were more likely to be a male if they were a step-parent of the abused child, or if the child victim suffered from a cognitive disability or behavioral problems. The age of both the male and female perpetrators ranged from 18 to 70 years of age, with the female perpetrators tending to offend between the ages of 27 and 39 years, and the male perpetrators between the ages of 20 and 42 years of age (McLeod, 2015).

Using this large dataset, McLeod and Craft (2015) also analyzed gender differences in the ways in which child protective and criminal justice systems responded to men and women who sexually offended against children. They found that women were more likely to be involved in child welfare services at the time of the abuse and to be receiving higher levels of mental health, substance abuse, family-centered, and economic services than their male counterparts. The women in the sample were also slightly more likely to be referred to the police following a substantiated report of child sexual abuse. However, after this initial referral, women were subject to farther-reaching diversion practices and ultimately represented only 1% of the sex offenders incarcerated for their sexually abusive crimes.

De Cou, Cole, Rowland, Kaplan, and Lynch (2014) recently presented an ecological process model of female sex offending and reported that 5% of all known sex offenders were female, but that women were implicated in up to 18.5% of sexual offenses identified in the United States each year (Bureau of Justice Statistics, 2010; Cortoni, Hanson, & Coache, 2010). They maintain that female sex offenders tend to offend while in the company of a co-perpetrator, and offend most often against known victims within the context of a care-taking role. Several other studies have confirmed that female offenders are more likely to offend against their own biological children, the children of relatives, or children in their care (O'Conner, 1987; Fehrenbach & Monastersky, 1988; Lewis & Stanley, 2000; Giguere & Bumby, 2007; Elliott et al., 2010; Wijkman, Bijeveld, & Henriks, 2010; Tsopelas, Spyridoula, & Athanasios, 2011).

ETIOLOGIES OF FEMALE SEX OFFENDING

DEVIANT SEXUAL AROUSAL

The cause of sexual offending in women is still largely unexplored, with no clear answers concerning whether women can experience a relatively exclusive pedophilic interest in children. Cooper et al. (1990) offered one case description of a 20-year-old woman, suggesting that she was a pedophile based upon a clinical assessment combined with psychological, psychometric, and physiological testing. The case report, however, suggested that the woman also suffered from borderline personality disorder with polymorphous eroticism colored by sadistic, masochistic, and pedophilic elements. Bouchard (1994) described the case of one woman whom she categorized as a fixated pedophile on the basis of psychological testing and assessment. By her account, the woman was egocentric and lacking in emotional development, with little concern for others. She was described as being sexually attracted to children but the case review failed to document whether she experienced comparable levels of arousal to adults of either sex.

Hindman (2000) reported on 21 women who were evaluated using photoplethysmography after being charged with a sexual offense against a child. The results indicated that only a small number of the subjects demonstrated sexual arousal to prepubescent bodies and that, when this did occur, the women also showed indications of arousal to either male or female adults. Larson and Maison (1987) described pansexual behavior among a group of women who were being treated for having sexually offended against children. They described the group as coming from families in which language was laden with sexual innuendo, clothing was designed to be sexually provocative, and continual touching of the sexual areas occurred. One woman in this group had engaged in sexual behavior with her adult children, their spouses, and her grandchildren. Another one of the women had offended against a number of different children, including a 2-year-old boy.

Nathan and Ward (2002) conducted a study of 12 female sex offenders and found that 41% of their sample demonstrated some level of deviant sexual arousal. Saradjian (1996) observed that female sex offenders who were initially coerced by their male partners did not exhibit significant levels of masturbatory fantasies involving children. Ford (2006) observed that different types of female sex offenders might manifest different levels of deviant sexual arousal, with those who offended alone or who treated their child victim as a surrogate partner possibly experiencing higher levels of arousal to the child. Suschinsky, Lalumière, and Chivers (2009) observed that female sexual arousal patterns were more emotionally determined and appeared to be motivated more by the desire to be wanted or by romantic feelings.

A recent study of a female pro-pedophile website found that the majority of the women contributors were frank about their sexual interest in children, but described themselves as "girl lovers" who were nurturing and loving in their involvement with children. According to Lambert and O'Halloran (2008) these women distinguished their sexual interest in children from that manifested by men whom they described as being predatory and misogynistic.

PSYCHIATRIC DISORDERS AND SUBSTANCE ABUSE

Sexual offending by women, as is true for men, is often associated with various types of behavioral health and personality disorders. Green and Kaplan (1994) reported on a small sample of 11 incarcerated female child molesters. Based upon structured diagnostic interviews, they found that, on average, these women suffered from 3.6 different personality disorders. The most common diagnoses were avoidant personality disorder, dependent personality disorder, and borderline personality disorder. Furthermore, Hislop found that 16 of the 43 women in her study met criteria for dependent personality disorder. They described or reported a neediness in their intimate relationships and a desire to be taken care of, combined with an exaggerated fear of abandonment or being alone. Perhaps one of the most common personality-related diagnoses found in the literature on female sexual offenders is borderline personality disorder, a condition that has been linked to experiences of personal victimization among cohorts of female sexual offenders (Christopher, Lutz-Zois, & Reinhardt, 2007).

Multiple studies have indicated high prevalence rates of posttraumatic stress disorder, anxiety, depression, and developmental disability among the female sexual offenders (Allen, 1991; Faller, 1995; Lewis & Stanley, 2000; Gao, Jiao, Zeng, & Zhang, 2002; Laque, 2002; Fazel, Sjöstedt, Grann, & Långström, 2010). Green and Kaplan (1994) reported on a sample of 11 incarcerated female child molesters, observing that 73% met full diagnostic criteria for posttraumatic stress disorder. West, Friedman, and Kim found that over a third of their sample of female sexual offenders had histories of psychiatric inpatient hospitalization, the majority of which was non-paraphilic in nature (2011).

Faller (1995) examined the substance-abuse patterns of 72 female child molesters and found that more than half of the women abused alcohol; she also found that 22% of her sample was developmentally disabled and met criteria for at least minimal cognitive disabilities. Similarly, Allen (1991) studied 65 women who had been charged with a sexual offense and found that 17% self-identified as alcoholics, while 26% reported that they had used drugs relatively often at some time in the past. McLeod (2015), however, compared the substance-abuse patterns of male and female perpetrators in his NCANDS dataset and found that while the female sexual offenders in his sample were described as having high levels of substance abuse in their personal histories, they did not abuse alcohol and/or other controlled substances at rates that were higher than the male sexual offenders.

DeCou, Cole, Rowland, Kaplan, and Lynch (2014), in their ecological process model of female sexual offending, noted the extensive psychiatric histories described by almost half of her 24 study participants. These reports included varied perceptual symptoms, use of psychotropic medication, psychiatric hospitalizations, and reports of suicidal ideation and attempts. Nearly all of the participants also reported substance use before and during the process of offending, chronicling the role it played in the disinhibition of their behavior with their child victims. Many women in the study also reported providing drugs and alcohol to their victims, ensuring that the youth would be responsive to their advances or those of their co-perpetrator.

In their clinical description of various motivational types found in sex offending by females, Warren and Hislop (2009) detail the case of a psychotic woman who killed her daughter by thrusting a large knife into her vagina. During her evaluation she described to a police interviewer how she came to understand there was "demon" in the child, and in an effort to assist her, her dead father advised her to "go for her privates."

Warren and Hislop note that one component of this motivational type gained considerable notoriety in the early 1990s as parents and communities became concerned about satanic ritualistic abuse. Such abuse allegedly exposed children to horrific and repeated forms of sexual abuse by multiple adults, who often held high positions in the community. These allegations often involved claims of sex with children paired with torture and cruelty, murder, cannibalistic consumption of infants, and sex acts paired with urine, feces, and other noxious substances. The assertions and the emotional fervor that accompanied them began in North America and circumnavigated the globe before the fantasy-based nature of these hysterical ideas began to be recognized. This change was spurred by court cases against therapists who had induced these ideas, often through the use of hypnosis, accompanied by the diagnosis of multiple personality disorder. These cases differ from those of the acutely psychotic individuals, as the fantastical nature of these beliefs could often be eradicated by clear boundary setting and the identification of the implausibility and lack of forensic evidence for any of the ideas or events that were being purported.

Cognitive Distortions

Building upon the initial work by Ward and Keenan, Gannon (2009) sought to compare the cognitions of female sex offenders with nonoffending women. Based upon these comparisons, Gannon concluded that it was possible to categorize the cognitions of female sex offenders using the five implicit theory headings, but found that the cognitions held by the female sex offenders differed in specific content from those found among male sex offenders. In particular, the women were found to believe that their specific victims, rather than children in general, were sexual; that sexual abuse by men was harmful while sexual abuse by women was not; and that men controlled the actions of women.

Recently, Gannon and Alleyne (2013) published a systematic review of offense-supporting cognitions found among female sex offenders. Based upon a full review of the research literature, the authors were able to identify 13 studies that included some quantitative measure of offense-supportive cognition and were either published in a peer review journal or contained unpublished data that included a control group. In this review, Gannon and Alleyne found that female sex abusers who offended alone tended to have more elevated levels of cognition that supported their offense behavior than women who offended in the company of a male; these offense-supportive cognitions tended to include schemas that attributed power to men but did not attribute sexual feelings to children. Further, rape myth acceptance and the acceptance of violence was not found among adolescent females who offended against children but rape myth acceptance was found among females who engaged in peer-on-peer sexual assault as were beliefs normalizing high levels of sexual activity among women. When empathy towards one's own victim was examined, female sex abusers were found to have more deficits in this arena relative to nonoffending controls, and women who offended with a male demonstrated deficits in empathy that were comparable to male sexual abusers.

Relational Offending

DeCou et al. (2014) found that approximately one half of their study participants reported offending with a co-perpetrator, these often being men with whom the women were involved in a romantic relationship. In these relationships, the women described limited emotional-interpersonal support, contemporaneous partner abuse, offending to please the co-perpetrator, and giving in to the insistence of their cooffender.

Gillespie et al. (2015) compared a group of 20 female sex offenders who offended alone with 20 female sex offenders who offended with a co-perpetrator. They found that both groups suffered from similar abusive developmental experiences but that the solo offenders had greater psychological vulnerabilities including mental health and substance abuse disorders, while the cooffenders had more environmentally based risk factors including being romantically involved with a man who was a known sex offender and being involved with other antisocial peers. Ashfield, Brotherston, Eldridge, and Elliott (2013) however, emphasize the importance of exploring the dynamics of offenses perpetrated by a dyad and not being premature in the assignment of women into the role of a passive and compliant victim, this being a more comfortable and culturally supportive image of sexually exploitive women.

Along similar lines, Warren and Hislop (2009) clinically described the behavior of the *facilitator* who engages in the sexual fantasy of their male partner. They note that this type of woman is willing over time to assist a man in the procurement of a victim and enactment of his sexual fantasy. This entering into or accepting the sexual request of the male partner may be attributed to a variety of different motivations, ranging from extreme dependency and frantic fear of abandonment to a daring wish to approach the forbidden and not be excluded from a seemingly inevitable sexual encounter. In research involving the consensual partners of sexually sadistic offenders, Hazelwood and Warren (1995) described women who assisted their romantic partners in obtaining victims for their sexually aggressive crimes and who over time began to display erotic pleasure in the activity, at times taking a lead role in sexual behaviors that eventually culminated in murder.

Another case encountered by one of the authors involved a woman who was sexually abused by both parents as well as others, some of whom used the child to make pornography. The mother, who was an alcoholic, continued to sexually abuse the child into adulthood after the death of the child's father. As an adult, this particular woman developed extreme experiences of dissociation that continued over many years of treatment.

DOMINATION AND CONTROL

Warren and Hislop (2009) identified a group of women whom they classified as the *instigating partner* in sexual crimes perpetrated against a child, adolescent, or adult—often for aggressive and retaliatory reasons—either alone or with a female or male partner. Saradjian and Hanks (1996) described a case in which a woman pressured her husband until he procured and raped a 14-year-old girl, allowing her to watch the sexual assault as an enactment of her own sexual fantasy. Kaufman, Wallace, Johnson, and Reeder (1995) examined the behavior of 53 female offenders and found that almost a quarter had offended sexually while accompanied by another adolescent or an adult peer. These instances commonly involved adolescent girls sexually offending against younger boys while babysitting, homosexual gangs raping other women as a sign of their revenge or dominance (Lane, 1991, personal report to author), and group sexual violence perpetrated by multiple women against a single male as a form of retaliation for some prior crime against one of the group members (Sarrel & Masters, 1982).

Larson and Maison's (1987) description of their prison sample included one woman who recruited men to gang rape a woman who had made reciprocated sexual advances to her boyfriend. She inserted a coke bottle into her vagina during the encounter. Another participant had initiated a sexual relationship with her 11-year-old son to avenge her husband's sexual interest in their daughter. Emerging research on prison rape and sexual coercion also indicates that sexual assaults can be perpetrated in prisons, often in retaliation for one inmate stealing the lover of another (Warren, personal reports). One of the authors evaluated a female inmate who had been charged with murder following the sexual abuse and murder of another woman. She was accompanied by other members of her homosexual gang. The victim had become involved with the partner of one of the homosexual gang members and her beating, which was intended to involve only sexual assault, escalated into murder.

In her research, Girshick (2002) described violent lesbian relationships in which sexual assault was part of a general pattern of violence within the relationship. One woman described being tied to a bed while a broom handle was inserted into her vagina. Another told of having her clothes torn off by her partner, after which a variety of objects were forced inside her.

ROMANTIC LOVE

Warren and Hislop (2009) identify the experience of the *female seducer/lover* who directs her sexual interest toward a particular adolescent and becomes romantically and often passionately involved with this young man or woman in a manner that is often enticingly provocative and yet dangerously disruptive of their adult lives. The older woman often experiences the relationship as a love affair with all the consuming feelings that are associated with this type of intimacy, and will describe a sweetly alluring form of innocence in the feelings that she has for her younger lover. Closer inspection, however, will often display heavy feelings of weariness experienced by the woman with the many responsibilities of her adult life, such as having biological children of her own. She often has a rather superficial and immature assessment of her own internal reasons for pursuing a relationship that is based on an illusory assessment of shared experiences and feelings. Prior exposure to incestuous experiences in childhood might also contribute to the appeal of this type of sexual boundary-crossing, and may be enacted with victims of the same age that the woman was when she was abused. The erotic and hidden nature of the passions ignited in these relationships also keeps the relationship from developing into one based upon shared experiences, and allows both the adult and the adolescent to experience a taboo form of sexuality that goes beyond the restrictions of more public and conforming patterns of intimacy.

Issues of consent can be difficult to disentangle in this type of relationship. While the behavior is clearly illegal and obviously exploitive because of the younger age and relative inexperience of the victim, the surface experience of the relationship can often seem mutually satisfying and appealing. In some instances, the young man or woman is not sexually naïve and the boundary-crossing can be experienced as a power-enhancing conquest of the slowly emerging adult sexuality. In others, the full expanse of the sexual experiences that emerge can be profoundly satisfying, leading to guilt, confusion, and exhilaration when compared with the more limited sexual experience of same-age companions.

One case, highly publicized in the media, involved a teacher who not only became involved with a 13-year-old sixth-grade student but also gave birth to his children over the course of the relationship. The woman was a married mother of four children when these events occurred. She was charged and convicted for her sexual relationship with the underage boy, and was sentenced to several years in prison. While serving time, she divorced her husband, continued in her relationship with the young man, and married him within days of being released from prison. This particular woman had experienced an incestuous relationship with her brother while growing up. Her father, who sired children with another woman, denied paternity of them, allowing both of them to be placed in an orphanage.

A less romantic variant of this same theme can be found in the cases of single women who find solace in promiscuous sexual encounters with multiple young men who often live within one community. Occurring in places where the young men can drink alcohol, use drugs, and be assured of easy, reciprocal sex, these encounters often become distorted and abusive as the young men are introduced to sexual variety that they often lack the maturity manage. In a case evaluation conducted by one of the authors, a 13-year-old boy reported providing a friend's mother with crack cocaine in exchange for allowing him to perpetrate sadistic sexual acts upon her, including urination, hair pulling, and various forms of assault. As his sexual fantasies continued to expand to include increasingly sadistic content, this behavior became disturbed enough to require a prolonged period of psychiatric hospitalization.

In some instances, these love affairs can occur with the youth's own mother. Faller (1987) described several cases in which single-parent females who lacked ongoing relationships with adult men placed the oldest child in the role of surrogate partner with adult responsibilities, including sexual contact. Faller noted that in many of these cases the women were not married to the fathers of their children and had children with multiple partners. As reported in a case study by de Young (1982), one young man experienced his incestuous relationship with his mother as both special and private, while also recognizing that she was mentally ill.

EMPIRICAL TYPOLOGIES OF FEMALE OFFENDERS

One of the first typologies that focused exclusively on female sex offenders was presented by Matthews, Mathews, and Speltz in 1989. It was based upon their interviews with 16 women undergoing treatment for sexual offending. Based upon clinical interviews augmented by a variety of psychological tests, they identified three primary types of female offenders: the teacher/lovers, the predisposed offenders, and the male-coerced perpetrators. The first group, the teacher/lovers, tended to deny the criminal aspects of their behavior. A woman in this group described herself as motivated by what she believed to be mutual feelings of romantic love. The second group, the predisposed offenders, was found to offend most often in the context of their own families during periods of isolation from other adults. This abuse tended to occur after chronic histories of sexual abuse during their own childhoods, often involving multiple members of their extended families.

The male-coerced group was described as passive and powerless in their interpersonal relationships, and increasingly acquiescent to the aggressive and exploitive demands of their partners or husbands.

Some years later, Vandiver and Kercher (2004) compiled information that had been garnered from the sex offender registry in Texas, a list that included 471 women who had been convicted of a sexually violent crime. They identified six distinct groups and differentiated between heterosexual and homosexual patterns of offending. These groups included the following:

- The *heterosexual nurturer* group ($N = 146$) was made up of women with an average age of 30 years who offended only against boys with an average age of 12 years. These women were found to be the least likely to be arrested for their behavior and they tended to experience the sexual experience as an expression of a love relationship that was not abusive. They were the group who were second least likely to be arrested for a similar type of crime.
- The *noncriminal homosexual* group ($N = 112$) was found to be on average 32 years of age and to become involved with female victims who on average were 13 years of age. They were found to have the lowest number of arrests and to be the least likely to be rearrested and were the least likely to commit sexual assault.
- The *female sexual predator* group ($N = 112$) were found to be slightly younger with an average age of 29 years and victims who on average were 11 years of age. These offenders were found to have a higher number of offenses and rearrest and were similar in characteristics to other female offenders and their sexual offending was thought possibly to be a part of their criminal disposition.
- The *young adult child exploiter* group ($N = 50$) was made up of the youngest women who were on average 28 years of age with both male and female victims who were on average 7 years of age. Over half of the offenders were related to their victims suggesting that a significant number were mothers who were sexually abusing their own children.
- The *homosexual criminal group* ($N = 22$) was on average 32 years of age with victims who were primarily females with an average age of 11 years. They had criminal histories of multiple arrests, displayed a variety of antisocial behaviors, and often forced their female victims into prostitution, which they used as a source of economic support. This group was the most likely to come in contact with the criminal justice system and had on average 10 prior arrests.
- The *aggressive homosexual offender* group ($N = 17$) was made up of older female offenders who sexually assaulted other women in the context of violent domestic relationships. They did not offend against children and had victims who were on average 31 years of age.

Sandler and Freeman (2007) sought to replicate the Texas research using 346 women registered in New York, a group that represented 2% of the sexual offenders identified by the registry since its inception in 1996. Using cluster analyses and hierarchical log linear modeling, they identified six offender groups that were differentiated using their choice of victim and level of risk for reoffense:

- The *criminally limited hebephile* group ($N = 158$) was made up of women in their early 30s who preferred adolescent victims around the age of 14 years. They offended primarily against male (70%) victims and appeared to have relationships with their victims that they considered to be romantic. These offenders were found to have a low rate of rearrest, with only 9% being arrested for any type of subsequent crime. They also had low rates of incarcerations terms (11%), drug arrests (2%), and supervision violations (4%).
- The *criminally prone hebephile* group ($N = 105$) were found to select a similar type of victim as members of the first group but differed significantly from this group in terms of their criminal histories and past antisocial behaviors. This group was found to have higher rates of rearrest (58%), more prior arrests (9%), more incarceration terms (52%), more drug

arrests (18%), and more supervision failures (42%). Offenders in this group also selected male victims in approximately two-thirds of the reported crimes.

- The *young adult child molesters* group ($N = 27$) was made up of women who were on average 28 years of age and who offended against male and female victims who were on average 4 years of age. They had few drug arrests (7%), low rates of prior crime (1%), and limited rates of incarceration (33%). None of the women in the group had prior supervision failures.
- The *high-risk chronic offenders* group ($N = 25$) had the highest rate of minority offenders who were on average 31 years of age and who abused male and female children who were on average 5 years of age. They tended to have chronic criminal histories (a mean of 15 prior convictions), high rates of rearrest (76%), consistent incarceration terms (72%), and the highest rate of supervision failures (64%).
- The *older nonhabitual offender* group ($N = 20$) was made up of women who were on average 50 years of age and who became sexually involved with victims who were on average 12 years of age. As a group, they had little prior criminal contact (mean of two prior arrests) and no prior involvement with drug arrests, rearrests, or supervision failures.
- The *homosexual child molester* group ($N = 11$) was found to exclusively target female victims who were on average 5 years of age. Offenders in this group had modest levels of prior arrests (4%), low rates of rearrest (18%) and these were combined with high rates of drug arrests (27%) and of incarceration (36%).

These studies represent a significant step forward in our empirical understanding of the criminal sexual offending behavior of women. They confirm that sexual offending by women is not uncommon, and suggest that the motivations for this type of criminal behavior are as diverse as, if not more so than, those found among male offenders. Embedded in these motivational typologies are varying degrees of romantic involvement with the chosen victim, combined with differing degrees of antisocial behavior and distinct patterns demonstrated by heterosexual and homosexual women. These data are obviously limited, however, due to the fact that they represent only the offense behavior of women who have been processed by the criminal justice system.

INVESTIGATORY SIGNIFICANCE OF THE PARADIGM

The research by McLoad (2105) offers for the first time a comparative platform for examining the sexual offending perpetrated by women as compared to men, at least within the context of the family and other care-taking relationships. Based upon an analysis of the substantiated cases entered into the National Child Abuse and Neglect Data System (NCANDS), McLoad found that there were 13,492 cases in 2010 of child sexual abuse in which a woman was identified as the primary perpetrator of the abuse. This was found to represent almost 21% of the sexual abuse reports substantiated by Child Protective Services (CPS) agencies nationally during the calendar year. These numbers suggest that the sexual abuse of children by women is a problem that is far more extensive than is commonly understood, and that the rates captured by the sex offender registries (2%) may reflect less than 10% of the crimes that actually occur on a yearly basis. These statistics illustrate the still limited nature of our understanding of these particular types of sexual offending and the importance of developing better identification and possible treatment strategies for these women. Similarly, the fact that many of these female perpetrators are mothers offending against their own children calls into question some of the incidence rates currently cited for child sexual abuse, as research indicates that children are less likely to disclose sexual abuse when it is being perpetrated by a parent.

The emerging research on female sex offenders also underscores the different patterns of sexual offending that can be found among women and the varying degrees of association that these patterns have with prior criminality and the risk for future offending. While it is not uncommon to portray male offenders as pedophiles or rapists, there is a tendency to portray women as victims who are inadvertently enticed into offending by past experience or through their relationships with a dominant male. While these influences may be operative and powerful, they also tend to mask the more chronic aspect of the personality style and/or lifestyle that can contribute to a risk for reoffense involving child sexual abuse or other forms of criminal offense. This risk also becomes difficult to manage given the ability of women to have children despite their past criminal history. The caseloads of social service agencies are replete with instances of women losing custody of one set of children, only to have more later in life, often with other partners who reflect a similarly high level of risk for harming the children through abuse or chronic patterns of neglect.

Certain high-profile cases have begun to illustrate the role that female offenders can also play in various types of sadistic serial crime. This type of partnering can be a pivotal part of the police investigation, as it creates the dyad that can be used to entice the one offender to provide information against the other, either based upon fear for his or her own safety or as part of a plea bargain once the couple has been apprehended. The possible role of women in the planning and/or executing of these crimes is often the missing link that explains the ability of the couple to acquire high-risk victims and transport them considerable distances without any apparent signs of struggle or resistance.

The tendency to underestimate the involvement of females in sexual crimes against children can diminish the reporting that could occur and curtail to some extent the nature of the investigation that follows it. All too often, when a female child has been found to be the victim of sexual abuse, the investigation stops and does not complete a full review of the cycle that could involve the victim's sexual contact with other children. It is not uncommon to discover that when one child is being sexually abused in a family, foster home, or residential setting, other children are also involved in sexual activity with each other. While there may be a cursory attempt to question other children in a home, the significance of this type of incidence as a risk factor for all the children in the home has yet to be adequately identified and addressed as part of social service investigations. When attempts are made to inquire further into these types of situations, there is also a tendency to assume that young males are the most likely perpetrators, thus missing the proximity of the child to other female children who may be abusing them.

The available research also suggests that the criminal justice system responds very differently to male and female sex offenders. For example, reports of female sexual offending that originate with law-enforcement agencies tend to involve older, adolescent victims who are predominately male, while reports originating with child protective service agencies tend to involve younger victims, offending behaviors that are less discriminate of victim gender, and higher overall levels of female offender involvement (Bader, Scalora, Casady, & Black, 2008; McLeod, 2015). The reporting dynamics of these cases also impacts the outcome of the investigations: evidence not only suggests female offenders receive more lenient sentences in court systems across the United States, but they also receive more extensive services including mental health treatment, substance abuse treatment, and social support from child welfare systems at higher rates than male offenders (Bunting, 2007; Franklin & Fearn, 2008; McLeod & Craft, 2015). The gender disparities in experiences that exist between these systems undoubtedly have profound influences on the behavioral and legal trajectories of offenders, and could influence the perspectives of those investigating and adjudicating these crimes.

In terms of prevention, the research on female sex offenders only serves to underscore the importance of timely interventions and treatment of children who are sexually abused or exploited. There is no longer any doubt that early abuse serves as a significant risk marker for abuse against others in adulthood. In particular, we need to identify the vulnerability of young men regardless of their implied level of consent. This is necessary to ensure that hidden forms of sexual abuse can be identified and investigated without the distortions implied by our outdated definitions of victimization and abuse. With antisocial women, we need to add to our repertoire of crime types their ability to exploit children sexually for their own and others' sexual purposes. We also need to better understand the role they can play in both seducing and using children in ways that are directly and indirectly sexual.

REFERENCES

American Humane Association (AHA). 1987. National study on child abuse and neglect reporting. In *History of Child Maltreatment Reporting*. American Humane Association, Washington, DC. Retrieved August 12, 2016 from https://www.acf.hhs.gov/sites/default/files/cb/nccan14_workshop_42.pdf.

Allen, C. 1991. *Women and men who sexually abuse children: A comparative analysis*. Orwell, VT: The Safer Society Press.

Ashfield, S., Brotherston, S., Eldridge, H., and Elliott, I. 2013. Female sexual offenders. In K. Harrison and B. Rainey (Eds.), *The Wiley-Blackwell handbook of legal and ethical aspects of sex offender treatment and management*, 321–337. Chichester, UK: John Wiley & Sons.

Bader, S., Scalora, M., Casady, T., and Black, S. 2008. Female sexual abuse and criminal justice intervention: A comparison of child protective service and criminal justice samples. *Child Abuse and Neglect*, 32(1), 111–119.

Barlow, D. H. 1974. The treatment of sexual deviation: Toward a comprehensive behavioral approach. In K. S. Calhoun, H. E. Adams, and K. M. Mitchell (Eds.), *Innovative treatment methods in psychopathology*, 121–147. New York: John Wiley & Sons.

Beech, A. R., Parrett, N., Ward, T., and Fisher, D. 2009. Assessing female sexual offenders' motivations and cognitions: An exploratory study. *Psychology, Crime & Law*, 15, 201–216. DOI: 10.1080/10683160802190921.

Bouchard, V. 1994. *Women who sexually abuse children: Phenomenological case studies of 11 women*. Unpublished doctoral dissertation. The Adler School of Professional Psychology. Chicago, IL. UMI Number 9822803. Copyright 1998.

Bunting, L. 2007. Dealing with a problem that doesn't exist? Professional responses to female perpetrated child sexual abuse. *Child Abuse Review*, 16(4), 252–267.

Bureau of Justice Statistics. 2010. Criminal victimization in the United States, 2008 (NCJ-2311730). Retrieved from http://bjs.ojp.usdoj.gov/content/pub/pdf/cvus08.pdf.

Cavanaugh-Johnson, T. 1988. Child perpetrators: Children who molest children. *Child Abuse and Neglect: The International Journal*, 12, 219–229.

Centers for Disease Control and Prevention. 2013. ACE study: Major findings. Retrieved from http://www.cdc.gov/ace/violenceprevention/acestudy/findings.html.

Chideckel, M. 1935. *Female sex perversions: The sexually aberated woman as she is*. New York: Eugenics.

Christopher, K., Lutz-Zois, C., and Reinhardt, A. R. 2007. Female sexual-offenders: Personality pathology as a mediator of the relationship between childhood sexual abuse history and sexual abuse perpetration against others. *Child Abuse & Neglect*, 31(8), 871–883. DOI: 10.1016/j.chiabu.2007.02.006.

Colson, M.-H., Boyer, L., Baumstarck, K., and Loundou, A. D. 2013. Female sex offenders: A challenge to certain paradigms. Meta-analysis. *Sexologies*, 22(4), e109–e117. DOI: 10.1016/j.sexol.2013.05.002.

Cooper, A., Swaminath, S., Baxter, D., and Poulin, C. 1990. A female sex offender with multiple paraphilias: A psychologic and endocrine case study. *Canadian Journal of Psychiatry*, 35, 334–337.

Cooper, I., and Cormier, B. 1990. In R. Blugrass and P. Bowden (Eds.), *Principles and practice of forensic psychiatry*. New York: Churchill Livingston.

Cortoni, F., Hanson, R. K., and Coache, M. È. 2010. The recidivism rates of female sexual offenders are low: A meta-analysis. *Sexual Abuse: Journal of Research and Treatment*, 22(4), 387–401.

Cozolino, L. 2010. *The neuroscience of psychotherapy: Healing the social brain*. New York, NY: Norton.

DeCou, C. R., Cole, T. T., Rowland, S. E., Kaplan, S. P., and Lynch, S. M. 2014. The ecological process model of female sex offending: The role of victimization, psychological distress, and life stressors. *Sexual Abuse: Journal of Research and Treatment*, 27, 1–22. DOI: 10.1177/1079063214556359.

de Young, M. 1982. *The sexual victimization of children*. Jefferson, NC: McFarland & Company.

Elliott, I. A., Eldridge, H. J., Ashfield, S., and Beech, A. R. 2010. Exploring risk: Potential static, dynamic, protective and treatment factors in the clinical histories of female sex offenders. *Journal of Family Violence*, 25(6), 595–602. DOI: 10.1007/s10896-010-9322-8.

Elliott, M. (Ed.). 1994. *Female sexual abuse of children*. New York: Guilford Press.

Faller, K. 1987. Women who sexually abuse children. *Violence and Victims*, 2(4), 263–276.

Faller, K. C. 1995. A clinical sample of women who have sexually abused children. *Journal of Child Sexual Abuse*, 4(3), 13–30.

Fazel, S., Sjöstedt, G., Grann, M., and Långström, N. 2010. Sexual offending in women and psychiatric disorder: A national case–control study. *Archives of Sexual Behavior*, 39(1), 161–167. DOI: 10.1007/s10508-008-9375-4.

Fehrenbach, P. A., and Monastersky, C. 1988. Characteristics of female adolescent sexual offenders. *American Journal of Orthopsychiatry*, 58(1), 148–151.

Felitti, V. J., Anda, R. F., Nordenberg, D., Williamson, D. F., Spitz, A. M., Edwards, V., et al. 1998. The relationship of adult health status to childhood abuse and household dysfunction. *American Journal of Preventive Medicine*, 14(4), 245–258.

Finkelhor, D., and Russell, D. 1984. Women as perpetrators: Review of the evidence. In D. Finkelhor (Ed.), *Child Sexual Abuse: New Theory and Research*, 171–187. New York: Free Press.

Foege, W. H. 1998. Global public health: Targeting inequities. *Journal of the American Medical Association*, 279(24), 1931–1932.

Ford, H. 2006. *Women who sexually abuse children*. Chichester, UK: John Wiley & Sons.

Franklin, C. A., and Fearn, N. E. 2008. Gender, race, and formal court decision-making outcomes: Chivalry/paternalism, conflict theory or gender conflict? *Journal of Criminal Justice*, 36(3), 279–290.

Freel, M. 1995. Women who sexually abuse children. *Social Work Monographs*, Norwich, England: University of Hull, Monograph 135.

Frey, L. 2010. The juvenile female sexual offender: Characteristics, treatment, and research. In T. Gannon and F. Cortoni (Eds.), *Female sexual offenders: Theory, assessment, and treatment*, 53–72. Oxford, UK: Wiley-Blackwell.

Fromuth, M., and Conn, V. 1997. Hidden perpetrators: Sexual molestation in a nonclinical sample of college women. *Journal of Interpersonal Violence*, 12(3), 456–465.

Gannon, T. A. 2009. Current cognitive distortion theory and research: An internalist approach to cognition. *Journal of Sexual Aggression*, 15(3), 225–246. DOI: 10.1080/13552600903263079.

Gannon, T. A., and Alleyne, E. K. 2013. Female sexual abusers' cognition: A systematic review. *Trauma, Violence, & Abuse*, 14(1), 67–79.

Gao, C., Jiao, Z., Zeng, T., and Zhang, Z. 2002. Risk factors of sexual wrong-doings in young females. [risk factors of sexual wrong-doings in young females.] *Chinese Mental Health Journal*, 16(4), 259, 263–264.

Giguere, R., and Bumby, K. 2007. *Female sex offenders*. Silver Spring, MD: Center for Effective Public Policy, Center for Sex Offender Management.

Gillespie, S. M., Williams, R., Elliott, I. A., Eldridge, H. J., Ashfield, S., and Beech, A. R. 2015. Characteristics of Females Who Sexually Offend A Comparison of Solo and Co-offenders. *Sexual Abuse: Journal of Research and Treatment*, 27(3), 284–301.

Girshick, L. B. 2002. *Woman-to-woman sexual violence: Does she call it rape?* Lebanon, NH: Northeastern University Press.

Green, A., and Kaplan, M. 1994. Psychiatric impairment and childhood victimization experiences in female child molesters. *Journal of American Academy of Child and Adolescent Psychiatry*, 33(7), 954–961.

Groth, N. 1979. Sexual trauma in the life histories of rapists and child molesters. *Victimology: An International Journal*, 4(1), 10–16.

Hazelwood, R., and Warren, J. 1995. The relevance of fantasy in serial sexual crime investigation. In R. Hazelwood and A. Burgess (Eds.), *Practical aspects of rape investigation*, 2nd ed., 127–138. New York: CRC Press.

Higgs, D., Canavan, M., and Meyer, W. Q. 1992. Moving from defense to offense: The development of a female sex offender. *Journal of Sex Research*, 29(1), 131–140.

Hindman, J. 2000. *Understanding the male victim and the female perpetrator. Sixteenth National Symposium on child sexual abuse*. Huntsville, AL: The National Children's Advocacy Center.

Hislop, J. 1999. Female child molesters. In E. Bear (Ed.), *Female sexual abusers: Three perspectives*. Brandon, VT: The Safer Society Press.

Jennings, K. T. 1998. *Female sexual abuse of children: An exploratory study* (Doctoral dissertation). University of Toronto. Retrieved from http://hdl.handle.net/1807/13063.

Kaufman, K., Wallace, A., Johnson, C., and Reeder, M. 1995. Comparing female and male perpetrators' modus operandi: Victims' reports of sexual abuse. *Journal of Interpersonal Violence*, 10(3), 322–334.

Knopp, F. H., and Lackey, L. B. 1987. *Female sexual abusers: A summary of data from 44 treatment providers for the Safer Society Program of the New York State Council of Churches*. Brandon, VT: The Safer Society Press.

Korbin, J. 1986. Childhood histories of women imprisoned for fatal child maltreatment. *Child Abuse and Neglect*, 10, 331–338.

Krafft-Ebing, R. 1886. *Psychopathia sexualis: A medico-forensic study*, trans. H. E. Wedeck. New York: G. P. Putnam's Sons.

Lambert, S., and O'Halloran, E. 2008. Deductive thematic analysis of a female pedophilia website. *Psychiatry, Psychology & Law*, 15, 284–300. DOI: 10.1080/13218710802014469.

Lane, S. 1991. Special offender populations. In G. Ryan and S. Lane (Eds.), *Juvenile sexual offending: Causes, consequences and correction*, 299–332. Lexington, MA: Lexington Books.

Laque, J. C. 2002. *Childhood traumas, substance abuse, and sexual experiences: A comparison study between incarcerated female sex offenders*. University of Houston. 85–134.

Larson, N., and Maison, S. 1987. *Psychosexual treatment program for female sex offenders*, Minnesota Correctional Facility-Shakopee. St. Paul, MN: Meta Resources.

Laws, D. R., and Marshall, W. L. 1991. Masturbatory reconditioning with sexual deviates: An evaluative review. *Advances in Behavior Research and Therapy*, 13(1), 13–25.

Laws, D. R., and Marshall, W. L. 2003. A brief history of behavioral and cognitive behavioral approaches to sexual offenders: Part 1. Early developments. *Sexual Abuse: Journal of Research and Treatment*, 15(2), 75–92.

Lewis, C. F., and Stanley, C. R. 2000. Women accused of sexual offenses. *Behavioral Sciences & the Law*, 18(1), 73–81. DOI: 10.1002/(SICI)1099-0798(200001/02)18:1<73::AID-BSL378>3.0.CO;2-#

Marques, J. K. 1984. *An innovative treatment program for sex offenders: Report to the legislature*. Sacramento, CA: California Department of Mental Health.

Marshall, W. L. 1971. A combined treatment method for certain sexual deviations. *Behavior Research and Therapy*, 9(3), 293–294.

Marvasti, J. 1986. Incestuous mothers. *American Journal of Forensic Psychiatry*, 7(4), 63–69.

Mathews, R., Matthews, J., and Speltz, K. 1989. *Female sexual offenders: An exploratory study*. Orwell, VT: The Safer Society Press.

McGuire, R. J., Carlisle, J. M., and Young, B. G. 1965. Sexual deviations as conditioned behavior: A hypothesis. *Behavior Research and Therapy*, 3, 185–190.

McLeod, D. A. 2015. Female offenders in child sexual abuse cases: A national picture. *The Journal of Child Sexual Abuse*, 24(1), 97–114. DOI: 10.1080/10538712.2015.978925.

McLeod, D. A., and Craft, M. L. 2015. Female sexual offenders in child sexual abuse cases: National trends associated with CPS system entry, exit, service utilization, & socioeconomics. *Journal of Public Child Welfare*, 9(4), 399–416. http://dx.doi.org/10.1080/15548732.2015.1064849.

McLeod, D. A., Natale, A. P., and Johnson, Z. 2015. Comparing theoretical perspectives on female sexual offending behaviors: Applying a trauma-informed lens. *Journal of Human Behavior in the Social Environment*, 25(8), 934–947.

Miccio-Fonseca, L. C. 2000. Adult and adolescent female sex offenders: Experiences compared to other female and male sex offenders. *Journal of Psychology & Human Sexuality*, 11(3), 75–88.

Nathan, P., and Ward, T. 2004. Female sex offenders: Clinical and demographic features. *Journal of Psychology & Human Sexuality*, 11(3), 75–88.

Nelson, C. A. 2003. Can we develop a neurobiological model of human social-emotional development? Integrative thoughts on the effects of separation on parent–child interactions. *Annals of the New York Academy of Sciences*, 1008, 48–54.

O'Connor, A. A. 1987. Female sex offenders. *British Journal of Psychiatry*, 150, 615–620.

Oliver, B. E. 2007. Preventing female-perpetrated sexual abuse. *Trauma, Violence & Abuse*, 8(1), 19–32. DOI: 10.1177/1524838006296747.

Perry, B. D. 2000. Sexual abuse of infants. *Trauma, Violence, & Abuse*, 1(3), 294–296. DOI: 10.1177/1524838000001003009.

Risin, L., and Koss, M. 1987. Sexual abuse of boys: Prevalence, and descriptive characteristics of childhood victimizations. *Journal of Interpersonal Violence*, 2(3), 309–323.

Rosencrans, B. 1997. *The last secret: Daughters sexually abused by mothers*. Brandon, VT: The Safer Society Press.

Sandler, J., and Freeman, N. 2007. Topology of female sex offenders: A test of Vandiver and Kercher. *Sexual Abuse: Journal of Research and Treatment*, 19(2), 73–89.

Saradjian, J. 1996. *Women who sexually abuse children. From research to clinical practice*. Chichester, UK: John Wiley & Sons.

Saradjian, J., and Hanks, H. 1996. *Women who sexually abuse children: From research to clinical practice*. New York: John Wiley & Son.

Sarrel, P., and Masters, W. 1982. Sexual molestation of men by women. *Archives of Sexual Behavior*, 11(2), 117–131.

Sheldrick, C. 1991. Adult sequelae of child sexual abuse. *British Journal of Psychiatry*, 158(Suppl. 10), 55–62.

Strickland, S. M. 2008. Female sex offenders. *Journal of Interpersonal Violence*, 23(4), 474–489. DOI: 10.1177/0886260507312944.

Suschinsky, K. D., Lalumière, M. L., and Chivers, M. L. 2009. Sex differences in patterns of genital sexual arousal: Measurement artifacts or true phenomena? *Archives of Sexual Behavior*, 38, 559–573.

Travin, S., Cullen, K., and Protter, B. 1990. Female sex offenders: Severe victims and victimizers. *Journal of Forensic Sciences*, 35(1), 140–150.

Tsopelas, C., Spyridoula, T., and Athanasios, D. 2011. Review on female sexual offenders: Findings about profile and personality. *International Journal of Law and Psychiatry*, 34(2), 122–126. DOI: 10.1016/j.ijlp.2011.02.006.

Vandiver, D. M., and Kercher, G. 2004. Offender and victim characteristics of registered female sexual offenders in Texas: A proposed typology of female sexual offenders. *Sexual Abuse: Journal of Research and Treatment*, 16(2), 121–137.

Ward, T., and Keenan, T. 1999. Child molesters' implicit theories. *Journal of Interpersonal Violence*, 14, 821–838.

Warren, J. I., and Hislop. J. 2009. Patterns of female sex offending and their investigatory significance to law enforcement and child protective services. In R. R Hazelwood and A. W. Burgess (Eds.), *Practical aspects of rape investigation*, 429–444. Boca Raton, FL: Taylor & Francis Group, CRC Press.

West, S. G., Friedman, S. H., and Kim, K. D. 2011. Women accused of sex offenses: A gender-based comparison. *Behavioral Sciences & the Law*, 29(5), 728–740. DOI: 10.1002/bsl.1007; 10.1002/bsl.1007.

Wolfe, F. 1985. Twelve female sexual offenders. Paper presented at the Next steps in research on the assessment and treatment of sexually aggressive persons (paraphiliacs). March, 1985, St. Louis, MO. [Cited in Mathews, Matthews, & Speltz, 1990.]

Wijkman, M., Bijleveld, C., and Hendriks, J. 2010. Women don't do such things! Characteristics of female sex offenders and offender types. *Sexual Abuse: Journal of Research and Treatment*, 22(2), 135–156. DOI: 10.1177/1079063210363826.

Wulffen, E. 1934. *Woman as sexual criminal*. New York: American Ethnological Press.

22 Drug-Facilitated Sex Assault

Michael Welner and Barbara Welner

CONTENTS

Introduction 355
Tracing the History of DFSA 356
The DFSA Perpetrator 357
What Makes the DFSA an Agent of DRSA? 358
Modus Operandi 360
    Components of the DFSA Modus Operandi 361
A Typology of DFSA 362
    Workplace Settings 362
    Health Care Settings 362
    Social Settings 363
    Accomplices and Conspiracies 363
    Intrafamilial DFSA 364
    Male-on-Male Offenses 364
    Sexual Deviance or Sexual Hunters 364
What Distinguishes DFSA Offenders from Other Sexual Criminals? 365
What Makes a Sound Investigation? 366
References 369
Further Reading 370

INTRODUCTION

For experts in sexual assault and its investigation, drug-facilitated sexual assault (DFSA) turns many preconceived generalizations about crimes and offenders upside down. DFSA is defined as the use of an agent, legal or illegal, to maneuver an unsuspecting and otherwise nonconsenting person to sex or to an otherwise psychosexually gratifying act. Not all DFSAs end in rape; the person manipulated, however, is unmistakably victimized by a person who absolutely exploits and calculatedly so.

Moreover, DFSA is perpetrated by offenders for whom elimination of toxicological evidence is essential to the selection of the drug they employ. As such, DFSA is specifically adapted to overcome current potentials of forensic investigation.

DFSA allows the exploitive and sexually self-indulgent to cross boundaries once limited to the violent who sexually assault. Force is not required to subdue victims of DFSA; struggle only happens, if at all, when the sedated victim awakens sooner than expected from a drug that has worn off.

DFSA thus differs dramatically from many rapes in that it is not typically a crime of physical violence (Welner, 2001b); it is a crime of sexual hedonism and entitlement. Not surprisingly, the gratuitous battering and mutilation carried out by the enraged and sadistic are not seen in DFSA. Were physical marks left behind, the perpetrator would defeat one essential purpose of DFSA: to exploit sexually without the victim's or investigator's detection.

Investigators should also be aware that perpetrators over age 60 have been found. DFSA enables sexual assault by older offenders whose criminal career would have otherwise passed because of their inability to contain a victim forcefully, especially one much younger and more able.

The criminal complaints against comedian Bill Cosby, beset with accounts from numerous women of having been drugged and assaulted them in incidents spanning many years, illustrates the many

355

facets of DFSA investigation. Indeed, the well-publicized accounts of many complainants evoke qualities noted in the research that informs this chapter to follow. But inconsistencies in some stories and the prospect of victims' secondary gain also highlight the discipline with which forensic examiners and investigators must approach such disputes. The very length of time passed before the reporting of the Cosby complaints highlights how ambivalence extends to some victims as well as investigators.

The ambivalence of both entities in suspected DFSA cases may feed off each other to contribute ironically to recidivism, through the perpetrator's confidence to recidivate and refining his modus operandi and his approach to later victims.

Research from emergency room populations has demonstrated the continuing rise in DFSA reports (Richer et al., 2015). This finding may reflect coercive rapists changing modus operandi to avoid detection, increased flow of information to those who fantasize to themselves offend, and/or increased sensitivity among the victimized to report and to get assistance. These trends underscore the importance of gaining investigative competence in the perpetrators, their modus operandi, and victim experiences in the aftermath.

TRACING THE HISTORY OF DFSA

DFSA charted its earliest territory in public awareness with the unsuspecting victim who was exploited in a business or professional setting and was clearly divorced from any sexual context. These exploitations would occur in the workplace when a drink would be given to the victim in circumstances that appeared to be celebratory (congratulations on a hiring or an achievement within the business). Furthermore, the employer had not necessarily been inappropriate at any point prior to the attack.

The earliest notorious cases of *sexual* exploitation through drugs and alcohol involved supervisors and employees, or doctors and patients (Welner, 2001a). DFSA in social settings inspired less sympathy for the victim as attitudes of many others at that time reflected the feeling that the victim should have known better. Today, DFSA in social settings assuredly represents the seizure of a nonconsenting victim through nonconfrontational means.

DFSA is honed by the evolution of cultural mores, including the inextricable linkage of drugs, alcohol, and sex. Contemporary claims of DFSA most commonly originate in settings where alcohol or drugs are readily consumed. Therefore, many DFSA claims struggle over issues of consent, rather than the use of drugs. With increased awareness of date rape, the civilized world now appreciates that forced sex does occur in settings that begin with a social relationship and different objectives for the encounter.

The dynamics of DFSA, namely a perpetrator exploiting a cognitively impaired person for sexual gratification, have long been recognized for their association with alcohol. Years before serious discussion of DFSA began, alcohol was the original DFSA agent. Alcohol contributes to the misinterpretation of interpersonal cues as sexual invitation and is associated with decreased coping and inability to defend against an attack (Rickert & Weimann, 1998). However, the use of drugs through the vehicle of alcohol is decidedly premeditated and schemed during sobriety. Unless alcohol alone is involved, research findings that demonstrate impairment in an accused's ability to perceive consent would therefore be irrelevant.

For all of the reasons that alcohol is exempt from the restrictions placed on other drugs, investigators and policymakers have talked around alcohol and its use in sexual exploitation. Medical studies on alcohol and victimization have shown nonspecific linkage between alcohol and victimization. More focused studies of sex assault victims, however, have demonstrated that among college students, those victimized have typically consumed alcohol in advance (Krebs, Lindquist, Warner, Fisher, & Martin, 2009). Recent trends of consuming energy drinks with alcohol have shown an increased association, among randomly surveyed college students, with being taken advantage of sexually (O'Brien, McCoy, Rhodes, Wagoner, & Wolfson, 2008).

DFSA drew more specific focus when it became clear to law enforcement that there were specific drugs being promoted among the underground drug culture for their immobilizing and memory-erasing effects on unsuspecting targets. Rohypnol and gamma-hydroxybutyrate (GHB), the drugs that drew earliest attention as DFSA agents in the late 1990s, were so effective that victims would not even know they had been victimized. DFSA consequently evolved into crimes of *no complaint* or *no evidence*, or events in which nothing apparently had happened. The frightening prospect of the perfect sexual crime spurred serious study of this area and creative initiatives for law enforcement and prosecution. A leader among these trailblazers was Robert Lipman, a Justice Department prosecutor who single-handedly promoted widespread awareness among law enforcement and who inspired the first author's sense of urgency to develop a typology of DFSA perpetrators.

More recent years have distinguished a variety of factors that clearly complicate the identification and investigation of DFSA cases and their prosecution. Manhood is increasingly promoted, especially among younger men, with the capacity to capture as many sexual partners as possible. Today marks a post-AIDS sexual revolution in which casual sexual encounters are accepted and encouraged by peers, particularly among those who go to clubs, where DFSA-applicable drugs may be readily available. Online dating, in turn, facilitates intimate encounters in settings that a perpetrator can control, with a victim who truly does not know him well enough.

At the same time, today's empowerment of females who make claims of sexual assault facilitates their undoing a regretted encounter while intoxicated with a false allegation that exaggerates the degree of their incapacitation during the encounter. Because these women are not victims, an already ambiguous crime becomes all the more inscrutable.

Presumptions of promiscuity as a universal gay trait contribute to a response to male victims' complaints with skepticism and indifference, although it is that same sexual predation that emboldens entitled homosexual hunters to prey through DFSA (Welner, 2001b). The personality issues and dynamics are the same, the sexual preference being the only distinction. However, studies have demonstrated DFSA victimization to constitute a particularly high percentage of cases among those men who present as having been raped (Richer et al., 2015).

THE DFSA PERPETRATOR

Law enforcement is in the uneasy middle—often focusing on quarry whose guilt is dangerously ascertained by no more than a hunch. The first author had consulted on a number of cases of DFSAs, both for prosecutors and for defense attorneys. This experience left him with the conclusion that DFSA is more widespread than identified and that confirmed offenders are most often identified as repeat perpetrators. That does not even account for the percentage of those who were apprehended after their first offense and before they could invariably recidivate. DFSA prevalence is unclear, but its perpetrators have every potential for recidivism until stopped and incarcerated.

Perpetrators of DFSA recognize that what they are doing is illegal; however, they do not feel it is wrong by their own morality. Pathological narcissism (Kernberg, 1989), exemplified by the exploitative abuse of power and control (Price, 1994), reflects the most clinically viable designation of the DFSA offender's personality. Pathological narcissists may be quite law-abiding otherwise, but they are so self-absorbed and motivated by entitlement as to trample over the boundaries of others (American Psychiatric Association, 1994) when they can.

DFSA is to its perpetrators a mode of acquiring immobilized sex partners. If sexual encounters with completely immobilized partners are charged elements of a perpetrator's fantasy life, that offender should be viewed with the risk for recidivism as would be an inveterate pedophile that hones and deftly carries out his modus operandi (Welner, 2001a, 2001b).

Unlike some compulsive offenders, DFSA offenders do not experience regret or show later empathy for their victims. They deny the crime and deny the victimization of their prey. Unlike many sexually deviant offenders, DFSA perpetrators offend only when opportunity presents itself. They strike when access, setting, and crime concealment are guaranteed.

DFSA perpetrators may be single or married. The same forethought and calculation that enables perpetrators to exploit victims enables them to maintain appearances of fidelity and happiness to unsuspecting spouses. This remorseless brazenness, reminiscent of psychopathy and pathological narcissism, includes people with no criminal record or history of violence who can nonetheless employ contradicting morality to successfully perpetrate DFSA. Witness the following case example:

> The defendant's wife testified that until mid-1996, she believed they had a strong marriage and she became pregnant with the couple's second child in July 1996. She testified that he was "thrilled" with the news. But, by early 1997 she and the defendant had separated. She went to their house (she was living in an apartment at the time) to get their video camera to record an upcoming family event. She viewed the videotape in the camera and saw the defendant having sex with three women, including her own younger sister.

DFSA perpetrators carry out their attacks in order to be able to do the same again. They are, therefore, an ongoing public health and safety risk and that is reason alone to prevent opportunity to offend and to stop labeling them with no more than *bad social judgment*.

DFSA requires familiarity with toxicology and behavioral science. For that reason, this chapter focuses on what investigators should know in order to guide their pursuit of DFSA cases: understanding the drugs involved, how victims are affected, challenges to the detection of given drugs, the perpetrators and their modus operandi, and strategies for investigation and identification of legitimate cases, and lastly, for the successful prosecution of true perpetrators.

WHAT MAKES THE DFSA AN AGENT OF DRSA?

To understand the "D" (drug) in DFSA, one must also focus on the "F" (facilitated). Drugs are chosen and utilized based upon their capacity to sedate and, if possible, to physically immobilize the intended victim. Moreover, agents that impair the formation of new memories also impact the victim's ability to identify details of an assault. The more sophisticated perpetrators of DFSA will choose agents that quickly metabolize to undetectable levels.

Rohypnol, or flunitrazepam (known by street names such as "roofies," "rope," "forget-me pill," "circles," "Mexican valium," "roopies," "roaches"; Welner, 1997), is the most recognized drug used in DFSA. A benzodiazepine, Rohypnol is a member of the same family as the more readily prescribed Valium, Librium, and Ativan and causes muscle relaxation and amnesia independent of its powerful and rapid (within 20 min) sedating effects. Once odorless and tasteless, the pharmaceutical firm Hoffman–La Roche modified its composition to include a blue dye that would make Rohypnol more difficult to conceal in beverages into which it is dropped. Rohypnol is not legally available in the United States and its import is banned (National Institute on Drug Abuse, 2006). (See Welner, 1997, for a more detailed review of the role Hoffman–La Roche played in the controversy over Rohypnol.)

Dizziness, visual disturbances, and urinary retention are among its side effects (Britt & McCance-Katz, 2005). Rohypnol may not be detectable in urine after approximately 72 h, although detection methods have become increasingly sensitive (Pope & Shouldice, 2001).

GHB, a powder or liquid that has a variety of uses and misuses, is known to produce sedation, increase libido, impair memory, and most importantly, rapidly clear from the system. GHB is even harder to trace before being completely metabolized than Rohypnol. It is cheap, more readily available, and popular on college campuses (Hensley, 2002).

With as little as a teaspoon dissolved into a drink, GHB can exert effects within 15 min. Tremors, seizure activity, bowel and bladder incontinence, and dizziness for as long as 2 weeks are side effects of GHB; history of these side effects may be the best evidence of such a medicine's being inappropriately given to a victim.

GBL, or gamma butyrolactone, relates closely in structure and effects to GHB. But unlike GHB, GBL is not subject to the regulatory barriers now in place to prevent GHB misuse. GBL may be found in a variety of more innocuous articles, such as liquid soap, super glue, or nail polish remover and is readily available online.

Chloral hydrate is an alcohol derivative that induces sedation rapidly. It does not provide the same muscle relaxation effects as those previously mentioned and is toxic in overdose. Chloral hydrate is even more toxic in interaction with other drugs, most dramatically demonstrated in the unexpected deaths of Marilyn Monroe and Anna Nicole Smith. However, chloral hydrate is easier to trace through toxicology than GHB or Rohypnol.

Those DFSA perpetrators unable to obtain the preceding drugs or who may have other drugs at their disposal may use high-potency benzodiazepines, such as Valium, known for their rapid onset. While Valium enhances muscle relaxation, sedation, and memory impairment, it remains in the system for so long that an unsuspecting victim would reflect Valium in his or her body for some time afterward. Less potent benzodiazepines do not begin to act with the speed for which an assailant would aim and therefore are not utilized.

DFSA, when most effectively perpetrated, is a crime in which victims are unable to recall the elements of the assault against them. In one reported case, the victim continued to trust the perpetrator, and he drugged and raped her a second time.

A victim may recall becoming very sleepy and weak, but remembers nothing until awakening, either while being attacked or even while being redressed after the assault. More than weakness, some drugs engender a feeling of paralysis that prevents victims from fighting an assailant even when they are aware of being assaulted.

After reviving, the victim may remain confused and have difficulty articulating his or her attack to responsible parties. Drug effects may persist beyond the sleep-inducing properties. Benzodiazepines, from Rohypnol to Valium, may leave their signatures through the victim's slurred speech after he or she awakens.

The sedating effects of GHB and Rohypnol can be abrupt and powerful (Greenblatt, Miller, & Shader, 1990; Welner, 1997, 2001a). Once the victim has ingested a spiked drink, he or she may soon be too sedated to walk. With increased awareness of DFSA, bars and their security men are increasingly sensitive to flag incapacitated female patrons being escorted "home" by seemingly concerned gentlemen. For this reason, many perpetrators try to drug their victims in settings within their complete control. This avoids the risks involved in moving a victim who is unable to walk.

Victims do not expect to be incapacitated, but sometimes do expect to be affected by what they ingest. While perpetrators may use water, coffee, or other nonalcoholic beverages, an additional drug is commonly concealed in alcoholic beverages.

In those instances, the victim generally knows he or she is ingesting one central nervous system (CNS) depressant—alcohol—but does not realize that he or she, in fact, is ingesting a second CNS depressant (e.g., GHB). The victim can account for an expected response to alcohol, but nothing more.

In other cases, the perpetrator may offer the intended victim a drug and encourage the victim to ingest it by telling her, "It will make you relax," "It will make you feel better," or "It will get you high." The victim may voluntarily ingest the tablet, but will not fully appreciate the contents or effects of the tablet—specifically, its ability to render her unconscious. Nor does he or she recognize the agenda of the perpetrator to carry out a sexual assault.

The perpetrator uses what he can obtain. Ketamine, a powder dissolved in drink, produces a sense of dissociation rather than sedation to unconsciousness and may also affect memory. Its use with animals makes ketamine more accessible to some, and it has been implicated in DFSA.

Not all DFSAs are so artfully carried out as to physically and mentally immobilize long enough or strongly enough. There are also identified cases of sedatives added to alcohol whose synergistic depressant effect on respiratory centers of the CNS unintentionally killed the victim. Such rare cases make for peculiar autopsy findings of evidence of consensual intercourse and polypharmacy on postmortem toxicology screening.

Some drugs may be associated with sexual exploitation, though they do not produce sedation. Crushed and then added to a drink, ecstasy or MDMA (3,4-methylenedioxy-methamphetamine) (also known as "XTC," "X," "E," "Adam," "clarity," and "lover's speed") enhances personal responsiveness and closeness. The person experiencing increased sexual responsiveness does not necessarily regret events in retrospect and will not feel the same sense of violation as someone rendered unconscious. Ecstasy use with alcohol has also been described to produce a state of stupefaction that overcomes the ability to resist physically and verbally (Eiden et al., 2013). Therefore, ecstasy use and possession is ambiguous and should be supplemented with an additional investigation of the calculation, cunning, and broader history of the suspect.

Not surprisingly, synthetic drugs or designer drugs are increasingly implicated in DFSA. Synthetic cathinones, known to most as "bath salts" (including methylone), have been found in testing of samples of unwitting rape victims (Hagan & Reidy, 2015). Methylone acts as a stimulant, is associated with a sense of well-being and profound insight, but can create a sense of confusion, especially when added to other drugs or alcohol. Some perpetrators may opt for bath salts such as methylone because it is promoted as a "love" drug.[*]

Use of bath salts may also fulfill the perpetrator's objective of drugging a victim with substances not typically tested for in drug toxicology panels. Inadequate testing is all the more problematic when a victim dies from overdose from an undetectable agent.

Advances in drug detection afford promise to investigative efforts. Research has demonstrated, for example, that different benzodiazepines, including Rohypnol, may be preserved for many days in collected alcohol from cups containing what may have been ingested (Gautam, Sharratt, & Cole, 2014). Zolpidem, a sleeping agent known to often impair memory that has been implicated in some cases of DFSA (most notably convicted former NFL star Darren Sharper), are detectable in hair and nails (Madry, Steuer, Binz, Baumgartner, & Kraemer, 2014).

MODUS OPERANDI

Variations within modus operandi reflect the perpetrator's occupation, social skills, and the setting (Welner, 2001a, 2001b). For most, delivery of the drug through alcohol or another drink is easiest, particularly if that drug is undetectable to the naked eye. One perpetrator was a celebrated chef–restaurateur who spiked a food dish he prepared for a waitress and her friend. This man, as did others, exploited the vulnerability in a relationship he had with the victims to gain trust and access to them. The victims would, of course, be more likely not to question an offer of food from him than an offer of a drink.

The perpetrator may be emboldened to incapacitate and sexually assault a victim even when others are nearby, as long as circumstances enable isolation of the victim. In one such case, a woman and the two men who accompanied her to a party were all given spiked drinks and incapacitated, after which she was raped.

As DFSA involves nonviolent isolation and then capture of victims, the perpetrator must use cunning and guile. In an effort to cover his tracks, the perpetrator may, after the rape, dress the victim while he or she is still under the influence of the drug. Reportedly, some victims first become suspicious that they were raped when, after gaining consciousness, they realize that their underwear is on backwards or that their clothes feel out of place.

The perpetrator often uses highly developed verbal and social skills to gain sufficient trust of a prospective victim to facilitate his or her isolation in order to commit the crime. After the crime, the offender may again rely upon social and verbal agility to persuade the victim, if he or she confronts him, that nothing happened or that the victim was a willing sexual partner or even an intoxicated aggressor. Another possibility—that the victim was raped while unconscious—may be so

---

[*] In the Hagan (2015) sample, some victims were forced to ingest the methylone; this represents a different form of DFSA, in which perpetrators use the pill to enhance the compliance or responsiveness of a conscious victim. While the focus of this chapter is on perpetrators who victimize the unconscious, such drug-facilitated rape deserves its own distinction and may ultimately denote how some rape can be all the more culpable because of agents used to enable and extend one's violation. Resolution of the legalities of such is one of tomorrow's challenges in the legal system and beyond the scope of this chapter.

disturbing that the victim employs protective denial and may accept the perpetrator's explanation. These devices advance the meme that no crime occurred.

The criminal's manipulation may include reminding the victim that he or she was drinking alcoholic beverages or voluntarily using illicit drugs, suggesting: "You got drunk [or were using marijuana, cocaine, etc.]—no one will believe you."

In some cases the perpetrator's modus operandi may include efforts to both enhance the vulnerability of the victim and destroy his or her potential credibility as a prosecution witness. For example, the criminal may offer the intended victim an illicit drug (cocaine, ecstasy, etc.) and also surreptitiously spike the victim's drink with a CNS depressant (such as a sedative).

In the event the victim reports the DFSA and testing is performed, all drugs might be detected but the drug profile would create the false impression that the victim is a drug abuser. The perpetrator's goal may be to destroy the credibility of the prosecution's most important witness: the victim. On the other hand, some victims may report posttraumatic stress disorder (PTSD) symptoms, even with memories impaired by amnestic drugs. The physical paralysis of DFSA is described by victims to heighten later the emotionally impactful powerlessness native to PTSD (Padmanabhanunni & Edwards, 2012).

Even if the victim reports the crime, prosecutors may be reluctant to bring charges because a jury may be hesitant to believe a victim who, at the time of the incident, may have been under the influence of an illicit drug that he or she took voluntarily.

A victim may be particularly reluctant to report the crime because his or her willing illicit drug use might be revealed publicly at a trial. The ambiguous circumstances of cases may also deter married victims or those in relationships who fear the perception of infidelity. These deterrents, along with public exposure, humiliation, and re-experiencing trauma, add to the obstacles rape victims already must overcome in exposing themselves to the rigors of a criminal justice system that affords vigorous cross-examination in the context of fair trial.

Components of the DFSA Modus Operandi

A perpetrator's modus operandi generally has four components (Welner, 2001a):

1. *Means:* access to sedating drugs and knowledge about their effects on a victim's consciousness, resistance, and memory;
2. *Setting:* an occupation, a residence, or other circumstance in which the perpetrator controls the environment to the extent that he can execute a plan in that environment without interruption or unexpected discovery;
3. *Opportunity:* the capacity to orchestrate a setting where the intended victim is alone and the crime will not be impeded, which generally requires establishing a degree of trust by the victim; and
4. *A plan to avoid arrest and prosecution:* includes exiting the premises before the victim awakens, redressing the victim, or creating alternate scenarios of the evening for the victim. When that is not possible because the victim has awakened prematurely, perpetrators commonly insist to the victim that consensual sex—or even no sexual contact—took place, to dissuade the victim from reporting the crime.

Of the components of the modus operandi, variability in setting accounts for opportunities to prevent DFSA in progress and to assist in its detection. Considerate thinking by those in drinking establishments, at fraternity houses, in private parties, for example, block isolation of the victim who is already vulnerable and can no longer exercise safe social judgment.

There is no characteristic DFSA victim. He or she may be assertive or meek, sophisticated or naïve, prim or promiscuous, cautious or adventurous. The DFSA perpetrator targets opportunistically and has the tools to render anyone primed for exploitation.

A TYPOLOGY OF DFSA

Perpetrators invariably use creativity and cunning to prevent the crime's discovery and DFSA is intended to be an opportunistic, nonconfrontational crime, no matter the setting. The drugs used to exploit the victim necessarily depend on what drugs the perpetrator can access. Therefore, a typology of DFSA is best distinguished by *settings* in which the attack takes place. Workplaces, medical facilities, and social encounters have all been used by perpetrators to exploit victims.

WORKPLACE SETTINGS

The more familiar scenario is that of an employer who takes a newly hired employee to dinner and a sexual assault occurs after the boss drugs the employee. The same dynamics apply in an aspiring applicant or in interactions with a mentor figure. The essential quality of these settings is the inherent power differential that enables a dominant person to control an applicant, aspirant, or employee.

The power differential is even more acute with an undocumented alien or another person who clearly needs to keep her job. The manipulative DFSA boss may provide financial or other incentives to promote obedience. Even when testing boundaries, there is established precedent for that victim following instructions and a willingness to go along with authority.

The dynamics of DFSA perpetrated by dominant landlords resemble those of the workplace. The key ingredient is again a power differential in the relationship that the landlord exploits in order to isolate and establish physical control over the victim.

A perpetrator who runs a business from his home maintains the ideal atmosphere for the crime. Drugs can be readily stored in unremarkable refrigerators and medicine cabinets, and beverages, which can be spiked, are handy. Victims can be positioned in such a way as not to witness tampering of a drink and so that the perpetrator may be alone with her or him. In such situations, even a perpetrator without significant social skills can isolate, drug, and sexually assault an intended victim who is there because he or she is at much needed work.

Not all workplace DFSAs involve employers and employees. In one reported case, a 48-year-old married man, while operating his housecleaning business, spiked the nonalcoholic drinks (tea, coffee, etc.) of his elderly clients. Once they were incapacitated, he would take sexually graphic photos of them and steal locks of their hair, nylon stockings, or tampons. Though this case has unusual aspects, its core features echo other DFSAs. The perpetrator targeted victims who needed him, he exploited them while they were drugged, and he acted in such a way as to avoid discovery and enable recidivism (Welner, 2001b).

HEALTH CARE SETTINGS

Physicians and paraprofessionals have also been implicated in drug-facilitated sexual crimes in distinctive, if familiar, fact patterns. Crimes involving doctors and dentists have characteristically taken place in private offices where the perpetrator/health care provider was in charge of the premises.

In these cases, perpetrators sedate and sexually assault patients while treating them. Such offenders may act professionally with most of their patients but carefully select others to victimize. In one case, for example, the victim was a new patient and the doctor arranged to be alone with her for an extended period in his office.

A health care provider who commits drug-facilitated sexual crimes may enjoy considerable respect in his neighborhood and among his colleagues, and he may also maintain an intact nuclear family. Patients and others in the community may be willing to attest to his professional skills and good character. The health care provider is therefore an example of how stature may insulate from prosecution for a considerable period of time.

Health care providers, especially those who perform procedures, are able to justify medically incapacitating their patients. Physicians and other health care professionals utilize the drugs they prescribe or administer in clinical practice, so nothing appears out of the ordinary—on the surface. Patients are administered sedatives during a consensual procedure and are sexually abused while sedated.

Depending on the circumstances, the defense would be expected to argue that the defendant, acting in the regular course of his practice, sedated the victim. The defense may further argue that, while sedated, the victim probably had a dream and, perhaps as a result of reaction to the drug, now innocently mistakes the dream for reality. This latter point is not entirely unfounded, for a DFSA victim's memory of the incident may resemble the fragmented recollection of a dream.

Notwithstanding the preceding obstacles, in some cases law enforcement authorities have been able to identify several victims and successfully prosecute the health care provider.

SOCIAL SETTINGS

Many perpetrators use social encounters to ensnare victims. Bars, clubs, parties, and dates are all effective staging areas to drug and incapacitate the victim. Drugs useful for DFSA are readily available in many clubs and bars. Recent studies have highlighted the mechanics of how college students are victimized by DFSA, particularly through alcohol and to a lesser degree with drugs (Krebs et al., 2009). Research has also distinguished between those women who are raped after voluntarily drinking to severe incapacitation versus those who are intoxicated against their will (Testa, Livingston, Vanzile-Tamsen, & Frone, 2003).

Some offenders in social settings are unable to seclude their victims before drugging them. In bars and clubs, these perpetrators may guide the intended victim away from the scene as quickly as possible. Consequently, security personnel can play an important crime prevention role. When a patron who is physically incapacitated is being removed by an apparently concerned and physically dominant person, responsible parties should query how well the two individuals know each other. Some suspicion and concern should follow that "Good Samaritan" who appears to be hurrying a person he just met out of a drinking establishment. Vigilance should be further heightened when the victim has difficulty walking and describes feelings of exceptional mental disorientation, a quick change in mental status, or physical incapacity to paralysis. These effects, while certainly representative of alcohol intoxication, are exceptional enough to prompt questions about whether more than alcohol is involved. Sending that impaired person home with more established friends is a safer directive because security in the club or bar may be the last responsible authority that can intervene before an attack takes place.

ACCOMPLICES AND CONSPIRACIES

More than one perpetrator may collaborate and conspire to commit DFSA. Confirmed cases, invariably occurring in social settings, have involved friends, a male and female couple, and even brothers as co-conspirators.

A perpetrator may use an accomplice who does not actually participate in the assault. For example, a female accomplice may be deployed to gain the trust of an intended female victim and engender in her a false sense of security and safety. The male who then orchestrates the con and primarily draws gratification from the ensuing attack is the dominant figure in the accomplice cases with male and female offenders.

Cases involving an accomplice or a co-conspirator evidence an exceptionally manipulative primary offender with an ingenious and elaborate modus operandi. Not surprisingly, such couples may victimize high numbers of women. The primary offender is remarkable for having the capacity to inspire an accomplice to engage in such outlandish activity when DFSA is not interesting or meaningful to the accomplice. The capacity to inspire the otherwise uninvolved to perverse crime is an identified element of a depraved crime.

Most male–female teams have histories notable for the use of recreational drugs (cocaine or ecstasy) and many have direct or indirect links to the pornography industry. As such, DFSA involving accomplices has been most frequently identified in Southern California and South Florida and other places where the industry flourishes.

Intrafamilial DFSA

It is hardly surprising that many intrafamilial DFSAs go unreported. Because the perpetrator may be the head of the house, each of the constraints confronting incest victims (threatened loss of family integrity, confusion over an act of aggression, vulnerability to psychological manipulation, self-blame, fear of eviction, lack of support of other family members) must be appreciated for its impact in lowering the reporting rate. Just as manipulative perpetrators can convince nonfamilial victims to remain silent from confusion and shame, similar dynamics are all the more powerful for the unique pressures confronting a child or other powerless victim of intrafamilial DFSA inside the home.

Male-on-Male Offenses

Cases in which a male perpetrator used drugs to exploit sexually another male have occurred almost exclusively in social or school encounters, rather than health care or workplaces. Power differentials may be a component of the exploitation and access, especially when the DFSA is perpetrated by an adult male against a child, an adolescent, or an economically vulnerable target.

Confirmed perpetrators of such male-on-male assaults have also included foster fathers and even men picking up hitchhikers. The latter are especially problematic to public health because the transient nature of the encounter makes it harder to identify an assaulter, especially when the DFSA perpetrator leaves the victim in an isolated area after the attack. Additional risk arises from a victim being abandoned while still under the influence of a DFSA drug. One such victim, abandoned by a road while still under the influence of the drug, was struck by a car and killed.

DFSA has generally not been described in crimes committed by heterosexual killers. However, sadomasochistic homosexual killers have employed DFSA as part of a homicidal agenda (Silvestrini, 2007). Jeffrey Dahmer and John Wayne Gacy, the notorious serial killers, verbally manipulated and then immobilized male victims through sedation before their sexual assaults. Dahmer used the benzodiazepine derivative Halcion (triazolam) and other drugs (Everything$_2$, 2001), and Gacy used chloroform (Bell & Bardsley, 2007).

Dahmer and Gacy, as with a number of non-murderous homosexual DFSA perpetrators, harbored strongly conflicted feelings about their private homosexuality (Stone, 1989). The preference for sex with a heavily sedated or essentially inanimate victim may, for some homosexual perpetrators, reflect continued conflicted feelings about relating intimately to the same sex. Gacy was married, a local businessman, and politically and socially active in a conservative community (Bell & Bardsley, 2007). As with a number of the perpetrators described earlier, Gacy lured victims with the promise of a job; he attacked the males in his home after he persuasively drew them there under false pretenses (Bell & Bardsley, 2007). Murder as an endpoint may also, for Dahmer and Gacy, have resolved conflict and self-loathing relating to their homosexuality.

Sexual Deviance or Sexual Hunters

Earlier sexual preferences of the perpetrator are worth noting. DFSA offenders appear to distinguish themselves into two groups of sexuality: those who are incompetent at finding sexual partners yet maintain a high degree of sexual interest; and those with sexual fantasies of complete domination and control of a partner.

The distribution of these groups crosses the socioeconomic, age, and educational spectrum, although DFSA offenders have been primarily male. In certain respects, particularly when examining someone's fantasy life, it is required to look beyond superficial or demographic details into the recesses of a person's private life if it is accessible. As previously mentioned, DFSA perpetrators may be personable, attractive, charming or not, and married or not. Those who have strong social and psychosexual skills may be manifesting, through their DFSA activity, the hypersexual stimulation seeking of psychopathy.

The possible link of consumption of Viagra, Cialis, Levitra, and related agents to antisocial and exploitative schemes among those seeking additional or unattainable partners has not yet been explored. DFSA, as a crime of hedonism and hypersexuality, would not be a factor in those with physiologically diminished sex drive.

WHAT DISTINGUISHES DFSA OFFENDERS FROM OTHER SEXUAL CRIMINALS?

DFSA perpetrators are distinguished from rapists as a group by generally well-developed communications and social skills (Scott, Cole, McKay, Golden, & Liggett, 1984; Welner, 2001a). This glibness assists the perpetrator to gain access to the victim and engender a sense of comfort. By contrast, many coercive rapists have numerous verbal neuropsychological abnormalities and more poorly developed social skills. Those poorly developed and isolating limitations are linked to problems in anger management that often contribute to violence as expressed through coercive rape (Hall, Hirschman, Graham, & Zaragoza, 1993).

Communications skills differ from social skills. A perpetrator armed with vocabulary could not effectively inspire potential victims to trust him. Social skills, on the other hand, enable one to persuade—to lure a potential victim to an isolated setting, to trick even a cautious person to accept a drink, even to convince a woman who has been drugged and raped that, in fact, no rape occurred.

Such manipulation may inspire the idea that those who engage in DFSA are the more sophisticated and more deliberate, cunning personalities. In many instances, that is the case. However, beyond their veneer and modus operandi, not all perpetrators of DFSA are cool and collected (Welner, 2001a).

DFSA may not allow for some elements of what makes sexual assaults appealing to rapists. Certainly DFSA does enable the fantasies of those who desire complete control and domination over a victim.

The capacity to establish workplace or landlord control over a victim underscores how DFSA offenders are *not* suffering from psychotic illness at the time of the assault. In these and social settings, bizarre behavior would frighten potential victims away from those offering them drinks or sedation. Forcible rape, by contrast, may be committed by someone especially irrational or responding to hallucinations (Smith & Taylor, 1999).

One rare example of a psychotic DFSA offender involved a 55-year-old clergyman–writer who placed want ads for assistance at his home office. He attempted to commit DFSAs on women who responded to the ads when he was experiencing a manic episode of his bipolar illness and even when his mood stabilized. He could never have qualified for an insanity defense, as he appreciated the wrongfulness of his actions, but when ill he was driven by the heightened sexual preoccupation of his mania.

Forcible rape affected by severe psychiatric distress is more likely to be impulsive (Phillips, Heads, Taylor, & Hill, 1999). DFSA is opportunistic, but is perpetrated through a modus operandi that involves planning the setting where the victim is to be drugged and assaulted.

Different DFSA perpetrators are not incapable of committing coercive rape any more than sex offenders may break the law in various ways. Cases have occurred of rapists who subsequently offended by DFSA when released from incarceration for their rapes. Violence is traditionally at the root of rape, but rapists released from custody modify their modus operandi to reduce the likelihood of being re-arrested. Furthermore, rapists who act impulsively earlier in life may have better impulse control (Welner, 2001a), yet the same antisocial or rape proclivities, at a more advanced age.

WHAT MAKES A SOUND INVESTIGATION?

Because successful DFSA also includes impairing the victim's recall, many DFSAs remain unreported. Reporting is further dissuaded by the perpetrators themselves and the daunting prospects of the victim's role in criminal prosecutions.

Investigation of DFSA is enhanced by immediate reporting because blood toxicology testing can then be undertaken to ascertain the presence of a DFSA agent in the victim. Delays in toxicology testing or mishandling of urine test samples routinely disadvantage DFSA investigations. GHB is not routinely tested in toxicology panels; when GHB intoxication is suspected, a urine sample should be taken. If the drug employed is Rohypnol or GHB, for example, testing the afternoon following an alleged DFSA may be fruitless.

Investigators do well to memorize the side effects of the DFSA drugs; questioning witnesses about such effects they may have seen in the victim provides an indirect source of evidence for ingestion. Referencing GHB, for example, there are not many drugs to which bladder or bowel incontinence can be attributed; Rohypnol, by contrast, produces the opposite: urinary retention, if anything.

Interviewers of the victim need to be mindful of the same obstacles confronting other rape victims, such as shame and guilt. However, no systematic study has compared DFSA victims with other sexual assault victims for specific vulnerabilities and potentials in the investigative phase. A victim may encounter poor support from her close associates but the responsiveness of a crisis counselor may facilitate an open communication of details relevant to solving the case.

The DFSA victim whose memory has been impaired to the point of erasure may not necessarily experience her assault in the same way or within the customary time frame of a person who consciously witnessed an assault to her body integrity (Padmanabhanunni & Edwards, 2012).

Agencies are well served by educating higher risk groups (such as students who socialize heavily around drinking and drugs) to seek assistance as quickly as possible and to ensure that toxicology testing is done during the window of drug detection.

Traditional techniques of sexual assault investigation—even seductive interviewing techniques such as minimizing the offense, joining the offender's vantage point, or blaming the victim—may not work. DFSA perpetrators are cunning, are often invested in jobs or lives in the community, and invariably never volunteer to the victim or to law enforcement that something unseemly has taken place. Appeals to their conscience do not work either.

Creative approaches for eliciting a confession may thus be necessary. Some law enforcement agencies convince a victim to contact the perpetrator on a pretext and to secure an admission to the drugging while police monitor the conversation. Also, investigators should be familiar with the different packaging and presentation of GBL before searching the offender's residence, office, or other property. Anything from "nail polish remover" to "car alloy cleaner" may warrant testing for the presence of GBL (Calman, 2006).

Profiling may be of limited benefit because of the diversity of perpetrators and variations in psychosexual motivation. Workplace and landlord DFSA perpetrators may be inept socially and often live alone, with poorly established intimacy with others. Some of these perpetrators exploit power differentials because they do not have the social skills for successful sexual attachment. For those with undeveloped capacity for intimacy, the opportunity to have sex with something (rather than someone) impersonal, compliant, and ephemeral may have been all they are emotionally capable of.

The existence of an internal drive to conquer sexually as much as possible demonstrates a narcissistic preoccupation with omnipotence, rather than the satisfaction of a compulsive or forbidden sexual need. In one case where male twins collaborated in numerous drug-facilitated rapes, the brothers would mug for the videotapes they took. One brother would brag to the other, "We have fucked more women than anybody." Despite the fact that some of their unsuspecting victims found them to be attractive, the brothers appeared to have had a greater interest in hunting new targets than in being with women they had already violated.

However, many confirmed DFSA perpetrators have well-developed intimate relationships. This speaks to gratifying forbidden sexual proclivities or frank sexual opportunism. Neither of these occurs exclusive of the capacity of intimacy. This is why perpetrators from social and health care settings and in male-on-male attacks may be adequately socially integrated.

Physical violence is less a part of DFSA offender histories than with other rapists, and DFSA offenders likewise do not carry out secondary robbery or destruction of property. Given the lack of even circumstantial links of evidence with which to work, DFSAs that lack toxicology evidence resemble probes of abuse allegations whose viability derives almost entirely from the complainant's credibility. Because DFSA offenders are so diverse, behavioral profiling alone (especially in the absence of a rich personal and behavioral history) may not resolve the competing later accounts of predation of the victim versus the complainant's potential secondary gain.

Consequently, DFSA investigation routinely requires creative, ambitious approaches. Some prosecutors or law enforcement officers may find elaborate stings or unorthodox approaches cumbersome and an unjustified use of resources, particularly when rape investigations do not routinely warrant such manpower or they even risk complaints of police harassment. Because DFSA perpetrators are a high risk to recidivate, however, public safety implications justify resourceful tenacity. This includes access to perpetrator and victim smart phones, which afford the most valid reconstructive evidence of motivations and choices before and after an event.

Health care providers suspected of DFSA may best be caught by undercover patients, in order to overcome arguments that sedatives are administered in the natural course of a procedure and that a patient's complaints of sexual assault reflect her confusion in emerging from sedation.

In one high-profile case, police obtained a court order authorizing them to place a hidden video camera in a dentist's treatment room. Then, the police recruited an undercover officer to pose as a patient. Like the three patients who had reported incidents to police, the undercover officer was young and female. During her appointment, the dentist sedated the officer and removed an abscessed tooth. He then lifted her blouse and began moving his hands across the upper part of her back and around toward her breasts. Officers who were monitoring the videotape in the basement signaled other officers to arrest the dentist. When one investigator first opened the door he observed that the dentist's thumbs were massaging the nipples of the victim's breasts. After the police officers entered the room, the dentist placed the "patient" back in the chair and asserted, "She's in respiratory distress—I was just trying to help her breathe and ventilate."

Employer and landlord perpetrators have the wherewithal to offend in different offices, businesses, and even across state lines. Investigations should solicit the input of former employees or tenants, who may have had unusual experiences or learned of them.

Today's generation of collegiate and young adults, who are increasingly connected through Internet chat rooms, instant messaging, Facebook, and WhatsApp, is far more open about sexuality than generations past. Locker room talk has advanced to the electronic media. It is far easier for investigators to cultivate relationships with a person of interest and to draw him or her into a discussion of sexuality and personal history. Because perpetrators of DFSA have far less willingness to experience their actions as wrong, investigators benefit from far easier accessibility of DFSA perpetrators who have an affinity for the electronic media, especially those who offend in social settings.

DFSA offenders who are otherwise sexually incompetent may also immerse themselves in the parallel universe of social media and electronic chats, where trust and friendships ignite with unusual speed and openness based on shared passions and reduced vigilance. In the authors' professional opinions, DFSA is one example of how cyberspace is to criminal investigation what cyber dating sites are to romance.

Networks of pedophiles, human traffickers, and other sex offenders have been exposed through their Web-based networking. DFSA tips are shared by posters to a variety of forums. Furthermore, underground websites promoting creative uses of drugs and pharmacology attract open-minded posters seeking to share and to refine their own uses of different agents for different purposes. These communities are appropriate pools in which to prospect and ferret out DFSA perpetrators, especially those fine-tuning their modus operandi.

Few DFSA offenders reflect evidence for an *uncontrollable* urge, although DFSA offenders rarely submit candid self-disclosure in their legal proceedings either. Nonetheless, some perpetrators of DFSA repeat the offense with astonishing frequency. Therefore, any investigation should explore the possibility of compulsive behavior relating to deviant sexual fantasy (paraphilia) contributing to the offending behavior.

In some cases, once the drug has rendered the victim unconscious, the perpetrator may exploit his control over the victim by acting out sexual fantasies. For example, he may violate the victim anally, shave her genital areas, or ejaculate on her face. Far more frequently, though, the perpetrator endeavors to conceal all signs of the crime.

Some perpetrators of DFSA reflect a persistent fantasy in their modus operandi. For example, in cases where the perpetrator prowled for victims who were either hitchhiking or in public places, or repeatedly telephoned prospective targets, the drive to offend appeared to be relentless in comparison with other cases. Further study is needed to determine the basis of exceptional drive to locate victims. DFSA perpetrators who organize their life's activities around victim acquisition, a quality observed in locked-in pedophiles, have not yet been described.

The perpetrator with the fantasy of sex with an immobilized victim may videotape the attack in order to relive the fantasy in later masturbation. Videotaping of drugged partners may also reflect narcissistic expression, especially likely when the perpetrator casts himself in the starring role of his own porn film. Consistent with this vanity, one videotaping rapist had a history of cosmetic surgeries, including liposuction.

Cases involving a victim to whom the perpetrator has ready access, such as a roommate, may involve multiple assaults over time, even videotaping. A victimized girlfriend, who would have already been sexually available to the perpetrator, speaks to a perpetrator's DFSA as the fulfillment of sexual fantasy.

The ease with which images can be captured and digitally stored, with relatively low technology, practically makes searching for recording equipment and image files mandatory. Backup hard drives, extra computers, and even flash drives are perfect places for perpetrators to preserve fantasy material. Roommate (victimized or not) or cohabiting family will better inform investigators whether and where videotaping and image collection (through pasted pictures, saved DVDs, and flash drives) are likely to be found.

Accomplices to DFSA are often involved through the social persuasion of the dominant offender and are not fueling a personal fantasy. The accomplice may be key to solving a DFSA or multiple DFSAs. Because accomplices are themselves often under the influence of substances when the crime is committed, their conscience may be more accessible when sober. Approaching accomplices requires patience. This is especially true because the accomplice may be the significant other of the dominant offender.

Alternatively, after a homicide, email and other electronic communications may represent the best evidence trail. Even though perpetrators of DFSA feel entitled to take advantage of their victims, death is unexpected and the stress may provoke incriminating correspondence.

A perpetrator may retain personal effects of victims to add to the intensity of a relived fantasy. Unlike videotapes, trophies or souvenirs only suggest that sexual contact may have taken place, not that sex happened with an incapacitated person. Trophies or souvenirs are more important for linking seemingly unrelated individuals—a situation in which a perpetrator might otherwise deny previous attacks.

It is easier to investigate the DFSA that occurs in a professional, vocational, or residential (landlord) setting. The perpetrator may be older, more socially isolated, and far more guarded.

However, his mode of victim acquisition is distinct (e.g., want ads for employees who desperately need work) and may be exploited by investigators acting undercover.

Some perpetrators may use sedatives, muscle relaxants, or pain relievers for which they have a prescription or which they have purchased illicitly either from drug dealers or via the Internet from overseas distributors.

Despite surprisingly well-integrated functioning in many DFSA perpetrators, one must remember that such offenders frequently obtain prescriptions the old-fashioned way: from doctors who treat them with sedatives characteristically prescribed for symptoms of anxiety or insomnia. Tracing the prescriptions may reveal a suspect who was specifically seeking a drug that had capacities more suited to DFSA than mere sedation. For example, suspicion is warranted for those who continue to fill and to use prescriptions without any evidence of insomnia.

Finally, there is a high probability that identifying the perpetrator's other victims will significantly enhance both the outcome of the prosecution and the sentence imposed. Whatever the ambiguity of DFSA investigations, multiple instances of completely unrelated complainants demonstrate that the more unusual an event, the more improbable such a repeated unusual scenario is innocuous and misunderstood. At some point, the reality of DFSA advances beyond the circumstantial because of sheer probability. Lurking even within multiple complainant cases, however, is the potential of one or more complainants whose opportunistic false charges can sabotage justice for all.

REFERENCES

American Psychiatric Association. 1994. *Diagnostic and statistical manual of mental disorders: DSM–IV*, 4th ed. Washington, DC: American Psychiatric Association.

Bell, R., and Bardsley, M. 2007. TruTV Crime Library, Retrieved from http://www.webcitation.org/getfile?fileid=0f4d40f7adde43eec178ae4c27cd58916a2fcfa9.

Britt, G., and McCance-Katz, E. 2005. A brief interview of the clinical pharmacology of club drugs. *Substance Use & Misuse*, 40: 1189–1201.

Calman, B. 2006. This graduate died after inadvertently drinking the date rape drug GHB. *London Daily Mail*, October 27, p. 42.

Eiden, C., Cathala, P., Fabresse, N., Galea, Y., Mathieu-Daudé, J-C., Baccino, E., et al. 2013. A case of drug-facilitated sexual assault involving 3,4-methylene-dioxy-methylamphetamine. *Journal of Psychoactive Drugs*, 45(1): 94–97.

Everything₂. 2001. Jeffery Dahmer. The Everything Development Co., http://www.everything2.com/index.pl?node_id=82125&lastnode_id=0.

Gautam, L., Sharratt, S, D, and Cole, M. D. 2014. Drug facilitated sexual assault: Detection and stability of benzodiazepines in spiked drinks using gas chromatography-mass spectrometry. *PLoS ONE*, 9(2): e89031. doi: 10.1371/journal.pone.0089031.

Greenblatt, D. J., Miller, L. G., and Shader, R. I. 1990. Neurochemical and pharmacokinetic correlates of the clinical action of benzodiazepine hypnotic drugs. *American Journal of Medicine*, 88(3A): 18S–24S.

Hall, G., Hirschman, R., Graham J., and Zaragoza, M. (Eds.). 1993. *Sexual aggression: Issues in etiology, assessment, and treatment.* Kent, OH: Taylor & Francis.

Hensley, L. 2002. Drug-facilitated sexual assault on campus: Challenges and interventions. *Journal of College Counseling*, Fall(5): 175–181.

Kernberg, O. F. 1989. The narcissistic personality disorder and the differential diagnosis of antisocial behavior. *The Psychiatric Clinics of North America*, 12: 553–570.

Krebs, C. P., Lindquist, C. H., Warner, T. D., Fisher, B. S., and Martin, S. L. 2009. College women's experiences with physically forced, alcohol- or other drug-enabled, and drug-facilitated sexual assault before and since entering college. *Journal of the American College of Health*, 57(6): 639–647.

Madry, M. M., Steuer, A. E., Binz, T. M., Baumgartner, M. R., and Kraemer, T. 2014. Systematic investigation of the incorporation mechanisms of zolpidem in fingernails. *Drug Testing and Analysis*, 6(6): 533–541.

National Institute on Drug Abuse. 2006, May. *Rohypnol and GHB*. Bethesda, MD.

Padmanabhanunni, A., and Edwards, D. 2012. Treating the psychological sequelae of proactive drug-facilitated sexual assault: Knowledge building through systematic case based research. *Behavioral and Cognitive Psychotherapy*, 41: 371–375.

Phillips, S. L., Heads, T. C., Taylor, P. J., and Hill, G. M. 1999. Sexual offending and antisocial sexual behavior among patients with schizophrenia. *Journal of Clinical Psychiatry*, 60(3): 170–175.

Pope, E., and Shouldice, M. 2001. Drugs and sexual assault. In *Trauma, violence, and abuse*, 51–55. London: Sage Publications.

Price, D. R. 1994. Personality disorders and traits. In J. J. McDonald, Jr. and F. B. Kulick (Eds.), *Mental and emotional injuries in employment litigation*, 93–140. Washington, DC: The Bureau of National Affairs.

Richer, Fields, L., Bell, S., Heppner, J., Dodge, J., Boccellari, A., et al. 2015. Characterizing drug facilitated sexual assault subtypes and treatment engagement of victims at a hospital-based rape treatment center. *Journal of Interpersonal Violence*, June 10: 1–19.

Rickert, V., and Weimann, C. 1998. Date rape among adolescents and young adults. *Journal of Pediatric and Adolescent Gynecology*, 11: 167–175.

Scott, M. L., Cole, J. K., McKay, S. E., Golden, C. J., and Liggett, K. R. 1984. Neuropsychological performance of sexual assaulters and pedophiles. *Journal of Forensic Science*, 29(4): 1114–1118.

Silvestrini, E. 2007. Drugging case ends with 2 convictions. *Tampa Tribune*, January 20.

Smith, A. D., and Taylor, P. J. 1999. Serious sex offending against women by men with schizophrenia. Relationship of illness and psychotic symptoms to offending. *British Journal of Psychiatry*, 174: 233–237.

Stone, M. H. 1989. Murder. *The Psychiatric Clinics of North America*, 12: 643–652.

Welner, M. 1997. Rapist in a glass: The big picture of the Rohypnol wars. *The Forensic Echo*, 1: 4–10.

Welner, M. 2001a. The perpetrators and their modus operandi. In M. LeBeau and A. Mozayani (Eds.). *Drug facilitated sexual assault*, 39–71. London: Academic Press.

Welner, M. 2001b. The drug facilitated sex offender: Distinguishing features and histories. Paper at the present. AAFS Annual Meeting, Seattle, WA.

FURTHER READING

Abarbanel, G. 2000. Assessing drug-facilitated rape: Learning from victims. *National Institute of Justice Journal*, 243: 11–12.

Alexander, M. A. 1999. Sexual offender treatment efficacy revisited. *Sexual Abuse: A Journal of Research & Treatment*, 11(2): 101–116.

Back, S., and Lips, H. M. 1998. Child sexual abuse: Victim age, victim gender, and observer gender as factors contributing to attributions of responsibility. *Child Abuse & Neglect*, 22(12): 1239–1252.

Berger, P., Berner, W., Bolterauer, J., Gutierrez, K., and Berger, K. 1999. Sadistic personality disorder in sexual offenders: Relationship to antisocial personality disorder and sexual sadism. *Journal of Personality Disorders*, 13(2): 175–186.

Black, D. W., Kehrberg, L. L., Flumerfelt, D. L., and Schlosser, S. S. 1997. Characteristics of 36 subjects reporting compulsive sexual behavior. *American Journal of Psychiatry*, 154(2): 243–249.

Blum, A. 2000. Seduction typology OK at sentencing: Testimony relevant on moral culpability of sex offender. *The Forensic Panel Letter*, 4(12), www.forensicpanel.com

Bownes, I. T., O'Gorman, E. C., and Sayers, A. 1991. Rape—A comparison of stranger and acquaintance assaults. *Medicine, Science, and the Law*, 31(2): 102–109.

Burgess, A. W., Hartman, C. R., McCausland, M. P., and Powers, P. 1984. Response patterns in children and adolescents exploited through sex rings and pornography. *American Journal of Psychiatry*, 141(5): 656–662.

Collings, S. J., and Payne, M. F. 1991. Attribution of causal and moral responsibility to victims of father–daughter incest: An exploratory examination of five factors. *Child Abuse & Neglect*, 15(4): 513–521.

Doren, D. M. 1998. Recidivism base rates, predictions of sex offender recidivism, and the "sexual predator" commitment laws. *Behavioral Sciences and the Law*, 16: 97–114.

Douglas, J. E., Burgess, A. N., Burgess, A. G., and Ressler, R. K. (Eds.). 1992. Rape and sexual assault. In *Crime classification manual: A standard system for investigating and classifying violent crimes*. New York: Lexington Books.

Du Mont, J., Macdonald, S., Rotbard, N., Asllani, E., Bainbridge, D., and Cohen, M. M. 2009. Factors associated with suspected drug-facilitated sexual assault. *Canadian Medical Association Journal*, 180: 513–519.

Fairstein, L. A. 1993. *Sexual violence: Our war against rape*. New York: William Morrow & Co.

Groth, A. N., Burgess, W., and Holmstrom, L. L. 1977. Rape: Power, anger, and sexuality. *American Journal of Psychiatry*, 134(11): 1239–1243.

Hagan, K. S., and Reidy, L. 2015. Detection of synthetic cathinones in victims of sexual assault. *Forensic Science International*, 257: 71–75.

Hanson, R. K., and Thornton, D. 2000. Improving risk assessments for sex offenders: A comparison of three actuarial scales. *Law and Human Behavior*, 24: 119–136.

Hazelwood, R. R., and Warren, J. I. 2000. The sexually violent offender: Impulsive or ritualistic? *Aggression and Violent Behavior*, 5: 267–279.

Henn, F. A., Herjanic, M., and Vanderpearl, R. H. 1976. Forensic psychiatry: Profiles of two types of sex offenders. *American Journal of Psychiatry*, 133(6): 694–696.

Horowitz, M. J. 1989. Clinical phenomenology of narcissistic pathology. *The Psychiatric Clinics of North America*, 12: 531–540.

Hucker, S., Bartlik, B., Moser, C., Berlin, F., and Quinsley, V. (Commentators). 2001. Cases in headlines: Sado-masochism. Harmless, or ominous? *The Forensic Panel Letter*, 4(12): 3–4. www.forensicpanel.com

Janus, E. S., and Meehl, P. E. 1997. Assessing the legal standard for predictions of dangerousness in sex offender commitment proceedings. *Psychology, Public Policy, and Law*, 3: 33–64.

Kafka, M. P. 1995. Sexual impulsivity. In E. Hollander and D. Stein (Eds.). *Impulsivity and aggression*, 201–228. Chichester, England: John Wiley & Sons.

Kaplan, H. I., and Sadock, B. J. 1993. *Pocket handbook of psychiatric drug treatment*. Baltimore, MD: Williams & Wilkins.

Kaplan, H. I., Sadock, B. J., and Grebb, J. A. 1994. *Kaplan and Sadock's synopsis of psychiatry: Behavioral sciences, clinical psychiatry*, 7th ed. Baltimore, MD: Williams & Wilkins.

Kushner, M. G., Abrams, K., Thuras, P., Thuras, P., and Hanson, K. L. 2000. Individual differences predictive of drinking to manage anxiety among non-problem drinkers with panic disorder. *Alcoholism: Clinical and Experimental Research*, 24(4): 448–458.

O'Brien, M. C., McCoy, T. P., Rhodes, S. D., Wagoner, A., and Wolfson, M. 2008. Caffeinated cocktails: Energy drink consumption, high-risk drinking, and alcohol-related consequences among college students. *Academic Emergency Medicine*, 15: 453–460.

Paris, J. 1997. Antisocial and borderline personality disorders: Two separate diagnoses or two aspects of the same psychopathology? *Comprehensive Psychiatry*, 38: 237–242.

Physicians' Desk Reference, 54th ed. 2000. Montvale, NJ: Medical Economics Company, Inc.

Pithers, W. D. 1993. Treatment of rapists: Reinterpretation of early outcome data and exploratory constructs to enhance therapeutic efficacy. In G. C. Nagayama Hall, R. Hirschman, J. R. Graham, and M. S. Zaragoza (Eds.). *Sexual aggression: Issues in etiology, assessment, and treatment*. Kent, OH: Taylor & Francis.

Pithers, W. D., Kashima, K., Cumming, G. F., Beal, L. S., and Buell, M. 1988. Relapse prevention of sexual aggression. In R. Prentky and V. Quinsey (Eds.). *Human sexual aggression: Current perspectives*, 244–260. New York: New York Academy of Sciences.

Raine, A. 1993. *The psychopathology of crime: Criminal behavior as a clinical disorder*. San Diego, CA: Academic Press, Inc.

Raj, A., Silverman, J. G., and Amaro, H. 1997. The relationship between sexual abuse and sexual risk among high school students: Findings from the 1997 Massachusetts youth risk behavior survey. *Maternal and Child Health Journal*, 4(2): 125–134.

Stone, M. H. 1993. *Abnormalities of personality: Within and beyond the realm of treatment*. New York: Norton.

Testa, M., Livingston, J., Vanzile-Tamsen, C., and Frone, M. R. 2003. The role of women's substance use in vulnerability to forcible and incapacitated rape. *Journal of Studies on Alcohol*, 64: 756–764.

Warren, J. I., Hazelwood, R. R., and Dietz, P. E. 1996. The sexually sadistic serial killer. *Journal of Forensic Science*, 41(6): 970–974.

Williams, C. D., and Adams-Campbell, L. L. 2000. Addictive behaviors and depression among African Americans residing in a public housing community. *Addictive Behavior*, 25(1): 45–46.

Witt, P. H., Del Russo, J., Oppenheim, J., and Ferguson, G. 1996. Sex offender risk assessment and the law. *The Journal of Psychiatry & Law*, Fall: 343–376.

23 The Criminal Sexual Sadist

Robert R. Hazelwood, Park Dietz, and Janet I. Warren

CONTENTS

Introduction..373
What Is Sexual Sadism?..373
Physical and Psychological Suffering..374
Sexually Sadistic Behavior 374
    Sadistic Fantasy...374
    Sadism toward Symbols...375
    Consenting or Paid Partners 375
Behavior Patterns Confused with Sexual Sadism 376
    Personalities Conflated with Sadistic Behavior 376
    Cruelty during Crime 377
    Pathological Group Behavior 377
    Sanctioned Cruelty..377
    Revenge-Motivated Cruelty 378
    Interrogative Cruelty 378
    Postmortem Mutilation..378
Study of Sadistic Offenders 379
    Offender Characteristics..379
    Crime Characteristics 380
    Evidence of Crime...381
Investigating Crimes of the Sexual Sadist...381
    Sources 382
    Search Warrants...382
Interviewing the Sexual Sadist...382
Summary..382
References..383

INTRODUCTION

Any investigator who has taken a statement from a tortured victim or who has worked the crime scene of a sexually sadistic homicide will never forget the experience. Human cruelty reveals itself in many kinds of offenses, but seldom more starkly than in the crimes of sexual sadists.

This chapter describes the more commonly encountered actions of sexual sadists and differentiates sexual sadism from other cruel acts. It also describes the common characteristics of sexually sadistic crimes and offers investigators suggestions that they should follow when confronted with the crimes of the sexually sadistic offender.

WHAT IS SEXUAL SADISM?

Sexual sadism is a persistent pattern of becoming sexually excited in response to another's suffering. Granted, sexual excitement can occur at odd times even in normal people. But to the sexually sadistic offender, it is the suffering of the victim that is sexually arousing.

The writings of two sexual sadists graphically convey their desires. One wrote:

> ...the most important radical aim is to make her suffer since there is no greater power over another person than that of inflicting pain on her to force her to undergo suffering without her being able to defend herself. The pleasure in the complete domination over another person is the very essence of the sadistic drive.

Of his sexually sadistic activities with a victim he killed, another offender wrote:

> ...she was writhering [*sic*] in pain and I loved it. I was now combining my sexual high of rape and my power high of fear to make a total sum that is now beyond explaining ... I was alive for the sole purpose of causing pain and receiving sexual gratification ... I was relishing the pain just as much as the sex....

Each offender's account confirms that it is the suffering of the victim, not the infliction of physical or psychological pain, that is sexually arousing. In fact, one of these men resuscitated his victim from unconsciousness so that he could continue to savor her suffering. Inflicting pain is a means to create suffering and to elicit the desired responses of obedience, submission, humiliation, fear, and terror.

PHYSICAL AND PSYCHOLOGICAL SUFFERING

Specific findings uncovered during an investigation determine if the crime committed involves sexual sadism. The critical issues are whether the victim suffered, whether the suffering was intentionally elicited, and whether the suffering sexually aroused the offender. This is why neither sexual nor cruel acts committed on an unconscious or dead victim are necessarily evidence of sexual sadism; such a victim cannot experience suffering. For this reason, postmortem injuries alone do not indicate sexual sadism.

Rapists cause their victims to suffer, but only sexual sadists intentionally inflict that suffering, whether physical or psychological, to enhance their own arousal. Neither the severity of an offender's cruelty nor the extent of a victim's suffering is evidence of sexual sadism. Acts of extreme cruelty or those that cause great suffering are often performed for nonsexual purposes, even during sexual assaults.

SEXUALLY SADISTIC BEHAVIOR

The behavior of sexual sadists, like that of other sexual deviants, extends along a wide spectrum. Sexual sadists can be law-abiding citizens who fantasize but do not act as well as individuals who fulfill these fantasies with freely consenting partners. However, it is only when sexual sadists commit crimes do their fantasies become relevant to law enforcement.

SADISTIC FANTASY

All sexual acts and sexual crimes begin with fantasy. However, in contrast to normal sexual fantasies, those of the sexual sadist center on domination, control, humiliation, pain, injury, and violence, or a combination of these themes, as a means to elicit suffering. As the fantasies of the sexual sadist vary, so does the degree of violence.

The fantasies discerned from the personal records of offenders are complex, elaborate, and involve detailed scenarios that include specific methods of capture and control, location, scripts to be followed by the victim, sequence of sexual acts, and desired victim responses. Sexual sadists dwell frequently on these fantasies, which often involve multiple victims and sometimes include partners.

CASE NO. 1

One offender, who is believed to have kidnapped, tortured, and murdered more than 20 women and young girls, wrote extensively about his sexually sadistic fantasies involving women. These writings included descriptions of his victims' capture, torment, and death by hanging. At the time of his arrest, photographs were found depicting the subject in female attire and participating in autoerotic asphyxia. The offender had apparently acted out his fantasies on both himself and others.

SADISM TOWARD SYMBOLS

Some individuals act out their sadistic desires against inanimate objects, most often dolls, pictures, and clothing, but sometimes corpses. As in the case of fantasy, the suffering in such activity is imagined. (See Chapter 4 for a more complete discussion.)

CASE NO. 2

A female doll was found hanging outside an emergency room of a hospital. Around its neck was a hangman's noose, and its hands were bound behind its back. Needles penetrated one eye and one ear. Burn marks were present on the doll, and cotton protruded from its mouth. Drawn on the chest of the doll were what appeared to be sutures. An incision had been made between the legs, creating an orifice to which hair had been glued and into which a pencil had been inserted. Nothing indicated that a crime had occurred.

Although it is commonly believed that sexual sadists are cruel toward animals, it has not been determined that such cruelty is related to sexual sadism. Violent men were often cruel to animals during childhood, but without sexual excitement. Cruel acts toward animals may reflect nonsexual aggressive and sadistic motives or may be sacrifices demanded by religious rituals or delusional beliefs. Someone who is sexually excited by an animal's suffering may indicate characteristics associated with both sexual sadists and zoophiles (one attracted to animals).

CONSENTING OR PAID PARTNERS

Sexual sadism may also be acted out with freely consenting or paid partners (i.e., prostitutes who specialize in role-playing the "submissive" for sexually sadistic clients). The nature of the acts varies from simulations of discomfort to actions that result in severe injury. A consenting partner turns into a victim when her withdrawal of consent goes unheeded or when an act results in unexpected injury or death. This is when such acts are likely to come to the attention of law enforcement.

Some sexual sadists cultivate "compliant victims" over an extended period of time (Hazelwood, Dietz, & Warren, 1993; Warren & Hazelwood, 2002)—that is, those who enter into a voluntary relationship but are manipulated into sadomasochistic activities for an extended time. These victims are likely to be wives or girlfriends who have undergone extreme emotional, physical, and sexual abuse over months or years of a relationship that began as an ordinary courtship. In these instances, the offenders shaped the behavior of the women into gradual acceptance of progressively deviant sexual acts and then, through social isolation and repeated abuse, battered their self-images until the women believed they deserved the punishments meted out by their "lovers."

CASE NO. 3

A woman in her 30s advised authorities that she had been coerced into an emotionally, physically, and sexually abusive relationship over an 18-month period. At first, she considered the offender to be the most loving and caring man she had ever known, and she fell deeply in love. Having occasionally used cocaine in the past, she was receptive to his suggestion that they use cocaine to enhance their sexual relations. Eventually, she became addicted. After 6 months together, he began to abuse her sexually. This abuse included forced anal sex, whipping, painful sexual bondage, anal rape by other males, and the insertion of large objects into her rectum. This abusive behavior continued for a full year before she made her initial complaint to the police.

These cases pose special problems to investigators because it appears as though the complainant "consented" to the abuse. However, the transformation of the vulnerable partner into a compliant victim resembles the process by which other abusive men intimidate and control battered women into remaining with their abusers. (See Chapter 25 for a more complete discussion.)

BEHAVIOR PATTERNS CONFUSED WITH SEXUAL SADISM

Many crimes involve the intentional infliction of physical and psychological suffering. Sexual sadism is only one of the several motives for such crimes. To avoid misinterpretation, investigators should be aware of those behavior patterns that appear to be sexually sadistic, but that, in fact, arise from different motives and contexts.

PERSONALITIES CONFLATED WITH SADISTIC BEHAVIOR

Persons with this condition usually exhibit cruel, demeaning, and aggressive behavior in both social and work situations, most often toward subordinates. They tend to establish dominance in interpersonal relationships and convey a lack of respect or empathy for others. Such individuals are often fascinated by violence; take pleasure in demeaning, humiliating, and frightening others; and may enjoy inflicting physical or psychological abuse. In this condition, the purpose of these behaviors is not that of becoming aroused.

CASE NO. 4

A woman left her husband because of his verbal abuse, control over her relations with family members, intimidating behavior, and violent outbursts when drinking. Vengeful that she left him, he lured her back to the apartment under the pretext of dividing their possessions. He then attempted to tie her to the bed, beside which he had arranged a variety of torture instruments. In the ensuing struggle, he told her of his plans to kill her as he stabbed her repeatedly. She eventually persuaded him that she wanted to reconcile and convinced him to summon medical assistance, whereupon he was arrested.

The husband did not have a history of sexual offenses or deviations and he did not show evidence of sexual sadism during the psychiatric examination. He denied any sexual arousal in response to the suffering and denied having any sexually sadistic fantasies. Although it is possible that the husband was a sexual sadist who only showed this tendency when he attacked his wife, the absence of evidence noting a persistent pattern of sexual arousal in response to suffering precluded this diagnosis.

CRUELTY DURING CRIME

While many crimes contain elements of cruelty, the acts are not necessarily sexually sadistic in nature.

CASE NO. 5

Two men, who recently escaped from a state prison, captured a young couple and took them to an isolated area. After repeatedly raping the woman, they severely beat the couple and locked them in the trunk of their car. They then set the car on fire and left the couple to burn to death.

Although these men intentionally inflicted physical and psychological suffering on their victims, there was no indication they did so for sexual excitement. They beat the couple after the rape and left as the victims were screaming and begging for mercy. Sexual sadists would have been sexually stimulated by the victims' torment and would have likely remained at the scene until the suffering ended.

PATHOLOGICAL GROUP BEHAVIOR

Cruelty often arises in offenses committed as a group, even where the individuals have no history of cruelty.

CASE NO. 6

A group of adolescents attacked a mother of six as she walked through her neighborhood. They dragged her into a shed where they beat her and repeatedly inserted a long steel rod into her rectum, causing her death. Some of her attackers were friends of her children.

Most likely, the participants in this attack tried to prove themselves to the others by intensifying the acts of cruelty. Although sexual sadism is possible among one or more of the perpetrators, investigators should also consider the socio-psychological dynamics of group offending and how factors such as peer acceptance and conformity may lead to excessive, ritualistic sexual violence that does not necessarily emanate from sadism.

SANCTIONED CRUELTY

History is replete with reigns of terror during which powerful institutions sanctioned atrocious behaviors. Consider the rape and plunder of defeated populations during the Crusades of the Middle Ages or the execution of women during the Salem witch hunts in colonial America. One of the most notorious times of cruelty occurred in the twentieth century, when millions of people fell victim to the Nazis during the Second World War.

CASE NO. 7

Commandant Koch, who headed the concentration camp at Buchenwald, punished a man who tried to escape by confining him in a wooden box so small he could only crouch. He then ordered that small nails be driven through its walls so that he could not move without being pierced. This man was kept on public display without food for two days and three nights until his screams ceased to sound human (Manvell & Fraenkel, 1967).

In all likelihood, sexual sadists volunteered to perform such deeds, but the widespread deployment of such tactics was politically and racially motivated.

REVENGE-MOTIVATED CRUELTY

Cruelty is often evident during acts that are inspired by an obsessional desire for revenge, either real or imagined.

CASE NO. 8

A physician married a show girl and came to believe that she was being unfaithful, even though there was no evidence to substantiate this. Eventually, his obsession overcame his logic, and he decided to ensure that no man would ever take her away from him. After lashing her to a table, he poured sulfuric acid over her body and face. She survived for 84 days in agony before succumbing to her injuries.

The offender in this case wanted to punish his wife and make sure that she would not be desirable to any man. His act was not designed to gratify him sexually, but was rather instrumental in achieving a nonsexual objective

INTERROGATIVE CRUELTY

Torture during interrogation may involve sexual areas of the body and is sometimes misinterpreted as being sexually sadistic in nature.

CASE NO. 9

A government agent was captured in another country. During his months in captivity, he was continually subjected to physical torture, including beatings with clubs and electrical shocks to all parts of his body, including his genitals.

The victim was tortured in this manner to obtain information concerning his government's activities in that country, not to enhance sexual arousal.

POSTMORTEM MUTILATION

The intentional mutilation of a victim after death is often mistakenly attributed to sexual sadism. However, in a majority of these cases, the offender kills the victim quickly and does not try to prolong suffering, which is in total contrast to the actions of the sexual sadist.

CASE NO. 10

A father bludgeoned his adult daughter to death. After her death, he attempted to dispose of the body. On the day of his arrest, he bought a food processor. Investigators found portions of her remains in the bathtub, the kitchen sink, in pots boiling on the stove, and in the refrigerator.

The man killed his daughter either in self-defense or because of his frustration over her disruptive and hostile behavior caused by her chronic mental illness. His actions were not intended to provide sexual satisfaction in seeing his daughter suffer. Postmortem mutilation was an attempt at concealing the body to avoid apprehension rather than for sexual gratification.

STUDY OF SADISTIC OFFENDERS

The authors studied 30 sexually sadistic criminals, 22 of whom were responsible for at least 187 murders (Dietz, Hazelwood, & Warren, 1990). Most of these cases had been submitted to the FBI's National Center for the Analysis of Violent Crime (NCAVC). Sources of information for the study included police reports, crime scene photographs, victim statements, statements by family members, confessions, psychiatric reports, trial transcripts, pre-sentence reports, and prison records. The authors also reviewed evidence created by the offenders themselves (i.e., diaries, photographs, sketches, audio tapes, videos, calendars, and letters). These materials, which recorded their fantasies and represented memorabilia of their crimes, provided windows into the minds of sexually sadistic offenders.

In addition, 5 of the 30 offenders were interviewed by the authors. When interviewed, these men revealed less about their sexual desires than they had in their writings and recordings of the offenses. This is consistent with our experience when interviewing subjects during ongoing investigations; that is, offenders speak much more readily about their violent acts than about their sexual acts or fantasies.

The 30 sexual sadists studied all intentionally tortured their victims. Their methods of physical torture included the use of instruments such as hammers, pliers, and electric cattle prods, and actions such as biting, whipping, burning, insertion of foreign objects into the rectum or vagina, bondage, amputation, asphyxiation to the point of unconsciousness, and insertion of glass rods in the male urethra, to name a few.

Some offenders used a particular means of torture repeatedly. Such actions could constitute an offender's signature, which shows that certain crimes are the work of a single offender. However, the absence of a common feature among crimes does not eliminate the possibility of a single serial offender, for he may be experimenting with various techniques in search of the perfect scenario or may be attempting to mislead investigators.

The 30 sexual sadists studied also inflicted psychological suffering on their victims. Binding, blindfolding, gagging, and holding a victim captive all produce psychological suffering, even if they are not physically painful. Other psychological tactics used included threats or other forms of verbal abuse; forcing the victim to beg, plead, or describe sexual acts; telling the victim in precise detail what was intended; having the victim choose between slavery and death; and offering the victim a choice of means by which to die.

Offender Characteristics

All 30 of the sexual sadists in the study were men and only one was nonwhite. Fewer than one-half were educated beyond high school. One-half used alcohol or other drugs, and one-third served in the Armed Forces. Forty-three percent were married at the time of the offense.

Sexual deviations are often associated with other sexual abnormalities, and this study confirmed this for sexual sadism. Fifty percent of the men participated in homosexual activity as adults, 20% engaged in cross-dressing, and 20% committed other sexual offenses, such as peeping, obscene phone calls, and indecent exposure.

CASE NO. 11

As a teenager, one sexual sadist "peeped" throughout his neighborhood, masturbating as he watched women undress or have sex. At home, he masturbated repeatedly to fantasies in which he incorporated what he had seen while peeping. As a young adult, he made obscene telephone calls, which led to his first arrest when he agreed to meet a victim who had informed the police.

He later exposed himself to a series of victims, which he eventually explained was for the purpose of eliciting their "shock and fear." He followed women home from shopping malls, determined how much cover was available for peeping and entering the residence, and eventually raped a series of women. In his early rapes, he depended on weapons of opportunity, but later carried with him a rape kit, which consisted of adhesive tape, handcuffs, pre-cut lengths of rope, and a .45 caliber handgun. He became progressively violent in his sexual assaults, torturing his victims by beating, burning, and pulling their breasts. His violence escalated to the point that he so severely assaulted one victim that she lost both breasts. He forcibly raped more than 50 women over the course of his criminal endeavors and was contemplating murder before he was finally apprehended.

Investigators should not be misled by the fact that the sexual sadist may have been involved in what are commonly referred to as "nuisance" sexual offenses. A history of such activity is common, but not universal, among sex offenders of all types. It is a myth that individuals who engage in nuisance offenses do not have a propensity for violence (Hazelwood & Warren, 1989).

Since the above-mentioned study by Dietz et al. (1990), there have been several other studies that have found interesting commonalities among sexual sadists. For example, Proulx, Blais, and Beauregard (2007) found that when compared to non-sadists, sexual sadists were more likely to report lower self-esteem, greater social isolation, and anger (as cited in Proulx, Blais, & Beauregard, 2006).

Although certain offender characteristics allow law enforcement to better distinguish sexual sadists from non-sadistic offenders, there is little agreement on diagnosis of the disorder itself. Thus, consideration of offense characteristics common to sexual sadists may aid investigators in making the distinction between the two types of offenders.

Crime Characteristics

Careful planning epitomizes the crimes of the sexual sadist, who devotes considerable time and effort to the offense. Many demonstrate cunning and methodical planning. The capture of the victim, the selection and preparation of equipment, and the methodical elicitation of suffering often reflect meticulous attention to detail.

The overwhelming majority of offenders studied by the authors used a pretext or ruse to first make contact with the victims. The sexual sadist would offer or request assistance, pretend to be a police officer, respond to a classified advertisement, meet a realtor at an isolated property, or otherwise gain the confidence of the victim.

Almost invariably, the victims were taken to locations selected in advance that offered solitude and safety for the sadist and little opportunity of escape or rescue for the victim. Such locations included the offender's residence, isolated forests, and even elaborately constructed facilities designed for captivity. Many of these findings were confirmed by a later study by Gratzer and Bradford (1995) which found that sadistic sexual offenders were more likely than non-sadistic sexual offenders to conduct careful and detailed planning of the offense, express detached effect, partake in intentional torture and assault of the victim, and take victims to preselected locations.

CASE NO. 12

A white male entered a respected modeling agency and advised that he was filming a documentary on drug abuse among pre-adolescents. He made arrangements to hire two young girls from the agency, and two elderly matrons accompanied them as chaperons. He drove to his trailer and, at gunpoint, bound the women and placed the girls in a plywood cell he had constructed in the trailer. The cell contained beds and additional mattresses for soundproofing. He murdered the women, placing their bodies in garbage bags. He terrorized the girls for more than 2 days before they were rescued.

Twenty-three (77%) of the offenders used sexual bondage on their victims, often tying them with elaborate and excessive materials, using neat and symmetrical bindings, and restraining them in a variety of positions. Eighteen (60%) held their victims in captivity for more than 24h.

The most common sexual activity was anal rape (22 offenders), followed in frequency by forced fellatio, vaginal rape, and penetration with foreign objects. Two-thirds of the men subjected their victims to at least three of these four acts.

Sixty percent of the offenders beat their victims. Of the men, 22 murdered a total of 187 victims; 17 of them killed 3 or more people. The manner in which they killed varied.

CASE NO. 13

Two men, who offended as a team, used a variety of methods to kill a series of victims. One victim was strangled during sex. Another was injected in the neck with a caustic substance, electrocuted, and gassed in an oven. A third victim was shot.

Twenty-nine of the thirty men selected only white victims. Eighty-three percent of the victims were strangers to the offender. While the majority of the men selected female victims, one-fourth attacked males exclusively. Sixteen percent of the men assaulted child victims only, and 26% attacked both children and adults.

A more recent examination of crime scene indicators by Healey, Lussier, and Beauregard (2013) demonstrates that humiliation, mutilation, and premeditation are key predictors of sexual sadism. They also suggest the possibility of two types of sexual sadists—sadistic sexual aggressors whose offenses are more often characterized by humiliation and sadistic sexual murderers who more often mutilate their victims.

EVIDENCE OF CRIME

These offenders retained a wealth of incriminating evidence. More than half of the offenders in the study kept records of their offenses, including calendars, maps, diaries, drawings, letters, manuscripts, photographs, audio tapes, video tapes, and media accounts of their crimes. For the most part, these secret and prized possessions were hidden in their homes, offices, or vehicles; kept in rental storage space; or buried in containers.

Forty percent of the men took and kept personal items belonging to their victims. These items, which included driver's licenses, jewelry, clothing, and photographs, served as mementos of the offense, and some of the offenders referred to them as "trophies" of their conquests. However, none of the offenders retained parts of their victims' bodies, though some kept the entire corpse temporarily or permanently.

INVESTIGATING CRIMES OF THE SEXUAL SADIST

The law enforcement community's legitimate concern rests with the criminal sexual sadist, who can be a noteworthy adversary. The sexual sadist is cunning and accomplished at deception. He rationalizes his actions, feels no remorse or guilt, and is not moved by compassion. He considers himself superior to society in general and law enforcement in particular. While he envies the power and authority associated with the police, he does not respect them.

SOURCES

Invaluable sources of information about suspects in sexual offenses are their former spouses and/or girlfriends. As noted previously, sexual sadists sometimes force sexual partners to become compliant victims (Hazelwood et al., 1993; Warren & Hazelwood, 2002). However, because of the embarrassing nature of the sexual acts involved, these individuals are often reluctant to divulge information.

SEARCH WARRANTS

Because offenders retain incriminating evidence and crime paraphernalia, these items should be listed in search warrant applications. This would include the records and mementos described previously, as well as photographic equipment, tape recorders, reverse telephone directories, and weapons or other instruments used to elicit suffering. Pornography, detective and mercenary magazines, bondage paraphernalia, women's undergarments, and sexual devices are other materials commonly collected by sexual sadists.

INTERVIEWING THE SEXUAL SADIST

Sexual sadists are masters of manipulation. Therefore, the investigator must be well prepared before conducting the interview. The investigator must know the suspect intimately and be aware of his strengths and weaknesses. Premature interviews of primary suspects often fail.

Despite their seeming sophistication, sexual sadists are likely to consent to interview, even after being advised of their rights. These offenders often have an exaggerated self-image and consider themselves intellectually superior to the police. They believe they are in no danger of divulging detrimental information about themselves. More importantly, they expect to learn more information from the officer than they provide during the interview. From the questions asked, they hope to determine how much the investigator knows and the current status of the investigation.

The interviewer should be of detective status or above, preferably older than the suspect, and superior to him in physical stature, personality, and intelligence. The interviewer must appear confident, relaxed, and at least as calm as the suspect. Any personal feelings about the crime or the suspect must be suppressed. The interviewer should not attempt to become "friends" with the suspect, as this will cause him to lose respect for the interviewer and provide him with an opportunity to manipulate the conversation. Instead, the interview should be conducted in a formal and professional manner.

Because these offenders enjoy attention, the interviewer should be prepared for an exhausting and lengthy interview. Questions should be thought out in advance and structured in such a way that the offender cannot evade a line of questioning with a simple "no" answer. For example, rather than asking the suspect if he likes to torture women, it is preferable to ask him his favorite instruments for torturing women. Posing questions in this manner reflects the interviewer's knowledge, does not provide additional information to the suspect, and may facilitate incriminating disclosures by the subject.

Above all, the suspect must not be allowed to provoke anger. In all likelihood, he will probably attempt to shock or antagonize the interviewer, and if the interviewer yields to human emotion, the suspect will score a significant victory.

SUMMARY

Sexually sadistic offenders commit well-planned and carefully concealed crimes. Their crimes are repetitive, serious, and shocking, and they take special steps to prevent detection. The harm that these men wreak is so devastating and their techniques so sophisticated that those who attempt to apprehend and convict them must be armed with uncommon insight, extensive knowledge, and sophisticated investigative resources.

REFERENCES

Dietz, P. E., Hazelwood, R. R., and Warren, J. I. 1990. The sexually sadistic criminal and his offenses. *Bulletin of the American Academy of Psychiatry and the Law*, 4, 163–178.

Gratzer, T., and Bradford, J. M. 1995. Offender and offense characteristics of sexual sadists: A comparative study. *Journal of Forensic Sciences*, 40(3), 450–455.

Hazelwood, R. R., Dietz, J. I., and Warren, P. E. 1993. Compliant victims of sexual sadists. *Australian Family Physician*, 22(4), 3–7.

Hazelwood, R. R., and Warren, J. I. 1989. The serial rapist: His characteristics and victims. *FBI Law Enforcement Bulletin*, February, 18–25.

Healey, J., Lussier, P., and Beauregard, E. 2013. Sexual sadism in the context of rape and sexual homicide: An examination of crime scene indicators. *International Journal of Offender Therapy and Comparative Criminology*, 57(4): 402–424. doi: 10.1177/0306624X12437536.

Manvell, R., and Fraenkel, H. 1967. *The incomparable crime: Mass extermination in the twentieth century—The legacy of guilt*. New York: G. P. Putnam.

Proulx, J., Blais, E., and Beauregard, E. 2006. Sadistic sexual aggressors. In W. L. Marshall, Y. M. Fernandez, L. E. Marshall, and G. A. Serran (Eds.). *Sexual offender treatment: Conversational issues*. Chichester, UK: Wiley.

Proulx, J., Blais, E., and Beauregard, E. 2007. Sadistic sexual offenders. In J. Proulx, E. Beauregard, M. Cusson, and A. Nicole (Eds.). *Sexual murderers: A comparative analysis and new perspectives*, 107–122. Hoboken, NJ: Wiley.

Warren, J. I., and Hazelwood, R. R. 2002. Relational patterns associated with sexual sadism: A study of 20 wives and girlfriends. *Journal of Family Violence*, 17(1), 75–89.

24 Sexual Sadists
Their Wives and Girlfriends

Robert R. Hazelwood

CONTENTS

Introduction 385
Genesis of the Research 386
Methodology 386
The Women 387
Their Relationships with the Men 387
The Transformation of the Women 388
    Selection of a Vulnerable Woman 389
    Seduction of the Woman 389
    Reshaping the Sexual Norms 389
    Social Isolation 389
    Punishment 389
Investigative Significance of the Research 390
    The Criminal 390
    Former Wives and Girlfriends 390
    Crime Behavior 391
Summary 391
References 391

INTRODUCTION

CASE NO. 1

Marie, a beautiful college woman, began dating a young man during her freshman year. No one could understand why they were dating. He was younger than she and certainly less attractive physically. She was a cheerleader and very popular, while he was a rather quiet person who participated in practically none of the school's activities. He had pursued her relentlessly since they were both in high school and she had repeatedly rejected him. The young man came from a wealthy family and he unsuccessfully tried to use his wealth to influence the woman. Eventually however, she became impressed with his singular dedication to her and consented to a date, beginning what would become 4 years of apparent happiness and love—with one notable exception. One evening while attending a party for the first time in their relationship, he became intoxicated. When they returned to his apartment, he insisted on sex and forced himself on her after she complained about his intoxicated state. However, because it was the only time in their relationship that he had exhibited such behavior, she accepted his apology.

    They married after she graduated and his parents provided them with a very large and expensive home on a lake about 150 miles from her family and friends. Within 3 days of their marriage, their entire relationship suddenly changed. He became less interested in "normal" sexual activities and instead, would force her to undress, beat her vagina with his fists and masturbate onto her face and body; displaying a much more deviant and abusive demeanor. He would berate her verbally, using profanity and sexual slang to describe her and to express his fantasy of having her raped by several of his friends while he watched. A year later, she had a child. After 2½ years of marriage, he brought his girlfriend home and wanted Marie to engage in sex with both of them—this was the final straw and she left him.

The author interviewed Marie after being introduced to her by her treating psychologist. She had obtained a divorce and was in counseling in an attempt to cope with the residual emotional trauma. She was interested in obtaining answers to the questions, "What was wrong with me?" "How could I have allowed this to happen?" "Were there any warning signs that I was oblivious to during the dating relationship?" Fortunately, this young mother was being counseled by a woman who not only had experience in dealing with battered spouses, but, more importantly, also was familiar with paraphilias in general and sexual sadism in particular. Furthermore, she was knowledgeable with the current research on sexually sadistic men and their relationships with wives and girlfriends (Dietz, Hazelwood, & Warren, 1990; Hazelwood, Dietz, & Warren, 1992, 1993; Warren, Hazelwood, & Dietz, 1996; Warren & Hazelwood, 2002).

GENESIS OF THE RESEARCH

In 1990, the author attended a presentation by Ms. Christine McGuire and Dr. Chris Hatcher on a crime that was recounted in the excellent book *Perfect Victim* (McGuire & Norton, 1988). The case involved a married couple by the name of Cameron and Janice Hooker, who captured a hitchhiking college student named Coleen Stans and kept her in sexual slavery for 7 years. Ms. McGuire, a career California prosecutor, tried the case and retained Chris Hatcher, a noted forensic psychologist (since deceased), as an expert witness.

Ms. McGuire and Dr. Hatcher narrated the terrifying story of Ms. Stans's confinement in a box kept beneath the couple's bed. They described physical torture by Cameron Hooker, Ms. Stans being forced to sign a "slave contract," and how she eventually became attached to and even dependent upon her captors. Needless to say, the audience was completely silent. Following the presentation, an attendee asked the author if he would like to interview Ms. Stans. The author responded that he would rather interview the wife, Janice Hooker. He wanted to learn about what kind of person she was, what kind of person her husband was, what the nature of their relationship was, and why she had participated in such aberrant behavior. As a result of this conversation, the author recognized an opportunity to learn much more about sexual sadism from a group that had not been queried before: the former wives and girlfriends of the sadistic men.

In 1991, the author, together with Dr. Park Dietz and Dr. Janet Warren, began the research that would study the relational patterns of sexually sadistic men and their spouses and/or girlfriends. This research would eventually result in the author's interview of 20 women, including the beautiful and unfortunate Marie. These were women who had lived and been intimate with the most cruel, intelligent, and, in many cases, criminally sophisticated offenders confronting the sexual crimes investigator.

METHODOLOGY

The research team developed an interview protocol more than 70 pages in length that included more than 450 questions. The protocol was designed to capture information about the woman's development from childhood, what she knew about the childhood and development of her sadistic mate, the development and continuation of their relationship, and the termination of that relationship.

The interviews were unstructured and conducted by the author and at least one additional FBI agent. All interviews were recorded by audiotape, but none were videotaped.

Eighteen of the participants were identified for the author by law enforcement or mental health professionals who were aware of the ongoing research; the remaining two women, who were incarcerated at the time, sought out the author for inclusion in the project. A statement of confidentiality was executed prior to beginning the interviews. The interviews ranged in length from 4½ to 15 hours. They were transcribed and the data from the protocols were analyzed.

THE WOMEN

It is important to note that while these women have been referred to as compliant victims (Hazelwood et al., 1993), the term is meant to reflect the acquiescence of the women in their own victimization and, in some cases, the victimization of others at the hands of their male partners. The use of this term is not intended to excuse the criminal behavior of the women in the study (Warren & Hazelwood, 2002).

As stated, 20 women were extensively interviewed and of that number, only 3 had been arrested prior to meeting the sadistic man. Each of those arrests involved minor theft (typewriter, check, tube of lipstick). Four of the women had some contact with mental health professionals prior to becoming involved with the sadistic males, but since leaving the men, all but one have been in therapy.

Nine of the women had been sexually abused as children and six had been physically abused. The formal education of these women ranged from 11 to 18 years and they were employed in a variety of occupations, including professional (elementary school teacher, fire system engineer), skilled (secretary), and unskilled (waitress) positions. Only two used drugs before meeting the men.

THEIR RELATIONSHIPS WITH THE MEN

Thirteen of the women married the men and the remaining seven dated them exclusively for a period of time. While with the men, 18 of the women were physically abused and all were emotionally and sexually battered. The men were able to convince the women to engage in a variety of deviant sexual practices, including bestiality, sex with other men and women, whipping, bondage, and hanging. The reader should note that if proper rapport is established with the woman, one can expect to be informed of painful and horrendous behaviors she has been subjected to by the sexual sadist. It is imperative that the interviewer not express either judgment or shock at the revelations.

Seven of the men killed at least 19 people and four of their wives were present during at least some of the murders. All four of the women were charged with crimes against persons.

CASE NO. 2

Stephanie dated a sexually sadistic male for a number of years, even while he was dating other women. She continued dating the man even though he became engaged to a woman named Lucy. Her devotion was so complete that Stephanie agreed to assist him in Lucy's "sex therapy class" and subsequently her murder. He brought Lucy to Stephanie's home and after forcing her to disrobe and engage in multiple sexual acts which Stephanie photographed, he killed her using chloroform. Together, they buried Lucy's body in Stephanie's back yard and her homicide remained unsolved for 2 years.

In another case, one of the women interviewed by the author was charged with being a co-conspirator in the murder of her husband.

CASE NO. 3

Sally had been married for more than 10 years to a sadistic male who had battered her physically, emotionally, and sexually. He forced her to have sex with the family dog on several occasions and she had been raped twice by different men who had been hiding in her home when she returned from shopping. Both times the rapists informed her they had been hired by her husband to commit the crime. On each occasion she called her husband to tell him of the assault only to have him laugh at her and demand that she not call the police. On the evenings of both occasions, her husband forced her to masturbate him while recounting the details of the rape.

After several years of abuse, Sally confided in a female friend who convinced her to retaliate by allowing the friend to enlist male acquaintances to beat up her husband. Sally agreed and one evening three men kidnapped the husband as he returned home from work and severely beat him with baseball bats. They then poured gasoline over the unconscious man and set him afire. He died and Sally was convicted of being a co-conspirator in his murder.

The women reported leaving the men for two primary reasons: fear for their lives and/or fear for their children's welfare.

CASE NO. 4

Clarissa, who was married to a sexual sadist for 7 years, was regularly forced to dress in a manner that sexually exposed her body. He took her to swinger clubs and forced her to approach and proposition men and women for sex. Her husband had a fantasy of torturing and murdering women and she was often forced to participate in the fantasy as the victim. After 6 years of marriage, she had a baby and he allowed her only 5 days to physically recuperate before he resumed sexually abusing her. One day he was beating her with his fists and their child, who was lying on a couch, began crying. She picked the baby up and attempted to comfort her. The husband grabbed the 1½-year-old girl by the arm and threw her back on the couch, stating, "That fucking kid isn't going to help you." A short time later, as he was eating breakfast, Clarissa retrieved a shotgun from the closet, held it a short distance from his head and considered shooting him. Despite her clear desire to end years of abuse, she relented and quietly put the gun away after considering the probable consequence of going to prison and having her baby taken from her.

She made her eventual escape one day soon after her husband had left for work, taking her child with her to an underground battered spouse shelter where she remained for 3 months. She has since obtained a college degree and remains in contact with the author.

THE TRANSFORMATION OF THE WOMEN

How is it that apparently normal women become involved with sexually sadistic men and are convinced to participate in sexual activities well outside the range of their experience and, in some instances, in violent criminal behavior against others at the man's urging?

It is important to understand that the ritualistic and heterosexual sexual sadist inherently believes that all women are evil—that they are all "bitches, whores, and sluts." Consequently, if and when they attempt to prove this hypothesis, they do not select prostitutes or drug addicts to become their wives or girlfriends, as such women have already proven the theory. Instead they select nice, apparently normal middle-class women. The reasons for why these women eventually became compliant with routine abuse reflects a complex interplay of the women's developmental characteristics, life circumstances, and vulnerabilities exploited by the sadist partner.

As the research interviews were accomplished, the team studied the results and noted a pat-terned method used by the men in transforming the women into becoming compliant victims. This process consisted of five identifiable steps: (1) identification of the vulnerable woman, (2) seduction, (3) reshaping of the sexual norms, (4) social isolation, and (5) punishment (Hazelwood et al., 1993).

SELECTION OF A VULNERABLE WOMAN

Extrapolating from the behavior described by the women, it appears that the sexual sadists had developed an ability to identify a naive, passive, and vulnerable woman. The majority of the women reported feeling bad about themselves at the time they were approached by the sadist. These feel-ings were either due to situational factors such as the breakup of a relationship or as a result of more chronic problems with self-esteem. The sexual sadists seemed able to assess this vulnerability and exploit it to manipulate these women toward interpersonal scenarios that would meet the men's needs for dominance, control, and sadistic sexual behavior. It seems likely that these men had attempted such activities with other women and failed.

SEDUCTION OF THE WOMAN

The women reported that their partners were initially charming, considerate, daring, unselfish, and attentive. They gave the women gifts unexpectedly and were constantly attentive to their desires. As one woman said, "He couldn't do enough for me." Another woman, who was experiencing marital problems, advised that the man she became involved with was available to her for advice day or night, or just to listen. The women were seduced by the men in a relatively quick period of time, even though they recognized a sinister side to them. The men related to the women in a romantic, seductive manner that was the antithesis of their eventual degradation and abuse. Like the pedo-phile, the sadist continued in this phase until he was confident in his ability to manipulate and use the woman in ways that were degrading to her and sexually gratifying to him. He cultivated the woman's affection for him before initiating the next step.

RESHAPING THE SEXUAL NORMS

The time devoted to the reshaping of the woman's sexual behavior depended on her vulnerability and susceptibility. Typically, the sexual sadist initially persuaded the woman to engage in a sexual activity that was just beyond her normal sexual repertoire. Once she had participated in such an act, the sadist then used positive reinforcement (gratitude, compliments, or attention) or negative reinforcement (pouting, ignoring, or rejection) techniques to obtain her compliance for progres-sively deviant activities. Over time, what began as atypical sexual behavior became the routine. Eventually, the men relied on threats and violence to maintain compliance of the women.

SOCIAL ISOLATION

Having shaped the women's sexual behavior, the sadists moved into the fourth phase of socially iso-lating the women from friends, family, and relatives. The men gradually became overly possessive and jealous of any activity that did not center around them, and they alienated those acquaintances who were not their own friends. Restrictive measures were used so that the world of these women became increasingly circumscribed and their circle of confidants greatly diminished. Eventually, there was no one left in the woman's world except the sadistic male.

PUNISHMENT

The fifth and final step in the transformation process involved physical and psychological pun-ishment. Having met, seduced, and transformed a normal woman into a sexually compliant and dependent individual, the sadist has validated his theory of women. The woman is now a subservient, inferior being who *allowed* herself to be re-created sexually and is now participating in sexual acts in which no decent woman would engage, thereby confirming his theory that she is a "bitch" and deserving of punishment. The woman's self-esteem is such that she has begun to believe that she is deserving of the punishment. In a desperate effort to prevent future harm, the victim sometimes attempts to adopt the perspective and beliefs of the abusive partner, in effect permitting her identity to be shaped by the sadist himself (Stevens, 2014). It is worth noting that *evil* was the most common word that these men wrote on the women's bodies with marking pens.

INVESTIGATIVE SIGNIFICANCE OF THE RESEARCH

It is appropriate to inform the reader how this research can be of practical value to the criminal investigator. The answer lies in the fact that it makes the investigator aware of an often overlooked source of information and prepares him or her to effectively interact with the compliant victim. Cases of domestic abuse are commonly evaluated by measuring the level of force or the amount of injuries sustained by the victim and are often focused less on the cumulative psychological and emotional implications of persistent assaults over an extended period of time. That said, measures of physical severity may not adequately encompass the various dimensions of abuse that become a routine experience of the victim. Abusive behaviors such as acts that deprive a victim of resources, liberties, personal autonomy, and self-regard may not leave physical impressions, but have long-lasting psychological effects that help explain why victims choose to stay and comply with the abusive partner (Stevens, 2014).

Any experienced investigator will agree that there are three primary sources of information about a criminal: the offender himself, those who know him, and his crime behavior.

THE CRIMINAL

When lecturing on sexually violent offenders, the author often begins by asking the audience what the *least* reliable source of information about an offender is. The answer, of course, is self-reported information—information provided by the criminal himself. It is a well-known fact that criminals lie, they *exaggerate* their accomplishments, they *minimize* their criminal behavior, they *deny* responsibility, they *project* blame for their failures, and then they *rationalize* their lies. In other words, they engage in the five defense mechanisms to protect themselves. Yet, some professionals, including mental health professionals, social workers, researchers, and even law enforcement, depend solely on what the *criminal* tells them in order to arrive at opinions about the *criminal*!

Invariably the author will be asked, either in a classroom or by an opposing attorney, whether he *ever* believes a criminal. The answer is "yes"—with qualification. If what the offender says can be validated with evidence, reliable witnesses, or his own criminal behavior, the author may have reason to believe him (Hazelwood, 2001).

FORMER WIVES AND GIRLFRIENDS

The former wife or girlfriend is an often overlooked, yet excellent, source of information. While the information provided by this source may not be as reliable as that learned from the behavior of the offender, these women can nevertheless prove to be extremely valuable to the criminal investigator and the researcher.

It is to be remembered that the author is specifically referring to women *formerly* in a relationship with the men. Legal ramifications aside, the *current* wife and/or girlfriend will probably be averse to speaking with investigators. Also, while former sexual partners are much more likely to participate in an interview, investigators should be on guard against exaggerations or even lies on the part of the woman in order to obtain revenge for wrongs suffered while with the sadistic male. The potential for lying or exaggerating can be minimized if the investigator thoroughly prepares for and remains alert to indications of excessive anger or hostility during the interview.

Perseverance is the key word in dealing with these women. They have information that deals with the most private, and potentially damaging, behaviors of the sexual criminal: his own sexual life. A former sexual partner can tell the investigator about the fantasies of the offender; his paraphilic interests; type and location of collections; record keeping habits; paraphernalia for use in crime; what makes him happy, sad, or fearful; what threatens him; what his strengths and weaknesses are; where he hides things; where and how he might travel while a fugitive; the type of investigative personality with whom he would most likely cooperate; and when (during the day or night) he is most vulnerable to interrogation.

CRIME BEHAVIOR

It is the author's opinion that the best source of information about an offender is his criminal behavior! Behavior simply does not lie. If the investigator is trained to recognize and capture significant behavior, he or she is well on the way to a true understanding of the sexual criminal. Trying to understand the offender without analyzing his criminal interaction with the victim is like asking a student to write a report on Thomas Harris's excellent book, *The Silence of the Lambs*, but not allowing that student to read the book or obtain any information about it.

It is important to re-emphasize that what an offender says to a victim, the type and sequence of sexual acts, and the amount of physical force the offender employs are very good indicators of what fantasies and motivations are operative in the mind of the man. Simply stated, the sexual offender is going to say and do those things that are sexually exciting to him.

SUMMARY

Twenty former wives and girlfriends of sexually sadistic men were identified and extensive interviews of the women were conducted. Three of these women had committed minor thefts and four had some contact with the mental health community prior to meeting the men. Four of these women assisted their husbands in committing murder and one additional woman was convicted of conspiracy in the murder of her husband. All of the women were sexually and emotionally battered and were convinced to engage in a variety of deviant and often criminal activities.

The sexually sadistic men engaged in a patterned method to transform these apparently normal women into becoming compliant victims. This transformation process involved selection, seduction, reshaping of sexual norms, social isolation, and physical and emotional punishment of the women.

There are three primary sources of information about an offender: the criminal, his former wife or girlfriend, and his behavior. The woman who was intimately involved in the life of the offender can be an excellent source of information for the investigator and it is vital to learn as much as possible about that woman to better enable effective interaction with her.

REFERENCES

Dietz, P. R., Hazelwood, R. R., and Warren, J. I. 1990. The sexually sadistic criminal and his offenses. *The Bulletin of the American Academy of Psychiatry and the Law*, 18(2): 163–178.

Hazelwood, R. R. 2001. Three sources of information. *National Academy Associates*, 3(1.6): 38–39.

Hazelwood, R. R., Dietz, P. E., and Warren, J. I. 1992. The criminal sexual sadist. *FBI Law Enforcement Bulletin*, February.

Hazelwood, R. R., Dietz, P. E., and Warren, J. I. 1993. The compliant victims of sexual sadists. *Australian Family Physician*, 22(4): 3–7.

McGuire, C., and Norton, C. 1988. *Perfect victim*. New York: Dell Publishing.

Stevens, P. 2014. Recent trends in explaining abuse within intimate relationships. *The Journal of Criminal Law*, 78(2): 184–193.

Warren, J. I., and Hazelwood, R. R. 2002. Relational patterns associated with sexual sadism: A study of 20 wives and girlfriends. *Journal of Family Violence*, 17(1): 75–89.

Warren, J. I., Hazelwood, R. R., and Dietz, P. E. 1996. The sexually sadistic serial killer. *Journal of Forensic Science*, 41(6): 970–974.

25 Sex Offenders of the Elderly

Ann Wolbert Burgess, Robert A. Prentky, and Mark Safarik

CONTENTS

Introduction 393
Background 394
Theories of Offending 394
Dynamics of the Offense 396
    Victimology 396
    Style of Approach 396
    Control of Victim 396
    Victim Resistance 397
    Multiple Assaults 397
    Types of Sexual Acts 397
    Classifying Sex Offenders of the Elderly 397
Typology and Examples 397
    Opportunistic 397
    Pervasive Anger 398
    Sexualization 399
    Nonsadistic Types 400
    Vindictive Motivation 401
Discussion 402
    Taxonomic Heterogeneity 402
    Policy and Investigative Implications 402
        Motive and Escalation in Serial Sexual Homicide 403
        Investigative Profiling and Risk Assessment 403
Conclusion 404
References 404
Further Reading 406

INTRODUCTION

Over the several past decades, the diversity of the expression of sexually coercive and aggressive behavior has been recognized in numerous studies that have focused on many subgroups of sex offenders, including abuse reactive children (Barbaree, Marshall, & Hudson, 1993; Elliott & Butler, 1994; Loar, 1994; Greenfield, 1996), juvenile sexual offenders (Pithers, Gray, Busconi, & Houchens, 1998; Becker & Hicks, 2003), female sexual offenders (Elliott, 1993; Adshead, Howett, & Mason, 1994; Larson & Maison, 1995; Anderson & Struckman-Johnson, 1998; Strickland, 2008), "impaired professionals" (Abel, Barrett, & Gardos, 1992; Loftus & Camargo, 1993; Haywood et al., 1996), internet sex offenders (Webb, Craissati, & Keen, 2007; Seto, 2013), and even such specific subgroups as stalkers (Meloy, 1996; Burgess et al., 1997).

The one remarkable omission has been any empirical focus on the rape of the elderly. These highly vulnerable, often incapacitated individuals appear to represent yet another category of "hidden" victims of sexual assault. Although there are no reliable incidence data on the sexual assault of the elderly, prevailing educated opinion is that "underreporting is significantly higher in this age group compared to other groups" (Hicks & Moon, 1984, pp. 195–196). Research on individuals who sexually assault elderly women has been relatively scant. A very early publication by Groth (1978) focused on the older rape victim and her assailant. In a 1988 study, Pollack compared five sex offenders who assaulted women aged 60 or older with seven offenders who assaulted younger women. By and large, the five men who assaulted older victims were more violent, more brutal, and more sadistic. Indeed, three of the victims were murdered or thought to be dead, and in the other two cases the victims were badly mutilated. Pollack concluded, moreover, that the greater evidence of psychotic features among those who assaulted the elderly suggested more severe psychopathology in that group. In a larger study that focused on the elderly victims of sexual assault, Muram, Miller, and Cutler (1992) compared 53 victims, aged 55 or older, with 53 victims, aged 18–45. The older victims were far more likely to sustain genital injury than the younger victims (51% vs. 13%, respectively). In a later study by Del Bove, Stermac, and Bainbridge (2006), 61 victims, aged 55–87 were compared with 73 victims, aged 31–54 and 78 victims, aged 15–30. They found that older female victims were more likely to present cognitive disabilities and heightened isolation and, as a result, made them particularly vulnerable to sexual assault. In contrast to previous studies, elderly victims were no more likely than younger victims to be assaulted by a stranger and it was found that there were no significant differences between the use of coercion or the severity of attacks (including physical trauma) between age groups. The finding that older female victims were no more likely than younger female victims to endure a greater degree of violence has also been supported by Ball and Fowler's (2008) empirical work on sexual offending against elderly females in the U.K.

The rape or sexual assault of an elder is a felony. In some states, the sentence for the crime carries special sanctions because of the victim's age. It is a crime reported and investigated by law enforcement and not by Adult Protective Services. A common question raised when describing elder rape victims is, "What would motivate someone to commit such an offense?" We sought to answer this question by studying 77 convicted rapists of women aged 60 and older and interviewing 25 of them in prison (Burgess et al., 1997). This chapter will report on the characteristics of these men and their crimes, classify them using the Prentky and Knight (1991) MTC:3R typology, and provide case examples of the subtypes.

BACKGROUND

One of the few contemporary studies published on elder sexual abuse victims was a British study. The project was sponsored in 2000 by the Nuffield Foundation to Professors Olive Stevenson and Katherine Jeary at the Nottingham University School of Sociology and Social Policy. The researchers, over 20 months and using a qualitative research design, studied 52 cases of 54 elder victims and 52 abusers (not of the 54 victims). Two major findings included minimal, if any, services offered to elderly victims with respect to coming to terms with their traumatic experiences, and little information on understanding the motivations of offenders and in identifying interventions to reduce the possibility of their re-offending.

THEORIES OF OFFENDING

Groth (1978) reviewed his clinical files of convicted sex offenders for sexual offenses where the victim was substantially older than the offender. He noted many offenders had difficulties in early adolescent adjustment, came from families with unstable parental relationships, and showed a lack of respect to the mother. The mothers were perceived (by the offenders) as high strung, overprotective, domineering, or provocative.

Pollack's study in 1988 reported just the opposite findings from those of Groth. Pollack, using study and control groups, observed no discernable differences in demographic details of marital, employment, psychiatric, or criminal history or in childhood behavior problems or adjustment. However, both Groth and Pollack commented on the offender of an elderly victim being more likely to use brutality or a weapon in the offense.

This view of brutality, however, is not supported in the early descriptive studies on genital trauma of victims. Muram and colleagues (1992) reviewed 53 elder cases compared with 53 younger victim cases. More injuries were found in the elder group (51%) compared with 13% of the younger group ($p < 0.003$). There was no observed significant difference found between the two groups in regard to type of assault or violence used during the assault. The authors concluded that the genital injury that was greater in the elderly women was due to the postmenopausal status of the genital anatomy rather than any offender-associated factors.

Genital trauma is stated to be more evident in the postmenopausal sexually assaulted woman than it is in her younger counterparts (Cartwright, 1987). However, as with those 65 and younger, rape may occur without obvious injury (Cartwright & Moore, 1989; Tyra, 1993). In one comparative study, medical and forensic records were reviewed between 1986 and 1991 from 129 women 50 years or older and 129 women from a comparison group ages 14–49 (Ramin, Satin, Stone, & Wendel, 1992). Trauma, in general, occurred in 67% of the older group and 71% of the younger group. Genital trauma was more common in older than younger victims (66% vs. 49%). Although forensic findings were similar in both groups, in the older group motile spermatozoa were seen only in those examined within 6 h of the assault.

Ball (2005) identifies two conceptual models emerging from the literature attempting to explain the motivation behind sexual abuse of the elderly. The first theory is based on sexual intent. In essence, the perpetrator is viewed as sexually deviant and the term *gerontophilia* is suggested. However, there has been no empirical study to support the view that most or even a significant number of offenders have a sexual preference for elders. Neither the studies by Groth (1978) nor those by Pollack (1988) reported on the sexual preferences of their samples. Nevertheless, two of the six cases presented by Ball et al. (1992) did demonstrate gerontophilic tendencies.

A second model of sexual offending of the elderly is a variation of a psychodynamic interpretation of rape. Groth referred to this variation as "anger rape." In this type of rape, the offender offends as a way to direct feelings of rage onto the victim. The offense is not primarily a sexual act, but rather one that occurs within a sexual context in which emotions of anger and control are put onto the victim. Groth continued to suggest that the object of the rage, the victim, represented an authority person who needed to be controlled, hurt, and degraded. Pollack's (1988) study supports this view in that the offender is acting out motives of rage and sadistic intent rather than motives of sexual desire. Lanyon (1991) has suggested that the victim becomes a substitute for the original source of the offender's anger, often noted to be the offender's mother. Safarik and Jarvis's (2005) examination of offenders who sexually assaulted and murdered their elder female victim found results similar to both Groth and Pollack as determined by the level of injury inflicted. Safarik, Jarvis, and Nussbaum (2002) found that these victims became surrogates for someone in the offender's life against whom he could not act out against. This was often a dominant female family member upon whom the offender relied for financial and social support.

In more recent work by Ball and Fowler (2008) using a large population sample of recorded sexual offences in the U.K., the authors revealed that their findings did not support previous depictions of individuals who sexually offended against elderly female victims as young adult males, unknown to their victims, whose sexual assault was severe and extensive. Rather, they found that offenders tended to be older than offenders who committed sexual crimes against younger victims with a mean age of over 50 years. Offences where the age gap between the offender and victim was 30 years or more were exceptionally rare and were found not to be associated with a large degree of sexual violence.

As reported in Chapter 4, clinical studies of elder sexual abuse cases range between 2% and 7% of all reported sexual assaults. It is not uncommon for a woman over 60 to become a victim. Sexual offending against the elderly is not a new phenomenon as it has been recognized in psychiatry since Krafft–Ebing's writings. However, any link with a specific paraphilia remains unclear and poorly understood. A substantial amount of work is necessary to provide theoretical explanations for offender motivation.

In continuing her study of adult protective services data, Ramsey-Klawsnik (1995) identified five types of elder sexual abuse: stranger or acquaintance assault, abuse by unrelated care providers, incestuous abuse, marital or partner abuse, and resident-to-resident assault in elder-care settings. She further delineated subtypes of marital and incestuous abuse (2003). Three patterns of marital abuse seen in clinical samples are (1) long-term domestic violence, (2) recent onset of sexual abuse within a long-term marriage, and (3) sexual victimization within a new marriage. Incestuous elder abuse involves cases perpetrated by adult children, other relatives, and quasi-relatives. Resident-to-resident sexual abuse has been substantiated in nursing homes, assisted-living facilities, board and care homes, and other settings that care for elderly people (Ramsey-Klawsnik, 1995).

DYNAMICS OF THE OFFENSE

VICTIMOLOGY

Victims, in general, may be categorized as low, moderate, or high risk in relation to their exposure to crime-threatening situations. Low-risk victims are not normally exposed to predator danger and are usually sought out by the offender. In contrast, high-risk victims' lifestyles or employment consistently exposes them to danger from criminal elements.

The majority of elderly victims residing in nursing homes or long-term care facilities were highly vulnerable by virtue of incapacitation, dementia, and fragility. They were residing in a 24-h care facility and few were able to ambulate without assistance. It was thus not surprising that many of the assaults occurred in the residents' own beds (despite having roommates). Other assault locations included the victim's wheelchair, a bathroom, an empty classroom, and a closet. Two residents were taken off a secure unit to another part of the nursing home.

For nursing home victims, one could argue that risk level should vary depending on the number of staff available. The nursing homes all operated on three shifts, with the day shift employing the largest number of nurses and nursing aides. For those cases where the time of the assaults was known, the offenses occurred during either the evening or the night shift and before the day shift arrived.

STYLE OF APPROACH

Offenders can be categorized by the method of approach and control exerted on the intended victim. Three approach styles have been described: (1) con: verbal manipulation or coercion to gain the victim's confidence; (2) blitz: injurious force used to physically control the victim; and (3) surprise: threats but no force, in which the intended victim is typically approached when incapacitated or unsuspecting (Hazelwood & Burgess, 2017). The confidence method was used only in cases where the victim was ambulatory ("Let's go for a walk." "It's time for your bath." "We're going to a party."). In cases with extensive physical injury, a blitz style assault was noted. There were also surprise style approaches where there was no physical force and the victim was sleeping or incapacitated.

CONTROL OF VICTIM

The manner in which the offender maintains control of his victim may occur in a variety of ways: mere presence, verbal threats, display of a weapon, and use of physical force. Mere presence was often the primary method of control exercised by offenders of elders. Given the frailty of the victims, control strategies employing greater force would have been unnecessary. Some victims, however, reported having been threatened with a knife as well as tied at the wrists.

VICTIM RESISTANCE

The victim, when confronted with the offender, may either comply or resist. When there is resistance, the offender may cease his demand, ignore the resistance, compromise, flee, or use additional force. Residents in nursing homes were overheard telling the offender to stop.

MULTIPLE ASSAULTS

In a few cases, there was verification of multiple assaults on the same victim. Verification was derived from either the offender himself or the victim. In additional cases, multiple assaults were suspected where Human papillomavirus (HPV) was detected. HPV is a viral infection that is passed between people through skin-to-skin contact. There are more than 100 varieties of HPV, but most emphasis is given to the 40 varieties that affect the genitals, mouth, or throat, that are passed through sexual contact. One 33-year-old woman, semicomatose from a gunshot wound to the head when she was 19, was found to be 6 months pregnant. An investigation of this case revealed that six teenaged male aides were having routine "sex parties" in her room. DNA revealed the father of her baby to be one of the aides.

TYPES OF SEXUAL ACTS

Although the type and nature of the sexual acts performed in an assault are often critical in attempting to understand motivation, obtaining this information was difficult given that many of the victims suffered from dementia and were unable to communicate what had happened. Despite the almost uniform lack of reliable self-report data, physical evidence clearly indicated the nature of the physical and sexual abuse in many cases.

In some cases, it was possible to reliably code the presence of preexisting sexual fantasy, suggesting degree of planning and premeditation. For example, a 31-year-old nursing aide was observed at 4 a.m. by another nursing aide at the bedside of a 95-year-old resident. The aide had his pants down and his penis exposed. He admitted that he was attempting sexual intercourse. He said that when he changed the victim she asked to have her back scratched or her legs rubbed and that she would moan and that would sexually arouse him. In another case involving fondling, a male resident was observed in the dining hall to have his hand inside the top part of the nightgown of another resident.

CLASSIFYING SEX OFFENDERS OF THE ELDERLY

Using the MTC:3R, the sex offenders in this study were classified (see Chapter 18).

TYPOLOGY AND EXAMPLES

OPPORTUNISTIC

Opportunistic motive refers to an impulsive rapist type who shows little planning or preparation. He usually has a history of unsocialized behavior and the rape serves as an example of the degree to which he lacks interpersonal awareness. These rapists show no concern for the welfare or comfort of their victims. The rape is for immediate sexual gratification rather than the enactment of a highly developed fantasy or sexualized ritual. The rape is in the service of dominance and power. The opportunistic offender in this elder sample differed from other rapists with this classification in that 8 of the 10 offenders claimed not to have penetrated the elder, but rather to have committed acts of fondling, kissing, and molestation. This classification is similar in the nature of the sexual act to some child molester acts.

CASE NO. 1

An 83-year-old female resident was observed being led off of a locked Alzheimer's Unit by MO, a 42-year-old maintenance employee. A search ensued, and the resident was located in an area far removed from her unit. She was fatigued, nonverbal, disoriented, barefoot, and disheveled (e.g., clothes unbuttoned). She was taken for a sexual assault examination.

MO said the resident asked him to take her for a walk but that she had to go to the bathroom, so he helped her remove her pants. MO said she started giving him a "sob story" that she appreciated his taking care of her, how her husband had died, and how she didn't feel whole. She didn't feel like she would have time "to play" a last time before she died; she felt she was a nobody. MO said he kept trying to wrestle with her to get her clothes back on, but she kept on kissing him. He got her up and then "It just happened; we had intercourse. I had to. I couldn't control it. I didn't ejaculate. I left her and she got up and she was satisfied. She grabbed me by the arm and she walked back pretending that it wasn't nothing. I unlocked the door and let her in. She said she hoped I'd come by to see her tomorrow." DNA evidence matched MO to the victim.

After identifying his real name, it was revealed that MO had a lengthy criminal history and that he was on probation at the time of being hired. MO told police that he was angry at his girlfriend, that he had been to her house and asked for sex but she would not give it to him because she had a yeast infection. She drove him to work and "kicked him out of the car." MO's girlfriend, who also worked at the nursing home, told police that she saw MO (on her unit) later that afternoon holding the hand of a blonde haired woman wearing a purple outfit. MO was classified as a Type 2 (opportunistic, low social competence).

PERVASIVE ANGER

A second classification in the MTC:R3 typology is termed *pervasive anger*. The degree of force used in this type of assault is excessive and gratuitous. The violence is an integrated component of the behavior even when the victim is compliant. Resistance from the victim is likely to increase the aggression and serious injury or death may occur. The rage is not sexualized, suggesting that the assault is not fantasy driven. The violence is a lifestyle characteristic that is directed toward males and females alike. The rape is but one feature in a history of unsocialized aggressive behavior noted across various social settings.

CASE NO. 2

CW, an 83-year-old resident of a nursing home, was observed closing the door after following a 76-year-old Alzheimer resident into her room. Two nursing aides watched CW digitally penetrate the victim, lie on top of her, and put his face into the woman's genital area while the woman cried, "Stop. It hurts."

CW told the police that he "went into the lady's room, because an aide told me she had a room to herself and wanted to show it to me." He was just helping her take down her pants when she grabbed his private area and pulled him down on her and was grinding. She told him that he was hurting her leg so he got off her, inserted his finger into her vagina because he thought she wanted him to (she was saying "help me"). He asked her if she climaxed, and she said she did. He also claimed he was not aware of what was going to happen when he entered the room and that he thinks he was set up.

The police report indicated that a physician said CW had no prostate, implying that he was impotent. The police report also noted that CW used a walker or wheelchair to get around, and that his mind was in good working order for his age. Although CW was known to be angry much of the time and to aggress and hit other residents, he was allowed free access to most areas of the facility.

SEXUALIZATION

Sexualization in the MTC:R3 typology essentially refers to a high degree of preoccupation with gratifying one's sexual needs. Sexual preoccupation is typically evidenced by highly intrusive, recurrent sexual and rape fantasies, frequent use of pornography, reports of frequent uncontrollable sexual urges, use of a variety of alternative outlets for gratifying sexual needs (e.g., massage parlors, X-rated movies, sex clubs, strip bars), and engaging in other deviant sexual behaviors (paraphilias), such as voyeurism, exhibitionism, or fetishism. The sexual assaults of these offenders are often well planned, as evidenced by a clear, scripted sequence of events, possession of assault-related paraphernalia, and an apparent plan to procure the victim and elude apprehension after the assault.

CASE NO. 3

A nursing aide walked into a resident's room and observed nursing aide TM with his penis exposed and making humping movements on an 82-year-old woman. The woman was lying across the bed without underwear. TM stated to the police that, "I went into the woman's room to change her brief, and I thought of having sex with her. Then I unzipped my pants and began having sex and someone walked into the room." His statement to the nursing assistant who caught him with his pants down was that he was looking for a bed sore.

Records on TM, a 16-year-old youth, noted that in elementary school, a family doctor diagnosed him with attention deficit disorder, prescribed Pamelor, and said his problems were due to depression. At age 13, he became sexually active with a 16-year-old girl who was living with his family and raising her 1-year-old child. The girl became pregnant by TM who testified that he was working 50–60 h a week to pay child support as well as attending high school. Cognitive testing revealed an average IQ (107).

The records also revealed sexual abuse by a male cousin when he was age 5. At the time of the assault he lived in a trailer with his parents and four younger siblings. His father had frequent charges of Driving while Intoxicated (DWI). He had no prior criminal record. The nursing home had received complaints of his using frequent sexualized language but there had been no reprimand. TM was convicted and sentenced to 7 years for the rape, although he continued to deny the act. TM was classified as a Type 7 (sexual, nonsadistic, low social competence).

The sexualization type is further subdivided into sadistic and nonsadistic subtypes. Both of the sadistic types show evidence of poor differentiation between sexual and aggressive drives, and a frequent co-occurrence of sexual and aggressive thoughts and fantasies. To be classified as an overt sadistic rapist, an offender's behavior must reflect his intention to inflict fear or pain on the victim and to manifest a high level of aggression. Moreover, because the defining feature of sadism is the synergistic relationship between sexual arousal and feelings of anger, there must be some evidence that the aggression either contributed to sexual arousal or at least did not inhibit such arousal. Because each of the two feelings (sexual arousal and anger) have equal ability to enhance or increase the other, the sexual acts may precede aggression or the aggression may precede the sexual acts. The cardinal feature, in either case, is the intertwining or "fusing" of the two feelings such that increases in one lead to increases in the other. As a group, overt sadistic rapists appear to be angry, belligerent people, who, except for their sadism and the greater planning of their sexual assaults, look very similar to the pervasive anger rapists. There were three cases classified as sadistic types.

CASE NO. 4

Joe, at age 19, broke into a woman's house (that he had been watching). The 62-year-old woman awoke to a light turned on, a small pocketknife placed to her throat, and a hand covering her mouth. Joe pulled down her pajamas and "shoved his hand into her vagina in a violent way." He grabbed her breasts and pinched the nipples telling her they were nice titties. He hit her on the right breast and she cried. He then raped her vaginally, anally, and then orally. He also inserted the barrel of a gun into her rectum. He was arrested after fingerprints were linked to him. This was his first arrest for a sexual offense. As a juvenile, he had a record for shoplifting, theft, robbery, and assault. He admitted to sadistic rape fantasies of both men and women. He described feeling "over-sexed." He was aroused by watching people urinate and by being around children. He was sentenced to 15 years.

To be classified as a muted sadistic rapist, there must be evidence that the victim's fear or discomfort, or the fantasy of violence, contributed to the offender's sexual arousal (or did not inhibit such arousal), and that the amount of physical force in the sexual assault did not exceed what was necessary to gain victim compliance. Symbolic expressions of sadistic fantasy characterize these offenders, who may employ various forms of bondage or restraint, noninjurious insertion of foreign objects, and other sexual "aids" such as vaseline or shaving cream. What is absent is the high level of expressive aggression that is clearly manifest in overt sadism. In general, muted sadistic offenders, except for their sadistic fantasies and their slightly higher lifestyle impulsivity, resemble the high social competence, of nonsadistic rapists.

CASE NO. 5

A 55-year-old married mother diagnosed with amyotrophic lateral sclerosis reported, using a communication board, that a short, fat, bearded man came to treat her. He pulled the privacy curtains around her bed. He lifted up her hospital gown, touched her breasts, twisted her nipples, spread her legs apart and inserted two fingers into her vagina. She was unable to scream, cry out for help, or fight him off due to her paralyzed condition. This happened two days in a row. The offender, a respiratory therapist, consistently denied that anything had happened. He had no prior criminal record. He *pled nolo contendere* in the criminal case and at the Department of Public Health Services hearing, which handled licensing issues, he received several restrictions on his license. The respiratory therapist was classified as a Type 5 (muted sadistic).

Nonsadistic Types

For the nonsadistic sexualized rapists, the thoughts and fantasies that are associated with their sexual assaults are devoid of the synergistic relationship between sex and aggression that characterizes the sadistic types. Indeed, these rapist types are hypothesized to manifest less aggression than any of the other rapist types. If confronted with victim resistance, these offenders may flee rather than force the victim to comply. Their fantasies and behaviors are hypothesized to reflect sexual arousal, distorted "male" cognitions about women and sexuality, feelings of social and sexual inadequacy, and masculine self-image concerns. Compared with the other rapist types, these offenders have relatively few problems with impulse control in domains outside sexual aggression.

CASE NO. 6

A 45-year-old man, dubbed the "Naked Burglar," wore a mask and no clothes when breaking into the homes of elderly women. He would cut the screen, cut the phone wires, and unlock the door. He forced oral and vaginal penetration on his victims. One 91-year-old victim testified that he asked her if she was "enjoying it" and that he bet she "hadn't had it for a while." Before he left, the man took the bed sheets, but the elder took a washcloth, scrubbed her face and vaginal area, and went to a nearby store to phone the police. The man had been previously arrested for peeping on a couple in their hot tub. Evidence on the man included a mask, gloves, a video camera, and house and car keys. His earlier victim was 89. He was sentenced to life.

VINDICTIVE MOTIVATION

The core feature and primary driving force for the vindictive types is anger at women. Unlike the pervasive anger rapist, women are the central and exclusive focus of the vindictive rapist's anger. Their sexual assaults are marked by behaviors that are physically injurious and appear to be intended to degrade, demean, and humiliate their victims. The misogynistic anger evident in these assaults runs the gamut from verbal abuse to brutal murder. As noted, these offenders differ from pervasive anger rapists in that they show little or no evidence of anger at men (e.g., instigating fights with or assaulting men).

Although there is a sexual component to their assaults, there is no evidence that their aggression is eroticized, as it is for the sadistic types, and no evidence that they are preoccupied with sadistic fantasies. Indeed, the aggression in the sexual assault is often instrumental in achieving the primary aim of demeaning or humiliating the victim (e.g., forcing the victim to fellate the offender). Vindictive rapists also differ from both the pervasive anger and overt sadistic offenders in their relatively lower level of lifestyle impulsivity (i.e., they have relatively fewer problems with impulse control in other areas of their lives).

CASE NO. 7

JG, a 33-year-old, 6-foot, 200-pound man with a criminal felony history and an outstanding health warrant for gonorrhea, applied to be a nurse's aide. Under state law, the facility was required to request a criminal history check, which it did, mistakenly classifying him as a female. A state record check of a female by the name of JG revealed no criminal history. Three weeks after he was hired, he was fired by the assistant director of nurses for repeatedly slapping a frail and helpless 87-year-old female resident.

After some period of time out of state, JG returned and applied to another facility within the same nursing home system. The required criminal check was done, but the facility submitted a form with JG's name written by hand. His last name apparently looked like a "C" instead of a "G." Again, the incorrect name came up clear of any criminal record and he was hired. The offense that came to staff attention occurred about a month after he was hired. While in a shower stall, JG raped a 63-year-old semi-paralyzed woman, and then returned her to her bed. Two nursing aides were alerted to a substance appearing to look and smell like semen and they reported their findings to the nursing supervisor. The resident was taken to the hospital emergency room where a sexual assault examination revealed bruising to her left thigh and vaginal area, which was tender to the touch and included a brown mucous discharge. According to the victim, she was assaulted several times and was told by the offender to shut up when she screamed and that he would kill her if she told anyone. JG told the detective that he and the resident-victim "were close." JG said that he discussed his personal problems with her, that he called her "mama," and that he was sorry he could not make his penis bigger. He admitted that he digitally penetrated her and inserted a shower head.

JG was classified as a Type 8 (vindictive, low social competence).

DISCUSSION

TAXONOMIC HETEROGENEITY

Although clearly it is impossible to draw any conclusions about the taxonomic characteristics of men who sexually assault elderly women based on the small convenience sample of incarcerated offenders examined in this study, several observations are noteworthy.

First and most importantly, based on this sample, the age of predator and motive for sexual assault of the elderly are varied. Second, many offenders in our sample had long histories of criminal offenses, a few had a prior history of sexual assault, and several offenders were hired by the nursing homes despite criminal checks. Third, prior employment history was not always checked. In one case, out of 10 nursing home employments, the offender had been fired from seven. Fourth, if there were any commonalties among the offenders, they fell into two categories: (1) many of the offenders were classified as low in social competence and (2) all of the offenders exploited victims who were frail and defenseless.

There are two principal areas of concern that are beginning to emerge from our initial inquiry into nursing home sexual assault. The first area concerns victimology and the second area concerns liability. Victimology was addressed in greater detail in the chapter on victims of elder sexual abuse. In brief, the victims of these crimes are, not surprisingly, quite advanced in age and suffering from some degree of dementia. As a result, not only is the examination and assessment process quite difficult—often conducted in the absence of a coherent victim report and in the presence of victim resistance (i.e., out of confusion and fear victims resist routine physical examinations after rape)—but the treatment and recovery process is also immeasurably more difficult. Indeed, in a review of just 20 nursing home cases, 11 of the 20 victims died within 12 months of the rape—not from physical injuries associated with the assault but from the impact of the trauma on a very frail constitution. The unique examination and recovery problems associated with these elderly victims were discussed in detail by Hicks and Moon (1984). It is imperative that alternative methods for examining and treating these elderly, often frail victims be developed; that nursing home policies and procedures incorporate these new methods; that all caregivers employed by nursing homes be properly trained in identifying and responding to cases of sexual assault; and that the medical personnel that respond to these victims be properly trained in more effective, humane methods of examination.

The second principal area of concern involves first- and third-party liability. Over the past two decades, an increasing number of suits have been brought by rape victims or their families against employers and property owners whose negligence in the face of foreseeable risks may have contributed to a sexual assault (Loggans, 1985). Liability may be imposed for punitive damages when it has been determined that the defendant acted with "utter indifference" or "conscious disregard" for the safety and welfare of the plaintiff (Loggans, 1985). In sum, "third-party liability for rape and sexual assault is clearly based upon the fact that such crimes are frequently caused or encouraged by the failure to protect against a known and identifiable risk of harm" (Loggans, 1985, p. 54).

POLICY AND INVESTIGATIVE IMPLICATIONS

A practical question is how this classification of rapists of elders and the predictors of the severity of such crimes can be useful to investigators and policy makers in the criminal justice field. There are two answers that will be discussed below: (1) motive in the escalation of rapists to sexual homicide and severity of crimes and (2) the forensic utility of classification of rapists of the elderly.

Motive and Escalation in Serial Sexual Homicide

FBI agents at the Behavioral Analysis Unit have conducted further work on serial sexual murderers, in particular those who prey on elderly women. Myers, Husted, Safarik, and O'Toole (2006) argue that authors who attribute the actions of serial sexual murderers to *anger* actually may have meant to use the terms *aggression* or *violence*. These two terms are not synonymous with anger. Certainly the behaviors of serial sexual murderers toward their victims can be considered aggressive or violent. However, the commission of aggressive acts does not mean the offender was angry.

Controversy exists in the literature and society regarding what motivates serial sexual killers to commit their crimes. Hypotheses range from the seeking of sexual gratification, to the achievement of power and control, to the expression of anger. Myers et al. (2006) argue that serial sexual murderers commit their crimes in pursuit of sadistic pleasure. The seeking of power and control over victims is believed to serve the two secondary purposes of heightening sexual arousal and ensuring victim presence for the crime. Anger is not considered a key component of these offenders' motivation due to its inhibitory physiological effect on sexual functioning. On the contrary, criminal investigations into serial sexual killings consistently reveal erotically charged crimes, with sexual motivation expressed either overtly or symbolically. While anger may be correlated with serial sexual homicide offenders, as it is with criminal offenders in general, it is not causative.

Investigative Profiling and Risk Assessment

The utility of classification for forensic examiners is in two important domains: investigative profiling and risk assessment.

Investigative Criminal Analysis

The taxonomic "profiling" of sex offenders essentially started with a deductive methodology using the systems first developed by Cohen and Groth in the 1960s and 1970s. The rapist system developed by Cohen and Seghorn, which was conceptually very similar to Groth's system, was put to empirical test by researchers at the Massachusetts Treatment Center in the 1980s. The current system for classifying rapists (MTC:R3) is the second major revision of the original Cohen/Seghorn system (cf. Knight & Prentky, 1990). MTC:R3 is the only known system to date that has been examined empirically with regard to efficacy in crime scene analysis.

An offender's motive is the purpose or intent for his committing the crime. The motive of a crime, including a violent crime or series of crimes, is more objective and may be inferred from a crime scene. Offenders can have multiple motives for a single offense. Motives may change as the crime proceeds. An offender may begin the crime with one primary motive that then becomes subsumed to another motive as the crime progresses. Safarik et al. (2002) noted that in over 70% of sexual homicides of elder women, the offender, after committing the sexual assault and homicide, redirected his attention to the theft of property. Financial gain becomes the new primary motive driving the offender's actions. In serial offenses motives can evolve over time (Safarik, Jarvis, & Nussbaum, 2000; Myers et al., 2006).

CASE NO. 8

In the early morning hours, after peeping through the front bedroom window, AW, threw a large seashell through the rear window of an 87-year-old woman as she slept. He entered the home and confronted the victim as she came to investigate the noise. He blitz attacked her, bound her wrists and ankles with dog leashes and sexually assaulted her. He used multiple weapons to kill her and she suffered numerous injuries. After her death he covered her with items which he dumped on her from several large bureau drawers. He proceeded to fill her car with numerous household items including her and her late husband's passports. The offender remained in the residence for a period of time removing her property. He eventually stole her car with the back seat and trunk filled with stolen items. AW was arrested early the next morning. He was convicted of sexual assault and murder and sentenced to death.

Motive, however, is not synonymous with the offender's affective or emotional state. Affective state—what the offender is feeling at the time of the crime—is much more difficult to discern. Despite this significant distinction, emotions are frequently identified as motives for crimes, particularly in violent crimes in which there is a great deal of violence and physical damage to the victim. In crimes involving extreme reactive violence, strong emotions, such as anger, rage, hatred, and hurt, likely underpin or fuel the offender's behavior (Safarik, 2006).

Informing Criminal Justice System Decisions

A parallel in elder abuse may exist between research findings in assessing child molesters and the strength of sexual preoccupation with children. On interview, many of the offenders described their sexual interest in an elder. Although there are various nonactuarial ways of assessing this variable (e.g., using penile plethysmography [PPG]), the most common method is to examine the strength or intensity of an offender's preoccupation with a specific age group as sexual objects (i.e., "fixation"). Strength of sexual preoccupation with children is repeatedly identified as a critical predictor of sexual recidivism (e.g., Proulx et al., 1997; Hanson & Bussiere, 1998). As noted, an offender's degree of preoccupation with children as sexual objects has often been measured using penile plethysmography to assess behaviorally the offender's sexual arousal to depictions of children of various ages. Although such a direct measure is appealing and sexual arousal patterns have been shown to predict sexual recidivism, it has its drawbacks, including the logistical problems of obtaining phallometric data, the cost of the assessment procedure, the invasiveness of the procedure, and the increased likelihood in forensic contexts that dissimulation may compromise the validity of the assessment.

CONCLUSION

In conclusion, this descriptive study of offender motivation in the rape of the elderly provides a beginning point on which to classify offenders. More research will be necessary to provide discussion as to whether such offenders constitute a new type of paraphilia. Regardless of the motive, however, investigators need to carefully interview the elder victim and the offender and to collect evidence that will assist in the successful prosecution of the case.

REFERENCES

Abel, G. G., Barrett, D. H., and Gardos, P. S. 1992. Sexual misconduct by physicians. *Journal of the Medical Association of Georgia*, 81: 237–246.

Adshead, G., Howett, M., and Mason, F. 1994. Women who sexually abuse children: The undiscovered country. *Journal of Sexual Aggression*, 1: 45–56.

Anderson, P. B., and Struckman-Johnson, C. 1998. *Sexually aggressive women: Current perspectives and controversies*. New York: Guilford Press.

Ball, A. 2005. Sexual offending on elderly women: A review. *The Journal of Forensic Psychiatry & Psychology*, 16(1): 127–138.

Ball, A., and Fowler, D. 2008. Sexual offending against older female victims: An empirical study of the prevalence and characteristics of recorded offences in a semi-rural English county. *The Journal of Forensic Psychiatry & Psychology*, 19(1): 14–32.

Ball, H. N., Snowdon, P. R., and Strickland, I. 1992. Sex offenses on older women: Psychopathology of the offender. *Journal of Forensic Psychiatry*, 3: 160–166.

Barbaree, H. E., Marshall, W. L., and Hudson, S. M. 1993. *The juvenile sex offender*. New York: Guilford Press.

Burgess, A. W., Baker, T., Greening, D., Hartman, C. R., Burgess, A. G., Douglas, J. E., et al. 1997. Stalking behaviors within domestic violence. *Journal of Family Violence*, 12: 389–403.

Cartwright, P. S. 1987. Factors that correlate with injury sustained by survivors of sexual assault. *Obstetrics and Gynecology*, 70: 44–46.

Cartwright, P. S., and Moore, R. A. 1989. The elderly victim of rape. *Southern Medical Journal*, 82: 988–989.

Del Bove, G., Stermac, L., and Bainbridge, D. 2006. Comparisons of sexual assault among older and younger women. *Journal of Elder Abuse & Neglect*, 17(3): 1–18.

Elliott, C. E., and Butler, L. 1994. The stop and think group: Changing sexually aggressive behavior in young children. *Journal of Sexual Aggression*, 1: 15–28.

Elliott, M. 1993. *Female sexual abuse of children*. New York: Guilford Press.

Greenfield, L. A. 1996. *Child victimizers: Violent offenders and their victims*. Washington, DC: Bureau of Justice Statistics.

Groth, A. N. 1978. The older rape victim and her assailant. *Journal of Geriatric Psychiatry*, 2: 203–215.

Hanson, R. A., and Bussiere, M. T. 1998. Predicting relapse: A meta-analysis of sexual offender recidivism studies. *Journal of Consulting and Clinical Psychology*, 66: 348–362.

Haywood, T. W., Kravitz, H. M., Wasyliw, O. E., Goldberg, J., and Cavanaugh, J. L. 1996. Cycle of abuse and psychopathology in cleric and noncleric molesters of children and adolescents. *Child Abuse and Neglect*, 20: 1233–1243.

Hazelwood, R. R., and Burgess, A. W. (Eds.). 2017. *Practical aspects of rape investigation*, 5th ed. Boca Raton, FL: CRC Press.

Hicks, D. J., and Moon, D. M. 1984. Sexual assault of the older woman. In I. R. Stuart and J. G. Greer (Eds.). *Victims of sexual aggression: Treatment of children, women and men*, 180–196. New York: Van Nostrand Reinhold Co.

Knight, R. A., and Prentky, R. A. 1990. Classifying sex offenders: The development and corroboration of taxonomic models. In W. L. Marshall, D. R. Laws, and H. E. Barbaree (Eds.). *The handbook of sexual assault: Issues, theories, and treatment of the offender*. New York: Plenum.

Lanyon, R. I. 1991. Theories of sex offending. In C. R. Hollin and K. Howells (Eds.). *Clinical approaches to sex offending and their victims*. Chichester: John Wiley and Sons, Ltd.

Larson, N. R., and Maison, S. R. 1995. Psychological treatment program for women sex offenders in a prison setting. *Acta Sexologica*, 1: 81–138.

Loar, L. 1994. Child sexual abuse: Several brief interventions with young perpetrators. *Child Abuse and Neglect*, 18: 977–986.

Loftus, J. A., and Camargo, R. J. 1993. Treating the clergy. *Annals of Sex Research*, 6: 287–303.

Loggans, S. E. 1985. Rape as an intentional tort. *Trial*, October: 45–55.

Meloy, J. R. 1996. Stalking (obsessional following): A review of some preliminary studies. *Aggression and Violent Behavior*, 1: 147–162.

Muram, D., Miller, K., and Cutler, A. 1992. Sexual assault of the elderly victim. *Journal of Interpersonal Violence*, 7: 70–76.

Myers, W., Husted, D., Safarik, M., and O'Toole, M. E. 2006. Aggression and anger in serial sexual murderers. *Journal of Forensic Sciences*, 51: 127–138.

Pithers, W. D., Gray, A., Busconi, A., and Houchens, P. 1998. Children with sexual problems: Identification of five distinct child types and related treatment considerations. *Child Maltreatment*, 3: 384–406.

Pollack, N. L. 1988. Sexual assault of older women. *Annals of Sex Research*, 1: 523–532.

Prentky, R. A., and Knight, R. A. 1991. Identifying critical dimensions for discriminating among rapists. *Journal of Consulting and Clinical Psychology*, 59(5): 643–661.

Proulx, J., Pellerin, B., Paradis, Y., McKibben, A., Aubut, J., and Quimet, M. 1997. *Sexual Abuse: Journal of Research and Treatment*, 9: 7–27.

Ramin, S. M., Satin, A. J., Stone, I. C., and Wendel, G. D. 1992. Rape in postmenopausal women. *Obstectrics and Gynecology*, 80(5): 861–864.

Ramsey-Klawsnik, H. 1995. Investigating suspected elder maltreatment. *Journal of Elder Abuse and Neglect*, 7(1): 41–67.

Safarik, M. E. 2006. Elder sexual homicide. In J. E. Douglas, Burgess, A. W. Burgess, A. G. Burgess, and R. K. Ressler (Eds.). *Crime classification manual*, 227–235. San Francisco: Jossey–Bass.

Safarik, M. E., Jarvis, J. P., and Nussbaum, K. E. 2000. Elderly female serial sexual homicide: A limited empirical test of criminal investigative analysis. *Homicide Studies*, 4: 294–307.

Safarik, M. E., Jarvis, J. P., and Nussbaum, K. E. 2002. Sexual homicide of elderly females: Linking offender characteristics to victim and crime scene attributes. *Journal of Interpersonal Violence*, 17(5): 500–525.

Safarik, M. E., and Jarvis, J. P. 2005. Examining attributes of homicides: Toward quantifying qualitative values of injury severity. *Journal of Homicide Studies*, 9(3): 183–203.

Seto, M. C. 2013. *Internet sex offenders*. Washington, DC: American Psychological Association.

Strickland, S. 2008. Female sex offenders: Exploring issues of personality, trauma, and cognitive distortions. *Journal of Interpersonal Violence*, 23(4): 474–489.

Tyra, P. A. 1993. Helping elderly women survive rape using a crisis framework. *Journal of Psychosocial Nursing*, 34(12): 20–25.

Webb, L., Craissati, J., and Keen, S. 2007. Characteristics of internet child pornography offenders: A comparison with child molesters. *Sexual Abuse: Journal of Research and Treatment*, 19: 449–465.

FURTHER READING

Acierno, R., Resnick, H., Kilpatrick, D., and Stark-Riemer, W. 2003. Assessing elder victimization: Demonstration of a methodology. *Social Psychiatry and Psychiatric Epidemiology*, 38(11): 644–653.

Aiken, L. H., Clarke, S. P., and Sloane, D. M. 2002. Hospital staffing, organization, and quality of care: Cross-national findings. *International Journal of Quality Health Care*, 14(1): 5–13.

American Nurses Association (ANA). 2002, May 9. ANA supports legislative proposal to improve staffing in nursing homes, http://www.nursingworld.org/pressrel/2002/pr0509.htm

Auslander, G. K., and Litwin, H. 1991. Social networks, social support, and self-ratings of health among the elderly. *Journal of Aging and Health*, 3(4): 493–510.

Bell, K. 1995. Tulsa sexual assault nurse examiners program. *Oklahoma Nurse*, 40(3): 16.

Brandl, B., and Horan, D. L. 2002. Domestic violence in later life: An overview for health care providers. *Women and Health*, 35(2–3): 41–54.

Burgess, A. W., Commons, M. C., Safarik, M. E., Cooper, R. R., and Ross, S. N. 2007. Sex offenders of the elderly. *Aggression and Violent Behavior*, 12: 582–597.

Burgess, A. W., Dowdell, E. B., and Prentky, R. A. 2000. Sexual abuse of nursing home residents. *Journal of Psychosocial Nursing and Mental Health Services*, 38(6): 10–18.

Crowell, N. A., and Burgess, A. W. 1996. *Understanding violence against women*. Washington, DC: National Academy Press.

Davis, L. J., and Brody, E. M. 1979. *Rape and older women: A guide to prevention and protection*. Rockville, MD: National Institute of Mental Health.

Du Mont, J., and Parnis, D. 2003. Forensic nursing in the context of sexual assault: Comparing the opinions and practices of nurse examiners and nurses. *Applied Nursing Research*, 16(3): 173–183.

Harrington, C., and Swan, J. H. 2003. Nursing home staffing, turnover, and case mix. *Medical Care Research and Review*, 60(3): 366–392 (discussion 393–369).

Hatmaker, D. D., Pinholster, L., and Saye, J. J. 2002. A community-based approach to sexual assault. *Public Health Nursing*, 19(2): 124–127.

Ledray, L. E., and Arndt, S. 1994. Examining the sexual assault victim: A new model for nursing care. *Journal of Psychosocial Nursing and Mental Health Services*, 32(2): 7–12.

Moseley, C. B., and Jones, L. 2003. Registered nurse staffing and OBRA deficiencies in Nevada nursing facilities. *Journal of Gerontological Nursing*, 29(3): 44–50.

Mueller, C. 2002. Nurse staffing in long-term care facilities. *Journal of Nursing Administration*, 32(12): 640–647.

Prentky, R. A., and Burgess, A. W. 2000. *Forensic management of sexual offenders*. New York: Kluwer Academic/Plenum Publishers.

Stermac, L. E., and Stirpe, T. S. 2002. Efficacy of a 2-year-old sexual assault nurse examiner program in a Canadian hospital. *Journal of Emergency Nursing*, 28(1): 18–23.

United States General Account Office. 2002. Nursing homes: More can be done to protect residents from abuse (report to congressional requesters). Washington, DC: United States General Accounting Office.

Woodtli, M. A., and Breslin, E. T. 2002. Violence-related content in the nursing curriculum: A follow-up national survey. *Journal of Nursing Education*, 41(8): 340–348.

26 Educator Sexual Misconduct
Grooming Patterns and Female Offenders

James L. Knoll, IV

CONTENTS

Educator Sexual Misconduct: The U.S. Department of Education Study 408
Female Perpetrators 409
General Sex Offender Grooming Patterns 409
Educator Sexual Abuse Grooming Patterns 411
Effects of Educator Sexual Abuse 413
Dilemmas 413
Case Example and Discussion 414
Toward Prevention 416
Conclusions 417
References 418

Teachers have a profound and life-long effect on their students. The student–teacher connection can create positive, transforming possibilities for the student (Gillespie, 2005). Conversely, the power imbalance present in this influential relationship may be abused, resulting in long-term trauma for the student. This is particularly the case for some sex offenders who use the profession of teaching to target victims (Sullivan & Beech, 2002). The topic of sexual abuse of students by their teachers has slowly been receiving increasing scrutiny. Prior to the 1990s, there was little formal research on this subject. In 1991, Wishnietsky conducted a survey of high school students, and found that 14% reported having engaged in sexual intercourse with a teacher (Wishnietsky, 1991). In 2015, a former U.S. Department of Education Chief of Staff began studying all cases of teacher sexual misconduct reported in the media (Abbott, 2015). This effort found that in 2014, there were 781 reported cases of teachers and other school employees accused or convicted of sexual relationships with students. It was concluded that, on average, 15 young people were sexually victimized by educators each week in the U.S.

Ratliff and Watson (2014) reviewed public records of 431 certified public school educators in the U.S. who had been arrested and charged with sexual misconduct between 2007 and 2011. The study identified 319 male and 112 female offenders. While male offenders were more likely to abuse younger victims (12 and younger), female offenders were more likely to abuse older victims (13 and older). Another difference between male and female offenders involved how they came to the attention of law enforcement. Male offenders were more likely to be caught due to a direct claim from the victim or discovery by school administration. In contrast, female offenders were more likely to be discovered when other students or the victim's parents reported their concerns.

Media focus on female teachers having sexual relationships with their students seems to have increased in recent years. The case of Mary Kay Letourneau captured national attention when she was convicted of second-degree child rape for having sex with her sixth grade student, Vili Fualaau, when he was 12 years old. Ms. Letourneau, who was 35 years old at the time, pleaded guilty and received a 7½-year sentence, which was suspended contingent on her completion of sex offender treatment and an 80-day jail sentence. At the time of her conviction in 1997, she had already given birth to Fualaau's daughter. In 1998, she was given prison time for violating her conditional release by having contact with Mr. Fualaau. Ms. Letourneau subsequently had another child by her former student, and eventually married him when she was released from prison.

High profile cases such as this have led to public outrage and inquiries into school credentialing procedures and termination practices for teachers (Schultz, 2005). The subject has fueled public debate over whether female teacher sex offenders receive more lenient sentences than their male equivalents (Saletan, 2006). While there is no clear answer to this question at present, some have noted a distinct difference in how the female teacher sex offender's crimes are described when compared to male teacher sex offender crimes. For example, it has been reported that the female offender's actions are commonly described as a "well-meaning," harmless initiation into sexuality (Denove, 2001). In a study of college students, men reported viewing female teacher–male student sexual relationships more positively than male teacher–female student sexual relationships (Fromuth, Holt, & Parker, 2001). Such findings raise the issue of socio-cultural biases at play in terms of how such sexually abusive relationships are perceived.

Such biases may be accounted for by a tendency to perceive a sexual relationship as more beneficial to a male subordinate than to a female subordinate. Research has established that men are expected to obtain greater social benefits (peer approval, social status) than are women for engaging in sexual acts (Sheeran, Spears, Abraham, & Abrams, 1996). In the case of student–teacher relationships, if the sexual misconduct was teacher-initiated, male teachers are more likely to be judged harshly than female teachers (Howell, Egan, Giuliano, & Ackley, 2011). Howell et al. (2011) also found that male students were perceived to benefit from a student–teacher sexual relationship to a greater extent than female students. Study participants used words such as "lucky, cool, and confident" to describe male students who had a student–teacher sexual relationship. Female students who had a student–teacher sexual relationship were described as "insecure, needy," and having "low self-esteem."

This chapter will review the literature on female teacher sexual misconduct, in addition to what is currently known about grooming patterns and warning signs. Dilemmas in resolving cases of educator sexual misconduct will be discussed, and basic prevention strategies will be recommended.

EDUCATOR SEXUAL MISCONDUCT: THE U.S. DEPARTMENT OF EDUCATION STUDY

To date there are few national level studies of educator sexual abuse. This is in spite of the "No Child Left Behind" act of 2001, which called for a national study of sexual abuse in schools. Most data on educator sexual abuse has come from newspaper reports. Shakeshaft performed a secondary analysis of data collected for the American Association of University Women (AAUW), (Shakeshaft, 2003). This data was drawn from a list of 80,000 schools surveyed in the fall of 2000 (AAUW, 2001). The secondary analysis revealed that 9.6% of all students in grades 8–11 report educator sexual abuse. This finding is similar to a study of secondary school students in Israel, 8% of whom reported being sexually maltreated by school staff (Khoury-Kassabri, 2006).

In an extensive synthesis of existing literature (Shakeshaft, 2004), the Ontario College of Teachers definition of educator sexual misconduct was used: "any behavior of a sexual nature which may constitute professional misconduct (p. 1)," (Ontario College of Teachers, 2002). The perpetrators of educator sexual abuse were described as falling into two patterns: (1) abusers with victims younger than seventh grade and (2) abusers with victims in late middle and high school (Shakeshaft, 2003). The abusers of children younger than seventh grade had a distinctly different public persona and modus operandi than those who abuse older children.

Educators targeting elementary school children were often high achievers in the profession who had been recognized with awards for their teaching efforts (Shakeshaft, 2004). The popularity and trust evoked by these educators may perplex school officials and community members when allegations of sexual misconduct are made. As a further complication, the teacher's professional reputation may result in a tendency to dismiss or ignore allegations. It was theorized that this type of abuser works at being recognized as a good teacher to secure trust and an irreproachable reputation in furtherance of their goal of sexual misconduct. For example, a highly regarded school band director in Texas was convicted of sexual misconduct with a student. It was found that he kept decades worth of pictures and notes as trophies (Henry, Griffith, & Goulas, 2006).

In contrast, educators who teach at the late middle and high school level target victims in this age range. They might be outstanding teachers, yet they may also be mediocre (Shakeshaft, 2003). Sexual abuse at this level may be less premeditated and planned, and more a result of bad judgment (Shakeshaft, 2004). For example, a case in New York State involved a married 33-year-old teacher who was abusing substances. The teacher reported feeling flattered that one of her 15-year-old male students found her attractive. Their affair "became public when the highly intoxicated teacher announced it to students and others nearby during a school basketball game" (Ramirez, 2007).

The majority of educators who abuse are classroom teachers (18%). The next most common abusers are coaches (15%), but bus drivers, administrators, and others affiliated with the school may also offend (Shakeshaft, 2003). Most sexual abuse of students by adults occurs in the school in empty classrooms, hallways, and in offices. It is common for teachers to target vulnerable or marginal students who feel especially gratified by the extra attention.

FEMALE PERPETRATORS

Most attention has focused on male teachers as the primary perpetrators; however, the scenario of female teachers sexually abusing their students is receiving increasing recognition (Thomas, 1999). In a study of 471 female offenders in Texas, Vandiver and Kercher (2004) reported finding six types of female sex offenders. The most common type was called the "heterosexual nurturer," who was also least likely to have an arrest for sexual assault. Another study followed up on this typology by examining 390 female sex offenders registered in New York State. It was concluded that female sex offenders, on the whole, are a heterogeneous group (Sandler & Freeman, 2007). A typology of "Teacher/Lover" has been proposed for the adult female who views herself as emotionally equal to her teenage victim (Mathews, Matthews, & Speltz, 1991). The victim of this type of offender is most commonly a troubled or needy adolescent seeking attention. The perpetrator conceptualizes the behavior as a "consensual" love affair, and often has difficulty seeing her actions as inappropriate.

Gannon, Rose, and Ward (2012) and colleagues have set forth a Descriptive Model of Female Sexual Offending (DMFSO), which recognizes different motivations for offending including intimacy, revenge/humiliation, sexual gratification, and financial gain. One type of female sexual offender, the Explicit-Approach type, is characterized by moderate–high levels of positive affect, offense planning, low levels of coercion, and moderate–high levels of self-regulation. A further study using DMFSO construct with 36 North American female sex offenders supported the Explicit-Approach type as one of three "offense pathways" (Gannon et al., 2014). Both the Explicit-Approach type and the Teacher/Lover type offenders seem to capture elements of the offending style of the female teacher sexual abuser.

GENERAL SEX OFFENDER GROOMING PATTERNS

"Grooming" is a term used to describe the process by which sex offenders carefully initiate and maintain sexually abusive relationships with children. Grooming is a conscious, deliberate, and carefully orchestrated approach used by the offender. The goal of grooming is to permit a sexual encounter, and keep it a secret. Correctly noting that there is no consensus definition for grooming, Bennett and O'Donohue (2014) critically evaluated the literature and proposed that grooming be defined as: "antecedent inappropriate behavior that functions to increase the likelihood of future sexual abuse." Indeed, a consensus definition will be needed for future research and prevention efforts. One challenge involves clearly distinguishing grooming from normal adult–child interactions. In an effort to minimize false positives, Bennett and O'Donohue (2014) opted to require that all grooming behaviors be "inappropriate" in and of themselves. However, these researchers struggled with vagueness of the term "inappropriate." Moreover, this requirement presents a significant limitation due to the fact that offenders may initially deliberately engage in grooming behaviors that would be considered "appropriate" for the purpose of establishing a rapport and trust with a victim and/or the victim's family. Thus, until research in this area makes more progress, the determination of whether grooming has occurred will require careful forensic assessment on a case-by-case basis.

The grooming process encompasses a variety of methods used by the offender during the preparatory stage of sexual abuse (Mcalindon, 2006). In addition, the methods help maintain the abusive relationship by ensuring the complicity and secrecy of the victim. Offenders carefully groom victims by systematically separating them from family and peers (Lawson, 2003). Once isolated, victims are more easily exploited and manipulated into sexual relationships. Ninety-one child sex offenders, who were not educators, were interviewed about how they selected and maintained their victims (Elliot, Browne, & Kilcoyne, 1995). Offenders reported using a variety of methods to select a victim, establish and maintain the sexual relationship. Victims were often selected because the offender perceived them as vulnerable, isolated and/or emotionally needy. Box 26.1 provides a list of sex offenders' common grooming strategies. Although these strategies were reported by child sex offenders who were not teachers, in the author's forensic experience the same general strategies are commonly used by teachers who groom to abuse students sexually. Additionally, use of these strategies by teacher sexual abusers has been confirmed by Moulden, Firestone, Kingston, and Wexler (2010) who found that Canadian teachers befriended students and gave them special attention and gifts in an effort to abuse students sexually.

BOX 26.1   SEX OFFENDER GROOMING STRATEGIES
(Elliot et al., 1995)

Targeting:
- Vulnerable (e.g., low self-confidence, low self-esteem)
- Less parental oversight
- Socially isolated or emotionally needy

Strategies:
- Caretaking (e.g., babysitting, teaching, tutoring)
- Form "special relationship"
- Become welcome in home/gain trust of parents
- Gifts, games, special times
- Isolate
- Seize on feelings of being unloved/unappreciated
- Emotional bonding and trust building
- Desensitize to sex (e.g., talking, pictures, pornographic videos)
- Use pretense ("teaching," "exploring," "closeness")
- Exploit victim's natural sexual curiosity or uncertainty

Maintenance:
- Bribes, gifts to ensure continued compliance
- Threaten dire consequences to ensure secrecy
- Threaten to blame victim
- Threaten loss of "loving" relationship

Offenders may also rely on a victim's natural sexual curiosity, or feed into a victim's feeling of being unloved or unappreciated. A study of 97 child sex offenders, who were not educators, revealed that the grooming process relies heavily on the offender gaining the trust of the victim (Bennell, Alison, Stein, Alison, & Canter, 2001). This often involves the offender exploiting the adult–child power imbalance in a variety of ways. Many child sex offenders believed that a "special relationship" was vital to obtaining victim compliance. For example, one offender stated, "I have to feel as if I am important and special to the child and giving the child the love she needs and isn't getting" (Elliott et al., 1995, p. 579). Once a trusting or special relationship is created, the offender may carefully test the victim's reaction to the topic of sex. This may be done by bringing up sexual matters in discussion, leaving sexually oriented materials out where the victim can see them and by subtly increasing sexual touching. In this way, the offender attempts to "normalize" sex and desensitize the victim.

During the maintenance phase, the offender may use a variety of strategies to ensure secrecy. For example, one offender stated, "secrecy and blame were my best weapons. Most kids worry that they are to blame for the abuse and that they should keep it a secret," (Elliott et al., 1995, p. 579). In addition, offenders may use intimidation, bribes, or threats to maintain secrecy (Shakeshaft, 2004). Paradoxically, the offender may represent the closest relationship the victim has, particularly if the victim is socially isolated or emotionally vulnerable. In such cases, the victim may be reticent to give up what he or she views as a "loving" relationship.

EDUCATOR SEXUAL ABUSE GROOMING PATTERNS

One central ethical theme of educator sexual abuse is the violation of professional boundaries. Research suggests that teachers generally recognize the importance of student–teacher boundary violations. In a study of teachers' opinions on ethical standards, teachers rated boundary violations as the single most serious ethical violation (Barrett, Headly, Stovall, & Witte, 2006). For educator sexual abusers, the process of grooming begins when an abuser selects a victim and subsequently employs a series of methods designed to "seduce" the student (Robins, 2000). Victim selection in educator sexual abuse is influenced by the compliance of the student and the likelihood of secrecy (Shakeshaft, 2003). Offenders tend to target students that they believe they can control. The sexual and psychological exploitation occurs within the perpetrator's subtle agenda of grooming and enticement. Most children respond to positive attention from an educator, and the praise of teachers can be quite influential (Nicaise, Bois, Fairclough, Amorose, & Cogerino, 2007). However, students who are estranged from their parents or who are experiencing some type of emotional difficulty are often targeted not only because they might be responsive, but also because they may be more likely to maintain silence (Shakeshaft, 2003).

The teacher may begin grooming by giving the student special attention, support, or rewards. The power of such rewards to affect the student should not be underestimated. Rewards from a teacher can have an influential effect on students' motivation and cognitions. Students' reward history is significantly related to their future motivation and performance (Davis, Winsler, & Middleton, 2006). Rewarding for the purposes of grooming may take place in the context of providing the student with additional help, mentoring, advisement on a project or opportunities for overnight outings. As this takes place, the teacher may be slowly introducing and increasing sexually related discourse. Next, the amount of touching and physical contact is gradually increased. At this point, the grooming assumes the purpose of testing the child's ability to maintain secrecy, and to desensitize the child through progressive sexual behaviors. This pattern is consistent with the findings of a study of Canadian sexual offenders who were in a professional position of trust which involved working or volunteering with children (Leclerc, Proulx, & McKibben, 2005).

Leclerc et al. (2005) found that "professional perpetrators" began by showing kindness, love, and attention to potential victims. They gradually desensitized victims to sexualized behavior, before proceeding to subtle forms of nonviolent coercion to ensure secrecy. A study of 113

Canadian male teachers (nine female teachers were identified, but excluded for statistical purposes) who had committed educator sexual abuse revealed that offenders used complex grooming strategies indicative of intact self-regulatory skills (Moulden et al., 2010). This sample of offenders used their positions of authority to befriend the victims, offer special assistance, or offer money and gifts.

The teacher may strive to provide the student with experiences that are valuable so that the student will be reticent to lose the relationship. Grooming may also involve the parents of the victim so that the offender can better gain their approval and trust. This will allow the offender greater access to the victim and enhanced ability to isolate the victim on outings. In the author's experience, it is not uncommon for parents to be appreciative of the extra attention from the teacher, who they perceive as a positive role model and authority figure to their child. Grooming patterns must be better understood if educator sexual misconduct is to be prevented or detected (Shakeshaft, 2003; Bennett & O'Donohue, 2014). Box 26.2 provides a list of some potential warning signs of educator sexual misconduct.

BOX 26.2   POTENTIAL WARNING SIGNS OF EDUCATOR SEXUAL MISCONDUCT

(Shakeshaft, 2004; Sutton, 2004; Leclerc et al., 2005; Educator's Guide to Controlling Sexual Harassment, 2006; Moulden et al., 2010; Abbott, 2015)

- Obvious or inappropriate preferential treatment of a student
- Excessive time spent alone with a student
- Excessive time spent with student outside of class
- Repeated time spent in private spaces with a student
- Driving a student to or from school
- Befriending parents and making visits to their home
- Acting as a particular student's "confidante"
- Giving gifts, cards, letters to a student
- After hours or excessive phone calls to a student
- Inappropriate texts, emails or social media messages to a student
- Overly affectionate behavior with student
- Flirtatious behavior or off-color remarks around a student
- Other students suspect, make jokes or references

Advances in technology represent new opportunities for sex offenders to engage in grooming. The term *electronic grooming* is used here to describe the use of methods such as online chatting, texting, and various forms of social media to facilitate the grooming process. For example, educator sexual abusers may use cell phone texting and/or Facebook messaging to engage a victim in the grooming process. Abbott (2015) reported finding that female teachers were slightly more likely than male teachers to use social media to engage victims. To date, there is little research focusing on computer-mediated communications used by offenders in the grooming process. Black, Wollis, Woodworth, and Hancock (2015) analyzed the communication transcripts of 44 convicted online sex offenders for strategies used and differences from face-to-face grooming. The study found support for basic grooming strategies in an online environment, but the pattern and timing of strategies appeared to be somewhat different than in face-to-face grooming. At the present time, there is no research data focusing on the analysis of communications by teacher sexual abusers who use electronic grooming methods.

EFFECTS OF EDUCATOR SEXUAL ABUSE

There is a large body of research on the adverse effects of childhood sexual abuse, yet there has been little focus on the long-term results of sexual abuse by educators. Findings that childhood sexual abuse is a strong predictor of suicidality (Moskowitz, 2001), depression, and low self-esteem (Griffing et al., 2006) would seem to hold for victims of educator abuse as well. Childhood sexual abuse is associated with an overall increase in disorders of mood, anxiety, substance use, and personality (O'Brien & Sher, 2013). As noted previously, new findings related to the effects of electronic grooming are beginning to emerge. Say, Babadağı, Karabekiroğlu, Yüce, and Akbaş (2015) conducted a study examining the rate and psychiatric correlates of sexual abuse in juvenile victims where the offender used on-line methods of grooming and abuse. The results showed that not only did the offender's use of electronic grooming aid the initiation and facilitation of the sexual abuse, but it was also associated with more severe psychiatric consequences for the victim.

Some have observed that educator sexual abuse has dynamics similar to incest, and the abuse results in a loss of trust in adults and authority figures (Finkelhor & Hashimma, 2001). Victims also have difficulty forming future intimate relationships, and suffer from a sense of betrayal and shame. Some abused students report that the abuse was particularly harmful because their trust was betrayed by someone whom they admired, saw as an authority figure, and felt comfortable confiding in.

Not surprisingly, the child victim's self-blame and guilt predicts self-reported symptoms of depression, poor social efficacy, and general abuse-related fears (Ligezinska et al., 1996). The psychological pain and struggles of the child invariably affect the parents (Modrcin & Robinson, 1991). Parents of children who have been victims of educator sexual abuse may suffer from intense guilt and emotional distress which may impair their ability to respond effectively to their children's post-abuse needs. Thus, there is a need to expand the clinical and research focus beyond child victims to the traumatized families (Manion et al., 1998).

In some cases, the victim may not be a student in the abusing teacher's class. The victim may simply be a student at the school where the educator holds a position of trust and responsibility (Shakeshaft, 2003). Within schools, teachers and other members of school staff have power over students, and students are taught from an early age to trust teachers. The abuse of power theory emphasizes that power hierarchies naturally put supervisors in a position to misuse their authority. A study focusing on this theory compared similarities and disparities between sexual harassment of students perpetrated by teachers and by peers (Timmerman, 2003). The study involved 2808 randomly selected adolescents at 22 secondary schools from two regions in the Netherlands. The study found that students felt less comfortable and reported more psychosomatic health problems when harassed by a teacher.

In considering the broader societal effects, there are the potential implicit lessons that may be transmitted to students. Teachers play an important role in transmitting cultural norms and values to students, and are expected to have a pedagogical relationship with their students. Thus, teachers serve as important behavioral models. In particular, they serve as models for acceptable social interactions. There is the theoretical risk that sexual misconduct by teachers will imply to students that this behavior is normative and/or acceptable. Even if not directly abused, there is the possibility that the student witnessing such behavior will have "learned his lesson," and proceed to carry this attitude into the adult work force.

DILEMMAS

Sexual abuse in New York City public schools cost taxpayers an approximate $18.7 million over a 5-year period (Campanile & Montero, 2001). Yet it is speculated that many cases go undetected, as few students tell adults and authorities about the abuse (Shakeshaft & Cohan, 1994). Only about 6%

of students report sexual abuse by a teacher or other staff member to someone who can do something about it (Denove, 2001).

Another dilemma involves questionable or inadequate sanctions. In a study of 225 cases of educator sexual abuse in New York, none of the abusers were reported to authorities, and only 1% lost the license to teach (Shakeshaft & Cohan, 1995). All 225 accused admitted to physical sexual abuse of a student, yet only 35% suffered any negative consequences. Fifteen percent were terminated, 20% received a formal reprimand or suspension, and 25% received no consequence or were spoken to informally. Approximately 39% chose to leave the district. Most of these individuals left with retirement packages or positive recommendations. Of the 54% who were terminated or retired, 16% were teaching in other schools. While the status of the other 84% was unknown, it has been observed that teachers who sexually abuse students may go on to abuse again (Zernel & Twedt, 1999). A nationwide Associated Press investigation found 2570 cases from 2001 to 2005, in which educators were punished, following allegations of sexual misconduct. Over the course of 5 years, the number of cases involving state action steadily increased (Associated Press, 2007).

Disciplinary actions against teachers often take lengthy periods of time, and educators accused of sexual misconduct may use defamation suits as a threat against employers. Teacher background checks typically go through the FBI and cover only felonies. These background checks will miss many sexual abuse charges that are reduced to misdemeanors through plea bargains or other negotiations. Offending teachers are able to retain their teaching certification and abilities as they go through the appeal process. This allows them to move to another state and use their certificates to get new teaching jobs. In states with serious teacher shortages, school districts experience pressure to quickly provide credentials to teachers. When this occurs, important warning signs or employment records may not be adequately scrutinized or communicated. In a case from New York, a man was sentenced to a minimum of 14 years for molesting two brothers, 8 and 10 years old, in their home. The Connecticut School District, which had fired him over sexual abuse accusations, gave him excellent recommendations to the New York School District (Moskowitz, 2001).

When charges of sexual abuse cannot be clearly established, school officials sometimes conclude that there was an "improper relationship" between the educator and student. However, this important information may not be passed on, or may be intentionally withheld. Even in cases where sexual misconduct was clearly established, school districts have been known to rid themselves of the problem by agreeing to keep quiet if the teacher moves on without initiating a civil suit against the school district (Moskowitz, 2001). Districts that have subsequently hired the abusers have begun suing the original districts for civil damages in those cases where the teacher was caught abusing students again. Additionally, when the victim's parents discover that the teacher had a past history of abuse which was or should have been known, there is an increased probability that they will seek legal restitution.

A salient and sometimes overlooked problem is the effect of abuse allegations on the school environment. It is not uncommon for teachers and parents in the school district to be greatly disturbed, not only by the allegations, but also by the devastation caused in the life of a well-liked teacher (McGrath, 1994). This has the unfortunate effect of creating a climate of fear among teachers, who may find themselves reducing contact with students. In a study of 515 New York state teachers, fear of abuse allegations was found to be a significant issue (Anderson & Levine, 1999). The majority of teachers (70%) advised against hugging or putting an arm around a student. In the wake of a teacher sexual abuse scandal, it may take the school district many years to recover from the stigma, and restore a pleasant work environment.

CASE EXAMPLE AND DISCUSSION

The following vignette describes the case of a female teacher sex offender who targeted a 15-year-old girl in her class.

Ms. T was a 35-year-old high school physical education teacher. When not teaching physical education or coaching the girls' basketball team, Ms. T would supervise a 10th grade study hall period. Ms. T's sexual orientation was lesbian, although she was not open about this with her teaching peers.

Ms. S was a 15-year-old student who played on the girls' basketball team, and was also in Ms. T's study hall. Ms. S's parents had been divorced for 2 years, and Ms. S had struggled emotionally since that time. Ms. S suffered from feelings of sadness, worthlessness, and felt neglected by her mother who had been actively dating. Although she had interest in dating boys her age, her low self-esteem caused her to shy away from going to social events where she would be likely to meet them.

One day after basketball practice, Ms. T struck up a conversation with Ms. S during which Ms. T was very complimentary of Ms. S's athletic ability. The conversation lasted several hours, and touched on a variety of other topics such as Ms. S's post high school plans. The conversation eventually led to a discussion of how Ms. S was coping with her parent's divorce. The following week, Ms. T gave Ms. S permission to leave study hall and go to a nearby coffee house so she could bring back coffee and pastries for Ms. T. Over the following months, their after practice conversations became routine, as did the special permission to leave study hall. Ms. T and Ms. S began having regular texting conversations on their cell phones, some of which would last late into the evening.

Ms. T and Ms. S began meeting on the weekends for extra technique and strength training at a local gym. This progressed to regular lunches afterward. Ms. S told her mother that Ms. T believed she could win a basketball scholarship to college, but it would require more intensive, private training. Ms. S's mother was happy and relieved to see her daughter's self-esteem and mood improving, and encouraged her daughter to invite Ms. T over for dinner one evening. After meeting Ms. T, Ms. S's mother began to view her as a welcome friend and tutor to her daughter.

Ms. T next invited Ms. S to a sports training seminar that was out of town and required an overnight stay. Ms. S's mother was not at all concerned when she learned that her daughter and Ms. T would be sharing a hotel room. The following week, Ms. S came home with a brand new "iPhone" that Ms. T had given her as a gift. This puzzled Ms. S's mother who then called Ms. T, mostly with concerns that she should offer to repay Ms. T for giving her daughter such an expensive gift. Ms. T explained that no payment was necessary, as she had obtained the phone at half price through a college female basketball recruiter she knew.

Ms. T and Ms. S continued to spend increasing amounts of time together outside of school hours. Ms. S's mother finally became quite concerned when a friend informed her that her daughter had seen Ms. T and Ms. S embracing each other in an empty classroom. When Ms. S's mother confronted her about this news, Ms. S became highly upset. After a lengthy, volatile argument, Ms. S openly proclaimed that she was "in love" with Ms. T, and wanted to live with her after graduating from high school.

Ms. S's mother complained to the school principal and threatened legal action if they did not take steps to remedy the situation. The school immediately began an investigation, in cooperation with the school district's attorneys. The investigation uncovered evidence suggesting that Ms. T had victimized at least two other female students over the past 5 years. Initially, Ms. T told the principal that she and Ms. S had been involved in a "mutually consenting relationship," and that no one was "harmed." When the principal began speaking in terms of her termination, Ms. T recanted and said that there was never any sexual activity between her and Ms. S. Subsequently, Ms. T hired an attorney and made known her intentions to sue the school district for defamation and wrongful termination should they decide to fire her.

This case presents some common themes observed in cases of educator sexual misconduct. Ms. T selected a student who suffered from low self-esteem and relatively less parental oversight than other students. In the wake of her parents' divorce and her mother's new focus on dating, Ms. S was highly vulnerable to Ms. T's efforts to make her feel special. Ms. T skillfully negotiated extra time with Ms. S, and began to win her trust and affection with gifts and praise. Ms. T also used electronic grooming by having texting conversations with Ms. S which occurred at inappropriate evening hours. Ms. T was able to groom Ms. S's mother by assuring her that she was a trustworthy adult who was interested in her daughter's future. Given her current situation, Ms. S's mother was only too happy to have an additional adult role model for her daughter.

Ms. T successfully isolated Ms. S on an overnight outing, and likely took advantage of Ms. S's natural sexual curiosity and uncertainty. Once Ms. T had established her relationship with Ms. S, Ms. S was vehemently opposed to giving up what she perceived as a "loving" relationship that had made her feel worthwhile. Thus, it is likely that Ms. S would refuse to testify or otherwise report the truth to authorities if it meant an adverse outcome for Ms. T. The long-term consequences of this type of sexual abuse for Ms. S will be difficult to predict, and will likely depend on factors such as her pre-abuse psychological vulnerabilities, as well as her post-abuse emotional support system. There will certainly be the risk that Ms. S might develop symptoms of depression and anxiety. She may also encounter difficulties trusting authority figures, and problems with sexual intimacy in her future relationships.

Besides the legal complexities presented by this situation, there is also the issue of the risk Ms. T may pose to future students. If Ms. T continues to teach, yet is unable to see her relationship with Ms. S as a violation of professional boundaries, her risk of repeating the behavior is likely to persist. Ms. T will continue to have a lack of insight into how she abused the power imbalance and trust inherent in her teacher role. Thus, as long as Ms. T views her behavior as a "consensual" love affair, her risk will remain unmitigated. There is also the possibility that Ms. T does have some insight into the inappropriateness of the relationship, but simply chooses to pursue it anyway. This type of mind-set suggests the presence of at least some psychopathic traits, which would also serve as a risk enhancing factor.

TOWARD PREVENTION

The acts of public school teachers within the course of their employment are considered to fall within in the "color of law" coverage of Title 42 USC §1983 (Valente, 1990). In cases of teacher sexual misconduct, the abuse may be argued as amounting to a deprivation of the student's constitutional right to bodily security. Thus, school districts and supervisors may be found liable for the sexual misconduct of teachers. Most plaintiffs cite Title IX of the Education Amendments of 1972 which prohibits discrimination on the basis of sex in any organization that receives federal funding (Sutton, 2004). In *Doe v. Warren Consolidated Schools* (2003), a school district was held liable under *both* §1983 and Title IX since administrators were found to have been aware of the teacher's long history of sexual misconduct, yet failed to act preventively (E.D. Mich. 2003). Therefore, school districts have a legal duty to safeguard students from educator sexual misconduct.

Cases of educator sexual misconduct are beginning to reach the state Supreme Court level. In *State v. Hirschfelder* (2010), the Washington state Supreme Court ruled that student age does not matter in teacher-sex cases, even if the student is 18 and considered an adult by other state laws. The case involved a choir teacher, Matthew Hirschfelder, who was charged with first-degree sexual misconduct with an 18-year-old choir member. Hirschfelder moved to have a lower-court dismiss the case because the girl was not a minor per Washington statutory law. The Washington Supreme Court held that the statute criminalized sexual misconduct between school employees and full time registered students 16 or older.

Since the issue of educator sexual misconduct has developed into a national child safety issue, some states are beginning to enact statutes directed at the problem. For example, New York State's senate passed legislation that would require immediate decertification, without pay, of teachers upon conviction of a serious crime against a child (S.6296). The bill also includes measures to provide better training to school districts on the issue, as well as improved prevention efforts.

School districts should consider developing and implementing sound prevention measures to prevent educator sexual misconduct. In particular, Title IX regulations require schools to publish policies on sexual discrimination and proper grievance procedures. District and individual school policies should explicitly define and prohibit educator sexual misconduct. Regular training and in-service programs should be established to educate staff, parents, and students about behaviors that are unacceptable, as well as potential signs of educator sexual misconduct. The details of mandatory reporting should be made explicit. School districts should carefully review and standardize employee screening and hiring practices. Box 26.3 provides a list of suggested prevention efforts to be considered by school districts, but should not be taken as exhaustive.

BOX 26.3   RECOMMENDED PREVENTION STRATEGIES

(Shakeshaft, 2004; Sutton, 2004; Fauske, Mullen, & Sutton, 2006; Moulden et al., 2010; Ratliff & Watson, 2014)

- District and School level policies prohibiting educator sexual misconduct
- Standardized hiring practices
- Standardized screening methods and criminal background checks
- Standardized investigative practices in response to allegations
- Development of a centralized reporting agency and registry
- Report all allegations to law enforcement and child protective services
- Regular training on educator sexual misconduct and prevention
- Enact state statutes on educator sexual misconduct and prevention
- Adopt policies on electronic and social media contact between teachers and students
- Enact anonymous reporting systems
- Consider forensic mental health consultation when appropriate

Attempts to prevent educator sexual abuse will most certainly have to deal with the fact that there is no clear central authority for tracking teachers accused of sexual misconduct. Thus, they may leave one jurisdiction, only to resume teaching in another. A national bulletin board run by the National Association of State Directors of Teacher Education and Certification, lists teachers whose licenses have been revoked or suspended, however, reporting is inconsistent (Schemo, 2002). One Internet news site has an extensive list of over 90 female teachers who have been accused or convicted of sexual misconduct with students (www.worldnetdaily.com).

Although the recidivism rates for female sexual offenders are typically quite low (Cortoni, Hanson, & Coache, 2010), there is insufficient research focusing on recidivism among teacher sex offenders, let alone female teacher sex offenders. Future research efforts in this area will help further guide screening, detection, and prevention methods. The fact that educator sexual misconduct is more likely to be revealed by discussion amongst other students (Ratliff & Watson, 2014) suggests the importance of school administrators listening carefully to students. Another potential option might be an anonymous reporting system whereby concerned students or family could notify the appropriate school administrators. Certainly, improved communication between relevant agencies in an effort to identify educators with a past criminal history, or past school board sanctions would seem warranted (Moulden et al., 2010). Very few organizations utilize forensic psychiatrists and/or psychologists, and those that do tend to use them well after the abuse has taken place. Forensic psychiatrists and psychologists with expertise in the area of educator sexual misconduct may be able to assist at multiple stages, from screening to evaluation of risk to testimony in court or administrative hearings.

CONCLUSIONS

Teaching is one of the most noble and time honored of professions. As such, a substantial amount of trust is granted to the profession. For the majority of their children's waking hours, parents hand over primary responsibility for shaping and modeling the latent potential of young minds. The vast majority of teachers work tirelessly to ensure the education of future generations. There are, however, a select few who use the power inherent in the teacher role to target vulnerable children for sexual abuse. School districts face serious dilemmas in cases of teachers who sexually abuse students. They often find themselves caught between the need to take decisive action against the offending teacher, and the teacher's threats of legal action against the school district.

While educator sexual misconduct has received increasing attention over the past decade, this attention has exposed a number of concerning issues, including a lack of formal research in the area, and difficulties in recognizing and prosecuting cases. Public responses to high-profile cases of sexual misconduct involving female teachers suggest that gender-biased views on sex offenders remain prominent in society, and this has been confirmed by social science research. In the future, it will be necessary for school administrators to give thoughtful attention to prevention strategies and legal liability issues concerning educator sexual misconduct.

REFERENCES

Abbott, T. 2015. More teachers are having sex with their students. Here's how schools can stop them. *Washington Post*, January 20, https://www.washingtonpost.com/posteverything/wp/2015/01/20/more-teachers-are-having-sex-with-their-students-heres-how-schools-can-stop-them/.

American Association of University Women. 2001. *Hostile hallways*. Washington, DC: AAUW, Educational Foundation.

Anderson, E., and Levine, M. 1999. Concerns about allegations of child sexual abuse against teachers and the teaching environment. *Child Abuse & Neglect*, 23(8): 833–843.

Associated Press: Sexual misconduct plagues US schools. http://www.msnbc.msn.com/id/21392345/.

Barrett, D., Headly, K., Stovall, B., and Witte, J. 2006. Teachers' perceptions of the frequency and seriousness of violations of ethical standards. *Journal of Psychology*, 140(5): 421–433.

Bennell, C., Alison, L. J., Stein, K. L., Alison, E. K., and Canter, D. V. 2001. Sexual offenses against children as the abusive exploitation of conventional adult–child relationships. *Journal of Social & Personal Relationships*, 18(2): 155–171.

Bennett, N., and O'Donohue W. 2014. The construct of grooming in child sexual abuse: Conceptual and measurement issues. *Journal of Child Sexual Abuse*, 23(8): 957–976.

Black, P. J., Wollis, M., Woodworth, M., and Hancock, J. T. 2015. A linguistic analysis of grooming strategies of online child sex offenders: Implications for our understanding of predatory sexual behavior in an increasingly computer-mediated world. *Child Abuse & Neglect*, 44: 140–149.

Campanile, C., and Montero, D. 2001. You pay for school assaults: Settlements cost city $18.7m over five years. *New York Post*, August 6.

Cortoni, F., Hanson, R. K., and Coache, M. È. 2010. The recidivism rates of female sexual offenders are low: A meta-analysis. *Sex Abuse*, 22(4): 387–401.

Davis, K., Winsler, A., and Middleton, M. 2006. Students' perception of rewards for academic performance by parents and teachers: Relations with achievement and motivation in college. *Journal Genetic Psychology*, 167(2): 211–220.

Denove, M. 2001. A culture of denial: Exploring professional perspectives on female sex offending. *Canadian Journal of Criminology*, 43(3): 313–329.

Doe v. Warren Consolidated Schools, WL 23315570 (E.D. Mich. 2003).

Educator's Guide to Controlling Sexual Harassment. 2006. 14(2): 5. Districts should appoint teacher-led teams to train staff about professional boundaries.

Elliot, M., Browne, K., and Kilcoyne, J. 1995. Child sexual abuse prevention: What offenders tell us. *Child Abuse & Neglect*, 19(5): 579–594.

Fauske, J., Mullen, C., and Sutton, L. 2006. Educator sexual misconduct in schools: Implications for leadership preparation. *University Council for Educational Administration Conference Proceedings for Convention 2006*, November, San Antonio, Texas.

Finkelhor, D., and Hashimma, P. 2001. The victimization of children and youth: A comprehensive overview. In S. White (Ed.), *Handbook of youth and justice*. The Plenum Series in Crime and Justice. Kluwer Academic Publishers: the Netherlands.

Fromuth, M., Holt, A., and Parker, A. 2001. Factors affecting college students' perceptions of sexual relationships between high school students and teachers. *Journal of Child Sexual Abuse*, 10(3): 59–73.

Gannon, T. A., Rose, M., and Ward, T. 2012. A descriptive offense process model for female sexual offenders. In B. Schwartz (Ed.), *The sex offender*, Vol. 7, 16.1–16.21. Civic Research: Kingston, NJ.

Gannon, T. A., Waugh, G., Taylor, K., Blanchette, K., O'Connor, A., Blake, E., et al. 2014. Women who sexually offend display three main offense styles: A reexamination of the descriptive model of female sexual offending. *Sex Abuse*, 26(3): 207–224.

Gillespie, M. 2005. Student–teacher connection: A place of possibility. *Journal of Advanced Nursing*, 52(2): 211–219.

Griffing, S., Lewis, C. S., Chu, M., Sage, R., Jospitre, T., Madry, L., et al. 2006. The process of coping with domestic violence in adult survivors of childhood sexual abuse. *Journal of Child Sexual Abuse*, 15(2): 23–41.

Henry, L., Griffith, K., and Goulas, F. 2006. Perspectives on sexual misconduct by educators: A call to action and a mandate for reform and solutions. *National Form of Teacher Education Journal*, 16(3E): 1–7.

Howell, J. L., Egan, P. M., Giuliano, T. A., and Ackley, B. D. 2011. The reverse double standard in perceptions of student–teacher sexual relationships: The role of gender, initiation, and power. *The Journal of Social Psychology*, 151(2): 180–200.

Khoury-Kassabri, M. 2006. Student victimization by educational staff in Israel. *Child Abuse & Neglect*, 30(6): 691–707.

Lawson, L. 2003. Isolation, gratification, justification: Offenders' explanations of child molesting. *Issues of Mental Health Nursing*, 24(6–7): 695–705.

Leclerc, B., Proulx, J., and McKibben, A. 2005. Modus operandi of sexual offenders working or doing voluntary work with children and adolescents. *Journal of Sexual Aggression*, 11: 187–195.

Ligezinska, M., Firestone, P., Manion, I., McIntyre, J., Ensom, R., and Wells, G. 1996. Children's emotional and behavioral reactions following the disclosure of extra familial sexual abuse: Initial effects. *Child Abuse & Neglect*, 20(2): 111–125.

Manion, I., Firestone, P., Cloutier, P., Ligezinska, M., McIntyre, J., and Ensom, R. 1998. Child extrafamilial sexual abuse: Predicting parent and child functioning. *Child Abuse & Neglect*, 22(12): 1285–1304.

Mathews, R., Matthews, J., and Speltz, K. 1991. Female sexual offenders: A typology. In M. Patton (Ed.), *Family sexual abuse: Frontline research and evaluation*, SAPP: London.

Mcalindon, A. 2006. Setting "em up": Personal, familial and institutional grooming in the sexual abuse of children. *Social & Legal Studies*, 15(3): 339–362.

McGrath, M. 1994. The psychodynamics of school sexual abuse investigation. *School Administrator*, 51(9): 28–30, 32–34.

Modrcin, M., and Robinson, J. 1991. Parents of children with emotional disorders: Issues for consideration and practice. *Community Mental Health Journal*, 27(4): 281–292.

Moskowitz, A. 2001. Assessing suicidality in adults: Integrating childhood trauma as a major risk factor. *Professional Psychology: Research & Practice*, 32(4): 367–372.

Moulden, H. M., Firestone, P., Kingston, D. A., and Wexler, A. F. 2010. A description of sexual offending committed by Canadian teachers. *Journal of Child Sexual Abuse*, 19(4): 403–418.

Nicaise, V., Bois, J., Fairclough, S., Amorose, A., and Cogerino, G. 2007. Girls' and boys' perceptions of physical education teachers' feedback: Effects on performance and psychological responses. *Journal of Sports Science*, 25(8): 915–926.

O'Brien, B. S., and Sher, L. 2013. Child sexual abuse and the pathophysiology of suicide in adolescents and adults. *International Journal of Adolescent Medicine and Health*, 25(3): 201–205.

Ontario College of Teachers. 2002. Professional advisory on professional misconduct related to sexual abuse and sexual misconduct. https://www.oct.ca//media/PDF/Advisory%20Sexual%20Misconduct/2002%20Professional%20Advisory%20on%20Sexual%20Misconduct%20EN%20WEB.pdf.

Ramirez, P. 2007. Female teacher accused of sex with upstate student. *The Post Standard*. December 11, 2007. http://blog.syracuse.com/news/2007/12/female_teacher_accused_of_sex.html.

Ratliff, L., and Watson, J. 2014. A descriptive analysis of public school educators arrested for sex offenses. *Journal of Child Sexual Abuse*, 23(2): 217–228.

Robins, S. 2000. Protecting our students. Ministry of the Attorney General. Ontario, Canada. S.6296. http://www.senate.state.ny.us/pressreleases.nsf/6d7ac8927bea79d085256b76006cc004/1802f3d50df06 1098525730100559f66.

Saletan, W. 2006. Are teachers sleeping with boys getting off? *Slate News*, Retrieved January 16, 2006, http://www.slate.com/id/2134158.

Sandler, J., and Freeman, N. 2007. Typology of female sex offenders: A test of Vandiver and Kercher. *Sexual Abuse: A Journal of Research and Treatment*, 19(2): 73–89.

Say, G., Babadağı, Z., Karabekiroğlu, K., Yüce, M., and Akbaş, S. 2015. Abuse characteristics and psychiatric consequences associated with online sexual abuse. *Cyberpsychology, Behavior, and Social Networking*, 18(6): 333–336.

Schemo, D. 2002. Silently shifting teachers in sex abuse cases. *The New York Times*, June 18. http://www.nytimes.com/2002/06/18/us/silently-shifting-teachers-in-sex-abuse-cases.html?pagewanted=all.

Schultz, M. 2005. State fails to stop teacher sex abuse. *The Detroit News*, April 24.

Shakeshaft, C. 2003. Educator sexual abuse. *Hofstra Horizons*, Spring, 10–13.

Shakeshaft, C. 2004. Educator sexual misconduct: A synthesis of existing literature. (U.S. Department of Education Document No. 2004–09).

Shakeshaft, C., and Cohan, A. 1994. In loco parentis: Sexual abuse of students in schools. What administrators should know. Report to U.S. Department of Education.

Shakeshaft, C., and Cohan, A. 1995. Sexual abuse of students by school personnel. *Phi Delta Kappan*, 76(7): 513–520.

Sheeran, P., Spears, R., Abraham, S. C. S., and Abrams, D. 1996. Religiosity, gender, and the double standard. *The Journal of Psychology*, 130: 23–33.

State v. Hirschfelder, 242p. 3d 876, 170 Wash. 2d 536 2010. The big list: Female teachers with students— young victims mostly male, while penalties often hand slap. http://www.worldnetdaily.com/news/article.asp?ARTICLE ID=53859.

Sullivan, J., and Beech, A. 2002. Professional perpetrators: Sex offenders who use their employment to target and sexually abuse the children with whom they work. *Child Abuse Review*, 11(3): 153–167.

Sutton, L. 2004. Preventing educator sexual misconduct. *School Business Affairs*, 9–10, December, http://www.asbointl.org.

Thomas, S. 1999. Dirty secrets chart: Pennsylvania teacher discipline cases, 1990–1999. *Post Gazette*, Retrieved November 2, 1999, http://www.postgazette.com/regionstate/19991102dschart3.asp.

Timmerman, G. 2003. Sexual harassment of adolescents perpetrated by teachers and peers: An exploration of the dynamics of power, culture, and gender in secondary schools. *Sex Roles*, 48(5/6): 231–244.

Valente, W. 1990. School district and official liability for teacher sexual abuse of students under 42 U.S.C.§1983. 57 ed. *Law Reporter*, 645: 1–12.

Vandiver, D., and Kercher, G. 2004. Offender and victim characteristics of registered female sexual offenders in Texas: A proposed typology of female sexual offenders. *Sexual Abuse: A Journal of Research and Treatment*, 16(2): 121–137.

Wishnietsky, D. H. 1991. Reported and unreported teacher–student sexual harassment. *Journal of Education Research*, 84(3): 164–169.

Zernel, J., and Twedt, S. 1999. Dirty secrets: Why sexually abusive teachers aren't stopped. *Post Gazette*, October 31. http://www.nospank.net/zemel.htm.

27 U.S. Military Sexual Assault

Cynthia T. Ferguson

CONTENTS

Introduction 421
Background 422
Advocacy: Assisting Victims of Sexual Assault 422
Military Forensics 423
Military Criminal Investigative Organizations 423
    Air Force Office of Special Investigations (AFOSI) 423
    Army Criminal Investigation Division (CID) 423
    Naval Criminal Investigative Service (NCIS) 424
Military Crime Lab: USACIL 424
Forensic Toxicology 424
Forensic Odontology in the Military 425
Sexual Assault Investigation Process 425
The Medico-Legal Sexual Assault Exam 425
The Development of a Forensic Nursing Specialty in the Military 425
Child Sexual Abuse 426
Uniform Code of Military Justice 426
The Military Courtroom 427
    The Investigation 428
    Sarah's Sexual Assault Exam 429
    Article 32 429
    The Court-Martial 430
Conclusion 430
Military Sexual Assault and Forensic Resources 431
    Military Criminal Investigative Commands 431
    Military Crime Lab 431
    Military Legal Offices 431
    Military Medical Sexual Assault Offices 431
    Military Sexual Assault Program Offices 431
    Military Toxicology 431
    Military Death Investigation 431
References 431

INTRODUCTION

The crime of sexual assault is not new in the U.S. military. It is, however, a crime that has high public visibility. This is particularly true since the *Denver Post* publicized reports of sexual assaults occurring in the deployed environment of Iraq in 2004 (Ferguson, 2008). The feature story titled, "Betrayal in the Ranks," caused a ripple effect that spread across the nation (Herdy and Moffeit, 2004). Suddenly voting constituents and advocacy groups were bombarding Congress with demands to actively address the issues of rape and sexual assault in the armed forces. This outcry for change resulted in the U.S. President issuing an order to the Secretary of Defense, Donald Rumsfeld, to globally assess the problem of sexual assault, make recommendations for improvement of prevention and response on military bases and installations, and to institute policies and programs that would ultimately change the face of sexual crime in the U.S. military forever.

BACKGROUND

In 1993, the U.S. Military received 94 reports of alleged sexual assault from soldiers in the regions of Iraq, Kuwait, and Afghanistan. The same regions generated approximately 24 reports in 2002 (DoD, 2004). Among advocacy groups and military leaders alike, it was suspected that the drop in numbers was due to soldier's fear of reporting the crimes. These reports covered only a small fraction of the global numbers of sexual assaults in the military ranks. According to the Pentagon, there were 901 alleged sexual assaults throughout the Defense Department in 2002 and 1012 in 2003 (DoD, 2004).

As illustrated above, sexual assault in the U.S. armed forces has been a major topic of discussion in Congress and the public media for well over a decade. In 2004, Secretary of Defense Rumsfeld commissioned a special task force to address this issue and examine how sexual assault victims were cared for and how their cases were investigated and adjudicated (DoD, 2004). Based on the task force recommendations and later that same year, Secretary Rumsfeld created the Joint Task Force for Sexual Assault Prevention and Response (JTF-SAPR) which was designed to serve as the single point of accountability for sexual assault prevention and response policy. The JTF-SAPR developed the first comprehensive sexual assault policy for the DoD, and collaborated closely with the U.S. Military Departments and Services to implement the directives and policies required for this critical program. The author of this chapter served on the JTF-SAPR as a subject matter expert and action officer for the Task Force, and assisted in writing the health care portions of the policy.

Two of the most important concepts that were developed within this sexual assault policy addressed the issue of confidentiality and the duties of the sexual assault response coordinator (SARC) and victim advocate (VA). The issue of confidentiality was addressed by what was termed a "Restricted Report." This is the policy that permits victims of sexual assault to receive medical care without triggering a criminal investigation. This is important because military health care providers were previously required to report knowledge of a sexual assault to their respective criminal investigative units. Today, medical personnel play an important role in protecting the identities of victims who opt for restricted reports, which allow for confidential reporting and a limited collection of forensic evidence and any necessary preventive medical care.

ADVOCACY: ASSISTING VICTIMS OF SEXUAL ASSAULT

When the JTF-SAPR was convened, it took action on several of the recommendations identified by the Care for Victims Task Force (CVTF), to provide safe and standardized care for military victims of sexual assault. One of the first actions was based on three findings and one recommendation:

Finding 12: There are barriers to reporting incidents of sexual assault. Some are consistent with those in the civilian community while others are unique in a military setting (DoD, 2004).

Finding 13: Generally, individuals are not aware of the full range of reporting options available to them (DoD, 2004).

Finding 20: DoD has not mandated requirements to provide advocacy for sexual assault victims (DoD, 2004).

Recommendation 4 (4.4): Providing specially trained and experienced medical, investigative, legal and advocacy personnel in all locations presents an ongoing challenge, given the mobility of the armed forces (DoD, 2004).

After reviewing the CVTF Report, and selecting their findings and the recommendation as one of their first target actions, the JTF-SAPR chose to build and develop a standardized advocacy network throughout the DoD. VAs could assist victims who reported sexual assault, and help them navigate through the sometimes convoluted investigation-and-trial procedures, while keeping them continuously updated on the status of their case.

The position of SARC was developed in order to organize advocate response to victims of sexual assault, to provide leadership and training for VAs at various bases and installations, and to develop a functional network to track and provide information regarding the status of sexual assault cases to JTF-SAPR. The SARC network, and the sexual assault victim advocacy system, was developed quickly across the military with planning and organizational assistance from civilian victim advocacy leaders across the nation. Within a matter of months, the DoD created an advocacy foundation that assisted in addressing more improvements in the U.S. military.

MILITARY FORENSICS

There are a number of individual offices that investigate, process, and analyze forensic information in the military system. They work to ensure fair, unbiased treatment of the suspect until the case goes to trial. Among these offices are Military Criminal Investigative Organizations (MCIOs), U.S. Army Criminal Investigative Command (Forensic Crime Lab), and the Forensic Toxicology Drug Testing Laboratory.

There are also a number of military professionals who contribute expertise to these investigations. These include: Sexual Assault Forensic Examiners (SAFE), medical personnel to include physicians, nurse practitioners, physician assistants, and registered nurses, Forensic Nurses, Forensic Psychiatrists, Forensic Odontologists, and Forensic Pathologists.

MILITARY CRIMINAL INVESTIGATIVE ORGANIZATIONS

Each of the military services has special investigative divisions and within those divisions are experts in a variety of fields. One of those fields is sexual crimes and specially trained agents are stationed at installations and deployed as needed to assist in the investigation of these crimes.

MCIOs include the U.S. Navy's Naval Investigative Service (NIS), The Army's Criminal Investigation Division (CID), and the U.S. Air Force Office of Special Investigations (AFOSI). When a sexual assault is reported, it is these investigators who are called to the scene, take statements from the victim(s) and suspect(s), and witnesses. In joint military environments, they work together to investigate sexual crimes. These professionals investigate a wide variety of sexual offenses (i.e., child pornography, rape, hate crimes involving sexual violence, sexual trafficking, sexual homicide).

AIR FORCE OFFICE OF SPECIAL INVESTIGATIONS (AFOSI)

The AFOSI was created on August 1, 1948 (AFOSI, 2011). This organization provides criminal investigations and counterintelligence services for the Air Force and works with other government investigative agencies worldwide (AFOSI, 2011). There are over 2000 federally credentialed special agents, some of whom specialize in sexual crimes. While conducting sexual assault investigations is only one part of AFOSI's responsibilities, it has become a critical part of their duties in the military's increasingly vigilant approach toward sexual violence.

ARMY CRIMINAL INVESTIGATION DIVISION (CID)

The U.S. Army has been very progressive in addressing issues related to sexual assault investigation. This investigative organization was officially formed in 1918 as a division within the Military Police Corps (USA CID, 2016). CID agents were tasked with investigating crimes committed by

American soldiers and by other nationals against World War I Allies. While successful, their progress was hindered by a lack of central leadership and direction. World War II caused an evolution of the CID and all plans and policies were coordinated between investigators at various commands via the Provost Marshal General's office. It wasn't until 1971 that the U.S. Army CID was officially recognized as an Army Command and centralized under one office. The Commander of CID answers directly to the Army Chief of Staff and the Secretary of the Army. The CID headquarters is located at Quantico, Virginia (CID, 2015).

NAVAL CRIMINAL INVESTIGATIVE SERVICE (NCIS)

In 1882, Secretary of the Navy William H. Hunt created the Office of Naval Intelligence in order to collect useful information on the naval powers around the globe (NCIS, n.d.). The Naval Investigative Service (NIS) became an independent unit in 1992, assigned to work under the direct supervision of the Secretary of the Navy thus ensured independence from the uniformed Navy during their investigations (NCIS, n.d.). Among NCIS investigators, there are individuals who specialize in sexual crimes and who use their training and experience to sort through these complex cases.

MILITARY CRIME LAB: USACIL

During World War II, the first U.S. military forensic lab was activated on October 1, 1943 (U.S. Army, n.d.). Today, the U.S. Army Criminal Investigative Laboratory (USACIL) is located at the Gilliem Enclave in Forest Park, Georgia. In 2013, it became part of the newly designated Defense Forensic Science Center, which also includes the Forensic Exploitation Directorate (FXD), the Office of the Chief Scientist (OCS), and the Office of Quality Initiatives and Training (OQIT) (U.S. Army, n.d.). USACIL is a crime lab that provides a multitude of forensic capabilities. It supports military criminal investigations globally, and includes forensic disciplines such as: Trace Evidence, DNA/Serology, Combined DNA Indexing System (CODIS), Latent Prints, Firearms and Toolmarks, Digital Evidence, Drug Chemistry, and Forensic Documents (U.S. Army, n.d.). In addition, it provides specialized forensic training to investigators and trial/defense lawyers and serves as the Executive Agent for DoD CODIS (U.S. Army, n.d.).

The USACIL not only processes sexual assault forensic exam kits from military cases around the globe, but their leading experts participate in education and policy development to ensure that investigators and military providers who conduct sexual assault examinations, understand how best to collect forensic evidence.

FORENSIC TOXICOLOGY

The Forensic Toxicology Drug Testing Laboratory (FTDTL) is located at Fort Meade, Maryland (AMEDD, 2016). This technologically advanced facility is recognized as a premier full-service toxicology laboratory, and is one of six in the Department of Defense Drug Testing Program (AMEDD, 2016). The Fort Meade laboratory is one of the largest within the Department of Defense and tests over 90,000 forensic specimens per month. It is the only DoD lab that is certified by the Substance Abuse and Mental Health Services Administration (SAMHSA) (AMEDD, 2016). The facility can perform drug screening for amphetamines, cannabinoids, cocaine, opiates, 6-acetlymorphine (heroin), ecstasy (3,4-methylenedioxymethamphetamine, MDMA), oxycodone/oxymorphone and phencyclidine (PCP) (AMEDD, 2016).

Toxicology samples from sexual assault victims and suspects are routinely sent to this lab, under strict chain of custody, for processing in cases that are reported to have involved alcohol or drug facilitated assault. In addition to testing for alcohol and illegal drugs that may have been used in a sexual assault, the lab can also test for over-the-counter medications and prescription medications that may have contributed to the incapacitation of a victim. This information may assist in determining "intent" of the suspect. A suspect who has no blood alcohol, drugs, or medications in his/her system would be under greater suspicion if the alleged victim was completely intoxicated, drugged, or heavily medicated.

FORENSIC ODONTOLOGY IN THE MILITARY

Military forensic odontologists are forensically trained dentists with expertise in identification of decedents via the deceased's dentition (type, number, and arrangement of teeth) and dental x-rays (Brannon, 1983; Chelko, 2004). They are also trained in identifying bite marks made by a perpetrator on a victim's skin. When sexual assault cases occur that include bite marks, every effort is made to ensure that a military forensic odontologist is brought in to examine the mark, photograph it and, if possible, make a casting of the mark. If there is not a military forensic odontologist immediately available, a civilian forensic odontologist may be asked to assist.

SEXUAL ASSAULT INVESTIGATION PROCESS

The investigative process of a sexual assault within the military can be complicated at times, however new policies and instructions in place have made it a much smoother process.

The victim of a sexual assault has the option to keep the report confidential providing he/she has not reported the alleged offense to anyone other than a VA, a Chaplain, or a member of the medical community. As mentioned, this confidential report is called a "Restricted Report," and allows for the individual to make the report and have the history of the assault recorded by the medical professional. They also have the option of providing forensic evidence to be held for 5 years in a repository in event they later decide to make their report "Unrestricted" and have it officially investigated. In addition, the victim has the option of obtaining medical care, which can include prophylactic antibiotics, to protect against potential sexually transmitted infections and (if female) emergency contraception to protect against potential pregnancy.

The VA is the victim's lifeline throughout the entire investigative process and keeps the person informed as to what is happening during the investigation. With the victim's permission, the advocate will accompany the person to a medical facility and be present during interviews, medical care, and forensic examination. The advocate will also accompany the victim throughout the legal process, including the court-martial if the case goes to trial.

THE MEDICO-LEGAL SEXUAL ASSAULT EXAM

The Sexual Assault Forensic Exam (SAFE) is a critical component of forensic evidence collection in a sexual assault case. It is a detailed and complicated examination that requires knowledge of forensic evidence collection from the body and forensic photography. The military services are now required to have SAFE capability at every military hospital. In areas where there is no military hospital available, the military is required to ensure that service members have access to trained forensic examiners in the local area. Over the past 12 years, the DoD has gone from having only a handful of knowledgeable SAFE examiners, to having hundreds.

THE DEVELOPMENT OF A FORENSIC NURSING SPECIALTY IN THE MILITARY

The use of Sexual Assault Nurse Examiners (SANEs) has been shown to be a benefit to civilian communities in the Continental United States (CONUS) (Ledray, 2001). The 2004 Task Force Care for Victims of Sexual Assault report specifically identified a need for the integration and implementation of SANE nurses by recommending that the military "Develop DoD-wide medical standards of care and clinical practice guidelines for treatment and care of victims of sexual assault" and

"Establish a Health Care Integrated Process Team to: Consider how to better incorporate SANEs within the Military Health System in both the Active and Reserve component force structure, and/or through contract support" (DoD, 2004).

In 2003, the sexual assault forensic exam courses taught at the Naval Hospital in Yokosuka, Japan, by then LCDR Lovette Robinson, U.S. Navy Nurse Corps, included the concept of the Sexual Assault Response Team (SART) and the process of sexual assault forensic examination (SAFE). Since that time, CDR (ret.) Robinson has developed similar training programs for U.S. military services worldwide.

In 2005, LT Col Susan L. Hanshaw (USAFR, NC), the Director of Medico-legal Education and Training with the Armed Forces Medical Examiner System, and LT Cynthia Ferguson (author), further developed the work of Robinson's and that of CAPT (ret.) Sue Rist, U.S. Navy Nurse Corps, to create the first comprehensive DoD SART training program. This multidisciplinary program was taught annually for 3 years, and trained over 450 military and civilian personnel on new DoD policy related to sexual assault and how to perform SAFEs.

CHILD SEXUAL ABUSE

As within any community, there are cases of child sexual assault, child pornography, and trafficking of humans in the military. These cases are complex and extremely sensitive in nature. Child pornography cases are proliferative and military sexual crime investigators spend a lot of their time on such matters and must rely on military professionals who have forensic expertise in the field.

The Armed Forces Center for Child Protection (AFCCP), is currently led by a forensic pediatrician (Dr. Barbara Craig, MD, CAPT, ret.). When the AFCCP is involved in a child sexual assault case, they may elect to bring the victim(s) to their facility at the Walter Reed Military Medical Center (WRMMC) for forensic interviews, and/or for physical examination. Interviews are conducted by highly trained personnel in rooms with state-of-the-art video and auditory equipment. It is important to note that child exams are very different from adult exams.

With children, it is not common to find acute injury as might be expected in adult cases and there is usually no speculum examination unless evidence of bleeding and fresh injury of the genitals is presented. Most cases of child sexual assault are perpetrated by pedophiles who take a great deal of time to groom their victims. Before any full physical contact takes place, they may slowly and gradually progress and consequently, the child's genital examinations may exhibit signs of long-term abuse (i.e., vaginal hymen that is worn away or nonexistent). In both boy and girl victims, there may be evidence of anal sphincter scarring and anal canals which no longer close properly (Giardin et al., 2003).

Additionally, it's the mission of AFCCP to educate and train military health care providers to understand and recognize physical signs of child sexual abuse, and to know how to properly proceed in an examination if necessary. The staff at AFCCP also provides consultation to military medical personnel around the globe and serve as expert witnesses, when a case goes to trial (WRNMMC, n.d.).

UNIFORM CODE OF MILITARY JUSTICE

The Uniform Code of Military Justice (UCMJ) is federal law that governs the U.S. military (Powers, 2011). It was enacted by the U.S. Congress, and requires that the President of the United States write the Manual for Courts-Martial which lists the specifics rules and regulations for implementing military law (Powers, 2011). The purpose of military law is "to promote justice, to assist in maintaining good order and discipline in the armed forces, to promote efficiency and effectiveness in the military establishment, and thereby to strengthen the national security of the United States" (Vergun, 2015).

THE MILITARY COURTROOM

Once the military investigation of a reported sexual assault is completed, the case is scheduled for an Article 32, which is much like a civilian Grand Jury hearing. The National Defense Authorization Act (NDAA) of 2014, states that the purpose of an Article 32 is "to determine whether probable cause exists to believe that an offense under the UCMJ has been committed and that the accused committed it" (Vergun, 2015). At the beginning of the Article 32, the accused is presented with the changes against him or her.

It is during this pretrial phase that an Investigating Officer (IO) will hear evidence from Judge Advocate General (JAG) officers who represent the Government (i.e., the prosecution) and JAG officers who represent the accused (i.e., the defense). After hearing all of the evidence the IO decides whether there is enough evidence to forward the case to a General Court-Martial (GCM). A GCM is the most severe of the military court-martials and is reserved for the most serious types of offenses (Vergun, 2015).

If a general court-martial is convened, the accused has the right to choose a civilian attorney to represent him/her, and may choose to have a military panel (jury) of at least five members. He or she can elect to dismiss the panel and opt for a judge to determine the verdict.

The following case is an example of the type that frequently occurs within the military community. Both the victim and offender were enlisted members, Caucasian, and had been drinking alcohol. The names have been changed.

CASE STUDY

Sarah's Statement: Sarah was a 19-year-old female who reported she had been sexually assaulted while attending a military school in May 2011. She was 5'5" and weighed 110 pounds. She accused a 20-year-old male (Bob) of the assault. Sarah had made friends with Bob and another member of their class (Jim). After breaking up with her fiancé a few days prior to the offense, the three of them made plans to get drinks and hang out at a hotel off base. On what she believes was a Friday, they went to a Wal-Mart and purchased two bottles of vodka, some Mountain Dew, and two cases of beer. Bob or Jim rented the hotel room.

They checked into their room, which had two queen sized beds, and decided to go swimming at the hotel pool. Sarah changed into a two-piece swimsuit, while the other two men changed into their swimming trunks. She stated she never felt uneasy around either Bob or Jim. They got into a hot tub, and Sarah reported that at no time did they have any physical contact. When they got out of the hot tub, the two men went swimming in the pool, while Sarah remained on the pool deck because she did not want to get her hair wet. Later, they went up to the room, Sarah showered and dressed in the bathroom. After everyone was dressed, she recalls having a total of 7 drinks, three of which were mixed using Mountain Dew and vodka and four mixed using Kool-Aid and vodka. She also drank three beers. Bob mixed the drinks for her and Sarah said that she never left her drinks unattended. After 3 or 4 h, she realized she was very drunk, and passed out on the bed closest to the window. Sarah remembers waking up once to find Bob kissing her shoulder. She told him to stop, but he tried to tickle her and he played with her belly-ring. She told him to stop again, and passed out.

She stated that she awoke a second time and found Bob asleep on top of her and his erect penis was inside her. The crotch of her panties had been moved to the side. She pushed him off her and could not recall if he was wearing a condom. Although she realized she'd been raped, she stayed in the same bed and eventually went back to sleep. She feared returning to the base without her "liberty buddy." The next morning there was very little conversation. When Sarah returned to her barracks room, she changed her clothing but did not shower. She contacted the duty driver, and had the driver take her to the military hospital for a sexual assault examination.

She stated that a couple of days after the examination, she threw away the underwear she was wearing at the time of the assault. It is not clear why she did this.

After the incident, she and Bob exchanged a few text messages. She advised that she did not share the facts of the incident with anyone else because she was embarrassed and ashamed.

Bob's Statement: Bob, a 20-year-old male, 5′6″ and 170 pounds, stated he met Sarah while attending the same military school in May 2011. At some point during his friendship with Sarah, she became engaged but still hung out with him and his friend Jim when they were away from the base. He stated he wasn't sure of the date, but stated he sent text messages to Sarah a few days prior to the time she had alleged the assault occurred. He recalls stopping at a Wal-Mart, where Jim bought 2 bottles of vodka, and a 12 pack of Budweiser beer (cans), as well as some cranberry juice. Bob said he purchased a case of Mountain Dew and some chips. They decided to stay at a hotel, Sarah recommended, and he paid for the room with his credit card. He stated he did not remember the name of the hotel, or the room number they stayed in.

When they arrived at the hotel, he said they each had a drink. Bob had a Mountain Dew mixed with vodka, and Sarah and Jim both had cranberry juice mixed with vodka. They all decided to go swimming. Bob recalled that Sarah wore a two-piece swimsuit. He stated, "At no time did I make any verbal comments that would be sexually suggestive about her attire. At no time did I make any physical contact with Sarah at this time."

They went to the pool area, and entered a hot tub. There was no physical contact at that time. After about 15 min, they got out of the hot tub, and Jim and Bob got into the pool while Sarah stayed out of the pool. They were in the pool for about 15 min, and then got out, and everyone returned to the room. Sarah took a shower, and Bob and Jim changed into their clothes, after which the men decided to go back to Wal-Mart so Jim could purchase a 12-pack of Blue Moon beer.

When they returned to the hotel, they all continued drinking. Bob stated that he had never seen Sarah drunk, but felt she was faking that she was getting drunk and stated that she never finished any of her drinks. Later, Jim climbed into one bed, and Sarah got into the bed closest to the window. She invited Bob to sleep in the bed. She wore a bra and panties, and he had shorts and underwear on. Bob stated that Sarah and he started "rubbing on each other" and that eventually he digitally penetrated her vagina asking her if it was okay. He reported that she said, "Yes" and after a few minutes started to fall asleep. He stated that at no time did he penetrate her vagina with his mouth or penis, and at no time did he have an erection or ejaculate. He did not think Sarah had an orgasm. There were condoms in his bag, but he never took them out.

In the morning, he woke to find Sarah on the other side of the bed. Jim had left the room. When Sarah woke up, she asked if they'd "done anything," and thinking she meant sexual intercourse, he told her they didn't have sex, but he told her that he'd "fingered" her. She told him her vagina felt sore. Jim returned, stating he was at Wal-Mart, and at 10:00 AM, they all left to go back to the base. As soon as they returned to the base, Sarah immediately left with another Sailor he did not know.

On Sunday, Bob was at the beach with a friend when two sailors approached him, and asked if he was "Bob." They told him they knew Sarah and that they'd heard the two of them had sex over the weekend, and that Sarah had bragged she'd had a good time.

THE INVESTIGATION

This case was investigated by the NCIS after Sarah reported the sexual assault. Official statements were taken from Sarah and Bob. Sarah consented to a forensic examination at a government hospital and a military nurse, trained as a sexual assault nurse examiner, performed the exam. Sarah's cell phone was taken as evidence by the NCIS investigator.

A forensic investigation was conducted in the hotel room where the alleged victim and suspect stayed. A search of Bob's barracks room took place and the shorts and underwear he'd worn that night were collected. His cell phone was taken and investigators took a DNA sample from him in the form of swabs. However, they did not swab his fingers nor was he given a sexual assault suspect exam that would have included retrieving penile swabs for evidence.

SARAH'S SEXUAL ASSAULT EXAM

A VA was present and confirmed that Sarah desired to have a sexual assault exam and medical treatment to protect against sexually transmitted infections and pregnancy. Sarah was given a complete sexual assault forensic exam, conducted by a military nurse who had attended a course on SAFE, but who had never personally completed a full sexual assault exam. During the interview portion of the exam, Sarah stated she had no memory of events after she "passed out." Her answers to questions about the assault were most often answered with, "I don't remember," or "I was passed out." The exception was to the question about whether or not Bob had penetrated her vagina. Sarah answered, "I woke up and his penis was inside me." She also stated that Bob had confessed that he'd put his fingers in her vagina.

The physical examination included collection of her clothing and photographs of her body including her genital region. The examination documented no findings of genital or nongenital injury. The examiner collected swabs from areas where Sarah thought Bob might have kissed her and collected swabs from her vaginal vault. No samples of blood or urine were submitted for toxicology. At the end of the examination, the evidence was handed to NCIS, and Sarah was escorted back to her barracks room by the VA.

ARTICLE 32

At the Article 32 hearing, the accused was presented with the following charges:

Charge I: Violation of Art. 92, UCMJ—Failure to Obey a Lawful Order or Regulation
This charge was levied, in part, due to the evidence that the accused was under the age of 21 and engaged in underage drinking of alcohol, which is prohibited.
Charge II: Violation of Art. 12, UCMJ—Rape, sexual assault, and other sexual misconduct.
Under this charge, there were three specifications: 1. Aggravated Sexual Assault in violation of UCMJ, Article 120(c)(2); 2. Abusive Sexual Contact in violation of UCMJ, Article 120(h); and 3. Wrongful Sexual Contact in violation of UCMJ, Article 120(m)

During the Article 32 hearing, in addition to Sarah's sworn testimony and that of witnesses, the government presented USACIL's test results of the SAFE which demonstrated that semen was found on the swabs taken from Sarah's vagina and that the DNA of that semen matched Bob's DNA sample. This evidence supported Sarah's claim that sexual intercourse had occurred.

Sarah's testimony concerning the number of alcoholic drinks she had and her description of passing out, or blacking out, illustrated her incapacitation and inability to consent to sexual intercourse.

A fellow student of Bobs who talked with him after the sexual assault was reported, stated that Bob told him he'd gotten "fucked up that night" and that when he woke up in the morning "his pants were down and his dick was out."

Jim invoked his 5th Amendment right against self-incrimination and did not testify.

A friend of Sarah, who met with her after the alleged sexual assault, testified that Sarah told him she'd "gotten very drunk at the hotel, and when she woke up someone was having sex with her."

Testimony for the defense included a witness who described Sarah as untrustworthy and had frequently provided false information in the past. He testified that in their training classes, Sarah had been reprimanded for dishonesty. One of Sarah's friends testified that Sarah had told the friend of the incident and this refuted her statement that she had not discussed the sexual assault with anyone.

NCIS attempted to gather text messages from the phones of Sarah and Bob, but they had been deleted. They attempted to retrieve them from the server, but the messages had not been preserved. However, the number of text messages each phone sent out, and to what numbers was available. Sarah had testified she'd only sent a couple of text messages to Bob after reporting the incident, but the records showed that she'd texted back and forth with Bob 33 times.

Based on evidence presented during the Article 32, the IO concluded that Bob was not so incapacitated that night that he was unaware of what occurred. He also decided to add the charge of Article 107, UCMJ, Making a False Official Statement, since it was clear, based on the forensic evidence, that Bob had sexual intercourse with Sarah and that he'd not solely "fingered her."

THE COURT-MARTIAL

The case continued to court-martial and evidence was introduced much like the Article 32, with the exception that the accused admitted to having sexual intercourse with the alleged victim and stated he had not been truthful due to his fear of being charged with sexual assault.

The Defense argued the case was based on "mistake of fact," explaining that Bob believed he was having consensual intercourse with Sarah and that she had likely "blacked out" and did not remember participating in consensual intercourse. They also argued that because Bob was also under the influence of alcohol, he did not correctly remember the events that transpired that night, and may likely have "blacked out" as well.

Since blood and/or urine was not collected during Sarah's forensic exam, there was no documented blood alcohol level or other toxicological evidence, A defense expert witness (toxicologist), was called to testify as to the difference between "passed out" and "blacked out" as a result of drinking alcohol. The expert testified that an individual who "passes out" either falls asleep from too much alcohol or they literally drink themselves unconscious. He stated that when a person's blood alcohol level is elevated to approximately 0.30%, a "black out" could occur. In a black out, the intoxicated individual can participate in events that he or she cannot remember later. This state is called, "alcohol-related amnesia." The individual may remember a few events, or have a "spotty" memory of what occurred, but others may perceive them as barely intoxicated.

The jury found Bob guilty of all the charges and he was sentenced to 12 years in prison and a dishonorable discharge. Upon release from prison, he will be required to register as a sex offender and will be so identified for the rest of his life.

CONCLUSION

Despite the many changes that have occurred in the military to improve sexual crime prevention and response, there remains much to be done. The violence of sexual crime still needs to be seen as a part of the larger public health problem in military communities. Today, it is frequently and improperly considered solely a women's issue, which reduces the scope and effectiveness of addressing the problem within the ranks of the armed forces. Sexual assault affects populations of men, children, the mentally and physically disabled, and the elderly, as well as the female population. Addressing its root causes requires a public health preventative approach as well as a carefully planned community response. Military services should consider basing their sexual assault programs under the larger umbrella of Violence Prevention and Response (VIPR), and placing that umbrella over the purview of their Armed Forces Public Health divisions. By so doing, the prevention of, and response to, interpersonal violence in the military can become more proactive in understanding the pathology and epidemiology of these crimes.

MILITARY SEXUAL ASSAULT AND FORENSIC RESOURCES

MILITARY CRIMINAL INVESTIGATIVE COMMANDS

U.S. Air Force Office of Special Investigations (OSI): http://www.osi.af.mil/
United States Army Criminal Investigation Command (CID): http://www.cid.army.mil/
U.S. Naval Criminal Investigation Service (NCIS): http://www.ncis.navy.mil/

MILITARY CRIME LAB

U.S. Army Criminal Investigation Command: http://www.cid.army.mil/usacil.html

MILITARY LEGAL OFFICES

U.S. Air Force Judge Advocate General's Corps: http://www.afjag.af.mil/
U.S. Army Judge Advocate General's Corps: https://www.jagcnet.army.mil/
U.S. Navy Judge Advocate General's Corps: http://www.jag.navy.mil/legal_services.htm
U.S. Marine Corps Staff Judge Advocate to the Commandant: http://www.hqmc.marines.
mil/sja/UnitHome.aspx

MILITARY MEDICAL SEXUAL ASSAULT OFFICES

Bureau of Navy Medicine (BUMED) Sexual Assault Prevention and Response Office
(SAPRO): http://www.med.navy.mil/bumed/Pages/SAPR.aspx
U.S. Army MEDCOM Sexual Harassment/Assault Response and Prevention Program
(SHARP): http://armymedicine.mil/Pages/SHARP.aspx

MILITARY SEXUAL ASSAULT PROGRAM OFFICES

DoD Sexual Assault Prevention and Response Office (DoD SAPRO): http://www.sapr.mil/

MILITARY TOXICOLOGY

Forensic Toxicology Drug Testing Laboratory: https://iftdtl.amedd.army.mil/ftmd/

MILITARY DEATH INVESTIGATION

Office of the Armed Forces Medical Examiner (OAFME): http://www.health.mil/Military-
Health-Topics/Research-and-Innovation/Armed-Forces-Medical-Examiner-System/
Armed-Forces-Medical-Examiner

REFERENCES

Air Force Office of Special Investigations (AFOSI). 2011. U.S. Air Force fact sheet. Retrieved from http://
www.osi.af.mil/library/factsheets/factsheet.asp?id=4848.
Army Medical Department (AMEDD). 2016. Forensic Toxicology Drug Testing Laboratory. Retrieved from
https://iftdtl.amedd.army.mil/ftmd/.
Brannon, L. 1983. Forensic odontology: An application for the army dentist. *Military Medicine*, 148: 655–659.
Chelko, L. 2004. Department of Defense Forensic Capabilities. Retrieved from http://sites.nationalacademies.
org/cs/groups/pgasite/documents/webpage/pga_049968.pdf.
Department of Defense (DoD). 2004. Task force report on care for victims of sexual assault. April 2004.
Department of Defense (DoD). 2012. Manual for courts martial: 2012 edition.
Ferguson, C. 2008. Caring for sexual assault patients in the military: Past, present and future. *Journal of
Forensic Nursing*, 4(4): 190.

Giardino, A., Datner, E., Asher, J., Giardin, B., Faugno, D., and Spencer, M. 2003. *Sexual assault victimization across the life span: A clinical guide and color atlas.* St. Louis: G.W. Medical Publishing, Inc.

Ledray, L. 2001. *Evidence collection and care of the sexual assault survivor: The SANE-SART response*; Violence Against Women Online Resources (August 2001).

NCIS. n.d. 1882. NCIS origin in the Office of Naval Intelligence. Retrieved from http://www.ncis.navy.mil/AboutNCIS/History/Pages/1882.aspx.

Powers, R. 2011. *Basic training for dummies*, 1st ed. Hoboken, NJ: John Wiley & Sons.

Taylor, R. 1998. Forensic nursing: Standard for a new specialty. *American Journal of Nursing*, 98(2): 73.

U.S. Army. n.d. U.S. Army Criminal Investigation Command. Retrieved from http://www.cid.army.mil/usacil.html.

Vergun, D. 2015. Legislation changes UCMJ for victims of sexual assault.

Walter Reed National Military Medical Center (WRNMMC), n.d., Armed Forces Center for Child Protection. Retrieved from http://www.wrnmmc.capmed.mil/Health%20Services/Medicine/Pediatrics/Armed%20Forces%20Center%20for%20Child%20Protection/SitePages/Home.aspx

28 Campus Sexual Assault

Raina V. Lamade, Ann Wolbert Burgess, Sarah M. Chung,
Shannon W. Spencer, and Robert A. Prentky

CONTENTS

Background 433
Media Reporting 435
Risk Factors Associated with College Student Perpetrators of Sexual Assault 436
The Perfect Storm: Converging Risk Factors 437
The Adjudicatory Process 438
Title IX Reporting of Sexual Violence on Campus 438
Prevention and Intervention 439
Pilot Data from Female Surveys 440
    Pilot Data 440
    Focus Group 441
Treatment 443
References 446

There has been a global explosion of literature, research, and policy reports that examine the prevalence, impact, and experiences of rape and sexual assault over the last four decades. It is in recent years that the focus has shifted to the problem of campus sexual assault, with reports and cases sparking major media coverage. In 2008, the American College Health Association (ACHA) recognized sexual violence as "a serious campus and public health issue" (ACHA, 2008, p. 5). In 2014, the White House Task Force to Protect Students from Sexual Assault was established to provide tools to assist colleges to respond to and address campus sexual assault, strengthen compliance with federal requirements, and raise public awareness.

Since sex crime investigations may be conducted by both campus police and local law enforcement, it is useful for investigators to have an overview of campus sexual misconduct. This chapter provides a brief history of campus sexual assault, summarizes key research, presents recent pilot data of female students' experiences with campus sexual assault, and presents two adjudicated cases.

BACKGROUND

Kirkpatrick and Kanin were one of the first teams to examine sexual aggression on college campuses (Kirkpatrick & Kanin, 1957; Kanin, 1969) and found that a significant proportion of college women (20%–25%) reported sexually coercive experiences involving their male collegiate peers (Kanin, 1957). Koss and colleagues published a series of landmark studies (Koss & Oros, 1982; Koss & Gidycz, 1985; Koss, Gidycz, & Wisniewski, 1987) demonstrating the problem of sexual assault on college campuses. Through the development of the Sexual Experiences Survey (SES), Koss and colleagues (1982, 1985, 1987) systematically studied the range and prevalence of campus sexual experiences and misconduct. The SES has evolved to include the mechanisms (e.g., use of physical force, verbal threats, etc.) that perpetrators use to facilitate acts of sexual aggression.

Although sampling differences (e.g., size, representation), the time frame (e.g., past year, throughout college) and the type of misconduct measured (e.g., attempted vs. completed; unwanted touching vs. sexual intercourse) impact rates, overall, studies find considerably high rates of sexual assault on college campuses (Abbey, 1991; Berkowitz, 1992). Ranges of any type of unwanted sexual contact, that includes unwanted kissing/fondling to sexual intercourse vary across samples from 27% (Gross, Winslett, Roberts, & Gohm, 2006) to 38% (Nasta et al., 2005), are about 19% when exclusively measuring oral, anal, or vaginal intercourse (Gross et al., 2006), and are about 6% when exclusively measuring completed rape defined as sexual activity through the use of or threat of physical force (Nasta et al., 2005). Fisher, Cullen, and Turner (2000) pro-tracted their annual victimization rate over the course of a typical college career (i.e., 5 years), and found that one-fifth to one-quarter of women are the victims of completed or attempted rape while in college. More recently, the National Institute of Justice sponsored Campus Sexual Assault Study found that in a sample of 5446 undergraduate women, almost 20% of undergradu-ate women have experienced attempted or completed sexual assault since entering college (Krebs, Lindquist, Warner, Fisher, & Martin, 2007, 2009). Kilpatrick and McCauley (2009) found that over 300,000 college women in the United States reported being sexually assaulted during the year prior to their 2006 survey (see Kilpatrick, Resnick, Ruggiero, Conoscenti, & McCauley, 2007 for study details). With respect to self-reports of sexual misconduct by male students, stud-ies have found self-reported perpetration rates ranging from 25% (within the past year) to 61% (from age 14 until present time in college) (Wheeler, George, & Dahl, 2002; Abbey & McAuslan, 2004; Parkhill & Abbey, 2008; Abbey, Wegner, Pierce, & Jacques-Tiura, 2012).

Significant gender differences have been found, with women reporting more unwanted sexual contact than men (e.g., 19.6% compared to 8.2%, Banyard et al., 2007). Although women are significantly more likely to experience unwanted sexual contact, there are male victims, and cam-pus sexual assault is not limited to heterosexual contexts. More research is needed to explore the experiences of gay, lesbian, bisexual, and transgender student victims and perpetrators of campus sexual assault. Furthermore, because of possible stigma encountered by gay, lesbian, bisexual, and transgender individuals, LGBTQ students may require additional support and resources, and may present with more complex treatment needs.

In addition to the academic community, private organizations and research groups have also joined the effort to investigate and report on campus sexual misconduct. An example is the Association of American Universities (AAU) Campus Climate Survey that surveyed 27 universi-ties and found that 21.2% of seniors endorsed experiencing nonconsensual sexual contact since first enrolling at their institution (Cantor et al., 2015). One-third of senior females and 39.1% of seniors identifying as transgender, genderqueer, nonconforming, questioning, or not listed (TGQN), reported experiencing nonconsensual sexual contact at least once (Cantor et al., 2015). In one aca-demic year (2014–2015), 11.0% of students reported being a victim of nonconsensual sexual con-tact, and 11.7% of students reported experiencing nonconsensual penetration or sexual touching by force or incapacitation since enrolling at the college/university (Cantor et al., 2015).

The Washington Post and Kaiser Family Foundation (2015) collaboratively developed a survey questionnaire and published the results online. The Post/Kaiser team polled over 1,000 individuals nationwide who had attended college within the past 4 years about sexual assault and campus cul-ture. In addition, interviews were held with over 50 women and men who responded that they had experienced unwanted sexual contact, or attempted or suspected unwanted sexual contact, while they were students (The Washington Post/Kaiser Family Foundation, 2015). The poll defined sexual assault to include five types of unwanted contact: forced touching of a sexual nature, oral sex, vaginal sexual intercourse, anal sex, and sexual penetration with a finger or object.

Based on this definition, 5% of men and 20% of women said they had been sexually assaulted in college. Their assailants either used force, threats of force, or they attacked while their vic-tims were incapacitated (Anderson & Clement, 2015). These percentages do not include attempted sexual assaults and suspected incidents where the victim was incapacitated (The Washington Post/Kaiser Family Foundation, 2015). The Post/Kaiser poll suggests that "sexual assault is often connected to factors woven deeply into campus culture" (Anderson & Clement, 2015, para. 4). Most notably, two-thirds of victims said they had been drinking alcohol just before the incidents.

Other potential risk factors that were identified included casual romantic encounters, known as "hookups," and the presence on campus of fraternities and sororities students (Anderson & Clement, 2015). Some of the poll results, including those highlighted by Anderson and Clement (2015), are as follows (The Washington Post/Kaiser Family Foundation, 2015).

- Students were divided in determining whether situations where both parties did not give clear agreement constituted sexual assault. When both parties have not given clear agreement, 47% of students identified this as sexual assault, 6% said it was not, and 46% said it was unclear.
- Thirty-seven percent of students identified sexual assault as a problem on college campuses, with only 12% identifying it as a "big problem." In contrast, 56% of students viewed alcohol and drug use as a problem.
- Students were generally confident in how their institution deals with sexual-assault complaints. Over two-thirds gave their institutions an A or a B rating on handling sexual-assault complaints, and 8% gave their schools a D or an F.
- When asked about what specific strategies/changes would be effective in preventing sexual assault on college campuses, the following were the top items endorsed by students as being effective:
  - 93% identified changes in attitudes (e.g., "men respecting women more")
  - 91% endorsed training students how to identify and intervene in potentially harmful situations
  - 86% endorsed physical self-defense training
  - 85% endorsed harsher punishments for those found responsible
  - 79% endorsed mandatory sexual assault prevention training for all students
  - 78% endorsed drinking less alcohol
  - 64% endorsed avoiding causal hookups
  - 47% endorsed stronger enforcement of alcohol restrictions on campus.

MEDIA REPORTING

In 2011, Gwen Florio, a reporter, wrote about a number of rapes involving University of Montana football players "that had gone unpunished by school or local authorities," that ultimately "led to a Justice Department investigation into the alleged mishandling of 80 reported rapes in Missoula over a period of three years" (Gray, 2015, para. 1). Although the "investigation resulted in settlements between the federal government, local law enforcement and university officials," Missoula continued to be referred to as America's "rape capital" (Gray, 2015, para. 1).

In 2012, the issue of campus safety was neither a national news story nor was it on the radar of filmmakers Kirby Dick and Amy Ziering who, at that time, were promoting their Emmy-award winning documentary on sexual assault in the U.S. military, *The Invisible War* (Dockterman, 2015, March 5). They, soon however, learned that issues of sexual misconduct afflicting the military were also occurring at institutions of higher education. This prompted them to produce *The Hunting Ground* where, in an interview with *Time*, "they critiqued the fraternity system, university officials who protect athletes accused of attacking women, politicians advocating for arming women on campus and even the White House for what they believed to be an insufficient campaign to keep students safe" (Dockterman, 2015, March 5, para. 3).

In November 2014, *Rolling Stone* published a story about a 2012 gang rape of a University of Virginia freshman, and the subsequent administrative mishandling of the incident. The article implied that schools often responded to student-perpetrated sexual crimes with indifference. As public outrage intensified, questions were raised about the author's failure to contact the alleged rapists and the criticism expanded to questionable journalism ethics (Hartmann, 2015). In the interim, investigators found significant problems at every stage of the reporting, editing, and fact-checking process, "which many critics said the story set back the clock decades on rape activism and advocacy" (Gray, 2015, para. 3). After the publication retracted the controversial story about the gang rape committed by some fraternity members, the University of Virginia chapter of Phi Kappa Psi reported that they were planning to sue *Rolling Stone* magazine (Gray, 2015). It was Jon Krakauer's book, however, that created a storm of controversy, even though it was reviewed as representing a corrective to the *Rolling Stone* story (Gray, 2015).

Media headline coverage also included criminal cases of college men. In January 2015, two former Vanderbilt University football stars were convicted by a Nashville jury of aggravated rape and aggravated sexual battery. The victim reported that she lost consciousness the night of the sexual assaults. The evidence included university surveillance videos of the players carrying an unconscious woman and graphic pictures of the assault retrieved from the players' phones (Dockterman, 2015, January 29). Within 6 months however, the two football players were given a new trial date after a judge declared a mistrial in the case. The judge ruled that one of the jurors was biased, after it was discovered that the juror was a victim in a statutory rape case, and failed to disclose this when asked during the jury selection process (Almasy, 2015). *Time* magazine made rape their cover story in 2015 and reported on books, movies, and court cases that provided the foundation for the focus on campus rape.

RISK FACTORS ASSOCIATED WITH COLLEGE STUDENT PERPETRATORS OF SEXUAL ASSAULT

A crucial component of prevention and intervention programs is to identify and target risk factors associated with sexual misconduct. Studies of risk to perpetrate sexual aggression among college students emerged in the 1980s, beginning with Malamuth's (1981) groundbreaking study on prediction of likelihood to rape. This line of research has shown that the large number of risk factors reported in the literature (e.g., Prentky & Knight, 1991) may be reduced to a more manageable number of key factors that may be meaningfully organized into two main dimensions labeled "Hostile Masculinity" and "Impersonal Sex" (Malamuth, 1986). The Hostile Masculinity Path reflects a personality profile combining two interrelated components: (a) an insecure, defensive, hypersensitive, and hostile-distrustful orientation, particularly towards women and (b) sexual gratification by controlling or dominating women. The Impersonal Sex pathway is characterized by a noncommittal, game-playing orientation towards sexual relationships. It is the *interaction* of two core dimensions that is most highly predictive of sexual aggression (Malamuth, Hald, & Koss, 2012). The galvanizing principle underlying most empirical studies on college student rape, often from different vantages, is the central pillar of cognitive distortions that support and justify sexual assault and minimize or trivialize its consequences for victims, ranging from the constellation of attitudes embodied in the Hostile Masculinity dimension (Abbey & McAuslan, 2004), to the Centers for Disease Control and Prevention's (CDC) recent broad review of 191 empirical studies examining risk and protective factors for sexual aggression (Tharp et al., 2012). Swartout (2013) found that perceived peer rape supportive attitudes and peer structure (i.e., tightly knit groups) significantly influenced individuals' hostile attitudes towards women.

Studies have found a strong association between alcohol consumption and sexual assault as both a correlate of (Abbey, 2002; Krebs et al., 2009) and a significant predictor of sexual assault (Carr and VanDeusen, 2004), with an average of at least 50% of campus sexual assault involving alcohol consumption (Abbey, 2002). When alcohol is involved, typically both the victim and perpetrator have been drinking (Abbey, 2002). In their review of empirical studies, Abbey, Wegner, Woerner, Pegram, and Pierce (2014) found a direct positive association between both proximal and distal measures of alcohol consumption and the perpetration of sexual assault. Furthermore, Locke and Mahalik (2005) found that men who engage in problematic drinking and conform to specific negative masculine roles (e.g., power, male dominance, being a playboy), tended to endorse rape myths and report sexually aggressive behavior. Overall, students who drink more frequently are more likely to experience unwanted sexual contact. Banyard et al. (2007) found an indirect gender effect, such that women tend to consume less alcohol, and those who drink less are less likely to experience unwanted contact.

The circumstances that commonly foster reluctance to report sexual assault are precisely the same circumstances that are most frequently encountered on college campuses—assaultive behavior that occurs in the context of a date or at a party, frequently involving alcohol. The Sexual Harassment & Rape Prevention Program (SHARPP) webpage about consent for the University of New Hampshire, a national leader in sexual-assault prevention states that "Alcohol is the No. 1 'date rape drug,' and is often used as a tool to commit an assault" ("Wildcats Get Consent," 2016, para. 18).

THE PERFECT STORM: CONVERGING RISK FACTORS

In sum, college students are in fact a notably high-risk group for rape (Koss, 1988; Kilpatrick & McCauley, 2009). Converging risk factors forge something of a *perfect storm* for rape on college campuses. The combined influences of individual and situational factors have been empirically supported (Abbey, Zawacki, Buck, Clinton, & McAuslan, 2001). Additionally, advocates have argued for more comprehensive models that consider how all of these variables operate in tandem and can be targeted through prevention programs (Banyard, 2014). Converging risk factors include:

1. The *age of the victims*: an abundance of young women who are open to socializing, "hooking up" and dating.
2. *Victim access*: numerous opportunities for easy access to potential victims; many of these opportunities are designed to promote socializing and hooking up.
3. *The social culture*: emphasizing informal, casual "dating" (e.g. hooking-up, friends "with benefits"). Abbey (1991) noted that, "More than 80% of the rapes that occur on college campuses are committed by someone with whom the victim is acquainted; approximately 50% are committed on dates" (p. 165).
4. The availability of *alcohol* to facilitate disinhibition, along with readily available "rape drugs" that produce anterograde amnesia, such as the benzodiazepine Rohypnol and the central nervous system (CNS) depressant GHB (gamma-hydroxybutrate).
5. *Coercion-supporting peer groups* that espouse and condone rape-supportive attitudes and attitudes characterized by hostile and negative masculinity, including the role of athletic and fraternities organizations (Crosset, Ptacek, McDonald, & Benedict, 1996; Adams-Curtis & Forbes, 2004; Jackson, Veneziano, & Riggen, 2004).
6. The *age of the offenders*: typically young men in the 18–21 year age range, that still possess the same psychosocial, psychosexual, cognitive, and neuro-cognitive immaturity of juveniles, with all of the predictable sequelae of risk taking, impulsivity, poor decision-making, increased proneness to disregarding or breaking the law, and intense, often poorly managed emotions.

Armstrong, Hamilton, and Sweeney (2006) emphasize the specific convergence of low level forms of coercion, the abundance of alcohol, and manipulation of the environment/situation so that women cannot leave (e.g., use of physical force, body weight, etc.) as being components of campus sexual assault. Despite a clear identification of the risk factors associated with campus sexual assault, risk assessment scales specific to young male college students have not been developed. Although adult scales could technically be used given the lower age cut-off of 18, it would make little sense because given the amount of static items (e.g., historic factors), an adult scale would fail to provide adequate differentiation. For example, almost all college students would be rated as "hi" risk on the age risk factor (most are below the age of 25) and "hi" risk on the relationship factor (failure to have co-habited with a partner for two years or longer). The juvenile risk assessment scales were also not developed for college students and fail to adequately capture the risk factors associated with sexual assault in college students. In sum, there are no existing risk assessment scales that include the core risk factors identified by research on college students that can be used with this population. It is clearly an area of need and future focus.

THE ADJUDICATORY PROCESS

It is important to recognize that a primary difference between sexual assault that occurs within the context of a higher education system versus that which occurs outside of such is that victims of campus sexual assault have access to two adjudicatory systems, the academic and criminal justice (DeMatteo, Galloway, Arnold, & Patel, 2015). The adjudicatory procedure may vary across institutions (e.g., prosecutorial model, investigatory model, etc.), with the most commonly used procedure involving a hearing board (87%), using a closed hearing process (92%) (Amar, Strout, Simpson, Cardiello, & Beckford, 2014).

Higher education institutions, along with all schools receiving any federal funding, must comply with the provisions of Title IX, which requires schools to respond "promptly and effectively to sexual violence against students." Accordingly, the Office for Civil Rights of the U.S. Department of Education has issued a document, "Questions and Answers on Title IX and Sexual Violence," to clarify schools' responsibilities (United States Department of Education. Office for Civil Rights, 2014).

Title IX requires schools to conduct their own investigations of sexual violence cases, separate from any criminal investigation by law enforcement, and to take action to address sexual violence. Title IX applies to both on- and off-campus incidents, and to both student-on-student and employee-on-student sexual violence, including the creation of a hostile environment that interferes with a student's ability to participate in the educational process. In 2014, the Department of Education released a list of 55 higher education institutions under investigation of possible Title IX violations (United States Department of Education, 2014).

"Prior to 1988, less than 4% of American colleges publicly reported crime that occurred on their campuses" (McMahon, 2008, p. 361). In response to the brutal campus rape of Jeanne Clery, legislation was introduced requiring mandatory reporting of campus crimes. The Jeanne Clery Disclosure of Campus Security Policy and Campus Crime Statistics Act (1990) requires higher education institutions to disclose information about campus crimes. The 1992 amendment requires institutions to develop prevention policies and provide certain guarantees to victims of campus sexual assault. To provide additional guidance, the Department of Education issued a "dear colleague" letter in 2011 wherein they defined sexual violence and set a preponderance of evidence standard (DeMatteo et al., 2015). For additional information about the reporting, investigatory, and adjudicatory practices of campus sexual violence, please see the 2014 report commissioned by Senator Claire McCaskill, entitled Sexual Violence on College Campuses (United States Senate Subcommittee on Financial & Contracting Oversight, 2014).

TITLE IX REPORTING OF SEXUAL VIOLENCE ON CAMPUS

When college students reveal they have been sexually victimized, the question of how to respond and to whom to report is complicated. In addition to informal disclosures to college personnel (who may or may not have a responsibility to report to someone else), a student can report to:

- Campus police,
- Local law enforcement,
- Campus Student Conduct or Judicial Affairs Office,
- Title IX Officer,
- In some cases, a student can make an anonymous online report, usually through a campus website.

PREVENTION AND INTERVENTION

The Violence against Women Act in 1994 established the Rape Prevention and Education (RPE) program at the Centers for Disease Control and Prevention, a primary prevention program that operates at the local, state, and federal levels. Prevention models have been the main tools used to help combat campus sexual assault. A detailed discussion of the specific programs that exist is beyond the focus of this chapter. Prevention programs target risk factors through psychoeducation, training, increased awareness, and services. Common elements include presentations and trainings for students, faculty, and staff, providing educational materials, including information about available resources, hosting speakers and events to raise awareness, and services such as counseling and guidance of the adjudication process for victims and family members. Awareness raising events and campaigns include "Take Back the Night," "Denim Day," "Sexual Assault Awareness Month," and most recently, 'It's On Us."

Although the emphasis has been on assisting victims, institutions have multiple considerations when implementing strategies that target sexual misconduct with the overall goals of maximizing safety and minimizing risk. These include complying with federal, state, and local statutes, maximizing victim support and resources, providing fair adjudicatory processes, and providing appropriate and fair recommendations/sanctions for students found responsible for sexual misconduct. Unfortunately, these factors do not always align, and can ultimately result in greater challenges to successfully resolving cases through agreement methods. For example, it is challenging for schools to talk about voluntary drinking by women as part of sexual-assault prevention programs because student activists object to programs that incorporate warnings about the risks of drinking heavily (Bazelon, 2015). Student activists argue that this is analogous to questioning a woman's wardrobe choice, and is essentially another form of victim blaming (Bazelon, 2015). Conversely, one can argue the merits of providing accurate facts about campus sexual assault that can empower women with knowledge to help guide decisions. This is particularly relevant because heavy alcohol consumption can place the consumer in a vulnerable state and potentially increase the risk of being the victim of a sexual assault.

In the past, others have advocated for incorporating self-defense training into programs aimed at combating sexual assault (Bazelon, 2015). For example, *The New England Journal of Medicine* published a study of a Canadian program (Senn et al., 2015) that cut the risk of rape by nearly half. This program focused on training female students to assess risk among male acquaintances, overcome obstacles to resisting coercion, practice verbal and physical resistance, and consider their own desires and values. Student activists voiced objections to this program, arguing that the burden should rest almost exclusively on men to stop sexually assaulting women, not on training women on how to keep themselves out of danger (Bazelon, 2015). One can argue that given the risk factors, a multifaceted approach is likely to yield better results than ones that exclusively target perpetrators. The problem with an approach that is exclusively directed toward male students is twofold. First, it may set serious limits on being comprehensive and effective. Secondly, it adopts a one-dimensional perspective that sexual violence exclusively occurs in a male perpetrator—female victim heterosexual scenario, and essentially ignores other scenarios (e.g., male victims, gay and lesbian contexts).

Although there is some evidence to suggest that prevention programs can be effective at targeting victim empathy and decreasing rape myths in male students (Bradley, Yeater, & O'Donohue, 2009), prevention programs have had a limited effect on lowering the incidents of campus sexual violence (Ashworth, Viada, & Franklin, 2015). Programs with multiple exposures, active engagement, peer delivery techniques, and content to increase empathy have been successful in producing behavioral change (Ashworth et al., 2015). Prevention programs are necessary but not sufficient. Bradley et al. (2009) recommended research that examines intervention programs with perpetrators. Banyard (2014) suggested exploring models that include the use of "multipronged prevention approaches," researching synergistic effects and moderating variables to understand and develop programs to target campus sexual assault. Up until recently, there has been little discussion of treatment interventions for perpetrators (Bradley et al., 2009). Developing risk assessment tools to be used with students found responsible of sexual misconduct can help guide decision making and treatment recommendations.

PILOT DATA FROM FEMALE SURVEYS

Because therapeutic sanctions may potentially have positive and negative effects on women's feelings of campus safety and willingness to report sexual assault, a survey of undergraduate women was piloted to provide insights that informed the final version of the survey. The final survey was administered to over 1000 women and data from this survey will be used to inform recommendations about sanctions for those found responsible of sexual misconduct and victim-sensitive policies and procedures.

Victims suffer from silent rape trauma (Burgess & Holmström, 1974) when a sexual assault is not reported or treated. The circumstances that commonly foster reluctance to report sexual assault are precisely the same circumstances that are most frequently encountered on college campuses—assaultive behavior that occurs in the context of a date or at a party, frequently involving alcohol. Whether victims fail to recognize that they have been raped, are in denial about having been raped and "re-frame" the experience as something other than rape, or make a deliberate decision not to report, the bottom line remains the same—a substantial proportion of victims are not coming forward. All three of the aforementioned possibilities must be addressed: education about what constitutes rape, including a responsibility to report to prevent future assaults against others; a clear message about "responsibility" under intoxication; and comfortable, safe, and confidential reporting conditions. A significant additional factor is the institutional response to sexual misconduct.

The sexual aggressors can repeat their behavior when a report is not made. The greatest challenge for colleges in the midst of increasing victim reports of sexual misconduct is to maintain a fair adjudicatory process, secure treatment for the victim, and administer appropriate justice to those found responsible of sexual misconduct. A corollary question is if this should include treatment sanctions for students found responsible of sexual misconduct. One could argue that if the student is to return to campus, then perhaps providing treatment is another way to enhance protecting the college community. When viewed from a larger public health perspective, it is sensible to offer treatment sanctions for those found responsible.

PILOT DATA

Each university has an Institutional Review Board (IRB), which is responsible for reviewing, approving and monitoring research projects in accordance with federal regulations to uphold ethical standards and to protect the rights and welfare of human participants of research studies.

Campus safety: The overwhelming number of students felt their campus was safe. Only 5% responding they did not feel the campus was safe both in day light and at night. A dozen students avoided certain areas of the campus during the day with a larger number saying they would avoid certain areas of the campus after dark. Almost half of the students reported having used campus police/safety resources (e.g., using the emergency phone services and/or using campus escort services). In terms of campus police, 25% were dissatisfied with over half neutral and 20% satisfied with police presence on campus.

When examining the relationship between living situation (i.e., on campus vs. off campus), and reporting, significant differences were noted on (1) would the university take a report seriously and (2) would students react negatively to the student reporting the incident. Students residing off campus were significantly more likely to endorse that the university would take the report seriously than students residing on campus, $p = 0.002$ (78.3% and 44.2%, respectively) while students residing off campus were significantly more likely to endorse that students would react negatively to the student reporting the incident $p = 0.005$ (30.4% and 5.2%, respectively), than students residing on campus.

In terms of incidents of sexual harassment, stalking, or assault, 30% of respondents reported being fondled at least once with 22 of them saying they were too drunk or out of it to stop what was happening, and 16% were forced to have oral sex 1 or more times with 13 of these respondents saying they were too drunk to stop what was happening.

To the question, "Someone had sex with me at a party after I had too much to drink, but I did not report it," 13% of the undergraduate women reported "yes" and 40%–45% of those who said "yes," endorsed feeling that they were partly responsible for their own victimization, they could not clearly remember the details and/or their victimization wasn't important enough to warrant reporting.

Some students said they did "report" it, but only to a roommate or a close friend(s). When asked why they decided not to report an incident of sexual misconduct, they responded with a variety of reasons that fell into the following categories:

- Lack of confidence that discretion would be exercised and confidentiality would be maintained; it would become public,
- Lack of confidence that they would be taken seriously or that something would be done,
- Embarrassed to report,
- Felt it was a private matter and wanted to deal with it alone,
- Did not know who to report it to,
- Did not want the perpetrator to get in trouble/go to jail,
- Did not have time to deal with it due to schoolwork and job,
- Fear of retaliation from the assailant,
- Fear of the legal process and going to court, or
- Concern that they would be punished for underage drinking.

Other reasons for not reporting included the student felt she would be blamed or held partly responsible, did not want to report it because of a prior sexual assault, felt too anxious or depressed to report it, could not remember, the details of the assault are unclear, had a bad experience with police in the past, had a bad experience with campus administration in the past, and did not report it because my family or friend(s) would be upset. One student replied that she "liked him so thought it was OK."

In this mini-survey, there are clear guidelines for the education component for women. For example, if their purse was stolen they'd report to campus police. This raises questions and concerns about why a violation of a material possession is likely to be reported, but not a more serious, harmful violation of one's body.

Focus Group

In addition to the pilot survey data, a focus group was held to test some questions. Some of the noteworthy responses from students are quoted:

In what context does sexual assault occur? (Male perpetrator, female victim at a party, etc.?)
"It happens primarily at events, like parties; places where alcohol is involved or there are a lot of people or things going on because it's very easy to feel anonymous in a sense where they can get away with something or slip through. Yes, it's more like drinking and things going on at night."

What do you feel will increase the likelihood that a female would report unwanted sexual behavior?
Two factors were frequently mentioned: the gray area and presence of a weapon. "If it was really traumatic or violent; if there's a knife involved. Or something that wasn't in the gray area."

Are females more *likely to report* less *severe unwanted sexual behaviors, and* less *likely to report* more *severe unwanted behavior?*

Again the gray area was identified. "It's not that clear cut. I think it's less likely to report [oral sex]. I think it's easier to chalk that up to 'oh I was just really drunk' or 'things just happen'... I think they'd think you were being petty to report."

"There's a big stigma attached to it, I think to reporting things like that. So if anyone's not sure about it and it's not clear cut like saying NO, there's a gray area where someone could say ... It's easier to victim blame in those situations."

"Exactly, yeah."

Let's say a male student was found responsible of sexual misconduct. What do you think would be a fair way of dealing with a male student found responsible of sexual misconduct? (How can this be handled on the campus level? In other words—what would be fair sanctions for this student?)

Students sided more with the legal approach. "All the school is going to do is give him suspension? That's not enough. Take it to court." Another suggestion was for the court to mandate it to the school? For example, "If someone's convicted of rape, the school should follow these steps to implement them on campus." Students suggested that this should be implemented on a national level. The students' rationale was that "sometimes people tell the school administration, and the administration will handle it, but they end up not doing anything. 'And that's why we have protests.' Another student argued, "I think the way administration handles it is confusing because they say we're here for you, but only THE COURT will do something about it."

Students were asked if a student was suspended after being found responsible for sexual misconduct and was allowed to return after a period of time, what would make them feel safer about this student returning to campus? Some students firmly said they did not want the offender to return back to the school where he committed the crime. The question "what should happen if the person returned to school?" was then posed. In such a situation, students suggested going into therapy or perhaps a mandatory sanction.

Students believed there should be some kind of consequence, irrespective of whether or not the offender was to return to campus. One student did not think that it was right to say he can never come back again.

One student gave an interesting analogy to stealing that created a debate: "It's like you steal something at a store, and they say that you can never come back here. But you just stole something— you're setting an environment where may be the person who committed the crime is still attending that school, what kind of psychological trauma is that person going to go through?"

Another student brought up the victim focus. "It's more so for the victim. If you stole something at Macy's and they said you can't come back. In a rape case you stole someone's trust, someone's emotional health."

In contrast, another student said, "I do think when it comes to education there's a lot more that is just than walking through a store again. Because you don't know the person's situation, opportunities, money, whatever it is. And an education is different than going to a store. I get the logic, what I want to say is I agree, but I just believe in second chances. As terrible as it is."

The focus group students agreed that was as long as the person experienced consequences and left for an extended period of time, the person could come back.

How would you feel if you knew a student who had been found responsible for sexual misconduct had to successfully complete a treatment program before returning to campus?

This question raised the issue of the victim. "The thing is maybe some people believe in second chances, and personally maybe I do too, but you are also forcing the victim to do that too. And yes, I believe that education is important, but education can be found elsewhere. Maybe they can have a program—where they don't have to pay more and credits can be transferred. But I feel that the student body is going to be forced to accept—what if the person committed more than one crime? I don't know. I feel that the people have to first be okay with the person who committed the crime to come back. If I were assaulted, and I saw this person on campus, but I didn't have a choice in that matter—can you put a restraining order? As the victim I think you'd be stressed all the time knowing that the person's there."

"Maybe the school/government believes in second chances, but what about the person who actually got assaulted? They'd have to live every single day knowing that that person still walking around and could potentially target them again."

"Yes, education is important, but second chances can be elsewhere. I don't think it would be as traumatic for them to go to another college."

TREATMENT

Although the high incidence of student sexual misconduct on college campuses has frequently been documented, it has not been adequately sanctioned with treatment. Existing scholarship on perpetrator risk and needs assessment and treatment focuses either on adjudicated juvenile or adult sex offenders. College students constitute a unique group that is not addressed by existing research on treatment. Therapeutic sanction of college students merits an approach tailored to the needs and correlates of offending in the college environment.

The following two actual campus sexual-assault cases will be analyzed by risk factors that predict sexual misconduct in college men, e.g., cognitive distortions/hostile masculinity, unhealthy sexuality, poor interpersonal skills, and unhealthy levels of alcohol and other drug use.

CASE 1

A freshman who was raped in front of onlookers at a "wildly out of control" campus fraternity party.

The freshman was an attractive, bright, articulate young woman. In high school she was "the best," the darling of the faculty, first in her class, excelled in three sports and in music as well as academically.

She left home for college and stated that she became aware on her first night at the university of how imbedded and pervasive sexual activity was in the social scene at her college. She said it was not uncommon for a female to be grabbed around the waist by an unknown male who would proceed to kiss her or grind against her. Social "mores" seemed to call for the female to say she didn't want to hook up and for the male to reluctantly release her. This made quite an impression on a young woman from a small high school in the midwest.

The incident: Approximately at 9 p.m. while looking for her friend with whom she had come to the Pledge party, the freshman says she was cornered by a pledge she knew of through mutual friends and had seen earlier in the day but had never officially met or spoken with. Students were packed in a room dancing. She described the pledge as about 6'2" wearing only a sock over his penis who had just completed dancing and who appeared intoxicated. When he started kissing her on the mouth, she told him to stop because she had a boyfriend back home. She says she had a full glass of wine in her hand and started to dance again when he put his hand down her pants and began penetrating her with his fingers. She spilled wine over herself and tried to push him off; she told him to stop and says she kept saying no to him. She was against a wall and he was backed up to a couch. "He turned us around and we fell over on the couch." She was pushed against the arm of couch with him on top of her directly behind where she was dancing, pulled her leggings and panties down, and inserted something into her. She pushed him off and ran out the closest door. Intoxicated and unsure what to do, she sent several text messages to her friend who met her at the student center. She called the University Public Safety and reported the incident. She identified the perpetrator from a Facebook photo.

Analysis: Although based exclusively on the victim's report, it is not possible to develop a reliable treatment plan based on his "risk and needs," we can draw a number of tentative conclusions. "Wearing only a sock over his penis" ought to be the first warning sign to the victim. Even at a party, such an extravagant display brings new meaning to hubris. It suggests a considerable dose of conceit and pompousness. Perhaps, in his case, the word is "cockiness." Narcissism is a characteristic reported in the literature as a feature found among college students held responsible for sexual misconduct. The fact that he appeared intoxicated should be the second clue. Intoxication is highly associated with campus sexual misconduct in the literature, implying the need in his case for treatment for alcohol use/abuse. The final clue was when "he put his hand down her pants and began penetrating her. "He is treating the victim as if she was an inanimate object. He neither recognizes nor cares that this is a human being that might not want be party to his advances. This is already a sexual battery offense. He is taking what he wants and perhaps what he thinks rightfully belongs to him (i.e., sex is his birth rite as a man). Everything that happens after this first assault while dancing is prelude to the remainder of the sexual assault.

The greatest treatment need is a rigorous course of therapy on: healthy sexuality, healthy masculinity, hostile masculinity, cognitive distortions around women, dating, relationships, and sexuality. Hostile masculinity is perhaps the core element in all models of sexual aggression by college students emerging from noxious role models, both caregiver and peer that define what it is to be a man and what "role" women "serve" in men's lives.

CASE 2   STUDY DATE

A sophomore male (SO) asked a junior female (JU), who was in his class, if she wanted to study with him and she agreed. They had a study date in the library. Over several days multiple text messages followed. JU stated that she had bad experiences with men in the past who had gotten the "wrong idea," for example, that she had been "groped at clubs" and had to push men away. SO asked if she was looking for fun or a relationship and she replied "fun" since she had just gotten out of a bad relationship. He acknowledged he sought the same thing and had also just ended a relationship.

Later that week, JU asked SO to come to his dorm to study. The following abstract of the encounter was provided for the hearing.

They hugged each other while she sat on his lap. He showed her his Facebook page, which had pictures of him modeling. He moved his hands over her body while their clothes were still on. She admitted she was calm and comfortable during this interaction. He kissed her on the neck; she said she liked it. She agreed to have her shirt and bra removed. He asked if they could "keep this between us" and not post anything on Facebook. She agreed.

They kissed. She took off the rest of his clothes. He put on a condom. She asked him to "go slow" because it had been a few months since she had sex. She said he did not go slowly and she had "never been in so much pain." The second time, she asked him not to put it in "all the way," but he did. They continued with intercourse for about 3 to 4 minutes and then stopped because she expressed being in pain. They actually tried to have sex for a third time and she pushed him off again.

He asked if the sex felt good and she said "no." She left his dorm and called her roommate to come pick her up. She further described sex with him as "not all the way consensual but not rape."

She later explained to the investigator that it was rape or sexual assault because for about 2 to 3 minutes it was not consensual. Both parties acknowledged that they were not under the influence of alcohol or drugs.

She finally decided to come forward about the incident a month or so later. She also stated that it took a few months to report the incident because she wanted to be comfortable with the consequences and would regret it if she did not.

Analysis of the Sophomore: SO obviously was attracted to JU and most likely had it in mind all along to have sex with her. Alcohol did not seem to be involved (a major risk factor) and other peers did not seem to be involved (another major risk factor). Unlike the first case, this student would have difficulty being criminally charged or being found responsible for sexual misconduct. JU later explains that "about two to three minutes it was not consensual." At each step, he asked permission, and she agreed. We can't tell if she felt pressured to agree, but she doesn't say that she did. She asked him to get off of her, and "he stopped immediately." Based on what she said, she obviously was in considerable pain but that wasn't always communicated to him. At best, he can be blamed for being persistent—which it appears that he was, certainly the third time he tried to have intercourse with her.

The "typical" treatment is called cognitive restructuring—a form of cognitive behavior therapy. SO might benefit from sensitivity training, thinking about the comfort and satisfaction of his partner before his own needs and satisfaction. The secondary issue that hopefully will improve with age and maturity, is rational decision-making and self-control (it arrives with the maturation of the prefrontal cortex—often not until age 25). Lastly, it involves perspective-taking (an element of empathy), thinking of someone other than yourself, thinking of someone's needs other than your own, etc.

Analysis of the Junior: For her part, decision making is relevant in this situation. After having said that she came out of a bad relationship with a guy, it was a risk going to his dorm room alone. If she voluntarily sat on his lap, that was a bigger risk—assuming she didn't want to have sex with him. Assisting her to recognize the importance for her to consider her needs and readiness to engage in physical contact beforehand could help shift her focus to prioritize her health and well-being. Engaging in painful sex three times and later reporting it as rape for 2–3 minutes is controversial.

In conclusion, renewed attention to the alarming rates of sexual assaults on campuses was registered by the government (White House Council on Women and Girls, 2014). Despite the high incidence of student sexual misconduct on college campuses, adequate treatment sanctions for offenders have not been implemented. College students fall within a developmental epoch referred to as *emerging adulthood* (Arnett, 2006). This transitional group has not heretofore been addressed in the scholarly literature on sexual offender risk analysis or treatment. The focus of risk analysis with college students must be on those acute and stable dynamic needs and risk factors that have time and again been demonstrated to predict sexual misconduct in college men, namely cognitive distortions/hostile masculinity, unhealthy sexuality, poor interpersonal skills, and unhealthy levels of alcohol and other drug use.

There are no existing risk assessment scales that include the core risk factors identified by research on college students. Therapeutic sanctioning of college students merits an approach tailored to the needs and correlates of offending in the college environment. Developing, implementing, and evaluating a multifaceted, empirically based approach to risk assessment and treatment of perpetrators will contribute significantly to the intent of these policies to respond to victim's needs, hold those responsible accountable, and prevent re-offending.

REFERENCES

Abbey, A. 1991. Acquaintance rape and alcohol consumption on college campuses: How are they linked? *Journal of American College Health*, 39, 165–169. DOI: 10.1080/07448481.1991.9936229.

Abbey, A. 2002. Alcohol-related sexual assault: A common problem among college students. *Journal of Studies on Alcohol*, 14, 118–128.

Abbey, A., and McAuslan, P. 2004. A longitudinal examination of male college students' perpetration of sexual assault. *Journal of Consulting and Clinical Psychology*, 72, 747–756. DOI: 10.1037/0022-006X.72.5.747.

Abbey, A., Wegner, R., Pierce, J., and Jacques-Tiura, A. J. 2012. Patterns of sexual aggression in a community sample of young men: Risk factors associated with persistence, desistance, and initiation over a one year interval. *Psychology of Violence*, 2, 1–15. DOI: 10.1037/a0026346.

Abbey, A., Wegner, R., Woerner, W., Pegram, S. E., and Pierce, J. 2014. Review of survey and experimental research that examines the relationship between alcohol consumption and men's sexual aggression perpetration. *Trauma, Violence & Abuse*, 15(4), 265–282.

Abbey, A., Zawacki, T., Buck, P. O., Clinton, A. M., and McAuslan, P. 2001. Alcohol and sexual assault. *Alcohol Res Health*, 25(1), 43–51.

Adams-Curtis, L. E., and Forbes, G. B. 2004. College women's experiences of sexual coercion. A review of cultural, perpetrator, victim, and situational variables. *Trauma, Violence & Abuse*, 5(2), 91–122. DOI: 10.1177/1524838003262331.

Almasy, S. 2015. Judge declares mistrial in Vanderbilt rape case in Tennessee. *CNN*. June 24, 2015. Retrieved from: http://www.cnn.com/2015/06/23/us/vanderbilt-rape-case-mistrial/.

Amar, A. F., Strout, T. D., Simpson, S., Cardiello, M., and Beckford, S. 2014. Administrators' perceptions of college campus protocols, response, and student prevention efforts for sexual assault. *Violence & Victims*, 29(4), 579–593. DOI: 10.1891/0886-6708.vv-d-12-00154.

American College Health Association. 2008. Shifting the paradigm: Primary prevention of sexual violence. Retrieved from: http://www.acha.org/documents/resources/ACHA_PSV_toolkit.pdf.

Anderson, N., and Clement, C. June 12, 2015. College sexual assault: 1 in 5 college women say they were violated, June 12, 2015. *Washington Post*. Retrieved from:http://www.washingtonpost.com/sf/local/2015/06/12/1-in-5-women-say-they-were-violated/?tid=a_inl.

Armstrong, E. A., Hamilton, L., and Sweeney, B. 2006. Sexual assault on campus: A multilevel, integrative approach to party rape. *Social Problems*, 53(4), 483–499.

Arnett, J. J. 2006. Emerging adulthood: Understanding the new way of coming of age. In J. J. Arnett and J. L. Tanner (Eds.), *Emerging adults in America: Coming of age in the 21st century*, pp. 3–19. Washington, DC: American Psychological Association.

Ashworth, L., Viada, J. A., and Franklin, C. 2015. Campus sexual assault: Prevention, response and aftercare. *Family & Intimate Partner Violence Quarterly*, 8, 245–252.

Banyard, V. L. 2014. Improving college campus-based prevention of violence against women: A strategic plan for research built on multipronged practices and policies. *Trauma, Violence & Abuse*, 15(4), 339–351.

Banyard, V. L., Ward, S., Cohn, E. S., Plante, E. G., Moorhead, C., and Walsh, W. 2007. Unwanted sexual contact on campus: A comparison of women's and men's experiences. *Violence and Victims*, 22(1), 52–70.

Bazelon, E. 2015. The return of the sex wars. *New York Times Magazine*, September 2015. Retrieved from: http://www.nytimes.com/2015/09/13/magazine/the-return-of-the-sex-wars.html.

Berkowitz, A. 1992. College men as perpetrators of acquaintance rape and sexual assault: A review of recent research. *Journal of American College Health*, 40(4), 175–181. DOI: 10.1080/07448481.1992.9936279.

Bradley, A. R., Yeater, E. A., and O'Donohue, W. 2009. An evaluation of a mixed-gender sexual assault prevention program. *Journal of Primary Prevention*, 30, 697–715.

Burgess, A. W., and Holmström, L. L. 1974. Rape trauma syndrome. *American Journal of Psychiatry*, 131(9), 981–986.

Cantor, D., Lee, H., Fisher, B., Bruce, C., Chibnall, S., Thomas, G., et al. 2015. *Report on the AAU campus climate survey on sexual assault and sexual misconduct*. Rockville, MD: Westat.

Carr, J. L., and Van Deusen, K. M. 2004. Risk factors for male sexual aggression on college campuses. *Journal of Family Violence*, 19(5), 279–289.

Crosset, T. W., Ptacek, J., McDonald, M. A., and Benedict, J. R. 1996. Male student-athletes and violence against women. A survey of campus judicial affairs offices. *Violence Against Women*, 2(2), 163–179. DOI: 10.1177/1077801296002002004.

DeMatteo, D., Galloway, M., Arnold, S., and Patel, U. 2015. Sexual assault on college campuses: A 50-state survey of criminal sexual assault and their relevance to campus sexual assault. *Psychology, Public Policy and Law*, 21(3), 227–238.

Dockterman, E. 2015. The Vanderbilt rape case will change the way victims feel about the courts. *Time*, January 29, 2015. Retrieved 1/3/16 from http://time.com/3686617/the-vanderbilt-rape-case-will-change-the-way-victims-feel-about-the-courts/.

Dockterman, E. 2015. The hunting ground reignites the debate over campus rape. *Time*, March 5, 2015. Retrieved 1/3/16 from http://time.com/3722834/the-hunting-ground-provocative-documentary-reignites-campus-rape-debate/.

Fisher, B. S., Cullen, F. T., and Turner, M. G. 2000. *The sexual victimization of college women*. Washington, DC: National Institute of Justice.

Gray, E. 2015. Jon Krakauer defends new book on college rape. *Time*, April 23, 2015. Retrieved 1/2/16 from http://time.com/3828787/jon-krakauer-defends-new-book-on-college-rape/.

Gross, A. M., Winslett, A., Roberts, M., and Gohm, C. L. 2006. An examination of sexual violence against college women. *Violence Against Women*, 12(3), 288–300.

Hartmann, M. 2015. Everything we know about the UVA rape case [Updated]. *New York Magazine*, July 30. Retrieved from: http://nymag.com/daily/intelligencer/2014/12/everything-we- know-uva- rape-case. html.

Jackson, A., Veneziano, L., and Riggen, K. 2004. Sexual deviance among male college students. Prior deviance as an explanation. *Journal of Interpersonal Violence*, 19(1), 72–89. DOI: 10.1177/0886260503259051.

Jeanne Clery Disclosure of Campus Security Policy and Campus Crime Statistics Act, 20 USC § 1092(f).

Kanin, E. J. 1957. Male aggression in dating-courtship relations. *American Journal of Sociology*, 63(2), 197–204.

Kanin, E. J. 1969. Selected dyadic aspects of male sex aggression. *The Journal of Sex Research*, 5(1), 12–28.

Kilpatrick, D., and McCauley, J. 2009. *Understanding National Rape Statics*. VAWnet.org, September 2009. Retrieved from:http://www.icasa.org/docs/misc/understanding%20national%20rape%20statistics.pdf.

Kilpatrick, D. G., Resnick, H. S., Ruggiero, K. J., Conoscenti, L. M., and McCauley, J. 2007. *Drug-facilitated, incapacitated, and forcible rape: A national study*. Charleston, SC: National Crime Victims Research & Treatment Center.

Kirkpatrick, C., and Kanin, E. 1957. Male sex aggression on a university campus. *American Sociological Review*, 22(1), 52–58.

Koss, M. P. 1988. Hidden rape: Sexual aggression and victimization in a national sample of students in higher education. In A. W. Burgess (Ed.), *Rape and sexual assault*, pp. 3–25. New York: Garland Publishing.

Koss, M. P., and Gidycz, C. J. 1985. The sexual experiences survey: Reliability and validity. *Journal of Consulting and Clinical Psychology*, 53, 422–423.

Koss, M. P., Gidycz, C. J., and Wisniewski, N. 1987. The scope of rape: Incidence and prevalence of sexual aggression and victimization among a national sample of students in higher education. *Journal of Consulting and Clinical Psychology*, 55, 162–170.

Koss, M. P., and Oros, C. J. 1982. The sexual experience survey: An empirical instrument investigating sexual aggression and victimization. *Journal of Consulting and Clinical Psychology*, 50, 455–457.

Krebs, C. P., Lindquist, C. H., Warner, T. D., Fisher, B. S., and Martin, S. L. 2007. *The campus sexual assault (CSA) study. final report*. (Document No.: 221153). NIJ Grant No. 2004-WG-BX-0010, December 2007. National Institute of Justice. https://www.ncjrs.gov/pdffiles1/nij/grants/221153.pdf.

Krebs, C. P., Lindquist, C. H., Warner, T. D., Fisher, B. S., and Martin, S. L. 2009. The differential risk factors of physically forced and alcohol- or other drug-enabled sexual assault among university women. *Violence and Victims*, 24(3), 302–321.

Locke, B. D., and Mahalik, J. R. 2005. Examining masculinity norms, problem drinking, and athletic involvement as predictors of sexual aggression in college men. *Journal of Counseling Psychology*, 52(3), 279–283.

Malamuth, N. M. 1981. Rape proclivity among males. *Journal of Social Issues*, 37, 138–157.

Malamuth, N. M. 1986. Predictors of naturalistic sexual aggression. *Journal of Personality and Social Psychology*, 5, 953–962.

Malamuth, N. M., Hald, G., and Koss, M. 2012. Pornography, individual differences in risk and men's acceptance of violence against women in a representative sample. *Sex Roles*, 66(7–8), 427–439.

McMahon, P. P. 2008. Sexual violence on the college campus: A template for compliance with federal policy. *Journal of American College Health*, 57(3), 361–365.

Nasta, A., Shah, B., Brahmanandam, S., Richman, K., Wittels, K., Allsworth, H., et al. 2005. Sexual victimization: Incidence, knowledge and resource use among a population of college women. *Journal of Pediatric Adolescent Gynecology*, 18, 91–96.

Parkhill, M. R., and Abbey, A. 2008. Does alcohol contribute to the confluence model of sexual assault perpetration? *Journal of Social and Clinical Psychology*, 27, 529–554. DOI: 10.1521/jscp.2008.27.6.529.

Prentky, R. A., and Knight, R. A. 1991. Identifying critical dimensions for discriminating among rapists. *Journal of Consulting and Clinical Psychology*, 59(5), 643–661.

Senn, C. Y., Eliasziw, M., Barata, P. C., Thurston, W. E., Newby-Clark, I. R., Radtke, H. L., et al. 2015. Efficacy of a sexual assault resistance program for university women. *New England Journal of Medicine*, 372, 2326–2335.

Swartout, K. M. 2013. The company they keep: How peer networks influence male sexual aggression. *Psychology of Violence*, 3(2), 157–171.

Tharp, A. T., DeGue, S., Valle, L. A., Brookmeyer, K. A., Massetti, G. M., and Matjasko, J. L. 2012. A systematic qualitative review of risk and protective factors for sexual violence perpetration. *Trauma Violence Abuse*, 14(2), 133–167. DOI: 10.1177/1524838012470031.

The Washington Post/Kaiser Family Foundation. 2015. *Survey of current and recent college students on sexual assault.* (Publication #8718-T). Retrieved from: http://files.kff.org/attachment/topline-methodology-survey-of-current-and-recent-college-students-on-sexual-assault.

Title IX of the Education Amendments of 1972, 20 U.S.C. §§ 1681 *et seq.*

United States Department of Education. 2014. U.S. Department of Education releases list of higher education institutions with open title IX sexual violence investigations. Retrieved from: http://www.ed.gov/news/press-releases/us-department-education-releases-list-higher-education-institutions-open-title-ix-sexual-violence-investigations.

United States Department of Education, Office for Civil Rights. 2011. Dear colleague letter: Sexual violence background, summary, and fast facts, April 4, 2011. Retrieved from: http://www2.ed.gov/about/offices/list/ocr/docs/dcl-factsheet-201104.html.

United States Department of Education. Office for Civil Rights. 2014. Questions and answers on Title IX and sexual violence. Retrieved from: http://www2.ed.gov/about/offices/list/ocr/docs/qa-201404-title-ix.pdf.

United States Senate Subcommittee on Financial & Contracting Oversight. 2014. Sexual violence on campus, July 9, 2014. Retrieved from: http://www.mccaskill.senate.gov/SurveyReportwithAppendix.pdf.

Violence Against Women Reauthorization Act of 2013, 42 U.S. C. A. § 13701, West 2013.

Wheeler, J. G., George, W. H., and Dahl, B. J. 2002. Sexually aggressive college males: Empathy as a moderator in the "confluence model" of sexual aggression. *Personality and Individual Differences*, 33, 759–775.

White House Council on Women and Girls. 2014. Women and girls of color: Addressing challenges and expanding opportunity. Washington, DC: The White House Office of the Secretary.

Wildcats Get Consent. 2016. Sexual Harassment & Rape Prevention Program (SHARPP). The University of New Hampshire. Retrieved from: http://www.unh.edu/sharpp/wildcats-get-consent.

Index

A

Abbey, A., 437
Abbott, T., 412
Abel, G., 69
Acid phosphatase (AP) test, 230
Acker, M., 321
Acute injury in children, 251–252
Adams, J. A., 262
Adam Walsh Child Protection and Child Safety Act of 2006, 333
Adaptation, psychosocial, 6–7
    false allegations and, 169–174
Adkinson, C., 274
Adult Protective Services (APS), 46–47, 394
African-American culture, 12
Age of rapists, 119, 437
Air Force Office of Special Investigations (AFOSI), 423
Akbas, S., 413
Albert Lea Nursing Home, 51–52
Alcohol abuse, 10, 436–437. *See also* Drug-facilitated sexual assault (DFSA)
    homicide and, 193–194
Alexander, M. A., 330
Alibi, false rape allegation as, 169
Alison, L. J., 171
Allegations, false. *See* False allegations
Allen, 343
Alleyne, E. K., 344
Alternate Light Sources (ALS), 207, 216, 226–227, 228, 229–230, 233
Alvarez, F., 273
American Association of University Women (AAUW), 408
American College Health Association (ACHA), 433
American Psychiatric Association (APA), 4
Amey, A., 31
Amstadter, A. B., 9
Anderson, N., 435
Anger excitation rapist typology, 107–108, 135–136
Anger rape, 395
Anger retaliatory rapist typology, 106–107, 135
Anger/revenge and false rape allegations, 168
Antirape movement, 26
Anxiety-based disorders, 5–6
Appearance and grooming of rapists, 120–121
Approach, method of, 83–84, 114, 396
Armed Forces Center for Child Protection (AFCCP), 426
Armstrong, E. A., 437
Army Criminal Investigation Division (CID), 423–424
Arrests of rapists, 14, 20
    history of, 119
Ashfield, S., 344
Asian cultures, 12
Assisted living, 57
Association of American Universities, 434
Astrup, B., 273, 279
Attention, false rape allegations and, 162, 168

Attitudinal change in rapists, 91–92, 116–117
Auenbrugger, Josef Leopold, 5
Autistic disorder, 11
Automated Palm Identification System (APIS), 207
Avoidance behaviors, 6

B

Babaagi, Z., 413
Bachman, R., 32
Backlog of sexual assault kits, 29–30
Bainbridge, D., 394
Baker, T., 47
Ball, A., 394, 395
Ball, H. N., 395
Banasr, A., 272
Banyard, V. L., 439
Barnes, G., 321
Bath salts, 360
Beauregard, E., 380, 381
Beck Depression Inventory II, 6
Becker, J., 69
Bedding evidence, 238
Beech, A. R., 339–340, 344
Behavioral-oriented interviews
    introduction to, 80
    on method of approach, 83–84
    motivation in, 80–81
    profiling the unidentified rapist through, 81–82
    questioning for behavior in, 82–94
Benzodiazepines, 359
Biological evidence
    advancements in analysis of, 226
    CODIS and, 225
    collecting, 227–228
    DNA preservation, 225
    locating, 226–227
    mitochondrial and Y-chromosome DNA, 225–226
    nuclear DNA, 224–225
    packaging, 228
    polymerase chain reaction (PCR) and, 225
Bishai, D., 31
Bite marks, 230–231
Black, P. J., 412
Blais, E., 380
Blitz approach in rape, 83
Blogs, online, 37
Blood evidence, 228–229
Boston City Hospital, 23
Botash, A. S., 262
Bouchard, V., 342
Bradford, J. M., 380
Bradley, A. R., 439
Brawley, Tawana, 161
Brion, F., 272
Brown, C. R. V., 31, 272, 273
Brown, G. L., 330

Brownmiller, Susan, 26
Bull, R., 156–157
Bundy, Ted, 143
Bureau of Alcohol, Tobacco, and Firearms (ATF), 43
Burgess, A. W., 3, 10, 20, 23, 47, 82, 106
    on rapist typologies, 103
    on sexual dysfunction during rape, 87, 88
    on types of sex acts by rapists, 89, 90
Bybee, D., 28

C

California v. Kenneth Bogard, 152
Campbell, R., 28, 30, 275
Campus sexual assault, 9–10
    adjudicatory process, 438
    background and statistics, 433–435
    converging risk factors in, 437–438
    focus groups on, 441–443
    media reporting of, 435–436
    pilot data from female surveys on, 440–443
    prevention and intervention, 437, 439
    risk factors associated with, 436–437
    social networking and, 37
    substance abuse and, 10, 436–437
    treatment after, 443–445
Carlisle, J. M., 338
Carretta, C., 10
Cartwright, P. S., 46, 271
Caspi, A., 321–322
Cathinones, 360
Centers for Disease Control and Prevention (CDC), 262, 282, 436
Chain of custody, 281
Chewing gum, 231
Chideckel, M., 338
Child Advocacy Center (CAC), 242
Child Molesters: A Behavioral Analysis, 142
Child pornography, 141–142, 310
Child Protective Services (CPS), 245, 348
Children, medical evaluation of sexually abused
    acute injury found in, 251–252
    anal folds, *256*
    children as not little adults and, 244–245
    chronic findings, 252
    colposcopy in, 249
    evidence for absence of physical findings in, 258–260
    examination findings, 251–260
    examination positions, 250
    forensic evidence collection and, 261–262
    hymen and, 250–251, 250–253, *253–255, 257, 258, 259*
    medical history in, 245–248
    multidisciplinary investigations in, 242
    patient's history in, 245
    pediatrician's role in, 242–243
    penetration, however slight, found in, 253–256
    physical examination in, 248–261
    scope of problem and, 243–244
    sequelae and, 265–266
    sexually transmitted infections and, 262
    why positive physical findings are uncommon in, 252–253
    written report on, 261

Children, sexual victimization of, 7, 317. *See also*
    Female sexual offenders
    collateral materials related to, 141–142
    contrasting factors in, 308–317
    criminal investigative analysis of, 316–317
    disclosure and interviewing process in, 313–314
    false allegations of, 315–316
    global perspectives on, 11
    introduction to, 305–308
    juvenile sexual offenders and, 320–321
    in the military, 426
    prevention of, 314–315
    relevance of consent in, 309–311
    scope of problem, 243–244
    sequelae in, 265–266
    sexual disorder of offender and, 312
    sexual motive in, 311–312
    terminology used in describing, 308–309
    use of violence in, 311
    victim access and number of incidents in, 313
Children and adolescents
    cyberbullying of, 41–42
    development and risky Internet behaviors, 36–37
    false allegations of sexual abuse made by, 262–265, 315–316
    Internet safety for, 39–41
    Internet use by, 35–36
    interviews of, 245–248, 313–314
    reporting Internet-related crimes against, 42–43
    risk assessment regarding technology and, 39
    romantic relationships and Internet use among, 38–39
    social networking sites and, 37–38
Chivers, M. L., 342
Chloral hydrate, 359
Chronic examination findings in children, 252
Ciancone, A. C., 27, 28
Cigarette butts, 231
Circumstantial evidence, 140
Clay-Warner, J., 86
Clearance rates, 20
Clement, C., 435
Clery, Jeanne, 438
Clothing, 67–68, 71, 88
    forensic examination of, 277
Clothing evidence, 237
CODIS (Combined DNA Index System), 225
Coerced-compliant false confession, 182–183
Coerced-persuaded false confession, 183
Coercion-supporting peer groups, 437
Cognitive distortions in female offenders, 344
Cold case investigations, 199, 207–208. *See also*
    Investigations
    case reactivation concerns and, 203
    case reorganization issues, 203
    crime reconstruction in, 204
    definitions in, 200
    four levels of prioritization in, 201–202
    interviews of nonfamilial persons in, 205–206
    investigative plan for, 204–205
    multi-agency team approach to, 202
    nontraditional investigative techniques used in, 206
    resource limitations and, 200
    reviewing original case files in, 203–204

solvability factors, 200
technology support in, 207
Cole, T. T., 341, 343, 344
Collateral materials. *See also* Evidence
  defined, 142
  educational, 143
  erotica, 142–143
  examples, 141–142
  intelligence, 144–147
  introspective, 143–144
  types of, 142–147
Collection
  forensic evidence, 139–140, 278
  phase, crime scene, 222–223, 227–228, 233–236
Collette, R., 27, 28
Colposcopy, 31–32, 271–272, 279
  used with child victims, 249
Combined DNA Index System (CODIS), 207
Community notification of juvenile sex offenders, 333
Comparison of physical evidence, 216–217
Compassion fatigue, 25
Compliant false confession, 182–183
Conditional ejaculation, 88
Conditional insufficiency, 88
Condoms and condom wrappers, 238
Confessions, false, 177–178
  compliant, 182–183
  consequences of, 183
  individual risk factors for, 181–182
  persuaded, 183
  police interrogations and, 179–180
  pre-interrogation investigations and, 178–179
  prevention of, 184
  problem of contamination and, 182
  risk factors for, 180–182
  types of, 182–183
  voluntary, 182
Con in rape attack, 83
Conn, V., 340
Consenting partners in fantasy, 72
Contamination, 182
  of physical evidence, 217–218
Control, method of, 84–85, 101–102, 114, 396
Cooke, C., 110
Cooper, A., 342
Cosby, Bill, 355–356
Cote, A. M., 161, 167
Courtney, G. M., 32
Craft, M. L., 341
Craig, Barbara, 426
Credibility of victims, 289–293
Crime Classification Manual, 52
Crime scene investigation (CSI). *See also* Evidence;
    Physical evidence
  collection phase, 222–223, 227–228, 233–236
  crime scene integrity and, 219
  CSI triangle and, 213
  documentation, 220–221, 223
  evidence packaging, 223, 228, 236
  exit photography, 224
  final phase, 223–224
  general approach, 218
  initial phase, 218–222
  interviews in, 219–220

measurements, 222
  mid-range and close-up photography, 222
  overall photography, 221
  preliminary scene survey, 220
  rough sketch, 221–222
Criminal experience of rapists, 92, 119, 402
Cross-examination
  defendant, 298–300
  victim, 296
Crowley, S., 31, 272, 273
Cullen, F. T., 9, 434
Culture and sexual assault, 11–14, 437
Cunningham-Rathner, J., 69
Curwen, T., 330–331
Cutler, A., 394, 395
Cyberbullying, 41–42

D

Dahmer, Jeffrey, 364
DeCou, C. R., 341, 343, 344
Defendants, cross-examination of, 298–300
De la Grandmaison, G., 272
Del Bove, G., 394
Delusional rape allegations, 167
Denver Post, 421
Department of Education, U. S., 408–409
Department of Justice, Office for Victims of Crimes,
    U. S., 30
Depression, 6
Descriptive Model of Female Sexual Offending
    (DMFSO), 409
De Young, M., 346
DFSA. *See* Drug-facilitated sexual assault (DFSA)
Diagnostic and Statistical Manual of Mental Disorders
    (DSM-5), 4, 69, 312
Dick, Kirby, 435
Dickson, N., 321–322
Dietz, P. E., 144, 386
Direct evidence, 140
Direct examination of victims in prosecutions,
    291–293
Disabled individuals, rape of, 10–11, 84
Disclosure. *See also* Reporting
  child sexual victimization and, 313–314
  rape, 9, 22
Diversity of rape victims, 9–11
DNA (deoxyribonucleic acid) evidence, 224–225
  advancements in analysis of, 226
  CODIS (Combined DNA Index System) and, 225
  collection of, 223, 278
  contamination of, 217
  known samples, 236–237
  mitochondrial and Y-chromosome, 225–226
  polymerase chain reaction (PCR) and, 225
  preservation, 225
  touch, 232
  in urine and feces, 232
  used in prosecutions, 297
  wearer, 231
Documentation
  crime scene, 220–221, 223
  evidence, 281
  medical examination of child victims, 261

Doe v. Warren Consolidated Schools, 416
Dolls, 70–71
Douglas, J. E., 150, 152
Drink ware, 231
Drug-facilitated sexual assault (DFSA). *See also*
    Substance abuse
  accomplices and conspiracies, 363–364
  distinguished from other sexual crimes, 365–366
  drugs used in, 358–360
  in health care settings, 362–363
  intrafamilial, 364
  introduction to, 355–356
  investigations of, 366–369
  male-on-male, 364
  modus operandi in, 360–361
  perpetrators of, 357–358
  physical evidence in, 238–239
  sexual deviance or sexual hunters and, 364–365
  in social settings, 363
  tracing the history of, 356–357
  typology of, 362–365
  in the workplace, 362
Duke, J. O., 47
Duke University, 162
Dunnuck, C., 271, 272
Durigon, M., 272

E

Ecstasy (drug), 359–360
Educational collateral material, 143
Education of rapists, 120
Educator sexual misconduct, 407–408, 417–418
  case example and discussion, 414–416
  dilemmas in dealing with, 413–414
  effects of, 413
  female perpetrators of, 346, 409
  general sex offender grooming patterns, 411–412
  prevention of, 416–417
  U. S. Department of Education study on, 408–409
Ego-building, 100
Elder sexual abuse, 45–46, 393–394
  Adult Protective Services (APS) and, 46–47, 394
  dynamics of, 396–397
  early recognition and detection of, 53
  intervention for family members of victims
    of, 58–59
  interventions for victims of, 55–56
  interviewing victims of, 53–55
  investigation barriers, 47–52
  literature on, 46–47
  living situations of victims of, 56–58
  in nursing homes, 47, 48, 49, 50–51, 58, 61–62
  policy and investigative implications, 402–404
  prevention of, 59–61
  problem scope, 46
  research on, 46–47, 50–51, 394
  selecting victims for studying, 52
  taxonomic heterogeneity in, 402
  theories of offending, 394–396
  type of crime in, 52–53
  typology and examples, 397–402
Eldridge, H. J., 344
Electronic grooming, 412

Elicitation of narrative in interviews, 126–127
Elimination samples, 238
Elliott, I. A., 344
Elliott, M., 339
Elomaa, K., 273
Employment of rapists, 120
Erectile insufficiency, 87–88
Erotica, 142–143
Everett, R. B., 271
Evidence. *See also* Crime scene investigation (CSI);
    Linkage analysis; Physical evidence
  case study, 144–147
  chain of custody, 281
  from child victims, 261–262
  circumstantial, 140
  collateral materials, 141–147
  direct, 140
  documentation, 281
  eyewitness, 140
  false, 181
  in false rape allegations, 172
  forensic, 139–140, 261–262, 278, 280–281
  items taken after rape, 93, 140
  in the online age, 140–141
  proper handling of, 280–281
  of sadistic crimes, 381
  traditional sexual crimes, 139–140
  types of, 212–213
Exonerations, 177
Experienced rapists, 92
Expert testimony, 293
Eyewitness evidence, 140

F

Facebook, 37, 38, 39, 41, 367
Factitious disorders and malingering, 171, 174
Faller, K. C., 343
False allegations, 159–160
  adaptation continuum and, 169–174
  by children, 262–265, 315–316
  classification of unfounded rape cases and,
    163–167
  components of, 165–167
  definition of, 160
  delusional rape allegations and, 167
  description of assailants in, 172
  emotional problems in need of attention leading to,
    162, 168–169
  evidence in, 172
  factors consistent with, 171–174
  impact on legitimate victims of rape, 161
  imprisonment of innocent persons due to, 160–161
  initial complaint, 171–172
  injuries in, 172–173
  motives for, 168–169
  personality and lifestyle considerations in, 173
  potential consequences of, 160–163
  problems confronting investigators and, 162–163
  second opinion in investigation of, 174
  sex-stress situations and, 163–165
  sexual assault report in, 172
  unusual behaviors to look for in, 173–174
  who makes, 167–168

False confessions, 177–178
  compliant, 182–183
  consequences of, 183
  individual risk factors for, 181–182
  persuaded, 183
  police interrogations and, 179–180
  pre-interrogation investigations and, 178–179
  prevention of, 184
  problem of contamination and, 182
  risk factors for, 180–182
  types of, 182–183
  voluntary, 182
False evidence, 181
Fantasy
  acting out of homicidal, 188–189
  as always perfect, 73–74
  clothing in, 67–68, 71, 88
  consenting partners in, 72
  enactment with wives and/or girlfriends, 74
  human sex drive and, 68
  inanimate objects in, 70–71
  intelligence and, 73
  investigative significance of, 73–76
  and the linking of cases, 74–75
  as paraphilia, 69
  photographs/magazine pictures in, 71
  pornographic videos in, 71
  prosecutive strategy and, 76
  rituals and, 152
  sadistic, 374–375
  search warrants and, 75
  sex as a sensory act and, 68–69
  in sexual crimes, 69–70
  sight and, 69
Feces and urine, 232
Federal Bureau of Investigation (FBI), 42, 98–99, 203,
    204, 207, 243, 403
Federal Rule of Evidence, 288–289
Feldman, M. D., 171
Female sexual offenders
  cognitive distortions in, 344
  deviant sexual arousal and, 342
  domination and control by, 345
  etiologies of, 342–346
  introduction to, 337
  investigatory significance of the paradigm of,
    348–349
  prevalence and patterns of, 340–342
  psychiatric disorders and substance abuse among,
    342–343
  relational offending by, 344–345
  romantic love and, 345–346
  teachers as, 346, 409
  theoretical perspectives on, 337–340
  typologies of, 346–348
Fiber and hair evidence, 232–236
  known samples, 237
Figley, Charles, 25
Figueredo, A., 320
Filipas, H. H., 13
Fingernail scrapings, 237
Finkelhor, D., 339. 341
Fisher, B. S., 9, 31, 434
Fisher, D., 339–340

Fleeing by rapist, 87
Flight or flight response, 5
Florio, Gwen, 435
Focus groups, 441–443
Ford, C. V., 171, 342
Ford, K., 28
Forensic evidence
  chain of custody, 281
  collection of, 139–140, 261–262, 278
  proper handling of, 280–281
Forensic examination, 276–277, 282–283
  clothing, 277
  detection of bodily injury in, 277–278
  drug and alcohol testing in, 281
  of genitalia, 279–280
  history in, 276
  proper handling of evidence and, 280–281
  rectal, 280
  role of examiner in, 275–276
  therapy and prophylaxis in, 282
Forensic services. See also Sexual assault nurse
    examiner (SANE); Sexual assault
    response team (SART)
  consent from victim in, 276
  elder sexual abuse and, 54–55
  forensic odontology in the military, 425
  military, 423
  role of the forensic examiner in, 275–276
  team approach to, 274–275
Forensic Toxicology Drug Testing Laboratory
    (FTDTL), 424–425
Forster, G. E., 32
Fowler, D., 394, 395
Fraser, I. S., 273
Freeman, N., 347
Freud, Sigmund, 5, 338
Friedman, S. H., 343
Fromuth, M., 340
Frost, T. H., 274
Fualaau, Vili, 407–408

G

Gacy, John Wayne, 364
Gamma butyrolactone (GBL), 358
Gamma-hydroxybutryate (GHB), 238–239, 357,
    358, 359
Gang rape, 109–110, 375
Gannon, T. A., 344, 409
Gardinier, L., 161, 167
Garrett, B., 182
Gawn, R. A., 169
Geberth, V. J., 151
General Court-Martial (GCM), 427, 430
Genital injury, 8–9. See also Injuries
  acute, in children, 251–252
  in assaults versus consensual sexual
    intercourse, 272–273
  colposcopy technique and, 271–272, 279
  forensic examination of, 279–280
  location of, 272
  overview of, 270
  photography of, 279–280
  prevalence, 270–273

Genital injury (*cont.*)
  role in criminal justice proceedings, 273–274
  staining techniques and, 271
  type, 273
  visual inspection of, 270–271
Gerson, L. W., 27, 28
Gilbertson, S. A., 330
Gillespie, S. M., 344
Girshick, L. B., 345
Global perspectives on rape, 11
Goodall, E., 279
Goodyear-Smith, F. A., 271
Gratzer, T., 380
Green, A., 342–343
Greer, Germaine, 26
Greeson, M. R., 275
Griffin, Susan, 26
Grooming patterns, educator sexual abuse, 411–412
Grossin, C., 272
Groth, A. N., 82, 87, 88, 106
  on female sexual offending, 341
  on older rape victims, 394, 395
  on rapist typologies, 103
Group counseling for elder sexual abuse victims, 56

H

Hagmaier, William, 143
Hair and fiber evidence, 232–236
  known samples, 237
Hamilton, L., 437
Hancock, J. T., 412
Hanks, H., 345
Hanrahan, N. P., 47
Hanshaw, Susan L., 426
Harris, Thomas, 391
Hatcher, Chris, 386
Hazelwood, R., 74, 80, 83, 142, 144, 344
  on change in rapists attitude during rape, 91
  on false rape allegations, 167
  on juvenile sex offenders, 321, 322, 323, 326
  on types of sex acts by rapists, 89, 90
  on unintentional murder of rape victim, 189
Healey, J., 381
Health care settings, DFSA in, 362–363
Heavey, C., 321
"Heterosexual nurturer," 409
Hibler, N., 160
High risk victims, 114
Hindman, J., 342
Hislop, J., 340, 343, 344, 345
History of psychological trauma, 4–5
Hofer, Johannes, 5
Hollin, C. R., 156–157
Holmstrom, L. L., 3, 20, 23, 82, 106
  on rapist typologies, 103
  on types of sex acts by rapists, 89, 90
Holt, M. G., 46–47
Homicide, 195–196
  acting out fantasy of, 188–189
  drug intoxication and, 193–194
  as impulsive reaction to victim resistance, 190
  monotony and boredom leading to, 194–195
  primary motivational themes, 188–195

  rape escalating to, 187–196
  seeking a psychosexual plateau and, 190–192
  serial sexual, 403
  unintentional, 189
  witness elimination through, 192–193
Hospital-based victim care service, 23–25
Hostile Masculinity Path, 436
Human papillomavirus (HPV), 397
Human sex drive, 68
Human trafficking, 309
Hunter, J. A., 320, 321, 322, 323, 326, 327, 330, 331
Hunting Ground, The, 435
Husted, D., 403
Hymen, 250–253, *253, 253–255, 257, 258, 259*
Hypothalamic-pituitary-adrenocortical (HPAC) biologic
  stress systems, 5

I

Identification of physical evidence, 213–218
Immigration and Customs Enforcement (ICE), U. S., 42
Impersonal Sex pathway, 436
Imprisonment, false, 160–161
Impulsive offenders, 152
Inanimate objects in fantasy, 70–71
Independent living by elders, 56–57
Indirect Personality Assessment, 207
Individual counseling for elder sexual abuse victims,
  55–56
Injuries, 269–270
  acute, in children, 251–252
  detection of bodily, 277–278
  false rape allegations and, 172–173
  forensic examination of, 274–275
  overview of genital, 8–9, 270
  prevalence of genital, 270–273
  role in criminal justice proceedings, 273–274
  types of genital, 273
Instagram, 37
Integrated Automated Fingerprint Identifcation System
  (IAFIS), 207
Integrity, crime scene, 219
Intelligence
  collateral materials, 144–147
  fantasy and, 73
Internet, the
  child development and risky behaviors on, 36–37
  cyberbullying on, 41–42
  evidence in age of, 140–141
  mobile access to, 37
  reporting crimes related to, 42–43
  risk assessment regarding, 39
  romantic relationships and, 38–39
  safety on, 39–41
  social networking sites on, 37–39
  use by children, 35–36
Internet Crimes Against Children Task Force (ICAC), 43,
  141
Interrogations, police, 179–180
Interrogative cruelty, 378
Interviewers, successful, 125–126
Interviews
  behavioral-oriented (*See* Behavioral-oriented
    interviews)

of child victims, 245–248, 313–314
in cold case investigations, 204–206, 206–207
crime scene, 219–220
of elder victims of sexual abuse, 53–55
of juvenile sex offenders, 326–327
of sexual sadists, 382
of suspects, 179–180, 206–207
of victims by prosecutors, 291
of wives and girlfriends of sexual sadists, 386–387
Interviews of rapists, 123–136
anger excitation typology and, 107–108, 135–136
anger retaliatory typology and, 135
developing plan for, 124–125
eliciting a narrative in, 126–127
offender-specific tactics in, 130–131
planting ideas in, 128
power assertive typology and, 131
power reassurance typology and, 131, *132–135*
question formulation for, 126
reading minds in, 127–128
test of commitment in, 130
theme development in, 129–130
tools for, 126–136
traits of successful interviewers and, 125–126
Introspective collateral materials, 143–144
Inventum Novum, 5
Investigations. *See also* Cold case investigations; False
      confessions; Interviews; Interviews of rapists;
      Prosecutions; Reporting
barriers with elder sexual abuse, 47–52
of child sexual victimization, 316–317
clearance rates and, 20
contamination of, 182
criminal analysis, 114–118
drug-facilitated sexual assault, 366–369
elder sexual abuse, 402–404
false confessions and, 184
false rape allegations and, 162–163, 174
items taken after rape and, 92–93
of juvenile sex offenders, 326–327
linkage analysis in, 149–157
military sexual assault, 423–426
physical evidence commonly identified in, 224–236
pre-interrogation, 178–179
profiling of offenders, 81–82, 98–99, 99–113,
      118–121
rapist typologies and, 103–110
search warrants in, 75, 382
selfish versus pseudo-unselfish behavior by rapists
      and, 99–103
of sexual sadists, 381–382, 390–391
significance of fantasy in, 73–76
Invisible War, The, 435
Items taken during and after rape, 92–93, 117, 140

J

Janet, Pierre, 5
Jarvis, J. P., 395
Jimerson, G. K., 271
Johnson, C., 345
Johnson, I. M., 9
Johnson, V. K., 87, 88
Johnson, Z., 340

Joint Task Force for Sexual Assault Prevention and
      Response (JTF-SAPR), 422–423
Jones, J. S., 88, 271, 272
Judge Advocate General (JAG) officers, 427
Jury instructions, 300
Juvenile sexual offenders
developmental issues and, 320–321
disposition decision making and management of,
      328–329
effective community programming to prevent,
      329–330
interviews of, 326–327
introduction to, 319–320
investigative issues with, 326–327
mental health examinations of, 327–328
modus operandi, 322–323
registration and community notification of, 333
treatment of, 330–333
typology research, 321–323
violent, 323–325

K

Kaiser Family Foundation, 434
Kaplan, M., 342–343
Kaplan, S. P., 341, 343, 344
Karabekiroglu, K., 413
Karhumen, P. J., 273–274
Karjane, H. M., 31
Kassin, S., 182
Katz, S., 160
Kauffmann, E. A., 169
Kaufman, K., 345
Keenan, T., 339, 344
Keller, A., 330
Kellogg, N., 262
Kemper, Edward, 143
Kercher, G., 347, 409
Ketamine, 238–239, 359
Kilpatrick, D. G., 9
Kim, K. D., 343
Kim, M., 47
Klein, A., 31
Knight, R. A., 321
Known samples, 236–237
Koss, M. R., 12–13, 342
Krafft-Ebing, R., 337, 338
Krakauer, Jon, 436

L

Lacarra, M., 273
Lahteenmaki, P., 273
Lalumière, M. L., 342
Lambert, S., 342
Lanning, K. V., 141, 142
Lanyon, R. I., 395
Larson, N., 342, 345
Lathrop, A., 7
Latino cultures, 12–13
Lauber, A. A., 271
Lauritsen, J., 273, 279
Le, G., 274
Leclerc, B., 411

Ledray, L., 31
Lee, W., 10
Lefer, H., 162
Lenehanm, G., 31
Lengthy interrogation and false confessions, 180–181
Leo, R. A., 182
Letourneau, Mary Kay, 407–408
Lewis-O'Connor, Annie, 25
Lexier, L. J., 327
LGBTQ persons, rape of, 434
Lichty, L. F., 30
Lighting techniques for physical evidence, 207,
          215–216, 226–227, 228, 229–230, 233
Linkage analysis. *See also* Evidence
     case example, 152–154
     computerized systems, 156–157
     introduction to, 149–150
     modus operandi in, 149–152, 155–156
     motive in, 154–155
     signature in, 152, 156
     steps in, 154
Linz, D., 321
Lira, L. R., 12–13
Lisak, D., 161, 167
Little, K., 31
Locard, Edward, 216
Locard's Theory of Exchange, 214–215, 219
Low risk victims, 114
Luminol, 229
Lussier, P., 381
Lynch, S. M., 341, 343, 344

M

MacCullough, M., 70
Macdonald, J., 46
Maguire, W., 279
Maison, S., 342, 345
Malamuth, N. M., 321, 436
Male on male rape, 10, 364, 434
Malingering, 171, 174
Maniglio, R., 71
Marchetti, C. A., 21
Marion, S. A., 274
Marital status of rapists, 119–120
Marshall, B. C., 171
Masochism, 338
Masters, W. H., 87, 88
Mathews, R., 346
Matthews, J., 346
Mazur, M., 160
McCabe, M. P., 102
McCartney, J. R., 51
McCauley, J. L., 9
McDowell, C., 160
McGarvey, E. L., 330
McGovern, S. K., 331
McGregor, M. J., 274
McGuire, Christine, 386
McGuire, R. J., 338
McKibben, A., 411
McLeod, D. A., 340, 341, 343, 348
MDMA (drug), 359–360
Measurements, crime scene, 222

Media reporting of campus rapes, 435–436
Medical testimony, 296–297
Medical therapy for victims, 282
Meloy, Reid, 189
Mental health examination of juvenile sex offenders,
          327–328
Mental states and false rape allegations, 169–171
Method of approach, 83–84, 114, 396
Method of control, 84–85, 101–102, 114, 396
Method of operation in paraphilias, 312
Methylone, 360
Mikrosil, 231
Military history of rapists, 120
Military sexual assault
     advocacy for victims of, 422–423
     Article 32 hearings, 429–430
     background, 422
     child sexual abuse, 426
     crime labs, 424
     criminal investigative organizations for, 423–424
     development of forensic nursing specialty in the
               military and, 425–426
     forensic odontology, 425
     and forensic resources, 431
     Forensic Toxicology Drug Testing Laboratory
               (FTDTL) and, 424–425
     General Court-Martial (GCM) and, 427, 430
     introduction to, 421–422
     investigation process, 425
     Joint Task Force for Sexual Assault Prevention and
               Response (JTF-SAPR), 422–423
     medico-legal sexual assault team, 425
     military courtrooms and, 427–430
     military forensics and, 423
     SANE/SART programs and, 425–426
     Sexual Assault Forensic Exam (SAFE), 425, 429
     Uniform Code of Military Justice (UCMJ) and, 426,
               429–430
Military sexual trauma (MST), 10
Miller, K., 394, 395
Mills, H., 70
Mind reading in interviews, 127–128
Minimization and false confession, 181
Mini-STR (Standard Tandem Repeat), 226
Minnesota Multiphasic Inventory, 143
Mishell, D. R., Jr., 273
Mitochondrial DNA, 225–226
Mittleman, M., 69
Moderate risk victims, 114
Modus operandi (MO)
     defined, 149–150
     in drug-facilitated sexual assault, 360–361
     juvenile sexual offenders, 322–323
     in linkage analysis, 154
     observations regarding ritual and, 151–152
     ritualistic behaviors in, 151, 155–156
Moffitt, E. E., 321–322
Molestation, child. *See* Children, sexual
          victimization of
Monotony and boredom leading to homicide,
          194–195
Monroe, Marilyn, 359
Moore, R. A., 46
Moore, T., 279

Morton, M., 330
Multi-agency team approach to cold case
        investigations, 202
Multiple assaults, 397
Munchausen syndrome, 169
Munn, C., 150, 152
Muram, D., 394, 395
Murder. *See* Homicide
Music therapy, 56
Muslim communities, 11
Myers, W., 403
Myspace, 37
Myth of Psychological Interrogation, 178

N

Napier, M. R., 167
Natale, A. P., 340
Nathan, P., 342
National Association of State Directors of Teacher
        Education and Certification, 417
National Center for Missing and Exploited Children
        (NCMEC), 39
National Center for the Analysis of Violent Crime
        (NCAVC), 99, 379
National Center for the Prevention and Control of
        Rape, 22
National Child Abuse Neglect Data System (NCANDS),
        341, 348
National Crime Victimization Study (NCVS), 47
National Defense Authorization Act (NDAA) of
        2014, 427
National DNA Index System (NDIS), 207
National Institutes of Justice, 434
National Intimate Partner and Sexual Violence Survey
        (NISVS), 19
National Registry of Exonerations, 177
National Sexual Violence Resource Center (NSVRC), 25
National Violence Against Women Survey
        (NVAWS), 9, 20
National Women's Study (NWS), 47
National Women's Study-Replication (NWS-R), 275
Naval Criminal Investigative Service (NCIS), 424
Nelson-Horan, C., 271
New England Journal of Medicine, The, 439
Nicksa, S. C., 161, 167
No Child Left Behind Act of 2001, 408
Noncoerced-persuaded false confession, 183
Nonprofane speech, 101, 116
Nonsadistic rapists, 400–401
Nontraditional investigative techniques in cold case
        investigations, 206
Nostalgia, 5
Novice rapists, 92
Nursing homes, 47, 48, 49, 50–51, 58, 61–62
Nussbaum, K. E., 395

O

Oblique lighting, 215
Observation and perception of physical evidence, 214
Occupational Safety and Health Administration
        (OSHA), 218
O'Donohue, W., 439

Offender-focused prosecutions, 287–289
Ofshe, R., 182
O'Halloran, E., 342
O'Neal, E. N., 162
Opening statements, 295–296
Opportunistic rapist typology, 109
        in elder sexual abuse, 397–398
Oral rinse, 237
Ostovar, H., 88
Otis, K. E., 331
O'Toole, M. E., 403

P

Packaging, evidence, 223, 228, 236
Page, A. D., 161
Paraphilias, 69, 190–192, 312
Parrett, N., 339–340
Passive resistance of victims, 86
Patel, H. C., 32
Pathological group behavior, 109–110, 375
Patriarchal societies, 12
Patterson, D., 28, 30, 275
Peck, R., 31
Pediatricians, 242–243
Pedophile paraphernalia, 141, 144
Pedophiles, 312
Penttila, A., 273–274
Perception and observation of physical
        evidence, 214
Perception of health, 8
Perfect Victim, 386
Perry, B. D., 340
Personal items taken after rape, 93
Personality disorders, 343
Personal protective equipment (PPE), 217
Persuaded false confession, 183
Pervasive anger typology, 398–399
Peterson, G. F., 274
Pew Research Center, 35
Phallometry (PPG), 404
Pharmacologists, 297–298
Phenolphthalein, 228–229
Photography
        of bodily injuries, 277–278
        crime scene, 221, 222, 224
        in fantasy, 71
        of genital injuries, 279–280
Physical evidence. *See also* Crime scene
        investigation (CSI); Evidence
        biological, 224–228
        blood, 228–229
        clothing as, 237, 238
        collection, 222–223, 227–228, 233–236
        commonly identified in sexual assault
                investigations, 224–236
        comparison of, 216–217
        contamination of, 217–218
        in drug-facilitated sexual assaults, 238–239
        forensic examination of, 276–280
        hair and fiber, 232–236, 237
        identifying, 213–218
        lighting techniques, 207, 215–216, 226–227, 228,
                229–230, 233

Physical evidence (*cont.*)
    observation and perception of, 214
    packaging, 223, 228, 236
    principle theory of exchange and, 214–215, 219
    proper handling of, 280–281
    recovery, 215
    recovery kits, 236–238
    safety precautions with, 218
    saliva, 230–231
    semen stains, 229–230
    touch DNA, 232
    types of evidence and, 212–213
    urine and feces, 232
    vaginal secretions, 230
    wearer DNA, 231
Physical examination of child victims. *See* Children,
        medical evaluation of sexually abused
Physical force in rape, 85, 87
    amount of, 114–115
    by juvenile offenders, 322–323
    selfish versus pseudo-unselfish behavior by rapists
        and, 101–102, 103
Physical resistance by victims, 86
Pinkerton, R., 330
Planting ideas in interviews, 128
Poey, E. L., 331
Police interrogations, 179–180
Pollack, N. L., 394–395
Polymerase chain reaction (PCR), 225
Pornography
    child, 141–142, 310
    in fantasy, 71
Postal Inspection Service, U. S., 42–43
Postmortem mutilation, 378–379
Post-traumatic stress disorder (PTSD), 4
    anxiety-based disorders and, 5–6
    childhood sexual abuse and, 7
    psychosocial adaptation and, 6–7
    substance abuse and, 6
Poulin, C., 342
Power-assertive rapist typology, 105–106, 131
PowerPlex Fusion DNA analysis, 226
Power reassurance rapists, 104–105, 131,
        132–135
Precautionary actions by rapists, 117
Pregnancy after rape, 7
Pre-interrogation investigations, 178–179
Preliminary scene survey, 220
Premature ejaculation, 88
Prentky, Robert, 189, 321
Presence of rapist as control of the
        victim, 84
Pretrial motions, 294
Prevalence. *See also* Reporting
    on campus, 433–435
    child sexual abuse, 243–244
    elder sexual abuse, 46–47, 50, 393–394
    female sexual offending, 340–342
    genital injury, 270–273
    juvenile sexual offending, 319–320
    in the military, 422
    rape, 19, 21
Prevention
    campus sexual assault, 437, 439

child sexual victimization, 314–315
    educator sexual misconduct, 416–417
    elder sexual abuse, 59–61
    false confessions, 184
    juvenile sex offending, 329–330
Principle theory of exchange, 214–215, 219
Prioritization of cold case investigations, 201–202
Profane speech, 102
Profiling of offenders, 81–82, 98–99, 118–121. *See also*
        Investigations
    age in, 119
    appearance and grooming in, 120–121
    arrest history in, 119
    case study, 110–113
    in drug-facilitated sexual assaults, 366
    education in, 120
    in elder sexual abuse cases, 403
    employment in, 120
    marital status in, 119–120
    military history in, 120
    personality characteristics in, 118–119
    race in, 119
    rapist typologies in, 103–110
    residence in, 120
    selfish versus pseudo-unselfish behavior in, 99–103
    transportation in, 120
Prophylaxis, 282
Prosecutions. *See also* Investigations; Rapists
    additional strategies for, 301
    clearance rates, 20
    closing arguments, 300
    conducting offender-focused, 287–289
    cross-examination of defendants, 298–300
    direct examination of victims in, 291–293
    DNA in, 297
    for educator sexual misconduct, 416–417
    enhancing victim's credibility in, 289–293
    and expert testimony regarding victim
        behavior, 293
    general trial strategies in, 294–297
    and imprisonment after false allegations, 160–161
    introduction to, 287
    jury instructions in, 300
    of juvenile sex offenders, 328–329
    medical testimony in, 296–297
    by the military, 427–430
    opening statements, 295–296
    preparation, 294
    pretrial motions, 294
    prosecutive strategy and fantasy in, 76
    role of genital injury in, 273–274
    toxicologist and/or pharmacologist in, 297–298
    victim cross-examination in, 296
    victim interviews and, 291
    voir dire, 294–295
    witness orders, 294
Prostitution, 72, 309
Proulx, J., 380
Pseudo-unselfish behavior, 99–103
Pseudovictims, 160, 171–174. *See also* False
        allegations
Psychobiology of trauma, 5
Psychopathia Sexualis, 337
Psychopathy, indications of, 89, 323

Psychosexual plateau and homicide, 190–192
Psychosocial adaptation, 6–7

R

Rambow, B., 274
Ramsey-Klawsnik, H., 46, 50, 396
Rape, act of
    criminal experience of rapists and, 91
    culture and, 11–13
    escalating to homicide, 187–196
    forced victim verbal activity during, 91
    global perspectives on, 11
    indications of psychopathy in, 89
    items taken during and after, 92–93, 117, 140
    method of approach in, 83–84
    offender's control of the victim in, 84–85,
        101–102, 114
    offender's reaction to resistance during, 86–87
    offender's use of physical force in, 85, 101–102
    precautionary actions by rapists and, 117
    prevalence of, 19, 21
    purpose of the assault, 117–118
    sexual dysfunctions during, 87–89
    in specific populations, 9–11
    sudden change in offender's attitude during, 91–92,
        116–117
    type and sequence of sex acts during, 89–90
    verbal activity by rapist during, 90–91, 116
    victim resistance during, 85–86
Rape, physical effects of
    general health effects, 8
    genital injury, 8–9
    perception of health and, 8
    pregnancy, 7
    sexually transmitted diseases (STDs), 7–8
    utilization of health services and, 8
Rape crisis centers/services, 22–23, 25
    antirape movement and development of, 26
Rape trauma syndrome (RTS), 3–4
    anxiety-based disorders and, 5–6
    childhood sexual abuse and, 7
    depression and, 6
    in elder sexual abuse victims, 55–56
    history of psychological trauma and, 4–5
    psychobiology of trauma and, 5
    psychosocial adaptation and, 6–7
    substance abuse and, 6
    victim care services and, 24
Rapists. *See also* Female sexual offenders; Juvenile
        sexual offenders
    amount of force, 114–115
    anger excitation, 107–108, 135–136
    anger retaliatory, 106–107, 135
    case study, 110–113
    control of victims, 84–85
    criminal experience of, 92, 119, 402
    indications of psychopathy in, 89, 323
    indications of targeting by, 93–94
    interviewing of, 123–136
    method of approach, 83–84, 114, 396
    method of control, 114, 396
    power-assertive, 105–106, 131
    power reassurance, 104–105, 131, *132–135*

precautionary actions by, 117
profiling of, 81–82, 98–99, 118–121, 403
purpose for assault, 117–118
reactions to resistance, 86–87, 115
risk factors associated with college student,
        436–437
selfish versus pseudo-unselfish behavior by, 99–103
sexual dysfunctions in, 87–89, 115
sudden change in attitude during rape, 91–92,
        116–117
type and sequence of sexual acts by, 89–90,
        115–116, 397
typologies, 103–110, 397–402
use of physical force, 85, 101–102, 103, 114–115
verbal activity by, 90–91, 100–101, 102–103, 116
victims drugged by (*See* Drug-facilitated sexual
        assault (DFSA))
Rationalization, projection, and minimalization
        (RPM), 130
Ratliff, L., 407
Ravn, P., 273, 279
Reading minds in interviews, 127–128
Recovery, evidence, 215
    kits, 236–238
Rectal examination, 280
Reeder, M., 345
Registration, juvenile sex offender, 333
Reid Method of interrogation, 178
Relevance of consent in child sexual abuse, 309–311
Reporting, 9, 19
    arrests after, 14, 20
    campus rape, 438
    of on campus rape, 435–436
    disclosure and, 9, 22
    false, 160
    global, 13
    Internet-related crime, 42–43
    problems in, 19–20
    rape prevalence and, 19, 21
    underreporting, 21–22, 275
ReproCAST, 231
Research
    on educator sexual misconduct, 408–409
    on elder sexual abuse, 46–47, 50–51, 394
    on juvenile sexual offenders, 321–323
    related to rape and culture, 12–13
    on sadistic offenders, 379–381
    on SANE/SART programs, 30–32
    on sexual sadists, 386–391
Residence of rapists, 120
Resistance
    homicide as impulsive reaction to, 190
    rapists' reactions to, 86–87, 115
    by victim, 85–87, 115, 397
Resnick, H. S., 9
Retarded ejaculation, 88
Revenge-motivated cruelty, 378
Risin, L., 342
Ritualistic behaviors, 151–152, 155–156
    in child sexual victimization, 316
Roberto, K. A., 47
Robinson, Lovette, 426
Rohypnol, 238–239, 357, 358, 359
Rolling Stone, 435–436

Rose, M., 409
Rosencrans, B., 338, 341
Rossman, L., 88, 271, 272
Rough sketch, crime scene, 221–222
Rouleau, J., 69
Rowland, S. E., 341, 343, 344
RTS. *See* Rape trauma syndrome (RTS)
Ruggiero, K. J., 9
Rumsfeld, Donald, 421–422
Russo, N. F., 12–13

S

Sadists, sexual, 385–386, 391
    behavior of, 374–376
    behavior patterns confused with those of, 376–379
    child sexual abuse and, 312
    consenting or paid partners of, 375–376
    crime characteristics, 380–381
    defined, 373–374
    evidence of crime by, 381
    homicide by, 194–195
    interviews of, 382
    investigating crimes of, 381–382
    investigative significance of research on,
        390–391
    offender characteristics, 379–380
    physical and psychological suffering caused
        by, 374
    rapes by, 399–400
    research on, 379–381, 386–391
    transformation of women in relationships with,
        388–390
    women in relationships with, 386–388
Safarik, M. E., 395, 403
Safety, Internet, 39–41
Safety precautions with physical evidence, 218
Saliva evidence, 230–231
Sanctioned cruelty, 377–378
Sandler, J, 347
SANE. *See* Sexual assault nurse examiner (SANE)
Santos, D., 331
Sapir, Avinoam, 130
Saradjian, J., 339, 342, 345
SART. *See* Sexual assault response team (SART)
Say, G., 413
Schwartz, N., 272
Search warrants, 75, 382
"Second assault" of victims, 26–27
Secret Service, U. S., 42
Self-blame, 7
Self-composition in fantasy, 72
Self-demeaning, 100, 116
Self-exploitation, 38, 41
Selfish versus pseudo-unselfish behavior by
        rapists, 99–103
Semen stains, 229–230
Sensory act, sex as, 68–69
Serial sexual murderers, 403
Severson, K., 51
Sex offenders and social networking sites, 37
Sex-stress situations, 163–165
Sexting, 38–39, 310
Sexual activity

in selfish versus pseudo-unselfish behavior by
        rapists, 101, 103
    as a sensory act, 68–69
    type and sequence of rapists', 89–90, 115–116, 397
Sexual Assault Forensic Exam (SAFE), 425, 429
Sexual assault kits backlog, 29–30
Sexual assault nurse examiner (SANE), 20, 236
    backlog of sexual assault kits and, 29–30
    child victims and, 243
    evolution of, 26–27
    in the military, 425–426
    past and present, 27–28
    research on, 30–32
    structure and operation of, 28–29
Sexual assault response coordinator (SARC),
        422–423
Sexual assault response team (SART), 20, 274–275
    access to, 275
    backlog of sexual assault kits and, 29–30
    evolution of, 26–27
    in the military, 426
    past and present, 27–28
    research on, 30–32
    structure and operation of, 28–29
"Sexual deviation as condition behavior: A
        hypothesis", 338
Sexual dysfunctions, 87–89, 115
Sexual Experiences Survey (SES), 433
Sexual harassment, 10
Sexual Harassment & Rape Prevention Program
        (SHARPP), 437
Sexualization typology, 399–400
Sexually transmitted diseases (STDs), 7–8
    in child victims, 262
Sexual sadists, 385–386, 391
    behavior of, 374–376
    behavior patterns confused with those of, 376–379
    consenting or paid partners of, 375–376
    crime characteristics, 380–381
    defined, 373–374
    evidence of crime by, 381
    homicide by, 194–195
    interviews of, 382
    investigating crimes of, 381–382
    investigative significance of research on, 390–391
    offender characteristics, 379–380
    physical and psychological suffering caused
        by, 374
    rapes by, 399–400
    research on, 379–381, 386–391
    transformation of women in relationships with,
        388–390
    women in relationships with, 386–388
Sharpton, Al, 161
Shell shock, 5
Sibille, I., 272
Sight, male sexual response and, 69
Sigler, R. T., 9
Signature in sexual crimes, 152, 156
Silence of the Lambs, The, 391
Silva, P., 321–322
Simmel, Georg, 9
Situational risk factors for false confession,
        180–181

Sketch, crime scene rough, 221–222
Slaughter, L., 31, 272, 273
Slesinger, D., 321, 322, 323, 326
Smith, Anna Nicole, 359
Snapchat, 37
Snowden, P., 70
Snowdon, P. R., 395
Social networking sites, 37–38
    cyberbullying and, 41–42
    drug-facilitated sexual assault and, 367–368
    romantic relationships and, 38–39
Solola, scott, 31
Sommers, M. S., 31
Souma, M. L., 271
South Dakota v. Robert Anderson, 152
Speltz, K., 346
Spohn, C., 162
Stanton, W., 321–322
Starzynski, L. L., 13
State of New Jersey v. Steven Fortin, 152
State v. Hirschfelder, 416
Statistics, rape. *See* Prevalence, rape; Reporting
Stereotypes, cultural, 12
Stermac, L., 394
Stone, T., 171
Stress-compliant false confession, 182–183
Strickland, I., 395
Student-teacher relationships. *See* Educator sexual
        misconduct
Substance abuse. *See also* Drug-facilitated sexual
        assault (DFSA)
    homicide and, 193–194
    in rape trauma syndrome, 6
    and sexual violence among college students, 10,
        436–437
Suicide, 413
Surprise in rape attack, 83–84
Suschinsky, K. D., 342
Swabs, 237, 279
Swaminath, S., 342
Sweeney, B., 437
Symbols, sadism toward, 375

T

TEARS (genital injury type), 273, 281
Teaster, P. B., 47
Technology, 35, 140–141. *See also* Internet, the
    computerized linkage systems, 156–157
    support in cold case investigations, 207
Tellis, K., 162
Test of commitment, 130
Theme development in interviews, 129–130
Thomsen, J. L., 273, 279
Threats by rapists, 87, 102, 116, 322–323
Time (magazine), 435, 436
Title IX U. S. Education Amendments of 1972,
        313–314, 438
Touch DNA, 232
Townsend, S. M., 13
Toxicologists, 297–298
Transportation used by rapists, 120
Trauma
    history of psychological, 4–5

    psychobiology of, 5
Treatment of juvenile sex offenders, 330–333
Tumblr, 37
Turner, M. G., 9, 434
Twitter, 37, 38
Typologies, offender, 103–110
    anger excitation, 107–108, 135–136
    anger retaliatory, 106–107
    case study, 110–113
    drug-facilitated sexual assault and, 362–365
    in elder sexual abuse, 397–402
    female, 346–348
    gang rape, 109–110
    juvenile, 321–323
    nonsadistic, 400–401
    opportunistic, 109, 397–398
    pervasive anger, 398–399
    power-assertive, 105–106, 131
    power reassurance, 104–105, 131, *132–135*
    sadistic, 194–195, 399–400
    sexualization, 399–400
    vindictive motivation, 401–402

U

U. S. Army Criminal Investigative Laboratory
        (USACIL), 424
Ullman, S. E., 13, 85
Ultraviolet lighting, 216
Underreporting of rape, 21–22, 275
Uniform Code of Military Justice (UCMJ), 426,
        429–430
University of Montana, 435
University of Virginia, 435–436
Urine and feces, 232
Utilization of health services, 8

V

Vaginal secretions evidence, 230
Valium, 359
Valuables taken after rape, 93
Vanderbilt University, 436
Vandiver, D., 347, 409
Vedros, D., 330
Verbal activity
    forced victim, 91
    by rapists, 90–91, 100–101, 102–103, 116
    in selfish versus pseudo-unselfish behavior by rapists,
        100–101, 102–103
Verbal resistance of victims, 86
Verbal threats against victims, 84
ViCAP system, 156
ViCLAS system, 156
Victim care services (VCS), 22. *See also* Rape crisis
        centers/services
    hospital-based, 23–25
    Joint Task Force for Sexual Assault Prevention and
        Response (JTF-SAPR), 422–423
    rape crisis centers, 22–23, 25
    SANE and SART, 20, 26–32
Victimology, 114, 396
Victims. *See also* Rape trauma syndrome (RTS)
    child (*See* Children, sexual victimization of)

Victims (*cont.*)
  consent for forensic services, 276
  credibility in prosecution proceedings, 289–293
  criminal investigative analysis of, 114
  cross-examination of, 296
  direct examination in court, 291–293
  drugged by offenders (*See* Drug-facilitated sexual
      assault (DFSA))
  expert testimony regarding behavior of, 293
  force verbal activity, 91
  forensic examination of (*See* Forensic examination)
  impact of false allegations on legitimate
      rape, 161
  indications of targeting of, 93–94
  interviews by prosecutors, 291
  items taken from, 92–93, 140
  LGBTQ, 434
  male, 10, 364, 434
  mere presence of rapist as control over, 84
  murder of (*See* Homicide)
  passive resistance by, 86
  physical force used against, 85, 87, 101–102, 103,
      114–115
  physical resistance by, 86
  postmortem mutilation of, 378–379
  pseudo-, 160, 171–174
  resistance by, 85–87, 115, 190, 397
  "second assault" of, 26–27
  self-blame by, 7
  of sexual sadism, 375–376
  verbal resistance by, 86
  verbal threats against, 84
Vindictive motivation typology, 401–402
Violence Against Women Act of 1994, 311, 439
Violent juvenile sex offenders, 323–325
Voir dire, 294–295
Voluntary false confessions, 182

W

Waite, D., 330
Walker, D. F., 331
Wallace, A., 345
Walter Reed Military Medical Center (WRMMC), 426

Ward, T., 339–340, 342, 344, 409
Warren, J., 74, 89, 144, 386
  on female sexual offenders, 343, 344, 345
Washington Post, 434
Watson, J., 407
Wauchope, M., 102
Weapons used in rapes, 84–85
Wearer DNA, 231
West, S. G., 343
WhatsApp, 367
White, C., 162
White House Task Force to Protect Students from
      Sexual Assault, 433
Wiebe, E., 274
Wieckowski, E., 330
Williams, R., 344
Wilson, C., 27, 28
Wilson, D., 31
Witness elimination, 192–193
Witness orders, 294
Wolitzky-Taylor, K. B., 9, 275
Wollis, M., 412
Women offenders. *See* Female sexual
      offenders
Wood, J., 70
Woodhams, J., 110, 156–157
Woodworth, M., 412
Workplace DFSA, 362
World Health Organization, 13
Worling, J. R., 330–331
Wrightsman, L., 182
Wulffen, E., 338
Wynn, B. N., 88, 271, 272

Y

Y-chromosome DNA, 225–226
Yeater, E. A., 439
Young, B. G., 338
Yüce, M., 413

Z

Ziering, Amy, 435